The Encyclopedia of Jewish Genealogy

The Encyclopedia of Jewish Genealogy

Volume I
Sources in the United States and Canada

edited by
Arthur Kurzweil and Miriam Weiner

JASON ARONSON INC.
Northvale, New Jersey
London

The editors and publisher gratefully acknowledge the following for permission to reprint material found in this book:

"Records of Immigration across the Canadian Border," courtesy of *The National Genealogical Society Newsletter*.

"Videodisc Program" is adapted from "People of a Thousand Towns," originally printed in YIVO News #172 (Autumn 1987). Reprinted with permission of the YIVO Institute for Jewish Research.

From *Avotaynu: The International Review of Jewish Genealogy:* "Jewish Records on Microfilm in the Library of the Genealogical Society of Utah" by John Henry Richter; "German–Jewish Records on Microfilm at the Genealogical Society of Utah"; "Hungarian–Jewish Records on Microfilm at the Genealogical Society of Utah"; "Polish–Jewish Records on Microfilm at the Genealogical Society of Utah"; "HIAS–New York" by Marsha Saron Dennis; "Archival Sources for Canadian Jewry" by Dr. Rolf Lederer; "Book Review: Jews of Toronto" by Zachary M. Baker; "Book Review: Genealogical Resources in Metropolitan New York" by Zachary M. Baker. Reprinted by permission.

"Immigration Records in the National Archives," by permission of Family Service World, P.O. Box 22045, Salt Lake City, Utah 84122.

The "Description of Resources" at Yeshiva University, YIVO, the National Archives/Northeast Branch, the New York Public Library, and the Jewish Theological Society of America Library was published in *Genealogical Resources in the New York Metropolitan Area*, copyright © 1989 by the Jewish Genealogical Society, Inc. Reprinted by permission.

From *Search*, Vol. 7, No. 4, Winter 1987: "Military Research." Reprinted with permission.

Library of Congress Cataloguing-in-Publication Data

The Encyclopedia of Jewish genealogy / edited by Arthur Kurzweil and
  Miriam Weiner.
      p. cm.
    Includes bibliographical references and index.
    Contents: v. 1. Sources in the United States and Canada
    ISBN 0-87668-835-0
    1. Jews—Genealogy—Handbooks, manuals, etc.   I. Kurzweil,
Arthur. II. Weiner, Miriam.
CS21.E53 1991
929'.1'089924073—dc20   90-24600

22057

Manufactured in the United States of America. Jason Aronson Inc. offers books and cassettes. For information and catalog write to Jason Aronson Inc., 230 Livingston Street, Northvale, New Jersey 07647.

For my parents
Evelyn and Saul Kurzweil
"One should revere his father and mother
as he reveres God,
for the three are partners in him."—Talmud

Arthur Kurzweil

To the memory of my grandparents
Moische Winikur and Malka Ochs
Alexander Rabkin and Miriam Odnopozov
who inspired me to walk in the footsteps of my ancestors.

Miriam Weiner

CONTENTS

Chapter 3
CANADA: GUIDE TO INSTITUTIONAL RESOURCES ARRANGED BY CITY

APPENDIXES

ACKNOWLEDGMENTS

This volume represents the combined efforts of many people—genealogists, historians, scholars, archivists, and librarians—all of whom worked hard to make this book as comprehensive and accurate as possible.

The contributing authors, through their professionalism and dedication to this project, made it possible for us to present this material in a manner that will enable thousands of people to discover and preserve their Jewish family heritage.

In developing the concept for Vol. I of the *Encyclopedia of Jewish Genealogy*, we turned to Alan Spencer and Scott Meyer of Chicago, who are not only very knowledgeable in the field of Jewish genealogy, but also have editorial experience as editors of *Search: International Journal for Researchers of Jewish Genealogy*. In their capacity as editors of the *Encyclopedia's* chapters on sources in the United States and Canada, we cannot say enough about the hundreds of hours, long weekends, short deadlines, and consistent high quality of the material produced by Alan and Scott, which far exceeds what we asked of them. Their meticulous attention to detail and dedication to this book is consistent with the quality of any project that involves them, and we welcome this opportunity to thank them for their hard work and special efforts on this book.

Material that originally appeared in *Search* was updated for this publication and, as an on-going feature of *Search*, these "locality guides" are a valuable contribution to the field of Jewish genealogy. For subscription information, write to *Search*, P.O. Box 515, Northbrook, Illinois 60065.

Many members of genealogy societies throughout the United States were responsive to requests for material, and we wish to acknowledge their contributions:

Norma Arbit, Heidi Farkash, Ted Gostin, and Carolyn Sherfy (California); Harry Boonin, Julian Falk, Elaine Kolinsky, and Jon Stein (Pennsylvania); Walter Cohen, Winnie Isaacs, and Joe Williams (Texas); Irwin M. Berent, Allan T. Hirsh, Jr., and Emmy Mogilensky (Maryland); Morris Fogel and Arlene Blank Rich (Ohio); Warren Blatt and William S. Rubin (Massachusetts); Dr. Robert Kravetz (Arizona); Gertrude Singer Ogushwitz (Connecticut); Annette Russman (Kentucky); Marsha Saron Dennis, Estelle M. Guzik, Loren Fay, Fern Mittleman, Muriel Selling, Steven W. Siegel, and Malcolm H. Stern (New York); Sylvia Kruger, Michelle Sandler, and Betty Proviser Starkman (Michigan); Chava Katibian (North Carolina).

Many people sent in tidbits of advice, suggested new source material, shared research experiences, and offered help throughout the project. Their names would extend this book significantly and delay the publication date! We gratefully acknowledge everyone who shared their research tips, and we regret the impossibility of listing each and every name.

Editors of many Jewish periodicals also contributed source information about their local communities, and we thank all of them for making their resources available. In particular we are grateful to Leon Brown of *The Jewish Times* in Philadelphia and Joel Roteman of *The Jewish Chronicle* in Pittsburgh for their special input.

Additionally, countless archives, libraries, organizations, institutions, Holocaust Resource Centers, and agencies were responsive to our requests for information, and we want to acknowledge the cooperation of their staff for guiding us through their holdings:

Baltimore Hebrew College (Judith Barrett); Brandeis University (Victor A. Berch); Ottawa Jewish Historical Society (Shirley Berman); Annenberg Research Institute (Claudia Bloom); National Archives—Northeast Region (Joel Buchwald); Jewish Cemetery Association of Massachusetts (Miriam Drukman); Yeshiva University (Dr. Roger S. Kohn); Jewish Historical Society of Hartford (Marsha Lotstein); Texas State Library (Colleen Munds); Arizona Jewish Historical Society (Pearl Newmark); New York Genealogical and Biographical Society (Betty Hall Payne); Library Of Congress/Hebraic Division (Peggy Pearlstein); American Jewish Archives (Dr. Abraham J. Peck and Rabbi Malcolm H. Stern); Jewish Community Center of Louisville (Annette Sagerman); Philadelphia Jewish Archives (Lilly Schwartz); Perry Castaneda Library/ University of Texas (Nathan Snyder); Leo Baeck Institute (Diane R. Spielmann); American Jewish Historical Society (Nathan Kaganoff and Bernard Wax); Holocaust Memorial Center/Detroit (Feiga Weiss); National Archives/Military Archives Division (Robert Wolfe); Nebraska Jewish Historical Society (Mary Fellman); Hebrew Immigrant Aid Society (Karl D. Zukerman); Jewish Historical Society of Western Canada, Inc. (Dorothy Hershfield); Canadian Jewish Congress (Dr. Stephen A. Speisman); Y.I.V.O. Institute (Dina Abramowicz, Zachary M. Baker, Marek Web); Temple Beth El/Detroit (Miriam E. Kushner); Jewish Community Council of Metropolitan Detroit (Sally Reinicke); Family History Library (David Mayfield and Daniel Schlyter).

Throughout our project, the staff at the Family History Library in Salt Lake City has shared information and source material and has generously provided artwork. We want to acknowledge their continuing cooperation and extensive input and, in particular, a special thank you to David Mayfield, Jayare Roberts, and Daniel Schlyter.

For the section of the New York Metropolitan Area, we provided excerpts from *the* genealogical source, *Genealogical Sources in the New York Metropolitan Area* (New York: Jewish Genealogical Society, 1989), edited by Estelle M. Guzik. With her book, genealogists now have a comprehensive guide to resources (see Appendix H). We are particularly appreciative to the Jewish Genealogical Society, Inc., for graciously allowing us to reprint excerpts here.

In the editorial department of Jason Aronson Inc., Muriel Jorgensen made frequent invaluable suggestions and demonstrated extraordinary patience with the complications caused by so many contributors of differing styles and geographic origins. Her enthusiasm and interest in the project made her a partner in the frantic days of completion. Also at Jason Aronson Inc., Marion Cino was always there to handle the administrative questions with a smile and her usual efficiency.

In discussing the proposed material for the Encyclopedia, it was clear that many articles published in *Avotaynu: The International Review of Jewish Genealogy* were appropriate for our publication. We are especially grateful to Gary Mokotoff, publisher, and Sallyann Amdur Sack, editor, for their continuing cooperation throughout the project, and we appreciate their permission to reprint articles from *Avotaynu.* Both Gary and Sallyann are among the leaders who have made significant contributions to the field of Jewish genealogy. A subscription to *Avotaynu* is $20.00 yearly and may be ordered from *Avotaynu,* P.O. Box 1134, Teaneck, New Jersey 07666.

David Zubatsky contributed numerous references to publications that ultimately became part of the bibliography. His friendship, knowledge, and continuing interest are deeply appreciated.

A book on Jewish genealogy is not complete without some input from Steven W. Siegel, Archivist at the 92nd Street "Y." Throughout the project, Steve was always there to answer a question or offer advice, and he was invaluable in his review of this volume's New York section.

The job of surveying Washington, D.C., and its many genealogical sources was expertly done by Suzan Fisher Wynne, a seasoned, long-time researcher of her Galician Jewish roots. Suzan merits our special gratitude for her comprehensive and informative article, which evolved from many long hours of research at the Library of Congress and the National Archives.

A special thanks goes to Gary Mokotoff and his right hand at Data Universal, Ms. Rose Ciecierski, both of whom provided extensive administrative input, graciously donating copying facilities and helping in ways too numerous to mention, but deeply appreciated.

Arthur Kurzweil and Miriam Weiner

Special Acknowledgment

When we discussed the many people who had direct influence on our "genealogy" lives, both of us were in total agreement about one very special person, Rabbi Malcolm H. Stern, who has nurtured and guided thousands of Jewish family historians by his lectures, workshops, and publications. He responds to voluminous correspondence and generously shares strategies and sources for documenting Jewish roots.

On a personal level, Rabbi Stern has been supportive of this project from its inception and has given freely of his time and advice throughout. His love of the subject and willingness to promote the efforts of others has endeared him to all of us. Additionally, he has had a unique impact on both of our careers, and we welcome this opportunity to publicly thank him, for ourselves and the rest of the genealogy world as well.

Arthur Kurzweil and Miriam Weiner

Personal Acknowledgments

It is my sincere hope that those who use this Encyclopedia will know that it would not exist without the countless hours of work as well as the remarkable resourcefulness of Miriam Weiner. Miriam is a major force in the world of Jewish family history and genealogy. Her passion for the subject is inspirational, her knowledge is truly encyclopedic, and her skills are many and impressive. Through her lectures, classes, newspaper columns, magazine articles, publications, and activities, Miriam has enriched and elevated the field of Jewish genealogy. She has assisted great numbers of people and is a generous soul, with a deep and profound love for the Jewish people.

When I pondered the question of who could join me in the task of producing this Encyclopedia, Miriam was clearly the person of choice. Thank you, Miriam, for your hundreds of hours of work, your amazing abilities, and the patience shown for your grateful co-editor.

Marion Cino, my secretary, colleague, and friend, deserves thanks and more thanks for the many ways that she helps me. Thank you, Marion, for your abundant assistance. You are a rare person, and your approach to life has been a light of wisdom for me.

Thank you to the entire staff at Jason Aronson Inc., for all you have done for this book and for the joy you give me daily. I would especially like to thank Muriel Jorgensen, Jane Andrassi, Dianna Walsh, Pamela Roth, and Dr. Jason Aronson.

Two of the most important leaders in this field are Gary Mokotoff and Sallyann Amdur Sack. Their contribution to Jewish genealogists worldwide has been and continues to be extraordinary. Among their many publications and activities, their journal, *Avotaynu,* is a most impressive and useful periodical. It is not surprising, therefore, that we looked to its pages for contributions to this Encyclopedia. Thank you, Gary and Sallyann, for your generosity, your cooperation, your helpful suggestions, and your permission to reprint material from your journal. I pray that you continue to be as active as you have been in helping so many of us with our research. The world of Jewish genealogy is infinitely richer because of you.

I want to express my gratitude and devotion to my teacher, Rabbi Adin Steinsaltz, for his guidance and his love. No single person has had as much an impact on my life as Rabbi Steinsaltz.

Most of all, I thank my wife, Rea, and our children,

Malya, Miriam, and Moshe, for the love, support, and encouragement with which they always shower me.

Blessed are you, Hashem, our God, King of the universe, Who has kept us alive, sustained us, and permitted us to reach this season.

Arthur Kurzweil

First and foremost, I am grateful to my co-editor, Arthur Kurzweil, for initially suggesting the project and asking me to join with him in producing this series, which has grown from a one-volume concept to the projected three-volume work. Arthur brought many invaluable components to this project, including his pioneer expertise in the field of Jewish genealogy, his many contacts throughout the United States, and his understanding of the relationship of genealogy to Jewish history. I thank you, Arthur, for the opportunity to develop this project with you and, most of all, for your friendship, guidance, and high standards that you set in this field. My copy of your invaluable book, *From Generation to Generation,* is tattered and worn from the many times I have referred to it. It holds a special place in my library, as it does in thousands of others.

Support for this project took many forms, and among the most important was through financial assistance, ongoing encouragement, and all around enthusiasm for my work. For all of this and so much more, I thank my dear parents, Edward and Helen Weiner, who have tolerated endless questions and requests for information while sharing in the euphoric highs of locating surviving family members in our small ancestral towns in the Ukraine, as well as other discoveries along the way.

It would not surprise me if Xerox and AT&T someday acknowledge the Weiner family for our extensive efforts in increasing their stock value.

To my first cousin once removed, Edward Leader, goes a special bouquet as the 95-year-old senior member of the Odnopozov family, who wanted to live long enough to see this book published! "Eddie" was one of my first discoveries almost twenty years ago in the beginning stages of my research, and he has continually cooperated by sharing his memories and memorabilia along with generous contributions to the "research fund."

Miriam Weiner

INTRODUCTION

"Why are you crying, Mother? Because the house is burning?"

"Yes."

"We shall build another, I promise you."

"It's not the house, son. If I cry, it is because a precious document is being destroyed before our eyes."

"What document?"

"Our family tree; it is illustrious you know."

"Don't cry. I'll give you another. I'll start anew, I promise you."

At the time, Dov-Ber was five.

–Elie Wiesel, telling of the Maggid of Mezeritch, a Chassidic master, in *Souls on Fire*.

The Encyclopedia of Jewish Genealogy is conceived and designed as a new reference tool in the continually growing number of publications whose purpose is to help the Jewish family historian in his or her research. It is not conceived as the definitive reference tool for its field; indeed, such a conception would be impossible. Rather, it is an ambitious attempt to bring together experts and specialists who can offer sound guidance for the Jewish genealogist.

By calling this work a "reference tool," its editors are profoundly aware that human experience has witnessed countless moments when tools have become weapons. And it was, of course, a mere generation ago, when a third of the Jewish population of the world was murdered and family trees were used by the perpetrators.

Our Sages teach us to be occupied with our genealogies. There is evidence of it everywhere: the Torah itself contains genealogies, and also includes, essentially, a family story, and one that we, as a family, retell over and over again. The Torah is a family history, and the command to its students is to join that family and be a part of its history. Family consciousness and an intimate knowledge of one's ancestors are clearly part of the basis of the experience of the talmudic Sages. Their appreciation and celebration of the spirit of the phrase *m'dor l'dor* (from generation to generation) is at the root of their method. Yet with all their occupation with lineage, a well-known passage from the Talmud states, "An educated bastard takes precedence over an ignorant High Priest."

The name a Jew is given at birth is actually a bit of a family tree itself, for the name is always at least two names, including a father's or mother's name, or sometimes both, as the basic name to be used at all important moments and rites of passage.

To be a Jew is to be aware of one's past, and it is not surprising in our generation to see an intensification of interest in genealogy precisely because our Tree has been severely damaged in recent decades, and the need for revival, for renewal, for a reconnection appears extremely urgent to many of us. We feel a deep responsibility not only to preserve the past, but to participate in its rejuvenation and become a part of its future. Not a third, but a vital third was all but destroyed, yet we who are engaged in the pursuit of Jewish genealogy seem to know, through every tiny effort with our little family trees, that our dedication is surely to connect with these departed souls. We wish to memoralize them, to become the gravestones they do not have, and to rediscover not only how they died as Jews, but how they lived as Jews. By knowing that the ancient tradition is now ours, we face the question of what to do with it. And it is our central prayer, the *Shema*, spoken twice each day, that guides us as it says, "Teach them diligently to your children."

The structure of *The Encyclopedia of Jewish Genealogy* is a necessary compromise, for there is no correct structure, and this fact stems from the nature of genealogy itself: it is highly individualized. Each researcher has his or her own goals, set of clues, combination of resources. One researcher will find nothing of use in the same resource where another will locate the missing piece to a decade's worth of hunting. As any experienced genealogist knows, everything has potential value as a research clue, and the route of one's search is filled with unexpected surprises.

The editors have therefore come up with what we think is the most practical structure for these volumes, the present volume being an in-depth look at Jewish genealogical resources in the United States and Canada. The contents and its authors speak for themselves, with the hope that this research tool will be a useful aid.

During the past 15 years, we have witnessed a remarkable growth in the field of Jewish genealogy. A number of specialized journals, a network of Jewish Genealogical Societies, a bibliography of how-to guides, new reference tools, newspaper columns, curriculums for Jewish schools and adult Jewish education as well, have all added to a burst of energy and creativity in this field. It is the sincere hope of the editors of this Encyclopedia that their work be welcomed as one more useful tool that can serve many researchers well.

When we ventured into the world of Jewish genealogy two decades ago, there was little help to be found even in the finest of libraries. There were no how-to books available for Jewish research, no groups publicizing their efforts in the field, and the only entry in the best of library card catalogs was the work of Rabbi Malcolm Stern. While Rabbi Stern has been a crucial figure in the Jewish genealogical developments over the past few decades, his own scholarship in the field has been confined mainly to families that arrived in the United States before the year 1840.

Rabbi Stern, however, provided encouragement as well his personal correspondence files for what would become the first concrete step in bringing individuals with mutual interest in Jewish genealogy together: the publication of *Toledot, The Journal of Jewish Genealogy.* Steven W. Siegel and Arthur Kurzweil joined forces in the late 1970s by publishing *Toledot,* and with over a dozen issues of the journal, began to contribute to the building of a network of people who could share sources, fellowship, and enthusiasm. At about the same time as the founding of *Toledot* came the publication of the first how-to Jewish genealogy book, *Finding Our Fathers* by Dan Rottenberg. The book received much publicity, in great part due to the fact that the general topic of genealogy was getting significant media attention because of the achievements of Alex Haley and his book (and TV series), *Roots.* Following shortly after the publication of *Finding Our Fathers* was Arthur Kurzweil's book, *From Generation to Generation: How to Trace Your Jewish Genealogy and Personal History.* It was an excellent commercial success, reflecting the rapidly growing interest among Jews in tracing their family histories, and continues to be the basic introduction to the field.

Those who have been intimately involved in genealogy in this country for decades quickly testify that until the publication of Alex Haley's *Roots,* family history was largely of interest to White Anglo-Saxon Protestants. This fact is clearly reflected in the activities of such groups as the Daughters of the American Revolution (DAR), as well as in the contents of the available books on the subject of genealogy, most of which directed their remarks with the assumption that the place for Americans to look for family history was in the British parish records.

The focus on the Bicentennial celebration, restoration of the Statue of Liberty, and recent reopening of Ellis Island have also directed attention to family history and the immigration experience, resulting in an avalanche of requests for such items as passenger lists and naturalization records.

Additionally, technology has also played a major role, from the invention of photocopy machines to the use of computers with their vast databases, which enable researchers to locate material once inaccessible by its sheer volume and vast dispersiveness of locations. Individuals now utilize home computers to organize their genealogical material and to "tap into" databases worldwide.

The next significant development for the field of Jewish genealogy was the founding of the first Jewish Genealogical Society, the brain child of Dr. Neil Rosenstein. Dr. Rosenstein's own work, at the time, centered around his extensive research into family trees of major rabbinic families in Europe. This research resulted in the publication of *The Unbroken Chain,* an impressive document consisting of detailed family trees of many of the great rabbinic families of Europe. But it was Rosenstein's invitation to a number of individuals who had expressed some public interest in the field that launched what is today a significant network of Jewish Genealogical Societies throughout the world. Out of this first gathering (which directly resulted in the founding of the Jewish Genealogical

Society of New York) there grew a number of similar groups, the result being that as of this writing there are over three dozen such groups throughout the United States, Canada, Europe, and Israel.

It was after the founding of the first Jewish Genealogical Society that rapid growth in the field became apparent. One direct result that Kurzweil felt personally was the great demand to be a public speaker on the "Jewish lecture circuit," speaking about Jewish genealogy, why it is important, and how one goes about doing successful research. Over the past 15 years Kurzweil has spoken before nearly 750 Jewish groups across the United States, including synagogues, Jewish Federations, Jewish Community Centers, Hillels, and just about every other kind of Jewish group. In each case the leadership of these organizations desired a lecture that would bring the possibilities of Jewish genealogical research to its membership.

A few years ago Weiner also joined the Jewish genealogy lecture circuit, and we both find that the demand for speakers on this subject continues at the same pace to this very day.

Over the years, a number of individuals have taken significant leadership roles within the Jewish genealogical community. Already noted are Rabbi Malcolm Stern and Steven W. Siegel. Rabbi Stern, an important personality in the general world of genealogy in the United States, has provided leadership, encouragement, and perhaps most of all, a fair-minded, dignified attitude. His grace, generosity, and professionalism have been an inspiration to countless numbers. Steve Siegel is a researcher's researcher and has provided his vast amount of knowledge as well as strong organizational and leadership skills to the Jewish genealogical community.

Two individuals who have established themselves as important leaders within the field are Dr. Sallyann Amdur Sack and Gary Mokotoff. Dr. Sack has published an important book, *A Guide to Jewish Genealogical Research in Israel,* and has been instrumental in efforts to gain access to important Jewish sources in the National Archives. She has also teamed up with Gary Mokotoff to publish *Avotaynu: The International Review of Jewish Genealogy,* an excellent journal in the field. Mokotoff brings his considerable expertise in computer science as well as his deep personal commitment to Jewish genealogical research to the growing field of Jewish family history. It is important to note that Sack and Mokotoff have been quite generous in granting reprint permission to the editors of this Encyclopedia for a number of pieces that originally appeared, sometimes in different forms, in the pages of *Avotaynu.*

The attempt to describe each of the key participants who have contributed to the burst of growth within the Jewish genealogical community these last several years is dangerous for many reasons, not the least of which is the fear that someone important will be forgotten. Suffice it to say that it is a personal privilege to be a part of the "movement" to bring Jewish genealogy to the entire community, and it is clear that a movement is always dependent upon many people. It is also clear that the most "famous" are not necessarily the most essential.

The contributors to this and the subsequent volumes have been invited by the editors, based on our confidence that each could provide reliable information on a specific aspect of Jewish genealogy research.

The contributing authors to the Encyclopedia come from diverse backgrounds throughout the world. While some of the authors are seasoned genealogists, others toil as historians, archivists, librarians, museum directors, and experts in a diversity of other fields. Their articles are based upon both research and personal experiences. Some articles are more personal than others, depending upon the topic. In some cases, more than one article makes reference to the same topic, resulting in overlapping material. The rationale for this is that one author provides an in-depth treatment of the topic while another author mentions it as part of a larger topic.

We do not imply by our selection of contributors that these are the only people who are knowledgeable about their topic, any more than we assume that we are the only ones who could make such a selection. Basically, we are passionate about our subject, we have between us many years of experience in the field, and we have as our only goal the dissemination of information that will help others, like ourselves, who have found genealogy to be deeply rewarding personally and spiritually.

There are bound to be inaccuracies in this volume, and the editors would be grateful for any corrections readers can provide. It is a given fact that with time these contents will become outdated, but a good researcher will be able to grasp the end of the string and persevere.

A few years ago, it became obvious that there was a growing demand and a growing need for wide access to Jewish genealogical information. The growth of Jewish genealogical societies, the successes of their excellent newsletters, the use of genealogy as a teaching tool within synagogue schools and Jewish day schools, and the importance of Jewish genealogy in the activities of *ba'alei teshuvah* (returnees to Jewish tradition) are but a few of the factors that evidence this need. After Kurzweil made a careful survey of the field, he engaged the assistance of Eileen Polakoff, an enthusiastic researcher and a leader in the Jewish Genealogical Society of New York. Kurzweil met her when she was a student of his in a course on Jewish genealogical research that he offered in a joint program between New York University and Hebrew Union College. Polakoff provided Kurzweil with a more detailed survey of the field and helped to build the foundation for this encyclopedia.

When it was clear to Kurzweil that a full partner was needed to create as ambitious a work as an encyclopedia, he turned to Miriam Weiner, who has established herself as a trail blazer in the field. Through her discoveries of new and important sources, her public seminars, her frequent lectures, her popular newspaper column, and her many other activities, Weiner has made an enormous impact and has touched the lives of thousands of people.

Our purpose here was *not* to write the definitive book on the National Archives and its branches, the Library of Congress, Family History Library, or the New York metropolitan area, as those books have already been written and are included as reference sources where appropriate.

As for genealogical sources in general, that subject, too, has been covered well. See *The Source: A Guidebook of American Genealogy,* edited by Arlene Eakle and Johni Cerny (Ancestry Publishing Company, Salt Lake City, Utah, 1984).

The amount of material per "state" entry is not uniform for all states, based upon several factors, including availability of material, size of immigrant population at the turn of the century during peak immigration periods, and interest in the locality. As an example, although some Jews probably trace their ancestors to Montana and Wyoming, they are in small numbers compared with states such as New York, Pennsylvania, Illinois, and Massachusetts.

We want the Encyclopedia to be "user friendly"— for both the novice and professional researcher. The book is designed to provide both source material and research methods.

As is common with encyclopedia projects, our structure changed from its original concept of one volume to a multi-volume series in order to accommodate the voluminous material collected. Volume I covers the immigration process and sources within the United States and Canada. Volume II will cover sources in Europe, South America, Australia, Israel, and South Africa, and Volume III will be arranged by topic, i.e., chapters on Rabbinic sources, Sephardic genealogy, Holocaust sources, family reunions and newsletters, publishing your family history, visiting your ancestral towns, and more.

As experienced researchers, we realize the importance of organizing source material by locality and topic. For instance, if a researcher is visiting the National Archives in Washington, D.C., he would want to know about all the genealogical sources to be found there. On the other hand, if he is researching "passenger records," he will want to know about places where they can be found other than in the National Archives. Consequently, the Encyclopedia is accessible by both locality and topic.

In structuring this book, we concentrated on sources for Jewish genealogy while including, in many cases, listings for general genealogy research, such as libraries, vital record offices, courthouses, and historical societies.

Most entries in the Encyclopedia include a select bibliography, which should be considered a starting place, but by no means the "last word" on the subject.

The Encyclopedia also contains maps, photographs, excerpts from books, and sample documents. Among the appendices are listings of Jewish Genealogy Societies, Jewish Historical Societies, Regional Federal Archives and Records Centers, and other detailed listings to guide the researcher in his quest.

Some believe that the search for family history is, at its deepest level, a spiritual longing. In his book *Teshuvah* (Free Press, 1982), an important guidebook for Jews who are seeking a stronger connection with Jewish tradition, Rabbi Adin Steinsaltz devotes a chapter to the importance of heritage and family. He writes:

The search for roots, even in the simplest genealogical sense, is likely to be a meaningful experience on both the personal and religious levels. But it is important to pursue it even if the meaning is elusive. Lineage is not just a matter of empty self-congratulation. All lineage, and not just that of nobility, carries with it a certain responsibility. A great person discovered among one's ancestors is not just a cause for bragging but something that must be related to and learned from. The sense of kinship with such a figure can be a source of strength and encouragement to one suffering spiritual distress or self-doubt. It need not be a famous or distinguished figure; even a person—remembered or reconstructed—who was at one with himself and with the world can serve as an anchor point and source of commitment. Such connections represent, in a sense, a broadening of the commandment to "honor thy father and thy mother," a commandment described through the ages in terms of the obligation of the "branch" toward the "root" from which it sprang and that nourished it. Honor of parents and of earlier generations of forebears is connected, in turn, with *kibbud hamakom,* honoring the source of all human life. Strengthening one's ties with one's own past is part of renewing one's connectedness with the sources of Jewish life in general.

Beyond the memories and quasi-memories of one's forebears, there is also a practical significance of recovering their particular traditions. Though one may not be able to reconnect fully with the particular community they belonged to, one can at least adopt certain of their practices. Halakhically, this would not constitute following *minhag hamakom* or *minhag mishpahah* (local or family custom), but it could be highly meaningful. The very knowledge that a certain custom, style, or version comes down to one from one's own ancestors makes it compelling and alive in a way that can be very important for sustaining observance. Certain details, insignificant in themselves, can give one the feeling of following in his ancestors' footsteps, and this adds a dimension of warmth and intimacy to what might otherwise be a mechanical act. The very fact that one is giving new life to something with which one has an inner connection is meaningful.

From another less obvious point of view, an individual's relationship to a particular manner of observance is determined by his family's relationship to it. The tribes enter the sanctuary through the gates designated for them, though there are other ways of getting in. A given Jewish community's insistence on a particular way of doing things is not just a matter of obstinacy. It reflects a prolonged, only partly conscious process of natural selection over many generations in which certain ritual affinities form and are strengthened. There is an inner connection between a particular community or family and its customs. Thus the *ba'al teshuvah,* returning to the primary sources of his Jewish being, is bound to feel an especially deep resonance with those forms of expression associated with his own origins, and these forms are likely to serve him best in his quest for himself.

The search for familial roots and customs can be pursued in a variety of ways. Sometimes one discovers a great many relatives one did not know he had and realizes, too, that his relationship to them can be more than casual. Such encounters can provide a person with new ways of seeing himself. One can also learn a great deal from books describing life in the localities where one's family lived.

Of course, one also must exercise caution. Carried away with the sense of identification, one can lose sight of the ineradicable distance between the generations caused by differences in time and place. The affinity one sometimes feels for certain forebears, or the warmth and "homyness" one experiences in certain company, do not necessarily signify complete identity with them. Appearances can be deceiving. One cannot always "return" to the past, however much one may wish to. Nonetheless, while one can live without roots, it is better to hold on to them. It is especially valuable for the *ba'al teshuvah,* who must sever so many of the connections in his life, to replace them with others. It is good for a Jew to know that, for all the loneliness his personal choice imposes on him, his life is nonetheless a continuation and an offshoot of a whole world that preceded him.

The editors of this volume and its many contributors join in hoping that the Encyclopedia will aid you in your family history research. We know in our hearts that we are not merely gathering facts to put on a family tree, but that we are rebuilding our shattered families and seeing where we come from to know where we are going.

Arthur Kurzweil
Miriam Weiner

Chapter 1

IMMIGRATION AND NATURALIZATION

INTRODUCTION

The only Americans who are not immigrants are native American Indians. The rest of us, the vast majority of us, arrived here a day ago, a year ago, a generation ago, a century ago. Each steamship that arrived in an American port carried not only new Americans, but also the spirit of the *Mayflower,* bringing people with hopes and dreams to their new home. This is what is special about America: in one way or another, most of us are newcomers, hoping for the peace and tranquility that can nourish a family.

Hidden within the files of archives and libraries throughout the United States are old pieces of paper testifying to the arrival of our ancestors. When the family historian discovers one of these documents, a silly piece of paper is transformed into a profound connection between past and future. [Eds.]

NATURALIZATION RECORDS: AN IMPORTANT GENEALOGICAL SOURCE

Arthur Kurzweil

Finding naturalization records is not like looking for a needle in a haystack. It can be worse. First, you have to find the haystack. (It's not easy to find the "haystacks" of naturalization records, since they are scattered all over the place, look different, and are often hidden under haystacks of other kinds of documents.) Once you find the haystack, looking for the needle (the papers that *you* want) requires you to have certain amounts of knowledge, skill—or luck. But the final problem is this: however difficult it might be to find a needle in a haystack, the saving grace is your assumption that the needle is in there somewhere. But in searching for naturalization records of an ancestor, you never know if you will find what you are looking for. In fact, you can never be sure that the documents even exist.

With that pessimistic introduction, we have to attempt to tackle the problem of naturalization records because they often are profoundly important sources

of information—genealogically. One personal illustration will suffice: after sending for my great-grandfather's naturalization records, I received a reply from the Immigration and Naturalization Service, which gave me my great-grandfather's birth date, place of birth (in Europe), place of last residence (in Europe), his first wife's name (she died in Europe and never came to America), the date of his arrival (this allowed me to get a copy of the passenger list of the ship), and the names and birth dates of all his children—some of whom were killed in the Holocaust and whom I would never have been able to learn much about!

How did I get the document that provided me with so much information? I simply sent a letter to the Immigration and Naturalization Service telling them what I wanted. They sent back a form. I filled it out. And in a few weeks I received the information. All for $15.00.

If it's that easy, then what was the "needle in a haystack" business all about?

The answer is that it can be easy, or it can be terribly difficult, depending on when your immigrant ancestor arrived in America and petitioned to become a citizen.

But let's start at the beginning. We are looking for naturalization records, better known as citizenship papers. On your family tree, only your immigrant ancestors might have naturalization records on file. Ancestors of yours who never came to America would not have become citizens, obviously, and those ancestors (or family members) who were born in the United States were automatically citizens—and therefore never had to fill out papers. But for your immigrant relatives, citizenship papers might very well be on file somewhere in the United States. As a genealogist, you should be interested in finding those records.

There are three different types of naturalization records. The first is the *Declaration of Intention,* which was filled out by an immigrant who wanted to become a citizen. This Declaration of Intention was commonly known as one's "first papers." Then there is the *Final Petition,* which was completed just prior to becoming a citizen. And finally there is the *Certificate of Naturalization,* which is the document given to the new citizen that declares that citizenship has been granted. (See also: National Archives, Passenger Arrival Records.)

Among old family papers you can often find the Certificate of Naturalization, but this is the least valuable document in terms of information about the individual. The Declaration of Intention and the Final Petition are the most valuable because they often asked several personal questions of genealogical interest, such as occupation, date and place of birth, name of ship and date of arrival, and details on spouse and children.

There are a few more things to know before we discuss the locations of naturalization records. While we may assume that immigrants became citizens (unless we know for sure that someone did not), it is possible that an immigrant ancestor of yours never applied for citizenship. Indeed, you may have a grandparent still alive who was an immigrant and who is not a citizen.

Also be aware of the fact that children under 16 automatically became citizens when their parents were naturalized, and furthermore that until 1922 a wife automatically became a citizen either by marrying a citizen or by the naturalization of her husband.

As odd as it may sound, the key date in the story of naturalization records is September 26, 1906. It was on that date that citizenship procedures became a federal function. If you are looking for the naturalization records of someone who was naturalized on or after September 26, 1906, you will usually have an easy time of searching. How do you know if your ancestor was naturalized on or after this date? You don't. But by asking a few questions within your family, you will probably have a good sense of when the immigration occurred and therefore when the naturalization could possibly have taken place.

If you have reason to believe that the naturalization of interest to you took place after this date, you are advised to write to:

U.S. Immigration and Naturalization Service
425 I Street NW
Washington, D.C. 20536

Ask them for a few copies of *Form G-641* (Application for Verification of Information from Immigration and Naturalization Service Records). Don't write them a long letter describing your great-grandmother and her trip to America or any other information of a personal nature. No matter what you write, however long, short, or interesting, if it has to do with naturalization records, they will send you Form G-639. So, you might as well ask for it right from the start. And again, ask for a few; it will save you time when you want more.

Fill out the form as best you can. Do not be alarmed when you find that you cannot fill out but 3% of the form. The Immigration and Naturalization Service has the nice policy of working with whatever information you can give them. If *all* you have is your ancestor's name, then fill that in and leave everything else blank. But the more you can fill out, the better chance you have of locating the document—or the right document. (Once, when all I knew was the person's name, I received the papers of someone with the same name, but of an entirely different individual.)

After you fill out the form and send your check (current fee is $5.00), you will wait a few weeks (sometimes more) and will hopefully receive the information you are looking for (see also pp. xx–xx, "Freedom of Information Act"). One thing I have yet to figure out is the Immigration and Naturalization Service policy on sending information. Sometimes I receive photocopies of the desired documents and sometimes I receive a letter containing a transcription of the information on the original documents.

What if you are sure that a person was naturalized but the Immigration and Naturalization Service tells you they have nothing? Then, either the person was

naturalized before September 26, 1906, or a clerk made a mistake. As far as a clerical error is concerned, all you can do is try again (unless you want to—and are able to—examine the documents yourself, which will be discussed in a little while). But if the person was naturalized before the key date, then the fun begins.

Before September 26, 1906, naturalizations were a local function, and naturalization proceedings took place in just about any court, federal, state, or local. Although naturalizations took place in courts around the country before September 26, 1906, it was only after that date that the courts were required to send the information to the federal government for processing and filing.

Besides the lack of centralization of these documents before 1906, the procedures also varied. Therefore, different questions were asked of the potential citizen and different records were kept. So, whereas the type of information on post-1906 naturalization records is basically standard, the pre-1906 information varies from next to nothing (person's name and country of origin) to varying amounts of data.

Let us say that you are looking for the naturalization records of someone who arrived in the United States well before September 26, 1906. I say "well before" because if the immigrant arrived shortly before that cutoff date, there is still a good chance that the naturalization took place after the 1906 date. It is here where excellent detective work is essential. What you must try to determine is where the immigrant whose papers you are looking for entered the United States (which port) and where he or she resided right after arrival.

Once you have determined this (to any degree of accuracy), you must try to determine to which court the immigrant might have gone to file "first papers." Of course, there is no guarantee that the immigrant filed for citizenship immediately upon arrival. He might have waited 10 years (at which time he could have been living in another city) or he could have never gotten around to becoming a citizen.

But we have to assume that the immigrant became a citizen, and we must also begin somewhere in our search. The best bet is to start at the location where the person entered the country and first resided. Finding the right court is not easy. It takes patience, time, and lots of letter writing—unless you can travel to the city in mind, in which case you might either get the search done quickly or you might reach a dead end. If this all sounds very negative, it is meant to.

The process of searching for pre-1906 naturalization records can be difficult, especially if you have little information to go on. Of course, if someone entered the United States in Boston and then spent all his life there, the search would not be too difficult. You would have the "field" narrowed, and it would just be a limited amount of leg work. But the more vague your information is, the more difficulty you will have.

An excellent book that tackles this very problem head-on is well worth the purchase or use if you are searching for naturalization records. This book is *Locating Your Immigrant Ancestors, A Guide to Naturalization Records,* by James C. Neagles and Lila Lee Neagles, published in 1975 (see Bibliography at end of chapter). The bulk of this volume is a state-by-state, county-by-county listing of courts and what records they have for what years. In addition, if the records are indexed, the book will indicate this. (The subject of indexing is quite important, since locating the court of a certain naturalization is not the same as locating the document that you want; if the documents are not indexed in some way, then you are looking for a needle in a barn!)

While we are on the subject of indexes, we might as well discuss a body of indexes of naturalization records that can save years of work, depending on the location you are dealing with. During the Great Depression, the Works Progress Administration (WPA) put people to work doing various interesting and unusual tasks. One of them was the mimeographing and indexing of pre-1906 naturalization records for certain locations. If the naturalization you are looking for took place in Maine, Massachusetts, New Hampshire, Rhode Island, or New York City, you're in luck. The National Archives and the regional branches in Bayonne, New Jersey, and Waltham, Massachusetts, have the Soundex indexes and photocopies for these New England states and New York City (see "District of Columbia" in Chapter 2, p. 000).

Since New York City was not only the entering point for most Jews to the United States but also the home of the greatest number of Jews, it would be justified to go into more detail here regarding naturalization resources for New York City.

The Federal Archives and Records Center located in Bayonne, NJ (Building 22 at the Military Ocean Terminal) has an excellent collection of naturalization records for New York City. (See next section for a summary of naturalization holdings in Bayonne.)

The holdings in Bayonne are a large, but not complete, collection of New York City naturalizations. For example, the county clerk of each county in New York has the records of those naturalizations that occurred in the State Supreme Court of that particular county. Other records are scattered elsewhere as well. In fact, this situation of the noncentralization of these records is a good example of what the researcher often has to face when trying to locate naturalization records.

A trip to the Records Center in Bayonne would be worthwhile for all people doing searches of these documents for the New York City area (see also under "New York" in Chapter 2, p. 000). If you are unable to travel to Bayonne, you can write them at:

National Archives and Records Service
Federal Archives and Records Center
Archives Branch
Building 22—MOT Bayonne
Bayonne, NJ 07002
(201) 858-7245

There is one important reason why a trip to the Records Center (or any archives) is worthwhile. A clerk will try to answer a specific question, but in my opinion, you and you alone can do an adequate search. You can look for a dozen alternate spellings of a name while a clerk will usually only check the spelling provided. In addition, every researcher knows that you always learn more than just what you are looking for—*if* you do it yourself!

Finding naturalization records is not easy but is certainly worthwhile. Be aware, of course, that the earlier the naturalization took place, the less information there is likely to be. However, you can never know what you might find until you try.

Adapted from *Toledot,* Fall 1977.

IMMIGRATION RECORDS IN FEDERAL COURT RECORDS
Arlene H. Eakle

There has been much emphasis on the immigration records to be found in local courts, including Declarations of Intent, Final Petitions, Certificates of Naturalization, and evidence of immigrant origins that appear in apprenticeships, voters' lists, and church and property records. Research guides and how-to books discuss these records by category and advise the genealogist to consult all courts, referencing local and state courts for the most part. Often overlooked are the federal courts in each state that have jurisdiction over naturalization as well as other matters.

See Appendix C (pp. 157–162), which lists federal courts by state and the dates and record categories they created: minutes books and court journals are included for some. Every court—district and circuit—kept minutes in which naturalization matters were referenced. For early years, the minutes entry may be the only documentation of your ancestor's citizenship, especially where separate volumes or loose papers do not begin until after 1850. These minutes books can be found in the National Archives and in the possession of the district court clerks today. A summary of such holdings has not yet been compiled, but see the bibliography at the end of the chapter for important references.

U.S. IMMIGRATION, PASSENGER RECORDS, AND STEAMSHIP RESEARCH
Michael Brenner

One of the most productive records for genealogists to research is the arrival records of immigrant ancestors. The National Archives, and its regional branches, many local research libraries, and the LDS Family History Library (see Utah, pp. 128–133) have microfilm copies of part or all of the arrival records. Additionally, they can be purchased or borrowed from various private companies. Passenger records for vessels arriving from approximately 1820 (1800 for Philadelphia) through the mid-1950s are available for the main ports on the East, Gulf, and West coasts. Lately, the National Archives has begun to make available records of persons who crossed the border from Canada, and for additional minor ports.

The collections are in two parts—earlier records called Customs Records and later records called Immigration Records. The following is a list of what records are available for the various ports and the indices for each:

Customs Records
1820–1873 *Various* Atlantic-Gulf of Mexico and (Great) Lake Ports
Alphabetical Index 1820–1874

3

1820–1897	*Baltimore Lists*
	Soundex Index 1820–1897
	Alphabetical Index 1833–1866
1820–1891	*Boston Lists*
	Alphabetical Index 1848–1849
1820–1902	*New Orleans Lists*
	Alphabetical Index 1853–1899
1820–1897	*New York Lists*
	Index 1820–1846
1800–1882	*Philadelphia Lists*
	Index 1800–1906

Immigration Records

1890–1924	*AL, FL, GA, and SC Lists*
	Index
1891–1909	*Baltimore Lists*
	Soundex Index 1897–1952
1891–1943	*Boston Lists*
	Index 1902–1906
	Index 1906–1920
	Crew Lists 1917–1943 (by date)
1918–1943	*Gloucester, MA, Crew List*
1898–1945	*Key West (no index) List*
1902–1942	*New Bedford List*
	Index 1902–1954
	Crew Lists 1917–1943
1903–1945	*New Orleans List*
	Index 1900–1952
	Crew List 1910–1945
1897–1957	*New York (incl. Crew List) Lists*
	Index 1897–1902
	Soundex 1902–1948
1883–1945	*Philadelphia Lists*
	Soundex 1883–1948
1893–1943	*Portland, ME, Lists*
	Index 1893–1954
1911–1943	*Providence Lists*
	Index 1911–1954
1906–1945	*Savannah Lists*

Recent Acquisitions

St. Albans, VT, District Records
    Canadian Pacific and Atlantic Ports
        Soundex 1924–1952
        Lists 1895–54
    Canadian Border Entries
        Soundex 1895–1924
        Lists 1929–1949
    Small Ports in VT
    Alphabetical Index 1895–1924
Detroit
    Lists 1906–1954
    Card Manifest 1946–1957
Galveston
    Index 1896–1951
    Lists 1896–1948
San Francisco
    Index 1893–1934
    Lists 1893–1957
        Various Lists and Indices
        Honolulu Separate
Washington
    Seattle Lists 1890–1957
    Pt. Townsend/Tacoma Lists 1894–1909

In addition to the customs and immigration lists with their various indices, there exists for selected ports a *book index*. These are microfilmed records kept or provided by the various steamship lines that alphabetically list the passengers on each ship, by class of passage. They can appear as ledger binders or, for later ships, as actual printed passenger list booklets given to the passengers. The National Archives filmed these by years, then alphabetically by name of the shipping line and then by ship, in order of its arrival at the port, then within each by class of service, i.e., 1st class, 2nd class, 3rd class, or steerage, and, finally, alphabetically within each class. These book indices are not complete for all ports and all years. Following is a list of the ports for which a book index exists and the dates of the collection:

Boston	1899–1940
New York	1906–1942
Philadelphia	1906–1926
Portland, ME	1907–1930
Providence	1911–1934

Since the publication of the source material used, the National Archives has begun to release additional years of passenger lists and lists from additional ports. Current information can be obtained directly from the National Archives (see pp. 31–33).

Some explanation is needed of what is in each of the different types of records. The earlier lists (customs lists) usually asked for only the passenger's *name, age, sex, occupation, country of origin,* and *destination country.* The lists beginning in 1893 were expanded by law, and additional questions included *marital status, ability to read and write, nationality (race), last legal residence,* and *name and address of person going to.* It was not mandatory for all shipping lines to switch to the expanded format and, as you research, you can find the use of the old form for years subsequent to 1893. In 1910, additional information was requested, and again not all shipping lines used the new forms immediately which asked all the above questions plus *language-could read and write, last permanent residence, name* and *address of nearest relative from whence came,* and *place of birth (city and country).*

One area usually neglected by researchers is a section at the end of the individual ship passenger and crew list for *detained passengers.* These begin with the opening of Ellis Island and list those passengers detained, the page and line number of the passenger list they can be found on, and the number of meals given to them. When researching a particular ship, if you cannot locate your ancestor, the detained list should be reviewed, since this portion is usually typed and is easier to read. If found, the entry will refer back to the page and line number for the person being sought. Also, when searching the index or Soundex (see District of Columbia, pp. 31–33) for the arrival records, if a particular person cannot be found, search for family members who traveled with them. The indices are not 100% complete; therefore, searching for traveling companions will increase your chance of success.

If research in person at the National Archives or other facility is not possible, then there is a mail-in procedure. Using National Archives *Form 81,* the staff of the National Archives will search the index, notify you if the record is found and request payment at that time. Passenger research can also be done for the port of embarkation. Records exist for the port of Hamburg and for the British ports. See *later in this chapter.*

Sources of Ship Name and Year Immigrated

The Federal Census for 1900 asked questions regarding year of immigration, number of years in the

Ship manifest for S.S. Numidian sailing from Glasgow to Boston, arriving on February 29, 1904, showing passenger Alexander Rapkin (last line) as a male, age 30, last residing in Chernigow, a Hebrew, $70 in possession, destined for brother-in-law in Boston.

United States, and whether naturalized. The 1910 census asked year of immigration and whether naturalized. Many state censuses also asked the same questions. If the census return shows that the person was naturalized, then the Declaration of Intent will show the date arrived, port, and ship name, immediately allowing you to go to the correct microfilm roll and review the passenger arrival record.

Passport applications also ask for date and port of arrival, and ship name. The pre-1906 passport applications are at the National Archives main building; those from 1906–1923 are held at the National Archives branch in Suitland, Maryland. For records of 1923 and later, you must write to:

U.S. State Department
Passport Office
1425 K Street, N.W.
Washington, D.C. 20420

Passports for most years prior to 1941 were not required; therefore, the record for an ancestor may or may not be in existence, depending on whether a passport was obtained (see pp. 35–36).

Least productive as a source of arrival date would be family legend or searching city directories for the first entry of the person sought. This will at least give the latest date to search. Do not overlook older relatives' scrapbooks, or boxes of family documents for passenger tickets, health certificates, or old photos of the voyage. If only a ship or port and year are known, the *Morton Allan Directory of Arrivals, 1890–1930*, can help (see later in this chapter). From this source, you can narrow the search down to specific dates within a year that ships arrived from a specific port.

Ship Research

A natural outgrowth of searching passenger lists is the desire to see a picture of the ship or at least read of its history.

Fortunately, there are societies that research and collect information on steamships. These societies can provide copies of the photos in their collection or provide a copy of these documents for a fee. Prior to contacting a society, you should do preliminary research about the ship. This research will give you the year built (to determine if you are researching the correct ship), since the same name can be used consecutively for different ships; a ship may go out of service, but the name could and would be used again. Also, if you have the history of a ship, you will know by what names it was known in different years and which shipping line owned it. If you cannot find a photo under the ship name you know it had when your ancestor sailed, you can then search under the name it may have been changed to. For example:

The SS *Westphalia*	Built 1868 as SS *Westphalia* (German owners)
	Sold 1887–1988, renamed SS *Atlantic* (British owners)
	Sold 1888–1889, renamed SS *Provincia di San Paulo* (Italian owners)
	Sold 1889–1890, renamed SS *Mentana* (Italian owners)
	Sold 1890–1901, renamed SS *Sud American* (scrapped in 1901)

If you are unable to locate a ship photo or details under the name *Westphalia* from German sources, it might be possible to locate it under the name *Atlantic* or *Provincia di San Paulo* from Italian or British sources.

Some excellent sources of ship history and photographs can be found in the following books: *North Atlantic Seaway* by N.R.P. Bonser; *Passenger Liners of the Western Ocean* by C.R. Vernon Gibbs; *Merchant Fleets in Profile* by Duncan Hawes; *Lloyds Register of Shipping*, published annually by Lloyds of London; *Ships of Our Ancestors* by Michael Anuta (photos only); *Passenger Liners of the World Since 1893* by Nicholas T. Cairis; and *Passenger Ships of the World: Past and Present* by Eugene W. Smith.

These books will give details of the ship, its history, and possibly a line drawing of the ship in profile. Some also have extensive photo sections.

Providing this information will help the various ship societies locate the material you want. The major American societies that have large photo collections are:

Steamship Historical Society of America
University of Baltimore Library
SSHSA Collections
1420 Maryland Avenue
Baltimore, Maryland 21201

(See also Baltimore, pp. 58–60.)

Mariners Museum
Newport News, Virginia 23606

Peabody Museum
East India Square
Salem, Massachusetts 01970

After describing the ship you are looking for and providing the year of interest, you will be advised by the society as to which photos they have and the cost of reproduction, which varies from library to library and is usually nominal.

There are also excellent sources available in Europe for information about the steamships that carried immigrants to this country. If they sailed from Bremen or Hamburg, Germany, they would have sailed on the Hamburg-American Line (Hamburg) or the Norddeutscher-Lloyd Line (Bremen). The successor company to these two world famous lines has a large archive of photos concerning their ships, and they have been extremely helpful in providing photos. You can write them at:

HAPAG-Lloyd A.G.
Postfach 102626
2000 Hamburg 1, Germany

For ship photos from other German lines, try:

Museum of Hamburgische Geschichte
D2000 Hamburg 36
Holstenwall 24, Germany

Deutsches Schiffahrts Museum
Van Ronzelen Strasse
2850 Bremerhaven-Mitte, Germany

The repository of information for ships that sailed for any of the Italian-owned lines would be:

Registro Italiano Navale
Cesella Postale 1195
Via Corsica 12
16128 Genova, Italy

Again, these resources will advise what information they have on the ship in question and the cost of reproduction. It is helpful, after your initial research of the history of the ship, to write to more than one of these sources and to advise them of the ship in question under the different names it was known and the year it held each name.

The greatest source of ship information is the National Maritime Museum located in England. It holds records of ships built in England and Scotland as well as ships owned by all British-controlled shipping lines. Prior to the 1880s most steamships were built by British shipbuilders. This museum is a major source of information on English and other European shipping companies.

The National Maritime Museum holdings include many photos, blueprints, and some ship histories. Correspondence should be addressed to:

National Maritime Museum
Greenwich Old Royal Observatory
London SE 10 9NF, England

Since almost all ships are insured by Lloyds of London, over the years they have also become a collector of information about the world's ships. Each year they publish the *Lloyds Register*, which lists alphabetically every registered ship in the world. This is a good secondary source of information about a ship and when it was built. If the ship sailed for English, Italian, or German owners, the information you need should be there.

Lloyds can also be a source of ship photos. Their address is:

Leed Librarian
Lloyds Shipping Register
Lime Street
London EC 3M 7HA, England

When all else fails, go the route of attending shows of your local postcard collectors club. Since postcards were an early form of advertising, many shipping lines used this medium to extoll the virtues of their ships, and color photographs were used extensively.

EASTERN EUROPEAN JEWISH EMIGRATION VIA THE PORT OF HAMBURG: 1880–1914

Jürgen Sielemann

Between 1880 and 1914, almost three million Jews left Eastern Europe, representing the most extensive migration in Jewish history since the expulsion of Jews from Spain at the end of the 15th century. Most of the emigrants fled from Russia, where, especially in 1881, 1903, and 1905, horrible pogroms had raged, and where the laws of Czar Alexander III had oppressed Jewish life. Another large number of Jews emigrated from Austria-Hungary and Romania where they left a world of poverty and hostility. Most of them came to the United States in search of freedom, peace, and prosperity.

In 1880, at the beginning of the extensive migration, almost four million Jews lived in Russia. Galicia was part of the Austria-Hungary empire at that time where the number of Jewish inhabitants amounted to about 800,000, whereas about 200,000 Jews lived in Romania.

A considerable number of European Jews emigrated via German ports. There are statistics for the period between 1905 and 1914 that indicate approximately 700,000 European Jewish emigrants sailed from Germany. Hamburg and Bremen were the most important ports of embarkation; almost five million people left Europe via these ports between 1890 and 1914. Other German ports were used less extensively. Only 7,000 passengers embarked from Emden, Wilhelmshaven, and Stettin in the years of their greatest importance as emigration ports (1888–1898).

The port of Hamburg was preferred for several reasons, most notably for its convenient geographic location and its traffic conditions. Since the 1880s, Hamburg had been connected with several Eastern European countries by a well-developed railway network. Another reason why so many emigrants decided to travel via Hamburg was the "Hamburg Amerikanische Packetfahrt-Aktiengesellschaft," abbreviated HAPAG. The HAPAG was a shipping company that specialized in the transfer of passengers to the United States and owed its rapid growth mainly to the vast numbers of Eastern Europeans who were emigrating here. Before World War I, the HAPAG became the greatest passenger line in the world. The agents of the HAPAG tried to engage as many passengers as possible by offering economical fares and by intensive propaganda techniques in Eastern Europe. When the government of Hungary proposed to direct the emigration across the Mediterranean port of Fiume in 1904, the HAPAG was powerful enough to prevent the plan, and Mediterranean and Russian ports were eliminated as competition for the HAPAG.

The exact number of European Jews who emigrated via Hamburg is unknown because there are no statistics based on the religion of the emigrants. Also, the passenger lists of the emigration ships, from 1850 to present, which are kept in the State Archives of Hamburg, do not state religion prior to 1920. We do know that 1,200,000 Russians emigrated between 1880 and 1914 and that 1,100,000 emigrated from Austria-Hungary. These figures are based on yearly statistics made up by the office that had control over emigration via the port of Hamburg.

In 1911, Samuel Joseph stated that 62% of the Russians who emigrated to the United States between 1886 and 1898 were Jewish. If we take this figure (62%) as a basis for the whole period, it can be determined that from 1880 to 1914 about 730,000 Russian Jews emigrated via Hamburg; this figure almost accounts for half of all Russian Jews who reached the United States in that period.

In a similar manner, the number of Jews who emigrated from Austria-Hungary via Hamburg can be calculated using the data of Michael Traub. According to Traub, 7.5% of all Austrian and Hungarian emigrants bound for the United States between 1899 and 1914 were Jewish. Taking this percentage as a basis for the whole period, then, 85,000 Jews emigrated from that monarchy via Hamburg between 1880 and 1914.

Therefore, together with the smaller number of Romanian Jews and those European Jews who had been living for a while in Germany before they left the continent, the total number of European Jews emigrating via Hamburg from 1880 to 1914 approaches 1,000,000.

After the horrible pogrom of 1881, when Czar Alexander III oppressed Jewish life by degrading laws, the number of emigrants rose continuously until 1891, the year of the expulsion of the Jews of Moscow.

The 1907 Hamburg-America Line. (Courtesy of Hamburg State Archives)

There were further pogroms in Russia in 1903 and 1905.

The lodging houses for Jewish emigrants awaiting departure of their ship were regulated in such a way that the travelers were allocated to licensed landlords, who were supervised and periodically inspected by the Board of Emigration in order to control transit, provide security for ships, prevent epidemics, provide travelers with information, and protect them from fraudulent practices of the so-called "Litzer." The "Litzer" worked for the clerks of the shipping companies, landlords, and for special stores selling useful and useless utensils for the voyage, and for money changers. They were paid a commission on each customer they brought. In the year preceding 1890, about 40 lodging houses with a total of 1,200 beds were licensed. As the emigrants did not arrive in a steady flow, but in very differing numbers, it sometimes was not easy to arrange accommodations. For instance, between October 1881 and October 1882, when masses of refugees fled from Russian pogroms, about 10,000 Jewish emigrants were brought with extra trains from the Galician town of Brody to Hamburg. Members of the Jewish community of Hamburg very quickly reacted to their misery. In 1881, they founded a relief organization for the Russian Jews, which took care of the emigrants from their arrival at the railway station to the departure of their ships. In 1892, there were 23 German committees that cared for Jewish emigrants from Russia. But who supported the Jewish emigrants coming from Galicia, other parts of Austria-Hungary, or Romania? It was Daniel Wormser, a teacher for the Hamburg Talmud-Torah-School who decided to stop the misery of the non-Russian Jewish emigrants in Hamburg as best he could.

One day he saw a crowd of about 400 non-Russians sitting helplessly in front of the Hamburg Jewish Community Office. Daniel Wormser succeeded in lodging them all. In 1884 he founded the "Israelitic Union for the Relief of Homeless People" which provided accommodations and food, paid for medical care and for ship tickets. Wormser did his best to collect the needed money, but it was not easy, and he never got enough to relieve all the emigrants' need. Fortunately, he became acquainted with an aristocrat who lived in Paris, Baron Moritz von Hirsch, who was not only very rich but also a very humane person. In the following

Dining hall of Gottschalck Lodging House, Hamburg, Germany. (Photo courtesy of Hamburg State Archives)

years, Moritz von Hirsch donated so much money to Daniel Wormser's union that Wormser was able to help thousands of emigrants.

In 1891 the Hamburg government ordered the Hamburg-America Line to better the housing situation of the emigrants. Indeed, the available overnight accommodation was not sufficient in the least.

On a site provided by the city on the America Quai, the HAPAG erected eight big sheds. There was room for 1,400 persons. The emigrants only had to pay one mark per day for accommodations and full board. The police authority took over the management of these huts. Daniel Wormser cared for the new emigration camp very eagerly. Through his activities, the Jewish emigrants could get kosher meals and attend services in a synagogue which was consecrated at the America Quai in 1896.

In July of 1892, the emigrant camp was ready for use. In late summer of that year, a terrible cholera epidemic raged in Hamburg. The conditions of emigration via Hamburg changed fundamentally. In the spring of 1892, cases of cholera had been diagnosed in southern regions of Russia, and now nearly everyone was sure the Russian emigrants carried the epidemic. Robert Koch, the famous explorer of the vibrio comma and in later days winner of the Nobel prize, visited the emigrant camp at the America Quai and stated that Russian emigrants caused the outbreak of cholera. Later research proved he was wrong. In actual fact, the cholera was introduced by French sailors.

However, the Russian emigrants were isolated as well as possible. The emigrant trains no longer stopped in the city, but were directed straight to the America Quai. Those who were in possession of steerage tickets were not allowed to leave the train before the emigration camp was reached.

There, the emigrants were medically examined and their clothing and baggage were disinfected.

After the outbreak of the cholera epidemic, every Russian emigrant was kept in quarantine for several days. The German border to Russia was closed for all those emigrants who intended to sail as steerage passengers. Nevertheless many were able to cross the border. In June 1893, the Hamburg authorities prohibited the embarkation of Russian steerage passengers completely.

The loss of the HAPAG ran into millions, and Albert Ballin, the famous managing director of the shipping company, tried to find a way out. He really was in a difficult situation, especially caused by very restrictive immigration laws of the U.S.A. Because of the laws in 1891 and 1893, neither very poor people (the so-called paupers) nor people suffering an epidemic or repugnant disease were allowed to immigrate. They had to return immediately, and the return-tickets were paid by the shipping company that sold the ticket for the voyage.

In 1900 Wormser died, but his work continued. Wormser had cared for the emigrants like a father. Of course, the missionary society of Hamburg tried to persuade many Jewish travelers to change their religion, sometimes by extortive methods. Wormser spared no pains to get all of them embarked without being baptized. Sometimes, in cases of undecided young people, he ordered their relatives to come to Hamburg. So, when suddenly the father appeared, the mind of the son often changed very quickly.

At the end of 1893, HAPAG and the shipping company, Lloyd of Bremen, offered the German government the opportunity to build control stations at the German-Russian border at their own cost. The purpose of these control stations would be to conduct medical examinations as well as determining whether the finances of the emigrants would be sufficient. The government agreed to this suggestion.

The control stations were established mainly at places where the Russian trains crossed the German border, for example in Bajohren, Eydtkuhnen, Tilsit, Illowo, Thorn, Posen, Ostrowo. The transfer to Hamburg or Bremen was only allowed to those emigrants who were in possession of a valid passport, a railroad ticket to the port of embarkation, and enough money in case their entry was refused in the US. They also had to enter into a contract with one of the German shipping companies, mainly HAPAG or Lloyd of Bremen, concerning their voyage. The control stations at the border were supervised by police authorities, but the shipping companies managed the control themselves.

The competitive struggle between HAPAG and Cunard had favorable effects for the emigrants. For example, in 1904 the HAPAG reduced the price for a ticket from Europe to the U.S. to 61 marks, which was equal to three English pounds at that time and really very cheap. Indeed, that price was not a great deal for the HAPAG, but the intention is quite clear as stated in a letter from HAPAG dated December 9, 1904. "If we don't make such a sacrifice, the passengers will be lost to England."

In 1900, the city required the emigration camp area for other purposes and HAPAG decided to build a completely new camp on an adjacent site in a district named Veddel. The camp was constructed in the form of pavilions. The pavilion system offered the advantage of better isolating persons with infectious diseases and made it possible to keep the sleeping rooms much smaller. Each of the pavilions contained dormitories for up to 40 persons, bathrooms, toilets, and a living room. The camp was opened in 1901 and offered space for initially 1,000 persons per day. After 1906, it could provide accommodations for 5,000 passengers daily.

After their arrival, the emigrants had a medical examination. If necessary, modern bathing and disinfecting facilities could be used for arriving guests, their clothing and luggage, prior to being transferred into the "clean" division. Emigrants suffering infectious diseases were taken to another division, an observation ward. A special kitchen prepared food strictly in accordance with Jewish ritual. The enormous capacity of the kitchens made it possible to serve more than 3000 meals per hour. There was not a wide choice of menu. Here is the daily bill of fare of 1907: In the morning: Tea or coffee with sugar, milk and white bread. At noon: Soup with meat and vegetable. In the evening: Tea or coffee with sugar, milk and white bread. The price for board and lodging amounted to 2 Mark per day. Normally the emigrants did not stay in the camp longer than five days.

HAMBURG PASSENGER LISTS

Daniel M. Schlyter

Introduction

During the last half of the 19th century and early 20th century, great surges of emigrants, including large numbers of German and eastern European Jews, left the European continent.

A great many of these Jews departed from Europe by way of Hamburg, Germany. The passenger lists of Hamburg are an excellent source of genealogical research. If your ancestor sailed from Hamburg, these passenger lists can provide much useful genealogical data, including the name of the town in Europe your ancestor came from. The passenger lists are available for the years 1850 to 1934. An extensive set of indexes makes these passenger lists easy to use (see Appendix D).

Of course, your ancestor may not have sailed from Hamburg. Hamburg is only one of several European ports from which Jewish emigrants sailed. Many European Jews embarked from Bremen, Le Havre, Amsterdam, Rotterdam, or Antwerp because those ports were easier to reach. The passenger lists of Le Havre have not yet been microfilmed by the Family History Library, and the records of the other ports have not been preserved.

Most of the European emigrants who departed through Hamburg went to the United States, but some emigrated to Australia, Argentina, Brazil, Canada, South Africa, and other places. If your ancestor went to any of these countries you can use the Hamburg passenger lists to determine exactly where he came from in Europe.

Research Value

In the passenger list you will find your ancestor with age, occupation, birthplace or last residence, the exact date of sailing, the name of the ship and the ship captain's name, as well as the ship's destination. Persons who traveled with your ancestor will be listed on the same page or at least in the same ship's passenger list. This can be very helpful to your research as it can provide names and ages of other family members, such as parents, brothers and sisters, and children, and the names of family friends.

The greatest value of the Hamburg passenger lists is that they always give a specific place of origin. In some cases, the place of origin recorded on these passenger lists is the town of last residence rather than the actual birthplace of the ancestor. But even last residence can be helpful to your genealogical research. It is true that you may be able to find your ancestor's place of origin by searching available records in the United States in the areas where he resided. However, American research sources often do not give a specific town or village of origin. Instead they often give only the country or province from where he came. In many cases, the Hamburg passenger lists, available at the Family History Library and its family history centers, are more readily accessible for research than many American sources.

European Emigration

The two most important ports for Jewish emigration were Hamburg and Bremen. Beginning about 1820, the small German city of Bremen developed a prosperous enterprise of shipping European emigrants to America. By 1845, Hamburg got involved in this profitable new business. Hamburg sent out agents to persuade emigrants to embark from Hamburg rather than Bremen.

Available statistics do not distinguish Jews from other emigrants. But between 1859 and 1891, 30 percent of all European emigrants departed from Hamburg. It was especially popular with emigrants from eastern Europe: East Prussia, Russia, Austria, and Hungary (including areas now in Poland and Czechoslovakia). Many Scandinavians also emigrated through Hamburg.

German Passenger Lists

During the periods of great emigration, the German authorities kept records of the departure of each person who left a German port. Shipping companies were required to submit a list of all emigrants leaving Bremen or Hamburg on ships with 25 or more passengers, but often lists were submitted with as few as one emigrant. These lists preserved such information as the passenger's name, home town, age, other family members, and occupation.

For Hamburg, these records have been gathered, bound, and indexed since 1850. The lists and indexes for Hamburg have been preserved and are available for research.

The Bremen passenger lists were not preserved. These lists were routinely destroyed every few years after statistical data was extracted. Beginning in the early 20th century, Bremen began preserving its passengers lists, but these surviving lists were destroyed in a World War II bombing raid.

Routes of Travel

European emigrants who left from Hamburg could sail either directly or indirectly to their destination. Most of those who embarked at Hamburg sailed directly to New York City. These emigrants are found on the "direct" Hamburg passenger lists. However, some emigrants chose the less expensive indirect route to America. These emigrants were recorded in the "indirect" passenger lists. Between 1850 and 1870, about 14 percent of all emigrants from Hamburg used indirect routes. Figures are not available for the years after 1870.

Most of the emigrants who traveled indirectly departed Hamburg for England, where they traveled overland to an English transatlantic port. Usually, these emigrants crossed England between Hull and Liverpool or between Leith and Glasgow. At Liverpool or Glasgow, they could book ship passage to New York. Other indirect routes took emigrants through London, Le Havre, and Antwerp.

Hamburg Passenger Lists at the Family History Centers

Because of the value of these records for locating European places of origin, the Genealogical Department of the Mormon Church became involved in various projects to obtain and preserve copies of the Hamburg passenger lists and indexes. In 1964, the Genealogical Library (now the Family History Library) received microfilms of the direct passenger lists and indexes. Then, in 1975, the library acquired microfilms of the indirect Hamburg passenger lists from the Hamburg Archives, thus completing the collection.

You can personally search for your ancestor in the Hamburg passenger lists using the microfilmed records available at the Family History Library or at any of its family history centers. If you don't want to conduct such a search yourself, you can arrange for a professional genealogical researcher to do it for you. You can get a list of accredited genealogists by writing to:

The Family History Library
35 North West Temple Street
Salt Lake City, Utah 84150

The original records are stored in the State Archives at Hamburg. In recent years, an Historic Emigration Office opened in Hamburg, which will search the passenger lists for you for a fee of approximately $30.00 per year.

Hamburg-Information GmbH
Neuer Jungfernstieg 5
D-2000 Hamburg 36
Germany

The Family History Library's collection consists of the following material on microfilm:

1. The *direct Hamburg passenger lists,* 1850–1934 (256 rolls of 35-mm microfilm).
   The direct lists for 1850 to 1854 are alphabetical. The surnames of heads of households are alphabetized by first letter only.
2. The *regular index* to the direct Hamburg passenger lists, 1855–1934 (126 rolls of 35-mm microfilm).
   The direct lists are indexed in small segments. Each index covers a year or part of a year. Surnames of heads of households are alphabetized by first letter only.
3. The *fifteen-year index* to the direct Hamburg passenger lists, 1856–1871 (ten rolls of 16-mm microfilm).
   This index includes the names of passengers sailing from Hamburg from 1856 to 1871 in one simple alphabetical listing. It is convenient to use, but is not complete.
4. The *indirect Hamburg passenger lists,* 1854–1910 (81 rolls of 35-mm microfilm).
   The indirect list for June–December 1854 is alphabetical. The surnames of heads of households are alphabetized by first letter only.
5. The *regular index* to the indirect Hamburg passenger lists, 1855–1910 (twelve rolls of 35-mm microfilm).
   The indirect lists are indexed in small segments. Each index covers a period of one or several years. Surnames of heads of households are alphabetized by first letter only.

How to Use the Passenger Lists

The following pages give detailed information on using:

- The fifteen-year index
- The regular indexes to the passenger lists
- The direct and indirect passenger lists

Fifteen-year index. The fifteen-year index is a card index made from the direct passenger lists for the years 1856 to 1871. It puts the names of passengers leaving from Hamburg during those years into one simple alphabetical listing. However, the index is incomplete. If you do not find your ancestor's name in this index, you will need to search the regular indexes.

To use the fifteen-year index:

1. Determine which film includes the section of the alphabet in which your ancestor's name should be listed. For example, if your ancestor was Anton Waltenspuel you would look on film number 884677.

2. Obtain the film and turn to the place in the alphabet where your ancestor's name should be listed. (*Note:* If your ancestor is not in the fifteen-year index, go on to the instructions for the regular indexes.)

3. The index card for Anton Waltenspuel gives the emigrant's name, age, occupation, and place of origin; family members are also listed. The index card also gives the year and page number of the original passenger list entry so that you can refer to the actual list. To find the original entry, see the section *Using the Passenger Lists.*

Using the Regular Indexes

Note: If your ancestor sailed from Hamburg between 1850 and 1854, skip this section and refer to the next section.

1. Using the register of film numbers for the direct index, determine the film number of the index for the date your ancestor departed. (The 1900 U.S. census can often provide year of arrival in United States.) In some cases, several volumes of material are on the same film (Bd [*Band*] volume). For example, both Bd 1 and Bd 2 are on film number 473070.

2. On the film, turn to the year your ancestor emigrated and the letter of the alphabet with which your ancestor's surname begins. (The year may be given at the beginning of each new letter or periodically throughout the index.) The names are only alphabetized by the first letter of the surname. Search through the names until you find your ancestor.

3. After you have found your ancestor's name in the index, write down the number following the name. This is the page number of the passenger list on which the name appears. (Sometimes the number is "dittoed" from the number above. Look at the top of the page and note the page number listed there. Then compare this with the page number by your ancestor's name.

4. Next, move back in the index from where the name is entered until you find the departure date (see the sample regular index entry). The dates are given in the order of day, month, year. For example 30/10/90 would be read as October 30, 1890. With the departure date and page number you are now ready to locate your ancestor in the actual passenger list.

5. If you do not find your ancestor in the alphabetical listing, he still may be listed in the index. Each letter of the alphabet was allotted a certain number of pages on which names could be indexed. When these pages were filled, the overflow names were continued under a letter of the alphabet that was not used much that year. For example, names beginning with "W" may have been continued at the end of the names beginning with "Q." Indication may or may not have been given when this occurred. Therefore, search at the end of other letters of the alphabet if your ancestor is not listed under the correct letter. If your ancestor's name begins with *Sch* check *after* the letter *S.* In some cases the *Schs* were alphabetized separately.

6. If you still do not find your ancestor in the index, follow these same instructions for the regular index to the indirect passenger lists.

Using the Passenger Lists

The passenger lists from 1850 through 1854 were arranged alphabetically so that there is no need for an index. Beginning in 1855, the lists are arranged by ship departure date.

1850–1854. If your ancestor departed during this period, proceed as follows:

1. Determine the film number of the passenger list for the time period in which your ancestor emigrated.

2. On the film, turn to the year your ancestor emigrated and the letter of the alphabet with which your ancestor's surname begins. The names are only alphabetized by the first letter of the surname. Search through the names until you find your ancestor listed.

1855–1934. If your ancestor departed during this time:

1. Depending on which index you found your ancestor listed in, use the direct or indirect lists section of this register to find the film number of the direct passenger lists for the time period when your ancestor departed.

2. Obtain the film. Turn to the page number given in the index and locate your ancestor's name on the page. (On some of the passenger lists there is a numbered page followed by one or more unnumbered pages before the next numbered page. If your ancestor's name does not appear on the numbered page given in the index, search the unnumbered pages following it.)

3. Several columns of information are given after the emigrant's name. These provide information useful to genealogists, including age, occupation, marital status, and place of origin or birthplace. However, the arrangement and titles of these columns vary according to the shipping line and year. A glossary of column titles used throughout the Hamburg passenger lists is provided below. By using this glossary and a German-English dictionary, it should be possible to determine what information the Hamburg passenger lists provide about your ancestor. The important information about your ancestor's place of origin is given in the third column. Please note that this is sometimes not the birthplace but rather the last place of residence.

Note: If you did not find your ancestor in the Hamburg passenger lists, there are several possible reasons:

Your ancestor did not sail from Hamburg. Other major ports were Bremen, Antwerp, Rotterdam, and Le Havre. The library has no passenger lists from these ports.

You failed to recognize your ancestor's name in the index or list. Repeat the process again more carefully. Many emigrants changed their names or the spelling of their names once they reached their new home. Search for all the possible alternative spellings of your ancestor's name if you cannot find it under the normal spelling. Also, children and wives are usually not indexed. Search the indexes for parents, guardian, or husband of your ancestor if he or she emigrated when young or married.

Glossary of Column Titles of Hamburg Passenger List

Alter: Age
Alter (in Jahren): Age (in years)
Alter-Jahre, Monate: Age—years, months
Anschrift in Deutschland: Address in Germany
Bd (Band): Vol. (volume)
(Bei deutschen Männern v. 17 bis 25 Jahren.) Ist die Entlassungsurkunde oder das Zeugniss 23 des Ausweges vorgelegt?: (For German men between 17 and 25 years.) Has the bill of release or testimony for Article 23 concerning a release been presented?
Bemerkungen: Remarks
Beruf: Calling, occupation

Beruf oder Beschäftigung: Calling or occupation

Bezeichnung des bisherigen Berufs: Indication of previous occupation

Bisheriger Stand oder Beruf: Previous status or occupation

Bisheriger Wohnort: Previous residence

Bestimmungsort: Destination

Datum d. Abgang: Date of departure

Davon sind: Of those the following are

Erwachsene: Adults

Erwachsene und Kinder über 8 Jahr.: Adults and children over 8 years

Familienstand (ledig, u.s.w.): Family status (single, etc.)

Geboren am: Born on, birth date

Geboren in: Born at, birth place

Geburts Datum: Birth date

Geburtsort: Birth place

Geburts und Wohnort: Birthplace and residence

Geschlecht—männlich, weiblich: Sex—male, female

Gewerbe: Profession, occupation

Herkunftsort: Place of origin

Im Staat oder in der Provinz: In the state or province

Kinder: Children

Konf.: Confirmed (Catholic, Lutheran, etc.)

Landes: From the country, nation (of)

Letzter Aufenthaltsort: Last place of temporary residence

Letzter Wohnort: Last place of residence

Name: Name

Name d. Schiffes: Name of the ship

Names des Vaters: Name of the father

Name und Vorname des Kindes: Surname and given name of the child.

Name—Zu, Vor: Name—last, first

Nationalität-Land, Volkstamm: Nationality–Nation and race

Ob kundig des Lesens, Schreibens: Whether knowledgeable of reading, writing

Ort: Place

Reiseziel in den Vereinigten Staaten (Staat und Stadt): Destination in United States (state and city)

Staatsangehörigkeit: Citizenship

Stand des Vaters: Occupation/status of the father

Stellung im Berufe: Position in profession

Strasse: Street

unter 1 Jahr.: Under one year

unter 8 Jahr.: Under eight years

Verheiratet oder ledig: Married or single

Vor und Familienname: Given and family name

Vorname: Given name

Vornamen: Given names

Wohin?: Where to, destination

Zahl der Personen: Number of persons

Ziel der Auswanderung, Ort und Land ist anzugeben: Destination, place and country should be given

Ziel der Auswanderung (Ort and Staat): Destination (place and country)

Ziel der Reise: Destination

Zivilstand: Marital status (married, single, etc.)

Zu and Vorname und Familie: Surname, given name, and family

Zuname: Surname

Material for this article was taken from *Register and Guide to the Hamburg Passenger List.* Copyright © 1987 by Corporation of the President of the Church of Jesus Christ of Latter-day Saints. Used by permission.

THE OTHER ELLIS ISLAND

Miriam Weiner

While the vast majority of our immigrant ancestors came through Ellis Island, from 1907 to 1914 thousands of East European Jews participated in a little-known episode in American Jewish history. They immigrated through the port of Galveston, Texas, and then were routed to towns throughout the Midwest, where lodging and jobs awaited them.

Because of the concentration of immigrant Jews in New York City and rising anti-Semitism in Russia around the turn of the century, Jewish leaders such as financier Jacob Schiff and the celebrated English writer Israel Zangwill felt that Jews should enter the United States through a port other than New York. Because of his knowledge of the railroads, Schiff proposed Galveston, which had good rail connections to points throughout the Midwest. He raised funds for the project including $500,000 from his own pocket.

In 1910, the Bureau of Immigration and Naturalization investigated the "Galveston Movement" to discover whether it was engaged in the illegal organization of immigration. The transcripts of these examinations are revealing. In the examinations, the immigrants—most of whom came from Russia—answered questions about their family origins, reasons for emigration, expectations of America, and their experiences on the voyage. Later, during interviews in their destination cities, they talked about their satisfaction (or lack of it) with conditions of employment.

In *Galveston: Ellis Island of the West* (1983), author Bernard Marinbach referred to 84 files he had examined as part of the research for his book. You can imagine my surprise and delight to discover that the last name on the list was Hirsch Zukerman—my grandmother's first husband! I quickly sent for a copy of the transcript and was mesmerized to read details of his voyage to Galveston.

> Q: Where did you obtain the money to purchase your ticket?
> A: My wife's mother sold her home and gave me the money.
> Q: What arrangements have you made for the support of your wife and children in Russia until such time as you are able to send them money?
> A: I left her without money.
> Q: How do you expect them to live?
> A: She will sell her clothes to buy something to eat.
> Q: Did she give you all the money resulting from the sale of her house?
> A: Yes.
> Q: How much did your mother-in-law receive for her house?
> A: 110 rubles.

This three-page interview revealed the desperate situation of my grandmother and her four young children. They were not to join Hirsch Zukerman for three long years. It is difficult to imagine how they survived during that time.

The interviews were conducted during the summer of 1910, both at the port of Galveston and in the cities where the immigrants settled. They contain a treasure of information about the immigrant and the family left behind.

According to Dr. Marinbach, the Industrial Removal Office in New York hired Morris D. Waldman to help oversee the settlement of the Galveston immigrants. Dr. Marinbach writes:

> In February (1908), Waldman embarked upon a tour of his own, to see for himself how bad conditions were throughout the West. Writing . . . from St. Louis, Waldman commented, "What I have seen thus far is enough to make one blue—men out of work everywhere, starvation staring them in the face. The charities here are crowded with applicants and some of them Galveston men." He concluded that it was useless at this time to persuade well-meaning communities to accept immigrants if these communities were actually unable to provide work.

Although the plan was controversial and short-lived, in its seven years, 10,000 Jews came through Galveston. The plan ended in 1914 because of new restrictions on immigration, rising anti-Semitism, and the threat of war.

These revealing transcripts can be found in the subject's immigration files (Record Group No. 85, Immigration File No. 52), and copies are available from the National Archives Records Center in Suitland, Maryland.

The actual ship's manifest records for the period 1895–1921, port of Galveston, are in the National Archives in Washington, D.C. Copies can be ordered from the National Archives, the Rosenberg Library in Galveston, and the Houston Public Library.

The Galveston Movement is the subject of a documentary film by Allen and Cynthia Salzman Mondell entitled *West of Hester Street* and has also been explored in numerous biographical works on Jacob Schiff.

MORTON ALLAN DIRECTORY OF EUROPEAN STEAMSHIP ARRIVALS

This work is intended as an aid in the use of the indexes to immigration passenger lists in the National Archives, which unfortunately are arranged by dates of vessels' arrival, thereunder by names of vessels or steamship lines, and only then by passengers' surnames.

The *Morton Allan Directory* provides something of a remedy to this problem. By year and steamship company, and thereunder by port of entry, it lists the name of the vessel the exact date of the vessel's arrival, and the port of embarkation, thus lowering the number of unknowns and making searching the indexes that much easier.

Reprinted from *Toledot*, 1981, Vol. 4, Nos. 1–2.

IMMIGRATION HISTORY TIDBITS
Suzan Fisher Wynne

United States legislation requiring the collection of immigrants' names was first passed in 1819. More detailed information was required in several later bills. Castle Garden, under the control of New York State, opened in 1855. Despite years of alleged abuses and mistreatment of immigrants, it wasn't until 1890 that the U.S. Treasury Department took control of New York's port for immigrants. A year later, Congress placed all immigration matters under federal control. New York refused to permit the federal authorities to use Castle Garden, and so, until Ellis Island opened in 1892, a temporary facility in Battery Park was used.

Also in 1892, the commissioner of the Immigration Service finalized an agreement with all steamship companies transporting immigrants to the United States to collect standard information about alien passengers. This questionnaire is actually the manifest that we now see at the Archives. A more stringent law was passed in 1902, and, a few years later, another law extended the information to be collected by a few items.

In 1897, Ellis Island burned, along with many immigration records stored in underground chambers. Until the new building opened in 1900, the Battery Park facility again served as the reception hall.

Many manifests were destroyed by water, fire, or mishandling and a listing in the *Morton Allan's Directory* is no guarantee that the manifest will be at the Archives. Unfortunately, when the films were taken during the Depression, the cards containing the indexed information were destroyed.

Bibliography

Allan, M. *Directory of European Passenger Steamship Arrivals for the Years 1890 to 1930 at the Port of New York and 1904 to 1926 at the Ports of Philadelphia, Boston & Baltimore.* Baltimore: Genealogical Publishing Co., Inc., 1979.

Bennett, M. *American Immigration Policies: A History.* Washington, DC: Public Affairs Press, 1963.

Brownstone, D. M., Frank, I., Brownstone, D. L. *Island of Hope, Island of Tears.* New York: Rawson, Wade Publishers, Inc., 1979.

Eakle, A., and Cerny, J. *The Source: A Guidebook of American Genealogy,* Chapters 6 (Court Records) and 15 (Tracing Immigrant Origins). Salt Lake City: Ancestry, Inc., 1984.

Filby, P. W., and Meyer, M. K. *Passsenger and Immigration Lists Index, 1538–1900.* Detroit: Gale Research Co., 1981–1986, 3 vols. (initial series), 5 vols. supplements. Index to printed sources only. *Bibliography of Passenger and Immigration Lists, 1538–1900* (Ibid., 1982–1985) lists the sources indexed, 2 vols.

Genealogical Research in the National Archives. Washington, DC: NARS Trust Fund Board, 1982.

Glazier, I. A., and Filby, P. W., eds. *Germans to America: Lists of Passengers Arriving at U.S. Ports, 1850–1855.* Wilmington, DE: Scholarly Resources Inc., 1988 (multi-vol.).

Handlin, O. *A Pictorial History of Immigration.* New York: Crown Publishers, Inc., 1972.

Heaps, W. *The Story of Ellis Island.* New York: Seabury Press, 1967.

Hutchinson, E. P. *Legislative History of American Immigration Policy, 1798–1965.* Philadelphia: University of Penn-

MORTON ALLAN
DIRECTORY

of

EUROPEAN PASSENGER STEAMSHIP ARRIVALS

FOR THE YEARS
1890 to 1930
AT THE PORT OF
NEW YORK
and
FOR THE YEARS
1904 to 1926
AT THE PORTS OF
NEW YORK, PHILA-
DELPHIA, BOSTON
and BALTIMORE

DISTRIBUTED BY

Immigration Information Bureau, Inc.,
-366 MADISON AVENUE   NEW YORK

MORTON ALLAN DIRECTORY   189

Year 1909

NORTH GERMAN LLOYD
Express Service
Bremen—New York
(Continued)

N. Y. Arrival	Steamer
May 11	Kronprinzes. Cecilie
May 18	K. Wm. der Grosse
May 26	Kaiser Wilhelm II
June 2	Kronprinz Wilhelm
June 8	Kronprinzes. Cecilie
June 16	K. Wm. der Grosse
June 22	Kaiser Wilhelm II
June 30	Kronprinz Wilhelm
July 7	Kronprinzes. Cecilie
July 13	K. Wm. der Grosse
July 20	Kaiser Wilhelm II
July 27	Kronprinz Wilhelm
Aug. 3	Kronprinzes. Cecilie
Aug. 17	K. Wm. der Grosse
Aug. 25	Kaiser Wilhelm II
Aug. 31	Kronprinz Wilhelm
Sept. 7	Kronprinzes. Cecilie
Sept. 14	K. Wm. der Grosse
Sept. 21	Kaiser Wilhelm II
Sept. 28	Kronprinz Wilhelm
Oct. 5	Kronprinzes. Cecilie
Oct. 13	K. Wm. der Grosse
Oct. 20	Kaiser Wilhelm II
Oct. 27	Kronprinz Wilhelm
Nov. 2	Kronprinzes. Cecilie
Nov. 16	Kaiser Wilhelm II
Nov. 30	Kronprinzes. Cecilie
Dec. 21	Kaiser Wilhelm II

NORTH GERMAN LLOYD
Regular Service
Bremen—New York

N. Y. Arrival	Steamer
Jan. 3	Rhein
Jan. 9	Brandenburg
Jan. 12	Main
Jan. 14	Pr. Fried'h Wilhelm
Jan. 25	Chemnitz
Jan. 28	Koenig Albert
Feb. 1	Neckar
Feb. 3	Grosser Kurfuerst
Feb. 13	Scharnhorst
Feb. 17	Brandenburg
Feb. 18	Pr. Fried'h Wilhelm
Feb. 19	Koeln
Feb. 27	Main
Mar. 2	Chemnitz
Mar. 3	Gneisenau
Mar. 15	Roon
Mar. 17	Scharnhorst
Mar. 23	Pr. Fried'h Wilhelm
Mar. 25	Rhein
Mar. 30	Brandenburg
Apr. 1	Yorck
Apr. 10	Wittekind
Apr. 11	Main
Apr. 14	Gneisenau
Apr. 23	Breslau
Apr. 27	Pr. Fried'h Wilhelm
May 5	Fried'h der Grosse
May 10	Berlin
May 18	Prinzess Alice
May 26	Bremen

NORTH GERMAN LLOYD
Regular Service
Bremen—New York
(Continued)

N. Y. Arrival	Steamer
June 1	P. Fried'h Wilhelm
June 9	Fried'h der Grosse
June 16	Grosser Kurfuerst
June 21	George Washington
June 30	Bremen
July 6	Pr. Fried'h Wilhelm
July 14	Fried'h der Grosse
July 20	Grosser Kurfuerst
July 26	George Washington
Aug. 4	Bremen
Aug. 12	Pr. Fried'h Wilhelm
Aug. 18	Fried'h der Grosse
Aug. 24	Grosser Kurfuerst
Aug. 30	George Washington
Sept. 7	Bremen
Sept. 13	Pr. Fried'h Wilhelm
Sept. 20	Main
Sept. 21	Fried'h der Grosse
Sept. 28	Grosser Kurfuerst
Oct. 4	George Washington
Oct. 13	Bremen
Oct. 19	Pr. Fried'h Wilhelm
Oct. 20	Neckar
Oct. 29	Barbarossa
Nov. 3	Grosser Kurfuerst
Nov. 11	George Washington
Nov. 12	Cassel
Nov. 17	Main
Nov. 25	Hannover
Nov. 26	Pr. Fried'h Wilhelm
Dec. 3	Rhein
Dec. 10	Neckar
Dec. 17	Breslau
Dec. 19	Zieten
Dec. 22	Roon
Dec. 28	Main

NORTH GERMAN LLOYD
Mediterranean—New York

N. Y. Arrival	Steamer
Feb. 8	Barbarossa
Feb. 19	Koenigin Luise
Feb. 27	Prinzess Irene
Mar. 4	Koenig Albert
Mar. 12	Neckar
Mar. 20	Barbarossa
Apr. 2	Koenigin Luise
Apr. 9	Prinzess Irene
Apr. 15	Koenig Albert
Apr. 21	Neckar
Apr. 24	Grosser Kurfuerst
Apr. 30	Barbarossa
May 13	Koenigin Luise
May 27	Prinzess Irene
June 4	Neckar
June 9	Koenig Albert
June 18	Barbarossa
June 22	Berlin
July 1	Koenigin Luise
July 8	Prinzess Irene
Aug. 3	Berlin
Aug. 18	Prinzess Irene
Sept. 2	Koenig Albert

NORTH GERMAN LLOYD
Mediterranean—New York
(Continued)

N. Y. Arrival	Steamer
Sept. 14	Berlin
Sept. 30	Prinzess Irene
Oct. 14	Koenig Albert
Oct. 27	Berlin
Nov. 11	Prinzess Irene
Nov. 25	Koenig Albert
Dec. 8	Berlin
Dec. 24	Prinzess Irene

NORTH GERMAN LLOYD
Bremen—Baltimore

Baltimore Arrival	Steamer
Jan. 6	Rhein
Jan. 15	Main
Jan. 29	Breslau
Feb. 5	Hannover
Feb. 14	Rhein
Mar. 1	Main
Mar. 5	Cassel
Mar. 13	Breslau
Mar. 27	Rhein
Apr. 2	Koeln
Apr. 12	Hannover
Apr. 22	Frankfurt
Apr. 25	Breslau
May 6	Rhein
May 19	Main
June 5	Koeln
June 10	Rhein
June 17	Breslau
June 24	Hannover
June 29	Main
July 15	Frankfurt
July 21	Cassel
Aug. 4	Breslau
Aug. 10	Main
Aug. 26	Chemnitz
Sept. 8	Cassel
Sept. 15	Rhein
Sept. 22	Main
Oct. 6	Breslau
Oct. 21	Neckar
Nov. 5	Chemnitz
Nov. 20	Main
Nov. 28	Hannover
Dec. 2	Brandenburg
Dec. 19	Breslau
Dec. 30	Main

NORTH-WEST TRANS-PORTATION LINE
Halifax—Rotterdam—Ham-burg—New York

N. Y. Arrival	Steamer
Feb. 21	Volturno
Mar. 20	Raglan Castle
Apr. 4	Volturno
Apr. 18	Uranium
May 8	Raglan Castle
May 16	Volturno
June 2	Uranium
June 23	Raglan Castle
July 4	Volturno

Morton Allan Directory of European Passenger Steamship Arrivals. Provides names of vessels and dates of arrival to New York, Philadelphia, Boston, and Baltimore during the early decades of the 20th century. Title page and samply entry.

sylvania Press, 1981.

Immigrant & Passenger Arrivals: A Select Catalog of National Archives Microfilm Publications. Washington, DC: National Archives and Records Administration, 1983.

Joseph, S. *Jewish Immigration to the United States from 1881 to 1910.* New York: AMS Press, Inc., 1967.

Marinbach, B. *Galveston: Ellis Island of the West.* Albany: State University of New York Press, 1983.

Neagles, J. C., and Neagles, L. L. *Locating Your Immigrant Ancestors: A Guide to Naturalization Records.* Logan, UT: Everton Publishers, Inc., 1975. New edition, 1986. Guide to local and state court holdings, based on questionnaires.

Novotny, A. *Strangers at the Door.* Riverside, CT: Chatham Press, 1971.

Pitkin, T. M. *Keepers of the Gate: A History of Ellis Island.* New York: New York University Press, 1975.

Stephenson, G. *A History of American Immigration,* 1820–1924. New York: Russell & Russell, Inc., 1964. (First published in 1926. Re-issued 1964 by arrangement with Ginn & Co.)

Szucs, L., and Leubking, S. H. *The Archives: A Guide to the National Archives Field Branches.* Salt Lake City: Ancestry Publishing, 1988.

Tepper, M. *American Passenger Arrival Records.* Baltimore: Genealogical Publishing Co., Inc., 1988.

Van Vleck, W. C. *The Administrative Control of Aliens: A Study in Administrative Law and Procedures.* New York: Commonwealth Fund, 1932.

Wynne, S. F. "On the History of Ellis Island," and "So Your Name Was Changed at Ellis Island," *Mishpacha,* the publication of the Jewish Genealogy Society of Greater Washington, Vol. 3, No. 1, Spring 1983.

Zimmerman, G. J., and Wolfert, M. *German Immigrants: Lists of Passengers Bound from Bremen to New York, 1863–1867.* Baltimore: Genealogical Publishing Co., Inc., 1987– (multi-vol.).

Chapter 2

UNITED STATES: GUIDE TO INSTITUTIONAL RESOURCES ARRANGED BY CITY

Scott E. Meyer and Alan Spencer, Editors

INTRODUCTION

Scott E. Meyer and Alan Spencer

Before You Start

The information contained in this section was provided to us by countless researchers over a period of many years. They have indicated those sources that have proven useful in their own investigations, and they have passed the material along as a way of aiding their fellow researchers.

The basis for much of the information presented in this chapter was originally compiled by Dr. Eli Grad. Dr. Grad amassed the material primarily in his role as Editor of the Guides to Area Research Sources, which have appeared for many years in *Search, International Journal for Researchers of Jewish Genealogy.*

In addition to contributions from Dr. Grad, the others submitted information in many and various formats. We received so much material, in so many different formats, that we struggled long and hard with the issue of how to present the information in a consistent, concise, yet comprehensive manner. Our goal was to compile an overview of available source material. The trick was to find a format that could be most easily accessed by researchers of Jewish genealogy at all levels of experience—the beginner as well as the more advanced.

We made the assumption that you have in mind an area of interest within North America. In order to learn what research materials may exist in that area, you have found your way to these pages. You will notice that we have chosen a familiar format: alphabetical by state or province within each country (United States and Canada) and then alphabetically by city.

Please do not expect to find every city, state, or province represented in this section. We included only those areas that were known to have significant sources for Jewish genealogical research. The New York City section refers frequently to the book *Genealogical Resources in the New York Metropolitan Area,* edited by Estelle M. Guzik and published by the Jewish Genealogical Society, Inc., in New York. You should be aware that her book also contains information regarding some genealogical sources (although none specifically Jewish) in northern New Jersey. If you are interested in resources located in that area, you are advised to consult Ms. Guzik's book.

Listed below each city we have included several important institutions (again arranged alphabetically). Within each institution's listing, we may include a summary of the holdings that could be of interest to you.

If the institution has indicated to us that they charge a membership or research fee, we pass that information along to you. A few may have noted that they are not able to respond to inquiries by mail; in those cases, we have mentioned that as well.

We have also included some sources that are not specifically Jewish but, nonetheless, contain information of value to researchers of Jewish genealogy. Therefore, you will find references to holdings of city directories, vital statistics, court records, and others.

Near the end of each city's entry, we may list cemeteries and/or funeral homes, newspapers, and synagogues with important holdings. Do not expect to see every institution that might be located in a particular city. We have only listed those that we have learned are useful in genealogical investigations.

An entire book could be written about sources in the cities across North America. As a matter of fact, a book could be written on the sources in just one city— or within one institution. Since books of that nature have often been written, we will point them out to you in the Bibliography section near the end of the cities' listings.

Before proceeding, we must point out what this section is not. It is not a directory of every public library, synagogue, Jewish cemetery, or Jewish funeral home in North America. It is possible that any one of these types of institutions could have information that could prove invaluable to your research. Due to space limitations, however, we have narrowed the scope of this section to only those sources that have proven useful to other genealogical researchers.

How to Use These Chapters

This is certainly not the first time that a list of sources has been organized in this way. Many others have found this a handy way to display information. But how can you profit by such a list?

1. Scan the chapters. It may not be necessary to read every word at this time, but scan the name of each institution in each chapter. In that way you'll familiarize yourself with the types of research sites that exist. Then you'll have a better idea of the questions to ask when you begin to explore the resources of a city not detailed here.

Explore the various types of information summarized under each place. Again, you'll have a better idea of what you should ask for or may expect to see in other locations.

2. Focus on a city. Say, for instance, that your grandfather lived for a time in Pittsburgh. What kind of information by and/or about him may exist in that city? His name might appear in city directories, vital statistics, burial society records, synagogue records, and so on. Look closer at the holdings of the institutions to see if the collections could be of benefit to you.

3. Focus on types of sources. If your grandfather contributed a few articles to some Jewish periodicals, copies of those articles might exist today in many different locations. Archives and libraries might have back issues of the publication. They may also have indexes to them—or those indexes may exist in a different location, perhaps in another city.

4. Call or write to the institution. You'll notice that we don't list a few things you may have expected to see: hours of operation, and the name of a contact person at a given place. These are items that are subject to change at a moment's notice or, all too often, without a moment's notice.

Unlike a newsletter, which is able to provide constantly updated information, this volume is meant to be of a more permanent nature. By not listing hours of operation and names of contact people, we are encouraging you to write or phone the institution for current information. We think this may save you some frustration.

Although we usually won't mention names of people to contact, we may list a contact person if the institution or the department in question is a one-person organization. In such cases, it is not unusual to find that the *individual* is the source. If he/she leaves the organization, the sources leave as well. Luckily, this rarely happens.

5. Ask questions. Be as specific as you possibly can. Narrow the focus of your questions. In fact, you're more likely to get a more immediate response if you limit the number of questions. The people who are in a position to respond to you usually have more to do than answer letters! It is almost never their primary function. If it looks as though it will take some time to read your request (let alone answer it), it may be put aside until they are less busy, and there's no telling when that might be.

When phoning, make sure to ask for the name of the person you're dealing with and write to or ask for them specifically the next time. People are likely to be more helpful if they have had positive dealings with you in the past.

6. Plan a visit. A firsthand view of the holdings of an institution is ideal. It is not uncommon to find things that you weren't looking for. Sometimes those found items will even be of benefit to you! You should first ask a few questions before venturing out.

Some institutions have been known to change their hours several times within a year. Remember: an institution's hours of operation may be different from day to day and season to season (many institutions have summer hours). Don't assume that, because they open at 9 a.m. on Monday, they will be open at the same time on Tuesday. In fact, they might even be closed. Make sure you ask for hours of operation for the day you plan to visit.

It is often helpful to ask if the person to whom you are writing (or talking) knows of any other institutions that may be of help to you. New places that will open their doors in the future are of course not included here. (Even a few "old" places may have escaped our notice.) Your contact person works in the area. Be sure to make use of their expertise.

7. SASE. If you expect a reply to a letter, be sure to include a self-addressed stamped envelope (SASE). Most researchers consider this common courtesy. It can only be common if we are all aware of the practice. Consider yourself aware!

8. A word about Jewish genealogical societies. Genealogical societies are wonderful sources in and of themselves, and Jewish genealogical societies have additional assets. Although many societies do not yet have actual research libraries, they will often have on hand such materials as the "Computerized Jewish Family Finder," a listing of over 20,000 entries representing surnames and placers being researched by Jewish family historians the world over. The societies' primary "holdings of interest," however, are their members.

These family researchers have struggled with the same types of problems that may be confronting you. Perhaps they have a success story and a few tips to share.

Unfortunately, these organizations do not usually have permanent offices, so correspondence is often sent in care of the societies' presidents or newsletter editors. Their addresses are subject to change as new officers of the societies are elected. This information is so changeable that we have not included each Jewish genealogical society within the listings by city. You will, find, however, a list of Jewish genealogical societies in Appendix A (pp. 151–152).

9. Come on back! Make regular trips back to these chapters (and back to this encyclopedia, as a matter of fact). Something that does not seem useful to you at first reading may not stick in your mind. Six months from now, however, your research may present you with a different set of problems. ("You mean I had relatives in Seattle—and Chicago—and Savannah?") Then you'll turn to this section, thumb through it, and the answers will just jump off the page. This can't be guaranteed, of course, but a little positive thinking couldn't hurt!

ARIZONA

■ MESA
(Phoenix Metropolitan Area)

Family History Center
Mesa Branch
464 East 1st Avenuc
Mesa, Arizona 85202
(602) 964-1200

■ PHOENIX

Arizona Jewish Historical Society
Greater Phoenix Chapter
2211 East Highland, Suite 112
Phoenix, Arizona 85016
(602) 957-7507

Arizona State Library
State Capitol
1700 West Washington
Phoenix, Arizona 85007
(602) 255-3942

Will do limited research over the telephone. Will copy and mail indexes. Genealogy Department has information from all over the United States.

- Lineage books
- Marriage, death, birth, military records, etc.

Health Services Department
Vital Records
1740 West Adams
Phoenix, Arizona 85007
(602) 255-1080 (recorded message)
(602) 255-1072 (information)

Must provide full name, country where born or died, approximate year, and your relationship to them. Write for fee schedule. Records since 1805.

Maricopa County Clerk
201 W. Jefferson
Phoenix, Arizona 85003
(602) 262-3253

Marriage and divorce records 1871 to present

Phoenix Central Library
12 East McDowell
Phoenix, Arizona 85004
(602) 262-4766

Cannot answer specific questions by phone. Arts and Humanities Desk has genealogical books and indexes.

Sinai Mortuary of Arizona
4538 North 16th Street
Phoenix, Arizona 85016
(602) 248-0030

Temple Beth Israel Library
3310 North 10th Avenue
Phoenix, Arizona 85013
(602) 264-4428

■ TEMPE
(Phoenix Metropolitan Area)

Arizona Historical Foundation
Hayden Library
Arizona State University Campus
Tempe, Arizona 85287

■ TUCSON

Leona G. and David Arthur Bloom Jewish Archives of the Southwest Center
On the campus of the University of Arizona
Tucson, Arizona 85721

Recently established Jewish archive, eventually expected to contain an assortment of

- Historic material
- Documents
- Photographs
- Oral histories (on tape)
- Materials from Jewish historical societies in Tucson and Phoenix, Arizona, San Diego, California, Albuquerque, New Mexico, and El Paso, Texas

Histories will eventually be transferred to computer.

Bibliography
Fierman, F. S. "The Drachmans of Arizona," *American Jewish Archives* 16:135–160, November 1964.
_____ . "The Goldberg Brothers: Arizona Pioneers," *American Jewish Archives* 18:3–19, April 1966.
_____ . *Guts and Ruts: The Jewish Pioneer on the Trail in the American Southwest.* New York: Ktav Publishing House, Inc., 1985.
_____ . *Roots and Boots: From Crypto-Jew in New Spain to Community Leader in the American Southwest.* Hoboken, NJ: Ktav Publishing House, Inc., 1987.
Glanz, R. "Notes on the Early Jews of Arizona," *Western States Jewish Historical Quarterly* 5:231–242, July 1973.
Marcus, J.R.., ed. "An Arizona Pioneer—Memoirs of Sam Aaron," *American Jewish Archives* 10:95–120, October 1958.
Rudd, H. L., *Mountain West Pioneer Jewry.* Los Angeles: Will Kramer, 1980.
Schmerler, H. *The Universal Jewish Encyclopedia*, 1st ed., S.v. "Arizona."

CALIFORNIA

■ BERKELEY
(San Francisco Metropolitan Area)

Western Jewish History Center
2911 Russell Street
Berkeley, California 94705
(415) 849-2710

The Western Jewish History Center is an archival research library concentrating on the contributions of Jews to the American West from the Gold Rush to the present.

The center will answer inquiries and will do research. The first half hour of research is free; after that, an hourly fee is charged.

The center's holdings include:

- Anglo-American newspapers published in the West since 1860
- Oral histories of Western America's Jewish personalities
- Photographs
- Organizational records
- Letters chronicling Western Jewish history
- An almost complete set of the *Emanu-El and Jewish Journal* and *Jewish Bulletin* in bound volumes or loose editions

The Judah L. Magnes Memorial Museum, whose purpose is to collect, preserve, and make available artistic, historical, and literary material reflecting Jewish life and cultural contributions throughout history, to encourage research and creativity through a program of exhibition, public education, research projects, and publishing. Today, the Magnes Museum is the third largest Jewish museum in the United States.

■ LAGUNA NIGUEL
(Los Angeles Metropolitan Area)

National Archives
Los Angeles Branch
24000 Avila Road
Laguna Niguel, California 92677
(714) 643-4241

■ LOS ANGELES

Hebrew Union College
Frances Henry Library
3077 University Ave.
Los Angeles, California 90007
(213) 749-3426

Letters of inquiry are answered if questions are clear, concise, and not too involved.
The library's collection contains:

* Yizkor books of Polish and Russian communities
* Microfilmed newspapers from the American Jewish Periodical Center
* American Jewish Community records, organizational minutes, personal correspondence, memoirs on microfilm from the American Jewish Archives

A 70,000 volume specialized collection: books, pamphlets, periodicals, microfilms, and other materials cover such subjects as Archaeology, Bible, Talmud, Midrash, Rabbinical Responsa and Codes, Philosophy, Theology, Liturgy, Hebrew Language and Literature, Jewish Education, Jewish Communal Studies, American Jewish Literature, Zionism, and Modern Israel.
Within the library is its recent four-volume publication, *Manuscript Catalog of the Archives*. It consists of some 90,000 entries pertaining to the growth and development of the American Jewish community.
Joseph Periodical Reading Room. 250 periodicals, in various languages, devoted primarily to scholarship and opinion relating to Jewish lore and learning.
Joseph H. Rosenberg Collection (American Jewish Archives). Microfilmed copy of a collection of the American Jewish Archives in Cincinnati, Ohio. Deals with the Jewish experience in the Western Hemisphere.

Family History Center
10777 Santa Monica Boulevard
Los Angeles, California
(213) 474-9990

Los Angeles County Assessor
500 West Temple Street, Room 205
Los Angeles, California 90012
The assessor can usually furnish you with a copy of the index indicating the name of the assessed owner, if you have the legal description or the street address of the property. There is a fee for this service.

Peter M. Kahn
Jewish Community Library
6505 Wilshire Boulevard
12th Floor
Los Angeles, California 90048
(213) 852-1234; Ext. 3202

The library is directed under the auspices of the Bureau of Jewish Education of the Jewish Federation Council. Of genealogical importance is its Archives Center, which houses documents and preserves the history of the Jews of Los Angeles from 1849 to the present. The archives also houses a microfilm collection of periodicals and newspapers, photographs relating to Jewry in Los Angeles, some individual genealogies, and some personal memoirs of the Holocaust and World War II.

* *Encyclopedia Judaica* (the old set)
* Vertical file of Californiana: miscellaneous materials including landsmanshaftn and donor information

Registrar-Recorder
Hall of Records, Room 5
227 North Broadway
Los Angeles, California 90012
(213) 974-6631

The Vital Records Division maintains permanent files of birth, death, and marriage certificates of persons who were born, deceased, or obtained a license to marry in Los Angeles County. Listed below are the years available for the above records.

* Birth 1866–Present
* Death 1877–Present
* Marriage 1856–Present

A vital records search for certified copies of birth, death, or marriage certificates can be obtained from this office. When a specific date of a record is not known, the registrar must be told which years to search. Write for a fee schedule.

Registrar of Voters Office
5557 Ferguson Drive
Los Angeles, California 90022

This office can furnish you with the address of any person who is currently a registered voter in Los Angeles County.

Simon Wiesenthal Center
Library/Archives
9760 W. Pico Boulevard
Los Angeles, California 90035
(213) 553-9036

There is an annual membership fee, and inquiries are answered.
The center and its library are located on the campus of Yeshiva University of Los Angeles and is named after the famous hunter of Nazi war criminals. The center holds lectures and classes which convey the story of the Holocaust. Group tours are available if

booked in advance. The center publishes *Response* and *Social Action Update.*

Multimedia presentations, including photographs and film footage from the Holocaust period, are being created. Original documents, periodicals, books, and oral histories are also being assembled into one of the most comprehensive facilities of its type in North America. Genealogical resources include:

- Rare Holocaust works
- Judaica collection
- Memorial volumes (Yizkor books) of various Jewish communities
- Deportation and Survivor Lists
- Family chronicles
- Sourcebooks on Jewish genealogy
- Historical atlas of Poland

Southern California Jewish Historical Society
6505 Wilshire Boulevard, No. 1108
Los Angeles, California 90048
Valuable source for the history of L.A. Jewry.

UCLA University
Research Library and Map Library
405 Hilgard Avenue
Los Angeles, California 90024
(213) 825-1544
Contact: Bibliographer Judaica (213) 825-2930.

The main building of the University Research Library houses 70,000 volumes of Judaica, with an additional 30,000–40,000 volumes stored in the Inglewood annex. In this library are memorial books, encyclopedias, biographies, periodicals, and a microfilm collection containing oral histories and Holocaust materials. Also included is a collection of German Jewish genealogical magazines.

An index titled *European Jewish Communities 1933–1945–Histories, Memoirs, Diaries, Memorial Books* is available in the library.

Map Library. The UCLA Map Library is the fourth largest collection of maps in the United States. The library's holdings include gazetteers, atlases, and geographical books.

A collection of map series on western Russia can be found here. Ranging widely in age, some of these maps were published in 1886, whereas others were printed in the late 1950s. There are several series compiled between 1912 and 1939, many of them in English and German. There are also extensive series covering Poland, Czechoslovakia, and Hungary.

Also available in the Map Library are all the United States government gazetteers, which cover virtually every country in the world. There are also numerous single-sheet maps covering entire countries. Many of these maps are pre-World War II, and some are pre-World War I. Several of them cover specialized subjects (for example, 1912 railroad map of Russia). Included are many historical maps from previous centuries.

University of Judaism
Jack M. and Bel Ostrow Library
15600 Mulholland Drive
Los Angeles, California 90077
(213) 476-9777 or 897-4114

The University of Judaism's library is affiliated with the Jewish Theological Seminary of America. The collection contains close to 140,000 volumes, which are listed in separate English and Hebrew card catalogs. Of particular interest are the uncataloged older periodicals and literary journals in the open stacks. There is a large collection of Holocaust materials and Yizkor books.

Yeshiva University of Los Angeles
9760 West Pico Boulevard
Los Angeles, California 90035
(213) 553-4478

The main campus library is developing a major collection in Biblical studies and Jewish law. It is broad-based in Jewish history, literature, Zionism, sociology, the Hebrew language, religion, philosophy, ethics, and education. Interested individuals are advised to contact the library to find out their lending procedures. See previous entry for Simon Wiesenthal Center.

Bibliography
Barth, L. M. *The History of Temple Israel of Hollywood, 1926–1931.* 1959.
Cogan, S. G. *The Jews of Los Angeles: 1849–1945. An Annotated Bibliography,* comp. 1980.
Glanz, R. *The Jews of California: From the Discovery of Gold Until 1880.* New York: 1960.
Gostin, T., and Gould, G., eds. *A Guide to Jewish Genealogical Resources in the Los Angeles Area,* unpublished, 1990. Order from: Jewish Genealogical Society of Los Angeles, P.O. Box 25245, Los Angeles, CA 90025.
Newmark, M. R. *Congregation B'nai B'rith (Wilshire Boulevard Temple) History, 1860–1947.*
Sass, S. J., ed. *Jewish Los Angeles: A Guide.* Los Angeles: Federation Council of Greater Los Angeles, 1982.
Stern, N. B., ed. *The Jews of Los Angeles: Urban Pioneers.* Los Angeles: Southern California Jewish Historical Society, 1981.
Vorspan, M., and Garner, L. P. *History of the Jews of Los Angeles.* 1970.

■ SACRAMENTO

State Bureau of Vital Statistics
410 "N" Street
Sacramento, California 95814

The State Bureau can supply information on deaths in California if given the approximate date of death. A fee is charged by the state for making each search and furnishing a certified copy of the record if found. If no record is found, the fee will be retained.

Bibliography
Wyatt, B. *The Jewish Settlement in Sacramento.* Sacramento: Jewish Federation, 1987.

■ SAN DIEGO

County Recorders Office
P.O. Box 1750
San Diego, California 92112
Write for copies of birth, marriage, and death certificates.

Jewish Community Center Library
4079 54th Street
San Diego, California 92105
(619) 583-3300

- Copies of *Heritage-Southwest Jewish Press* from 1962
- Copies of *Israel Today, San Diego edition* from 1980
- Copies of *Western States Jewish Historical Quarterly* from 1970
- *Who's Who in the West*

Of more general genealogical interest, the library also has:

- *Universal Jewish Encyclopedia*, published in 1939
- *The Jewish Encyclopedia*, published in 1907
- *Encyclopedia Judaica*, published in 1972
- American Jewish Yearbook from 1914 (not all years)
- Jewish newspapers from all over the United States and Israel
- Extensive Holocaust collection including the complete proceedings of the Nüremberg War Criminal Trials

San Diego Public Library
820 E Street
San Diego, California 92101
(619) 236-5800

California Room has city and county directories dating from 1886, plus old maps of San Diego County.
Newspaper Room has the *San Diego Herald* (now the *Union*) on microfilm from its inception in 1951.
The Genealogy Room has the following books:

- "Index to the 1850 Census for the State of California"
- "California Pioneer Register and Index, 1542–1848"
- "A History of San Diego and San Diego County," published in 1922

Cemeteries
Home of Peace
3668 Imperial Avenue
San Diego, California 92113
Established 1882; office is at:

6363 El Cajon Boulevard
San Diego, California 92115
(619) 286-1867

Greenwood Cemetery
I-805 and Imperial Avenue
San Diego, California 92113
(619) 264-3131
Jewish section established in 1954.

Cypress View Mortuary and Mausoleum
Home of Peace Sanctuary (Jewish Section)
3953 Imperial Avenue
San Diego, California 92113
(619) 264-3168
Established 1950.

Mount Hope Cemetery
3751 Market Street
San Diego, California 92102
(619) 264-3151
The oldest cemetery in San Diego, it was established in 1869.

Synagogues
Temple Beth Israel
2512 Third Avenue
San Diego, California 92103
Reform congregation founded in 1877.

Tifereth Israel Synagogue
6660 Cowles Mountain Boulevard
San Diego, California 92119
Orthodox congregation when founded in 1905, it is now Conservative.

■ SAN FRANCISCO

California Genealogical Society
300 Brannon Street Suite 409
San Francisco, California 94102
(415) 777-9936 or 989-5441
Extensive well-balanced library collection contains well over 10,000 books, more than 1,800 family histories, 1,500 reels of microfilm, and numerous reference indexes, periodicals, and maps. Although some of their collection is international in scope, most of their materials cover the United States. Reader's fee: $5.00 per day for nonmembers. Membership: $20 per year. Publishes bimonthly newsletter. Phone: (415) 625-4280. Will answer inquiries.

California Historical Society Library
2099 Pacific Avenue
San Francisco, California 94109
(415) 567-1848
There is a membership fee and a per-day research fee for nonmembers. Written inquiries are not accepted. Research must be done in person or by hired researcher.
The Society library has many manuscripts and photographic collections, as well as published collections about Jews in California.

City Hall
County Clerk's Office
400 Van Ness Avenue
San Francisco, California 94102
(415) 558-3275
Room 317, (415) 558-3705, contains indices and files for:

- Probate cases
- Civil cases (which include divorce cases)

Probate indexes contain four microfilms 1906–77, microfiche, 1978–81, computer printout of alphabetical index to books for each year, 1982 et seq.
Civil case indices contain cartridge microfilm reels. Some older probate and civil files are in a warehouse. The warehouse files may take several days to access, and if there is a large number of files ordered at the

same time, there is a per file charge. Therefore, a call should be made in advance of going to the Clerk's office to order an older file.

Jewish Home for the Aged
302 Silver Avenue
San Francisco, California 94112
Records, dating back to 1923 and some as far back as 1914, are kept in the home's basement.

Judah L. Magnes Memorial Museum
(See Western Jewish History Center, Berkeley, California)

San Francisco Archives
San Francisco Room. 3d Floor
same building as the Public Library
(415) 558-3949
- *San Francisco Examiner* morgue (1906–1980)

A morgue is the clipping library of a newspaper, alphabetized by name or subject. They frequently contain marriage announcements and other information that is not otherwise readily available.

It takes three days to get a holding from storage into the library. Therefore, call in advance to see if the Archives have any envelopes for the names in which you are interested. Then, call back three or four days later to make sure it is in. If it is, ask them to hold it until the date you plan to come in and do research. They will usually hold it for about three days.

San Francisco Historic Records Index
City Hall Historian
Room 167, Mezzanine Level
San Francisco, California 94102
(no telephone calls, please)
Write for a copy of the information request form.

The main effort being made by the San Francisco Historic Records Index is to create a single computer database for pre-1906 genealogical, biographical, and historical data. Materials of particular interest are naturalization and name-change records. Virtually all significant pre-1906 records of genealogical importance for San Francisco residents are here, including:

- (Reconstructed) birth records, marriage records, and death records
- Births, marriages, and death records from all 58 counties of California, all counties in Oregon, Washington, and Baja California, British Columbia, Alaska, and Hawaii. Indexing is not yet complete

Although this office routinely keeps and indexes records of Jewish families, they do not keep them apart from records of other ethnic groups.

San Francisco Public Library
200 Larkin Street at McAllister Street
San Francisco, California 94102
(415) 558-3191
Newspaper Room: Third Floor (415) 558-3206.

- Contains newspaper microfilms
- Index to the *San Francisco Chronicle* since 1976
- Hard copies of San Francisco city directories
- California telephone books

The Society of California Pioneers
456 McAllister Street
San Francisco, California 94102
(415) 861-5278
The society maintains a reference library for the public where all phases of research may be carried on by genealogical researchers.

- Several books on Jews in California including biographies
- A photo collection of California pioneers identified by surname
- Collection of pictures, paintings, lithographs, prints, and photographs, with some 12,000 negatives from which prints may be made for a nominal fee

Western Jewish History Center
(See Berkeley, California)

Newspapers
Northern California Jewish Bulletin
88 First Street, 3rd floor
San Francisco, California 94105
(415) 957-9340
Cannot answer inquiries. Researchers are allowed to do research from the bound volumes of past issues.

The Jewish newspaper of record for San Francisco is *Northern California Jewish Bulletin* (changed name from the *San Francisco Jewish Bulletin* in 1981). It began publication about 1895 as the *Bulletin of Emanu-El Temple* and later evolved into a general Jewish-community newspaper.

Western Jewish History Center
(See Berkeley, California)

Cemeteries
Unlike other cities with large Jewish populations, San Francisco has a highly structured and organized system of Jewish cemeteries, and they are relatively easy to research. There are four Jewish cemeteries for San Francisco, all located in Colma, California, right next to each other.

A researcher should not expect to find inscriptions of Hebrew names.

Eternal Home Cemetery
Colma, California 94014
(415) 755-5236

Hills of Eternity Jewish Cemetery and Mausoleums
(including Portals of Eternity and Gardens of Eternity)
240 El Camino Blvd.
Colma, California 94014
(415) 756-3633

Owned and operated by Sherith Israel Congregation (415) 346-1720.

Home of Peace Cemetery and Emanu-El Mausoleum
(including Garden of Peace Mausoleum)
Colma, California 94014
(415) 755-4700
Owned and operated by Emanu-El Temple. Records are available and inquiries are answered at Emanu-El Temple. One record book from before the San Francisco Earthquake of 1906 survives.

Salem Memorial Park and Garden Mausoleum
Colma, California 94014
(415) 755-5296
Owned and operated by Congregation Beth Israel-Judea.

San Francisco National Cemetery
Presidio of San Francisco
San Francisco, California
(415) 561-2211, 2208, 2986
This is a military cemetery, and Jewish veterans are buried there. It is known in San Francisco as the Presidio Cemetery.

Funeral Homes
Until the late 1930s, Jewish funerals were conducted by N. Gray and Company, which subsequently merged with Halsted Mortuary.

Halsted has voluminous records. However, it requires a letter of inquiry and a substantial fee. Since 1937, practically all Jewish funerals have been handled by:

Sinai Memorial Chapel
1501 Divisadero
San Francisco, California 94115
(415) 921-3636

This chapel has extensive records. Sinai is a not-for-profit organization owned by the Jewish community. Prior to 1937, there was a *Chevra Kadisha*, which was established about 1905. It is unclear if the records of the *Chevra Kadisha* exist, but a book about it was written by Dr. Abe Bernstein.

Sinai owns and operates the fourth Jewish cemetery.

Synagogues
There are three major historic old congregations in San Francisco. Each of these owns and operates a cemetery. For further details, see the list of Jewish cemeteries of the San Francisco Bay area.

Congregation Beth Israel-Judea
The Temple on Brotherhood Way
625 Brotherhood Way
San Francisco, California 94132
(415) 586-8833
This is a Conservative synagogue. Beth Israel was founded in 1860. Known in the old days as the Geary Street Shul, it was the standard Orthodox synagogue of the Russian immigrants years ago. It merged with Temple Judea, a Reform Temple. Beth Israel-Judea does not have many historic synagogue records other than its cemetery records.

Emanu-El Temple
Arguello Boulevard and Lake Street
San Francisco, California 94118
(415) 751-2535
Contact: Cemetery Records Specialist
This was a classic Reform Temple founded by German Jews of Bavarian origin in 1850.

Sherith Israel Congregation
2266 California Street
San Francisco, California 94115
(415) 346-1720
This is a Reform congregation founded by Jews of Polish and English background in 1850.

■ SANTA MONICA (Los Angeles Metropolitan Area)

Western States Jewish Historical Quarterly
2429 23rd Street
Santa Monica, California 90405
(213) 399-3585
Evenings: (213) 450-2946
WSJHQ contains a vast amount of genealogical material on Jews west of the Mississippi River, including Alaska, Hawaii, Baja California, Western Canada, etc. WSJHQ answers only those inquiries sent by subscribers or those wishing to subscribe.

WSJHQ has published *A Twelve Year Index of the Western States Jewish Historical Quarterly (1968–1980)*, compiled by Suzanne de Beaulieu Nemiroff. This WSJHQ index is a guide and tool for the pursuit of the personalities, organizations, locales, affiliations, businesses, occupations, social and religious life of pioneer Western Jewry. Included are such topics as Zionism, congregations, anti-Semitism, Jews in politics, agriculture, art, entertainment, and transportation.

As a genealogical aid, the index presents leads to thousands of personalities in all major cities and hundreds of remote places across the full range of the West.

It also contains an author index, listing the studies written by each, and a guide that gives the titles and locations of all photographs and other graphic materials published.

■ STANFORD (San Francisco Metropolitan Area)

Stanford University Libraries
Department of Special Collections and University Archives
Stanford, California 94305
(415) 723-4054
A limited amount of research is provided without a fee. There is no membership fee for the Department of Special Collections.

This facility contains three collections that may prove very useful to researchers of Jewish genealogy:

- Meyer Lissner Papers
- Moses Schallenberger Papers
- The Pacific Slope Collection

Letters of inquiry are answered, and all collections are available for scholarly use.

Bibliography

Cogan, S. G. *The Jews of San Francisco and the Greater Bay Area, 1849–1919.* Western Jewish Americana Series, 1972.

Congregation Sherith Israel. Program: 90th Anniversary 1850–1940, 1940.

First Hebrew Congregation: 75th Anniversary of Temple Sinai (Oakland) 1950.

Narell, I. *Our City: The Jews of San Francisco.* San Diego: Howell-North, 1981.

Rafael, R. K. *Guide to Archival and Oral History Collections.* Berkeley, CA: Western Jewish History Center/Judah Magnes Museum, 1987.

Rischin, M., ed. *Jews of the West: The Metropolitan Years.* Waltham, MA: American Jewish Historical Society, 1979.

Rochlin, F., and Rochlin, H. *Pioneer Jews: A New Life in the Far West.* Boston: Houghton Mifflin Company, 1984.

Rosenbaum, F. *Architects of Reform: Congregation and Community Leadership, Emanu-El of San Francisco, 1849–1980.* Berkeley, CA: Western Jewish History Center, 1980.

COLORADO

■ DENVER

Clerk and Recorder
Room 200
City and County Building
Denver, Colorado 80202
(303) 575-2628, 575-2641, 575-5964

There is a fee for search of marriage licenses and for a certified copy of an application or certificate.

- Denver marriage licenses

The Colorado Historical Society
1300 Broadway
Denver, Colorado 80203
(303) 866-2305

- Complete microfilm set of *The Intermountain Jewish News*

The Stephen S. Hart Library

A special noncirculating library that focuses on Colorado and western history. The library is free and open to the public. The library will provide a "Basic Reference Package" that includes up to one-half hour search time, up to five copies documenting the search, and all postage and handling fees. Write for fee schedule.

- Over half a million photographs, including 10,000 glass plate negatives taken by pioneer photographer William Henry Jackson

- 1,500 manuscript collections, which consist of personal papers, ledgers, journals and corporate records, rare books, maps, oral history interviews, newspapers, Denver City Directories and Denver Census records.

Colorado Genealogical Society
P.O. Box 9671
Denver, Colorado 80209
(303) 573-5152, Ext. 207

Denver General Hospital Vital Statistics Department
605 Bannock
Denver, Colorado 80204
(303) 893-7436

- Denver birth and death records (since 1964)

Denver Public Library Genealogy Department
1357 Broadway
Denver, Colorado 80203
(303) 571-2074 or 571-2077

Rocky Mountain Jewish Historical Society Center for Judaic Studies
University of Denver
University Park
Denver, Colorado 80208
(303) 871-3020, 871-3022

State Department of Health Vital Records
4210 E. 11th Avenue
Denver, Colorado 80220
(303) 320-8474

- State-wide birth and death records

Newspaper

The Intermountain Jewish News
1275 Sherman Street, Suite 214
Denver, Colorado 80203
(303) 861-2234, 861-8333

- A complete set of back issues (microfilm)
- Bound volumes from 1934

Synagogues

B.M.H. Congregation
560 S. Monaco Parkway
Denver, Colorado 80224
(303) 388-4203

Beth Joseph
825 Ivanhoe Street
Denver, Colorado 80220
(303) 355-7321

The Rabbi will respond to a reasonable number of written inquiries without charge.

Archives contain:

- Old membership lists
- Applications for membership, which include vital statisitcs and the like

The Congregation does not maintain a cemetery.

Congregation Hebrew Educational Alliance
1555 Stuart Street
Denver, Colorado 80204
(303) 629-0410
Will respond to written inquiries on a limited basis.

- Family census records from 1960s

The synagogue is the administrator of the Golden Hill Cemetery (established 1908). Burial records are available.

Temple Emanuel
51 Grape Street
Denver, Colorado 80220
(303) 388-4013
Will to respond to written requests on a limited basis.

- Maintains archives (no material may be removed)
- Maintains cemetery with extensive records available

Zera Abraham
1560 Winona Court
Denver, Colorado 80204
(303) 825-7517

Zera Israel
3934 W. 14th Avenue at Perry
Denver, Colorado 80204
(303) 571-0166

Cemeteries
United Hebrew Cemetery Association
63 South Fairfax
Denver, Coloado 80222
Operates:

Rose Hill Cemetery
P.O. Box 11335
930 South Monaco
Denver, Colorado 80224
(303) 322-0438
Records showing the names, dates of death (some are dates of burial) and location of the graves.
Write for fee schedule.
All records prior to 1950 are stored at the Jewish Historical Society.

Bibliography
Breck, A. D. *A Centennial History of the Jews of Colorado: 1859–1959.* Denver: Hirschfeld Press, 1960.
Rudd, H. L. *Mountain West Pioneer Jewry.* Los Angeles: Will Kramer, 1980.

CONNECTICUT

■ BLOOMFIELD

Family History Center
1000 Mountain Road
Bloomfield, Connecticut 06002
(203) 242-1607

Hartford Stake serves the north central and northeastern areas of the state. (Moved to Bloomfield from Manchester in 1986.)

Rabbi Haskel Lindenthal
4 Puritan Road
Bloomfield, Connecticut 06002
(203) 242-2521
Mohel for forty-six years. Send date of birth and surname of circumcised boy.

Funeral Directors Association
89 Brewster Road
West Hartford, Connecticut 06117
(203) 527-3890
Can provide names of mortuaries that serve clientele throughout Connecticut.

Bridgeport Public Library
925 Broad Street
Bridgeport, Connecticut 06604
(203) 576-7403
Extensive collection includes:

- Voter registration cards, Bridgeport, 1822–1963
- Tax assessments 1890–1960
- U.S. Census for Connecticut 1900 and 1910
- Bridgeport obituary index 1978–1983
- City directories from 1855 to date
- Directories of other Connecticut cities 1935 to date
- Connecticut newspapers on microfilm 1861 to date

Colchester Historical Society
School Road
Colchester, Connecticut 06415
A great number of Jewish farmers were settled in Eastern Connecticut by the Baron de Hirsch Society and others. Colchester had a very large Jewish population during the first half of this century.

Hebrew Funeral Association
(Chesed Shel Emeth)
124 Hebron Road
Glastonbury, Connecticut 06033
(203) 566-2750
Out of business as of April 1, 1987, but will reply to queries concerning years 1950–1987.

■ HARTFORD

Charter Oak Temple
Restoration Association
21 Charter Oak Avenue
Hartford, Connecticut 06106
(203) 249-1207
Connecticut's oldest synagogue, being restored and used as a cultural center. Research limited to original Beth Israel Temple congregation and the Charter Oak neighborhood.

Connecticut Historical Society
1 Elizabeth Street
Hartford, Connecticut 06105
(203) 236-5621
Responds to queries. Resources include *Connecticut, a Bibliography of Its History* (see Bibliography). Index includes listings for synagogues, towns, and cities, and mentions names of Jewish residents.

Connecticut State Health Services
150 Washington Street
Hartford, Connecticut 06106
Vital records:

• Births and deaths: (203) 566-2334
• Marriages: (203) 566-1123

Note: Connecticut law allows access to vital records by genealogical societies legally incorporated in Connecticut.

Connecticut State Library
231 Capitol Avenue
Hartford, Connecticut 06106
(203) 566-3692
• Probate records: most probate estate papers prior to 1850, and about half up to 1900
• Military records: Connecticut State Military Census of 1917 lists all males (ages about 10 to 30, with some under age included)
• Land records: microfilmed collections of deeds, mortgages, and related records to 1850, land records to ca. 1900 are now being microfilmed
• Court records: updated guides for civil and criminal court records for Connecticut after 1850
• Census, State of Connecticut: information on Connecticut State Military Census taken in 1917; all males from ages 20 to 30, with younger males sometimes included; automobile owners, aliens (friendly and enemy), and nurses; also agricultural stats (unique: done only in Connecticut)
• Census, federal: Federal Census schedules for Connecticut from 1790 to 1880, 1900 and 1910; index to schedules from 1790 to 1850; Soundex index on microfilm of the 1880 and 1900 schedules available for Connecticut; 1910 is not indexed for Connecticut; local town librarians can borrow through interlibrary loan program
• Cemetery records: master index of individual names compiled from tombstones in over 2,000 cemeteries in Connecticut by the WPA in the early 1930s; 59 volumes, typed, and file-card drawers; cemeteries listed alphabetically, sometimes by their names, sometimes just as "Jewish cemeteries"; individual names are listed thereunder, last name, first name, date of death, age at death, sometimes both, sometimes neither; individual names are not listed alphabetically; Hebrew not translated.

Open Door Society of Connecticut, Inc.
999 Asylum Avenue
Hartford, Connecticut 06101
(203) 522-4636
Adoption records up to ca. 1900 are open for research. Records of adoptions ca. 1900 to date are closed to the public.

Trinity College Library
300 Summit Street
Hartford, Connecticut 06106
(203) 527-3681
Excellent reference library.

U.S. Immigration and Naturalization Service
450 Main Street
Hartford, Connecticut 06103
(203) 249-4222
Office in Hartford services entire state.

Wadsworth Atheneum
600 Main Street
Hartford, Connecticut 06103
(203) 278-2670
Has a costume collection (currently in storage). Curator of costume might be able to identify period clothing.
Museum has recently acquired objects (i.e., Torah covers, contemporary textiles) from the recently closed Congregation Ados Israel, in Hartford.
Museum's bookstore has many books of interest.

Family History Center
275 Warpas Road
Madison, Connecticut 06443
(203) 245-4986
Serves south central Connecticut.

■ MIDDLETOWN

Godfrey Memorial Library
134 Newfield Street
Middletown, Connecticut 06457
(203) 346-4375
Will answer short queries by mail concerning immigrants who arrived prior to 1880. Private library (open to the public), devoted to genealogy (primarily early New England).
Gale Publishing Company's indexes to passenger and immigration lists (edited by William Filby and Mary Meyer), useful to about 1850; later years are not indexed.

Olin Library at Wesleyan University
Wesleyan University
Middletown, Connecticut 06457
(203) 347-9411
Private library, open to serious researchers; fairly extensive collection of Holocaust literature, Jewish history, Judaica.

Polish Genealogical Society of Connecticut, Inc.
(See New Britain, Connecticut)

Family History Center
682 South Avenue
New Canaan, Connecticut 06840
(203) 966-9511
Yorktown Stake, serves southwestern (Stamford) area.

■ NEW BRITAIN

Polish Genealogical Society of Connecticut, Inc.
c/o Jonathan Shea
8 Lyle Road
New Britain, Connecticut 06053
(203) 229-8873
Incomplete collection of both Christian and Jewish obituaries of people born in Poland, taken from newspapers in Connecticut, Rhode Island, and Massachusetts. Obits must say deceased was born in Poland. Willing to help however they can.

■ NEW HAVEN

Family History Center
(See Trumbull, Connecticut)

Video Archives for Holocaust Testimonies
Yale University
New Haven, Connecticut 06520
(203) 432-1879
The people who come to be interviewed are volunteers who want to have their story told. The archive uses standard terminology to describe volunteers: victim, survivor, perpetrator, bystander, witness, partisan, in hiding, emigrated before war, etc. Over 1,000 Holocaust victims have volunteered to be videotaped. Collection of testimonies will continue as long as there are volunteers who want to contribute.

Tapes can be viewed by appointment weekdays except holidays. Limited viewing facilities. Tapes are indexed geographically and entered into RLIN data base (Research Libraries Information Network, a subgroup of RLG). Can be accessed at any good research or university library. Names of those interviewed are not released. Of the 1,000 testimonies that have been taped, 200 are in the data base. They expect to have 300 entered soon. Almost all tapes available now are narrated in English; those done in Israel are in Hebrew, and some—in Romanian and Italian, for example—have translated explanations in English. Available research can also be accessed through RLNR.

Donations are appreciated to facilitate the archive's work.

Weller Funeral Home Inc.
425 George Street
New Haven, Connecticut 06051
(203) 624-6912
Will reply to queries.

Rabbi David Zurasky
310 Dyer Street
New Haven, Connecticut 06515
(203) 387-5554
Mohel. Send surname, date of birth. Usually practices in southern part of state, but sometimes travels further.

■ NEW LONDON

The Jewish Leader
302 State Street
New London, Connecticut 06320
(203) 442-7395

Published since 1972. Serves southeastern Connecticut towns that border Long Island Sound.

Family History Center
Dunbar Road
Quaker Hill, Connecticut 06375
No phone
Write for an appointment. New London area, serves southeastern part of state.

■ STAMFORD

The Stamford Program in Judaic Studies
University of Connecticut at Stamford
Scofieldtown Road
Stamford, Connecticut 06903
(203) 322-3466
Books, pamphlets, reports, and publications, among them books by a survivor, Prof. Nechama Tec, who is a member of the University of Connecticut faculty at Stamford.

■ STORRS

Center for Judaic Studies
University of Connecticut
Box U-68
Storrs, Connecticut 06268
(203) 486-4289
Books, pamphlets, reports, and publications, among them books by Professor Tec (see above).

Homer Babbidge Library
University of Connecticut
Box U-5H
Storrs, Connecticut 06268
(203) 486-4636

■ TRUMBULL

Family History Center
30 Bonnie View Terrace
Trumbull, Connecticut 06611
(203) 364-7444
Serves New Haven area, not staffed continously

■ WEST HARTFORD

Beth Israel Temple Library
701 Farmington Avenue
West Hartford, Connecticut 06119
(203) 236-4571
Library of this Reform temple contains books and pamphlets about Connecticut Jews, including

- 3 volumes concerning Jews of New Haven
- Rabbi Silverman's, *Jews of Hartford, 1659–1970*
- A volume on the Jews of Connecticut (published early in the twentieth century)

Beth Israel Temple Library
701 Farmington Avenue
West Hartford, Connecticut 06119
(203) 233-8215
Small museum of items belonging to members in the past, of value to descendants of former members. Collection indexed; will respond to queries.

The Connecticut Jewish Ledger
P.O. Box 1688
West Hartford, Connecticut 06144
(203) 233-2148
Published since 1929, covers complete state.

Jewish Historical Society of Greater Hartford
335 Bloomfield Avenue
West Hartford, Connecticut 06117
(203) 236-4571
Brief written inquiries handled without charge, but will not perform research (researcher requests forwarded to the Connecticut Historical Society). Photocopies of records provided on request.

Visitors should make an appointment with the director. The society, founded in 1971, maintains photographs and oral histories of Greater Hartford Jewish families.

Publications: *Hartford Jews: 1659–1970* by Rabbi Morris Silverman.

Their holdings include:

- 500 photocopies of documents
- 800 photographs
- 200 tapes of interviews
- 240 tapes
- 60 tape transcriptions
- 290 slides
- Press clippings and books

University of Hartford
Mortensen Library
200 Bloomfield Avenue
West Hartford, Connecticut 06117
(203) 243-4264
- Excellent reference library, maps, atlases, etc.
- Collections of Judaica, Jewish history, Holocaust literature
- Complete transcripts (fifty volumes) Nuremberg Trials.

Weinstein Mortuary
640 Farmington Avenue
West Hartford, Connecticut 06105
(203) 233-2675)
Will respond to mail request, prefers no phone calls for genealogical information.

Bibliography
Genealogy and Local History in New London County Libraries. New London: Southeastern Connecticut Library Council, 1982.

Goldberg, A. *The Jew in Norwich, Connecticut: A Century of Jewish Life.* Rhode Island Jewish Historical Notes 7: 79–103, November 1975.

Gordon, M. L. *The History of the Jewish Farmer in Eastern Connecticut.* Ph.D. dissertation, Yeshiva University, 1974.

Gustafson, Don, ed. *A Preliminary Checklist of Connecticut Newspapers 1755–1975.* Hartford: Connecticut State Library, 1975.

The Jew in Norwich: A Century of Jewish Life. Norwich: Norwich Jewish Tercentenary Committee, 1956.

Kemp, T. *Connecticut Researcher's Handbook.* Detroit: Gale Publishing Company, 1982.

Koenig, S. *An American Jewish Community: The Story of the Jews in Stamford, Connecticut.* WPA Typescript, 187 pp., 1940. (Connecticut State Library Archives RG 33 Box 102).

———. "The Social Aspects of the Jewish Mutual Benefit Societies." Social Forces 18:268–274, 1939.

Lindberg, M. W., ed. *Genealogists Handbook for New England Historical Society,* 1985.

Marcus, J. R. "Light on Early Connecticut Jewry." *American Jewish Archives* 1:3–52, 1948.

Mittelstein, R. "Mutual Aid Societies." WPA Typescript, 1939. (Connecticut State Library Archives RG Box 85).

Parks, R., ed. *Connecticut, A Bibliography of Its History.* University Press of New England.

Silverman, M. *Hartford Jews 1659–1970.* Hartford: Connecticut Historical Society, 1970.

Sperry, K. *Connecticut Sources for Family Historians and Genealogists.* Logan, Utah: Everton Publishers, 1980.

DISTRICT OF COLUMBIA

■ VITAL RECORDS

Birth and death records
Marriage License Bureau
500 Indiana Ave. N.W.
Washington, D.C. 20001
Marriage records; fee charged for a search of the indexes. To obtain old records, it is best to go in person.

Martin Luther King Library
Washington Room, 3d floor
8th and G Streets, N.W.
Washington, D.C. 20001

- Contains census index up to 1870
- Archival material about DC, newspapers, plat maps, city directories, and material from the Jewish Historical Society of Washington and the Washington Historical Society
- Staff is knowledgeable and eager to help

National Archives Records Center
4205 Suitland Road
Suitland, Maryland 20409
Probate records; earliest (up to 1966) are in large, bound books. Records from 1967 to the present are at the Probate Office in the District of Columbia government building. Records before 1967 may be stored at the Federal Records Center at Suitland, Maryland, but you must obtain permission to view them at 500 Indiana Avenue. Call (202) 879-1010 for information.

Naturalization records are stored in Suitland. Records through 1926 are open to the public by appointment. Write to National Archives, Washington, D.C. 20409 or call (301) 763-7410. Records post-1926 may be seen only with permission from the Clerk of the Court (District or Superior) or by arrangement with the Immigration and Naturalization Service, 425 I Street N.W., Washington, D.C. 20536, (202) 633-2441.

The National Genealogical Society
4527 17th Street, North
Arlington, VA 22207
(703) 525-0050

- Offers home study courses
- Publishes "The NGS Newsletter" six times per year
- Sponsors annual conference
- Collects and preserves genealogical, historical, and heraldic data
- Maintains library and archive
- Membership benefits and discounts

Vital Statistics Branch
Department of Human Services
425 I Street N.W.
Washington, D.C. 20001
(202) 727-5314

Cemeteries

Jews who died in Georgetown and in the District of Columbia before the founding of Washington Hebrew Congregation (WHC) may have been buried in the Home of Peace Cemetery in Alexandria, Virginia, or perhaps in nonconsecrated ground. WHC was the earliest Jewish congregation, and its cemetery opened soon after the founding in 1858. The oldest section of the Washington Hebrew cemetery is just to the right of the gate at the entrance on Alabama Avenue S.E., in the Anacostia section of the District of Columbia. The earliest Jews buried there were mostly from Germany.

Adas Israel Congregation was established in 1873 by a group from WHC, and its cemetery adjoins Washington Hebrew. There is a separate entrance gate, however. Two other large cemeteries adjoin those of WHC and Adas Israel. They are for Ohev Shalom–Talmud Torah Congregation and for the Elesavetgrad Burial Society.

In this century, a number of congregations and burial societies established cemeteries in the metropolitan Washington area. There are many synagogues, and each would have to provide information about its cemetery.

Bibliography

Altshuler, D. *The Jews of Washington, D.C.* Chappaqua, NY: Rossel Books/Jewish Historical Society of Greater Washington, 1985.

Babbel, J.A. *Lest We Forget: A Guide to Genealogical Research in the Nation's Capital.* Annandale, VA: Annandale Stake of The Church of Jesus Christ of Latter-day Saints, 1965 (1982 ed. by C.S. Neal).

Marans, H. *Jews in Greater Washington.* Washington, DC: Self-published, 1960.

Wynne, S. "District of Columbia Research." *Mishpacha,* Vol. 8, No. 2.

■ THE NATIONAL ARCHIVES
Suzan Fisher Wynne

National Archives and Records Service
8th and Pennsylvania Avenue N.W.
Washington, D.C. 20408

Overview

The National Archives and Records Administration is not in one building, but in many, scattered throughout the Washington metropolitan area and in branch offices throughout the United States (see Appendix M, pp. 216–217). (The address above is the principal office.) Before the year 2000, the National Archives will have consolidated its Washington area collections and research facilities in a new facility on the grounds of the University of Maryland. For now, the main branch will be our major focus (unless specified), for it is here that genealogists gather to pursue information about their ancestors. The vast majority of the material housed at the National Archives concerns people coming to or living in the United States. However, we will note a few collections about citizens of other countries.

The National Archives research facility must be entered through the Pennsylvania Avenue entrance. Visitors to the public exhibit enter on the opposite side of the building. Room 400, the hub of genealogical activity, is where much of the material we will discuss is on microfilm. Room 203 is the library and the main research room for records and materials not on microfilm.

Current security measures are fairly stringent. You must submit your hand luggage to a search upon entering or leaving the building. Having a research card will enable you to enter during the day without signing in at the lobby desk. Obtaining a research card requires only that you have a piece of identification with your photo.

As noted above, the Archives has two other facilities in the Washington area, which can be reached by shuttle van from the main building several times during the day. To obtain a current schedule of hours and shuttles and *to obtain all forms and publications*, unless otherwise noted, write to the *National Archives, Washington, DC 20408.*

The National Archives publishes a very useful book, *Guide to Genealogical Research in the National Archives* (1985). This is available by mail order or in the bookstore in the public section of the National Archives. Prices for the paperback and hardcover edition are under $50.

Each regional branch of the National Archives has a catalog of the records available there, either in original or microfilmed form. Although always out of date, since new material is continually being acquired, these catalogs are an excellent source of information about the availability of information. For holdings of the regional archives, see *The Archives: A Guide to the National Archives Field Branches* by Loretto Dennis Szucs and Sandra Hargreaves Luebking. This comprehensive volume includes descriptions of the individual field branches, listings of microfilm copies held by all branches, printed descriptions and inventories, histories of the agencies and their records, cross-references to microfilm holdings, and suggestions for research topics.

National Archives staff will search ship records for a fee if sufficient information is provided. For instance, if you want a passenger record found and no index for the period exists, you must know the date and port of arrival and port of embarkation or name of the ship, port of arrival, and date. Similarly for census records, if no index exists, you must have the address of the party, although, for a rural area, a town or county will probably be acceptable. To request a search, obtain *Form 81* for each record desired, from References

Services Branch (NNIR) at the above address. The Census Bureau has issued a new form, BC-600, to use in requesting a search of the 1900–1980 censuses. The cost if $25 for age and citizenship information and $31 for a copy of the full schedule for a household.

Military service, pension, and bounty-land records can be searched by requesting *Form 80* for each person of interest. Money will be requested after the search is done.

Genealogical Resources

The purpose of the National Archives is to collect and store records of importance to the nation and to the national interest. Obviously, this formidable task presents some giant management problems. In order to preserve material and, at the same time, make records available to researchers, much material of interest to genealogists is on microfilm and must, generally, be seen this way when that is the case.

The National Archives, operating under laws created by Congress, receives old records from all agencies of the federal government. Not all records must be given to the National Archives. Some agencies, especially if they continue to answer many public requests for information, prefer to maintain their old records in active status. The Social Security Administration is a good example of this. Some agencies have their own archival storage facilities in order to retain access to specific information they might need. The Immigration and Naturalization Service retains most records pertaining to naturalization and alien registration in the 20th century.

The records housed by the National Archives are not all open to the public. Some records have restrictions for a time period, and others are given with the understanding that only approved researchers will have access to the records. Some military records are still classified long after being received by the National Archives. Not all material is retained by the National Archives. Some material is discarded through a very complex process of review after it is determined that it is of no value.

Genealogists generally use a small portion of the material held by the Archives. The most common records used by genealogists are census, ship records, passports, and land and military records. Land records will not be covered in this article, since these records affect only a small percentage of Jews and the subject is well covered in most general genealogy books. However, this article will cover records not usually of interest to genealogists, including diplomatic records, materials captured from the Germans at the end of World War II pertaining to the Holocaust, and materials taken from the Russian Embassy in 1933 pertaining to Russian citizens living in the United States and Canada from 1846 to 1926.

Census Records

The federal government has conducted a census of all residents of the United States every ten years since 1790. These censuses have not all survived intact, and they differ widely in terms of quality of information. Later censuses are considerably more informative than those from the earlier years. The 1890 census burned except for a few counties. A few states and cities also conducted a census in 1890 or 1895 which can help to supplement the unfortunate loss in these areas. By law, the public is not to have access to records until they are 72 years old. In 1982, microfilms of the 1910 census became available for public research; the 1920 census will be available in 1992.

There are many good basic genealogy books that discuss, in considerable detail, the questions asked in each census. Commercial firms have indexed virtually all existing censuses from 1790 to 1870.

During the Depression, one of the projects of the Works Projects Administration was to hire people to index the 1880 and 1900 censuses. The 1880 census index included all families with children under 10 years of age. It is important to keep in mind that if there were no such children in the household, the people were *not* included. The 1900 census was completely indexed, although there are certainly errors and omissions.

The 1910 census is partially indexed. The National Archives ran into budget problems in the middle of creating an index to this census so that only some states are indexed. New York and New Jersey are not among those indexed. Described below are a few aids to help the researcher locate people in nonindexed states.

First, it is important to understand that all censuses were organized by "enumeration district," that is, by a number given to an area on a map and assigned to an enumerator who went from door to door literally writing down information about the persons in each household. Thus, if you know that a family lived in Missouri in 1870, but don't know the county, you would have to search every enumeration district in Missouri. But if you know that they lived in St. Louis, you would only have to search that city's enumeration districts—still a formidable task, but within the realm of possibility.

There is an excellent publication that can help a great deal with determining which county your ancestor might have lived in between 1790 and 1920, since some county lines changed and many new counties were formed as population grew. The book, entitled *Map Guide to the U.S. Federal Censuses, 1790–1920*, was written by William Thorndale and William Dollarhide. It is available in many libraries, but if you want to order it, write:

Genealogical Publishing Co., Inc.
1001 N. Calvert Street
Baltimore, Maryland 21202-3897

City directories were used by businesses to aid in mailing advertisements to local residents. They served as a means of finding people in a community as well, prior to the telephone directory. While some people were missed, these directories serve as an excellent means to finding addresses. (They also provide occupational information and occasionally the names of wives. They are extremely useful for determining the likelihood of a relationship or finding missing names of children as they became young adults because our forebears tended to live in very close proximity.) Some are organized so that they include several small communities, and some cover entire counties in rural areas. City directories are not available for every community in the country, even at the Library of Congress, which has a huge collection of them. Directories can be found in state, historical, and county libraries and at some universities.

Another aid to obtaining an address may be a birth, marriage, or death record. The Census Bureau oper-

MICROFILM ROLL NUMBER 965				1910 ~~1900~~ CENSUS — UNITED STATES																			
STATE New York				**TOWN/TOWNSHIP** Brooklyn										**SUPV. DIST. NO.** 301			**SHEET NUMBER** 1B						
COUNTY Kings				**CALL NUMBER** (drawer T624)						**DATE** April 15, 1910				**ENUM. DIST. NO.** 350 (part of Ward 16)			**PAGE NUMBER**						
LOCATION				**NAME**	**PERSONAL DESCRIPTION**										**NATIVITY**			**CITIZENSHIP**			**OCCUPATION**		**EDUCATION**	
Street	House Number	Dwelling Number	Family Number	of each person whose place of abode on June 1, 1900, was in this family	Relation to head of family	Color	Sex	Month of birth	Year of birth	Age	Single, married, widowed, divorced	Number of years married	Mother of how many children	Number of these children living	Place of birth	Place of birth of father	Place of birth of mother	Year of immigration to United States	No. of years in U.S.	Naturalization	dress goods	Number of months not employed / Attended school (months)	Can read	Can write / Can speak English / Home owned or rented / Home owned free or mortgaged
	51	11		FREEDMAN, Harris	H	W	M			42	M	25			Russia	Rus	Rus	1890		A	Retail/ Merchant			Y Y
				Fannie	W	W	F			41	M	25	3	1	Russia	Rus	Rus	1891			none			Y Y
				Rebecca	D	W	F			22	S				Russia	Rus	Rus	1891			piano teacher			Y Y

NATIONAL ARCHIVES TRUST FUND BOARD   NATF form 53F

Transcript of 1910 U.S. census return.

ated from maps that delineate the enumeration districts. Copies of these maps can be seen at:

Cartographic and Architectural Branch
841-5 S. Pickett Street
Alexandria, Virginia 20408

This branch will be discussed more fully later. (There is one major exception; the map for New York in 1910 has disappeared.) Copies of these maps can also be ordered from the Cartographic Branch. Additionally, the boundaries of each enumeration district were also written, and those written boundaries have been filmed.

Shortly after the 1910 census was released, the Bureau of the Census in Pittsburg, Kansas, discovered a small document that provided enumeration districts for each block in the 50 largest cities in 1910. This document was placed on microfiche and can be found in Room 400. The cities covered were Akron, Atlanta, Baltimore, Canton, Charlotte, Chicago, Cleveland, Dayton, Denver, Detroit, Washington, Elizabeth (NJ), Erie, Fort Wayne, Gary, Grand Rapids, Indianapolis, Kansas City, Long Beach, CA, Los Angeles, Newark (NJ), New York City (Brooklyn, Bronx, and Richmond included but not Queens), Oklahoma City, Omaha, Paterson, Peoria, Philadelphia, Phoenix, Reading, Richmond, San Antonio, San Diego, Seattle, South Bend, Tampa, Tulsa, Wichita, and Youngstown. (A cautionary note: Some of the enumeration districts provided for Baltimore and New York City are not correct.)

Census Indexing System

The National Archives uses a Soundex system, based on Western language sounds, to index census and ship records. Using a code system, surnames are grouped according to similar sounding consonants (like d and t). Vowels and a few other letters are not coded. The system places names like Greenstein, Grunshtein, and Greenstone in the same code group. The file is then organized alphabetically by first name. The National Archives has a pamphlet to instruct researchers how to Soundex surnames. The system is not foolproof, particularly for Eastern European names, which are based on non-Western languages that use different sounds for some letters.

The National Archives sells paperback publications describing each census, which provide complete information about which rolls of film cover sections of the Soundex, particular enumeration districts, counties, cities and, in the case of the 1910 census, which states are indexed. The publications are available by mail to facilitate your planning. You may request that the National Archives staff search a particular record, provided that you have either an address or other suitable locator information. You may also purchase any copy of the microfilmed censuses or indexes for $20 by writing to the National Archives.

Bibliography

A Century of Population Growth: 1790–1900. Orting, WA: Heritage Quest Press, 1989.

"Searching Census Records," *Dorot* (Journal of the Jewish Genealogical Society, Inc.), Summer 1987.

Thorndale, W., and Dollarhide, W. *Map Guide to the U.S. Federal Censuses, 1790–1920.* Baltimore: Genealogical Publishing Co., 1987.

U.S. and Special Censuses Catalog. Ancestry, Inc., P.O. Box 476, Salt Lake City, UT 84110.

Passenger Arrival Records (see also Chapter 1)

All persons who entered the United States from other than land masses attached to our continent entered by ship until the airplane came into common use. The majority of the records available to researchers are from 1820 to 1945. The records from 1820 to 1897 are called "customs lists" and were created in response to an 1819 act of Congress that required the master of a ship to file a list of passengers with the district collector of customs. The lists were created at the port of entry and include such information as the port of embarkation, the date of arrival, passenger, age, sex, occupation, and country of origin. Occasionally, a "customs list" will provide a town as well as a country of origin and may give additional information like a birth that occurred on board or how many passengers died of disease.

Before 1891, states with ports controlled their own immigration entry process. As a first step toward federalization of the process, in 1882, Congress directed the Secretary of the Treasury to coordinate a program of registration through existing state commissioners, boards, or officers, using state forms for information collection. Legislation in 1891 placed immigration under federal control, but retained some state involvement. Legislation in 1893 standardized the registration process and increased the informational content. From this point on, the lists began to be created at the point of embarkation.

Legislation in 1903 placed the immigration process under the newly created Department of Commerce and Labor. By 1907, the content of the registration lists had greatly expanded to include, among other items, town of birth, physical description, and previous U.S. residence if he or she had been here before. The paper used for information collection had gone from a few columns on a narrow sheet in 1820 to two wide pages in 1907.

Beginning in 1891, shipping companies were required to give all prospective passengers a medical exam before they were permitted to board, to reduce the number of people being refused entry into the United States. If a person was denied entry, the shipping company had to absorb the cost of the return passage. This practice ended in 1921 when new legislation shifted responsibility from the shipping companies to the American consulates. Although very few immigrants traveled first or second class, those who did were generally inspected and cleared on board ship and were free to leave the ship when it docked at the pier.

In June Babbel's *Lest We Forget* (see Bibliography), the editor/compiler reminds us that many ships deposited and collected passengers at multiple ports in the United States and that the ship's manifest was left at the first port of entry. Thus, the manifest may be filed in Boston even though relatives debarked in Philadelphia. Immigrants left the inspection station with a card pinned to their clothing indicating whether the person was being admitted or held. Those who were not admitted had cards with letters denoting heart trouble, eye diseases, and so forth. These immigrants were required to have an interview with a Board of Special Inquiry or a more detailed medical examination.

Barriers in the search for ship records. In order to be successful in finding a relative in ship records, there are several things you must know. Most critically, you must know the surname, since the name on the manifest was the name as it was *prior* to entry into the United States—usually the name that appeared on identification papers that all Europeans had to carry. This name may have been changed at the port of entry or shortly thereafter, or to make matters more confusing, the relative may have entered the United States with false papers. The Russian military draft was so feared and hated that families would do almost anything to ensure that a young male would not have to serve. Among the strategies for avoiding military service was the purchase of false papers to facilitate leaving the country.

Another barrier is not knowing the name of the ship, the port of entry, or the date of arrival. A further and fatal barrier is that the manifest of interest did not survive the perils of fire, water, and insects. The port of New York was served by Castle Garden, a facility in Battery Park from 1855 through 1891 when the new facility on Ellis Island opened, though it was not finished until June 13, 1897. The following day, fire broke out, destroying the new building along with many of the records from 1855 to that date. The reconstructed building on Ellis Island did not reopen until late 1900.

Resources for overcoming barriers. Post-1906 Petitions for Citizenship can provide important clues including the original name of the immigrant, current address, port and date of entry, and the name of the ship, birth date and place, occupation, and the names of two witnesses. At some point, Petitions also included the maiden name of the mother and recent places of residence other than the current address. Pre-1906 naturalizations are less reliable for this type of information, but sometimes contain arrival information, birth data, and occupation.

The 1900 and 1910 censuses include information about year of arrival in the United States. While this is sometimes inaccurate, the information can help to narrow the search (see earlier in this chapter).

Indexes to ship records, when they are available, are a quick route to locating an individual's arrival. Ship records and indexes are organized by port, and each group has been indexed in part. There are three types of indexes to ship records: alphabetical, Soundexed, and "book indexes." Early indexes tend to be alphabetical, leaving more room for error because of spelling problems. Soundexed indexes collapse all versions of the same name into one code, thus ensuring a more thorough search (see earlier in this chapter).

Book indexes were created by the shipping companies themselves. They are alphabetical listings of the passengers on each run of each ship in the line for a quarter of a year. The films of these indexes are organized by shipping company and time period. For instance, the Cunard Line created an alphabetical list of passengers for each ship in their line for January–March 1909. This kind of index is useful if you know, for instance, that a person arrived on the *Lusitania* between 1908 and 1910. You simply scroll through Cunard's entries for all of their ships during that time period. The limitation of the book index is that some of the lists are incomplete, particularly with respect to cabin passengers. The Soundexed lists were probably compiled from the book indexes and therefore reflect the same flaw. Book indexes are available for five ports for the following time periods:

Boston: 1899–1940, except 1901
New York: 1906–1942
Philadelphia: 1906–1926
Portland, ME: 1907–1930
Providence, RI: 1911–1934

The National Archives sells *Immigrant and Passenger Arrivals: A Select Catalog of National Archives Microfilm Publications* (1983), which lists the available passenger lists on microfilm by type of list and port and year, and provides information about the availability of indexes.

New York was the port where most Jewish immigrants debarked, from 1880 onward, although certainly other ports were used—Boston, Philadelphia, Charleston, Baltimore, Seattle, San Francisco, Galveston, and others. There were many minor ports along the Atlantic and Gulf of Mexico coasts. Baltimore was much used by German shipping companies. Philadelphia, for a time from 1840 to 1870, was a port favored by Germans. Charleston was a popular port in the late 18th and early 19th centuries.

Recently, the Immigration and Naturalization Service discovered repositories of manifests long thought to be lost. These have been filmed and are now available at the National Archives. These include records of immigration through Canadian border-crossing stations. Since these new film series do not appear in any current National Archives publication, they are reproduced on pp. 138–139 for the reader's convenience.

The National Archives' indexes for the New York port do not include the period 1847–1897. Two commercial firms have begun to fill that gap by indexing particular groups of immigrants such as Irish, Dutch, and German nationals during their peak immigration years. The list of Dutch and German immigrants, of course, will include Jews. Another project is underway to index the 1880s for all immigrants. The filmed index cards for 1897 to June 1902 are very informative, but almost half of the films are virtually unreadable, and the original cards were destroyed after filming.

The index for July 1902 to 1942 is really two index series merged into one. The cards for 1902 to about 1910 provide the name of the ship and the date of arrival as well as substantial data about the immigrant. After that, most cards provide no more information than a volume number with some vague locator information that can mean something different for different ships. A volume can have as many as 15 ships' manifests, although generally only two or three are from European ports. Obviously, the lack of information can lead to many hours of frustrating search when there are multiple entries for a name.

The index for the port of Baltimore is in three separate groups: city lists and two groups of federal lists. All are poor and obviously incomplete. Note that the newly filmed Baltimore records are not indexed.

All of the indexes have various problems associated with them, but they are better than no indexes at all.

Another avenue to finding information about an arrival is Morton Allan's *Directory of European Passenger Steamship Arrivals for 1890 to 1930 at the Port of New York and 1904 to 1926 at the Ports of Philadelphia, Boston, and Baltimore* (see Bibliography). This can serve to verify a date on an index card, which is sometimes very difficult to read. Information in the Morton Allan book is not always correct, because ship arrival dates were not necessarily the same dates manifests were logged. (Unfortunately, the Archives does not have a list of the ships that appear in each volume so you may have to look at a few rolls to find the correct one.) This directory is also useful if you know the name of the ship and have a rough idea about arrival time.

One other avenue might be the immigration indexes created by William Filby (see Bibliography). They are merged indexes compiled from hundreds of sources, mostly genealogists who have voluntarily indexed ship records. The Filby indexes now go up to 1900, but the vast majority of those listed are arrivals in an earlier period and very few of those listed appear to be Jewish. However, it is worth a try. The indexes are at many large libraries.

What we can learn from the manifest. From 1897 on, the ship manifests begin to be fairly informative. Information improves after 1903 and becomes excellent after 1907, when we can learn who paid for the passage, the nearest relative left behind in Europe, with the name of a town, birth place, where the immigrant last lived, how much money the person had, where and to whom he or she was going, physical description, and health status. Early lists generally include name, age, occupation, and country of origin.

Frequently, immigrants were detained for varying periods of time and for a number of reasons. When this occurred, the immigrant is relisted at the end of the manifest section. The detention section provides the number of meals consumed and the date of actual entry into New York from the island. It appears that many immigrants arrived with out-of-date addresses for their relatives, and in the detention section, the corrected address is provided with a more legibly written name. Indeed, sometimes, a wholly different relative is given in this section.

In the detention section, codes will be written by most names. "LPC" stands for "likely to be a public charge." Other codes denote health problems or "political undesirables" (see Immigration and Naturalization, p. 4).

There are scattered numbers and notes throughout the manifest itself, most of which are self-explanatory. One set of numbers on the manifest itself may be mysterious. Written very close to the name of the immigrant is the naturalization number and sometimes a date for when the manifest was checked. After 1906, as part of the federal naturalization process, clerks were instructed to verify entry information to be certain that entry was legal and that applicants had been in the United States five years.

The handwriting on many manifests is difficult to read. In some cases, the writing is close to old German script; in other cases, there appear to be vertical lines of various lengths, which obscure the letters; mercifully, in some cases, the writing is beautifully round and clear. Often, a mixture of writing will be found on a single manifest.

Some tips for a successful search. Each roll of microfilm contains from one to three volumes. After 1897, the volumes are preceded by a list of the ships appearing in that volume. The volumes may overlap somewhat in terms of arrival date, particularly in a period of heavy traffic. Thus, if you do not find the ship of interest in one volume, it may be in the previous volume (on another roll of film) or in the one following, in which case you simply scroll forward. There is a black area between the volumes to aid the user in knowing when to slow down.

It may be easier to ignore the group and list numbers, as they rarely seem to correspond with anything on the manifest and scroll from the beginning to the end of a manifest. The beginning is generally where United States citizens are listed. Foreign cabin passengers follow and then steerage passengers. Since the ship may have stopped at more than one port of embarkation, this listing pattern follows throughout for each port. The end of the manifest contains the detention list discussed above. If you are unsure whether you are searching the right ship or if you have scrolled through and cannot find the person, check the detention list. Sometimes the passenger only shows up on this list.

Arrivals in the period 1820 to about 1880 are less well organized on film. Ships are listed in approximate date order, but there is no volume listing of the ships and information about each ship only appears on a scrap of paper just prior to the manifest. Searching these volumes takes considerable patience for a rather paltry payoff.

One irritating aspect of this frustrating search process is that many users fail to scroll back to the beginning of a roll. If you put a roll on the machine and can't make heads or tails of it, chances are you are in the middle of the roll. Scroll to the beginning. And when you are finished, scroll back to the beginning again.

The Canadian border. Canada was a route of arrival for many immigrants beginning in the late 19th century. Railroad connections made it fairly simple to debark at one of the Canadian ports and transfer to a rail line that connected to an official border crossing point into the United States. There were two advantages to this route, one being that many of the ships left from British ports, a less expensive method of travel. The second advantage was that the medical inspection was less rigorous at the border crossing points.

The films for the Canadian border crossings are somewhat misleadingly labeled. In fact, all of the indexes except for the one marked "Detroit" are for immigrants who entered at points all along the border from the Atlantic to the Pacific.

The films of the actual entry records provide information obtained by United States immigration inspectors at border crossing points, along with what appears to be ship manifests, listing the name of the ship on which the immigrants arrived plus personal data. The cards appear to be for people who had spent some time in Canada before crossing, while the manifests concern groups of ship passengers who were headed immediately for the United States. The indexes are easy to use, but trying to find an individual on the manifest films from the indexes is difficult.

The entry records are organized by date and then provide grouped records from specific entry points along the border. Unfortunately, because these films are so new, the National Archives has not yet provided a finding aid to each of the volumes, and this hampers the researcher in using the series efficiently.

Bibliography

Babbel, J. A. *Lest We Forget: A Guide to Genealogical Research in the Nation's Capital.* Annandale, VA: Annandale Stake of The Church of Jesus Christ of Latter-day Saints, 1965 (1982 ed. by C. S. Neal).

Glazier, I. A., and Filby, P. W., eds. *Germans to America: Lists of Passengers Arriving at U.S. Ports, 1850–1855.* Wilmington, DE: Scholarly Resources Inc., 1988 (multi-vol.).

Marinbach, B. *Galveston: Ellis Island of the West.* Albany: State University of New York Press, 1983.

Morton Allan Directory of European Passenger Steamship Arrivals. Baltimore: Genealogical Publishing Co., Inc., 1980.

Tepper, M. *American Passenger Arrival Records.* Baltimore: Genealogical Publishing Co., Inc., 1988.

Zimmerman, G. J., and Wolfert, M. *German Immigrants: Lists of Passengers Bound From Bremen to New York, 1863–1867.* Baltimore: Genealogical Publishing Co., Inc., 1987 (multi-vol.).

Naturalizations

Naturalization after September 26, 1906, was carried out in three stages. First, the individual filled out a Declaration of Intention (better known as "first papers") to become a United States citizen. The second stage involved filling out a Petition for Citizenship, which provided very good genealogical information, including the original name of the immigrant, birth date and place, maiden name of mother, occupation, arrival information, last place of foreign residence, the person in the United States to whom the immigrant was coming, and the initial place of destination, plus other items of lesser interest. This petition was filed prior to becoming a citizen and was used by naturalization officials to verify information provided on the ship record, the petitioner's contention that he had been in the United States at least five continuous years, and that other facts were correct as given. The final stage of the naturalization process was the granting of a Certificate of Naturalization, which contained no information except the date and court of naturalization and the country of origin of the newly-naturalized citizen.

In addition to these documents in post-1906 Immigration and Naturalization Service (INS) files, there were also stubs and Certificates of Arrival, which are useful. When applying for naturalization papers, it is important to ask for the whole file.

Prior to the 1906 law, state law may have required a person to file "first papers" or a Final Petition, but often these papers were only partially completed or missing altogether and in general were not reliable as sources of information about arrival or even birth date. However, one can never predict what will be on file. A person may have been asked to provide proof of residence for the required period of time (this differed over time), and the material that they offered would still be on file in the form of hospital, school, or work documents, letters, or even scraps of paper from the inspection at port of entry.

The Archives publication *Genealogical and Biographical Research* (currently available for $2.00) provides an overview of what the National Archives system has in the way of naturalization records along

Declaration of Intention for Morris Weiner, Monroe, County, Iowa, September 13, 1918.

Immigration and Naturalization Service

FOIA/PA Section
425 I Street N.W.
Room 5114
Washington, D.C. 20536

Request one copy of *Form G639* for each person for whom you need information. The phone number is (202) 514-3278.

Copies of all naturalization records are available to the person on whom the file exists and members of the public. The person whose file it is must file under the Privacy Act, submitting proof of identity. Others can file under the Freedom of Information Act. Form G639 is used for both kinds of requests.

While you are requesting naturalization information, on that same form, ask for all material the INS has on that individual. The INS has a file on virtually every person who entered this country after 1906. The information they have includes post-1921 visa material, alien registrations for people who had not become citizens at the time of World War I, and then again in the World War II era, as well as other material that the INS maintained at various times.

When making a request, provide as much identifying information as possible to facilitate the search. If the person you are tracing could still be alive (by date of birth), you may be required to present a death certificate. No money will be required with this application. The first 100 copies of a person's file are provided free of charge. If there are charges, you will be billed and required to pay before you receive any material.

INS is required to confirm receipt of your request within ten days, but the search may take quite a long time. Be patient, and you may be well rewarded.

Bibliography

Neagles, J. C., and Neagles, L. L. *Locating Your Immigrant Ancestors: A Guide to Naturalization Records.* Logan, UT: Everton Publishers, Inc., 1986. (A guide to local and state court holdings based on questionnaires.) $7 from the publisher, P.O. Box 368, Logan UT 84321.

Wynne, S. "Naturalization and Visa Records at the U.S. Immigration and Naturalization Service." *Avotaynu*, Vol. V, No. 1, Spring 1989.

Military Records

The National Archives publishes *Military Service Records in the National Archives* (current price is $2.00). There are many other excellent sources of information about these records. Records for those who served in the military are not in the public domain for 75 years. Before then, the record must be for yourself or a close relative who has died, and then proof of death and relationship must be offered.

This section will focus on records for those who served in World War I, since these are available, and this war was the first in which substantial numbers of Jews served. This is also a collection of material not often described well in existing publications.

More than 24 million draft registrations in 1917–1918 are on file for males born between 1873 and 1900. The records are arranged by state, county, and (within the county) the draft board. The registration cards for each board are arranged alphabetically by surname. The cards provide the registrant's birth date, birth place, citizenship, race, address, occupation/employer, and name of person to be notified in an emergency.

The requirement for registration pertained to all

with records pertaining to land, taxes, civilian government employees, resident aliens, and so on. Newly filmed material is being acquired all the time at the regional level so you shouldn't assume that what you are looking for is not in the system.

The National Archives has some information about pre-1906 naturalization records. The pre-1906 naturalization records for New England and other regions were collected and indexed during the era of the Works Progress Administration. An index to these records is in Room 400 at the main branch and in the regional branch. Similar projects were carried out for the boroughs of the New York City area and New Jersey, and this index is at the Federal Archives and Records Center in Bayonne, New Jersey. The main branch also has other early naturalization records including those for South Carolina (1790–1906), Eastern (Philadelphia), (1790–1951) and Western (Pittsburgh) Pennsylvania (1790–1906), Maryland (1797–1951), California, Northern District (1852–1928), and Montana (1868–1929).

The branches of the National Archives are the repositories of naturalization records for states in their regions and new material is continually being acquired. (See Appendix C.)

Requesting post-1906 naturalization information. Post-1906 naturalizations were handled by federal courts. To obtain records of these proceedings, write directly to:

males who were citizens or who had filed first papers or a Declaration of Intention to become a citizen. However, some draft boards ignored the legal requirements and contacted men who had not filed first papers. In some cases, these men were drafted. Although some of these men were successful in appealing for a release from military service, others served in the war.

One incentive to serving was that final citizenship would be arranged, and many draftees did, in fact, become citizens in the federal court closest to their basic-training camps.

The National Archives Main Branch has a complete file card index to the names of men who became naturalized during World War I. The staff will search this index for all names provided.

A search of the draft registration records can be done by mail for a $5 fee for each individual. To locate a registration card, a researcher must be able to provide a birth date and residence in 1917 or 1918. In a rural area, the county is sufficient, but for a metropolitan area, it is necessary to have a street address. A mail search requires a form for each individual. Contact the branch below for the necessary forms. Research can also be done by visiting the Southeast Region research room:

National Archives Southeast Region
1557 St. Joseph Avenue
East Point, Georgia 30344
(404) 763-7477

(See East Point, Georgia, p. 49.)

Copies of the records for relevant states have been distributed to the regional branches and can also be seen at these facilities. For instance, the Southeast Region branch in Denver has records from Colorado, Montana, North Dakota, South Dakota, Utah, and Wyoming.

The records are scheduled to be filmed by the Family History Library in Utah and will eventually be available through this alternate system. Additionally, some state and university libraries have copies of films relevant to the area. The Hillman Library of the University of Pittsburgh, for instance, has all of the films relevant for draft boards in the Pittsburgh area.

Another source of information about World War I draftees is, curiously enough, the Russian Consular Records, which will be discussed in some detail later in this article. The records, particularly those from Philadelphia, specifically pertain to Russian citizens (Jews as well as non-Jews) who were drafted although they had not filed first papers.

The large number of draftees who appealed their draft status generated another collection of records, most of which, unfortunately, were destroyed in a fire. The files consist of transcripts of interviews with those who were appealing. The only records to survive the fire were those for people with surnames A through part of D. Copies of these interviews are also in the Atlanta branch (Southeast Region) and are also at the Federal Records Center in Suitland, Maryland, a facility near Washington and accessible by shuttle from the main branch.

Other military records. Other military records can be obtained by requesting copies of *NATF Form 80* from the National Archives. If a file is found, you will be notified and will have 30 days to send $5.00.

Passport and Visa Applications

The National Archives has passport applications issued by the State Department from 1810, although the majority of applications are for the period after World War I. Passport applications from 1810 to February 1906 are in the main building. Those from 1906 to 1925 are stored at the Suitland facility.

The Family History Library in Utah has completed filming of indexes to applications as well as the applications themselves. A microfilmed index for 1810 to February 1906 (series M1371) is now in Room 400 in the main building. Thus far, there are nine rolls for regular passport applications from December 21, 1810, to February 1906; two rolls for emergency passport applications from June 1874 to 1906; one roll for special passport applications for the period 1829–1894; and one roll for passports issued by the New York Passport Office in 1861 and 1862 along with a register of miscellaneous applications, 1835–1869.

The early indexes for the first two groups of records are organized by the first letter of the surname and the date of application. Gradually, the index becomes easier to use when surnames are grouped by the first few letters. No Soundex system was used for this index.

Later indexes will be available on film as soon as they are processed. In the meantime, inquiry can be made of the staff at the Suitland facility regarding the existence of a passport application after February 1906.

Emergency passport applications. As a rule, regular passports were issued by federal clerks based in the United States to people who were citizens of this country, but emergency passports were also issued to people living or traveling abroad. They were issued by authorized persons on the staff of a United States consulate or embassy when a person could prove he held United States citizenship and needed or wanted a passport.

Prior to September 1922, women acquired citizenship through their husbands or fathers. Minor children, too, acquired citizenship through their fathers. (Children born in this country were citizens as a matter of course.) This arrangement led to the legal conclusion that women and children of naturalized citizens living abroad were entitled to United States citizenship, and if they held a United States passport, they could enter this country as citizens, thus avoiding the immigration inspection process at the port of entry. Their applications at United States consulates around the world, complete with photos, are on file at the National Archives.

Emergency passports became especially important after World War I broke out and after the conclusion of the war. Women and children who were technically United States citizens, since the husband or father had been naturalized, were trapped in Europe without funds or protection. Men who had returned to Europe for various reasons were also trapped there for the duration of the war, and many applied for these passports. Many names appear in these records several times since they had to renew their passports annually. It is possible to trace their movements, because they sometimes renewed at different consulates.

After the war, the applications increased as participation in military service had been instrumental in expanding the number of new citizens. There was also a new group of applicants. Many immigrants had not been impressed with life in the United States and had returned to Europe, but not before having children in the United States. These children were citizens in their own right and were therefore entitled to return to the United States.

The State Department created indexes for the emergency passport applications up until 1915, but no index could be found for the period of 1915 to 1925. A team of volunteers from the Jewish Genealogy Society of Greater Washington (JGSGW) created an index of Jews appearing in the records for those years. The index undoubtedly misses some people and certainly includes some people who are not Jewish. The index can be obtained by sending a check for $15.00 to:

JGSGW
P.O. Box 412
Vienna, Virginia 22183-0412

How to gain access to passport applications. For a fee, the National Archives will respond to a mail request for a search of the indexes and will copy the correct record for you. A negative of the photograph attached to an application can be made by a photographic process that costs $5.00 and takes about six weeks. If you would like to arrange for this, include this request in your original letter. The National Archives does not need elaborate information about the relative you are researching, but it would be helpful to indicate a year (of application) or as small a time frame as possible, country of origin, and other identifying data that would differentiate him from others of the same name.

Post-1926 passport applications remain with the State Department. The name of the applicant, place and approximate date of application should be supplied. These requests should be addressed to:

Passport Office
U.S. Department of State
Washington, D.C. 20520

Information from the passport applications. Passport applications are now simpler than they used to be. Old applications requested much more personal data. At a minimum, the application for a naturalized citizen provided birth date and birth place, the date and place of naturalization, and sometimes the original date and port of entry into the United States, mother's maiden name, name of father, occupation, and current address. Emergency passport applications after 1906 almost always provided information about the naturalized person's date and place of naturalization, United States address, notes about the applicant's appearance, circumstances, and often the name of the ship and date of arrival of the naturalized person as well as birthplace and birth date.

Visas. Visa applications and supporting material are at the INS. They can be obtained by the applicant or by members of the family if the applicant is deceased. This is extremely rich material, consisting of birth and marriage records, family trees, affidavits from the applicant's town of residence attesting to good character, school records, and so on. It can be assumed that visa material will yield much of interest to Jewish family historians.

To request visa material, ask the INS (see p. 34 for address) for one copy of *Form 1115-0087* for each person for whom you would like information. *Keep in mind that visas only came into use after July 26,* 1917. Every member of the family had to have a visa application with supporting documents.

You will be asking the INS for information under the Freedom of Information Act if you are a relative of the applicant. You may be asked to supply proof of death of the applicant if the individual could still be alive.

The National Archives has some State Department correspondence pertaining to visa applications from 1921 to 1926. Since these records were only recently released for public inspection, little is known about them from a genealogical point of view. Some of the records were to have been destroyed many years ago, but it now appears that most of the visa files remain intact.

Indexes to the records at the National Archives exist. They are organized by the name of the person applying for a visa, but this was not always the would-be immigrant himself.

Diplomatic Records
Two publications are available describing what the National Archives has on film regarding its extensive collection of diplomatic materials. One publication (write Scholarly Resources, Inc., 104 Greenhill Avenue, Wilmington, Delaware 19805) is entitled *Official Records of the U.S. State Department.* The other (write National Archives Trust Fund Board, Dept. 732, P.O. Box 100793, Atlanta, Georgia 30384) is entitled *Diplomatic Records: A Select Catalog of National Archives Microfilm Publications* and was compiled by John H. Hedges. This publication currently sells for $5.00 plus $3.00 for shipping.

There are several groups of State Department records that may be useful for Jewish family historians. These records are being indexed by volunteers from the Jewish Genealogy Society of Greater Washington.

Consular post records. All United States consular posts maintain files that eventually are bound by year. These bound volumes, in the custody of the National Archives, are a permanent record of business transacted by the consular post and include correspondence, memos, and daily logs. Consulates transact all manner of business on behalf of citizens living or visiting in the host country, including issuing emergency passports or visas, advancing a loan to a United States citizen, providing legal assistance, or assisting in arrangements connected with the death of a citizen who died abroad. The records contain names and details about the circumstances surrounding a request for assistance from the consulate.

The material is currently being indexed by JGSGW for the period 1880–1926. The original material may be viewed by requesting the desired years from a consultant in Room 208 or by contacting the diplomatic branch in Room 13E, main branch. This material will be moved to the new building.

Records from the decimal file. The State Department maintained a decimal classification system for its central files from 1906 to 1963. The system is highly complex, but a simplified explanation is provided in a free pamphlet, *Purported Lists for the Department of State Decimal File, 1910–1963.* The files were indexed by name, and this index continues to exist on 3×5-inch cards in the diplomatic branch of the National Archives. The cards may be viewed by applying in Room 13E. The files themselves are accessible to researchers in two forms: Many records are now on microfilm and more are being filmed all the time; those not on film can be ordered and examined in Room 203, the Central Research Room. Ordering time: one half-hour to more than one hour.

Each portion of the decimal file system is accompanied by an elaborate daily log which briefly describes the event (letter, telegram, etc.) and the names mentioned. It is not as satisfactory as an index, but can be read through fairly quickly, and it does provide locator information, which saves the researcher from having to hunt through all the files or the name card index. These logs can be viewed on microfilm.

One such group of materials has already been indexed by volunteers from the JGSGW. These records concern the protection of interests of relatives of American citizens—at first glance, an odd matter for the U.S. State Department to be involved with. At the start of World War I, family members in the United States became concerned about relatives still living in war-torn Europe and appealed to politicians, attorneys, and to the State Department directly, for assistance in obtaining information and transmitting money and boxes of food and clothing. As the war continued, there were new requests for information about pris-

oners of war, displaced refugees whose present whereabouts were unknown, and information about friends as well as relatives. The State Department became the conduit for thousands of such requests.

Records of the consular post in Jerusalem.
Part of the consular post records, this group needs to be addressed separately, because virtually every page has some relevance to Jews. In 1880, Americans living in Palestine numbered about 100, but this changed quickly. Hundreds of Jews, mainly from Russia, emigrated to the United States long enough to become citizens and then reemigrated to Eretz, Israel, then under Turkish rule. These families depended on the United States consulate as its government abroad. Indeed, there was a special United States court attached to the consulate from 1873 to 1934. Records in six volumes address wills, divorces, adoptions, land transactions, and civil disputes.

Jerusalem Court Records, 1877–1925, 2 volumes.

Probate Records and Registers of Wills, 1910–1929, 75 cases.

Misc. Correspondence and Other Records Regarding Estates and Consular Court Cases, 1873–1890, 1 volume.

Civil Docket, 1911–1934, 1 volume.

Criminal Docket and Record Book, 1921–1925, 1 volume.

American citizens in Palestine had to register annually with the consulate. These registrations are recorded in two volumes covering 1867 to 1928 (marriages for 1888–1894 are also included) and books for 1910–1914, 1919–1928, 1923–1928 (indexes included), and 1925–1929 (no index included). There is a slim volume of miscellaneous records for 1919–1921, which includes scattered records about transactions of the period.

Additionally, the National Archives recently filmed U.S. State Department records for Palestine for 1930–1944 (M1037).

FBI Records

The National Archives has recently released investigation files from the Federal Bureau of Investigation. There are about 900 rolls of film for this collection of material from 1908 to 1922 (the agency was then known as the Bureau of Investigation). The material is indexed, although it is difficult to go smoothly from the index to the material itself. Much of the material consists of written reports from agency employees and agents, transcripts of interviews, and other investigative records. Many of the targets of investigation were people suspected of being subversives because of union activities or membership in other groups, including those favoring open immigration.

Another group of those investigated were men who had failed to register for the 1917 and 1918 draft calls, many of whom were immigrants. There are also numerous files for people requesting visas to attend international conferences abroad.

Russian Consular Records

In 1917, the government of Russia underwent the first in a series of radical upheavals, and as a result of the change, the United States withdrew its recogni-

Entry from State Department files at the National Archives documenting execution of Israel Abramovich Odnopozov in 1930 as a "counter-revolutionary damager."

tion of the government. Representatives of the Russian government in the United States and Canada, former employees of the czarist regime, continued their duties in the belief that the regime would soon be restored and in an effort to maintain continuity with Russian citizens living in the United States and Canada. Funds for their salaries were supported, for a time, by the wealthy refugees who fled Russia immediately after the Revolution. These funds eventually dried up, the offices were closed, and the records collected for storage in the embassy in Washington. Despite the lack of contact between consular employees and the official government of Russia, Russians living abroad continued to receive assistance and services almost as though nothing had changed.

Some files of these consular offices dated back to 1848, although most material had been sent periodically to Russia for handling and storage there. Correspondence tended to be retained in the offices while political and economic material was sent to Russia. Naturally, after 1917, all material was retained in the United States or Canada.

Consulates functioned in the late 19th century in areas where significant numbers of Russian immigrants had settled. The location and number of offices changed frequently over the years, depending on many factors, including the availability of suitable staff. Most consular "officials" were attorneys, born in this country as a rule, who served the Russian government on a part-time basis. Most performed consular services for several countries, in addition to practicing law. Most of these consular officials did not speak or read Russian and had to rely on translators for assistance with case and clerical work. The exception was the New York consular office, which functioned as the primary consulate in North America and which always employed Russian citizens exclusively.

Consulates then served much the same function as they do today. In addition to representing their governments in political and economic matters on a local level, they provided a wide range of services to their citizens living abroad. It must be remembered that many Jews from Russia did not become United States citizens and so continued to need assistance from a consulate nearest to their place of residence.

In the ordinary course of events, the files from these consular offices would have reverted to the new representatives of the Soviet regime, which was recognized by President Roosevelt in 1933. However, the President, in consultation with General Douglas MacArthur, concluded that it was in the interests of the United States to confiscate the material as part of a larger collection of material from the Russian Supply Committee, a cooperative venture between the United States and Russia during World War I. This confiscation took place on November 17, 1933, the eve of the day the new Soviet ambassador arrived in Washington. The material had been stored in huge boxes that were subsequently moved a number of times while in the custody of the State Department. The Soviets, under the watchful eyes of guards, could examine the material and were given permission to take a couple of boxes of records. An early inventory of the records was apparently lost, but correspondence between the State Department and the Russian custodian of the records shows the extent of the records at that time. The State Department handled their custodianship of these files with disregard for their future value, discarding some and mixing material indiscriminately. When the Na-

tional Archives eventually acquired the remaining records in 1949, they were already crumbling, faded, and in a highly disorganized state. Still in their original, highly acid folders, the papers were placed in archival boxes and left to sit on shelves, unexamined until the late 1970s, when the Soviet Union asked for the return of the records. Plans were made to film the records, and an archivist was hired to arrange the records and to prepare finding aids to assist researchers in using the material. The archivist left after a short period of time, and the funds for his job were absorbed by other, more immediate needs.

In late 1981, the JGSGW learned of the collection through Zachary Baker and Rabbi Malcolm Stern from the New York-based JGS. After determining that the records were, indeed, of great value to Jewish family historians, funds were raised to continue the task of both organizing and creating a name index to the material. This was completed in 1986. The Mormons (Family History Library) subsequently microfilmed the material, and it is now available for research in Room 400 of the National Archives and through the Family History Library ordering system.

Much of the material is, of course, in Russian. However, other languages are represented, including Polish, Finnish, occasionally Hebrew, German, Lithuanian, and Ukrainian. Some material is in English. The records cover the period 1848–1926, with the vast majority from the period 1914–1926.

The consulates and vice-consulates for which we have material are: New York, Philadelphia, Chicago, San Francisco, Portland (Oregon), Seattle (includes Alaska), and Honolulu. We know there were other consulates or vice-consulates in Boston, Pittsburgh, Detroit, locations in West Virginia, Alabama, and the Midwest, because they are referred to in correspondence, and there are scattered letters from other consulates. However, this material has disappeared. There is no way of determining how much material the State Department destroyed or whether they discarded material from one or more of the missing consulates.

In addition to extensive correspondence files, there are:

- Applications for renewal of passports, which often include old passports, some with photos, names of wives and children, and information about travel on that passport
- Applications for visas to travel or to return to Russia that generally include much family data and photos
- Forms authorizing transmittal of money to savings accounts set up by the consulates for the benefit of relatives in Russia
- Requests for certificates of Russian citizenship, which transmit birth, marriage, circumcision, and school records
- Letters (particularly in the Philadelphia files) that request assistance in resisting efforts of World War I draft boards from drafting men who were not United States citizens

The San Francisco, Seattle, and Portland files include much material relating to legal transactions requiring a transfer of power of attorney. All of the consulates devoted considerable time to cases involving the deaths of Russian citizens in this country, requests for information about people whose relatives

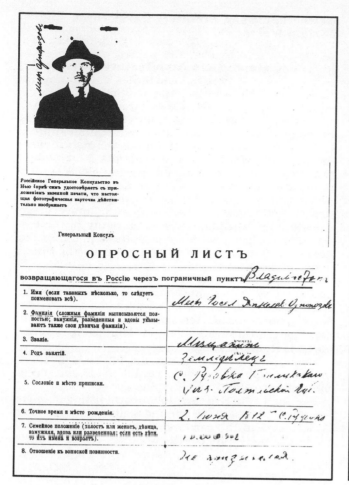

Application of Meyer Yankel Odnopozov for visa to return to Russia, April 23, 1918. (Courtesy of Russian Consular Records Collection, National Archives)

TRANSLATION

Photo signed by Meyer Odnopozov

The Russian General Consulate in N.Y. certifies that the above photo is that of applicant

APPLICATION FORM

(applicant . . . .
is returning to Russia via border corssing at Vladivostok

1. First name		Meyer Iosel Yankelev
2. Last Name		Odnopozov
3. Status		Bourgeois
4. Occupation		Farmer
5. Place of domocile		Village of Rudovka, District of Priluksk Prov. of Poltava
6. Date and place of birth		June 2, 1892, Rudovka
7. Family status		bachelor
8. Draft status		Was not called
9. Draft class of		1913
10. Present residence		
11. Place of residence during last 5 years		America
12. Residence of parents		Rudovka, District of Priluksk Prov. of Poltava
13. Religion		Jewish
14. Nationality		Hebrew
15. Citizenship		Russian
16. Parents' citizenship		Russian
17. Did you change citizenship, if so, when		
18. Destination in Russia		Central Province
19. Purpose of trip and supporting documents		Returning home for permanent residence
20. Relatives in Russia and their address		Rudovka, Priluksk, Prov. of Poltava
21. Trips abroad during the last 3 years		

April 23, 1918

signed Meyer Odnopozov

Translation of application of Meyer Yankel Odnopozov.

were unable to contact them in the United States, and people who got into difficulty with the police. San Francisco's consulate was heavily involved in rescuing a large group of Russian families from involuntary indentured servitude on Hawaiian plantations.

The consulate in Hawaii, for the most part a political office with diplomatic functions, is documented in this collection from 1848 forward, with some gaps in service. The files are primarily reports on activities or correspondence and contain, in English, a fascinating history of Hawaii and the early years of its royal family. Russian economic and political interests in Hawaii are clearly documented in this material.

Working with a team of highly qualified translators, the entire collection was indexed for names by the JGSGW. The index was Soundexed using a unique system devised for East European names by two Jewish genealogists, Randy Daitch and Gary Mokotoff. The index was published by Garland Publishing in 1987.

Questions regarding the Russian consular records should be addressed to:

Civil Reference Branch NNRC
National Archives
Washington, D.C. 20408
(202) 501-5410

Bibliography

Baker, Z. "The Russian Consular Collection at the Public Archives of Canada: Genealogical Implications." *Toledot,* Vol. 4, No. 3.

Brown, J. H. "The Disappearing Russian Embassy Archives 1922–49." *Prologue:* Journal of the National Archives, Spring 1982.

Sack, S. A., and Wynne, S. F. "Russian Consular Records to be Indexed." *Avotaynu: The International Review of Jewish Genealogy,* Vol. 1, No. 2, July 1985.

———. "The Russian Consular Records index and Catalog." New York: Garland Publishing, Inc., 1986.

Weiner, M. *Sources for Military Records.* Secaucus, NJ: Self-published, 1987.

Still Pictures Research
Miriam Weiner

Still Pictures Research Room
8th and Pennsylvania Avenue N.W.
Room 18N
(202) 523-3010

Still pictures number over five million and collection headings include

- National Archives Collection of World War II War Crimes Records (RG 238)
- *Records of the United States Information Agency* (RG 306)
- The photographic file of the Paris bureau of the *New York Times,* 1900–1950. This contains photographs (663,998) covering a broad range of subject matter including World War I, the opening phases of World War II, and activities of Allied and Axis armed forces, the liberation and Allied occupation of Europe following the war, atrocities, and cities. Material is accessible through topic/subject index in finding aid on premises. Photocopy machine and fee schedule for photographs on premises

Cartographic and Architectural Records
Miriam Weiner

Cartographic and Architectural Branch
841 S. Pickett St.
Alexandria, Virginia 22304
(703) 756-6700

Housed in the Cartographic and Architectural Branch (CAAB) are approximately one million prints of aerial photographs taken by the German military during World War II. Many of the prints are annotated to indicate military installations and defenses; other prints are marked to show potential bombing targets. Although the scale and quality of the photographs in this collection vary considerably, the imagery provides unique wartime coverage of many of the contested areas. The photos were captured at Tempelhof Airport in Berlin at the end of the war by the British and Americans.

Some of the photos were taken at a low enough altitude to show buildings, streets, rivers, landmarks, and details of the town. Frequently, when shown these aerial photos, former residents have pointed out the exact location of their house and identified many other portions from the photo.

Each time a town is researched for the availability of an aerial photo, an index card is made and put on file at the CAAB.

See Appendix E for an alphabetical listing of towns from the index card file referred to above. If your town is not listed in the card index file, it is necessary to follow the procedure below:

1. Look up name of town in index to AMS (Army Map Service) 1:250,000 Eastern Europe Series N501 or Western Europe Series M501 map se-

Aerial photo of Shepetovka and Sudilkov in the Ukraine c. 1941. (Courtesy of the National Archives)

ries. Note coordinates and map number from index.

2. Request map by number from archivist.
3. Archivist will bring map and box of plastic overlays.
4. Place overlays on map until you identify which photo(s) you want to see and note identifying numbers on plastic overlays.
5. Request box of photos (by number) from archivist.
6. Review photos and place order, if desired.

Note: In many cases, the AMS maps have town plans on the reverse side.

Aerial photos are also available for the Warsaw Ghetto and the concentration camps at Auschwitz and Mauthausen.

Aerial photos for the United States cover 1930–1960. A fee is charged for reproducing maps.

Military Archives Records
Miriam Weiner

Military Archives Division
8th Street and Pennsylvania Ave. N.W.
Room 13W/Military Reference
Room 400/Microfilm Research
Washington, D.C. 20408

Many German records were seized by the U.S. Army during and after World War II. These records were subsequently microfilmed, and include records of the Reich leader of the SS and chief of the German police relating to various aspects of the Holocaust. Various documents deal with treatment of the Jews by the SS in concentration camps, pogroms, and deportations. In some cases, photos are mentioned in the microfilmed records and can be ordered along with copies of the documents.

The microfilm collections constitute one of the largest groups of Holocaust records in the National Archives, and they are described in detail in a series of finding aids, which include an alphabetical index at the end of each guide.

See Bibliography: *Guides to German Records Microfilmed at Alexandria, Virginia* Nos. 32, 33, 39, and 81.

These records are under the jurisdiction of the Military Archives Division, with the actual microfilms, finding aids, and guides available in the Microfilm Research Room (Room 400) of the National Archives.

A portion of these records were translated into English for use as evidence in the Nüremberg trials. A joint publication by YIVO and Yad Vashem, *The Holocaust*, includes a digest, index, and chronological tables.

Prior to his death, Dr. John Mendelsohn, a supervisory archivist in the Modern Military Headquarters Branch, published two articles in *Prologue*, the National Archives journal: "Genealogy and the Holocaust: Selected Sources at the National Archives" (1983) and "The Holocaust: Records in the National Archives on the Nazi Persecution of the Jews" (1984). Dr. Mendelsohn also edited *The Holocaust: Selected Documents in Eighteen Volumes*. (See Bibliography.)

Dr. Mendelsohn said, "The core of the records are concentration camp personnel records, including entry registers, 'deathbooks' [*Totenbücher*], and postwar personnel records . . . amounting to almost 150 volumes and over 200 rolls of microfilm and camera

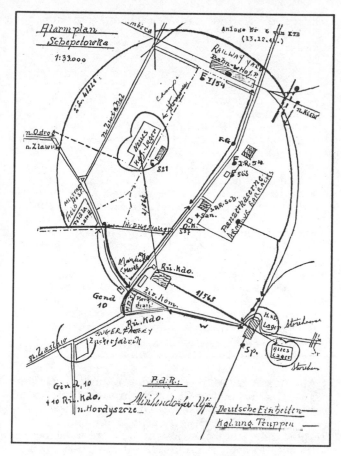

Alarm plan of Shepetovka, Ukraine. (Reprinted from *Guide to German Records Microfilmed at Alexandria, Virginia*; Courtesy of National Archives)

TRANSLATION OF DOCUMENT SUBMITTED IN EVIDENCE AT NUREMBERG TRIAL

Translation of Declaration Under Oath

I, Wilhelm Kueffner, swear, depose and state that:

1.   I was born on 5/11/1904 in Nuernberg and attended there 8 grades of public school and during the following 3 years a business-oriented high school. During this time, I also worked as an apprentice in the law office of Dr. Hans Marx. Because of an eye disease, I had to interrupt my studies there and worked for a while in an export business in Nuernberg. After completion of my studies, I was unemployed for a considerable time. In 1939, after a 3-month course in Finance, I passed an examination for an assistantship, found such a position in Nuernberg-West, and was transferred to Vienna shortly thereafter. I worked there until March 1942, when I was drafted into the "Landesschuetzen-Ersatz-Company" 3/17. We were stationed in the Ukraine, Frontstalag 358 in the town of Schepetowka.

2.   On 1/12/1929, I joined the NSDAP (National Socialist German Workers Party -- the Nazi party).

3.   On a day in August, 1942, while I was stationed in Schepetowka, Stalag 357, I heard a series of shots in quick succession, which seemed to originate in a small forest near the camp. Upon inquiring who would be doing any shooting here, I was told that now the remaining Jews in the neighboring area were being liquidated. To confirm this, I walked in the direction of the shooting. In front of the small forest was a group of people, amongst whom were SD people, distinguishable by the special insignia on their arm-bands. I came through the barrier and saw from a distance of roughly 250 meters a row of 400-500 people slowly moving towards a ditch. They were mostly women, some with children in their arms, who were taken from them by the SD. A group of women were already undressed. The women were led to the ditch in groups of 2 or 3 by 2 SD's, where they were shot with machine guns by soldiers sitting behind a wooden shield. I was told later that the "Sturmbannfuehrer" or "Obersturmbannfuehrer", who directed the extermination, was hit in the face by a Jewish woman with a knife.

The headquarters of the SD-group who perpetrated this execution, was at that time in Rowno.

I have read the above statement, consisting of two pages in the German language, and declare that, to the best of my knowledge and belief, it is the full truth. I have had the opportunity to make changes and corrections. I have made this declaration freely, without any promise of reward, and without any threat or force.

/s/ Wilhelm Kueffner

Translation of document submitted in evidence at Nuremberg Trial.

film." Work still needs to be done with the filmed material to make it suitable for public use, Mendelsohn noted. That work continues, but much progress has been made since 1983.

In his 1984 article, Dr. Mendelsohn indicates that the following material can be found in the microfilmed records:

- Concentration camp personnel records, entry registers, deathbooks
- Index of Jews whose German citizenship was annulled
- Material on the *Kristallnacht* pogrom
- List of Jews expelled from professional organizations
- Transport lists of Jews deported from Berlin and other German cities
- Concentration camp documents for Mauthausen, Natzweiler, Buchenwald, Flossenburg, Dachau, and Sandbostel
- Records of Reichsmusikkamer (musicians' organization), which expelled "non-Aryan" members in 1934
- Lists of victims in Germany
- Lists of persons whose personal property was confiscated
- Lists from postwar displaced persons camps
- Operational records from Occupied Eastern Territories
- Records of German field commands

Although most of the material is not indexed in any way and some of it will for a time continue to be restricted for public use because of privacy regulations, the deathbooks, primarily from Mauthausen, are not under such restrictions and are available on National Archives Microfilm Publication T990. The two rolls of microfilmed volumes for Mauthausen are arranged numerically in rough chronological order.

Microfilmed index cards containing approximately 30,000 names of Jews whose German citizenship was annulled are arranged alphabetically by surname and contain such information as birth date and place, address, and sometimes occupation. This material is on nine rolls in M1355 and is not subject to privacy restrictions.

The transport lists for Berlin and other cities are on five rolls in Record Group 242, the record group containing all of the seized documents. Most of the Jews on the Berlin lists were transported to the Riga Ghetto or the Trawniki labor camp. This material is the source of information for military and other actions, including mass killings, in Eastern Europe. Although personal names are not mentioned, it is possible to obtain specific dates of massacres and some details surrounding these actions.

Note: The original of the microfilmed German records are held by

Bundesarchiv-Abt. Militärarchiv
Wiesentalstrasse 10
7800 Freiburg am Breisgau
Germany

Bibliography

Darrish, M. B. "Gazetteers and Maps of Eastern Europe." St. Louis: Jewish Genealogy Society of St. Louis, 1985.

Gellert, C. L., comp. *The Holocaust, Israel and the Jews: Motion Pictures in the National Archives.* Washington, DC: National Archives and Records Administration, 1989.

Genealogical Research in the National Archives. Washington, DC: National Archives Trust Fund Board, 1983.

Grant, S.A. *Scholar's Guide to Washington, D.C.: Russian/Soviet Studies (The Baltic States, Byelorussia, Central Asia, Moldavia, Russia, Transcaucasia, The Ukraine).* Washington, DC: Smithsonian Institution Press, 1983.

Guides to German Records Microfilmed at Alexandria, VA, Nos. 32, 33, 39, 81, 83, and 84. Washington, DC: National Archives Records Administration, 1961–1985.

Mendelsohn, J., ed., comp. *Nuernberg War Crimes Trials, Records of Case 9 Einsatzgruppen (United States of America v. Otto Ohlendorf, et al.).* Washington, DC: National Archives and Record Service, 1978.

_____ , ed. *The Holocaust: Selected Documents in Eighteen Volumes.* New York: Garland Publishing Co., 1982.

_____ . "Genealogy and the Holocaust: Selected Sources at the National Archives." *Prologue: The Journal of the National Archives,* Fall 1983.

_____ . "The Holocaust: Records in the National Archives on the Nazi Persecution of the Jews." *Prologue: The Journal of the National Archives,* Spring 1984.

Robinson, J., and Sachs, H. *The Holocaust: The Nuremberg Evidence (Part One: Documents).* Jerusalem: Yad Vashem and YIVO Institute for Jewish Research, 1976.

Szucs, L. D., and Luebking, S. H. *The Archives: A Guide to the National Archives Field Branches.* Salt Lake City: Ancestry Publishing, 1988.

Weiner, M. *Sources for Military Records.* Secaucus, NJ: Self-published, 1987.

Numerous pamphlets and brochures published by NARAS are available at no charge along with extensive guides which can be purchased on-site or by mail.

■ THE LIBRARY OF CONGRESS
Suzan Fisher Wynne

The Library of Congress is exactly what its title implies. This library, one of the largest in the world, contains much material of interest to Jewish family historians. The trick is understanding how the Library of Congress is organized so that you can make the best use of your time and the library's resources.

The Library of Congress, or LC, is currently comprised of three buildings: the Jefferson Building, the oldest of the three and the one generally depicted as *the* Library of Congress, Adams, a small building located just behind Jefferson, and Madison, the newest building, located on Pennsylvania Avenue between 2nd and 3rd Streets S.E.

Overview

At this writing, the LC is undergoing extensive renovation in two of its three buildings. Locations are provided within this article to indicate where collections normally are and where they will be after the renovation. For current locations, check with the reference librarians on duty.

The LC publishes excellent general reference guides that cover the rules and services of the library, including copying services, stack pass privileges, the National Union Catalog, the use of typewriters and tape recorders, hours, and so forth. Each reading room and division is briefly described as well. To obtain information by mail, write:

Library of Congress
Central Services Division
Washington, D.C. 20540

If you plan to visit the LC, avoid driving. The complex is well located for both bus and subway lines. The rear entrance of the Madison Building is across the street from the Capitol South Metro stop, which is on the blue and orange lines. The three buildings are linked by an underground tunnel system and may be used to advantage in poor weather.

There is a small cafeteria in the tunnel level of the Madison Building and a very large cafeteria on the sixth floor of the building. Both serve good, reasonably priced food and provide smoking and nonsmoking sections.

Copying material is extraordinarily difficult, given the general availability of excellent photocopy machines in our society. The machines are poor, and there are far too few for the demand. Expect to wait for up to one hour for an available machine. One problem is that library users flagrantly ignore copyright laws and use the machines to copy whole books one dime at a time. You can request that material be copied for a fee by the Photoduplication Service located on the ground floor of the Adams Building. This service can also make a photostat of special materials such as maps, photos, and other materials you may wish to preserve.

Catalogs

All material in the English language cataloged through 1968 is listed in the card catalog, which is slowly being entered into the library's computer system. Material acquired since 1968 is generally accessible by the computer system. There are classes to teach people how to use the computer system, and reference librarians can be of assistance. For those comfortable with computers, self-service instructions also are posted. Materials are entered into the system even before the library receives them, so you can determine whether something has been ordered, when it was received, where it is in the lengthy cataloging process (up to two years), and all relevant information about the material.

Telephone Directories: United States and Foreign (Jefferson Building)

Current telephone directories for all localities are generally housed in a stack area just off the Central Research Room.

Biographic Reference (Jefferson Building)

In one section of the Central Research Room, you will find a very large collection of biographic materials, including United States and foreign *Who's Who* books, indexes, and materials covering people belonging to particular occupational groups. If biographic material on an individual is published anywhere, chances are excellent that you will find the reference among the indexes in this area. The Local History and Genealogy Division also has material of this type and foreign language materials are in the appropriate divisions.

Hebraic Section, African and Middle Eastern Division (Adams, first floor)

The Hebraic Section primarily includes material in Hebrew, Yiddish, Ladino, and other foreign languages related to Jewish history. However, there is some English language material as well. It is important to note that most English language materials are in the general collection.

The Hebraic Division shares a small reading room where books can be put on reserve for readers. Mate-

Title page of 1969 Leningrad telephone book at the Library of Congress.

Entry from Leningrad telephone book. Last three entries, right column, for individuals named "Odnopozov" previously unknown to editor Weiner and subsequently determined to be family members.

rial acquired by the section prior to 1968 is cataloged, primarily in foreign languages, in the section's reference room. The small staff is well acquainted with the interests of Jewish genealogists, and they have made every effort to provide material and assistance.

Ellen Murphy, a former reference librarian in the section, compiled a bibliography of genealogically useful materials. This bibliography was published in *Toledot* and a copy of this journal can be found in the reference room.

The reference room also houses Jewish encyclopedias and general books about Jews in various countries and some towns in the United States and other countries. They have a copy of the 1917 *Directory of Jewish Organizations* in New York which describes hundreds of Jewish organizations, burial societies, landsmanshaftn, and synagogues in the Greater New York area along with names of staff and officers.

The staff is making every effort to collect a copy of every memorial book published. Commonly known as Yizkor books, these are books compiled by Holocaust survivors about their towns in Europe. The books are still being produced, but the vast majority were written by groups and individuals within twenty years of the war's end. They generally include a history of the town with respect to Jewish settlement, religious life, including biographical information about rabbis, economic life, education, Zionist activity, and so forth. Those who were killed by the Nazis are often memorialized in some fashion, including by photograph. Some Yizkor books are indexed for names and subject. Most are written solely in Hebrew or Yiddish or a combination of the two, since most were written and published in Israel. A few books have English sections.

It should be remembered that the books do not always mention every family in the community. Since they are written by survivors in Israel, there is a natural tendency for remembrance of those involved in Zionism, but there is also a matter of memory and not everyone was known or remembered by the authors.

A list of the Yizkor books held by the Hebraic Section is in the reference room.

The section also has a collection of Yiddish newspapers, which are not indexed, but which can be seen in paper or microfiche form.

Additionally, for those researching rabbinic families, the section's resources are excellent.

Genealogy and Local History (Jefferson, second floor)

This division is useful to Jewish genealogists for some of its local history books, general biographical

Magyar Zsidó Lexikon was published in 1929 in Budapest. It is a one-volume encyclopedia of Hungarian Jewry.

Entry from *Magyar Zsidó Lexikon*.

reference materials, ship passenger indexes, census indexes, city directories, and old phone directories. The vast majority of genealogical materials are books written by non-Jews. There is a small reference section on ethnic genealogy, including Jewish genealogy.

The division has many census indexes and most of the ship arrival indexes that have been published. The period 1880–1920 rarely appears in these indexes, but researchers with German ancestry may find items of interest.

City directories are described in the census portion of the discussion of the National Archives (see p. 29). Briefly, they were compilations of residents of a community or of several adjoining communities done by commercial organizations supported by advertisers. These directories do not exist for every community, and they do not reliably include residents from year to year, particularly those from poor areas. However, they provide useful information for those listed, including addresses and occupations. The year of a man's death can often be determined, because his wife will be listed as a widow in the issue subsequent to his death. Further, city directories can assist in making connections among family members or learning the names of children in a family group. Most large city directories have been placed on microfilm and may be viewed in the reading room area or in the microform room one floor below. Other directories can only be seen by ordering them or by obtaining a stack pass. This is also true of old phone directories. A stack pass can be issued for one day to three months depending on how long you need access. On the application form, be sure to indicate that you need the pass because the directories you want cover many years and many small communities. If you are successful in obtaining a stack pass, you will find that there are no chairs or desks in the stacks. Dress comfortably so you can sit on the floor to record what you learn.

Although not all communities had city directories, those that exist are organized alphabetically by the first letter of the community's name, not by state. This can be a little tricky when several communities are combined, so be sure to check the card catalog in the reference area/reading room before you begin your search.

European Reading Room (Jefferson, second floor)

This is a well-stocked and potentially useful division if you are prepared to cope with languages other than English since the small staff is not generally able to render much translation assistance. There are encyclopedias, biographical dictionaries, community and country histories, and books about Jews. Though some of the material is in English, these tend to be books readily available from other libraries.

The division has a large collection of city and business directories from Russia in the nineteenth and early twentieth centuries. These directories, in Cyrillic, include many Jews and cover all of the Russian territories for that period.

Microform Room (Jefferson, first floor)

This room is filled with microform readers, and there is a card catalog to help you learn what is available on microform.

A most useful source for Jewish genealogists with roots in England is the *London Chronicle*, both the index and published issues. This appears to be the only source for this set in the United States.

Newspaper and Current Periodical Reading Room (Madison, first floor)

This large room houses all newspapers collected by the Library of Congress with the exception of some materials held by the European Reading Room.

The material is either on film or in bound volumes, consisting of a complete set of films for *The New York Times* and the *Washington Post* as well as a few other papers. Materials in bound volumes must be ordered, which can take an hour or several days.

The Reading Room has a large reference section that includes indexes of newspapers and periodicals. It has listed its newspaper holdings in bound volumes by time period and community. It should be noted that the Library of Congress does not have all newspapers published in this country. Most local, state, and historical libraries are better sources for early issues of community newspapers.

The Reading Room has custody of all current unbound serials and periodicals except those in music and law. Bound volumes are in the general collection.

Manuscript Division (Madison)

The former head of this Division, Gary J. Kohn, developed *The Jewish Experience* (see Bibliography), a valuable source for historians and genealogists.

The book lists more than 800 items, including papers written by individuals, materials from institutions and organizations, and other items such as oral history interviews conducted by the Works Progress Administration, captured German documents on the Nazi era, a 1937 list of Jews living in Stuttgart, and Bremen passenger lists from 1908 and 1913–1914.

There is also a collection of surveys of churches and synagogues done by the Works Progress Administration in 1937–1938.

Geography and Map Division
Miriam Weiner

James Madison Memorial Building
Room LM B01
101 Independence Avenue, S.E.
Washington, D.C. 20540
(202) 707-6777

Mail Inquiries:

Library of Congress
Geography and Map Division
Washington, D.C. 20540

The Geography and Map Division is known for the world's largest collection of reference material, including more than 4 million maps, 50,000 atlases, and 8,000 reference works. Even with all of these wonderful resources, however, Jews who have only the Yiddish name of an Eastern European town will still need to rely on the *Shtetl Finder* (located on the shelves in this division) or a similar resource to help identify the official name. Once that is established, you can begin to locate the community on a map.

For a comprehensive description of the holdings, see *Gazetteers and Maps of Eastern Europe in the Library of Congress* by M. B. Darrish (see Bibliography), available in Geography and Map Division and also at Hebraic Section (Adams Building).

Title page of *Shtetl Finder Gazetteer*, by Chester G. Cohen. Provides basic information on hundreds of pre-Holocaust towns in Eastern Europe.

Entry from *Shtetl Finder Gazetteer*.

To locate maps for specific towns in this collection, it is necessary to determine its current name and country. In some cases, you will need the coordinates.

The Board of Geographic Names has standardized the spelling in Romanized English of every community in the world. Place names no longer in use are often cross-referenced to present-day names. These names are listed with their coordinates in place-name gazetteers based on current national borders. To determine which modern-day country your town is located in, it may be necessary to use gazetteers, historic atlases, and other aids to guide you. For instance, your information may indicate that your family came from Austria, but you are unable to find the town on any Austrian map. Chances are good that your town is now within the borders of Poland, Czechoslovakia, Hungary, or the Soviet Union. The Austro-Hungarian Empire was enormous prior to World War I. Germany too held land which now lies mostly in Poland, and a small area of what was East Prussia is within Soviet borders today.

These kinds of changes in political control occurred with some frequency until the end of World War II. Your relative could have been born in Hungary in 1900, lived in Czechoslovakia in 1920, and in the Soviet Union in 1946, all the while living in the same house.

For the purpose of identifying the location of place names, the division has a detailed (circa 1:100,000 scale) Polish, German, Austro-Hungarian, and Russian map series that covers most of Eastern Europe and the Western Soviet Union. The maps in these series were produced in the late 19th and early 20th centuries.

Numerous general gazetteers and atlases, Jewish resources, and Polish and related resources, along with gazetteers of Eastern Europe, are available to help you pinpoint the exact location of towns.

The division is well equipped and well lighted, and has a highly knowledgeable staff willing to be of assistance. On your first visit, after signing in at the front desk, ask a reference librarian to help you find your way around. Or, if you prefer, you can wander around the reading room and explore the division's reference collection on your own.

Town Plans

Russia—Individual Maps. Individual town plans (more than 800) for Russia are cataloged in Classed Catalog drawer 9, and they include maps from various sources such as AMS maps from World War II, some aerial photos, and other sources. In some cases, it is

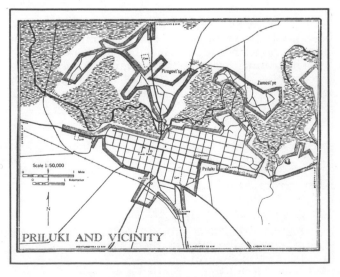

Town plan of Priluki, Ukraine.

possible to identify buildings, shaded business districts, streets by name, railway stations, rivers, cemeteries, breweries, flour mills, and other landmarks.

The index cards in Drawer 9 provide place name, call number, country where prepared, preparer, series title and sheet identification, place and date published, size and description, scale, language, and such features as street indexes, other cities and vicinities on the reverse, and detailed inserts of even larger-scale maps. Town plan scales are generally 1:7,500–50,000, with some inserts 1:5,000. (See Appendix F, pp. 171–173.)

Individual maps are filed in folders in closed stacks. A reference librarian will bring the maps to you, and you can then photocopy them, if you desire, at copy machines in the Reading Room.

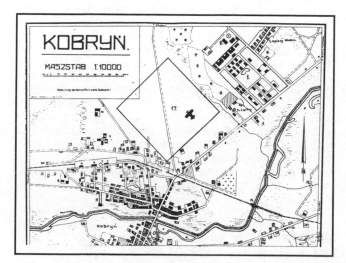

Key to town plan of Kobryn

1. Kasernon, durch russische Truppen belegt.
2. Ziegelei in Lepiosy, Außer Betrieb.
3. Sägewerk.
4. Bahnhof von Kobryn.
5. Gutermagasin.
6. Verladerampe mit Güterschuppen.
7. Wasserturm.
8. Sägewerk.
9. Waserpumpuerk für die Versorgung der Eisenbahn.
10. Ziegelei, außer Betrieb.
11. Ziegelei, außer Betrieb.
12. Wasserdurchlaß unter Straße (Betonröhre).
13. Eisern eingleisige Eisenbahnbrüoke, 60 m lang, grau gestrichen. Brückenköpfe aus Stein.
14. Chaussee-Brück über den Euchawico.
15. Wasserdurchlaß unter Straße (Betonröhre).
16. Wasserdurchlaß unter Straße (Betonröhre).
17. Flugplats von Kobryn, ohne Gebaude.

Town plan of Kobryn, U.S.S.R., with key.

Poland—Individual Maps. There are 11 drawers of Polish town plans (in closed stacks) including two drawers each for Gdansk and Warsaw. There is no index or finding aid available in the Geography and Map Division for identifying these maps and the procedure is to ask the reference librarian to bring any maps available for a specific town. (See Appendix G, p. 174.)

Austria and Hungary—Individual Maps. The division has comparable holdings for Austria and Hungary.

Requests for maps, including town plans, can be made by mail. You will be sent an order form for computing the cost and ordering photodirect print reproductions from the Photoduplication Service of the Library of Congress.

Bibliography

Darrish, M. B. "Gazetteers and Maps of Eastern Europe." St. Louis: Jewish Genealogy Society of St. Louis, 1985.

Kohn, G. J. *The Jewish Experience: A Guide to Manuscript Sources in the Library of Congress.* Cincinnati: American Jewish Archives, 1986.

Murphy, E. R. "Jewish Genealogical Materials in the Library of Congress." *Toledot: The Journal of Jewish Genealogy,* Vol. 4, No. 3, 1982.

Neagles, J. C. *The Library of Congress: A Guide to Genealogical and Historical Research.* Salt Lake City: Ancestry Publishing, 1990.

GEORGIA

■ ATLANTA

Georgia Department of Archives and History
330 Capitol Avenue SE
Atlanta, Georgia 30334

- County records on microfilm to circa 1900 (except for Cobb, Coffee, and Wilkinson counties and the superior courts of Hart, Lowndes, and Quitman counties)
- Municipal records including copies of almost all city directories for Georgia to 1900 (microfilm)
- State and private records relating to Georgia's Civil War soldiers and civilians
- Georgia state pensions (given to Confederate veterans and their widows residing in Georgia without regard to the state in which the soldier served), on microfilm with index
- National Archives microfilm of the compiled service records and rosters of the Georgia Confederate servicemen
- 1867 state voter registration books for each Georgia county and major city, with the exception of Haralson County. (Can provide naturalization, place of birth, and residency information for males)
- Statewide genealogical journals for Georgia and local interest quarterlies and newsletters
- Birth-death records for 21 Georgia counties for 1875–76 (microfilm)

- Tax records from the various offices in Georgia's courthouses (microfilm)
- "Georgia Military Affairs, 1775–1832" (indexed typescripts of miscellaneous military records)
- State copies of county tax digests for each Georgia county from 1872
- Plats to headright and bounty grants containing the names of neighbors and chain carriers (who are possible relatives of the grantees)
- Extensive, general genealogical collection. Special emphasis on the states from which the major migrations came to Georgia
- Saftall Papers of the American-Jewish Historical Society (microfilm copy of the guide, index)
- Family Exchange Cards (a free query service that can be participated in by mail)
- Family folder
- Name File (a card catalog to the genealogical holdings and to many names found in various state records)
- DAR collection (over 300 typescripts of Georgia records)

Georgia Surveyor General Department. Floor 2V. Map collection consists of more than 15,000 items. Copies of historical maps of Georgia available. More than 1 million land grants issued in Georgia (1756–1909).

Georgia Department of Human Resources
Vital Records Unit
Room 217-H
47 Trinity Avenue
Atlanta, Georgia 30334
Death certificates can be obtained for fee. (Birth certificates restricted.)

Historic Preservation Section
Georgia Department of Natural Resources
Floyd Tower East, Suite 1462
205 Butler Street SE
Atlanta, Georgia 30334
Has a list of 100 local historical organizations.

Jewish Community Archives/Heritage Center
Atlanta Jewish Federation
1753 Peachtree Road NE
Atlanta, Georgia 30309
(404) 873-1661

- More than 1,000 photographs, plus collection of artifacts
- 50 different collections of papers

Free Kindergarten and Social Settlement. Minutes, 1906–1915. One of the first Jewish social service organizations in Atlanta.

Georgia Farm School and Resettlement Bureau, Inc. Records, 1939–1943. The social historian interested in Jewish relief activities, immigration efforts in the early days of World War II, and the resettlement and assimilation of Jewish refugees into a Southern community will find this collection of special interest.

Roseland Cemetery. Records, 1910–1966. One of the oldest Atlanta cemeteries to have a Jewish section. Causes of death as well as the birth and death dates of the deceased.

Stanford E. Moses. Journal, 1934–1939. The journal traces the history of the Raphael Moses family, one of the first Jewish families of the South.

Atlanta Jewish Federation. Records, 1906–1986. The history of Jewish social services in Atlanta; also, the records of predecessor agencies, the Atlanta Federation of Jewish Social Service, the Atlanta Jewish Welfare Federation, and the Jewish Community Council.

Joseph Cuba Family. Papers, c. 1920–1985. The papers reflect upon the lives and careers of Max and Joseph Cuba who were instrumental in the establishment and successful operation of many of the major Jewish organizations in Atlanta.

Southern Israelite. Records, c. 1937–1984. The collection of photographs is voluminous and is representative of the diversity of the Atlanta Jewish community.

Herman Heyman Family. Papers, 1886–1950. The collection contains material relating to both the Heyman and Joel families, who were among Atlanta's leading first Jewish families. Of special interest are the diaries written by 14-year-old Josephine Joel Heyman from 1914 to 1915. The diaries, kept by an affluent young Jewish girl, are indicative of the type of lifestyle members of the German Jewish community led in the first part of this century. Reference is also made to the Leo Frank case.

Raphael J. Moses. Autobiography, 1890. The Moses family was one of the first Jewish families to settle in Georgia.

Oscar Strauss Family. Papers, c. 1860–1960. Material relating to the Strauss, Rich, Weil, Hirsch, and Sartorius families, all of them pioneering Jewish families in Atlanta. Of special interest is the material relating to the Rich family, founders of Rich's Department Store.

The Jewish Progressive Club. Records, 1923–1970. One of the first and most successful Atlanta Jewish social clubs.

Herbert Taylor Family. Papers, 1915–1982. Both Herbert and his wife Edith were active members of Atlanta's Jewish community. The papers reflect upon those activities.

Congregation Beth Hamedrash Hagodel Anshi S'fard. Records, 1939–1960. Founded in 1913, this is Atlanta's only Hasidic Congregation.

Edward M. Kahn. Papers, c. 1925–1976. Director of the Atlanta Federation for Jewish Social Service, the Jewish Community Council, and the Atlanta Jewish Welfare Fund for twenty-five years.

Jacob Elsas Family. Papers, 1888–1926. Jacob Elsas was the founder of the Fulton Bag and Cotton Mill, one of Atlanta's oldest and largest companies.

Standard Club. Records, 1854–1950. Established in 1867 as the Concordia Club, it is the oldest Jewish social club in Atlanta.

Rabbi Harry H. Epstein. Papers, 1907–1984. Rabbi of Congregation Ahavath Achim, the largest Conservative Jewish congregation in the South for over fifty years.

Congregation Beth El. Records, 1956–1959. Established in the 1950s, this Conservative Jewish congregation lasted only a few years.

Arthur and Josephine Shulhafer. Guest book,

1923–1938. Autographs of friends and relations who visited the Shulhafer home from 1923 to 1938.

Nathan Saltzman Family. Papers, 1873–1950. Pioneer Atlanta Jewish families. The correspondence is of special significance as it is very descriptive of the kind of life-style that affluent members of the Jewish community were leading in the early 1900s.

Eugene Oberdorfer, Sr., Family. Papers, 1901–1946. Pioneer German Jewish family, they established the Oberdorfer Insurance Co.

B'nai B'rith Women (Atlanta Branch). Records, 1944–1976. Women's division of one of the oldest and largest Jewish charitable organizations in the South.

David Alterman Family. Papers, 1910–1976. The Alterman brothers established one of the largest food-store chains in the Southeast.

Louis J. Levitas Family. Papers, 1910–1982. Louis and Ida Levitas were long-time Atlanta residents active in organizations such as B'nai B'rith, the Jewish Educational Alliance, Hadassah, and the Jewish Welfare Board.

Rosenfeld/Sommerfield Family. Papers, 1879–1950. The Rosenfeld family was one of the first Jewish families to settle in Atlanta, and helped to found The Temple. Dr. Julius Edward Sommerfield was family physician to most of the German Jewish population in Atlanta and was instrumental in bringing the diphtheria serum to the United States from Germany. Of special interest is a collection of unpublished photographs from the 1939 opening of the movie *Gone with the Wind*.

Alexander Family. Papers, ca. 1850–1967. One of the first Jewish families to settle in the South, eventually making Atlanta its home.

Hebrew Academy of Atlanta. Scrapbook, 1953–1962. Private Jewish Day School.

The Temple. Records, 1874–1987 (on loan). Oldest congregation in Atlanta.

Leon Eplan Family. Papers, ca. 1914–1959. Leon Eplan was a founding member of Congregation Ahavath Achim and Beth Israel.

Isadore Leff. Photographs, 1906–1928. Atlanta public school class photographs.

Helen Alperin Family. Papers, 1926–1958. The papers reflect upon the activities of Helen Alperin who was an active participant in Jewish youth activities such as Young Judaea and the Intercollegiate Zionist Federation during the 1940s.

Note: This list does not include over forty vertical file items which have been cataloged and made available to researchers.

National Archives, Southeast Region
(See East Point, Georgia)

Southern Jewish Historical Society
Valdosta State College
P.O. Box 179
Valdosta, Georgia 31698

Newspaper

Atlanta Jewish Times
P.O. Box 250287
Atlanta, Georgia 30325
(404) 352-2400

■ EAST POINT

National Archives, Southeast Region
1557 St. Joseph Avenue
East Point, Georgia 30344
(404) 763-7477

Records from the World War I draft system. Approximately 24 million registration cards, (1917–1918) from men throughout the United States born 1873–1900, whether actually drafted or not. (May provide information on registrant's birth date, birthplace, citizenship, race, address, occupation/employer, and name of person to be notified.) Forms on which to request copies of the cards are available on request. There is a fee for copies.

■ SAVANNAH

Chatham County Health Department
2011 Eisenhower Drive
P.O. Box 14257
Savannah, Georgia 31412-1257
- Birth records
- Death records 1803–1890

The CEL Regional Library
2002 Bull Street
Savannah, Georgia 31499
(912) 234-5127

The library serves Chatham, Effingham and Liberty Counties. It will respond to short and specific inquiries.

World War I draft registration for Alexander Rabkin, Tulsa, Oklahoma.

- *Jewish Burial Grounds* (1773 to 1935). Historical Research Association. RG 929.5 H
- *Savannah's Old Jewish Community Cemeteries.* B.H. Levy. RG 975.8724 Levy
- Substitutes for Georgia's Lost 1790 Census. RG 929.3758 S
- Georgia Census Indexes: 1820, 1830, 1840, 1850 in separate volumes. RG 929.3758 G
- 1850 Census of Georgia (hard copy, incomplete) Rhea Otto RG 929.3758 O
- 1860 Census of Chatham County (Includes complete place of birth). Georgia Historical Society. RG 3758 G
- Georgia Census Schedules on Microfilm: 1820, 1830, 1840, 1850, 1850 slave schedules, 1860, 1860 slave schedules, 1870, 1880, 1900, 1910
- Georgia Soundex 1880, 1900, and 1910 Note: 1880 Soundex—Families with children under ten years of age. 1880 and 1900 Soundex do not have birthplace of parents (included in census)
- Index to the 1830 Census of Georgia. Alvaretta Register. RG 929.3758 Regi

Congregation Mickve Israel
20 East Gordon Street
Savannah, Georgia 31499

Third-oldest synagogue in the U.S. Congregation established 1735.

The Federation
P.O. Box 23527
Savannah, Georgia 31403

Publishes *The Savannah Jewish News*, the local Jewish paper.

The Georgia Historical Society
501 Whitaker Street
Savannah, Georgia 31499

The society's library is open to individual researchers. There is no charge except for copying costs. The library will respond to simple genealogical queries. If appropriate, it will refer the inquirer to local professional genealogists.

- Georgia censuses (1820–1880)
- Census indexes (1820–1850)
- Savannah city directories (1858–) The years are scattered until 1880. From then on, there are very few years missing
- Digest (index) of Savannah newspapers (1763–1891, 1936–1984; 215 volumes)
- Large manuscript collection

Probate Court
Chatham County
P.O. Box 8344
Savannah, Georgia 31412
- Marriage licenses (from 1806)
- Wills (from 1742)

Bibliography (Savannah)
Levy, B. H. *Savannah's Old Jewish Community Cemeteries.* Macon, GA: Mercer University Press, 1983.
Levy, M. A. "Savannah's Old Jewish Burial Ground." *Georgia Historical Quarterly,* Vol. 34, 1950.

Morgan, D. T. "The Sheftalls of Savannah." *American Jewish Historical Quarterly,* Vol. 42, No. 4, pp. 348–361, June 1973.
Rubin, S. J. *Third to None: The Saga of Savannah Jewry 1733–1983.* Savannah, GA: Congregation Mickve Israel, 1983.
Stern, M. H. "New Light on the Jewish Settlement of Savannah." In *The Jewish Experience in America,* vol. I. New York: Ktav Publishing House, Inc., 1969.
_____ . "The Sheftall Diaries: Vital Records of Savannah Jewry (1733–1808)." Publication of *The American Jewish Historical Society,* Vol. 54.

Bibliography (Georgia)
Beton, S., ed. *Sephardim and a History of Congregation Or Ve Shalom.* 1981.
Brook, T. O. *Georgia Cemetery Directory.* 1985.
Davis, R. J., Jr. *Research in Georgia: With a Special Emphasis on the Georgia Archives.* Easley, SC: Southern Historical Press, 1981.
Dorsey, J. E. *Georgia Genealogy and Local History: A Bibliography.* Spartanburg, SC: The Reprint Co., 1983.
Evans, E. N. *The Provincials: A Personal History of Jews in the South.* 1973.
Georgia Citizens and Soldiers of the American Revolution Easley, SC: Southern Historical Press, 1979.
Georgia Local and Family History Sources in Print. 1982.
Hemperley, M. R. *Military Certificates of Georgia, 1775–1800.* Atlanta: Georgia Surveyor General Department, 1983.
Hertzberg, S. *Strangers Within the Gate City: The Jews of Atlanta 1845–1915.* 1978.
Historical Collections of Georgia. 1859. (reprint edition Danielsville: Heritage Papers, 1968).
Index to Probate Records of Colonial Georgia. R. J. Taylor, Jr., Foundation. Spartanburg, SC: The Reprint Co., 1983.
Kaganoff, N. M., and Urofsky, M. I., eds. *Turn to the South: Essays on Southern Jewry.* 1979.
Marx, D. *A History of the Hebrew Benevolent Congregation of Atlanta . . . Fiftieth Anniversary.* 1917.
"1987 Guide to Jewish Life in Atlanta." *The Atlanta Jewish Times,* Special Edition, November 1987.
Passports of Southeastern Pioneers, 1770–1823. Easley, SC: Southern Historical Press, 1982.
Rothschild, J. O. *As but a Day, The First Hundred Years.* The Temple, 1967.
_____ . "The Jews of Augusta." *Ancestoring,* Vol. 12, Augusta Genealogical Society, Inc., 1987.
_____ . "The Jews of Augusta." *Ancestoring* 40, pp. 29–34.
Steinberg, J. J. *United for Worship and Charity, A History of Congregation Children of Israel.* 1982.

ILLINOIS

■ CHICAGO

American Jewish Congress
22 West Monroe Street, Suite 2102
Chicago, Illniois 60603
(312) 332-7355
- Publishes a guide to Jewish Chicago

Chicago Genealogical Society
P.O. Box 1160
Chicago, Illinois 60690

Chicago Historical Society
North Clark Street & North Avenue
Chicago, Illinois 60610
(312) 642-4600

The Chicago Historical Society Research Library is located on the third floor. Researchers must obtain a pass at the information desk to use the Library.

- Chicago city and phone directories
- Records of Jewish Community Centers of Chicago 1904–1982
- Records of Jewish Home for the Aged (BMZ) 1899–1971
- Hundreds of books on Chicago Jewry

Chicago Jewish Historical Society
1640 East 50th Street
Chicago, Illinois 60615
(312) 493-7938

Chicago Municipal Reference Library
121 N. LaSalle
Chicago, Illinois 60602

Chicago Public Library
Social Sciences and History Division
400 North Franklin
Chicago, Illinois 60610
(312) 269-2830

The Central Library of the Chicago Public Library has been temporarily housed since 1975. In the future, holdings will be housed at the Harold Washington Memorial Library beginning in 1991. [As of publication date, the address had not be assigned.]
Holdings include:

- Census schedules with personal name information for Cook County, Illinois, 1850–1880 and 1900
- Chicago City Directories 1839, 1843–1917, 1923, 1928/1929
- Telephone Books
  Chicago Telephone Directories, 1878–1971 (with 1972 to date available in hard copy)
  Current Telephone books for approximately 2,500 U.S. cities and for foreign countries
- Newspapers and Periodicals
  Complete runs for Chicago newspapers
  Chicago Tribune 1849–present
  (indexed 1972–present)
  Chicago Daily News 1875–1978
  Chicago Record Herald (indexed 1904–1912)
  Chicago Sun-Times
  (indexed 1976–present)
- Chicago and Illinois Biography Sources
  *The Book of Chicagoans** 1905, 1911, 1917 (was continued as *Who's Who in Chicago and Illinois*)
  Who's Who in Chicago and Illinois 1926, 1931, 1936, 1941, 1945, 1947, 1950
  Who's Who in the Midwest 1947, 1949 to the present
- 1980 Biography and Genealogy Master Index
- Military Registers
  Army Register, Navy Register 1814–1947, 1948–1949, 1950–
  Air Force Register 1950–
- Official Register 1816–1861, 1861–1905, 1907–1932, 1932–1959
- Several books on Chicago Jewry

Chicago Public Library's Government Publications Department has some registers that may be of interest to the genealogist.

Chicago Public Schools Division of Records Services
1819 West Purshing Road, 2C(n)
Chicago, Illinois 60609
(312) 890-7722, 890-8748, or 890-8444

Write for application form. There is fee for copies of Chicago Public School records.

Cook County Bureau of Vital Statistics
118 North Clark Street
Chicago, Illinois 60602

Cook County Medical Examiner's Office
2121 W. Harrison Street
Chicago, Illinois 60612

Cook County Recorder of Deeds
118 North Clark Street
Chicago, Illinois 60602

Hebrew Immigrant Aid Society (HIAS)
1 South Franklin Street
Chicago, Illinois 60606
(312) 444-2869

Richard J. Daley Center
50 West Washington St.
Chicago, Illinois 60602
(312) 443-7935

Cook Country Circuit Court, Chancery Division Room 802
Cook County Circuit Court, Law Division, Room 1201
Cook County Circuit Court, Probate Division, Room 1202

- Naturalization Records from Cook County Courts from October 1871 to September 30, 1906
- Circuit and Superior Court Records granting naturalizations to Janurary 31, 1929
- Records of Cook County adoption and law cases

Federal Records Center—Chicago Branch
7538 South Pulaski Road
Chicago, Illinois 60629
(312) 581-7816, 353-0164

Searches of the index are made either from phone or written requests. If several names are involved, they ask that you write.
Naturalization Records of The U.S. Courts Region 5 (NARS):

- U.S. District Courts
  Northern District of Illinois, Chicago
  Eastern District of Illinois, East St. Louis and Danville
  Southern District of Illinois, Springfield
  Southern District of Illinois, Peoria
  Northern District of Indiana, Hammond
  Southern District of Indiana, Indianapolis
  Western District of Michigan, Marquette
  Western District of Michigan, Grand Rapids
  Eastern District of Michigan, Detroit

Minnesota, Duluth Division
Northern District of Ohio, Cleveland
Northern District of Ohio, Toledo
Southern District of Ohio, Cincinnati
Southern District of Ohio, Columbus
Western District of Wisconsin, Madison
Eastern District of Wisconsin, Milwaukee
- Records of the Immigration and Naturalization Service (INS)

LDS (Mormon) Family History Centers
(See: Chicago Heights; Naperville; Schaumburg; and Wilmette, Illinois)

Newberry Library
60 West Walton
Chicago, Illinois 60610
(312) 943-9090

The Newberry Library is a private reference and research library containing one of the most extensive collections of local history and genealogy in the country.

Newberry Library books may not be checked out, nor do they circulate on interlibrary loan. Photocopying service is provided for materials not covered by copyright.

A reasonable attempt is made, however, to answer specific, limited mail inquiries.

- Resources for genealogical research in the Midwest, New England, and the mid-Atlantic, southern and border states
- Historical materials on all other regions of the United States and Canada
- Over 16,000 printed family histories
- Extensive collection of county and town histories and published local records, such as birth, marriage and death registers, tax lists, land records
- All major genealogical periodicals, including the *New England Historical and Genealogical Register*, *New York Genealogical and Biographical Record* and the *National Genealogical Society Quarterly*, and *Search*, an international quarterly for researchers of Jewish genealogy
- United States census records from 1790 to 1910, as well as directories for many American cities and towns before 1920
- Published military records form another important component of genealogical resources at the Newberry
    rosters, pensions records, and regimental histories for the American Revolution, War of 1812, and the Civil War
- Multi-volume biographical and genealogical works
    Dictionary of American Biography
    Cyclopedia of American Biography
    American Genealogical-Biographical Index
- Lineage books, rosters, annual reports, and periodicals from patriotic and hereditary societies
- Published passenger lists prior to the twentieth century
- One of the most comprehensive heraldry collections in the country
- Some genealogical and local history materials for Great Britain and Ireland

- Genealogical materials for continental Europe dealing primarily with nobility and heradry
- Maps and atlases, military histories, biographies, and church histories

The Genealogical Index of the Newberry Library (4 volumes, Bostin, G. K. Hall, 1960), which is available at many libraries, is a massive surname index to a large number of volumes in the Library. (Compiled from 1896 to 1918, it contains no reference to any book published after 1918.)

Northwestern Memorial Group Archives
1516 West 36th Street
Chicago, Illinois 60609
(312) 908-3090
- Records of some of the older and also some nonexistent hospitals
- Collection includes birth records
- Finding aids

Spertus College of Judaica
Norman and Helen Asher Library
618 South Michigan Avenue
Chicago, Illinois 60605
(312) 922-9012
One of the largest libraries of Judaica in the Midwest.

- Rabbinic genealogical sources
- Yizkor books
- Sources on Chicago Jewish History
- Chicago Jewish periodicals
- Microfilm of early 20th-century Yiddish newspapers

Also included in the library are the Chicago Jewish Archives containing:

- Large unindexed collection of manuscripts
- Collections of papers from Chicago Jewish organizations and other material about Jewish life in and around Chicago

Viewing of materials in these archives is *only* by appointment.

United States District Court—Chicago
219 South Dearborn, Room 2062
Chicago, Illinois 60604
(312) 435-5697
- Index to naturalizations at U.S. District Court-Chicago from 1871 to present
- Naturalizations at U.S. District Court-Chicago since 1959

Newspapers
J.U.F. News
1 South Franklin Street
Chicago, Illinois 60606
(312) 346-6700
- Obituaries
- Individuals sought by HIAS in Chicago
- Several in-depth articles on Chicago Jewish neighborhoods, past and present

The Sentinel
175 West Jackson Street
Chicago, Illinois 60604
(312) 663-1101

Published since 1912.

Back issues available at Spertus College of Judaica's Asher Library.

Funeral Homes
Piser Weinstein Menorah Chapel
5206 Broadway
Chicago, Illinois 60640
(312) 561-4740

Piser Weinstein is one of the oldest Chicago area Jewish funeral homes. Over the years it has merged with other local funeral homes, including Gratch-Mandel and Hartman-Miller. Will respond to telephone and written inquiries.

The funeral home publishes, as a public service, the *Piser Original Weinstein & Sons Menorah Chapels Cemetery Guide of Jewish Cemeteries and Non-Sectarian Cemeteries with Jewish Sections in the Chicago Area and Map of Jewish Waldheim Cemeteries.* This fourteen-page publication (with map of the Jewish Waldheim Cemeteries) was produced with the assistance of the following cemetery maintenance organizations: Free Sons of Israel Cemetery Association; Barnett Joseph & Son; Lebovitz & Company, Inc.; Schwarzbach & Company; Silverman & Weiss; and Woodlawn Cemetery Association.

The book includes names, addresses, and phone numbers of Chicago area cemeteries, as well as the synagogues and burial societies that have sections in each cemetery. The area known as Jewish Waldheim is composed of over 300 cemeteries, and several cemetery maintenance companies serve as sextons. The book lists each cemetery and notes the entry gate and sexton. There is no charge for the publicaton.

Bibliography
Ahern, M. L. *Political History of Chicago.* Chicago, 1886.
American Jewish Congress. *A Guide to Jewish Chicago.* Chicago, 1973.
Associated Jewish Press Bureau. *Jewish Directory of Chicago: Containing a Full and Complete List of Congregations, Their Ministers and Members, Also a Complete Manual of the Various Jewish Lodges in the City.* Chicago, 1884.
Andreas, A. T. *Hisatory of Chicago.* 3 vol. Chicago, 1884–1886.
Bernheimer, C., ed. *The Russian Jew in the United States.* Philadelphia, 1905. (Deals with Russian-Jewish life in Chicago, Philadelphia, and New York).
Bregstone, P. P. *Chicago and Its Jews: A Cultural History.* Chicago, 1933.
Chicago Jewish Community Blue Book. Chicago: The Sentinel Publishing Co., ca. 1918.
Chicago und sein Deutchthum. Cleveland, 1901–1902.
Cromie, R. A. *The Great Chicago Fire.* New York, 1958.
Cutler, I. "The Jews of Chicago: From Shtetl to Suburb." In *Ethnic Chicago,* ed. Jones, P. A., and Holli, M. G. Grand Rapids, MI: William B Eerdmans, 1981.
Eakle, A., and Cerny, J. *The Source: A Guidebook of American Genealogy.* Salt Lake City, UT: Ancestry Incorporated, 1984. (Jewish-American Genealogy, pages 602–649).
Grossman, R. *Guide to Chicago Neighborhoods.* Piscataway, NJ, 1981.
Gutstein, M. A. *A Priceless Heritage: The Epic Growth of Nineteenth Century Chicago Jewry.* Chicago, 1953.
Heimovics, R. B. *The Chicago Jewish Source Book.* Chicago: Follett Publishing Co., 1981.
Jewell, F. *Annotated Bibliography of Chicago History.* Chicago, 1979.
Jones, P. d'A., and Holli, M. G. *Ethnic Chicago.* Grand Rapids, MI: William B Eerdmans, 1981.
Korey, H. "The History of Jewish Education in Chicago." M.A. thesis, University of Chicago, 1942.
Krug, M. M. "History of the Yiddish Schools in Chicago (1912–53)." *Jewish Education* 25 (Fall 1956), pp. 67–73.
Mayer, H. M., and Wade, R. C. *Chicago: Growth of a Metropolis.* Chicago, 1969.
Meites, Hyman, ed. *History of the Jews of Chicago.* Chicago, 1924. Reprinted 1990, Lake Bluff, IL: Wellington.
Pacyga, D. A., and Skerrett, E. *Chicago: City of Neighborhoods.* Chicago, 1986.
Rawidowicz, S., ed. *The Chicago Pinkas.* Chicago, 1952.
Rosenthal, E. "Acculturation without Assimilation? The Jewish Community of Chicago, Illinois." *American Journal of Sociology* 46 (Nov. 1960), pp. 275–288.
Szucs, L. D. *Chicago and Cook County Sources: A Genealogical and Historical Guide.* Salt Lake City: Ancestry Publishing, 1986.

■ CHICAGO HEIGHTS
(Chicago Metropolitan Area)

LDS (Mormon) Family History Center
402 Longwood (Inside Church Chapel)
Chicago Heights, Illinois 60411
(708) 754-2525

■ NAPERVILLE
(Chicago Metropolitan Area)

LDS (Mormon) Family History Center
Ridgeland Road & Naperville Road (Inside Chapel)
Naperville, Illinois 60540
(708) 357-0211

■ SCHAUMBURG
(Chicago Metropolitan Area)

LDS (Mormon) Family History Center
Family History Center
1320 W. Schaumburg Road
Schaumburg, Illinois
(708) 882-9889

mailing address:
1014 Boston Circle
Schaumburg, Illinois 60193

■ SKOKIE
(Chicago Metropolitan Area)

The Hebrew Theological College
7135 Carpenter Road
Skokie, Illinois 60076
(708) 674-7750

Houses the Saul Silber Memorial Library.

- Sources for Rabbinic genealogy
- Books of Chicago Jewry
- Holocaust materials including *The Blackbook of*

Localities Whose Jewish Population Was Exterminated by the Nazis
- Yizkor books

■ SPRINGFIELD

Illinois State Archives
Springfield, Illinois 62756

- Name index to early records
- Records of the sales of public domain lands
- War indexes
- Veterans burial lists
- Civil War Military enrollments
- Muster rolls
- World War I draft registrations
- Supreme Court case files
- Criminal records
- Illinois Historical Records Survey of the WPA

Bibliography
Irons, V., and Brennan, P. C. *Descriptive Inventory of the Archives of the State of Illinois.* Springfield, IL: Illinois State Archives, 1978.

■ WILMETTE
(Chicago Metropolitan Area)

LDS (Mormon) Family History Center
2801 Lake Avenue
Wilmette, Illinois 60091
(708) 251-9818

IOWA

■ DES MOINES

Adjutant General's Office
State House
Des Moines, Iowa 50319
Military records for those serving from Iowa in the Civil War and the Spanish-American War, World War I, and for members of the Iowa National Guard.

Clerk of the District Court
Polk County Courthouse
Des Moines, Iowa 50309

Poland

SERIAL NUMBER	LOCALITY	NUMBER OF JEWISH RESIDENTS	SERIAL NUMBER	LOCALITY	NUMBER OF JEWISH RESIDENTS
70	Parzynów ob.dw.	1	7	Szamotuły	264
1	Pauliny	1	8	Szklarka Myślniewska	5
2	Pawłówek	1	9	Szkółki	1
3	Piaski	1	10	Szubin	77
4	Pleszew	116	1	Śmieszkowiec	4
5	Pniewy	99	2	Śmigiel	13
6	Pobiedziska	24	3	Śrem	103
7	Podgaj	1	4	Środa	80
8	Podzamcze	28	5	Tarnowo Podgórne	3
9	Pogorzela	7	6	Tarnówko	1
80	Pożajewo	37	7	Trębaczów	2
1	Poniec	4	8	Trzcinica	3
2	Poznań	2088	9	Trzemeszno	37
3	Radzicz	10	20	Ujście	21
4	Rakoniewice	22	1	Wapienno	2
5	Raszków	7	2	Wartosław	6
6	Rawicz	139	3	Wągrowiec	206
7	Rogowo	47	4	Wąsowo	8
8	Rogoźno	264	5	Wieleń	54
9	Rudna	1	6	Wielichowo	2
90	Rychtal	5	7	Więckowice	3
1	Ryczywół	79	8	Winiary	6
2	Rzegnowo	1	9	Witkowo	46
3	Sadki	2	30	Wolsztyn	64
4	Sierakowo	1	1	Wójcin	2
5	Sieraków	24	2	Wronki	187
6	Skalmierzyce Nowe	12	3	Września	151
7	Skierszewko	2	4	Wyrzysk	18
8	Skoki	66	5	Wysoka	2
9	Sokolec	7	6	Zaniemyśl	12
700	Solec Kujawski	33	7	Zbąszyn	54
1	Sołeczno	1	8	Zduny	8
2	Strzałkowo	13	9	Żnin	134
3	Strzelno	61			
4	Sulmierzyce	3		WOJ.STANISŁAWOWSKIE	
5	Swarzędz	61	40	Akreszory	4
6	Szamocin	44	1	Albinówka	8

159

Title page and sample entry from *Blackbook of Localities Whose Jewish Population Was Exterminated by the Nazis.* Provides population figures for the number of Jewish residents in the thousands of towns affected by the Holocaust.

This office has Polk County records only. Birth records: 1880–1920, July 1941 to the present date. Marriage records from 1846. Death records from July 1941 to the present date.

Iowa Department of Public Health
Lucas State Office Building
Vital Records Section
Certified Copy Unit
Des Moines, Iowa 50319

This office has no birth, death, or marriage records before July 1, 1880. (Marriage records before that date may be obtained from the county in which the event occurred.) Birth records from 1920 to 1941 will have to be obtained from the Vital Records Office. Any birth that occurred out of wedlock will also need to be obtained from State Vital Records, and any person adopted must obtain the birth record from the State.

Any death prior to 1891 cannot be searched without the date and place of death. The parentage is not listed on any death record until July 1904. State-wide indexes (which cover all of Iowa) are by year and begin as follows: births: July 1, 1800; deaths: January 1891; marriage: July 1, 1916.

Iowa's mandatory registration law was enacted in July 1921. Prior to 1921, less than 50 percent of the vital events were registered, and the percentage decreases the further back in time the event occurred.

Write to request a fee schedule. (Fees are nonrefundable.)

The Iowa Department of History and Archives
East 12th Street and Grand Avenue
Des Moines, Iowa 50322

Contains over 62,000 volumes of historical and genealogical materials, plus the largest newspaper collection for local papers in the Midwest, over 85,000 volumes. Also a large collection of newspapers published in Iowa from the early 1840s.

State Historical Society of Iowa
East 7th Street and Court Avenue
Des Moines, Iowa 50319
(515) 281-5111

- State Archives (515) 281-3007:
  Land Records
  Tract books
  Patents
  Plats
  Surveyors' field notes (subdivisions and township lines)
- School records:
  Annual report of county superintendents
  High school normal training records.
- Election records:
  Election returns
- Military records:
  Grand Army of the Republic (GAR) post minutes and roster books. The index to the GAR records is available for use at the Newspaper and Census Library in the Historical Building (East 12th and Grand, Des Moines, Iowa). This index contains information on family history that is not found in the minutes and roster books
    Persons subject to military duty
    Clothing books
    Reports

Correspondence
Original muster rolls
Certificates of service
- Cities and towns:
  Articles of incorporation of Iowa cities and towns
  Fire Insurance Maps (also known as Sanborn Maps)
  Childrens' Services Institutional Records
  Governors' Executive Clemency Records
Legal records:
  Attorney General Case Files
  Supreme Court Case Files
  Court of Appeals Case Files
  Abstracts and Arguments and Opinions.
  The record copy is held by the State Archives; however, the Law Library has a case name index.

State Historical Society of Iowa
Census Library
Historical Building
Des Moines, Iowa 50319

- 1836 Dubuque and Des Moines counties
- 1840 Clayton, Clinton, Cedar, Dubuque, Des Moines, Delaware, Henry, Johnson, Jefferson, Jackson, Jones, Linn, Lee, Louisa, Muscatine, Scott, VanBuren, Washington
- Mortality schedules 1850, 1860, 1870, 1880 (for the state of Iowa by county)
- 1856
- Censuses:
  1880 (plus Soundex)
  1885
  1895 (This gives the company, regiment, state, infantry or cavalry for Civil War service)
  1900 Census (plus Soundex)
  1905
  1910
  1915 (indicates church affiliation)
  1925

State Historical Society of Iowa
Bureau of Library and Archives
East 12th and Grand
Des Moines, Iowa 50319
(515) 281-5472

Write to request an application for census search and fee schedules.

Iowa State Historical Department
East 12th Street and Grand Avenue
Des Moines, Iowa 50319
(515) 281-5111

- Des Moines city directories 1871–present
- Other large town directories for scattered and few years
- Newspapers will be searched if an exact date of an event is given
- Newspaper microfilm is available in interlibrary loan through your local public library
- Many of the census and mortality schedules are available on interlibrary loan

Mortuary

Dunn's Funeral Home
2121 Grand Avenue
Des Moines, Iowa 50312

Cemeteries

Glendale Cemetery
4909 University Avenue
Des Moines, Iowa 50311

Woodland Cemetery
2019 Woodland Avenue
Des Moines, Iowa 50312

Synagogues

Beth El Jacob Synagogue
945 Cummins Parkway
Des Moines, Iowa 50312
(515) 274-1551

Children of Israel Congregation
1338 9th Street
Des Moines, Iowa 50314
(515) 288-8335/277-8601

Temple B'nai Jeshurun
51st Street and Grand Avenue
Des Moines, Iowa 50312
(515) 274-4679

Tifereth Israel Synagogue
924 Polk Boulevard
Des Moines, Iowa 50312
(515) 255-1137

Newspaper

Des Moines Jewish Press
910 Polk Blvd.
Des Moines, Iowa 50312

Research Addresses

Iowa Genealogical Society
P.O. Box 3815
Des Moines, Iowa 50322

Iowa Genealogical Society Library
6000 Douglas Street
Des Moines, Iowa 50322

■ IOWA CITY

Library
State Historical Society of Iowa
402 Iowa Avenue
Iowa City, Iowa 52240
(319) 335-3916

Offers conservation lab services: polyester, encapsulation, washing and aqueous deacidification, nonaqueous deacidification, blueprint restoration (washing and flattening). Dry cleaning, tape removal, mending, backing, and flattening are available as schedule allows. Write for a fee schedule.

Bibliography

Andreas, A. T. *Illustrated Historical Atlas of the State of Iowa.* Chicago: Lakeside Press, 1875.
Annals of Iowa. Des Moines, IA: Iowa Department of History and Archives, 1893–

Ayer, N. W. *Ayer Directory of Newspapers and Periodicals.* Philadelphia, annual publication.
Beth El Jacob: 1885–1985. Beth El Jacob, 1985.
A Bibliography of Iowa Newspapers, 1836-1976. Iowa City, IA: State Historical Society of Iowa, 1979.
Cole, C. *A History of the People of Iowa.* Cedar Rapids, IA: Torch Press, 1921.
Glazer, S. *The Jews of Iowa: A Complete History and Accurate Account of Their Religious, Social, Economical and Educational Progress in This State; A History of the Jews of Europe, North and South America in Modern Times, and a Brief History of Iowa.* Des Moines, IA: Koch Brothers Printing Company, 1904.
Hawkeye Heritage. Des Moines, IA: Iowa Genealogical Society, 1865-
Iowa: A Guide to the Hawkeye State. Federal Writers' Project. New York: Viking Press, 1938.
Peterson, W., Jr. *A Reference Guide to Iowa History.* Iowa City, IA: State Historical Society of Iowa, 1942.
Rosenthal, F. *The Jews of Des Moines: The First Century.* The Jewish Welfare Federation of Des Moines, Iowa, 1957.
Sabin, H. *The Making of Iowa.* Chicago: A Flanagan, 1900.
75th Anniversary 1873–1948. Temple B'nai Jeshurun, 1948, 1975.
Wolfe, J. *A Century with Iowa Jewry: As complete a History as Could be Obtained of Iowa from 1833 through 1940.* Des Moines, IA: Iowa Printing & Supply Company, 1941.

■

KANSAS

■ OVERLAND PARK
(Kansas City, Missouri, Metropolitan Area)

The Jewish Community Foundation
5801 West 115th Street
Overland Park, Kansas 66211
(913) 469-1340

Oral history tapes and other materials used in the preparation of the book, *Mid-America's Promise,* edited by Professor Joseph P. Schultz (1982).

The Jewish Education Council
5801 West 115th Street
Overland Park, Kansas 66211
(913) 345-8815

Will respond to inquiries. There is a charge for reproductions of audio cassettes.

- Oral Histories describe life in Kansas City in the 1940s, and include rabbis, Jewish professionals and lay leaders
    Audio cassettes
    Videotaped Holocaust survivors histories

The Jewish Federation of Greater Kansas City
5801 West 115th Street, Suite 201
Overland Park, Kansas 66211
(913) 469-1340

Kehilath Israel Synagogue
10501 Conser
Overland Park, Kansas 66212
(913) 642-1880

PRAIRIE VILLAGE
(Kansas City, Missouri, Metropolitan Area)

Congregation Ohev Shalom
5311 West 75th Street
Prairie Village, Kansas 66208
(913) 642-6460

SHAWNEE MISSION
(Kansas City, Missouri, Metropolitan Area)

Congregation Beth Torah
9401 Nall
Shawnee Mission, Kansas 66207
(913) 341-2212

Temple Beth El
8301 Lamar
Shawnee Mission, Kansas 66207
(913) 642-8707

Newspaper

The Jewish Chronicle
7373 W. 107th Street
Shawnee Mission, Kansas 66212
(913) 648-4620

Bibliography

Schultz, J. P., ed. *Mid-America's Promise: A Profile of Kansas City Jewry.* Overland Park, KS: Jewish Community Foundation, 1982. (The book is a history of the Jewish community of Kansas City. The oral history tapes and other materials used in the preparation of the book are now on deposit with the Jewish Educational Council.)

KENTUCKY

LOUISVILLE

Cabinet for Human Resources
Department of Health Services
Vital Statistics
Division of State Health Planning
275 East Main Street
Frankfort, Kentucky 40621

- Birth and death records dating from 1911
- Marriage records dating from 1958

Application forms required. There is a charge for copies of birth records.

The Kentucky Historical Society
Old State House, P.O. Box H
Frankfort, Kentucky 40602
(502) 564-3016

Upon request, a Staff Genealogical Researcher will comb the Historical Society's collections in an effort to answer individual requests. There is a charge for this service (for nonmembers). Write for fee schedule. Photo duplication charges extra.

The Historical Society library has:

- Kentucky Federal Consuses 1810–1880, 1900 and 1910 (microfilm with soundex index for 1880 and 1900)
  Will send copies from indexed census records, but will not search microfilm
- Kentucky vital statistics on microfilm:
  Births, marriages, deaths (1852–1861); card index available (1874–1878)
- Indexes (in book form) for births and deaths 1911–1969
- County court records on microfilm:
  Wills and marriages, from the formation of the counties to 1900 when available
- Thousands of published genealogies (no general index to Kentucky genealogical records)
- Local histories
- City directories
- Military lists
- Biographical materials and manuscripts

The Louisville Historical Society
Filson Club
1310 S. 3rd Street
Louisville, Kentucky 40208

The Society responds to written inquiries, when possible.

- Louisville City Directories (from 1832)
- Kentucky Census records (1810–1910)
- Many genealogical archives

Louisville Public Library
4th and York
Louisville, Kentucky 40202

The staff responds to written inquiries on a limited basis. There is a charge for copies.

- Louisville City Directories from 1832 to present
- Census records 1810–1910 (no index for 1870)
- Many genealogical archives

Louisville and Jefferson County Clerk
400 East Gray Street
Louisville, Kentucky 40202

- Marriage records prior to 1958
- The school census (from 1888), a source of birth dates of individuals who attended Louisville public schools

The National Society of the Sons of the American Revolution
Genealogical Library
1000 South Fourth Street
Louisville, Kentucky 40203
(502) 589-1776

Fee for nonmembers.
Limited to American Revolutionary War histories, genealogies, state, local, and county histories.

Newspapers

Community (bi-weekly)
3620 Dutchmans Lane
Louisville, Kentucky 40205
(502) 451-8840

Kentucky Jewish Post and Opinion (weekly)
1551 Bardstown Road
Louisvill,e Kentucky 40205
(502) 459-1914

Synagogues
Adath Israel Congregation (Reform)
834 South 3rd Street
Louisville, Kentucky 40203
The state's first synagogue, founded in 1842 and chartered the following year.

Adath Jeshurun Congregation (Conservative)
2401 Woodbourne Avenue
Louisville, Kentucky 40205
(502) 458-5359

Congregation Anshei Sfard (Orthodox)
3700 Dutchmans Lane
Louisville, Kentucky 40205
(502) 451-3122

Chabad Lubavitch (Orthodox)
2607 Landor Avenue
Louisvill,e Kentucky 40205
(502) 459-1770

Keneseth Israel Congregation (Orthodox)
P.O. Box 5295
Louisville, Kentucky 40205
(502) 459-2780

Temple Shalom (Reform)
4220 Taylorsville Road
Louisville, Kentucky 40220
(502) 458-4739

The Temple (Reform)
5101 Brownsboro Road
Louisville, Kentucky 40222
(502) 423-1818

Funeral Directors
Herman Meyer & Son, Inc.
1338 Ellison Avenue
Louisville, Kentucky 40204
(502) 458-9569

Bibliography
Duff, J. M. *Inventory of Kentucky Birth, Marriage and Death Records.* Frankfort: Department of Library and Archives, Commonwealth of Kentucky, 1980.
Hinds, C. F. "Kentucky Records, How to Use Them and Where They Are Located." *National Genealogical Society Quarterly,* Vol. 59, p. 3, 1971.
Landau, H. "Adath Louisville."
Schweitzer, G. K. "Kentucky Genealogical Research." Knoxville, TN, 1985.

MARYLAND

■ ANNAPOLIS

Maryland State Archives, Hall of Records
P.O. Box 828
Annapolis, Maryland 21404
(301) 269-3914
There is no membership fee, but there is a $5 search fee, and researchers must complete a registration form and present proof of identity. The collection includes probate, land, court, and other state and local public records dating from 1634 to present.

Maryland State Law Library
Courts of Appeal Building
361 Rowe Boulevard
Annapolis, Maryland 21401
(301) 269-3395
There is no research or membership fee. The library will answer letters of inquiry (they ask that researchers be as specific as possible).

■ BALTIMORE

Baltimore City Archives & Records Management
211 East Pleasant Street, Room 201
Baltimore, Maryland 21202
(301) 396-4861 or 396-4863
Write for a fee schedule. Sources include:

- WPA-HRS alphabetical name index (1756 to 1938) to personal names appearing in documents such as petitions, licenses, bonds, police reports, correspondence, applications, and Civil War records
- 2d name index covers ships' passengers arriving in Baltimore from 1833 to 1866. Entries arranged alphabetically, include names of accompanying passengers, age, sex, occupation, nationality, name of vessel, date of arrival, and destination in United States
- "Indexes to Naturalization Petitions to the U.S. District Court and District Courts of Maryland" (1797–1951). Indexes cover only those aliens who sought naturalization in these courts for the district of Maryland, which were located in Baltimore

Bureau of Vital Statistics
201 West Preston Street
Baltimore, Maryland 21201
Birth and death records for Baltimore City, 1875 to present; for the rest of Maryland, 1878 to present. All marriage records from 1951 to present. There is a fee.

Genealogical Publishing Company
1001 North Calvert Street
Baltimore, Maryland 21202 `
(301) 837-8271
The company's catalog contains numerous titles which will be of assistance in tracing Jewish–

American and European Jewish forebears. (See Bibliography.) Publications include a reprint edition of *Finding Our Fathers*, by Dan Rottenberg, the first book specifically devoted to Jewish ancestry, Sallyann Amdur Sack's book *A Guide to Jewish Genealogical Research in Israel*, and numerous other books on genealogy, immigration and local history. The company expects to publish Jewish source records in the future. Write to request a catalog of publications.

Hebrew Immigrant Aid Society
(Social Service Building of Jewish Charities)
5750 Park Heights Avenue
Baltimore, Maryland 21215
(301) 542-6300
Records date back to 1911 and include:

- Individual records of Hamburg ship passengers
- Naturalization records
- Indemnification claims against Germany

Genealogical Council
Jewish Historical Society of Maryland
15 Lloyd Street
Baltimore, Maryland 21202
(301) 732-6400
Though there is no research fee, there is a membership fee. The society will answer letters of inquiry.

The bulk of the society's collection dates from 1880 to present and includes:

- 100 linear feet of manuscripts
- 12,000 photos
- 210 oral history tapes
- 11 drawers of vertical files

Maryland Historical Society Library
201 West Monument Street
Baltimore, Maryland 21201
(301) 685-3750
There is a fee for membership and for nonmembers conducting research. Letters of inquiry answered. Research may be requested by mail.

Since 1844, the Maryland Historical Society has been serving those interested in the history of Maryland and its citizens as the largest single repository of the state's cultural history. A private, nonprofit public service organization, the society has always been dependent on memberships, gifts and grants for the support of its programs and the enrichment of its collections.

The library of the society is divided into three divisions.

1. Manuscript Division: The holdings of the Manuscript Division—2,583 collections of manuscript and other unpublished materials—are described in the Society's 1981 *Guide to the Research Collections of the Maryland Historical Society*.

2. The Reference Division: The Reference Division has about 60,000 volumes, as well as countless clippings, newspapers (both in original form and in microfilm) and assorted material relating to Maryland and its people. Local history and genealogy are the greatest strengths, especially in terms of eighteenth and nineteenth centuries.

3. Special Collections:

- Genealogical index: key to the collection of unpublished genealogical materials

- Large collection of small groups of unpublished genealogical notes
- Dielman-Hayward File, made up of biographical material, usually copied or cut from newspapers, on Maryland since 1800
- Oath of fidelity index lists men who signed the Maryland Oath of Fidelity of 1778 (a rough approximation of a census of the state, though it lists only males of military age)
- Genealogical journals
- Wilkins file provides an index for standard Maryland histories whose original indexes were either incomplete or nonexistent
- Vertical file includes newspaper clippings on various aspects of Maryland life and history (contains no biographical information)

Research Services: The library offers two services by mail. Basic service covers one search from the following sources (write for fee schedule):

- Dielman-Hayward file
- *Maryland Historical Magazine* index
- Index to Passenger Lists of Vessels Arriving in Baltimore, 1820–1897
- Revolutionary soldiers of Maryland index

Basic service: a professional genealogist associated with the library will search any and every source at the Historical Society which holds the requested information.

Neither service can guarantee results or offer refunds.

The library publishes the *Maryland Historical Magazine* (quarterly) as well as *News and Notes* (bimonthly).

Peabody Library of The Johns Hopkins University
17 East Mount Vernon Place
Baltimore, Maryland 21202
(301) 659-8179
There are no research or membership fees. The library will answer letters of inquiry.

Peale Museum
(part of the Baltimore City Life Museums)
225 Holliday Street
Baltimore, Maryland 21202
(301) 396-1149/1164
The Peale Museum collects and exhibits objects pertaining to the history of Baltimore. Its photographic collection includes several quality images of Jewish neighborhoods of the past.

The museum staff will attempt to answer brief letters of inquiry.

Steamship Historical Society Collection
University of Baltimore Library
1420 Maryland Avenue
Baltimore, Maryland 21201
(301) 625-3134
Though not primarily a genealogical source, the collection contains material relating to immigrant steamships and steamship lines, postcards, ship histories, etc. The collection contains no material pertaining to sailing vessels and no passenger or crew lists.

Research fees are flexible. There is a membership fee. The staff will attempt to answer brief letters of inquiry (SASE appreciated).

Other sources include (1) Photo Bank Information sheet, (2) SSHSA Membership brochure.

Synagogues
Baltimore Hebrew Congregation
500 Park Heights Avenue
Baltimore, Maryland 21208

The congregation has a list of Jewish marriages from 1850 to 1985. They are indexed in chronological order (you must, therefore, know the date).

The congregation is in the process of computerizing cemetery records dating back to the middle 1800's.

Publications include *A History of the Baltimore Hebrew Congregation, 1830–1905,* 1905; *The One Hundredth Anniversary,* 1930; *1830–1955 125th Anniversary,* 1955.

Beth Jacob Congregation
5713 Park Heights Avenue
Baltimore, Maryland 21215
(301) 466-1266

Publication: *1979–65th Anniversary,* 1979.

B'nei Israel Congregation
27 Lloyd Street
Baltimore, Maryland 21202
(301) 732-5454

Publications include *100th Anniversary,* 1973; *Diamond Jubilee 5708–1948,* 1948.

Chizuk Amuno Congregation
8100 Stevenson Road
Baltimore, Maryland 21208
(301) 486-6400

This is a founding congregation of the Conservative movement in the United States. Minute books are available from 1871 to 1922, and from 1924 to the present.

Arlington Cemetery of Chizuk Amuno (Jewish Community Center) 1945 to present. Lot owners and cross references of deceased.

Shearith Israel Congregation
Park Heights and Glen Avenue
Baltimore, Maryland 21215
(301) 466-3060

Temple Oheb Shalom
7310 Park Heights Avenue
Baltimore, Maryland 21208

Biblioghraphy
Blum, I., ed. *The Jews of Baltimore.* Baltimore-Washington, 1910.

Directory: Hebrew Cemeteries in the Baltimore Area. Sol Levinson & Bros., Inc., Funeral Directors. Copies available without charge. (301) 358-1700.

Fein, I. M. *The Making of an American Jewish Community: The History of Baltimore Jewry from 1773 to 1920.* Philadelphia: Jewish Publication Society of America, 1971.

Marcus, J. R. *Early American Jewry 1655–1790.* Philadelphia: Jewish Publication Society of America, 1953.

MASSACHUSETTS

■ BOSTON

Boston Public Library
Research Division Copley Square
Boston, Massachusetts 02117
(617) 536-5400

- Various genealogical handbooks
- Collective biographical dictionaries
- Works of peerage and landed gentry
- Numerous heraldic works
- Journals
- Many useful reference works on Boston
- All of the published vital records of Massachusetts cities and towns
- A number of town histories (usually of eastern Massachusetts towns)
- The printed Massachusetts Bay and Plymouth Colony records

In addition to the printed materials already referred to, the genealogical collection also contains other very useful materials located in the Microtext Department. Some of these are:

- Obituary index collection from Boston and New York newspapers—1709 to the present (except for a few small gaps)
- Passenger lists of arrivals at the Port of Boston and other ports—1820–1921 (with gaps)
- All available Federal census reports for the New England states (1790–1880)
- The Veterans census of 1890
- Jewish historical journals
- Genealogical handbooks
- Collective genealogy
- Some individual genealogies (both United States and foreign)
- City directories (pre-1901)
- Boston city directories (1789–1978)
- Boston telephone directories
- Newspapers

The following Jewish newspapers (weekly unless otherwise noted) are available:

Southern Israelite (Atlanta)
January 2, 1959–December 31, 1971

National Jewish Post and Opinion (Indianapolis)
September 21, 1945–November 11, 1965

Boston Advocate/Jewish Advocate (Boston)
May 5, 1905+

Boston Hebrew Observer (Boston)
January 5, 1883–January 29, 1886

Jewish Herald (Boston)
June 2, 1893–August 31, 1894

Jewish World (Boston)
January 6, 1939–December 11, 1942

Jewish Weekly News (Springfield, Massachusetts)
March 28, 1952–January 10, 1974

Jewish Civic Leader (Worcester, Massachusetts)
January 7, 1960–December 28, 1967

Daily Forward (New York)
January 1, 1957–December 25, 1965

Carolina Israelite (Charlotte)
February 1944–February 1968 (monthly, bimonthly)

Jewish Post (Winnipeg)
January 4, 1968–June 26, 1969
Jewish Chronicle (London)
November 12, 1841 + Index 1841–1890
Palestine Post/Jerusalem Post (Jerusalem)
January 1, 1949 (daily)

Massachusetts State Archives
Columbia Point
220 Morrissey Boulevard
Boston, Massachusetts 02125
(617) 727-2816

- Noncurrent records of the state—all the vital records not located at the downtown Registrar of Vital Statistics office, 1841–1895 plus the indexes
- Massachusetts State Census returns for 1855 and 1865
- City directories
- Abstracts from state and local court naturalizations 1885–1931. (These abstracts can then lead you to the location of the original records.)
- Names of immigrants who arrived by ship to Boston in 1848 and continued until 1891, alphabetical name index
- Forty drawers of microfilm reels (most are copies of the LDS filming projects in Massachusetts). Microfilms include Suffolk County (City of Boston) birth indexes (1841–1971), marriage indexes (1841–1971), death indexes (1846–1971). (These are separate from the state returns.) Statewide returns include birth registers (1841–1890), marriage registers (1844–1890), death registers (1841–1851, 1852–1899)

Massachusetts Military Division
Adjutant General's Office
War Records, Room 1000
100 Cambridge Street
Boston, Massachusetts 02202
(617) 727-2964

Military Records
Massachusetts State Library
341 State House
Beacon Street
Boston, Massachusetts 02133

- Local histories
- Indexes to all Boston papers
- Massachusetts city and county atlases and maps
- Complete telephone directories for Massachusetts, fifty state capitals, and other major cities and some foreign cities
- Current and historic city directories for Massachusetts cities and towns back to 1789

New England Historical Genealogical Society
101 Newbury Street
Boston, Massachusetts 02116
(617) 536-5740

Founded in 1845 for the purpose of collecting, studying, and preserving New England family and local history. As the oldest and largest society of its kind, it maintains a research library of nearly 300,000 books, pamphlets, and family papers relating to these fields.

Membership fee; research fee for nonmembers.

The library publishes *The New England Historical and Genealogical Register*. Though its Jewish genealogical collection is not extensive, it does have some bibliographical materials.

The collection of finding aids such as city directories, maps, and other basic reference materials is impressive.

Probate Court or Registry of Deeds
Old Court House
Pemberton Square
Boston, Massachusetts 12108
(617) 725-8575

Registrar of Vital Statistics
150 Tremont Street, Room B-3
Boston, Massachusetts 02111
(617) 727-0110

Statewide birth, marriage, and death records (alphabetical indexes in five-year compilations).

Bibliography

Ehrenfried, A. *A Chronicle of Boston Jewry from the Colonial Settlement to 1900*. Boston: Privately printed, 1963.

Fein, I. M. *Boston—Where It All Began: An Historical Perspective of the Boston Jewish Community*. Boston: Boston Jewish Bicentennial Committee, 1976.

Feldman, S., ed. *Guide to Jewish Boston and New England*. Cambridge, MA: Genesis 2, 1986.

Kliman, B. S. "The Jewish Brahmins of Boston: a study of the German Jewish immigrant experience, 1860–1900" [senior thesis]. Waltham, MA: Brandeis University, 1978.

Schindler, S. *Israelites in Boston: A Tale Describing the Development of Judaism in Boston*. Boston: Berwick and Smith, 1889.

Schoeffler, W. H. *Genealogical Research at the Boston Public Library*. Massachusetts Genealogical Council, Publication #5.

Wieder, A. A. *The Early Jewish Community of Boston's North End*. Waltham, MA: Brandeis University, 1962.

■ BROOKLINE

Hebrew College
Jacob and Rose Grossman Library
43 Hawes Street
Brookline, Massachusetts 02146
(617) 232-8710

The library will answer letters of inquiry. It contains:

- Complete records of the *Boston Jewish Advocate* (1905–present)
- Archives of the Hebrew College
- Boston Communal Survey 1930, 1967, and 1977
- Yearbook of the Jewish philanthropies
- Histories, yearbooks, etc. about the Boston Jewish Community
- Records of individual synagogues and Jewish centers
- Some 400 photographs, tapes, records, press clippings

Microfilm collection includes:

- Special collections of the Jewish Theological Seminary of America
- IDC collection, Palestine, sixteenth–nineteenth centuries

The college publishes *The Hebrew College Bulletin*.

There is also an annual borrowing fee. Written inquiries are handled without charge.

Hebrew College is an institution created by American Jewish society for the academic study and teaching of Jewish culture. It has a particular commitment to those aspects of Jewish culture whose vehicle of expression is the Hebrew language. It is apolitical and nondenominational. Hebrew College is grounded in the belief that Judaism finds its richest expression in educational work, in studying and teaching, and in the continuous endeavor to improve the arts of Jewish living. Its 75,000 volume library contains manuscripts, records, and other archival material.

The archival collection in the library of greatest importance are those relating to the development of the Hebrew College and Boston Jewry from 1920 onward. Manuscripts of Solomon Zucrow, 1920–1930, and Abraham Charak, 1905–1909, prominent Jewish educators in the Greater Boston area are included in the manuscript collection.

■ CAMBRIDGE

Harvard University Baker Library
Harvard University
Graduate School of Business Administration
Cambridge, Massachusetts 02163
(617) 495-6411

The archives of the R. G. Dun & Co. (half of Dun and Bradstreet). 2,600 volumes of confidential credit reports on over 2 million people for the period of 1841–1890. Organized by state and then by county with a name index for almost every volume extant.

Anyone who operated a business was probably investigated by the Dun Company, plus other professional people. An article in *American Jewish History* said, ''A separate file was kept on doctors and lawyers. Men who were commercially active in a community, whether they were merchants, manufacturers, brokers or bankers, were almost certain to be included.''

■ LYNN

The North Shore Jewish Historical Society
31 Exchange Street
Lynn, Massachusetts 01901
(617) 593-2386

The Society's collection includes published books and unpublished manuscripts on Jewish families in the Boston area. It has also started a funded archives project that will serve to reconstruct and preserve the history of the large and vibrant Jewish communities in Lynn, Salem, Peabody, and Beverly, Massachusetts. Special emphasis will be given to explaining the economic centrality of the shoe trades within these North Shore communities, which were the national leaders in women's shoe production.

There is a membership fee. A newsletter is published semi-annually.

■ NEWTON CENTRE

Jewish Cemetery Association of Massachusetts
1340 Centre Street
Newton Centre, Massachusetts 02159
(617) 244-6509

A booklet listing member cemeteries is available upon request. The *Guide to Jewish Cemeteries*, including cemetery maps, is available annually.

■ WALTHAM

American Jewish Historical Society
2 Thornton Road
Waltham, Massachusetts 02154
(617) 891-8110

The AJHS is located on the campus of Brandeis University. It will try to answer questions if SASE is provided. Can recommend local students who will do research for a fee.

The library staff is able to do a limited amount of research in response to written inquiries, but is unable to handle extensive requests.

Request brochure describing collections and how to use material.

Holdings: Approximately 6 million items, mostly in English, but some in German, Hebrew, Yiddish, French, and Russian. In addition to the AJHS Library, housing more than 80,000 volumes and thousands of newspapers and periodicals, there is a collection of approximately 2,000 photographs.

The AJHS has a wealth of materials which may be used in doing genealogical research. In general, this material deals exclusively with American Jewry and consists of standard reference works (encyclopedias, biographical dictionaries, periodicals from local, national, and foreign Jewish historical societies), as well as manuscript collections, periodicals, and books. These materials are available for use at the society and, in some cases, by interlibrary loan.

- Card index to nineteenth century American Jewish periodicals (all of which the society has for use as originals on microfilm)
- Index in manuscript form, containing references to articles of American interest which appeared in European periodicals
- Index of articles of Jewish interest which appeared in American and non-Jewish newspapers published before 1850
- Several hundred individual family histories or genealogies

Local and synagogue histories and communal groups, as well as printed material on many such organizations.

Manuscript collection: over five hundred cataloged manuscript collections in the library:

- Detailed index to nineteenth century Anglo-Jewish periodicals and hundreds of Jewish weekly newspapers.
- Early communal histories
- Records of the Industrial Removal Office (relocation records)
- Original incorporation papers, incorporated between 1848 and 1920 in New York City—fully indexed. Landsmanshaftn (Sephardic and East European) and Jewish organizations (synagogues, communal groups, fraternal orders, clubs, unions)
- HIAS, Boston collection, including individual arrival records, arranged alphabetically, for immi-

grants arriving in Boston or Providence between 1882 and 1929. (Also, incomplete chronological lists of ship arrivals and passenger lists 1904–1953.)

- Mayor's court records (New York City), 1674–1860 (civil cases); insolvent debtors and bankruptcy proceedings, 1787–1861; inventories of wills of Jews in the early nineteenth century; and divorces from the 1850s to the 1930s. Early nineteenth century state and county courts' naturalization records
- Hebrew Orphan Asylum of the City of New York—administrative records 1844–1941 (including admittance, discharge, school, and conduct records)
- Woodbine Colony records (colony established in 1891 as a center of Jewish agricultural settlement by the Baron de Hirsch fund)
- Census for 1934 Pittsburgh, published by the Pittsburgh Hebrew Institute
- *Chevra Kadisha* records from Boston and Fall River, Massachusetts, from the nineteenth and twentieth centuries
- Lists of those honored at religious services at Congregation Shearith Israel, New York City
- Jewish marriage notices from the newspapers of Charleston, South Carolina, 1775–1906, compiled by Barnett A. Elzas
- Publications of Jewish historical societies from around the United States (some with recollections of family members and genealogies)
- Genealogies (several hundred)
- Over 300 cataloged manuscript collections dealing with individuals or families

National Archives—New England Region
380 Trapelo Road
Waltham, Massachusetts 02154
(617) 647-8100

Prior to the twentieth century, any immigrant could be naturalized in any Massachusetts court.
Holdings include:

- Superior Court records
- Records of Federal nationalizations, after 1906
- Common Pleas Court records
- U.S. District Court records
- Passenger arrival lists for port of Boston

Some declarations of intention and naturalization records may still be found in county courthouses.

Brandeis University Library
P.O. Box 9110
Waltham, Massachusetts 02254
(617) 736-4685

Brandeis University Libraries house a collection of close to 100,000 volumes of Judaica. The genealogical researcher will find much material of interest including some of the following types of materials:

- Genealogical handbooks, collective and individual genealogies
- Biographies, autobiographies, biographical dictionaries
- Histories of local Jewish communities including an extensive collection of Yizkor (memorial) books

- Cemetery records including books with data on tombstones in Jewish cemeteries
- Geographical material
- Scholarly periodicals
- Local Jewish newspapers

The library has among its special collections the following archival material:

- French-Jewish Community (Consistoire Israélite) ca. 1750–1910 (12 boxes)
- Theresienstadt Concentration Camp—one box of German camp bulletins

Bibliography
A Genealogist's Handbook for New England Research. Lynnfield, MA: New England Library Association Bibliography Committee, 1980 (rev. 1985).
"Researching Your Family's History at the State Archives." *American Jewish History,* Vol. 72, No 3 (March 1983) p. 333. Waltham, MA: American Jewish Historical Society.

MICHIGAN

■ BIRMINGHAM
(Detroit Metropolitan Area)

Temple Beth El
Leo M. Franklin Archives
7400 Telegraph Road
Birmingham, Michigan 48010
(313) 851-1100

The state's most extensive collection of Michigan Jewish History. Temple Beth El will answer brief inquiries if accompanied by a self-addressed stamped envelope. The archives' holdings include:

- Historical and some pictorial records of early Detroit and Michigan Jewry
- Historical and pictorial information regarding all synagogues in Detroit and most of Michigan
- A collection in miniature of Detroit and world synagogues
- Records of Detroit, American, and European Reform Jewish History
- Records of Lafayette Street Cemetery (Detroit's oldest Jewish cemetery)
- Burial records of Beth Olam Cemetery (Detroit's second-oldest Jewish cemetery)
- Birth, marriage, and death records of Temple Beth El membership
- Other material regarding members from 1850 to present

■ BLOOMFIELD HILLS
(Detroit Metropolitan Area)

Family History Center
Bloomfield Hills Branch
425 North Woodward Avenue
Bloomfield Hills, Michigan 48013
(313) 647-5671

- Vast Polish holdings (because of large local Polish-American community)
- Detroit probate records through 1900
- U.S. census records through 1910
- Research aids from many countries
- Excellent research aids for the Hamburg passenger ship lists (microfilm of the lists from the Family History Library in Salt Lake City may be ordered here)

■ DETROIT

Detroit Office of Vital Records
1151 Taylor Street
Detroit, Michigan 48202
(313) 876-4133 (recorded message)
(313) 876-4135 (further information)

Vital records of the state of Michigan. Write for fee schedule. Allow three to six weeks via mail (the office discourages mail inquiries).

Only individuals whose names appear on the records in question, or can prove relationship to those individuals, can obtain copies.

Detroit Public Library
Burton Historical Collection
5201 Woodward Avenue
Detroit, Michigan 48202
(313) 833-1480

The genealogical collection is an integral part of the local history collection and is served by a staff of eight librarians. Burton Library will do preliminary research of local history topics for in-depth requests for individuals writing papers or books, and then recommend graduate students or genealogists. They cannot carry out genealogical research through the mail.

Listed below are some of the library's holdings:

- United States Census records through 1910
- Hamburg, Germany passenger lists
- Detroit city directories 1837–1974
- Old and out-of-town telephone directories
- Detroit Jewish historical records (most uncataloged)
- Landsmanshaftn records (most uncataloged)
- Records of the Jewish Welfare Association.
- *Jewish News,* an English language weekly publication containing birth, marriage, death information and other Jewish news from the greater Detroit area (1942–present date; microfilmed)
- Interlibrary loans (microfilm) from National Archives (catalog of materials available)
- Local historical books and records
- Books, journals, and articles regarding genealogy
- Holdings of the Polish Genealogy Society of Michigan
- Temple Beth El Archives
- Papers of the Jewish Historical Society of Michigan

Holocaust Memorial Center
(See West Bloomfield)

Jewish Historical Society of Michigan
(See Southfield)

Family History Center
(See Bloomfield Hills)

Probate Court
1305 City County Building
Detroit, Michigan 48226
(313) 224-5720, 224-5722

Records up to 1900. The Family History Center has these records on microfilm.

Recorders Court
Frank Murphy Hall of Justice
1441 St. Antoine Street
Court Clerk
Detroit, Michigan 48226
(313) 224-2500

Records from 1852 to 1906. The Burton Historical Library has these records on microfilm.

Wayne County Clerk's Office
201 City County Building
Detroit, Michigan 48226
(313) 224-5536

The office has Wayne County, Michigan, records excluding Detroit

- Birth records after 1905
- Marriage after 1940 (approximately)
- Death records after 1910 (Some of these records may have restricted access. Call or write the office for details.)

Synagogues

Most synagogues in the greater Detroit area kept marriage and death records which may be obtained by correspondence.

Temple Beth El
(See Birmingham, Michigan)

Congregation Shaarey Zedek
27375 Bell Road
Southfield, Michigan 48037
(313) 357-5544

Second oldest Detroit congregation, established 1861. They have archives and photographs, birth, marriage, Bar Mitzvah, confirmation, and death records of members.

Members' genealogies are being computerized by the synagogue. They hold records of Beth Olam and Cloverhill Cemeteries.

Bibliography
Adat Shalom. *Story of the Synagogue.* 1952.
Beth Abraham-Hillel-Moses. *Dedication Journal.* 1958.
B'nai David. *75th Anniversary of Congregation B'nai David.* 1966.
B'nai Moshe. *Congregation B'nai Moshe.* 1982.
_____. *Dedication Volume Four.* 1960.
_____. 75th Anniversary. 1987.
Chapin, A. W. "History of the United Jewish Charities of Detroit, 1899–1949." Typescript. Jewish Welfare Federation of Detroit.
Edgar, I. I. "The Early Sites and Beginnings of Congregation

Beth El." *Michigan Jewish History*, pp. 5–11, November, 1970.

———. *A history of early Jewish physicians in Michigan.* 1984.

Franklin, L. M. *History of Congregation Beth El, 1900–1910.* Detroit, 1910.

Franklin, M. M. "Jews in Michigan." *Michigan History Magazine*, Vol. 33, No. 1, 1939.

Grad, E., and Roth, B. *Congregation Shaarey Zedek.* Detroit: Congregation Shaarey Zedek, 1982.

Heineman, D. E. Jewish beginnings in Michigan before 1850. *Publications of the American Jewish Historical Society*, pp. 47–70, 1950.

Katz, I. I., and Marcus, J. R. *The Beth El Story: With a History of the Jews in Michigan before 1850.* Detroit: Wayne State University Press, 1955.

———. *The Jewish Soldier from Michigan in the Civil War.* Detroit: Wayne State University Press, 1962.

Lederer, P. "A Study of Jewish Influences in Detroit" [M.A. thesis.] Detroit: Wayne State University, 1947.

Rockaway, R. A. "Ethnic conflict in an urban environment: The German and Russian Jew in Detroit, 1881–1914." *American Jewish Historical Quarterly*, Vol. 60, pp. 133–150, December 1970.

———. The Eastern European Jewish community of Detroit, 1881–1914. *YIYO Annual of Jewish Social Science*, Vol. 15, pp. 133–150, 1974.

———. "The Industrial Removal Office in Detroit." *Detroit in Perspective*, pp. 40–49, Spring 1982.

———. *The Jews of Detroit: From the Beginning 1762–1914.* Detroit: Wayne State University Press, 1986.

Shaarey Zedek. *Congregation Shaarey Zedek, 1861–1981.* 1982.

Temple Beth El. *Congregation Beth El. A History . . . 1850–1900.* 1900.

———. *A History . . . 1900–1910.* 2 vols. 1910.

———. *An Outline History of Congregation Beth El from 1850 to 1940. The Beth El Story.* 1955.

———. *110 Years of Temple Beth El.* 1960.

Temple Beth Jacob. *Dedication Volume.* 1955.

Temple Emanu-El. *Temple Emanu-El: 25 Year Anniversary.*

Temple Israel. *Silver Anniversary Album.* 1966.

Young Israel of Oak-Woods. *Silver Anniversary.* 1980.

■ LANSING

Library of Michigan
P.O. Box 30007
735 East Michigan Avenue
Lansing, Michigan 48909
(517) 373-1593

The library of the Michigan Board of Education. The staff may answer brief inquiries regarding their holdings, but cannot do research.

- Michigan Census records on microfilm through 1910
- Michigan birth, marriage and death records
- Many books about Jewish genealogy; also journals and articles

The following English/Jewish newspapers are available on microfilm and contain birth, marriage, and death notices:

- *Jewish Chronicle* (Detroit)
  March 3, 1916–July 13, 1951
- *Jewish Herald* (Detroit)
  May 25, 1927–January 13, 1928
- *Jewish News* (Greater Detroit)
  Recent years also contains Flint, Michigan,

March 27, 1942, to date. In 1951 they absorbed the *Jewish Chronicle*.

Michigan Department of Public Health
Office of the State Registrar
Vital Statistics and Records Section
3500 North Logan Street
P.O. Box 30035
Lansing, Michigan 48909
(517) 373-1387

- Birth, marriage, and death records from 1867. Some of these records may have restricted access. Call or write the office for details. Birth records prior to 1906 are handwritten in large ledgers. They have spaces to indicate birth date, birth place, parents' names (not mother's maiden name), and parents' place of birth; however, some records are incomplete.
- Divorce records from 1897

The following records are found in similar handwritten ledgers:

- Death records prior to 1897
- Marriage records prior to 1926
- Divorce records prior to 1924
- Photocopying of these early records is not possible (documents recorded in oversize ledgers). However, the staff will, for a fee, transcribe the material to the best of their ability (parts of original documents may be illegible). Copies of records after the dates mentioned above are reproductions of the actual documents on file.
- Many of the above records may also be obtained from the County Clerk in the county where the event took place. Interested researchers should write for the Application to Request a Vital Record for Genealogical Research, which includes the current fee schedule.

Michigan State Archives
Research Department
3405 North Logan
Lansing, Michigan 48918
(517) 373-0512

Before 1906, people could file a Declaration of Intent (first papers) in any Michigan court. Most, however, were filed in the Wayne County Circuit Court. After 1906, all Declarations were filed in the Circuit Court. Until recently Circuit Court records were kept in the Old County Building in Detroit. They were moved in 1986.

Written inquiries will be answered for a nominal fee per page. You must have a Certificate of Naturalization number for post-1906 records. A handwritten set of Declarations of Intent is cross-indexed by year and certificate number.

■ SOUTHFIELD
(Detroit Metropolitan Area)

Jewish Historical Society of Michigan
29699 Southfield Road, #217
Southfield, Michigan 48076

Not equipped to answer inquiries. This organization was established in 1957 and has 450 members. They meet monthly and publish a journal twice a year. Their purpose is to gather Jewish historical data in Michigan. Their archives are stored at the Burton Historical Library (see above). They have helped designate Jewish historical sites throughout Detroit and Michigan. They have also established the Michigan Jewish Genealogical Index (see Midrasha College, below).

Midrasha College of Jewish Studies Library
21550 West Twelve Mile Road
Southfield, Michigan 48076
(313) 354-3130

This library is part of the United Hebrew Complex in Southfield. The staff will answer inquiries if accompanied by a self-addressed stamped envelope. The Library's holdings include the following:

- Some memorial (yizkor) books mostly in Yiddish
- An edited English copy of parts of the David Horodoker Memorial Book
- Extensive collection of Jewish historical and reading material
- Holdings of the Genealogical Branch of the Jewish Historical Society of Michigan, including "Computerized Family Finder"
- Michigan Jewish Genealogical Index. Organized by the Michigan Jewish Historical Society, the Index incorporates the birth and death records of all of Michigan's Jewish communities. It draws on a number of sources for information, including newspapers, synagogue and community records, and burial lists. To date, the Index contains over one thousand entries. The Index lists burial records of three Bay City Jewish cemeteries, birth records of Congregation Beth El of Flint, and a burial list of Beth Olem of Hamtramck, Michigan. In addition to the above, some records of the Jewish communities of Ann Arbor, Grand Rapids, Houghton, Jackson, Kalamazoo, Lansing, and Mount Pleasant are also listed. This genealogical aid is continually growing, as the Michigan Jewish Historical Society microfilms data from the Jewish communities throughout the state and the records of old Jewish publications.

Synagogue
See Detroit, Michigan, p. 64.

■ WEST BLOOMFIELD (Detroit Metropolitan Area)

Holocaust Memorial Center
6600 West Maple Road
West Bloomfield, Michigan 48033
(313) 661-0840

Over 10,000 items in its multilingual collection of books, microforms, documents, manuscripts, photographs, sound recordings, computer files, videos, visible files, and maps. Included are:

- Extensive memorial book collection
- Holocaust trial proceedings
- Major National Archive collections on the Holocaust: Gestapo transport lists; Berlin documentation concerning Jews; Mauthausen death books;

name index of Jews whose nationality was annulled by Nazi regime; U.S. State Department records
- Detroit *Jewish News*
- Survivor oral histories on video and cassette with computerized index of persons and places
- Film documentaries
- East European geographical finding aids
- Newsletters of national genealogical societies
- Numerous survivor, deportation, transport, and death lists

Jewish Genealogical Society of Michigan
c/o Bruce Finsilver
4987 Bantry Drive
West Bloomfield, Michigan 48322

Funeral Homes
Hebrew Memorial Chapel
26640 Greenfield Road
Oak Park, Michigan 48237

Ira Kaufman Chapel
18325 W. Nine Mile Road
Southfield, Michigan 48075
(313) 569-0020

Landsmanshaftn Society
Jewish Community Council
163 Madison Avenue
Detroit, Michigan 48226
(313) 962-1880

Cemetery
Betty Provizer Starkman
1260 Stuyvesant Road
Birmingham, Michigan 48010

Mrs. Starkman has compiled a Table of Detroit Area Jewish Cemeteries. She is a source for information about landsmanshaftn, cemetery, and mortuary records in the Detroit area.

■ MINNESOTA

■ MINNEAPOLIS

The Center for Jewish Studies
University of Minnesota
178 Klaeber Court
320 16th Avenue S.E.
Minneapolis, Minnesota 55455

A research project (founded in 1980) is examining Jewish settlement in Minnesota from 1880 to 1924. The project is co-sponsored by the University of Minnesota and the National Conference of Christians and Jews. The CJS is engaged in:

- Cataloging artifacts: documents, papers, diaries, pictures, ceremonial/household materials and objects, and artwork (cataloging involves locating, photographing, and recording relevant information about artifacts)

- Writing a history of Jewish life in Minnesota for the five decades being studied. The publication will deal with several aspects of history including family (genealogy is included here), religion, work, culture, and politics
- Computerizing the material and making it available to scholars and researchers
- Over eighty-five oral interviews with individuals throughout the state and the Twin Cities area
- Photographing and/or reproducing its artifacts and documents
- Field trips to Hibbing, Chisholm, and Virginia, Minnesota
- Research has also been conducted in:
  Archives of the Minnesota Historical Society
  Iron Range Interpretative Center
  YIVO in New York
  The American Jewish Historical Society at Brandeis University
  The archives and collections of local synagogues and cemetery associations
- Over 500 names of rural Jewish settlers have been compiled

■ ST. PAUL

Immigration History Research Center
University of Minnesota
826 Berry Street
St. Paul, Minnesota 55114
(612) 373-5581

The center was founded to document the new migration from Eastern, Central, and Southern Europe beginning in the 1880s, and therefore, its Jewish collection is mainly East European.

Several hundred books, pamphlets, serials, and newspapers:

- A mixture of recent scholarly and popular works
- Pamphlets published by such organizations as: B'nai B'rith and the American Jewish Committee
- Self-published autobiographies and family histories
- Older reprints of the Yiddish American press
- Limited holdings of about two dozen serials and newspapers (mainly recent publications such as *American Jewish Archives Studies in American Jewish Literature*)

Minnesota Jewish Historical Society
313 Bush Library
Hamline University
St. Paul, Minnesota 55104
(612) 641-2407

Ongoing project is to document Jewish settlers in rural Minnesota. Also of help is their genealogical index of births and deaths from weekly newspapers dating from the turn of the century.

Bibliography

Chiat, M. J., and Proshan, C. "German Jews in Minnesota: 1845–1910." In *A Heritage Fulfilled: German-Americans*, pp. 168–181. Concordia College, 1984.

Danenbaum, R. "A History of the Jews of Minneapolis." *Reform Advocate*, pp. 7–40. Chicago, Nov. 16, 1907.

Frankel, H. D. "The Jews of Saint Paul." *Reform Advocate*, pp. 41–53. Chicago, Nov. 16, 1907.

"A Legacy of Pride: The American Jewish World." Minneapolis: American Jewish World, 1986.

Lipman, E. J., and Vorspan, A. *A Tale of Ten Cities*. New York: Union of American Hebrew Congregations, 1962.

Plaut, G. W. *Mount Zion, 1856–1956: The First Hundred Years*. Mt. Zion Hebrew Congregation, 1956.

MISSOURI

■ JEFFERSON CITY

Missouri Division of Health/Vital Records
P.O. Box 570
Jefferson City, Missouri 65102
(314) 751-4119

Official copies of state birth and death certificates since 1910 (indexed).

■ KANSAS CITY
(also see Kansas)

Bureau of Vital Statistics
21st Floor, City Hall
414 East 12th Street
Kansas City, Missouri 64106
(816) 274-2000

Write for fee schedule.

- Records of births and deaths that took place in Kansas City

Department of Records
Jackson County Court House
415 East 12th Street
Kansas City, Missouri 64106
(816) 274-2000

Write for fee schedule.

- Marriage records 1881 to date

When making a request, state name of groom, maiden name of bride, as well as month and year of marriage.

Kansas City Public Library
311 East 12th Street
Kansas City, Missouri 64106
(816) 221-2678

Missouri Valley Special Collection

No fee is charged for the use of the facilities, nor is a library card required.

The collections are reference collections and do not circulate.

There is a cost for microfilm and xerox copies, as well for postage and handling.

For individuals wishing more extensive research, the Library makes available a list of local professional researchers.

The Genealogy Collection

Primarily composed of materials on Missouri and those parts of the U.S. from which the majority of 19th-century immigrants came to Missouri: Kentucky, Tennessee, Virginia, the Carolinas, the Middle Atlantic states, New England, Ohio, and Pennsylvania.

- Pre-20th century transcripts of records of marriage, births, deaths, wills, court records, tax lists, land records, and tombstone inscriptions
- Family histories, county histories, ship passenger lists, military records, hundreds of rolls of microfilmed census records, and an extensive collection of indexes to these census records

The Local History Collection

Primarily composed of information related to Missouri, particularly the Kansas City area. The Kansas City segment includes:

- Books and periodicals
- Maps
- City directories (1859 to date)
- Vertical files
- Photograph files
- Newspaper clipping file (1900 to the present)
- Local newspapers:
    Kansas City Jewish Chronical—
      January 1920 to date
    Kansas City Star—
      September 1880 to date
    Kansas City Times—
      August 1871 to date
    Kansas City Journal—
      October 1857–September 1928
    Kansas City Post—
      March 1906–October 1928
    Kansas City Journal Post—
      October 1928–March 1942

Synagogues

(The following synagogues maintain their own archives and burial records.)

Beth Israel Abraham & Valiner Congregation
8310 Holmes
Kansas City, Missouri 64131
(816) 444-5747

B'nai Jehudah (The Temple)
712 East 69th
Kansas City, Missouri 64131
(816) 363-1050

- Kansas City's oldest congregation, organized in 1870
- Published *Roots in a Moving Stream*, by Frank Adler, a centennial history of the congregation (lists the names of most member families to and beyond the turn of the century)

Beth Shalom Congregation
9400 Wornall Road
Kansas City, Missouri 64114
(816) 361-2990

Formed in 1878.

The New Reform Temple
7100 Main at Gregory
Kansas City, Missouri 64114
(816) 523-7809

Bibliography

Adler, F. *Roots in a Moving Stream.* Kansas City, MO: Congregation B'nai Jehudah, 1972.
Schultz, J. P., ed. *Mid-America's Promise: A Profile of Kansas City Jewry.* Kansas City: Jewish Community Foundation of Greater Kansas City/The American Jewish Historical Society, 1982.

■ ST. LOUIS

Except as noted, all records and indexes are open to walk-in researchers, and copies may be requested by mail for a fee.

Board of Election Commissioners
208 South Tucker Boulevard, 1st Floor
St. Louis, Missouri 63102
(314) 622-4201

- Current city voter rolls
- Ward and precinct maps since 1908

City Hall
Tucker Boulevard and Market Street
St. Louis, Missouri 63103
The following are located within City Hall:

Assessor's Office
Room 114
(314) 622-3212

- Deed abstract books for tracing back property owners to the 1860s

The Microfilm Section of the Assessor's Office:

- Copies of deeds and indexes through 1900 (which may be transferred to the recorder of deeds)
- Deed abstract books
- Real estate tax lists since 1818 (which include poll tax records to the 1850s)
- Building permit cards since the 1860s

Marriage License Bureau
4th Floor
(314) 889-2180

- Records of all county marriage applications since 1876
- Complete male and female card index (cross-referenced by both parties' names)

Microfilm Section
Room 1
(314) 622-4275

- Microfilm copies of many city records cited below
- All original registers and certificates
- Statewide birth indexes since 1910
- Poll books 1896–1936 (recorded by ward and precinct)
- Canceled voter affidavit cards since 1937 (alphabetically indexed)

Access to some materials may be restricted.

Recorder of Deeds
Rooms 126-128
(314) 622-4610

- Property transfer records since 1804 (and earlier French and Spanish deeds), indexed by the grantor (who transfers) and grantee (who receives)
- Deed indexes 1804–1854
- Hard-copy record books and indexes through 1980 (thereafter computerized) in an open basement vault

Rooms 127 and 128:

- Indexed survey and plat books since the 1830s (for locating properties)
- Microfilm copies of marriage registers, licenses, and indexes

St. Louis County Government Center
The Administration Building
41 South Central Avenue
St. Louis, Missouri 63105

Board of Election Commissioners
(street level)
(314) 889-2242 and 889-2243

Photocopying not allowed, but researchers can abstract information, which includes:

- Naturalizations until 1982
- Current and inactive county registrations since 1938 are retained, indexed
- Registrations inactive for more than three years have been microfilmed.

Division of Mapping Services
3rd floor
(314) 889-2237

- Provides photocopies of current plat books

Real Estate Department
3rd floor
(314) 889-2225

- The assessor's current plat books, property descriptions, and valuations

Recorder of Deeds
Administration Building, 4th floor
(314) 889-2182

County records (all are open to the public):

- Deed books from 1877, microfilmed since 1967
- Grantor and grantee indexes
- Original plat books
- Recorded surveys

Courts Building
7900 Carondelet Avenue
St. Louis, Missouri 63105

Circuit Clerk's Office
Room 550
(314) 889-3028

- Divorces, name changes, and civil cases (the last twenty-five years)

- Criminal cases (last fifty years)
- Existing records and their indexes are open (unless sealed by a judge or statute)
- Court reporters' notes (dating back before the retained records) not stored on site, but may be requested

Probate Court
Room 549
(314) 889-2629

The records and indexes are open to the public.

- County wills and probate records since 1877 of decedent and guardianship estates
- All active county estate records (in hard copy)
- All closed estate records, active indexes, and closed indexes are on microfiche (except for occasional vault items now being microfilmed)

Division of Health/Vital Records
634 N. Grand Boulevard, Room 306
St. Louis, Missouri 63103
(314) 658-1134

Staff will check birth indexes by mail:

P.O. Box 14702
St. Louis, Missouri 63178

Periods of access to the death indexes are very limited (only a typescript is provided before 1910).

- City birth register books since 1863
- Birth certificates (mandatory statewide since 1910)
- Death registers since 1850
- Death certificates since 1876 (mandatory statewide since 1910)
- Death indexes since mid-nineteenth century are open to public (birth indexes since 1910 are closed)

Health Department/Vital Statistics
801 S. Brentwood Boulevard, Room 310
St. Louis, Missouri 63105
(314) 854-6684 through 6687

Staff will search closed indexes upon walk-in or written request.

- County births and death records since 1883 (including nonmandatory registers and some certificates to 1910, required certificates since 1910; these parallel city records)

Marriage License Bureau
City Hall Room 129
(314) 622-3257

- City marriage registers since 1808
- Licenses and short applications since 1881
- Open marriage indexes since 1806
- Detailed applications since 1947 (request originals from staff)

St. Louis Genealogical Society Library
Housed at University City Public Library
6701 Delmar Boulevard, 2d Floor
St. Louis, Missouri 63130

- Microfilmed marriage indexes through 1925
- Master indexes to marriages 1804–1859 and 1860–1876 (published by the society in 1973)
- St. Louis and St. Louis County, Missouri, Probate Records, Volume 1 (through 1849) (published by the society in 1985):
    Abstracted wills and probate filings 1804–1876 (with additional entries 1766–1804) including a name index
- Closed estate index
- Indexes of city residents in the 1850 (1969) and 1860 (1984) federal censuses (published by the society)

The Circuit Clerk's Office
Civil Courts Building, 3d Floor
(314) 622-4405

Staff will check Soundex card indexes for case numbers.

- City legal records: divorces, name changes, lawsuits

Archives
2nd floor
(314) 622-3551 and 3569

- Original Circuit Court records
- Materials of Land Court, Court of Common Pleas, and Chancery Court
- Old chronological alphabetical book indexes

Separately indexed court records held by the archives include:

- Naturalizations through September 26, 1906
- Religious and fraternal group incorporation papers

Probate Court
File Room (10th Floor)
(314) 622-4300 and 4238

- Wills and probate since 1804
- Open card indexes to decedent and guardianship estates (Records 1878–1931 must be requested in advance.)
- Wills since 1896, identified by estate number, may be filed separately (those to 1896 should be ordered in advance)

Family History Center
10445 Clayton Road
St. Louis, Missouri 63131
(314) 993-2328

Mercantile Library
510 Locust Street
P.O. Box 633
St. Louis, Missouri 63188
(314) 621-0670

Opened in 1846—largely a membership resource.

- Extensive private papers
- Archival and early newspaper (650 bound volumes)

- Local histories and genealogies (primarily through the nineteenth century)
- Special collections: focus on railroads and inland waterways
- Materials on early Jewish settlers: Joseph Philipson's daily business journal 1807–1809

Missouri Historical Society
Library and Archive
Jefferson Memorial Building
Forest Park
St. Louis, Missouri 63112
(314) 361-1424

There is a daily on-site research fee for non-members. Referrals to a list of paid researchers provided upon request.

- Archival records and published works on St. Louis and Missouri history
- Missouri county records and histories
- St. Louis official records, private papers, and manuscripts through the nineteenth century
- *Gateway Heritage* (formerly *Glimpses of the Past* and *Missouri Historical Society Bulletin*) is its illustrated quarterly.
- City censuses 1847–1866
- Nonpopulation federal census schedules for Missouri 1850–1880
- Old newspapers (microfilm and hard copy) in English and German
- 125,000 to 200,000 accessible print and photo collection items
- St. Louis maps, atlases, fire insurance maps, and privately published plat books

For Jewish research:

- Many of the community history monographs cited above
- Several congregation jubilee books
- Papers of the Pioneers (Reform Jewish women's group of the last quarter of the nineteenth century)
- Twentieth century Yiddish newspapers

Olin Library
Washington University
Lindell and Skinker Boulevards Campus
St. Louis, Missouri 63130
(314) 889-5410 (reference desk)

- Basic local and European histories
- Approximately 85 Yizkor (memorial) books
- Sizable Yiddish and Hebrew holdings

St. Louis Center for Holocaust Studies
12 Millstone Campus Drive
St. Louis, Missouri 63146
(314) 432-0020

A constituent agency of the Jewish Federation, located in the Federation Kopolow Building.

- Taped oral history collection; may provide leads to local Holocaust survivors and resources

St. Louis County Library Headquarters
1640 South Lindbergh Boulevard
St. Louis, Missouri 63131
(314) 994-3300

- Federal census complete for St. Louis
- Lengthy runs of some major newspapers since the mid-nineteenth century
- *The Jewish Light*

St. Louis Genealogical Society
1695 South Brentwood Boulevard
Suite 210
St. Louis, Missouri 63144
(314) 968-2763

A 2,200 member group which focuses on genealogical research in St. Louis and Missouri, other states irregularly, and Europe, particularly Germany.

The society provides a limited research service for a fee and referrals to paid researchers. It publishes a monthly newsletter, *News 'N Notes, a Quarterly*, primarily of transcribed and indexed Missouri records (public, newspaper, church, and cemetery), and the other indexes noted above.

The society library is housed in the University City Public Library.

St. Louis Jewish Archives
Federation Kopolow Building
12 Millstone Campus Drive
St. Louis, Missouri 63146
(314) 432-0020

Located in the Saul Brodsky Jewish Community Library. Archives are open to researchers upon request during library hours but do not provide a research service for genealogical inquiries by mail.

Continues to gather and preserve local Jewish community records:

- Microfilmed newspapers: *Der Vorsteher* and *The Jewish Record*
- Congregation jubilee books
- Minutebooks of the Beth Hamedrosh Hagodol and Roumanische synagogues
- Partial typescripts of cemetery minutes and death registers
- Records of the Hebrew Benevolent Society (incorporated in 1847)
- Records of the YMHA, the JCCA, and other benevolent and social organizations

St. Louis Public Library
1301 Olive Street
St. Louis, Missouri 63103
(314) 241-2288

History and Genealogy Department holdings include:

- City directories
- Early St. Louis maps
- United States, out of state, Missouri, and Jewish Genealogical publications
- Defense Mapping Agency maps of Eastern Europe and 1:100,000 maps of Poland and Germany.

Holdings in closed stacks include:

- Congregation and Jewish community histories
- *The Modern View*, Reform Jewish newspaper 1908–1943

- Extensive genealogical compilations for Missouri and states east of the Mississippi River
- Standard local and genealogical texts
- Jewish community monographs

Microfilm holdings include:

- Various states' United States censuses and some indexes through late nineteenth century
- United States censuses of Missouri and all available indexes through 1910
- Ship passenger lists and indexes generally to 1890s, except New York index, which ends with 1846
- Military records of Missouri volunteers through Civil War (Union and Confederate), some later records of officers and enlisted men
- Early St. Louis newspapers, including *St. Louis Jewish Light, St. Louis Daily Record* (the paper of legal record since 1890) *St. Louis Countian*, paper of legal record since 1902

U.S. District Court
Clerk's Office, Room 302
Tucker Boulevard and Market Street
St. Louis, Missouri 63101
(314) 539-2315

Walk-in and mail requests are answered. No photo copies are permitted, but the researcher may transcribe information. The staff will search the card index and brings records from the vault.

- Federal declarations, petitions, and certificates since September 27, 1906

University City Public Library
6701 Delmar Boulevard
St. Louis, Missouri 63130
(314) 968-2763

Houses the holdings of the St. Louis Genealogical Society:

- Regularly updated *Book List*, including microfilm
- St. Louis histories and family histories
- Microfilmed marriage license indexes
- St. Louis County closed probate estate indexes (microfiche)
- St. Louis and other cities' directories
- Genealogical guides and compilations
- Other states' genealogical indexes and periodicals

The Jewish genealogy section includes:

- Local guides
- Other cities' Jewish Genealogical Society quarterlies

Cemeteries/Monuments
Beth Hamedrosh Hagodol
9125 Ladue Road
St. Louis, Missouri 63124
(314) 991-0264

Primarily Lithuanian origins. All records are at the cemetery, indexed since 1937.

- 1902–1937 records (originals destroyed by fire) reconstructed, and recorded in plot books which are kept current
- Brief accounts in the golden and diamond jubilee books

B'nai Amoona
930 North and South Road
St. Louis, Missouri 63130
(314) 725-2033

Chesed Shel Emeth
7570 Olive Street Road
St. Louis, Missouri 63130
(314) 721-4658
and
650 White Road
Chesterfield, Missouri 63017
(314) 469-1891

Chevra Kadisha
Adas B'nai Israel Vyeshurun
1601 North and South Road, at Page Boulevard
St. Louis, Missouri 63130
(314) 427-0160
- Indexed records and plot maps since 1922

Mount Sinai Cemetery Association
- The original German minutes since 1868 (and an English typescript, also at the St. Louis Jewish Archives), listing burials and including the identified removals in 1872
- A reconstructed single graves book which gives name and location, beginning with the earliest burials
- A death register, indexed by initial, with entries starting in 1853

All but the minutes were microfilmed in 1972, and the American Jewish Archives holds a copy.

New Mount Sinai
8430 Gravois Road
St. Louis, Missouri 63123
(314) 353-2540

Ohave Sholom
7400 Olive Street Road
St. Louis, Missouri 63130
The most recent Jewish cemetery established in the city, primarily serving German immigrants, Holocaust survivors, and their families. Burials began in 1942, with fewer than 200 burials to date in the enclosed cemetery (the Rosenbloom map identifies many of those interred). Records are available through association president.

Rosenbloom Monument Company
7501 Olive Street Road
St. Louis, Missouri 63130
(314) 721-5070
A major source of monuments for the Jewish community in this century.

- Purchase orders 1918–28
- Work cards since 1922 indexed on microfiche

Records provide cemetery location, monument purchasers (with addresses), and inscription, which often includes the Hebrew name, father's name, and birth and death dates.

Work cards are regularly cross-referenced to other family members' stones.

- Card file index 1922 to the late 1970s (newspaper death notices often attached)
- Single sheet maps for all Jewish cemeteries but *Chevra Kadisha*

United Hebrew
7855 Canton Avenue
at North and South Road
St. Louis, Missouri 63130
(314) 727-9524
The congregation and trustees' minutes record all early burials; the indexed cemetery death register, at the synagogue, records, burials, beginning in 1849 to the present.

It includes the names of those removed in 1880, when the cemetery was cleared, who were transferred to the current UH cemetery (called Mount Olive until 1960). (The cemetery has a partial copy and card abstracts of the death register, which has not yet been microfilmed.)

The St. Louis Genealogical Society published an extensive and useful transcription of United Hebrew Congregation tombstone inscriptions in the older section of the current cemetery in *Old Cemeteries*, Vol. 1, 1982.

Newspapers
The Missouri Jewish Post and Opinion
(or various similar titles over the years)
9531 Lackland Avenue, Suite 207
St. Louis, Missouri 63114
(314) 423-3088
Jewish weekly (since 1948), strong on local, social, and individual news, including births, engagements, marriages, and death notices, as well as organization promotions and some historical articles. A local supplement to a national section edited in Indianapolis, it is invaluable for that period but has not been microfilmed by the AJPC. The only complete run available in St. Louis is the series of bound volumes at its office.

St. Louis Daily Record
612 North 2d Street
St. Louis, Missouri 63102
(314) 421-1880
The paper of legal record since 1890.

St. Louis Jewish Light
Federation Kopolow Building
12 Millstone Campus Drive
St. Louis, Missouri 63146
(314) 432-3353
Supported as an autonomous constituent agency of the Jewish Federation, it began as a house organ 1947–1962. It then broadened its coverage, shifted from largely monthly to bi-weekly publication (weekly 1982). It regularly includes community events, per-

sonal milestones, and in recent years a steady flow of historical articles.

The 1947–1978 microfilm is held by the Missouri Historical Society and St. Louis County Library Headquarters, while the Saul Brodsky Jewish Community Library has bound volumes to date.

The Watchman Advocate
200 South Bemiston Avenue
St. Louis, Missouri 63105
(314) 725-1515

Paper of legal record since 1881 held on microfilm by the St. Louis Public Library since 1953.

All existing Jewish newspapers (except the *Missouri Jewish Post and Opinion*) are held on microfilm by the American Jewish Periodical Center.

A series of English language weeklies for the most part edited by Rabbi Moritz Spitz of B'nai El, from 1879 to the 1920s with some gaps:

The Jewish Tribune 1879–1884
The Jewish Free Press 1885–1887
The Jewish Voice 1888–1920 have been microfilmed (regularly published historical articles, archival records, and death notices with data on longtime residents).

The Modern View, an illustrated weekly, which chronicled the Reform community and its members (including the charitable and educational establishments) from 1901 to 1943. The AJPC has filmed 1913–1940, but other libraries (such as the St. Louis Public Library, which has 1908–1943) hold additional volumes.

Der Vorsteher (The Representative), about 1906–1910 (the daily issues for all of 1907–1908 survive). Covered the East European immigrant community in great detail. The Library of Congress Hebraic Section, Missouri Historical Society, and St. Louis Jewish Archives all have copies of the microfilm.

The Jewish Record or *Der Yiddisher Record*, 1913–1951. The main long-term chronicler of the non-Reform community. The surviving run begins in 1916, as a Yiddish weekly, becomes daily for part of 1927–1928, and then again weekly. An English page introduced by the 1920s was gradually increased to an English section, and by 1946 the paper was entirely in English. The microfilm is also held by the Missouri Historical Society and St. Louis Jewish Archives.

Synagogues (surviving 19th century)
Beth Hamedrosh Hagodol
1227 North and South Road
St. Louis, Missouri 63130
(314) 721-1037

Founded in 1879.

- Golden and diamond jubilee books 1933 and 1954
- Historical sketch by Averam B. Bender in *Missouri Historical Society Bulletin*, October 1970
- Yiddish minutes 1900–1926 are held by the St. Louis Jewish Archives

B'nai Amoona
324 South Mason Road
St. Louis, Missouri 63141
(314) 576-9990

- *B'nai Amoona for All Generations*, by Rosalind Bronsen, a history published in 1982
- A golden jubilee book appeared in 1932

Few early minutes of documents other than cemetery records have survived:

- A synagogue archive is currently being assembled by Elaine Ginsberg
- Fairly detailed death register at the synagogue begins in 1895
- The cemetery holds a short entry register 1888–1895 (records 1872–1887 are lacking) and recent large plot maps which locate all identifiable graves from existing monuments and records

Some records are at the cemetery, particularly for locating burials by date and name and for finding graves, but the synagogue has complete records indexed by name, date, and plot.

B'nai El
11411 North Outer 40
St. Louis, Missouri 63131
(314) 432-6393

The Reform-minded Emanu El or German congregation, founded 1847, and the Bohemian B'nai B'rith Congregation, begun 1849, merged in 1852, by 1855 erected the first synagogue west of the Mississippi.

(B'nai El's minutes through 1886 held by the American Jewish Archives.)

Chesed Shel Emeth
700 North and South Road
St. Louis, Missouri 63130
(314) 727-7585

Founded by 1919.

- Golden jubilee book 1938

Shaare Emeth
11645 Ladue Road
St. Louis, Missouri 63141
(314) 569-0010

Reform groups withdrew from B'nai El in 1868–1869 to form this congregation. Holds a comprehensive archive with family data and temple records.

Temple Israel
10675 Ladue Road
St. Louis, Missouri 63141
(314) 432-8050

Published a golden jubilee history in 1937 and Samuel Rosenkranz's *A Centennial History . . .* in 1986 (does not focus on the early years).

United Hebrew Congregation
(Polish order of worship)
13788 Conway Road
St. Louis, Missouri 63141
(314) 469-0700

The congregation and trustees' minutes (1841–59) are held on microfilm by the American Jewish Archives, and include burials, some marriages, and considerable information on early Jewish settlers.

Bibliography

Abrams, Z. *The Book of Memories.* 1932.

Bush, I. "The Jews in St. Louis." 1883. Reprinted in *Missouri Historical Society Bulletin*, October 1951.

Compton, R. J., and Dry, C. N. *Pictorial St. Louis.* 1875.

Jewish Light. A weekly.

Makovsky, D. I. *The Philipsons: The First Jewish Settlers in St. Louis (1807–1858).*

_____ . "The Origin and Early History of the United Hebrew Congregation" [master's thesis]. St. Louis: Washington University, 1958.

Primm, J. N. *Lion of the Valley.* 1981.

Rosenwaike, I. "The Mussina Family: Early American Jews?" *American Jewish History*, April 1986.

Tibbits, R. K., comp. *Checklist of Printed Maps of the Middle West to 1900, Vol. 9: Missouri.* Boston: G. K. Hall & Co., 1981.

NEBRASKA

■ OMAHA

The Genealogy Room
F. Dale Clark Library
215 South 15th Street
Omaha, Nebraska 68102
(402) 444-4840

The availability of staff to respond to written inquiries is very limited. There is a fee for photocopies. (Write for fee schedule.) Materials cannot be borrowed through interlibrary loans.

- Omaha city directories since 1866.
- Census records: 1854–1856, 1860, 1870, 1880, 1890 (partial), 1900, and 1910

Congregation Beth Israel
1502 North 59th Street
Omaha, Nebraska 68132

The congregation runs the Jewish Funeral Home.
Very extensive cemetery records for all its members since the early days of the Jewish community of Omaha. All congregational records are accessible to the individual researcher at no charge.

Douglas County Historical Society
Fort Omaha, P.O. Box 11398
Omaha, Nebraska 68111
(402) 451-1013

Will respond to inquiries by mail on a limited basis, but will not lend material through interlibrary loan.

- City directories: 1866–1982 (partial)
- *The Jewish Press:* 1947–1950
- Records of Jewish families
- *The Omaha World Herald* clipping file 1907–1983

Douglas County Offices
Civic Center
1819 Farnam Street
Omaha, Nebraska 68183

Department of Vital Statistics
(402) 444-7204

Birth and death records.

Department of Marriage Licenses
(402) 444-6745

Marriage records.

Carol Gendler
910 South 111th Plaza
Omaha, Nebraska 68154

A professional genealogist, Ms. Gendler will answer inquiries and has an hourly fee (write for fee schedule). She holds extensive files on the Omaha Jewish Community, including Nebraska and Council Bluffs (Iowa) papers of the Industrial Removal Organization.

The Jewish Federation Library
333 South 132nd Street
Omaha, Nebraska 68154
(402) 334-8200, Ext. 30

Maintained and operated by the Jewish Federation of Omaha, the library has a genealogy collection (primarily general information rather than specific to Nebraska).
The Omaha Jewish Press with index (microfilm).

The Jewish Press
333 South 132nd Street
Omaha, Nebraska 68154

Established in 1921.

The Nebraska Jewish Historical Society
333 South 132nd Street
Omaha, Nebraska 68154

Will answer questions related to material in their repository at no charge; however, there is a charge for copies and handling. Appointments for research are suggested.
Noncirculating material related to Nebraska Jewish families:

- Correspondence
- Documents
- Photos
- Genealogical trees of Nebraska families

Publishes an annual *Memories of the Jewish Midwest* and a newsletter biannually.

Omaha History Museum
801 South Tenth Street
Omaha, Nebraska 68108-3299
(402) 444-5071/5072

Library is not generally available to outside researchers, will not do research or handle interlibrary loan.
The volunteers in Photo Archives will occasionally search for photographs for distant inquiries for a fee. There are also charges for reproductions of photographs (send for fee schedule). Some photographic

archives contain material relevant to Jewish genealogy.

Photographic collections:

- Louis R. Bostwick (Omaha residents and scenery, late 19th early 20th century)
- John Savage photographic archives. Photos for the *Omaha World Herald* (the 1920s–1970s)

Bibliography

Auerbach (Fleishman), E. *Jewish Settlement in Nebraska.* 1927.

Bittner, D. "Hebraic Mortar: The Strength of a Community." *Memories of the Jewish Midwest,* Vol. 2, No. 1, Summer 1986.

Gendler, C. *The Jews of Omaha: The First Sixty Years.* 1968.

The Golden Book, B'nai Israel Synagogue 1904–1954. Council Bluffs, IA.

Somberg, S. R., and Roffman, S. G. *Consider the Years 1871–1971.* Omaha: Congregation of Temple Israel.

NEW YORK (OUTSIDE NEW YORK CITY)

■ ALBANY

Albany County Hall of Records
250 South Pearl Street
Albany, New York 12202
(518) 447-4500

- Marriage records 1870–1936
- Naturalizations 1827–1973
- Declarations of Intention 1827–1973
- Deeds 1652–present
- Index to the Public Records 1630–1894 (includes lists by grantee and grantor)
- Mortgage books 1630–1905
- Military discharges 1917–1919, 1943–1976
- Wills 1691–1835
- Index to Wills and Letters of Administration 1787–1895
- Slave Manumission Register 1800–1829
- New York State Census Rolls 1915 and 1925
- City of Albany Assessment Rolls 1813–1976
- City of Albany Directories 1830–1983
- Supreme Court Records 1793–1919
- Church Records 1790–1900
- Register of Voters 1899–1966
- Atlas of Albany by G. M. Hopkins 1876
- Sanborn Insurance Maps 1892, 1909, 1934, 1974

There is a charge for copies and the search. Write for fee schedule.

Albany Public Library
161 Washington Avenue
Albany, New York 12210
(518) 449-3380

The Bureau of Vital Statistics
State Dept. of Health
Albany, New York 12208

Bureau of Vital Records
State Department of Health
ESP Tower Building
Albany, New York 12237
(518) 474-2005
Note: Call for appointments, which are scheduled at two-hour intervals.

Bureau of Vital Statistics
City of Albany
Room 107, City Hall
24 Eagle Street
Albany, New York 12207
(518) 434-5045
Birth and death records, 1870 to present.

Capital District Genealogy Society
Box 175
Empire State Plaza Station
Albany, New York 12220

City of Albany
City Clerk
Room 202, City Hall
Albany, New York 12207
(518) 434-5090
Note: Duplicate vital records from 1914 on are at State Offices.

County Clerk's Office
Albany County Courthouse
16 Eagle Street, Room 128
Albany, New York 12207
(518) 445-7642
1818–present (index only)
Note: Original deeds/mortgages are also in County Clerk's Office. Surrogate's Office (County Clerk) has estate/probate records.

Holocaust Survivors and Friends in Pursuit of Justice
P.O. Box 8867
Albany, New York 12208
(518) 459-8000 or 438-7858

Immigration and Naturalization Service
U.S. Post Office and Court House
445 Broadway, Room 227
Albany, New York 12207
(518) 472-2434

New York State Archives
Cultural Education Center
Empire State Plaza, Room 11D40
Albany, New York 12230
(518) 473-1203

New York State Holocaust Center/ Exhibit at the Museum
New York State Cultural Education Center
Albany, New York 12230
(518) 474-5801

Synagogues/Cemeteries

B'nai Sholom (Reform)
420 Whitehall Road
Albany, New York 12208
(518) 482-5283

Chabad Lubavitch
(Orthodox)
122 Main Street
Albany, New York 12208
(518) 482-5781

Congregation Beth Abraham-Jacob
(Orthodox)
66 Hackett Boulevard
Albany, New York 12209
(518) 449-7813
Has information on United Brethren and Beth Abraham Jacob cemeteries.

Congregation Ohav Sholom (Conservative)
New Krumkill Road
Albany, New York 12208
(518) 489-4706
For cemetery information:

E. Joe Brown
15 Prospect Terrace
Albany, New York 12208
(518) 489-1335

Shomrai Torah (Orthodox)
463 New Scotland Avenue
Albany, New York 12208

Temple Beth Emeth (Reform)
100 Academy Road
Albany, New York 12208
(518) 436-9761

• Extensive library and archives. Records date back 100 years

For cemetery information:

Norman Paul
222 Heritage Road
Guilderland, New York 12084
(518) 456-7076

Temple Israel (Conservative)
600 New Scotland Avenue
Albany, New York 12208
(518) 438-7858
For cemetery information:

Charles Morse
59-D Knights Bridge
Guilderland, New York 12084

Nassau Farmers
Western Avenue
Guilderland, New York
For cemetery information:

Martha Proskin
41 State Street
Albany, New York 12207
(518) 436-0775 or 436-7734

Hebrew Tailors
Western Avenue
Albany, New York
For cemetery information:

Jerry Lipfeld
115 Daytona Avenue
Albany, New York 12203
(518) 482-7276

People's Cemetery
Fuller Road
Albany, New York
For cemetery information:

Raymond Markman
179 Tampa Avenue
Albany, New York 12208
(518) 489-1961

Funeral Home
Levine Memorial Chapels, Inc.
649 Washington Avenue
Albany, New York 12206
(518) 438-1002

Newspaper
The Jewish World
1140 Central Avenue
Albany, New York 12205
(518) 459-8455

Libraries
University of New York at Albany (SUNY)
University Library
1400 Washington Avenue
Albany, New York 12227
(518) 442-3600
Yizkor (memorial) books at SUNY.

Family History Center
Loudonville Branch
(See: Loudonville, New York)

Bibliography
Gateway to America: Genealogical Research in the New York State Library. Albany, NY: New York State Archives.

Gerber, M. O. *Pictorial History of Albany's Jewish Community.* 1986.

Howell, G. R., and Tenney, J., eds. *History of the County of Albany from 1609 to 1886.* New York: W.W. Munsell & Co., 1886.

Kennedy, W. *O'Albany.* New York: Viking Press, 1983.

McEneny, J. J. *Albany: Capital City on the Hudson.* Albany Institute of History and Art, 1981.

Munsell, J. *Annals of Albany* (ten volumes). Albany, NY: Munsell & Rowland, 1850–1859, 1869–1871.

_____ . *Collections on the History of Albany* (four volumes). Albany, NY: J. Munsell, 1865–1871.

Rubinger, N. J. "Albany Jewry of the nineteenth century—historic roots and communal evolution" [unpublished Ph.D. thesis]. New York: Yeshiva University, 1971.

■ BUFFALO

Buffalo and Erie County Historical Society Library
25 Nottingham Court
Buffalo, New York 14216
(716) 873-9644
- Marriage notices up to 1880 culled from Buffalo newspapers, arranged alphabetically by names of both man and woman (microfilm)
- Name index to all forty volumes of Buffalo Historical Society Publications in one alphabet
- Death file covering Erie County prior to 1880; selected notices after 1880
- An extensive microfilm collection of most of the early newspapers of Buffalo:
  The Buffalo Times
  December 13, 1833–January, 1933
  The Buffalo Daily Courier
  November 1, 1842–June 13, 1926
  Buffalo Morning Express
  January 15, 1846–June 13, 1922
  The Courier Express
  June 13, 1926–September 19, 1982

A full collection of the *Jewish Review*—November 1918–December 1968 on microfilm; December 1968 to present in the original.

Buffalo and Erie County Public Library
Lafayette Square
Buffalo, New York
(716) 846-7102
The genealogy and local history collection consists of approximately 30,500 volumes in the related subject fields of local history (25,000 volumes) and genealogy (5,500 volumes).
Holdings include:

- New York State Census for Buffalo and Erie County: 1855, 1865, 1875, 1892, 1905, 1915, and 1925.
  (microfilm 225)
- Early newspapers; to the present, but with some gaps in the collection (microfilm)
  Buffalo Evening News—April 1881–present
  Buffalo Times—August 3, 1857–July 30, 1939, some boxed, some microfilm, with gaps
  Jewish Review—January 6, 1961–present
- Holdings of the Federal Decennial Census:
  1790 (complete)
  1800
    Seven New York State counties in existence in 1800
  1810 (complete)
  1820 (complete)
  1830
    Only New York State counties for 1830 and a few scattered counties for Ohio and Vermont
  1840
    Only the New York State counties for 1840 and a few scattered counties for Ohio and Michigan.
  1850 (plus index)
  1860
    Only New York State Counties
  1880
    Only New York State counties, plus Soundex

City Clerk
Room 1308, City Hall
Buffalo, New York 14202
Marriages in Buffalo from January 1880 to December 1907

Erie County Hall
Franklin Street
Buffalo, New York 14202
Erie County Clerk

- Marriages in Buffalo and Erie County from the 1850s through April 1915 (mostly justice-of-the-peace marriages)
- Buffalo and Erie County divorce records before 1960
- Land records (deeds, etc.)
- Births and deaths in Buffalo since 1914 or after
- Marriages in Buffalo and Erie County since May 1915
- Buffalo and Erie County Divorce records since January 1, 1963
- Births and deaths in Erie County since 1880

Division of Naturalization Records

- Naturalization records

Will and Probate Division

Family History Center
(See Williamsville, p. 78)

Registrar of Vital Statistics
Room 913, City Hall
Buffalo, New York 14202
(716) 855-4111
For births and deaths in Buffalo before 1914.

Selig Adler Archives
State University College at Buffalo
1300 Elmwood Avenue
Buffalo, New York 14222
(716) 878-6302

Western New York
Genealogical Society
(See Hamburg, p. 78)

Cemeteries
Forest Lawn Cemetery
(Administration Office)
1411 Delaware Avenue
Buffalo, New York 14209
Burial records with some genealogical information. Fees are charged for information. Inquiries may be directed to:

Jewish Center of Greater Buffalo
787 Delaware Avenue
Buffalo, New York 14209

Beth El Cemetery
(See Tonawanda, p. 78)

Holocaust Research Center
(See Getzville)

Jewish Federation of Greater Buffalo Cemetery Corporation
787 Delaware Avenue
Buffalo, New York 14209
Formed by the North Park Society and the B'nai Israel Cemetery. North Park Society records are cross-referenced with alphabetical listing of burials, including a map with the details.

Newspaper

Buffalo Jewish Review
15 E. Mohawk Street
Buffalo, New York 14203
(716) 854-2192
Founded 1918; replies to requests for information.

■ GETZVILLE
(Buffalo Metropolitan Area)

Holocaust Research Center
Jewish Center of Greater Buffalo-Amherst Building
2640 North Forest Road
Getzville, New York 14068
(716) 688-7020

■ HAMBURG
(Buffalo Metropolitan Area)

The Western New York Genealogical Society
P.O. Box 338
Hamburg, New York 14075

■ LOUDONVILLE
(Albany Metropolitan Area)

Family History Center
Loudonville Branch
411 Loudonville Road (Route 9)
Loudonville, New York 12210
(518) 462-3687
Mailing address:

79 Euclid Avenue
Troy, New York 12180

■ SYRACUSE

Bibliography
Concord: 1839–1939. 1939.
Marcus, J. R. *Early American Jewry, Vol. I: The Jews of New York, New England and Canada, 1649–1794.* 1953.
Rudolph, B. G. *From a Minyan to a Community: A History of the Jews of Syracuse.* 1970.
The Temple Society of Concord. History, 1839–1964. 1964.

■ TONAWANDA
(Buffalo Metropolitan Area)

Temple Beth El Archives
2360 Eggert Road
Tonawanda, New York 14150
(716) 836-3702
Buffalo area's oldest synagogue, 1847–1887; extensive collection of materials, including photographs from 1800s.

Beth El Cemetery
Temple Beth El of Greater Buffalo
2360 Eggert Road
Tonawanda, New York 14150

■ WILLIAMSVILLE
(Buffalo Metropolitan Area)

Family History Center
Williamsville Branch
1424 Maple Road
Williamsville, New York 14221

━━━━

NEW YORK CITY/NEW JERSEY

New York City, genealogically speaking, is in a class by itself. Its many institutions, agencies, libraries, archives (both private and governmental), counted in the hundreds, make it a central repository for Jewish family research, with some repositories physically located in New Jersey.

■ INTRODUCTION TO NEW YORK METROPOLITAN AREA
Miriam Weiner

In the United States, the New York metropolitan area is the central repository of numerous sources for Jewish family research. There are literally hundreds of institutions, agencies, libraries, and archives, both private and governmental.

For those researching their family history in the greater New York/New Jersey area, the task is made much easier because the vast number of resources have been researched, compiled, described, and published under the auspices of the Jewish Genealogical Society of New York. This monumental work—*Resources for Genealogy in the New York Metropolitan Area*—was arduously and capably edited by Estelle M. Guzik, with the help of a myriad of dedicated volunteers who personally visited most of the institutions covered in the book.

The book includes a description of the resources available, finding aids, fees, hours of operation, and transportation directions to the locations.

The material is organized geographically so that those conducting on-site research can coordinate their visits to facilities within a particular area. A map is included for each area. See Appendix H (pp. 175–176) for a complete listing of the Table of Contents of *Resources for Genealogy in the New York Metropolitan Area.*

■ BOOK REVIEW: *Genealogical Resources in the New York Metropolitan Area*
Zachary M. Baker

Estelle M. Guzik, ed., *Genealogical Resources in the New York Metropolitan Area.* New York: Jewish Genealogical Society, Inc., 1989. Price: $24.95. Publisher's address: P.O. Box 6398, New York, NY 10128.

Genealogical Resources in the New York Metropolitan Area, compiled and edited by Estelle M. Guzik, is a revised, reprinted, and updated edition of the editor's earlier *Resources for Jewish Genealogy in the New York Metropolitan Area.* This substantial reference work has assumed its rightful place among other classic volumes of its kind.

New York's importance as a center for genealogical research derives from the city's 19th and early 20th century role as the principal port of entry for arriving immigrants and from the concentration there of major research libraries and archival repositories. In addition, for Jewish genealogists, New York's significance assumes extraordinary dimensions because nearly half of all American Jews resided in the metropolitan area at the time that strict immigration quotas were imposed in 1924. (Now the figure is closer to 35 percent.) Most American Jews can claim some family connection to Greater New York City.

By including both general, public as well as private, and Jewish facilities, *Genealogical Resources* has underscored the importance of New York records to both Jewish and non-Jewish genealogists alike. As the editor notes in her introduction, of the 104 agencies covered in the book, "only 18 (17%) are specifically Jewish in character. Some of these Jewish repositories have records of interest to non-Jewish researchers." In overall terms then, *Genealogical Resources* represents an attempt at comprehensive coverage of the genealogical holdings of public repositories, including the New York Public Library (NYPL), private, non-Jewish genealogical and historical societies, and Jewish libraries, archives, and cemeteries in the New York metropolitan area.

Readers who are familiar with the 1985 *Resources* guide will find that the 1989 successor volume continues the earlier publication's approach to publicly held records. In Queens County, for example, articles on the following government agencies are included:

- Board of Elections—voter registrations
- City Clerk's Office—Marriage License Bureau
- City Register's Office—real property records
- Civil Court of the City of New York—name change records; this was *not* included in the 1985 edition
- County Clerk's Office—State Supreme Court, Queens County—naturalizations, New York State Census, matrimonial records, i.e. divorces, separations and annulments, military discharge records, court cases, business records, incompetency and conservatorship records, name changes, town records, adoptions, and surrenders of children

- Surrogate's Court—probate, administration, and guardianship records

Counterparts to these agencies are described in the chapters for New York City's other four boroughs. The three New York State counties outside of New York City that are included here have listings for their respective County Clerk's Offices and Surrogate's Courts only. The three New Jersey counties included here have varied levels of coverage for the government agencies described.

Extension of the New York metropolitan area's boundaries to include Albany, 150 miles away, and Trenton, which is closer to Philadelphia than to New York, enhances the reference value of the volume under review here. The chapter on Albany includes descriptions of the following New York State agencies:

- New York State Education Department, Office of Cultural Education:
  (a) New York State Archives and Records Administration—state census, military, court, naturalization, land, Governor's Office, State Board of Charities, Division of Youth, Department of Correctional Services, State Education Department, Department of State, and Legislature records
  (b) New York State Library—U.S. and New York State censuses, city directories, church and cemetery records, wills, D.A.R. records, maps and atlases, print collection, county histories, military records, genealogies, passenger reords, newspapers
- New York State Health Department, Vital Records Section, Genealogy Unit—birth, marriage, death records, *except* records filed in New York City, and City of Brooklyn, and some early records filed in Albany, Buffalo, and Yonkers

In New Jersey, certain types of records are centralized in Trenton, warranting coverage of the resources of that state's capital:

- New Jersey State Department of Health, Bureau of Vital Statistics—birth, marriage and death records
- New Jersey Department of State, Division of Archives and Records Management, New Jersey State Archives—earlier vital records, matrimonial records, wills and other probate records, US census, New Jersey tax ratables, property records, military records, tavern licenses, Justice of the Peace docket books, naturalization records, newspapers, court records, slave records, road returns
- New Jersey State Library, New Jersey Reference Services—Jerseyana, genealogy, maps and pictures, newspaper clippings, city directories, government documents
- Superior Court of New Jersey—court cases, name change, matrimonial, adoption, incompetency, and probate records

Warning: Before booking a trip to either Albany or Trenton, readers of this review will need to consult *Genealogical Resources . . .* for the detailed information that it contains relating to the specific topical, geographical, and chronological area of coverage of the respective state agencies just enumerated here.

As in the 1985 edition, the present work includes chapters on the holdings of a number of historical and genealogical societies, libraries and archives, Jewish and non-Jewish alike.

Several repositories not previously included are

described now as well, including the American Gathering of Jewish Holocaust Survivors, which maintains a computerized data base of over 65,000 survivors and their children in the United States and Canada, the American Jewish Joint Distribution Committee, the Bund Archives of the Jewish Labor Movement, the Archives of Hadassah—the Women's Zionist Organization of America, the New York Academy of Medicine Library, the Tamiment Institute Library and Robert F. Wagner Labor Archives of New York University's Elmer Holmes Bobst Library, and the Archives of the 92nd Street Y, to mention new listings just for Manhattan.

For further details, see the listing of the contents in Appendix H.

Genealogical Resources represents an important advance in our knowledge of the relevant holdings of the New York area's repositories. Its appearance is a tribute to the persistence and professionalism of its editor, the vision of its publisher, and the spirit of voluntarism and cooperation prevailing among the members of the JGS and the staffs of the facilities surveyed here. The publication of this book marks yet another milestone in the annals of the Jewish Genealogical Society and stands as a sign of the maturation of American Jewish genealogy.

Excerpted from *Avotaynu*, Vol. V, No. 1, Spring 1989.

■ THE HEBREW IMMIGRANT AID SOCIETY

HIAS, Inc.
200 Park Avenue South
New York, New York 10003
(212) 674-6800

Introduction

HIAS was formed in 1909 through the merger of the Hebrew Sheltering House Association (founded in 1884) and the Hebrew Immigrant Aid Society (1902), as the Hebrew Sheltering and Immigrant Aid Society and has long been the most important Jewish migration agency, helping uprooted families obtain visas and secure passage, settlement, and employment. HIAS has offices throughout the world, including Asia. Over the years, it has affiliated with many other similar agencies, and finally in 1954, it merged with the United Service for New Americans (USNA) and the Migration Service of the Joint Distribution Committee.

Few Jewish families in this country have *no* members who were helped by HIAS when they arrived in the New World. Records of these activities, including those of their cooperation with local *Gemeinden* (community organizations that gave services to immigrants) were kept in all the overseas offices, both records of a general nature and individual case files for every single family needing aid. These records are often helpful to genealogists.

HIAS has subject files and control cards for passengers who arrived in *any* United States entry port under HIAS auspices or sought the agency's aid. These give names, ages, family members overseas and in the United States, and occasionally other information. These records date from 1911. Some are on microfilm and are organized by ship and date. HIAS also maintains a tracing serivce for Jewish families overseas.

See also "HIAS Records at YIVO," pp. 107–108.

Location Department

Requests for information should include the individual's name (as spelled at the time of arrival) and, if known, the year of arrival, port of entry into the United States, and the names of other members of the household with whom the immigrant was traveling. Additional information such as date of birth and last known address would be helpful in corroborating that the record is that of the individual sought. HIAS uses the following indexes to locate records:

* Arrival Index Cards, 1909–1979 (1909–1964 on microfilm). Index cards, 1909–1949, are arranged by year of arrival and within each year alphabetically by the name of the head of the traveling party. Cards, 1950–1979, are arranged by HIAS' Case Name Indexing (Soundex) System.
  Index cards include the case number, and may include dates/places of birth, names and family relationship of people traveling together, last place of residence, destination, and details of arrival. (The actual files no longer exist for cases pre-1937. The index card is all that remains for these earlier years.)
* Master Card Index, 1950–1979. This is a cross-reference index identifying all members of the traveling party that appear on the arrival cards.
* For 1980 to the present, HIAS has a computerized index of HIAS-assisted arrivals.
* Index cards of arrivals, 1939–1950, of families assisted by the National Refugee Service and the United Service for New Americans, which merged into HIAS in 1954. These cards are organized by HIAS' Case Name Indexing (Soundex) System and are stored in HIAS' warehouse.
* Joint Distribution Committee (JDC) index cards. The originals are in HIAS' warehouse, but a microfilm copy is available at the office. This index is arranged alphabetically.
* Record cards are also in HIAS' warehouse for children brought to the United States immediately following World War II by the European Jewish Children's Aid.

Note: HIAS is in the process of placing *all* index cards in one computerized system, and there is a search fee.

Reprinted from *Genealogical Resources in the New York Metropolitan Area.*

■ HEBREW UNION COLLEGE— JEWISH INSTITUTE OF RELIGION (THE KLAU LIBRARY)

1 West 4th Street
New York, NY 10012
(212) 674-5300

The following is a bibliographical sampling of works available for genealogical research at the library. Call numbers are in brackets.

Cemetery Records

Algiers. Bloch, Issac. *Algiers Cemeteries.* Paris, 1888. [HS/210]

Austria. Eisenstadt, Mattersdorf, Zielheim, Kobersdorf, Lackenbach, Frauenkirchen, Kittsee. Goldstein, Moshe. *Maamar sheva kehilot* [Command of seven communities]. Tel Aviv, 1956. [HS/189]

Austria. Graz. Herzog, David. *Die juedischen Friedhofe in Graz*. Graz, 1937. [HS/609.2]

Barbados. Shilstone, E. M. *Jewish Monumental Inscriptions in Barbados*. New York, 1956. [HS/1260]

Curaçao. Emmanuel, I. S. *Precious Stones of the Jews of Curaçao: Curaçaon Jewry, 1656–1957*. New York, 1957. [HS/1257]

Czechoslovakia. Prague. Jerabek, L. *Der alte prager Judenfriedhof* [The old Jewish cemetery of Prague]. Prague, 1903. [HS/190]

Prague. Lion, Jindrich. *Der alte prager Judenfriedhof* [The old Jewish cemetery of Prague]. Prague, 1960. [HS/191]

Prague. Lieben, Koppelman. *Grabensteininschriften des prager israelitischen alten Friedhofs* [Gravestone inscriptions of the Old Prague Israelite cemetery. Contains the most complete record of epitaphs - in German gothic type]. Prague, 1856. [HS/190]

Denmark. Copenhagen. Margolinsky, Julius. *Jodiske Dodsfald 1693–1976* [Jewish cemetery]. Copenhagen, 1978. [HS/1206]

Greece. Salonika. Emmanuel, I. S. *Gedole Saloniki le-dorotam* [Leaders of Salonika in their generations; 500 inscriptions, 1500–1660]. Tel Aviv, 1936. [HS/755]

Salonika. Emmanuel, I. S. *Matsevot Saloniki* [Epitaphs of Salonika]. 2 vols. Jerusalem, 1963. [HS/889]

Salonika. Molcho, Michael. *Bet ha-alamin shel yehude Saloniki* [The Jewish cemetery of Salonika]. Salonika, 1975. [HS/889.2]

Hungary. Scheiber, Sandor. *Jewish Inscriptions in Hungary from the 3rd Century to 1686*. Leiden, 1983. [DS135 H9 S29 1983]

Budapest. Scheiber, Alexander. *Newly found Jewish tombstones at Buda*. Budapest, 1953. [HS/415]

Israel. Jerusalem. Cohen, Shear Yashub. *Har ha-zetim* [Mt. of Olives]. Jerusalem, 1969. [LB]

Lithuania. Vilna. Klausner, Israel. *Korot bet ha-olamin ha-yashan be-Vilna* [History of the old cemetery in Vilna]. 1935. [HS/928.2]

Netherlands. Amsterdam. de Castro, Henriques. *Keur van Grafsteenen op de Nederl. Portug. Israel. Begraafplaats te Oudekerk* [Record of epitaphs of the Dutch Portuguese-Jewish Cemetery at Oudekerk, the oldest Sephardic cemetery in the Netherlands]. Leiden, 1883. [HS/645.1]

Amsterdam. Vega, L. Alvares. *Het Beth Haim van Oudekerk . . .* [The cemetery at Oudekerk: images of a Portuguese Jewish cemetery in Holland]. Assen, 1975. (Dutch and English) [DS135 N5 0937 1975]

St. Thomas. Margolinsky, Julius. *299 Epitaphs from the Jewish Cemetery of St. Thomas, V.I., 1837–1916*. (mimeographed) Copenhagen, 1957. [HS/1229]

Spain. Cartera & Millas. *Las Inscripciones Hebraicas de Espana* [Hebrew inscriptions of Spain]. Madrid, 1956. [HS/756]

United States. Charleston, SC. Elzas, B.A. *The Old Jewish Cemeteries at Charleston, S.C.* Charleston, 1903. [F279 C4 E5 1903]

Galveston, TX. Dreyfus, A. Stanley. *Hebrew Cemetery No. 1 of Galveston, TX*. (mimeo-graphed) [ALU]

New York, NY. de Sola Pool, David. *Portraits Etched in Stone: Early Jewish Settlers, 1632–1831*. New York, 1952. [HS/1254]

Savannah, GA. Levy, B. H. *Savannah's Old Jewish Community Cemeteries*. Macon, 1983. [F294 S2 L47 1983]

West Germany. Frankfurt am Main. Hulsen, Julius. *Der alte Judenfriedhof in Frankfurt a.M.* [The old Jewish cemetery in Frankfurt am Main]. Frankfurt, 1932. [HI/472.3]

Rheinpfalz. Friedmann, Hugo. *Merischonim loachronim: Verstorbenlisten der juedischen Gemeinden der Mittelmosel von Wintrich bis Enkirch* [From first to last: Death lists of the Jewish communities of the central Mosel valley, from Wintrich to Enkirch]. (typescript) Berncastel-Cues, 1929. [HS/407]

Wuerttemberg. *Juedische Gotteshaeuser und Friedhofe in Wuerttemberg* [Jewish synagogues and cemeteries in Wuerttemberg]. Stuttgart, 1932. [HS/440]

Vital Records and Lists

England. London. Barnett, L.D. and G.H. Whitehill. *Bevis Marks Records* (Sephardic Congregation). v.1: Early history of the congregation; v. 2: Marriages, 1687–1837; v.3: Marriages, 1836–1901. London, 1940, 1973. [HS/337]

Portugal. Coimbra. Bivar Guerra, Luiz de. *Inventario dos Processos da Inquisicao de Coimbra (1541–1820)* [Catalog of the trials of the Inquisition of Coimbra, Portugal, 1541–1820. Names are indexed in vol. 2]. Paris, 1972. [HS/772]

Genealogies

United States. Stern, Malcolm H. *First American Jewish Families; 600 Genealogies, 1654–1977*. Cincinnati and Waltham, 1978. [ALU (RBR)]

West Germany. Frankfurt am Main. Dietz, Alexander. *Stammbuch der Frankfurter Juden* [Genealogies of the Jews of Frankfurt am Main]. Frankfurt, 1907. [HS/605]

Communal Histories and Yizkor Books (Pre- and Post-World War II)

The following books are in addition to those listed in Appendix A of *Genealogical Sources in the New York Metropolitan Area*.

Bavaria. Weinberg, M. *Die Memorbuecher der juedischen Gemeinden in Bayern* [Memorial books of the Jewish communities in Bavaria]. Frankfurt, 1937–1938. [HS/323]

Salfeld, Sigmund. *Das Martyrologium des Nuernberger Memorbuch* [Martyrology of Jews in Bavarian towns]. Berlin, 1898. [HS/350]

Brest-Litovsk. Brzesc nad Bugiem (Brisk) *Ir Tehilah* [Brisk, City of Prayer]. Warsaw, 1886. (Hebrew) [HI/912]

Busk. *Toldot yehudim* [History of the Jews]. Tel Aviv, 1962. [HI/926.3]

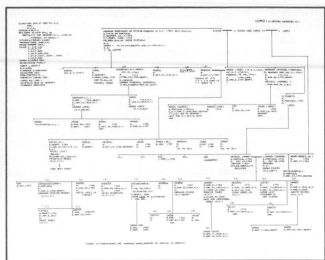

First American Jewish Families: 600 Genealogies, 1654–1977, compiled by Malcolm H. Stern, is Rabbi Stern's magnum opus. It documents Jewish families in America before 1840 and traces them to the present.

Sample genealogy from *First American Jewish Families: 600 Genealogies, 1654–1977*.

France. Klarsfeld, Serge. *Memorial to the Jews Deported from France, 1942–1944* [Registers of the dead]. New York, 1983. [DS135 F83 K4313 1983]

Kalisz. *Toldot yehude Kalish* [History of the Jews of Kalisz]. Tel Aviv, 1961. [HI/909.3]

Krakow. Friedberg, B. *Luhot zikaron* [Tablets of Memory]. Frankfurt am Main, 1904. [HI/929.1]

Lithuania. *Da'at kedoshim* [Religion of the holy. 1658 pogrom. Mentions these families: Eisenstat, Bachrach, Ginzberg, Heilprin, Morwitz, Mintz, Friedland, Katzenelbogen, Rapoport and Rokeach]. St. Petersburg, 1897/1898. [HI/921]

Dubnow, Simon. *Pinkas ha-medinah Lita* [Ledger of the province of Lithuania]. Berlin, 1925 (photocopy). [HI/917]

Lodz. *Kehilat Lodz* [The community of Lodz]. Jerusalem, 1948. [HI/905]

Ha-yehudim be-Lodz [The Jews in Lodz]. Warsaw, 1893. [HI/926.1]

Yasni, A. Wolf. *Die geshikhte fun yidn in Lodz* [The history of the Jews in Lodz]. Israel, 1960. [HI/922.3]

Lublin. Balaban, Majer. *Die Judenstadt von Lublin* [The ghetto of Lublin]. Berlin, 1919. [HI/907] and Hebrew edition [HI/907.2]

Lwow. *Zydzi Lwowscy* [Jews of Lwow]. Lwow, 1909. (Polish) [HI/903.2]

Anshe shem [Men of renown]. Krakow, 1895. (Hebrew) [HI/904]

Die Lemberger Juden Pogrom Nov. 1918–Jan. 1919. [HI/910]

Minsk. Eisenstadt, Ben Zion b. Moses. *Ravnei Minsk* [Chief Rabbis of Minsk]. Vilna, 1898. [HI/921.1]

Ostraha/Ostrov. *Mazkeret li-gedole Ostraha* [Memorandum of the Leaders of Ostraha]. 1907. [HI/906]

Pinsk. Aharoni, Avraham. *Maftehot shemot ha-ishim ve-ha-yishuvim shel sifre Pinsk* [Indexes of the names of the men and settlements of the records of Pinsk]. Haifa, 1982. [DS135 R93 P5433 1982]

Russia. *Juden Pogrome in Russland* [Jewish pogroms in Russia—giving the story of each community]. 2 vols. Koeln/Leipzig, 1910. [HP/100]

Ukraine. Revyuk, E. *Polish atrocities in the Ukraine*. 1931. [HP/73]

Vilna. Fein, Rabbi Samuel Joseph. *Kiryah Ne'emanah* [Faithful City]. Vilna, 1915. [HI/926]

Haivrit b'Vilna. *Toldot ha-kehilah* [History of the Community]. Vilna, 1935. [HI/923.2]

Zolkiew. *Sefer Zolkiew* [The book of Zolkiew]. 1843. [HI/905]

Gazetteers

Cohen, Chester G. *Shtetl Finder Gazetteer*. Los Angeles, 1980. [REF DS135 R9 C58]

Szajkowski, Z. *Analytical Franco-Jewish Gazetteer, 1939–1945.* New York, 1966. [HP/166]

Biographical Dictionaries

Who's Who in American Jewry. 1926, 1928, 1938–1939, 1980.

Who's Who in World Jewry. 1955, 1965, 1972, 1978, 1980.

Whittemore, Henry. *Progressive, Patriotic, and Philanthropic Hebrews of the New World* [Biographies of leaders of the NYC community with a history of their philanthropic institutions]. New York, 1907.

Periodicals

Allgemeine Zeitung des Judenthums [General Newspaper of Jewry], 1837–1922.

American Jewish Historical Society: *Publications, 1892–1947, American Jewish Historical Quarterly, 1947–1977, American Jewish History, 1977–0000.*

American Jewish Archives, 1949–0000.

American Jewish Year Book, 1899–0000. Of interest to genealogists:

Lists of every Jewish organization in the US: 1900–1901, 1907–1908, 1919–1920.

Biographical sketches of rabbis and cantors: 1903–1904, 1904–1905.

Biographical sketches of communal workers: 1905–1906.

Necrologies—every volume.

Individual biographies of prominent Jews.

Canadian Jewish Year Book, 1939–1941.

Chicago Jewish Forum, 1942–1969.

The Jewish Forum, 1918–1960.
Jewish Times, 1869–1872.
The Occident (edited by Isaac Leeser), 1843–1868.
Western States Jewish Historical Quarterly, 1968 +.

Periodicals on Microfilm

The American Hebrew, New York, 1879–1884, 1890–1900, 1926–1941.
The Reform Advocate (edited by Emil G. Hirsch), Chicago, 1891–1922.
The Israelite (edited by Isaac Mayer Wise, now *The American Israelite*), Cincinnati, 1854–1913.

American Jewish Archives (AJA) Microfilms

Portions of the holdings of the AJA in Cincinnati are on microfilm in the library. These include some congregational records, family histories and other data. The following are the records of genealogical interest. Film numbers are in parentheses.

Amsterdam. Portuguese Congregation ketuboth, 1690–1893. (833–840)
Barbados. Ledger books and burial records, 1696–1887. (822)
Efroymson-Feibleman-Kahn genealogy. (2764)
Hamburg, Germany. Sephardim, 1672–1682. (751)
Jamaica, West Indies. Wills, 1692–1798. (140)
Lisbon, Portugal. Inquisition records: New Christians, America to Lisbon. (606–650, 736–745, 842–847); Mexico. (720–722); Brazil to Lisbon. (783–794)
Mexico. Inquisition records, 1597–1718. (856–859)
St. Thomas, V.I. Vital records, 1786–1956. (125)
Surinam. Portuguese congregation records, 1754–1920. (67–67o)
Portuguese Community records. (176–198)
Records of the Portuguese Jews. (527–527t)
United States. American Jewish Joint Distribution Committee, papers, 1918–1980. (2798)

- Atlanta, Georgia. Hebrew Benevolent Congregation (The Temple), vital records, etc., 1890–1950. (552)
- Charleston, South Carolina. Congregation Beth Elohim, minutes, 1838–1850. (84)
- Cincinnati, Ohio. Judah Touro Cemetery, 1856–1970. (2160–61)
  United Hebrew Cemetery, records, 1850–1951. (48)
  United Hebrew Cemetery, burials, 1850–1930, 1951–1959. (439–439a)
- Erie, Pennsylvania. Congregation Anshe Chesed, minutes, etc. 1875–1936; cemetery records, 1865–1920. (3066–3069)
- Nashville, Tennessee. Vine Street Temple, marriages and deaths, 1881–1928. (592)
- New Orleans, Louisiana. Touro Synagogue and Hebrew Rest Cemetery, 1846–1955. (221–222)
- New York, New York. Congregation B'nai Jeshurun, records (marriages, 1825–1930, deaths, 1853–1928). (493–493h)
  Congregation Shearith Israel (Spanish and Portuguese), records, 1706–1949. (1–1g)
  New York Herald Tribune, Index, 1875–1906. (3–3b)
- Philadelphia, Pennsylvania. Association for the Protection of Jewish Immigrants, 1884–1921. (137–137d)

Reform Congregation Kneseth Israel, minutes, 1847–1880. (90)
- Piqua, Ohio. Anshe Emeth Congregation records, 1874–1956. (560)
- St. Louis, Missouri. Mount Sinai Cemetery, 1859–1972. (861)

Reprinted from *Genealogical Resources in the New York Metropolitan Area.*

■ JEWISH THEOLOGICAL SEMINARY OF AMERICA

Archives of Conservative Judaism

Archives, Jewish Theological Seminary
3080 Broadway
New York, New York 10027
(212) 678-8869

These records of Conservative congregations and rabbis, although housed in the Rare Book Room, constitute a separate collection. It is currently being assembled and already has material of value to genealogists. These include:

Congregation B'nai Jeshurun (New York City). Marriage certificates (twelve volumes), 1826–1973, and wedding book, 1897–1902; registers of deaths, including name, age, date, 1853–1928; cemetery burial permits, 1914–1934; perpetual care lists (index at 1972, 1975 and 1978); cemetery account ledgers, 1882–1926; minutes of the Joint Cemetery Committee (B'nai Jeshurun and Shaaray Tefila), 1857–1901; a "Book of Life" which includes *yahrzeit* (anniversary) dates of benefactors of B'nai Jeshurun, 1862–1965; eight files on estates and burial plots of congregants; correspondence concerning condolences, 1953–1954, and congratulatory correspondence, 1950–1952.

Also available is the Religious School register, 1855–1919 (listing name, address, parents' names, and attendance of students), and 1946–1947 (listing names and addresses of students); a Bar Mitzvah Information Book (including name, parents' names, and address), 1945–1953; and a copy of *The Clarion,* the B'nai Jeshurun Religious School Year Book, 1952.

There are members' dues ledgers, 1904–1923; lists of congregation members (names and addresses), 1928–1931, 1935–1946, 1949–1951, and 1957; seat deeds, 1886–1958; contribution acknowledgements, 1947–1954; minute books of the congregation, 1825–1966 (gaps); correspondence of its rabbis, cantors and officers; and rabbis' letters and applications for a pulpit position, 1917.

Baith Israel Anshei Emes—Kane Street Shul (Brooklyn). A list of marriages, 1913–1917 (included in the financial records of the synagogue); seat books, 1908–1949 (gaps), 1975–1981; membership receipts, 1922–1923; membership lists and contributions, 1930; scrapbook, 1955–1956; souvenir journals, 1916–1986 (gaps); and centennial banquet book, 1956.

Includes the Baith Israel Sunday School Register of Pupils, 1889–1890; and Talmud Torah Anshei Emes tuition book, 1922–1924; records of plots in Beth El, Washington, and Mount Carmel cemeteries, c.1919, and Cemetery Board records, 1919–1930.

Temple Beth Zion—Beth Israel (Philadelphia). Includes eight volumes on the congregation's history; typed *History of 100 years of Temple Beth Israel, 1840–1940;* centennial celebration book, 1940, and five notebooks of names on memorial tablets.

Includes records of donations, 1840–1895; a book of Board Managers, 1901–1960; account books, 1842–1900, showing seats, pew rents, offerings and/or membership; cemetery account book, 1934–1948; account book for receipts and disbursements, 1949–1963; minute books, 1873–1907 (annual general meetings), and 1926–1940 (Board of Managers meetings).

Temple Shomrei Emunah (Montclair, New Jersey). Includes minute books of general meetings, 1905–1955 (gaps); Sisterhood meetings, 1940–1948; Board of Trustees meetings, 1951–1969; congregational correspondence, 1929–1940; newsletter, 1936–1969; and fifth anniversary bulletin, 1955.

Chisuk Emuna Bnai Russia Congregation (Harrisburg, Pennsylvania). Includes cemetery lot records, 1937–1968; cemetery correspondence, sale of lots, perpetual care and legal papers, 1879, 1884, 1904, 1931, 1949–1974; blueprint of plots, 1945; fiscal records of membership accounts, 1926–1949; holiday honors, 1935–1949; and congregational minutes, 1893–1897 and 1929–1970 (gaps).

Other Collections. Recently acquired and currently being organized, these include the Brooklyn Jewish Center, Anshe Chesed (New York), and Shaarey Zedek (New York).

Rabbinical Records. Include biographical material, sermons, and correspondence of Rabbi Ben Zion Bokser, Rabbi Abraham Hurvitz, Rabbi Ario Hyams, Rabbi Nathan Kollin, Rabbi Israel H. Levinthal, Rabbi Louis Levitsky, and thirty other rabbis.

Rabbi Isaac Klein's collection includes also the Jewish divorces given or held by him; wedding sermons, Buffalo and Springfield; revised ketubah material (in which Rabbi Klein was involved); and eulogies.

Library, Archives, and Rare Book Room

Seminary Library. The library has a large collection of Yizkor books and rabbinic biographies. Its collection includes hundreds of histories of local Jewish communities throughout the world. The Periodical Collection includes local Jewish newspapers from communities in Europe, America, North Africa and the Near East. These include such diverse titles as:

- *Ami d'Israél,* Strasbourg, April, 1841 (microfilm), 1851–1858, 1862
- *The Canadian Jewish Chronicle,* 1914/1915–1930, 1941–1948
- *Davar Aher,* Calcutta, 1918
- *Emanu-el,* San Francisco, 1903–1930
- *Esra,* Vienna, 1919–1920
- *The Jewish Chronicle,* London, 1841–1842, 1844–1899, 1900–1939 (gaps), 1956–1988; index, 1841–1880 (on microfilm, except 1900–1939)
- *Jewish Daily Bulletin,* New York, 1924–1935
- *Jewish Times,* Baltimore, 1869–1951
- *Judische Rundschau,* Berlin, 1902–1906, 1924–1938 (microfilm), 1933, 1936

Rare Book Room. The bulk of the material in the Rare Book Room located on the fifth floor is of a literary-religious character. However, the collection includes:

- Communal record books (*pinkasim*) from Europe and the United States such as the *pinkasim* of the *Chevra Kadaisha* of the following places (call numbers in parentheses):
  - (3873) Alsace
  - (8537) Askenaz, 1729–1782
  - (3874) Eisenstadt, 1775–1869
  - (4028) Krotoschin
  - (3872) Lissa, 1833–1854
  - (8956) Lithuania, 1828, some communities
  - (9286) Louisville, Kentucky, 1892
  - (8499) Madi, Hungary, 1793–1890
  - (3947) Pesaro, Italy (cemetery)
  - (8513) Trinbach
  - (8510) Sultz
  - (8601) Sziget, Hungary, 1884–1922

The Rare Book Room has many other *pinkasim* listed in the catalog (Hebrew). In addition, there are other *pinkasim* in the collection still uncataloged and inaccessible to researchers.

- Nearly 300 ketuboth (Jewish marriage contracts). Most are from Italy and the Levant (North Africa, Egypt, Russia and Syria), but there are some from America, Great Britain and Europe. The majority date from the seventeenth to nineteenth centuries. A few are from the twentieth century.
- A collection of approximately 100 genealogical charts (uncataloged) of European and American families including the Rothschilds, the Caro Rabbinic dynasty, the Oppenheimer family (Frankfurt), the Phillips family (London and America) and the Yehya family (Spain).

Archives. The archives are located on the fifth floor with the Rare Book Room. The holdings include:

- Personal papers of communal leaders and scholars.
- Communal and organizational records (most uncataloged, but retrievable):

  The American Jewish History Center, for Cleveland (Anshe Chesed minute books, 1907–1920), Milwaukee (several congregations, periodicals), Philadelphia (Congregation Beth Israel)
  France. Consistoire records, 1808–1905
  France. Jewish communities records 1669–1940s
  Historical Documents, fifteenth–twentieth centuries (Jewish communal records—German, French and Italian communities)
  Morocco. Jewish community records, twentieth century (Fez mostly, but also Meknès, Rabat, Safi, Salé, Sefrou and Tangier)
  New York. Independent Slonimer Benevolent Association records, 1935–1936
  Paris. Temple Israélite, minute books, 1851–1875

- Print and Photograph Collections; includes portraits of individuals, Jewish communities, synagogues, cemeteries, and maps.

Reprinted from *Genealogical Resources in the New York Metropolitan Area.*

■ LEO BAECK INSTITUTE— GERMAN–JEWISH RESOURCES

Sybil Milton

German–Jewish genealogical research involves a number of unusual obstacles. The geographical amalgam called Imperial Germany (1871–1918) contained places like Strassburg, Breslau, and Königsberg, now located in France (Strasbourg), Poland (Wroclaw), and Russia (Kaliningrad). The German Empire consolidated over 300 sovereign states, which had existed independently prior to 1803. This geographical fragmentation resulted in archival decentralization; public records repeatedly changed their citizenship with boundary changes, transfers during wartime and military occupations, and the creation of new states.

Thus, archives located in Alsace were ceded to Germany in 1871, and were again returned to France in 1918 under the Treaty of Versailles. Historical archives were transferred en masse from the Austro-Hungarian Monarchy to the successor states of 1918: Hungary, Czechoslovakia, Poland, Yugoslavia, and Romania.[1] World War II and the Holocaust led to the further destruction and dispersal of documentary sources. Cemeteries and synagogues were irrevocably destroyed; public and private archives in occupied European countries were looted and transferred to Germany, and subsequent to the Allied victory in 1945, they were returned to their places of origin or to successor institutions in Israel, Canada, the United States, and elsewhere.[2]

The idiosyncrasies of German geography and political history are also reflected in the patterns of German–Jewish family history. The French Revolution and the Napoleonic era created the first steps toward Jewish civil emancipation and equal status. Civil registration for all births, deaths, and marriages was introduced in the French-occupied west bank of the Rhine, and in many states, Jews adopted German surnames. Jewish community records, kept intermittently since the 17th century, became more systematic as the administrative organization of the modern German state evolved during the 19th century. However, only in January 1876 was national civil registration (of all births, deaths, and marriages irrespective of religion) introduced. These registers were kept at the Standesamt (municipal civil registry), usually located at local city halls.[3]

Jewish records were not always complete or accurate. This was occasionally deliberate, a way of evading military conscription, residence restrictions, discriminatory fees, professional restrictions by craft guilds, and onerous taxation. There were also a large number of migrant Jews among the largely rural Jewish population at the beginning of the nineteenth century, who were probably included sporadically in official records. (The process of Jewish urbanization occurred during the second half of the century.)

Because of restrictions on the growth of Jewish population, younger sons of a large family were forbidden to marry in Bavaria under the *Familiengesetze* (legal infringements on newly granted citizenship for Jewish residents) between 1813 and 1861. Thus, clandestine (unregistered) marriages and births may have occurred. Circumcision registers recorded only male births; female children were systematically included in birth registers only by the end of the 18th century. Errors often entered the vital statistical registers by accident. Copyists made mistakes in transcribing earlier Jewish communal records for the state during the 19th century.

Many surviving Jewish registers carry the swastika stamp of the Reichsstelle für Sippenforschung (National Office for Kinship Research). An ironic byproduct of the Nazi pseudoscience of racial biology was the need to preserve Jewish vital registers. Nazi racial laws required all citizens to trace their genealogy back to the third paternal and maternal great-grandparents. This lineage was written up in the *Ahnenpass* (ancestral passport). The Nazi requirement that all Jews add the names "Israel" and "Sara" to all vital records in many instances led to the preservation of old Jewish vital registers. Furthermore, the Reichsstelle für Sippenforschung microfilmed many Jewish birth, death, and marriage records in 1944. These documents are available today at the Personenstandsarchiv (Personal Records Archives) in Brühl (near Cologne), West Germany.[4]

Various types of Jewish genealogical records are available in the Archives and Library of the Leo Baeck Institute (LBI) in New York. The LBI was founded in 1955 by the Council of Jews from Germany "for the purpose of collecting material and sponsoring research about the life and history of the Jewish community in Germany and other German-speaking countries, from the Emancipation to the Nazi persecution." The archives and library of the LBI comprise one of the largest documentary collections in this field, containing over 2,000 linear feet of archives, a specialized library of 50,000 volumes, over 600 periodicals and newspapers, 500 memoirs, and an art collection. The materials are mostly in German, although French, Swedish, Czech, Italian, Hebrew, Yiddish, Russian,[5] and English are occasionally found in the collections.

A selection of several especially interesting collections for the genealogist in the LBI Archives is listed below. This list is not comprehensive and comprises about 25 percent of the archives' holdings of relevance to genealogists. LBI Library holdings consisting of communal histories and newspapers are described at length in the LBI published catalog, volume I.

Adoption of German Surnames

Several collections at the LBI Archives help document the change from patronymics to surnames in early 19th century Germany. Thus the literary estate of Berthold Rosenthal (1875–1957) includes about 500 pages of detailed notes on the name changes and family names adopted by the Jews of Baden in 1809. His volumes are organized alphabetically by town name. The collection includes copious historical material about the history of Jews in Baden and the Palatinate as well as 70 family trees.

The literary estate of Jacob Jacobson (1888–1968) includes substantial remnants of the *Gesamtarchiv der Deutschen Juden* (Archives of German Jewry) established in Berlin in 1905 as the central Repository for the records of German-Jewish communities and organizations. Jacobson was forced to stay on as archivist under the Nazis, and succeeded in copying numerous files for the future. His wife and son were permitted to emigrate to England, and were able to smuggle out the Berlin segment of the records. The Jacobson collection includes the following registers of name changes and naturalizations. Numbers in parentheses identify the particular item in the collection.

- Berlin files contain lists of Jewish families living legally in Berlin on March 24, 1813, lists of family names taken in 1812, and a list of Jews who had taken family names and Christian first names before 1812 (379 entries). (I:51, I:58, and I:82.)
- Lippe-Detmold, 1810, list of family names. (III:50.)
- Marienwerder district, West Prussia, 1845, lists of family names. (III:88 and VIII:61.)
- Posen, alphabetical register of Jews naturalized, copied by Isidor Hirschberg, Bromberg, 1836. (III:32.)

These examples are multiplied by numerous individual identity certificates, passports, certifications of municipal citizensip, rights of domicile documents, certificates of name changes, etc. Individual family histories tell stories like the Straus Family history (AR 4492). Lazarus Straus was born in Otterberg in 1725; his son is listed in the French 1797 census as Jacques Lazare. Under the decree of the Department of Donnersberg to adopt family surnames, he changed his name in 1808 to Straus.

Name changes also occurred during subsequent emigration to the United States. Thus, the elder of two emigrant brothers, Seligmann Heilner, originally from Urspringen, Bavaria, changed his name to Ed D. Cohen in the United States, while the other retained the family name Heilner (AR 4471).

SPECIFICATION

Dererjenigen Juden/ welchen in Ihro Königlichen Majestät in Schweden Fürstl. Hessischen Erb-Fürstenthumen und denenselben incorporirten Landen, der Landes-Herrliche Schutz bis hierhinzu, Allergnädigst verwilliget, und die dahero an nachbenamten Orten mit ihren Familien, biß zu anderwärter Verordnung gedultet werden mögen.

I. Classe Cassel. Diemol-Strohm.

Stadt Cassel

1. Benedix Simon Goldschmidt.
2. Hesse Goldschmidts/ Rel.
3. Abraham David.
4. Jacob Gans.
5. Marcus Levi/ Rel. Namens Hinb.
6. Israel Hertzen/ Rel.
7. Lazarus Wallach.
8. Löb Gottschald.
9. Nathan Selig.
10. Ruben Joseph Levi.
11. David Salomon Israel.
12. Gumbrecht Meyer.
13. Michael Oppenheim.
14. Löb Weil.
15. Samuel Elkam/ Vorsinger.
16. Hertz Gans.
17. Hertz Wallach.
18. Isaac Itzig Wallach.

Excerpt from 1744 list of Hessen *Schutzjuden* (Jews with protected status and legal domicile rights). Many Jews already have German surnames. (From the Jacob Jacobson Collection III:43.) (Reprinted with permission from *Toledot*, Spring 1979)

Circumcision and Birth Records

It must be remembered that circumcision registers (*Mohelbücher*) are not registers of all male children born in a specific town or region; they are the private record kept by an individual Mohel (circumciser). The optimum amount of information they contain is the name of the child, his father and mother, the day and hour of birth, the date of circumcision, name of circumciser, and whether the child was legitimate. The following communities and years are represented by circumcision registers in the LBI Archives. JJC refers to Jacob Jacobson Collection.

- Aurich, 1758–1806. (JJC III:4)
- Berlin, 1714–1840. (JJC I:1–4, I:19, I:55, I:75–76, and I:96) Also alphabetical birth registers, 1813–1840. (JJC I:42–43)
- Filehne: Register, 1812–1850, of Rabbi A. Wreschner, containing 200 entries from Filehne and thirty-two entries from other places, and register, 1817–1864, of the Rabbinical Judge Aron Lazarus, containing 335 entries. (AR 2470/No. 1–2)
- Frankfurt am Main: Register, 1698–1836, kept by the ancestors of Moritz Abraham Stern, 63 pages. (AR 380/No. 233)
- Fürth: Registers, 1761–1806, of Benjamin Berlin and Mordechai Jafe, handwritten copy in German. (JJC III:20)
- Munich: Register, 1826–1874, of Rabbi Hirsch Aub, including entries for Prag, 1816, and Baiersdorf, 1819; registers, 1840–1878 and 1834–1885. (Ernst Kitzinger Collection, AR 3086/I:1–3)
- Munich: Register, 1913–1938, by Jewish community official Heinrich Glaser, 300 entries (AR 143/No. 11–13)
- Prague, Worms, Pfalz, 1782–1823. (JJC III:65)
- Randegg/Baden: Register, 1828–1881, of Baruch Bloch, copy with explanations by Dr. S. Moos-Moore, 1972. (AR 2483/No. 9)
- Schildberg/Posen: Register, 1866–1906, of Elkan Lewy, 376 entries. (Elkan Lewy Collection, AR 3126/No. 1)
- Schildberg, 1838–1866, and Bunzlau, 1867–1887, photocopies of register of Abraham Unger. (JJC III:76)
- Schleswig-Holstein, 1775–1817. (JJC III:77)
- Württemberg, 1882–1908. (AR 147/No. 18)

Among other community and family collections in the LBI Archives are numerous examples of individual birth certificates and announcements.

Marriage Records

The LBI Archives contain marriage registers of communities, contracts (ketuboth), individual engagement and wedding announcements, as well as special newspapers issued for weddings. The following communities and years are represented by marriage registers in the LBI Archives:

- Berlin, list of marriages (*Trauungsliste*), 1759–1813. (JJC I:12)
- Berlin, register, 1813–1829, 1830–1837, 1837–1847, 1847–1851, photocopies made by the Reichsstelle für Sippenforschung. (JJC I:9–10, I:12, I:40–41, I:46–47, and I:63)
- Breslau, 1789–1818. (JJC III:10)

- Dresden, table of births, marriages, and deaths, 1786–1819/20. (JJC I:2 and I:55)
- Nürnberg, 1872–1912, including four pages of marriages in Switzerland. (AR 1706/No. 3)

Death Records

Individual death certificates include the date and cause of death, and the name, age, and profession of the deceased. Additional death records for communities and individuals are also found in the papers of burial societies (*Chevra Kadisha*), memorial books (*Memorbücher*), and cemetery registers. Wills, testaments, and probate records add information about family relationships and individual identities. Tombstone inscriptions exist in both manuscript and photographic form. The quantity of information on these records varies widely, depending on the accuracy of the local scribe, and the degree of destruction caused by World Wars I and II.

It is important to remember that rights of domicile were not always synonymous with burial privileges. Thus, no Jew could be buried in Breslau until 1671. Jews from Breslau were buried in Krotoschin, Zülz, and other outlying communities; the death certificates are therefore filed with these towns rather than with Breslau records. The following communities and years are represented by death records in the LBI Archives.

- Allersheim near Würzburg, list of deceased, 1799–1903, typed in German. (JJC III:1)
- Altstrelitz, cemetery register, ca. 1740–1923. (JJC III:2)
- Arnswalde, miscellaneous tombstone inscriptions and documents, earliest ca. 1780, mostly from 19th century. (JJC III:3)
- Berlin, death registers, 1751–1813, 1818–1829, 1830–1837, 1847–1855. (JJC I:5–6, I:34, I:44)
- Berlin, inscriptions from grave monuments in the old Jewish cemetery, Grosse Hamburgerstrasse 26, by L. Landshuth, 2,767 entries, mainly in Hebrew, 13 volumes. (JJC I:20–32)
- Bretten/Baden, *Memorbuch*, 1725–1884. (AR 2799/No. 6–9)
- Düsseldorf, *Memorbuch*, 1714. (JJC III:13)
- Dyhernfurth, *Chevra Kadisha* records, 1782–1807. (JJC III:14)
- Frankfurt am Main, death register, 1805–1808. (JJC III:17)
- Gnesen, record book (*pinkas*) of the *Chevra Baalei Hamisakim Ubikur Cholim* (burial society and society for visiting the sick), including list of deaths, 1841–1892. (JJC III:22)
- Haigerloch, photographs of Jewish tombstones. (JJC VIII:57)
- Hannover, *Memorbuch*. (JJC III:29)
- Harburg, *Memorbuch*. (JJC III:30)
- Königsberg (today Kaliningrad, U.S.S.R.), requests for birth, marriage, and death certificates, 1847. (JJC III:39)
- Krotoschin, *Chevra Kadisha* and death records, 1785. (JJC III:41a)
- Potsdam, Jewish tombstone inscriptions, 1746–1836, typed list. (JJC I:54)

Deportation Lists

For those families trying to trace missing and murdered individuals affected by the Third Reich and the Holocaust, the two best resource centers are Yad Vashem in Jerusalem and the International Tracing

Excerpt from 1851 Hamburg Jewish wedding register, made in 1934 for an *Ahnenpass*. The document contains the following information.

Bridegroom: Jacob Salomensen, born in Copenhagen, 30 years old, assistant merchant.

Date of marriage banns: 29 November 1851.

Date of wedding: 17 December 1851.

Bride: Pesche Pauline Danziger, single woman, born in Hamburg, 20 years old.

Bridegroom's parents: Sally Salomonsen and Ernestine née Philip.

Bride's parents: Selmann Danziger and Ricka née Polack.

(From the Rudolf Simonis Collection III:6.) (Reprinted with permission from *Toledot*, Spring 1979)

Service in Arolsen, West Germany. There have also been numerous memorial publications in West Germany; many of the volumes contain lists of deported and killed Jewish residents of individual towns and regions.[6] The LBI Archives contain several deportation lists, as follows:

- Baden: eleven Gestapo lists: Jews still resident in Baden on February 1, 1941, including full Jews and those living in mixed marriages, 840 names from twelve or more towns; Jews who moved to the East, Easter 1942, seventy-eight names; Jews who moved to the East, summer 1942, forty-five names; Jews who "emigrated" from Baden to Theresienstadt, August 22, 1942, 139 names, and addenda, ninety names; Jews deported from Baden-Baden, Freiburg, Heidelberg, Mannheim, etc. on August 22, 1942; Jews expelled from Baden on March 1, 1943. (AR 2037/No. 1–11)

- Koblenz: four Gestapo lists, 1942, of Jews deported from Koblenz and the region, especially Bendorf-Sayn (printed by the Jewish community, ca. 1947–1948). (AR 7085/No. 1)
- Konstanz: names, dates of birth, and last residence of the Jews of Konstanz, deported to Gurs (Vichy France) in 1940 (photocopies of Nazi documents). (AR 2165/No. 2)
- Pfalz: two Gestapo lists, undated, 220 names; also a list for transports from Rheinpfalz, undated, eleven names. (AR 2039/No. 1–3)
- Regensburg: deportees who arrived in Theresienstadt, September 24, 1942, 117 names. (AR 1425/No. 6)
- Würzburg: transport II/26 of Jews who arrived in Theresienstadt, September 24, 1942, 610 names. (AR 3788/No. 1)

Several other lists of Jews deported to Gurs and Theresienstadt are located in the LBI Archives in the Bernhard Kolb, Karl D. Darmstädter, and Max Plaut Collections.

Other Collections with Regional Materials

The following collections at the LBI Archives also contain material of particular interest to the genealogical researcher:

- Michael Berolzheimer Collection: over fifty family trees for the families Männlein Berolzheim, Berolzheimer, Offenbacher, Rindskopf, Gosdorfer, Besels, Wertheimer, Brilin, and Simon Wolf Oppenheim (Oppenheimer). The papers include copies of Jewish community registries from eighteenth- and nineteenth-century Bavaria, copies of the Fürth *Testamentenbuch* (register of wills, estates, and death dates of selected members of the community—translated by Rabbi Max Freudenthal), a *Schutzgeldliste* (tax list for rights of residence of protected Jews) from Fürth for 1716–1718, and other valuable genealogical notes.
- Max Markreich Collection: extensive typed manuscripts about the Jewish communities in Aurich, Ostfriesland, and Bremen. Markreich was head of the Jewish community in Bremen and emigrated to the United States by way of Trinidad. His collection contains material as diverse as original documents on the Jewish community of Leer, 1748–1749; the Aurich *Mohelbuch;* items on Jewish life in Trinidad, 1939–1940, and papers of Congregation Shaare Zedek of Astoria (New York City), 1942.
- Karl D. Darmstädter Collection: unusually rich in materials about Jews from Mannheim and their fate in Nazi Germany. The documentation about Mannheim, Baden, and Worms includes photocopies and photographs of cemeteries in Prag and Neckarbischofsheim.
- Vierfelder Family Collection: a six-generation history of the Vierfelder family from Buchau. The collection also includes 52 photographs of the Jewish community in Buchau and copious newspapers and historical clippings about Buchau.
- Rudolf Simonis Collection: several hundred

family trees, family histories, and related correspondence for Berlin, northern Germany, and Sweden. There is also a copiously illustrated Simonis family tree.

- Arthur Czellitzer Collection: personal and family papers as well as information on the genealogical society he created, the Gesellschaft für Jüdische Familienforschung. A full set of this organization's periodical, 1924–1938, is available in the LBI Library.
- The Berthold Rosenthal and Jacob Jacobson Collections referred to earlier in this article are obviously rich in vital statistical and historical data for the genealogist.

Conclusions

Written genealogical inquiries may be sent to the LBI, or you may call in person. To be fully and adequately processed, the inquiry must contain reasonably precise family and geographical information, as well as some indication of a price limit on relevant photocopies when such material is available.

There is a great deal of luck involved in any genealogical research. However, without certain minimum amounts of information, a search of records would be futile. A detailed location of family origin is exceedingly important. A recent inquiry to the LBI concerned a family from Fischbach (literally, fishing brook). In this instance, detail did not help, since there are twenty-eight different villages called Fischbach, several in Bavaria, one in Silesia, etc. Details, such as the administrative district of this village, can always help to solve a problem, since with the administrative or court district, it would have been possible to find out which village was the "real" Fischbach.

Despite the complexities of research into German–Jewish genealogy, the interested person has an excellent chance of partial success. It may be possible to discover the world of an 18th century Jewish ancestor and to trace his periginations to the present.

Notes

1. Charles Kecskemeti, *Archival Claims* (Paris: UNESCO, 1977): Ernst Posner, "Effects of Changes of Sovereignty on Archives," in *Archives and the Public Interest* (Washington, D.C., 1967), pp. 168–181; and E. Posner, "Public Records under Military Occupation," in *Archives and the Public Interest*, pp. 182–197.
2. Daniel J. Cohen, "Jewish Records from Germany in the Jewish Historical General Archives in Jerusalem," in *Leo Baeck Institute Year Book I* (1956), pp. 331–345; and Bernhard Brilling, "Jewish Records in German Archives: Results of a Scientific Journey, 1955–1956," in *Leo Baeck Institute Year Book I* (1956), pp. 346–359. [The Jewish Historical General Archives is now known as the Central Archives for teh History of the Jewish People.]
3. Recent publications on German-Jewish communal history include massive reference works on specific regions such as: Baruch Zwi Ophir in collaboration with Schlomo Schmiedt and Chasia Turtel-Aberzhanska, *Pinkas Hakehillot Germany—Bavaria* (Jerusalem, 1972); Paul Arnsberg, *Die jüdische Gemeinden in Hessen*, 2 vols. (Frankfurt am Main, 1971); and Bernhard Brilling, *Die jüdischen Gemeinden Mittelschlesiens* (Stuttgart, Berlin, Köln, Mainz, 1972). A comprehensive review of these communal history publications is found in a three-part article by E. G. Lowenthal, "In the Shadow of Doom: Post-War Publications on Jewish Communal History in Germany," in *Leo Baeck Institute Year Books XI* (1966), pp. 306–335, *XV* (1970), pp. 223–242, and *XXIII* (1978),

pp. 283–208. Further data on German-Jewish record-keeping practices are found in "Registration of Births, Deaths and Marriages in European Jewish Communities, in Palestine and Israel," in *Archivum*, vol. 9 (1959), reproduced in part in Leslie G. Pine, *The Genealogist's Encyclopedia.*

4. Personenstandsarchiv Brühl, D-504 Brühl, Schloss Nordflügel, West Germany. This archive is particularly strong on the Rheinland provinces and the administrative district of Düsseldorf. It includes church and religious registers, as well as civil registers, for many individual towns in this region. The Bundesarchiv (West German National Archives) in Koblenz contains microfilmed Jewish vital statistical records from numerous towns today located in East Germany, Poland, and Russia. Further information may be obtained from the Bundesarchiv, D-54 Koblenz, Am Wöllerschof 12, Postfach 320, West Germany. The best address directory to German-language archives is *Archive im deutschsprachigen Raum, Minerva Handbücher*, 2 vols. (Berlin and Elmsford, NY, 1974).

5. In addition to unpublished finding aids available at the LBI, detailed information on its holdings is also found in a number of sources: Leo Baeck Institute, *Inventory List of Archival Collections*, Brochures I and II (1971 and 1976), *LBI Library and Archives News*, no. 1--(Feb. 1975--), and *LBI News*, no 1-- (1960--); Max Kreutzberger, in collaboration with Irmgard Foerg (eds.), *Leo Baeck Institut, New York, Bibliothek und Archiv. Katalog*, vol. I (Tübingen, 1970); and U.S. Library of Congress, *National Union Catalog of Manuscript Collections*, vol. 1-- (1959--). The publication of a detailed catalog of the LBI Archives is now in preparation.

6. Further information about deportations and the Holocaust may be gleaned from published works such as: Hans-Joachim Fliedner, *Die Judenberfolgung in Mannheim, 1933–1945*, 2 vols. (Stuttgart, Berlin, Köln, Mainz, 1971), and Jörg Schadt, *Verfolgung und Widerstand unter dem Nationalsozialismus in Baden. Die Lageberichte der Gestapo und des General-staatsanwalts Karsruhe, 1933–1940* (Stuttgart, Berlin, Köln, Mainz, 1976). Other volumes include lists of Jewish residents, their fate, and sometimes even earlier historical data about the Jewish residents, e.g., Arno Herzig, *Die judische Gemeinde Iserlohn* (Iserlohn, 1970), contains a list of 1834 Jewish residents of Iserlohn, the community members who paid taxes for a rabbinical salary in 1852, name and address list of the Jewish community and their professions in 1866, and a list of Jewish residents deported to concentration camps, slave-labor camps, and ghettos.

Reprinted from *Toledot*, Spring 1979.

■ NATIONAL ARCHIVES, NORTHEAST REGION

National Archives, Northeast Region
Building 22
Military Ocean Terminal
Bayonne, New Jersey 07002
(201) 823-7568

Although the National Archives was not established until 1934, its major holdings date back to 1775. The National Archives, Northeast Region, is one of 11 regional repositories for historically valuable records of the federal government. These records represent only 2 percent or 3 percent of those generated by federal agencies. The holdings of this branch of the National Archives are chiefly of regional interest but also include microfilm copies of many of the most important records in the National Archives, Washington. The Federal Records Center (FRC), a sister agency

which is part of the National Archives and Records Administration, stores current records of federal agencies. After a period of time, the FRC transfers records designated for permanent keeping to the National Archives. The following describes the records of the National Archives, Northeast Region. Related record groups in the FRC are noted.

Census Records (microfilm). All existing population schedules are available for the following years: 1790, 1800, 1810, 1820, 1830, 1840, 1850, 1860, 1870, 1880, 1900, and 1910. The 1890 Census was destroyed by fire for most states. The only surviving fragments covering the New York metropolitan area are Jersey City, New Jersey; Eastchester, New York (in Westchester County); and Brookhaven Township, New York (in Suffolk County).

Special schedules available include all existing mortality schedules, 1850, 1860, 1870, and 1880.

Immigrant and Passenger Arrivals (microfilm). These include passenger lists of vessels arriving at:

- New York harbor, 1820–August 14, 1905 (indexes 1820–1846, June 16, 1897–June 30, 1902), 1943–1952 (Soundex index 1944–1948). There are *no* lists for the 1905–1942 period in the Archives
- Atlantic and Gulf Coasts and ports on the Great Lakes, 1820–1873
- Canadian Pacific port entries, 1929–1949 (Soundex index 1924–1952 for Canadian Pacific port *and* Atlantic port entries)
- Canadian border entries through small ports in Vermont, index, 1895–1929
- Galveston, Texas, 1896–1948 (index 1896–1951)

The Archives also has (on microfilm) registers of vessels arriving at the port of New York from foreign ports, 1789–1919; and a subject index to correspondence and case files of the Immigration and Naturalization Service, 1903–1952.

Military Records (microfilm). These include Veterans Administration, War Department and Adjutant General's Office records as follows:

- Civil War Union Veterans and Widows of Union Veterans, enumeration schedules, 1890
- Civil War, index to compiled service records of volunteer Union Soldiers who served in organizations from the States of New Jersey and New York
- Revolutionary War rolls, 1775–1783
- Revolutionary War, compiled service records of soldiers who served in the American Army, Navy, and members of the Departments of Quartermaster General and the Commissary General of military stores
- Revolutionary War pension and bounty-land-warrant applications files, 1800–1900
- War of 1812, index to service records of volunteer soldiers

Naturalization Records. These are available for the following Courts in Federal Region 2 (New York, New Jersey and Puerto Rico):

- "Old Law" naturalization records for New York City: photocopies of naturalization records filed in federal, state and local courts in New York

City, 1792–1906. Any naturalization completed prior to October 1906 in *any* New York City court should be found in this group of records. These courts include the following:

Federal Courts:

U.S. Circuit Court, Southern District, New York, 1846–1876

U.S. District Court, Southern District, New York, 1824–1906

U.S. District Court, Eastern District, New York, 1865–1906

State and Local Courts:

Court of Common Pleas for the City and County of New York, 1792–1895

Marine Court of the City of New York, 1806–1849

Superior Court of the City of New York, 1828–1895

Supreme Court, 1st Judicial District, formerly Supreme Court, City and County of New York, 1868–1906

City Court of Brooklyn, 1836–1894

County Court, Kings County, 1856–1906

County Court, Queens County, 1799–1906

Surrogate's Court, Queens County, 1888–1898

County Court, Richmond County, 1869–1906

- U.S. District Court for the Eastern District of New York (covers Kings, Queens, Richmond, Nassau, and Suffolk Counties)

Naturalization records, 1865–1957

Declarations of Intention, 1865–1959

NOTE: Naturalizations, 1958–1985, and Declarations, 1960–1979, are in the custody of the Federal Records Center in Bayonne (not the Archives). See "U.S. District Court–Eastern District of New York" for later records.

- U.S. District Court for the Southern District of New York (covers Manhattan, Bronx, Westchester, Putnam, Rockland, Orange, Dutchess, and Sullivan Counties. However, most records are for residents of Manhattan and the Bronx. Residents of other jurisdictions, e.g. Brooklyn, may also have been naturalized in this Court.)

Naturalization records, 1824–1929

Declarations of Intention, 1842–1940

Note: Naturalizations, 1929–1940, and Declarations, 1967–1976, are in the custody of the Federal Records Center in Bayonne (not the Archives). Declarations, 1941–1966, are missing and presumed to have been destroyed.

- U.S. Circuit Court for the Southern District of New York (now defunct)

Naturalization records, 1906–1911

Declarations of Intention, 1845–1911

- U.S. District Court for the District of New Jersey

Camden Office—Naturalizations and Declarations of Intention, 1932–1981

Camp Fort Dix—Naturalizations filed by soldiers, May 1918–September 1919 and May 1942–December 1946

Newark Office—Naturalizations, 1914–October 1982, and Declarations of Intention, 1914–June 1982

Trenton Office—Naturalizations, 1838–September 1906

Note: Newark Office records, 1982 to the present, are in the U.S. District Court—Naturalization Section, Newark, New Jersey. For Trenton Office records, 1930 to the present, go to 304 East State Street, Room 301, Trenton, N.J. (Mail address: Clerk, U.S. District Court, P.O. Box 575, Trenton, NJ 08603). The records are in the basement. Camden Office records, 1982 to the present, are at 401 Market Street, Room 405, Camden, NJ (Mail address: Clerk, U.S. District Court, P.O. Box 2797, Camden, NJ 08101). There were no naturalizations filed in the Trenton Office, 1906–1929. The Newark office was opened in 1911 and began naturalizations in 1913. The Camden office opened in 1926.

- U.S. District Court for Puerto Rico
Naturalization petitions and related records, 1917–1929

Other Court Records. Court cases filed, 1789–1967 (RG 21) in the U.S. District Courts in New York State, New Jersey, and Puerto Rico; the Court of Appeals—Second Circuit (cases appealed from New York State, Connecticut, and Vermont); and all Circuit Courts in New York State and New Jersey. Dates vary for each court. (Note: The functions of the Circuit Courts were absorbed by the U.S. District Courts in 1911.)

The cases filed in these courts include legal proceedings in bankruptcy, and criminal, admiralty, and civil actions.

Income Tax Records. Post-Civil War income tax records relating to business and corporate taxes for the following district offices are available: Albany, 1910–1917; Buffalo, 1862–1917; Lower Manhattan (Second Collection District), 1910–1917; Lower Manhattan (Third District), 1913–1917; Newark, 1917; Syracuse, 1883–1917. In addition, the Archives has Assessment Lists for New York State, 1862–1873, and New Jersey, 1868–1873.

Internal Revenue Service (IRS) Employees. Registers of individuals employed by the IRS in Brooklyn, 1885–1919, and Buffalo, NY, 1875–1919, are available. These include employee name, position title, compensation, date of appointment, date and reason for termination of service, place and year of birth, and information concerning the employee's prior civil and military service.

Chinese Re-entry Permits. Case files (RG 85), 1880s–1944, of some 30,000 Chinese immigrants who applied for reentry permits under the Chinese Exclusion Acts of 1882 and 1902 are located here. The case files include correspondence, reports, transcripts of interrogations, and testimony, as well as the original identification forms issued by the Immigration and Naturalization Service.

Reprinted from *Genealogical Resources in the New York Metropolitan Area.*

■ NEW YORK PUBLIC LIBRARY

Central Research Library
General Research Division
Fifth Avenue at 42nd Street
New York, New York 10018

The New York Public Library (NYPL) was established in 1895 and moved into its current location on 42nd Street in 1911. Today, the library consists of the Central Research Library, the Performing Arts Research Center at Lincoln Center, the Schomburg

Center for Research in Black Culture, and the Annex, as well as the branch libraries. The Central Research Library includes eight divisions and five special collections including the Jewish Division, the Map Division, the Miriam and Ira Wallach Division of Arts, Prints, and Photographs, the Slavic and Baltic Division, the U.S. History, Local History, and Genealogy Division, and the Microforms Division. The General Research Division, with over 2,000,000 volumes in the arts and humanities, administers the Public Catalog Room, the Main Reading Room, the DeWitt Wallace Periodical Room, and the Astor Hall Information Desk of the Central Research Library.

The General Research Division is responsible for more than one-half the total book holdings of the research libraries. The Main Reading Room houses over 36,000 books on open shelves. Items of interest to genealogists include:

1. *Biographies:* The collection is rich in collective and individual biographies, as well as biographical dictionaries. These include [NYPL classmarks (call numbers) are indicated in parentheses]:
   Biography and Genealogy Master Index. 17 vols., 1981–1988. (*R-AA; South Hall, east wall 7)
   Contemporary Authors. 123 vols., 1964–1988. (*R-AB; South Hall, east wall 11–12)
   Dictionary of Scientific Biography. 16 vols, 1970–1980. (*R-AB; South Hall, east wall 12–14)
   Dictionary of Literary Biography. 71 vols., 1978–1986. (*R-AA; South Hall, east wall 12–13)
   The New York Times Index. September 1851–0000. (*R-*A). *Personal Name Index to the New York Times Index, 1851–1974* and supplement, *1975–1984.* (*R-*A 80-3601; North Hall, east wall 164–167)
2. *Telephone directories:* Current phone directories for most United States cities are available in paper copy in the North Hall. Current foreign directories, such as Paris, Great Britain, and Germany, may be ordered from the stacks.
3. *Cole Directory,* a reverse directory by address and by phone number, is available from 1970/1971 to the present for Suffolk County; from 1971 for Nassau County and for all New York City counties; and from 1973 for Westchester and Putnam counties. [Current year, South Hall, east wall 1; earlier years, Stack 7 (County)]
4. *Foreign City Directories* such as the *Berliner Address Book,* 1896–1939 [BAZ+]; *The Post Office London Directory,* 1799–1967 (gaps), and *Kelly's Post Office London Business Directory,* 1968–1984. [CO (London Post Office Directory)] See also later under "U.S. History, Local History, and Genealogy Division and Microforms Division" for additional London City Directories on microfilm. The current *Kelly's London Business Directory* is available in the Economic and Public Affairs Division of the Library.
5. *Voter Registration Lists,* New York City, include *List of Enrolled Voters,* 1899–1975 (missing: 1915, all boroughs; 1919–1922, Manhattan) (*SYA+); and *Registry of Voters,* 1881–1903 (*SYA+).

U.S. History, Local History, and Genealogy Division, and Microforms Division

Fifth Avenue at 42nd Street
Rooms 315N and 315M
New York, New York 10018
(212) 930-0828 (Genealogy)
(212) 930-0838 (Microforms)

The Genealogy Division has a vast collection of materials of interest to genealogists. Some of the materials, on microfilm or microfiche, are in the adjacent Microforms Division. The Information Desk in the Genealogy Division can advise researchers on these materials. The following listing includes key holdings of both divisions. Materials on microfilm are so noted. (NYPL classmark is indicated in parentheses).

1. *U.S. Census* (microfilm)
   New York State, New Jersey, and Connecticut, 1790–1880
   New York State only, 1900 (*ZI-263) and 1910 (*ZI-349)
2. *New York State Census* (microfilm)
   1855 census, 41 counties. Among those missing are Kings (Brooklyn), Queens, Westchester, and Dutchess Counties. (*ZAN-G124)
3. *Canadian Census* (microfilm)
   1871 (*ZI-353)
4. *City Directories*—New York City (all on microfilm)
   New York City Directories (generally Manhattan and parts of the Bronx), 1786–1933/1934
   Brooklyn City Directories, 1796, 1802/1803, 1811/1812, 1822–1826, 1829–1910, 1912/1913, 1933/1934
   Trow's Directory for Queens, 1898, 1912
   Polk's New York City Directory, Boroughs of Queens and Richmond, 1933/4
   Webb's Consolidated Directory of the North and South Shores of Staten Island, 1886, 1888, 1890/1891, 1892/1893
   Standard Directory of Richmond County, 1895/1896
   Trow's Business and Residential Directory of the Borough of Richmond, City of New York, 1898
   Standard Directory of Richmond Borough, 2906
   Note: There are two reverse New York City Directories arranged by street addresses: 1812 (Reel A6) and 1851 (Reel A14).
5. *Other City Directories* (microfilm/microfiche)
   The Microforms Division has City Directories for about 300 major U.S. cities, 1752–1860 (*XMG-156) and 1861–1935 (*ZAN-G67); and London City Directories from the Guild Hall Library, 1677–1855 (gaps) (*ZAN-G68)
   See also earlier under "Central Research Library, General Research Division" for additional foreign City Directories and the Annex for additional U.S. and Canadian City Directories.
6. *Telephone Directories* (microfilm/microfiche)

	White Pages	Yellow Pages
Manhattan	1878–1924	–
Manhattan (includes Bronx)	1924–1928	1928
Manhattan	1929–current	1929–1976/77
Bronx	1929–current	1931–1976/77

Brooklyn, Queens, SI	1924–1928/29	–
Brooklyn	1929–current	1944–1976/77
Queens	1927–current	1957–1976/77
Staten Island	1927/28–current	(Combined with White Pages)
Rockaway (Queens)	1928–1976	(Combined with White Pages)
Rockaway (Queens) and 5 Towns	1977	(Combined with White Pages)
Nassau	1913–current	1957–1976/77
Suffolk	1928–current	1957–1976/77
Suffolk, Nassau, Queens	1910–1947	–

The Microforms Division has a complete set of Phonefiche for telephone books around the country. Phonefiche copies start in 1976, but not all cities were included from the start. See earlier under "Central Research Library, General Research Division" for

paper copies of current telephone directories.

The New York Public Library Annex has pre-1976 telephone directories in paper copy for cities other than those in the New York City area.

7. *Address Telephone Directories for NYC* (microfilm)

Bronx, Brooklyn, Manhattan, Queens	1929–1980, 1986
Staten Island	1952–1980, 1982, 1986
Westchester (Southern)	1956–1980, 1986

See earlier under "Central Research Library, General Research Division" for additional address directories (*Cole Directory*).

8. *New York City Vital Records*
   Records (microfilm)
   Deaths (Manhattan only), 1798–1865
   (*ZI-201)
   Indexes
   The Library has the New York City Health Department indexes spanning the following years:

Births	August 1888–1982
Deaths	August 1888–1982
Marriages (grooms)	August 1888–1937

Brooklyn, Queens and Staten Island (Richmond) are not included until 1898 in the birth, marriage, and death indexes. Beginning in 1937 all boroughs of New York City are merged in one alphabetical listing. Prior to that year, separate listings (or volumes) were made for each borough. Marriage index volumes, 1911–1937, are on open shelves inside the entrance of the Genealogy Division.

Because of the aging condition of the indexes,

City directory of Albany, New York, 1913.

Certificate of Death provided by the Bureau of Vital Records, Department of Health, City of New York. Morris Adnopoz, born 1870 Russia, died April 6, 1937, Brooklyn, New York.

the library is in the process of microfilming them. The following are on microfilm or microfiche:

Births   August 1888–1915, 1922 (*ZI-328), 1898–1975 (Fiche, *XMG-1108)
Deaths   August 1888–1945 (*ZI-348)
Marriages August 1888–1910, 1913–1914, 1921, 1928 (*ZI-329)

The birth indexes, 1898–1909 (microfiche), are arranged according to the New York City Health Department Soundex system. The copies on microfilm are arranged in alphabetical order. This Soundex system was used again from 1943 to 1945 in both the microfiche and paper copies of the birth indexes. See pp. 31–33 for an explanation of this system.

The library will withdraw paper indexes from circulation for microfilming as necessary. Researchers should check in advance on the availability of those volumes not yet microfilmed.

9. *Marriage Announcements*
Marriages Taken from the Brooklyn Eagle (Index), October 27, 1841 to December 31, 1880. (APRN) (On open shelf)
New York Evening Post Marriages (Index), November 16, 1801 to December 31, 1890. (APRN) (On open shelf)
New York Marriage Bonds 1753–1783, by Dr. Kenneth Scott, 1972. (APRN 78-3023)
Names of Persons for Whom Marriage Licenses Were Issued ... Previous to 1784, New York State. (*R-APR New York State) (On open shelf)
Index to Marriages and Deaths in the New York Herald, 1835–1855, by James P. Maher, 1987. (APR)

10. *Obituaries*
New York Evening Post, New York City, Deaths (Index), November 16, 1801 to December 31, 1890, by Gertrude A. Barber, 1933–1947. (APRN) (On open shelf)
Deaths Taken from the Brooklyn Eagle (Index), October 27, 1841 to December 31, 1880, by Gertrude A. Barber, 1936–1966. (APRN) (On open shelf)
The New York Times Obituaries Index: 1858–1978. 2 vols. (At the Information Desk)
Boston Evening Transcript. The Index to Obituaries, 1875–1899, 1900–1930 (APK+)
New York Tribune. Obituaries 1875–1897 (APK+) (At the Information Desk).

11. *Cemeteries*
Fairchild Cemetery Manual, 1910 (*ZI-266)
Directory of United States Cemeteries, Vol. I only, 1974 (APK 75-1060)
Local Cemeteries in New York (APM 84-92)

12. *Wills and Administrations—Abstracts and Indexes*
Manhattan
New York Historical Society. *Abstracts of Wills on File in the Surrogate's Office, City of New York, 1665–1800.* 17 vols. + index. [APRN (New York)]
Sawyer, Ray C. and G. A. Barber. *Abstracts of New York County Wills, 1801–1856.* 19 vols. [APRN (New York)]
Sawyer, Ray C. *Index of Wills for NY County, NY, from 1851–1875 inclusive.* NY, 1950–51. (APRN)
Barber, Gertrude A. *Index of the Letters of Administration filed in NY County from 1743–1875.* NY, 1950–51. (APRN)
Brooklyn
Thomas, Milton H. and C. Shepard. *Index to the Wills, Administrations, Guardianships of Kings County, NY, 1650–1850.* Washington, DC, 1926. [APR (Kings County)]
Barber, G.A. *Index of Wills Probated in Kings County, NY Jan. 1, 1850–Dec. 31, 1890.* 3 vols. (typescript, 1949) [APR (Kings County)]
Queens
Surrogate's Court Records in the Office of the County Clerk, Jamaica, Long Island, NY—1680–1781. Wills and administrations, guardians, and inventories. Brooklyn, 1918. [APR (Queens County)]
Queens County, NY Surrogate Records at Jamaica, NY—1787–1835. Brooklyn, 1905–1918. [APR (Queens County)]

13. *Passenger Records and Indexes*
Passenger lists of vessels arriving at New York harbor from 1820 to April 5, 1906. These lists are arranged in order of arrival. (*ZI-131)
Indexes: 1820–1846 (*ZI-80); June 16, 1897 to June 30, 1902 (*ZI-333), and July 1902 to December 1943 (*ZI-333A). There is no name index from 1846 to June 15, 1897.
German Immigrants: Lists of Passengers Bound from Bremen to New York, compiled by Gary J. Zimmerman and Marion Wolfert, 1985–. (Lists only passengers with places of origin.) Vol. 1, 1847–1854. (APK 85-3230) Vol. 2, 1855–1862 and Vol. 3, 1863–1867 are on order.
Germans to America: Lists of Passengers Arriving at U.S. Ports, 1850–1855, edited by Ira A. Glazier and P. William Filby, 1988. (Passenger lists are derived from original ship manifest schedules and are published in their entirety in chronological order of arrival date at United States East Coast ports. The

Certificate and Record of Marriage, City of New York, April 13, 1905. Alexander Rabkin and Miriam (Marrie) Adnopoz.

determining factor for inclusion of a particular list is the presence of 80% or more passengers with German surnames.) Of the 10 volumes planned, Vol. 1, Jan. 2, 1850 to May 23, 1851 and Vol. 2, May 24, 1851 to June 1852, have been issued and are on order.

The library has the following lists of vessels to assist the researcher in locating a passenger record:

Register of Vessels Arriving at the Port of New York from Foreign Ports, 1789–1919. (microfilm) (*ZI-391)

Morton Allan Directory of European Passenger Steamship Arrivals for the years 1890–1930 for the Port of New York, and 1904–1926 for the Ports of Philadelphia, Boston and Baltimore. (79-906, 80-974) (At the Genealogy Division Information Desk)

14. *Veterans* (microfilm)

Revolutionary War Pension and Bounty Warrant files (*ZI-132)

1812 War Pension Index (*ZI-234)

Mexican War Pension Index (*ZI-388)

Civil War Veterans—index to the Compiled Service records of the Volunteer Union Soldiers who served in Organizations from the State of New York. (*ZI-411)

For additional resources, consult "Selected Military Sources for United States Genealogy: Rosters, Regimental Histories and Handbooks—Pre-World War II," a bibliography compiled by Asa Rubenstein. (At the Genealogy Division Information Desk)

15. *Name Indexes*

American Genealogical Biographical Index [name index to many genealogies, mostly non-Jewish]. (APG) (On open shelf)

British Biographical Archive. Biographical sketches in one alphabetical listing of 324 English-language biographical reference works published between 1601 and 1929. (Fiche, *XM-16,823)

Daughters of the American Revolution, New York Master Index—Genealogical Records [APRA]. Most of the 600-volume set is available either in hard copy or microfilm.

Dau's NY Blue Book. 1907–1935 (gaps). Lists name, address and household members of "prominent" New Yorkers (includes many Jewish families). (Film, *ZAN-4605)

International Genealogical Index (IGI) published by the Genealogical Department of the Church of Jesus Christ of Latter-Day Saints, Salt Lake City, 1988. Available in paper copy (*XMG-1041+) or microfiche (*XMG-1041)

Family Registry—Index published by the Genealogical Department of the Church of Jesus Christ of Latter-Day Saints, Salt Lake City, 1984. (Fiche *XMG-1117)

The *International Genealogical Index* and *Family Registry* microfiche are located in file drawers near the three microfiche readers in the Genealogy Division.

16. *Genealogy Guides*

The library has an extensive collection of "how-to" books. Among those available on open shelves or at the Genealogy Division Information Desk are:

Bailey, Rosalie Fellows. *Guide to Genealogical and Biographical Sources for NYC (Manhattan) 1783–1898.* New York, 1954. (APRN)

Beard, Timothy F. and Denise Demong. *How to Find Your Family Roots.* New York, 1977. (APB 78-817)

Eakle, Arlene and Johni Cerny. *The Source: A Guidebook of American Genealogy.* Salt Lake City, 1984. (APB 84-1480)

Everton, George B. *The Handy Book for Genealogists, 1981.* (APB 82092)

Gnacinski, Jan and Len. *Polish and Proud: Your Polish Ancestry.* Wisconsin, 1979. (APB 80-1324)

Hoff, Henry B. "Research in New York Downstate," *Tree Talks,* March 1982. (APR New York)

Kronman, Barbara. *Guide to NYC Public Records.* New York, 1984 (3rd edition). (IRGV 84-2902)

Kurzweil, Arthur. *From Generation to Generation.* New York, 1980. (APB 80-3575)

Rottenberg, Dan. *Finding Our Fathers.* New York, 1977. (APB 77-1002)

Smith, Clifford N. and Anna P.C. Smith. *Encyclopedia of German–American Genealogical Research.* New York, 1976. (ATA 80-950)

Smith, Jessie C. *Ethnic Genealogy; A Research Guide.* Westport, CT, 1983. (APB 84-208)

United States Works Progress Administration. *Guide to Vital Statistics in the City of New York, Church records.* [Location of church records.] New York, 1942. (APRN)

Wellauer, Maralyn. *Tracing Your Polish Roots.* Wisconsin, 1979. (APB 80-800)

Wellauer, Maralyn. *Tracing Your German Roots.* Wisconsin, 1978. (APB 80-1696)

17. *Photo Collections—NYC*

Photographic Views of New York City 1870s to 1970s (microfiche). The collection had its origins in the 1920s and includes some 54,000 photos of streets and buildings in New York City. Each photo is accompanied by a description (street, cross street, date, direction of photo, and name of building, if known). This collection is available both in the Genealogy Division and the Microforms Division.

Lloyd Acker Collection—Views of New York City buildings from 1935 to 1975 by Lloyd Acker, a commercial photographer who photographed specific buildings and indexed them by address. Photos are not dated. (*ZI-300)

Eugene Armbruster Collection of Long Island photographs, 1890s–1930s (being organized).

Check with the librarian at the Genealogy Division Information Desk for a complete listing of photograph collections that may be of interest to genealogists.

18. *Newspapers* (microfilm)

New York Times
September 18, 1851 to present

New York Post
May 1967 to present

World Journal Tribune
September 1966 to May 1967

19. *Other:* In addition to the above, the Genealogy Division has an extensive collection of genealogical periodicals, newsletters, family histories, and published genealogies, and county, town, and village histories.

Jewish Division

The Jewish Division has one of the great collections of Judaica in the world. It was established in 1897, just two years after the formation of the library. Today, the division contains some 227,000 books, microfilms, manuscripts, newspapers, and periodicals from all over the world. The collection includes 40 15th-century works and over 1,500 16th-century works.

Below are items of interest to genealogists (NYPL classmark is indicated in parentheses).

1. *Census.* Jews in Alsace, 1784: *Dénombrement Générale des Juifs* (*PXP+ 80-4713).
2. *Rabbinic Responsa.* These books of answers provided by rabbis to questions on halakhic matters usually make some reference to the rabbi's lineage on the first page or may have an introduction that was added posthumously, providing some bibliographical information.
3. *Newspapers.* An extensive collection of periodicals printed in Europe and America in the last two centuries, including:

The Jewish Daily Forward (New York, Yiddish), 1887–present (complete collection) (*ZAN-*P142)

The Day (New York, Yiddish), 1914–1967 (*ZY-*P2)

Freie Arbeiter Stimme (New York, Yiddish), 1890–1892, 1899–1952, 1963–1977 (*ZAN-*P183)

4. *Marriage Records.* 20 Italian ketubot from the 17th and 18th centuries.
5. *Holocaust Sources.* The second largest collection of Yizkor books in New York City, including *Yad Vashem Archives of the Destruction: A Photographic Record of the Holocaust* (microfiche; *XMH-2067).
6. *Community History.* Books on Jewish communities around the world.
7. *Gravestone Inscriptions*

De Sola Pool, David. *Portraits Etched in Stone: Early Jewish Settlers 1682–1831.* New York, 1951. [*PXY]

Hock, Simon. *Mishpahat KK Prague.* Pressburg, 1892. [*PXT]

Klein, Samuel. *Juedisch-Palaestinisches Corpus Inscriptionum* [Tombstones in Palestine]. Hildesheim, 1974. [*PWN 72-1014]

Hebrew Subscription Lists

With an Index to 8,767 Jewish Communities in Europe and North Africa

By

BERL KAGAN

THE LIBRARY
OF
THE JEWISH THEOLOGICAL SEMINARY OF AMERICA
AND
KTAV PUBLISHING HOUSE, Inc.
NEW YORK—1975

Hebrew Subscription Lists, by Berl Kagan, is an index to subscription lists appearing in thousands of books published in Europe. Included is an index to 8,767 Jewish communities.

Sample listing from *Hebrew Subscription Lists*.

Kober, Adolf. *Jewish Monuments of the Middle Ages in Germany* [110 tombstone inscriptions from Speyer, Cologne, Nuremberg and Worms 1085-c. 1428]. New York, 1944–1945. [*PBL—American Academy for Jewish Research Proceedings, Vols. 14–15]

Molho, Michael. *Matsevot bet ha-olamim shel yehude Thessalonika* [Tombstones in Thessalonika]. Tel Aviv, 1974. [*PWN 78-5700]

Weiss, Izak. *Sefer avne bet ha-yotser* [Tombstones in Bratislava]. Jerusalem, 1970. [*PWN 75-759]

8. *Biographies and Genealogies*
An extensive collection of biographical texts and genealogies such as:

Azulai, Joseph D. *Shem ha-gedolim ha-shalem* [An encyclopedia of 1300 rabbis in the 18th century]. Jerusalem, 1905. [*PWR]

Bader, Gershon. *Medinah ve-hakhamehah* [Biographies of leading Jews in Galicia]. New York, 1934. [*PWR]

Balaban, Majer. *Di yidn-shtot Lublin* [The Jews of Lublin]. Buenos Aires, 1947. [*PWZ]

Chones, Shimon. *Toldot ha-poskim* [Rabbinic authorities and their works]. Warsaw, 1921. [*PWR]

Cohen, Israel. *Vilna*. Philadelphia, 1943. [*PWZ]

Dembitzer, Chaim. *Kelilat yofi* [Rabbis of Cracow and Lwow]. Cracow, 1888. [*PWR]

Eisenstadt, Ben Zion. *Dor rabanav ve-sofrav* [Generations of Rabbis and Authors]. Warsaw, 1895–1905. [*PWR]

Eisenstadt, Ben Zion. *Dorot ha-aharonim* [Recent Generations]. New York, 1913, Brooklyn, 1936–1941. [*PWR]

Eisenstadt, Ben Zion. *Hakhme Yisrael be-Amerikah* [Israel's Scholars in America]. New York. 1903. [*PWR]

Federbusch, Simon. *Hokhmat Yisrael be-ma'arav Eyropah* [Science of Judaism in Western Europe]. Jerusalem, 1958–1965. [*PWR]

Frumkin, Arieh L. *Sefer toldot hakhme Yerushalayim*. Jerusalem, 1910. [*PWR]

Ghirondi, Mordechai and Ch. Nepi. *Toldot gedole Yisrael u-geone Italyah* [History of the Scholars of Israel and the Sages of Italy] and *Zekher tsadikim le-verakhah*. Trieste, 1853. [*PWR]

Halachmi, David. *Hakhme Yisrael* [Biographies from the 13th to 20th century]. Tel Aviv, 1958. [*PWR]

Halperin, Raphael. *Atlas ets hayim* [Encyclopedia of rabbis and Jewish scholars]. 14 vols. published of 20 projected. Tel Aviv, 1978–. [uncataloged]

Horodetzky, Samuel. *Keren Shlomo* [Solomon Luria]. Drohobycz, 1896. [*PWZ]

Lifschutz, Arieh L. *Avot atarah le-banim* [Katzenellenbogen, Wahl, Lifschutz, and related families]. Warsaw, 1927. [*PWZ 80-2207]

Schwartz, Sigmund. *Shem ha-gedolim le-gedole Hungaryah* [Encyclopedia of Hungarian Sages]. Brooklyn, 1959. [*PWR]

Stern, Abraham. *Sefer melitse esh* [2000 medieval and modern rabbis and scholars]. Jerusalem, 1974. [*PWR 77-3833]

Unger, Menashe. *Admorim she-nispu be-shoah* [Biographies of rabbis who perished in the Holocaust]. Jerusalem, 1969. (Hebrew) [*PWR]. Also in Yiddish as *Sefer Kedoshim*. New York, 1967. [*PWR]

Walden, Aaron. *Shem ha-gedolim he-hadash* [An encyclopedia of rabbis in the 19th century]. Warsaw, 1879. [*PWR]

Wininger, Salomon. *Grosse Juedische National-Biographie* [An international biographical dictionary of Jews from the Middle Ages to the 20th century]. Czernowitz, 1925–1936. [*PWR]

For a list of additional biographical books, many of which are in the collection of the Jewish Division, see *Toledot*, Vol. 4, No. 3, pp. 3–15, "Jewish Genealogical Materials in the Library of Congress" by Ellen Murphy; or David Einsiedler, "Rabbinic Genealogy Sources: A Bibliography by Type," printed for Jewish Genealogical Society Seminars, Israel and Los Angeles.

9. *Name Indexes*
Gorr, Shmuel, joint venture with Gary Mokotoff. *Palestine Gazette Name Changes, 1921–1948* [List of 27,000 Jews whose name changes were published in the *Palestine Gazette*]. 1984. [microfiche; uncataloged]

Kaganoff, Benzion. *A Dictionary of Jewish Names and Their History*. New York, 1977. [*P-*PWP 79-67]

Kaufman, Isidore. *American Jews in World War II: The Story of 550,000 Fighters for Freedom* [Lists Jewish soldiers who died in their country's service or who received awards/recognition of valor]. 2 vols., New York, 1947. [*PXY]

Singerman, Robert. *Jewish and Hebrew Onomastics: A Bibliography*. New York, 1977. [*PCL 77-3586]

Zubatsky, David S. and Irwin M. Berent. *Jewish Genealogy: A Source Book of Family Histories and Genealogies*. New York, 1984. [*PWO 85-614]

Map Division

The Map Division has the most extensive collection in New York City of gazetteers and maps (including pre-19th century maps and world atlases), produced in both the United States and Europe, dating from the 1800s through the present. The collection includes 375,000 maps and 14,000 atlases and books.

Gazetteers. *U.S. Board on Geographic Names Gazetteer.* Despite the post-World War II dates, these gazetteers are particularly useful for locating very small towns in Poland and the U.S.S.R. that are thought not to exist since the war. They provide latitude and longitude for every place name and also indicate place name changes in such countries as:

Austria, 1962
Czechoslovakia, 1955
East Germany, 1959
France, 1964
Hungary, 1961
Italy, 1956
Poland, 1955
Romania, 1960
Syria, 1983
U.S.S.R., 1970
West Germany, 1960

Ritters Geographisch-Statistisches Lexikon. 1874 (1983 reprint), 1905, 1906, and 1910 (in German).

Columbia Lippincott Gazetteer of the World. 1880, 1898, 1906, 1952, and 1960.

Defense Mapping Agency/Army Map Service— *Index to Names on AMS 1:250,000 Map of Eastern Europe* (Series N501). Provides latitude and longitude.

Austria–Hungary 1913 Index. A detailed place name index, based on *Stieler's Hand Atlas,* is kept at the reference desk. The accompanying map is available.

Shtetl Finder Gazetteer. A copy is also found in the Jewish Division.

Rand McNally Commercial Atlas. This has the most detailed place name index for the United States. It lists all communities, even those with zero population. It is published annually, and the Map Division has back editions since the 1880s. While not all editions are available, there is at least one per decade, usually for the year of (or following) the census, in order to provide accurate population data.

Bartholomew Gazetteer of the British Isles. This place name index that describes each location is available for 1887, 1893, 1943, 1955, and 1970.

The London Times Atlas of the World. The latest edition of this classic British atlas, 1985, with its valuable A-to-Z gazetteer (with latitudes and longitudes) is available along with some back editions starting in 1895 (gaps).

In addition to the gazetteers in the Map Division, the Slavic and Baltic Division (Room 217) has the 15-volume *Slownik Geograficzny* (geographical dictionary), which provides detailed late-19th-century information on most East European communities (in Polish); and the Jewish Division has resources in addition to the *Shtetl Finder.*

Maps. Greater New York area—road maps, national atlases, New York City geographical maps from the 1600s to date, and New York City property maps. These include maps such as Sanborn Fire Insurance, Sanborn Land Books, E. Belcher Hyde, Bromley or Perris for:

Bronx—1870s to 1959, 1969, 1987
Brooklyn—1885–1929, 1988
Manhattan—1850 to present
Queens—1901–1904, 1928–1973, 1988
Staten Island—1874–1917

Sanborn Property maps for cities in Connecticut, New Jersey, and New York are available on microfilm from the 1880s through the 1950s.

New York (*City*) *Boroughs,* tax maps and ownership information, indexed three ways—by street address, block and lot number, and alphabetically by owner's name, produced by Real Estate Data, Inc. (REDI), on microfiche for Brooklyn, the Bronx, Queens, and Staten Island, 1987 and 1988 (*XLK 88-4531).

The New York Public Library, Economic and Public Affairs Division (room 228), has a paper copy of the *Real Estate Owner's Directory of Manhattan* issued by REDI.

United States and Canada—road maps, national atlases. The Map Division maintains an extensive historical file of maps of all 50 states going back to the 1700s as well as an extensive Canadian collection.

Military Surveys of Europe—detailed surveys from the mid-19th century to the present.

1:250,000 AMS (Army Map Service) for Eastern Europe (N501 Series) and Western Europe (M501 Series)

1:200,000 set for Central Europe

1:100,000 AMS series for Poland and Germany (nearly complete set)

1:75,000 AMS series for Austria-Hungary

Generally complete map sets for the Soviet Union on scales greater than 1:250,000

Country Map Files. The division has extensive files of general maps for individual countries during different time frames. These are particularly good for reviewing a country's borders and assessing the geopolitics during particular historic eras.

Stieler's Hand Atlas. Several editions of this world atlas are available. It has good coverage of Europe, particularly in the 19th century. There is a detailed place name index. German spellings are used throughout.

Austria–Hungary 1913 map—a large, detailed map of this region has been reproduced from *Stieler's* and is kept at the reference desk. A place name index in book form is also available.

Slavic and Baltic Division

The Slavic and Baltic Division (formerly the Slavonic Division) has over 300,000 books and other materials in 12 Slavic and Baltic languages. No Estonian, Hungarian, Romanian, or Albanian materials are kept here, since these belong to other language groups. English- and German-language materials on Slavic and East European studies can be found in the General Division (Main Reading Room). Judaica in the Slavic languages are usually found in the Jewish Division. Books with classmarks beginning with [*R] can be found on open shelves. The following are some of the resources of interest to genealogists in this division:

1. *Guides to Archives/Libraries*
   Cracow Archiwum Aktow Dawnych Miasta Krakowa (Catalog of the Krakow Archive). 1907–1915. (Polish) (*QR)
   Grant, Steven and John H. Brown. *The Russian Empire and Soviet Union: A Guide to Manuscripts and Archival Material in the US.* 1981. (*R-Slav.Div. 83-43)
   Grimsted, Patricia. *Archives and Manuscript Repositories in the USSR.* 3 vols., 1976–. These volumes cover Moscow and Leningrad; Estonia, Latvia, Lithuania, and Byelorussia; Ukraine and Moldavia. These books provide geographic place names as well as listings of the holdings of various archives. (*R-Slav.Div. 82-829, 82-830, 82-1212)
   Grossman, Iu. *Spravochnik nauchnogo rabotnika* (Handbook for Scholars). 1979. Lists the archives of the USSR with addresses. (Russian) (*R-Slav.Div. 84-2615)
   Lewanski, Richard C. *Guide to Polish Libraries and Archives.* 1974. (Desk-Slav.Div. 83-1169)
   Magocsi, Paul R. *Ucrainica at the University of Toronto Library: A Catalogue of Holdings.* 1983. 2 vols. A guide to Ukrainian material at the University of Toronto Library. (Desk-Slav.Div. 86-1866)
   Mehr, Kahile B. and Daniel M. Schlyter. *Sources for Genealogical Research in the Soviet Union.* 1983. (uncataloged)

Moskva. 1962. Address book of Russian institutions. (Russian) (*R-Slav.Div.)

Odessa: Tzentral'na Naukova Biblioteka (Odessa Public Library Catalog). 1927–29. (*QGAA)

Sturm, Rudolf. *Czechoslovakia, A Bibliographic Guide*. 1967. (F-11/5001)

2. *Gazetteers and Related Works*

Atlas, U.S.S.R., 1969. Includes maps from 1:1,500,000. (*R-Slav.Div.)

Horecky, Paul L. *East Central and Southeast Europe*. 1976. A guide to basic publications about each country. (Desk-Slav.Div. 78-139)

Akademie der Wissenschaften und der Literatur. *Russisches Geographisches Namenbuch*. 10 vols., 1962–78. A German-language gazetteer of the Russian Empire. Place names are in Cyrillic script. (*R-Slav.Div.)

Semionov-Tyan-Shanski, Piotr. *Geografichesko Statisticheskii Slovar' Rossiiskoi Imperii* (Geographic Dictionary). 5 vols., 1863–1885. (Russian) (*R-Slav.Div.)

Slownik Geograficzny. 1900. A 16-volume geographical dictionary which provides detailed late 19th-century information on most East European communities. (Polish) (*R-Slav.Div. 78-445)

3. *Newspapers*

Karlowich, Robert. *Russian Language Periodical Press in New York City from 1880–1914*. 1981. (English) (Desk-Slav.Div.)

4. *Census*

Tzentralnyi Statisticheskii Komitet. *Obshchii svod, 1–2*. 2 vols., 1897. This is a statistical summary of the 1897 census of the Russian Empire by region/city. (Russian-French) [*QB (Russian)]. Of particular interest are the tables which provide by Oblast/City, the following:

Table IV, religion of the population;
Table XI, number of cemeteries by religion; and,
Table XII, number of synagogues and churches.

5. *Cemetery Lists*

Nicholas, Grand Duke of Russia. *Moskovskii Nekropol* [Tombstone Lists Moscow Area]. Non-Jewish; Pre-Russian Revolution. 1907–1908. (*QE)

6. *Name Indexes*

Sack, Sallyann and Suzan F. Wynne. *The Russian Consular Records Index and Catalog*. 1987. (*R-Slav.Div. 87-4638)

Unbegaun, Boris O. *Russian Surnames*. 1972. (*R-Slav.Div. 85-4708)

7. *Encyclopedias*

Evreiskaia Entsiklopediia (Russian Jewish Encyclopedia). 16 vols., St. Petersburg, 1906–1913. (*QAC).

Brockhaus, F.A. and I.A. Efron, eds. *Novyi Entsiklopedicheskii Slovar* [New Encyclopedia—lists cities and shtetlach, and, in some cases, the Jewish population as of the 1897 census]. 1904. (Russian) (*QAC)

8. *City Directories* (Russian Business Directories) A sample of available directories which list names of individuals are those for:

Ekaterinoslav, 1912
Gomel, 1908

Moscow, 1915, 1929
Odessa Gubernia, 1926, 1927
Omsk, 1911
Russia, 1899, 1903, 1911/12
St. Petersburg/Leningrad, 1894–1935 (gaps)
Saratov, 1911
Siberia, 1924
Southwestern Region (Kiev, Podolsk, and Volinsk Gubernia), 1913

In addition, the division has business and organization directories for various localities.

1. *Dictionaries* (on open shelf)
This Division has dictionaries of all Slavic and Baltic languages (Russian, Polish, Ukrainian, Bulgarian, Czech, Lithuanian and Latvian) to English.

Reprinted form *Genealogical Resources in the New York Metropolitan Area*.

■ YESHIVA UNIVERSITY

Archives

Yeshiva University
500 West 185th Street
New York, New York 10033
(212) 960-5451

The Archives (located in Room 405, 2520 Amsterdam Avenue) consist of 540 linear feet of records comprising some 240 collections of mostly Orthodox Jewish institutions and individuals. These are primarily organizational records, letters, memoirs, newspaper clippings, genealogies, and photographs. The major collections of interest to genealogists are described below. Researchers should consult with the archivist to determine whether other collections have documents related to their family histories or genealogy:

The Central Relief Committee Collection (1914–1959). Records, 1914–1918, include the following information: yeshivoth in interwar Europe; correspondence concerning requests to locate missing relatives, 1914–1916 (Boxes 10, 14); correspondence requesting funds for transportation of relatives from Palestine to the United States, 1916–1917 (Box 13); lists of Palestine (Boxes 15–19) and Russian remittances, 1916 (Box 25); and general correspondence with individuals (Boxes 30–40).

Records, 1919–1929, contain questionnaires filled out by yeshivoth in Eastern and Central Europe. Most are from Poland but Austria, Czechoslovakia, Romania, Germany, Hungary, Yugoslavia, the Baltic states, and Soviet Union are also covered. The collection includes mostly institutional information. Some lists of students are included.

Mordechai Bernstein Collection, 1605–1965. Includes original documents of 58 Jewish communities in Germany and photocopies of documents of thirty-eight Jewish communities. The earliest original document includes five records from the rabbinical court in Pappenheim, 1605–1619, on questions of heritage. Also included are a handful of marriage contracts, deeds of divorce, and court records from such communities as Brakel, Castell, Darmstadt, Eppendorf, Lübeck, Petershagen, Mülhausen, Warburg, and Zinnwald. The documents include the following: general meetings of the Jewish community of Esslingen on the Neckar (in Judeo-German), 1816–1825; a 1819–1843 volume of the burial society of Laupheim; excerpts of records of charitable endowments to the Jewish community of Laupheim, 1869–1872 (in German); a volume containing handwritten entries of circumcisions performed in an unidentified city, 1772–1796, and in Königsberg, 1852–1875; an account book of a burial society in Altenmuhr, 1845–1870, and a list of the Jewish residents of Fulda before 1933, with their location after 1945; documents regarding the Jewish cemetery and living in Schiltz, 1935–1947; and a list of the Jewish residents of Stuttgart, 1940–1941.

Includes the following: photocopies of the Memorbücher from Koblenz, 1610–1850, and from Ehrenbreitstein, 1703–1883; photocopies of community records from Mikulow (Nikolsburg) in Moravia, 18th century; the records of a burial society in Prague, 1785–1870; and photographs of buildings, cemeteries, and tombstones in over fifty Jewish communities in Germany, Czechoslovakia, Italy, and Poland. This subseries contains a folder of transcriptions of the Hebrew text of tombstones in the Jewish cemetery of Sinsheim, 1891–1938.

Of note, this collection includes 115 inventories of Jewish records in Staatsarchivs in the following German communities:

Amberg	Koblenz (Coblenz)
Amorbach	Landshut
Ansbach	Ludwigsburg
Assenheim	Lübeck
Bamberg	Marburg an der Lahn
Birsteien	Memmingen
Braunschweig	Munich
Castel	Neuburg
Coburg	Neuenstein
Darmstadt	Neumarkt (Oberpfalz)
Donaüschingen	Neuwied
Düsseldorf	Nuremberg
Esslingen	Oberehrenbreitstein
Floss	Pappenheim
Frankfurt	Regensburg
Friedberg	Reugland
Fürstenberg	Reutlingen
Göttingen	Schweinfurt
Gunzenhausen	Sigmaringen
Hamburg	Speyer
Hameln	Stuttgart
Hannover	Weikersheim
Hesse	Wertheim
Hildesheim	Wiesbaden
Hüttenbach	Wiesentheid
Jebenhausen	Wolfenbüttel
Karlsruhe	Würzburg

National Council of Jewish Women, Service to the Foreign Born. Includes an estimated 350,000 records on individuals and families who came through the port of New York and whom the National Council helped to become citizens. The records include the New York Section, 1939–1968, and Brooklyn Section, 1942–1955. Some restrictions on use.

Vaad Hatzala Collection (1939–1963). Includes information on the rescue efforts of the Union of Orthodox Rabbis of the United States and Canada (Agudath Ha Rabbonim). The files include the following: correspondence, lists, visas, and affidavits of sup-

port concerning rabbinical and student refugees, 1941–1948 (Boxes 4, 13–16, 19, 26–30, 38, 42–43); searches for missing relatives, 1944–1948 (Boxes 17, 40, 44); lists of nonquota immigrants, 1947, lists of sponsors, 1946, and lists of applicants for rabbinical positions, 1948 (Box 17); lists of refugees in concentration camps (Bergen-Belsen—Box 18; Dachau—Box 30), in Displaced Persons Camps (Box 18), in Camp Vittel, France (Box 26), and elsewhere (Boxes 18, 22, 31, 38, 39); identification papers (including photos) issued by the Vaad in Katowice, Poland (Box 18); list of students of the Windsheim Yeshiva transported from Frankfurt, Germany, to Lyons, France, 1948 (Box 31); lists of Jews of various nationalities who arrived in Sweden, 1945 and n.d. (Boxes 34, 40); list of 1,200 persons who left Theresienstadt for Switzerland, n.d. (Box 35); lists of refugees to be transferred to Paris (Box 40); and lists of Jews authorized to enter Tangier.

Louis Rittenberg Collection. Includes biographical data on famous American Jews. These data were accumulated for the preparation of the *Universal Jewish Encyclopedia* (1939–1944). These papers also include documentation of Jewish life in New York from the 1930s to 1960s, especially the rise of the Jewish community in Washington Heights.

Rescue Children, Inc. Collection (1946–1985). Includes files documenting the rescue of children who survived the Holocaust. RCI set up special centers in France, Belgium, Sweden, and Germany. The organization supported 2,200 orphans between 1945 and 1948, and identified or located the families of more than two-thirds of the children. The bulk of the archival material is from information supplied by the children through interviews seeking biographical information and recollections of people in their home towns. Some restrictions on use.

Yeshiva University Records (1895–1970). Contains records of the university, including the following: biographical files on Presidents Bernard Revel, Samuel Belkin, Norman Lamm; on Deans Pinchos Churgin, Moses Issacs, 1930–1970 and personal (family) files of Dr. Shelley R. Saphire, 1914–1960; applications for faculty positions at Yeshiva University and the High School, 1926–1952; faculty files, 1926–1946; files on foreign faculty, 1939–1941; Teacher's Time Book (Talmudical Academy) English Department, 1915–1921; and lists of faculty members and administrators, 1947, 1954–1955, 1957.

Records on students include the following: grades, Talmudical Academy, 1917–1919, and Yeshiva College, 1936–1937; applications for admission, withdrawn or rejected applicants, 1926–1942; student (registration) cards 1924–1949; applications for stipends, dormitory applications or dormitory residents, 1929, 1943–1944, 1946–1947; lists of students, 1949–1950, 1957; and graduate school mailing list, 1946. This record group also includes alumni questionnaire replies, 1935–1936; a file on Talmudical Academy Alumni, 1942–1954; questionnaires, B. Revel Graduate School, 1930–1946; and records of donations with names/addresses of donors, by year, 1909–1934. Access to some files is restricted.

Institutional Synagogue Records (1917–1967). Includes annual membership meetings, 1928, 1929, 1938 and 1941, regarding election of Board members, Fanny Henning will, 1937, and a bound volume of the synagogue's bulletin, *The Institutional*, 1933–1940 (with gaps).

Shelley Ray Saphire Collection (1890–1970). Includes personal correspondence with his future wife and other family members, applications for teaching positions at the Talmudical Academy, the High School Department of Yeshiva University, 1944–1950.

Henry S. Morais Collection (1860–1935). Contains biographical sketches of eight persons mentioned in his book, *The Jews of Philadelphia:* Col. Mayer Asch, Victor Caro, Joseph Chumaceiru, Col. Max Friedman, Dr. Samuel J. Gittleson, Abraham Jacob, Rev. Lee Reich, and one signed "S.S.C." Also, invitations to weddings and correspondence, mostly incoming, covering his years as a journalist and rabbi in Philadelphia and New York.

Jamie Lehmann Memorial Collection: Records of the Jewish Community of Cairo (1886–1961). Contains the records of three major institutions: the Sephardic Jewish community, the Ashkenazi community, and the B'nai B'rith Lodges (Cairo Lodge and Maimonides Lodge). The collection contains account books, case files, certificates, correspondence, minutes, and photographs. Most of the original documents were created between 1920 and 1960.

The records of the Jewish Community Council include the following: proceedings of meetings, 1925–1934 (Box 1); minutes of meetings of the B'nai B'rith Lodges, 1911–1928 (Box 11); and proceedings of meetings of the Administrative Committee supervising the Cairo synagogue, which include letters from synagogue personnel and ritual slaughterers (Box 8). General correspondence, 1926–1957, includes a list of rabbis and employees of the Chancellerie, with their nationality (no date); correspondence regarding the Abraham Btesh school and its personnel; and correspondence on personal matters such as deeds of marriage and divorce, 1953 (Box 2).

Passport forms (in Arabic), are available for 1919, containing name, age, date and place of birth, father's citizenship, father's profession, date of arrival in Egypt and length of stay in Egypt, profession, address, previous country of residence, place of destination, and reason for travel. Some contain photographs of individuals or families (Box 2).

The records of the Chief Rabbinate include general correspondence, 1941–1959 (Box 3). The correspondence deals with Palestinian Jewry regarding personal status and assistance to war prisoners. Correspondence with Alexandria, 1936–1946, includes deeds of marriage and divorce and the status of foreign Jews. Outgoing letters, 1947–1950, include letters about Jewish political detainees and complaints about attacks against Jews (Box 5). A list of butchers in Alexandria, 1945, is in Box 4.

Register of Deeds Regarding the Personal Status of Private Individuals, 1944–1946. Includes birth, marriage, and death certificates or affidavits (in Arabic). Each entry lists the name of the person involved in Arabic and French. The entries for Attestation of Personal Status, 1886, 1936–1937, 1947 (registration of requests for certificates) include the name of the person, date, and a statement of purpose. The most frequent purposes attested to were birth, celibacy, betrothal, marriage, divorce, widowhood, death, notarization of judicial sentences, and passport (Box 5).

Accounting documents of the Chancellerie, 1946, include the following: salaries of the staffs of the Rabbinate and the Arikha; a (Hebrew) list of ritual slaughterers in Cairo; and for 1949–1950, a ledger containing accounts of individuals, associations, and schools in Cairo (Box 6). Account books of contribu-

tions to the Ba'al Hanes Synagogue, 1890–1909 (Box 8), and of the Synagogue Al Ostaz al Amshati in al Mahalla al Kubra (no date), are also available. Records of the Ashkenazi Community of Cairo, 1933–1955, list funds distributed to indigent families, 1947, and include accounting records for 1950 (Box 10).

Identification records (five booklets) include entries for date, name, date and place of birth, profession, address, name of father, destination, spouse's name and place of birth, and names of children, 1946–1947. Most entries also have a photograph (Box 7).

The collection includes completed forms (in French) prepared by the Cairo Jewish Hospital on patients, 1959–1961, and forms (in Arabic and French) prepared by the Italian Hospital of Abbassieh, 1960–1961 (Box 9).

An unidentified register (may be assisted families) contains names of individuals living in Cairo neighborhoods. Each entry (in French) provides the name, number of persons in the family, and address. An additional list, providing name, age, and profession is scribbled on the back of a registration form of Yeshiva Ahaba Veahva in Cairo (Box 9).

French Consistorial Collection (1809–1939). Also includes also records of the Consistories of Rome, Italy, 1809–1810, and Treves and Koblenz, Germany, 1810–1812. The latter include the following: tax exemption requests from individual Jews; lists of young men serving in the army; the decision of the mayor of Treves to expel Isaac Levy from that city, 1810; and letters by Simon Samuel, a British prisoner of war, to the Central Consistory, 1812 (Box 1).

Extracts from the census of Parisian Jews, 1809, list all Jewish professionals and soldiers. Includes proceedings of the first meetings of the Consistory of Paris, 1909 and the records of the welfare committee containing certificates for foreign Jews, 1811–1813 (Box 1).

The records of the Administrative Commission for the Synagogues in Paris contain lists of synagogues' seat owners, 1834–1835, 1851, and 1853, and a contract hiring Cantor Israel Loevy, 1823 (Box 2). Consistory of Paris, Central Administration records include lists of funeral processions in Paris, 1834–1839, 1884, and 1886, circumcisions, and members of benevolent societies (Box 3).

The Ritual Bath folder contains the certificates of many converts to Judaism, 1880–1885. The Rabbinical Seminary folder contains certificates of Lazard Wogue, 1817–1897, and Lazard Isidore, 1814–1888, attesting that converts underwent the ritual immersion in a mikvah. Correspondence of the Central Consistory includes a letter from Rabbi Emmanuel Deutz, chief rabbi of the Central Consistory, to Rabbi Abraham Andrade of Bordeaux concerning the marriage of a Jew from Bordeaux, 1936. The records include complaints against rabbis, cantors, and ritual slaughterers (Boxes 3 and 4).

The collection includes a list showing the Jewish population of the following communities: Auxerre, 1810, Dijon (n.d.), La Orleans, c.1810s, 1872, Reims, 1837, Tours (n.d.), Le Havre, c.1835, Reims, 1838, 1851 (Box 4).

Records of the Association Consistoriale Israélite de Paris include elections, 1908, and proceedings of meetings, 1924 and 1939 (Box 4). Records of the Departmental Consistories include a register of pupils at the Jewish vocational school in Marseilles, 1830, letters from Oran, Algiers, regarding Moroccan refugees, 1859, Consistory of Strasbourg elections, 1835–1860, and Bordeaux elections, 1810–1812 (Box 5).

Gottesman Library of Hebraica-Judaica

The library includes the following in its holdings:

- An extensive collection of rabbinic materials, including rabbinical responsa and rabbinic lexicons
- Family histories, biographies, and genealogies.
- Jewish community histories, including a collection of Yizkor books
- Orthodox German weekly newspapers from the 1860s to the 1930s, such as *Der Israelit*, 1864–1937, and *Jeschurun*, 1854–1870
- Books with information on tombstones in Jewish cemeteries
- Hebrew periodicals from Eastern Europe that included news items as well as scholarly articles, such as *Ha-Meilits*, 1878–1899 and *Ha-Tzefirah*, 1874–1918, printed in Russia

---

Reprinted from *Genealogical Resources in the New York Metropolitan Area.*

■ YIVO INSTITUTE FOR JEWISH RESEARCH

Archives

YIVO
1048 Fifth Avenue
New York, New York 10028
(212) 535-6700

YIVO Archives contain extensive materials relating to Eastern European Jewry, including more than 1,100 collections of records from organizations and papers from individuals. For the most part, the individuals are people who were famous and/or published authors in Eastern Europe.

Do not go to YIVO with unrealistic expectations. Many of these materials are in Yiddish, Hebrew, Polish, and/or Russian. Some are handwritten in Hebrew or Cyrillic script, often illegible even to the YIVO staff. Your degree of success in utilizing YIVO's collections is directly related to your ability to read these languages. Members of YIVO's staff are available to help *find* materials (and their assistance is invaluable), but they cannot provide translations.

A sample of the collections of importance to students of genealogy and family history follows. Record Group numbers are in parentheses.

Otzar Harabanim: Rabbis' Encyclopedia, by Rabbi Nathan Zvi Friedmann. This one-volume encyclopedia provides brief biographical information on nearly 20,000 personalities from the year 970 to 1970.

Sample entry from *Otzar Harabanim.*

The Landsmanshaftn Archives. YIVO has gathered material from more than 800 societies, arranged in 303 collections. According to *A Guide to YIVO's Landsmanshaftn Archive* (1986), the archives contain:

> minutes . . . ; financial records, including membership dues books; records of special committees (relief, burial, loan fund, old age . . .); membership records (application lists, cards, censuses); burial records (golden books listing names, dates of death, records of interments, endowments, cemetery maps, burial permits); anniversary celebrations and banquet programs, menus, journals, photographs; correspondence, meeting announcements, and bulletins; honorary certificates and citations; memorial (Yizkor) books, publications, manuscripts, and materials; . . . personal immigration records and papers of society members.

Additional acquisitions since the publication of the *Guide* in 1986 include the records of:

Chevra Anshe Antipole, 1950–1980
Apter Workmen's Circle Branch No. 566, 1934–1957
Horodoker Benevolent Society, 1936, 1940–1953
Kolomear Friends Association, 1945–1947
Kurlander YMBA Society, 1938–1939
Molodetzner YMBA, 1914–1965

United Meseritzer Relief, 1948–1952
Independent Orler Benevolent Society, 1946
New First Sandez Society (Nowy Sacz)
Slutsker YMBA, 1925, 1954
Stoliner-Lubashover and Lulinetzer, Workmen's Circle Branch No. 531-231-481, 1961–1982
Tetiever Relief Fund, 1919

HIAS (Hebrew Immigrant Aid Society) Collection (RG 245). Most of the HIAS records in YIVO's collection are administrative and are of historic rather than genealogical interest. There are, however, the following materials about which researchers should know:

1. *HIAS Ellis Island Bureau Records, 1905–1923* (RG 245.2). Troublesome cases involving deportation, illness, or detention requiring the services of the HIAS Ellis Island Bureau. These records consist of twenty-six rolls of microfilm, arranged alphabetically by name of person being detained or about to be deported.

2. *HIAS Office and Organizational Files.* YIVO has many HIAS historical files, 1910–1950s, containing interoffice memos, correspondence, etc. They do not include individual case files. An individual might be mentioned in a letter or memo, but retrieving this information is extremely difficult and time-consuming, as the material is not indexed by name.

3. *HIAS Case Files after 1937.* There are thou-

A Guide to YIVO's Landsmanshaftn Archive, by Rosaline Schwartz and Susan Milamed. Provides a description, town by town, of documents in the YIVO collection.

PROBEZHNA
(Pol. Probuzna)
Ternopol province,
Ukrainian SSR*

176. First Probuzna Sick and Benevolent Society
Records, 1942-1975, 2½" (RG 1017)
Organized and incorporated in 1904.
Certificate of incorporation, 1904; constitution; minutes, 1947-75.

PROSKUROV
Kamenets-Podolski province,
Ukrainian SSR

177. United Proskurover Relief
Records, 1920-1974, 5" (RG 1083)
Established in 1916 to unite Proskurover *landsmanshaftn* in aid for war victims in Proskurov. Sent delegates to town after pogrom in 1920 to bring relief. Published memorial book to memorialize pogrom victims, 1924. Reestablished in 1939 to work with the United Jewish Appeal to support Palestine. Affiliate organizations were: Proskurover Zion Congregation K.U.V., Proskurov-Yarmolinitzer Br. 355, W.C., New Nook Ass'n., Independent Proskurover Society, Inc. and Sisterhood; First Proskurover Y.M.P.A., Ladies Auxiliary of the First Proskurover, Proskurover, Proskurover Ladies Society, Evans Family Circle.

Record book carried by delegate to Proskurov in 1920 with names of donors and recipients; memorial book, 1924; souvenir journals, 1959-76; taped interviews with delegate, 1979, 1980; records of affiliate organizations: New Nook Association, First Proskurover Y.M.P.A., Proskurover Ladies Benevolent Ass'n., Independent Proskurover Society; photographs.

PRZEMYSL
Rzeszow province,
Poland

178. Congregation Tifereth Joseph Anshei Przemysl
Records, 1917-1967, 7½" (RG 793)
Originally organized in 1891 for the purpose of founding a synagogue; chartered in 1892. Was affiliated with the United Przemysler Relief, organized in 1938 to help *landslayt* in Przemysl.

Constitution (German); certificate of incorporation, 1892; minutes, 1945-65; correspondence, 1930's-40's, also regarding Nazi war crimes testimony and material claims against Germany, 1960's; personal materials relating to Przemysl, 1930's-40's; announcements; anniversary journal, 1941; photographs; memorial book, 1964; materials of the United Relief for Przemysl, 1946.

179. First Przemysler Sick Benefit Society
Records, 1906-1965, 3' 10" (RG 932)
Founded in 1889 to "create a spirit of good fellowship." Maintained a loan fund; supported the Lemberger Home for the Aged, New York.

Constitutions; legal documents, including certificate of incorporation, Przemysler Central Relief Society, Inc., 1919; minutes, 1947-57; cemetery materials; membership records, 1908-64; financial records, 1920-60; photograph; memorial book, 1964.

Sample entry from *A Guide to YIVO's Landsmanshaftn Archive.*

sands of case files from 1937 to the 1960s, most from 1945 through 1950. These files are not on site and are difficult to retrieve from the warehouse where they are kept in original order by the agency that processed the files—e.g., National Refugee Service, German Jewish Children's Aid, New York Association for New Americans, European HIAS, etc. (These files are part of YIVO's HIAS collection because the other agencies were merged into the United HIAS Service.) Permission to see a case file is usually needed from HIAS and is provided only for an individual's own file or for a very special reason.

4. *HIAS Index Cards*, 1909–1979. HIAS index cards are available at YIVO in three series of films:

- Arrival Index Cards (approx. 110 reels), 1909–1949
- Master Index Cards (six reels), 1950–1979
- Joint Distribution Committee (JDC) Index (six reels), post-WWII

5. *Photographs Relating to HIAS.* These are mainly of the Ellis Island Bureau, HIAS offices, citizenship classes, etc., rather than of individuals. Individuals in photographs are not identified.

JDC (American Jewish Joint Distribution Committee) Records (RG 335). Includes the records of the JDC Landsmanshaftn Department. Many of these societies were formed in response to a particular disaster (such as a pogrom) and worked closely with the JDC to provide disaster relief. The records are arranged by town in two series: (1) 1937–1939; (2) post-1945.

Records of Vaad Hayeshivot (RG 25). This was an office in Vilna, Lithuania, that arranged for financial support of seventy yeshivas and their students throughout Lithuania. It had contact with about 350 towns that sent students to the yeshivas. The correspondence, written in Yiddish script, is mainly from the 1920s and 1930s.

Territorial Photo Collection. YIVO's photographs of life in Eastern Europe include:

1. *The Polish Collection.* For purposes of this collection, "Poland" is defined as those areas that were politically part of Poland between 1919 and 1939.
   1. Poland photographs between 1864 and 1939 are under the curatorship of Lucjan Dobroszycki. An appointment with Dr. Dobroszycki is necessary to research this collection.
   2. Poland photographs taken after 1945 are available in the Archives.
2. *The Russian/Soviet Union Collection.* YIVO has been adding photographs in this area as part of a special project. The collection is divided into two main parts with different finding aids but both are available in the Archives. Russia I includes all photographs that were in YIVO's collection prior to the inception of the special project. Russia II are those photographs that were collected for the new project.
3. There are also photographs of Jewish life in other European countries and the United States, e.g. Jewish agricultural settlements, immigration period, labor movement, etc.

4. *The Slide Bank.* The Archives has a large slide collection of images of Eastern Europe, religious artifacts, synagogues, and scenes of towns.

French Holocaust Archives. Contains over 200,000 documents, including the full records of the French Judenrat (RG 210), the Kehiles Hahareydim (RG 340), the underground Lubavitch children's rescue project in France, and Rue Amelot (RG 343), another underground rescue agency. The records contain lists of people in camps and people receiving assistance.

Collection on Genealogy and Family History. The following names, taken from the card catalog, represent genealogies and family histories in the archives. Where available, the town, country, or time period covered by the collection is shown:

Abramoff, Samuel (Vasilkov, Bialystok)
Albert, Ruth
Bendovid, Morton and Anna (Kremenchug, Brudne)
Buck, Miriam
Cantor, Max
Cohen, Abraham (1839)
Craig, Margrit L.
Dall (Yoniskas, Lithuania)
Dunkelman, David
Edelman, Hannah
Effron, Jacob (Kharkov)
Eisenberg, Samuel and Hershl
Fehl, Gertrude
Fichtner (Zloczow)
Fishman, Samuel (Kishinev)
Fried
Friederike, Meyer
Fricdkas, Joseph (Vienna, Lwow, Pinsk, Czernowitz)
Getzel, Eliokum
Gildesgame, Leon L.
Goichberg-Greenberg (Russia, England, U.S., 1910/1920)
Goldman, Moshe
Goldnadel, M. (Zivolen)
Gorbulov, Khayim
Greenberg, Jacob
Grenadier, Israel (Uman district, Kiev)
Grossgott, Sy
Hadra, Edmund/Josefa Rubin (1943)
Halevi (Olszanica)
Henigson, Abraham (Suwalki)
Herbst, Sydney (Sedziszow)
Herbstein, Regina

Jewish old age home in Priluki, Ukraine. (Photo courtesy of YIVO Institute for Jewish Research, Inc.)

Herz, Rosel
Hoffman, Frances B.
Holtz, Zalmen (Skierniewice)
Kalnitsky, Mini (Russia)
Kagan, Khane, Ziml (Vilna, Lininetz, Slovetchne)
Kaplan, Moshe
Klein, Elaine (Zidok, Lithuania, 1920/30)
Kling, Henry
Krarastan, Abraham
Kussy and Abeles families
Kweskin, Sam (Vilkija)
Lager, Lafzitsky, Lagrzitski families
Leanid, Gan (Korsk)
Lederman
Levine, Benjamin
Lipshitz, B. (1886)
Lourie, Anton/Landau, Alfred
Lowensohn, Amalia
Mendelson, Herman/Tsvi (1906–1967)
Minkin, Yehuda (1920–1940)
Morgenstern, Moshe (Wlodawa, 1937)
Myslobodsky (Bialystok, Sluck)
Nagel/Nogelberg, Ivan (Rohatyn, Galicia)
Nelkin, Edna and Morton, Telechin family
Oshrin, Joyce Schneider, Szeynersnayer family
Ostroff, Shmuel and Leah
Poliakoff, Michael (Russia)
Porter, Max
Rabinowicz, M. (Brzostowice, 1888, 1892)
Rappaport, Sam
Rassas, Abraham (Konotop, Russia, 1885)
Reiser, Lea
Resnick, Moshe (1896)
Richter (Zbaraz, Poland, 1906)
Rabbiner, Lillian and Delatiner, Debra: photos of
Moshe Cyna from Lodz and Mendel Cina of Glasgow;
Ida Kapilow family (Minsk, 1928)
Ring, Jacob and Lovinsohn, Rosa
Rosler, Solomon and Bayla (1914–1947)
Rosenberg, Rywka (Minsk, 1936)
Safier, Israel and Ollda Serka Safier (1872)
Salamanov-Rabinov, Khayim (Mogilev, Stary)
Schuster, Wolf (Biala Podolska, 1933)
Segal, Phillip (Poland, 1913–1960)
Shapiro, Lillian (1895–1976)
Spivack
Spiwack, Miriam (Talin, Estonia, 1920s, 1930s)
Sutro, Samuel (The Hague, 1930–1941)
Taub/Terkeltaub (Poland, Hungary, 1901–1936)
Taussig, Harry
Taylor, Libby (Pinsk, 1930s)
Teitelbaum, Meyer (Nikolayev, Voznesink, Ukraine,
1872–1910)
Tzitlenk, Nochomov (Niezhin, Russia, 1901)
Uttal
Volarsky, A. (Mlava, 1920s, 1930s)
Vordren
Vulcan, P. and Finkelstein family (Otwock, Poland)
Wayman, Samuel (Warsaw Ghetto, Soberoa, Pales-
tine, 1925–1947)
Weinshel, Shmuel-Pesach (Uscilvy, Wolhynia,
1900–1923)
Weinstock, Bennett
Wiesenfeld, Leon (Rzeszow, Poland, 1920s, 1930s)
Winik, Doris (Pinsk, Domatchevo, 1920s)
Witkin-Kaufman, Laura (Slutsk)
Yahuda, Abraham Shalom (Lisbon, 1904–1922)
Zalzman, Pinchask, Yechiel, and Chava
Zucker, Pinchas

Collection of Autobiographies (RG 102). Includes 350 autobiographies (mostly in Yiddish) prepared by immigrants in response to a YIVO-sponsored contest in 1942. The contestants describe why they left Europe and what they accomplished in America. Family backgrounds are included.

National Desertion Bureau (RG 297). This New York-based organization assisted Jewish families in which a parent had deserted, by attempting to locate the parent. The collection covers roughly 25,000 families from the 1920s to the 1950s. Some restrictions on use.

Records of Displaced Persons (DP) Camps and Centers (RG 294). Some 300,000 pages including correspondence, minutes of meetings, leaflets, and posters on Displaced Persons camps have been placed on microfilm. The documents show how survivors of the war ran their daily affairs as they were relocated in dozens of DP camps in Germany, Austria, and Italy. Lists of people are occasionally included. The collection includes material on those camps that were under the supervision of the American Army and agencies established by the United Nations.

Hebrew Technical Institute (RG 754). Includes detailed alumni career records of the oldest vocational school for Jewish boys in New York City. The career of each individual student was recorded as he moved from position to position. The records include annual reports and catalogs (9 volumes); alumni career records, class years, 1886–1939 (13 volumes); class standing records, 1884–1939 (34 volumes); and roll books, mainly 1896–1939 (27 volumes).

Records of the Jewish Community Council of Minsk, 1825–1921 (RG 12). This collection contains fragmentary registers of births, marriages, and deaths. The records are handwritten in Cyrillic.

Records of Lithuanian Jewish Communities, 1844–1940 (RG 2). These are mainly community records, 1919–1924, such as minutes of council meetings about tax collections or elections in those towns that were part of the independent Republic of Lithuania. Most of the material in the collection was generated by the Ministry of Jewish Affairs and is in Yiddish or Lithuanian.

Records of Jewish Communities of Ostrowo (RG 13), *Krotoschin* (RG 14), and *Briesen* (RG 15).

Borenstein-Eisenberg Collection on Early Jewish Migration (RG 406). A few passenger lists from the late 1880s and early 1890s.

Tcherikower Archive (RG 80–89). Contains miscellaneous records on Jewish life in the Ukraine and includes lists of victims of Ukrainian pogroms. Thorough knowledge of Yiddish and Russian script is required to use this collection.

Monika Krajewska Photo Collection (RG 1137). Exhibit prints and contact sheets of photos, 1974–1986, taken in preparation for Monika Krajewska's book on Polish cemeteries, *Czas Kamieni* [Time of Stones], Warsaw, 1982. The collection includes photos of tombstones in almost 100 cemeteries, an article about the Jewish cemetery in Sieniawa written in September 1982 (Polish), and information and photographs of some synagogues.

Resources

For the genealogical researcher, the following materials are of interest (call numbers are in parentheses):

Memorial or Yizkor Books. YIVO has one of the most extensive collections in the world of memorial books. Included are both the better-known Yizkor books commemorating communities destroyed by the Nazis and the lesser-known books written after World War I, about towns desecrated by pogroms. Most Yizkor books are in Hebrew and/or Yiddish. Some contain small sections in English. About 80 percent of the books do not have indexes.

Geographical material. YIVO has many items that will help locate small towns, verify the spelling of their names, and give descriptions of the towns or the areas in which they are located. Here are some examples:

- *Slownik Geograficzny* (Polish gazetteer). 1885–1891. (Polish). A 16-volume gazetteer that gives the name of the town, its population, what district it belongs to, etc. (DK403 S5)
- *Evreiskaia Entsiklopediya* (Jewish encyclopedia). St. Petersburg, 1906–1913. (Russian). Contains entries about cities and many small towns in Russia. (DS102.8 E7)
- *Yahadut Lita* (Lithuanian Jewry) 4 vols., 1959–1984. (Hebrew). Volume 3 includes descriptions of these communities and, in some cases, photographs of them. (DS135 L5 Y3)
- *Pinkas Ha-Kehillot* (an encyclopedia of communities). 1969–. (Hebrew). There is a volume on each of the following: Romania (2 volumes), Hungary, Poland (Lodz region), Poland (Eastern Galicia), Poland (Western Galicia), Poland (Warsaw region), Yugoslavia, Latvia and Estonia, The Netherlands, Germany (Bavaria), and Germany (Württemberg, Hohenzollern, Baden).
- *Books on synagogues,* such as *Wooden Synagogues* by M. and K. Piechotka (12/51537), often contain both photographs of the synagogues and descriptions of the town they were in.
- *Old maps.* YIVO has maps and atlases of Poland from the period between the two World Wars.

Rabbinic Material. These sources may be used both to trace rabbinic ancestors and to gather information about the religious heritage of the towns ancestors were from. Among these sources are the following:

- Wunder, Meir. *Meorei Galicia* (Encyclopedia of Galician Rabbis and Scholars). 1978–. (Hebrew). Includes biographical sketches of rabbis and sometimes their family trees. Three volumes in this series have been published to date. (BM750 W8)
- Friedmann, Nathan Zebi. *Otzar Harabanim* (Rabbis' Encyclopedia). 1975. (Hebrew). Contains about 20,000 entries, alphabetized by the rabbi's first name. Gives the rabbi's year of birth or death, father, son or son-in-law, a general

Meorei Galicia: Encyclopedia of Galician Rabbis and Scholars, by Rabbi Meir Wunder. This multi-volume encyclopedia is not yet complete. Thus far, it provides a significant amount of detailed information on rabbinic personalities in Galicia.

Sample entry from *Meorei Galicia: Encyclopedia of Galician Rabbis and Scholars.*

description of who the rabbi was, and a list of his works. (BM750 F7)

- Gottlieb, Samuel Noah. *Ohole-Shem.* 1912. (Hebrew). List of rabbis in Eastern Europe and the United States in 1912. [BM750 G6]
- Alfasi, Yitshak. *He-hasidut.* 1974. (Hebrew). Contains information on Hasidic rabbis from the Ba'al Shem Tov to the present and has an index of towns and an index of rabbis (by their first names). [BM198 A5]

Holocaust Sources: YIVO's library contains an important collection of material relating to the Holocaust in addition to the Yizkor books noted above. For example:

- *Blackbook of Localities Whose Jewish Population Was Extinguished by the Nazis.* 1965. Published by Yad Vashem. (English). Lists communities in the Soviet Union and Europe and gives the Jewish population for each town. The sections on Poland and Germany are arranged by province. [D810 J4 Y2]

- *Gedenkbuch: Opfer der Verfolgung der Juden, 1933–1945.* Koblenz: Bundesarchiv, 1985. 2 vols. This book lists all Jews of Germany who perished, with birth place, how they died and where; appendix gives data on each concentration camp. [9/80818]
- *Guide to Unpublished Materials of the Holocaust Period.* 1970–. (YIVO has vols. 1–5). A series of books that list, by town, original documents in the Yad Vashem archives. An entry might include documents relating to deportations, war criminals, refugees, orphanages, etc. Researchers can write to Yad Vashem to determine the cost of copying documents. [D810 J4 G8]
- Klarsfeld, Serge. *Le Mémorial de la Déportation des Juifs de France.* 1978. (French). English ed.: *Memorial to the Jews Deported from France, 1942–1944.* 1983. Lists transports of Jews to concentration camps, including both those that originated in France and those that passed through France. Information relating to about 90 transports is given. The names of victims are

He-hasidut, by Yitzhak Alfasi. This biographical directory of hasidic masters from the Baal Shem Tov to the present includes an index by town, by first name. Hundreds of portraits are also included.

Sample entry from *He-hasidut*.

listed alphabetically for each transport and, when known, the birth date and place of birth are included. Also given are the number of people who survived each transport and its destination. YIVO has similar books for other countries, such as Belgium and Germany. [9/76780-French; 9/79227-English]

- *Register of Jewish Survivors in Poland.* 1945. Like Yad Vashem and the International Tracing Service, YIVO has a collection of lists giving the names of survivors, the places where they registered, and (when known) their ages. Among the lists in YIVO's collection, in addition to Poland, are those for Warsaw, Riga, Lublin, Italy, and Yugoslavia. [3/22766A]

Name Indexes

- Lifschutz, Ezekiel, Compiler. *Bibliography of American and Canadian Jewish Memoirs and Autobiographies in Yiddish, Hebrew and English.* New York, 1970. [E36 L5]
- Sack, Sallyann and Suzan F. Wynne. *The Russian Consular Records Index and Catalog.* 1987. [CS856 J4 S23]
- Zubatsky, David S. and Irwin M. Berent. *Jewish Genealogy: A Source Book of Family Histories and Genealogies.* 1984. [Z6374 B5 Z79]

Miscellaneous Sources: Includes much material describing Jewish life in Eastern Europe. Among items of interest are memoirs, historical commentaries, histories of communities, and fiction that describes Jewish life and culture.

Reprinted from *Genealogical Resources in the New York Metropolitan Area.*

HIAS Records at YIVO
Marsha Saron Dennis

Currently, the collection is divided into two sections, a voluminous group of microfilms, which al-

Shepetovka Landsmanshaftn Society group photo in front of new cemetery gate in Shepetovka, Ukraine, c. 1924. (Photo courtesy of the YIVO Institute for Jewish Research, Inc.)

ready have been cataloged, and a second, as yet uncataloged set of 120-plus newly acquired microfilms. From 1948 through 1974, HIAS in New York donated vast quantities of its archives to YIVO. Included were records acquired by HIAS as other American and European agencies working with Jewish immigration eventually merged into the United HIAS Service. Represented are the United Service for New Americans (USNA), the Jewish Colonization Association (JCA), HICEM, a joint agency of HIAS, and Emigdirect, the National Coordinating Committee for Aid to Refugees (NCC), and the National Refugee Service (NRS).

Individual record groups sometimes overlap chronologically and geographically. Generally, they are clustered according to the agency from which they came. Correspondence is in many languages, especially in the European records, but a foreign language document frequently is followed by an English translation.

Cataloged Material. Most of the cataloged material is not valuable to genealogists in its present state. Many documents pertain to HIAS business and are minutes of meetings, financial matters, correspondence among HIAS offices and related agencies, correspondence with other Jewish organizations, public relations materials, brochures, reports from investigators on field trips, which include general statistics, and so forth.

It is a gold mine for the social historian writing the history of HIAS, especially focusing on ways it adapted to the changing needs of twentieth century Jewish refugees. However, the odds are not in favor of the genealogist seeking particular people in specific places at certain times.

Close to 1,200 reels of 35-mm film have been made from the material in addition to at least 2,500 feet of files, and YIVO has a double finding aid to help you use it. Before describing the finding aid, I must first dampen expectations. Although a random sampling of microfilms repeatedly yielded interesting correspondence about individual families, especially during World War II, there is no index to this material. Not only would it be hard to find these references, but I don't know how anyone researching such families would even know that he should look for them here.

To work at the YIVO archives, first consult the loose-leaf notebook containing the Record Group Inventory entitled "The United HIAS Service Archives (HIAS)." Each record group (RG) is described concisely in this directory of more than eighty pages. The first page of each RG provides a general description of the group (or subgroup) contents, plus such other information as the number of microfilm reels (from 1 to 299), dates covered, origin, restriction on use if any, finding aids, date material was cataloged, references to other, related records, and such notes as "Inventory is arranged alphabetically by country *in Yiddish:* microfilm is arranged alphabetically by country *in English....*" Not every RG comes with all this information, but each begins with a title page on which such data can be entered. Descriptions generally tell what records one can find and sometimes information that "the records were microfilmed in 1976 and discarded thereafter."

The key to the cataloged materials is a double finding aid. The first step is the Record Group Inventory, which summarizes each set of microfilms. If one finds a record group that seems relevant, the next steps are the Individual Inventories for the collection.

These very detailed inventories, kept in a series of binders, not only list all documents within a RG, but are the key to which microfilm reel to read. I was interested in an entry in RG 245.4.12 that said, "List of Jewish families in Amsterdam, 1943." Expecting a sizable list, I hoped families were listed alphabetically. Instead, I learned from the Individual Inventory that it was only one letter which included a "list of ten Jewish families in Amsterdam and Rotterdam."

The above cautions notwithstanding, materials do include assorted lists of people at various times and places, as well as some specific passenger lists that are itemized in the inventories. To use the lists, it is well to have an inkling of what you are seeking. There are lists of passengers leaving Lisbon in 1941, so if you have reason to believe that a relative might have passed through that city about that time, it would make sense to wade through the microfilm.

Other lists are sprinkled through the material. RG 245.4.12 includes a list of Jews from Riga killed by the Germans (150 people, dated July 1943), a list of non-Belgian Jewish refugees in Belgium (1945), lists of 120 Luxembourg Jews in Barcelona, in camps, 1941. Other record groups include lists of Jewish soldiers in the French Foreign Legion, or lists of deportees from Camp Gurs in France in 1942.

Much of the material has confidentiality restrictions. In such cases, usually anything having to do with individual case files, access is limited to researchers with a bona fide reason to view the material; permission generally must be obtained from HIAS and/or the individuals named in the document.

In summary, there is material of value to a genealogist in the cataloged HIAS holdings. The two-tiered finding aid is an excellent way to discover what might be of interest, and then what is worth following through to the microfilm.

Cards have the potential of giving not only dates and places of birth, and names and family relationships of people traveling together, but also the last place of residence, destination and details of the arrivals. The post-1937 case files are difficult to retrieve and are subject to strict confidentiality restrictions. YIVO itself houses case files until 1950; those from 1950 through 1977 are in the warehouse, and case files since 1977 are at the HIAS office itself. Since case files came not only from HIAS itself, but also from the related agencies which merged with HIAS, some groups of files at YIVO extended further into the 1950s than others.

Master Cards. Master cards are the cross-reference index to all the names that appear on the arrival records cards. If you are looking for say, Aunt Belle Cohen, but didn't know that she had arrived in a traveling party headed by her brother-in-law, Sam Levy, the Master Card index would refer you to Levy's arrival record to find her.

Six reels of microfilm marked "JDC" appear to be an index of people helped by the Transmigration Department of the Joint Distribution Committee immediately following World War II. YIVO already has the records of this department, as well as a finding aid.

Although no one can be certain until the cataloging is finished, it is assumed that this filmed index will be helpful, though not absolutely necessary, to access the JDC files. Remember that the JDC Transmigration Department merged with HIAS in 1954.

Original index cards up to about 1950 were discarded after microfilming; there is no possibility of refilming any improperly photographed cards from that period. Although the microfilms are negatives, much is legible. In many cases, however, the original handwriting already had faded by the time of filming and some reels have shadows or are blurry. These are 16-mm films, so one must use YIVO's magnifying reader. I also found it useful to carry a big magnifying glass. Because YIVO's machine is a reader only, it is not possible to make copies of their microfilms.

The first group of materials was filmed and cataloged by YIVO. The second group, the index cards, was microfilmed by HIAS, which gave YIVO a duplicate copy. One of the major differences between using YIVO and HIAS is that HIAS is not organized for the individual genealogist to do his own research; it can only be done by a HIAS staff member. On the other hand, if one wanted copies of index cards on microfilm, he could not get them at YIVO. HIAS also has the microfilms in negative, but makes positive prints. It might make sense to do research at YIVO and then write to HIAS (200 Park Avenue South, New York, New York 10003) for a print of the microfilm if you find a valuable index card.

In addition to the microfilmed index cards, the HIAS office has other records, such as a computerized index of HIAS-assisted arrivals from 1980 to the present. At its warehouse are index cards of arrivals for families assisted by the National Refugee Service and the United Service for New Americans between 1939 and 1950, record cards of children brought to the United States by the European Jewish Children's Aid immediately after World War II. NRS became part of the USNA in 1946, which in turn merged with HIAS in 1954.

"HIAS Records at YIVO" is adapted from *Avotaynu*, Vol. II, No. 3, October 1986.

Videodisc Program

Thanks to a grant from the Charles H. Revson Foundation initiated in 1981, YIVO recently began the process of selecting over 17,000 photographs from its archival collections of Jewish life in Eastern Europe, preserving these images on a laser disc and developing a computerized cataloging system for the collection. The project is called "People of a Thousand Towns," and its results, as described by the program's director, Joseph Waletsky, will be to free "thousands of images of East European Jewish life . . . from the confines of archival folders and place [them] before the eyes of millions of potential viewers."

This first phase is now complete. The next task for Waletzky is developing the various ways in which the videodisc can be utilized by educational institutions and researchers of all kinds. Waletzky explains, "The videodisc will not only make these photographs more accessible to a greater number of people, it will also serve as a kind of visual encyclopedia of Ashkenazic life in Eastern Europe. It will help us learn how to read the images of the culture."

"Videodisc Program" is excerpted from *YIVO News*, No. 172, Autumn 1987.

NORTH CAROLINA

■ CHAPEL HILL
(Raleigh Metropolitan Area)

Walter Royal Davis Library
University of North Carolina, Chapel Hill
Chapel Hill, North Carolina 27514
(919) 962-1356
The Davis Library has over 1 million volumes:

* Census records
* City directories (southeastern United States)

Wilson Library
University of North Carolina, Chapel Hill
Chapel Hill, North Carolina 27514
(919) 962-1172
* Family history collection (including Jewish family histories)
* Census records
* City directories
* Church records
* Military records
* Bibliographies
* Indexes
* Issues of *The Carolina Israelite* (1945–1968)
* Extensive newspaper clippings

■ DURHAM
(Raleigh Metropolitan Area)

William R. Perkins Library
Duke University
Durham, North Carolina
(919) 684-2034
Judaica and a genealogy section include reference books and city directories from across the country. A pamphlet about the genealogical holdings is available upon written request.

■ RALEIGH

Walter Royal Davis Library
(See Chapel Hill)

Department of Human Resources
Division of Health Services
Vital Records Branch
P.O. Box 2091
Raleigh, North Carolina 27602
(919) 733-3526
* Birth records: 1913–present
* Death records: 1930–present
* Marriage records: 1962–present

Genealogical Services Branch
North Carolina Department of Cultural Resources
Division of the State Library
Raleigh, North Carolina 27611
(919) 733-3952

The Genealogical Services Branch is a centralized repository of primary North Carolina materials in original form and on microfilm.
Private manuscript collections:

* North Carolina Jews
* Family genealogies
* Abstracts of county records of North Carolina and other states
* County histories
* Bibliographies
* Indexes and other guides

The State Archives Search Room has original county and state records, including:

* Census records
* Tombstone inscriptions
* Wills
* Estate papers
* Bible and church records

North Carolina State Archives
109 East Jones Street
Raleigh, North Carolina 27611
(919) 733-3952
Letters of inquiry are answered. Write for fee schedule.
Official vital statistics were not required before 1913 in North Carolina. For records before 1913, correspondence should be directed to the county in which the death or birth occurred.

* Death records 1913 to 1929
* Original marriage bonds 1790–1862 (1858–1959 on microfilm)
* Naturalization records 1824–1908 For records since 1906, apply to the Justice Department. The form can be obtained from the nearest federal courthouse. Records for years prior to 1906 are scattered. However, they can generally be found in the superior court of the county in North Carolina where naturalization occurred.

Registrar of Deeds
Wake County
Raleigh, North Carolina 27609
Write for fee schedule. The registrar keeps records for marriages performed in Raleigh 1850–1962. For other years, write to the registrar of deeds in the county seat where the couple was married.

Family History Center
5100 Six Forks
Raleigh, North Carolina 27609
(919) 781-1662

North Carolina Genealogical Society
P.O. Box 1492
Raleigh, North Carolina 27602
The society does not have a library, nor does it have a staff of researchers. Its primary focus is the publication of the *North Carolina Genealogical Society Journal,* a quarterly publication consisting of articles of general genealogical value, source data from original

documents, and other material from previously unpublished sources. The society also publishes material of general interest for North Carolina research.

Wake County Courthouse
Raleigh, North Carolina 27602

Letters of inquiry are answered. Request should contain name, place and date of death or birth of the individual being researched, and a check or money order.

Wake County Genealogical Society
P.O. Box 17713
Raleigh, North Carolina 27619

Holdings include a small circulating library, a monthly newsletter, and *The Heritage*, a general interest historical volume of current and former Wake County residents. The society also publishes a group of special publications relating to Wake County.

Wilson Library
(See Chapel Hill)

William R. Perkins Library
(See Durham)

Funeral Home
Brown-Wynne Funeral Home
300 St. Mary's Street
Raleigh, North Carolina
(919) 755-1480

Bibliography
Edwards, E. R. *A History of North Carolina's Association of Jewish Women.* 1961.

_____. *Jewish War Record.* Goldsboro, NC, 1945.

Freund, I. L. *Brief History of the Jews of North Carolina.* Typescript in the North Carolina Collection, University of North Carolina Library, Chapel Hill.

Goldberg, D. J. *An Historical Community Study of Wilmington Jewry, 1738–1925.* Typescript in the North Carolina Collection, University of North Carolina Library, Chapel Hill.

Golden, H. *Jewish Roots in the Carolinas.* Charlotte, NC: The Carolina Israelite, 1955.

Huhner, L. "The Struggle for Religious Liberty in North Carolina with Special Reference to the Jews." *Publication of the American Jewish Historical Society* 16, pp. 37–71, 1907.

Litwack, C. *Recollections.* Raleigh, NC: 1976.

OHIO

■ BEACHWOOD
(Cleveland Metropolitan Area)

The Temple—The Branch
26000 Shaker Boulevard
Beachwood, Ohio 44122
The Abba Hillel Silver Archives and Library

College of Jewish Studies Library
26500 Shaker Boulevard
Beachwood, Ohio 44122

Vast collection of reference material and books of Judaica.

■ CINCINNATI

Cincinnati Historical Society
Eden Park
Cincinnati, Ohio 45202
(513) 241-4622

- General genealogical sources
- Hamilton County records
- Manuscript holdings (personal papers, business archives, social agencies)
- Map collection
- Vital statistics file from local newspapers, etc.
- General
- Local and family histories
- WPA Church Records Survey (Southwestern Ohio)
- Extensive photograph collection (Greater Cincinnati area)
- City and county directories (1819 to date)
- Southwestern Ohio census records

Send for details.

City of Cincinnati
Department of Health
Vital Records
1525 Elm Street
Cincinnati, Ohio 45210
(513) 352-3120

- Birth certificates from June 1874 (incomplete)
- Death certificates: from January 1865 (incomplete)
- Certificates (for people who lived in Cincinnati only)

No marriage, naturalization, or probate records at this office.
Send for fee schedule.

Hamilton County Courthouse
Court and Main Streets
Cincinnati, Ohio 45202
(513) 632-6500

No telephone requests to the courthouse. All requests not given in person must be in writing. Enclose SASE.

Probate Court, Room 537, above address

- Wills (1791 to present)
- Administration of estates
- Application records and guardianship records

Room 549, above address

- Early birth certificates (1846–1908)
- Marriages (1817 to present)
- Deaths (1882–1899)

- Index to naturalization records (1869–1884)
- Some Declarations of Intention

Common Pleas Court, Room 329, above address

- Naturalization records (1850–1893)
- Lawsuits
- Divorce records (1884 to present)
- Criminal records
- Declarations of Intent, 1842+

Real Estate, Room 304
County Administration Building
138 East Court St.
Cincinnati, Ohio 45202

- Real estate tax records
- Permanent and duplicate cards
- Owners' and address indexes
- Plat maps (1940 to date)
- Field cards indicate date buildings erected and first taxed

Records before 1940 in storage; inquire as to availability.

Treasurer's Office, Room 402, above address

- Property tax records (1883 to present)

Recorder's Office, Room 205, above address

- Deeds (1794 to date)
- Mortgages and leases
- Original subdivision maps
- Atlases
- Soldiers' discharges (beginning with Civil War)
- Veterans' (military) grave locations (Revolutionary War to present)

The Hamilton County Courthouse was destroyed during the Courthouse Riot of 1884. Many records were lost and gaps were caused in others.

Hamilton County Vital Statistics
Room 604, above address
(513) 632-8452

- Birth and death certificates (1909 to present)

Write for fee schedule.

Hebrew Union College–Jewish Institute of Religion
Klau Library
3101 Clifton Ave.
Cincinnati, Ohio 45220
(513) 231-0810

There is no research fee or membership fee. The library will answer letters of inquiry.

- Outline of genealogical sources for Jewish ancestry
- City directories; the library has an extensive collection for most American cities, fairly complete through 1880—available on microfiche and/or microfilm in the American Jewish Periodicals Center
- Yizkor books
- *Deutsch Index;* nineteenth and twentieth century periodicals and books for detailed biographical citations
- Inventories to the special collections—numerous official and community records on individual families

American Jewish Archives
(513) 221-1875

There are no research or membership fees. The archives will answer letters of inquiry.

The American Jewish Archives located on the campus of the Hebrew Union College, Jewish Institute of Religion, is a depository created to keep alive for future generations the important historic records of Jews on the North American continent.

The collection (dating back to 1654) documents the early religious, social, and economic life of Jewry in the Western Hemisphere, primarily the United States, Canada, and Mexico. It contains:

- Memoirs
- Letters
- Wills
- Unpublished papers

The collection of over a thousand volumes of minute books, both originals and copies, reflects the growth and development of the early congregations and Jewish societies. The Archives personnel seek out valued papers and arrange their acquisition through photo duplication.

The Archives also publishes books and articles in American Jewish history, including its semi-annual journal, *American Jewish Archives.*

The American Jewish Periodical Center
(513) 221-1875

There are no research or membership fees. The center will answer letters of inquiry.

Located on the campus of Hebrew Union College, the center is in the process of filming every Jewish periodical published in America from 1823 to 1925, as well as a sampling of serials published since 1925.

An initial catalog of its available periodical materials was issued in 1957 under the title *Jewish Newspapers and Periodicals on Microfilm* (a supplement appeared in 1960). Publications available include items in eight languages: English, German, Hebrew, Yiddish, Ladino, Serbo-Croatian, Polish, and Hungarian. They range from Solomon Jackson's New York monthly, *The Jew* (first published in 1823), to current periodicals.

The center also publishes several free brochures including *Tracing Your Jewish Roots* by Malcolm H. Stern (1977) and *How to Write the History of an American Jewish Community* by Jacob R. Marcus (1953).

Public Library of Cincinnati and Hamilton County
800 Vine Street
Library Square
Cincinnati, Ohio 45202-2071
(513) 369-6900

There are no research fees. The library will try to answer brief letters of inquiry.

- "How-to-do-it" books for the beginner
- Local history and family name indexes
- City and county directories (1819+)
- Newspapers, obituaries; local newspaper index
- City, county, and state histories
- Family histories
- U.S. census microfilm for 1800–1870 (Ohio only for 1870–1910)
- Many state and U.S. census indexes
- Extensive genealogical and historical periodical collections
- Military records (unit histories, rosters, indexes)
- Maps, historical gazetteers, cadastral (real-estate ownership) county atlases
- "How to Research the Newspaper and Census Collections of the Public Library"
- Published vital statistics

A videotape, "Genealogy Research at the Main Library," is available in the Films and Recordings Center for loan to interested individuals or groups. Introduces genealogist and family researchers unfamiliar with the library's collections to techniques for using the genealogical resources of the Public Library of Cincinnati and Hamilton County.

University of Cincinnati Central Library
Clifton Campus
Cincinnati, Ohio 45221

Regional archives
Archives and Rare Books Department
808 Blegen Library
(513) 475-6459

Part of a statewide program to preserve local government records of historical value.

- County and municipal records: Adams, Brown, Butler, Clermont, Clinton, Hamilton, Highland, and Warren Counties
- JP dockets
- Youth and voter enumerations
- Court records
- Tax records

Ohio Genealogical Society
Hamilton County Chapter
P.O. Box 15851
Cincinnati, Ohio 45215

The chapter's quarterly publication, *The Tracer,* contains in each issue, in addition to genealogical records:

- Chapter news
- A list of recent acquisitions of the public library of interest to the genealogist
- Chapter exchange publications placed in the public library collections

Send SASE for details about the chapter, its publications, and information on placing queries in *The Tracer.* The chapter also provides upon request (SASE) a list of persons in this area who do research for a fee.

Cemeteries/Funeral Homes
Spring Grove Cemetery
4521 Spring Grove Avenue
Cincinnati, Ohio 45232

One of the largest burial grounds in the country, this cemetery has excellent records.

United Jewish Cemetery
8501 Ridge Road
Cincinnati, Ohio 45236
(513) 891-1770

The cemetery answers letters of inquiry. It holds funeral records for six Jewish cemeteries in the Greater Cincinnati area (from 1821).

Weil Funeral Home
3901 Reading Road
Cincinnati, Ohio 45229
(513) 281-0178

Founded January 1, 1912.

Newspaper
The American Israelite
906 Main Street, Room 505
Cincinnati, Ohio 45202
(513) 621-3145

Oldest English-Jewish weekly in America, founded July 15, 1854, by Isaac M. Wise. Has bound volume of most editions.

■ CLEVELAND

Abba Hillel Silver Archives and Library
The Temple
University Circle at Silver Park
Cleveland, Ohio 44106
(216) 791-7755

Contains the writings, works, papers, letters and photos of Rabbi Abba Hillel Silver and a vast collection of other reference material.

Cleveland Board of Elections
2925 Euclid Ave.
Cleveland, Ohio 44115
(216) 443-3200

Researchers may request the following information by telephone:

- Whether or not an individual was registered to vote in Cuyahoga County
- Number of naturalization certificate
- Court where naturalization certificate was issued

Cleveland Jewish Archives
(see Western Reserve Historical Society)

Cleveland Jewish News
3645 Warrensville Center Road
Suite #230
Cleveland, Ohio 44122

College of Jewish Studies Library
(See Beachwood)

Cuyahoga County Archives
2905 Franklin Boulevard
Cleveland, Ohio 44113
Records may be found for aliens naturalized in Common Pleas Court.

- Petitions (1906 to approximately 1931); these records are also on microfilm at the WRHS library; the petition provides information similar to petitions found in federal court
- Declarations of Intention; 1818–1905—date of arrival, date of declaration, and country of origin. 1906–1971—information nearly equivalent to petitions. Only the date of completed naturalization is excluded
- Indexes to Declarations of Intention (1818–1971); lists all those who filed for naturalization in Common Pleas Court
- Card file index (1818–1931); includes only the persons who completed the naturalization process and filed petitions
- Extensive family history sources: birth, marriage, death, and election records from the nineteenth and twentieth centuries, plus court records from the same period

Jewish Community Federation
1750 Euclid Avenue
Cleveland, Ohio 44115
Publishes: *Guide to Jewish Cleveland.*

Old Federal Courthouse
201 Superior Avenue, Room 100
Cleveland, Ohio 44114
(216) 522-4200
For aliens naturalized in federal court, records include

- Petitions (from 1907); those dated prior to 1907 are available from the Immigration and Naturalization Service, Washington, D.C. 20536.
- Card file index to all petitions filed in federal court (from 1855); persons who failed to complete the naturalization process may also be included in this file.

Cleveland Public Library
A325 Superior Avenue
Cleveland, Ohio 44114
(216) 623-2800

- Extensive map collection
- Genealogy books

Newspaper Room
623-2904
The library offers a Necrology Service, and will check files since 1850.

City Directories Department
(216) 623-2864
- City Directories since 1837

The department will answer phone requests for up to three listings.

Family History Center
(See Kirtland and Westlake)

Western Reserve Historical Society
History Library
10825 East Boulevard
Cleveland, Ohio 44106
(216) 721-5722
Contact librarian or Documents & Manuscripts Section of the library. No admission charge to members of the society.

- Indexes (in book form) for Ohio census, 1820–1860, and Soundex (microfilm) for 1880 and 1900 Ohio census
- Necrology File (Cleveland newspaper death notices) 1850–1975
- 1810–1941 microfilm index to marriage records and the auditors tax duplicate, 1819–1869
- City directories:
  Cleveland (1837–1972)
  Other United States cities (late nineteenth–early twentieth centuries)
- Entire U.S. census (1790–1900)
- Entire Soundex (1880–1900)
- 1907 Cuyahoga County voter-registration book (all twenty-six Cleveland wards are indexed)

The library also houses the Cleveland Jewish Archives and intains the best overall collection of books, documents, manuscripts, business records, and genealogical information for the Jewish family researcher in the Cleveland and northeastern Ohio area.

Synagogues

Fairmount Temple
(Euclid Avenue Temple)
23737 Fairmount Boulevard
Cleveland, Ohio 44122
(216) 464-1330

Heights Jewish Center
14270 Cedar Road
Cleveland, Ohio 44121
(216) 382-1958

14274 Superior Road
Cleveland, Ohio 44118
(216) 932-7424

Park Synagogue
3300 Mayfield Road
Cleveland Heights, Ohio 44118
(216) 371-2244
Published: *75th Anniversary Book,* 1944; *Oral History,* Henry Rocker, 1966, 17 pages; *Oral History,* Myron Guren, 1966, 26 pages; *Oral History,* Myron Guren, 1980, 44 pages.

Temple on the Heights
(B'nai Jeshurun)
27501 Fairmount Boulevard
Cleveland, Ohio 44124
(216) 831-6555

Temple Emanu-El
2200 South Green Road
Cleveland, Ohio 44121
(216) 381-6600

The Temple
University Circle and Silver Park
Cleveland, Ohio 44106
(216) 791-7755
Fiftieth Anniversary Services, 1900, 26 pages; *The Temple: 1850–1950,* 1950, 39 pages.

The Temple—The Branch
(See Beachwood)

Bibliography

Gartner, L. P. *History of the Jews in Cleveland.* 2nd ed. Cleveland, OH: Western Reserve Historical Society and the Jewish Community Federation of Cleveland, 1987.

Guide to Jewish Cleveland. Cleveland, OH: Jewish Community Federation.

Vincent, S. Z., and Rubenstein, J. *Merging Traditions—Jewish Life in Cleveland.* Cleveland, OH: Western Reserve Historical Society and the Jewish Community Federation of Cleveland.

Weisenfeld, L. *Jewish Life in Cleveland in the 1920's and 1930's: The Memoirs of a Jewish Journalist.* Cleveland, OH: Jewish Voice Pictorial.

■ FAIRVIEW PARK
(Cleveland Metropolitan Area)

Cuyahoga County Public Library
Fairview Park Regional
4449 West 213th Street
Fairview Park, Ohio 44126
(216) 333-4700
Large genealogical holdings.

■ KIRTLAND
(Cleveland Metropolitan Area)

Family History Center
8901 Chillicothe Road
Kirtland, Ohio 44904
(216) 256-8808

■ NORWOOD
(Cincinnati Metropolitan Area)

Family History Center
5505 Bosworth Place
Norwood, Ohio 45212
(513) 531-5624

Norwood Health Center
2059 Sherman Avenue
Norwood, Ohio 45212
Some birth records before 1908; all after 1908.

■ READING

Reading City Hall
100 Market Street
Reading, Ohio 45215
Birth records 1899 to date.

■ ST. BERNARD

St. Bernard City Hall
110 Washington Street
St. Bernard, Ohio 45217
St. Bernard birth records available only for persons who were born at home or who died at home (from 1889). All other birth and death records available at City of Cincinnati Vital Records.

■ WESTLAKE
(Cleveland Metropolitan Area)

Family History Center
25000 Westwood Road
Westlake, Ohio 44145
(216) 777-1518

■ YOUNGSTOWN

Jewish Community Center
Youngstown Jewish Archives Project
505 Gypsy Lane
Youngstown, Ohio 44504
(216) 746-3251
Youngstown is collecting family genealogies, histories, memorabilia, manuscripts, photographs, etc., tracing the history of the Jewish community in Youngstown. The collection was begun in 1987 and is an ongoing project.

Mahoning County Court House
120 Market Street
Youngstown, Ohio 44503
Naturalization records.

Temple Rodef Sholem
Elm Street and Woodbine
Youngstown, Ohio 44505
(216) 744-5001
One of the oldest Reform congregations in northeastern Ohio. This temple was established in 1864. A 100th anniversary book was published listing names and other important information about the congregation that may be of genealogical value to the researcher.

Cemeteries

Knox Street Cemetery
South Avenue at Knox Street
Youngstown, Ohio 44502
Records dating back to 1910 are kept at the Youngstown Jewish Community Center.

Todd Cemetery
2200 Belmont Avenue
Youngstown, Ohio
(216) 743-3194
Includes Rodef Sholem section.

Bibliography
Bell, C. W. *The Ohio Genealogical Guide. 3rd ed.*
County by County in Ohio Genealogy. Columbus, OH: Ohio State Library, 1977.
Golden, H. *Travels through Jewish America.* Garden City, NY: Doubleday, 1973.
Lipman, E. J., and Vorspan, A. *A Tale of Ten Cities.* New York: Union of American Hebrew Congregations, 1962.
Sperry, K. "Genealogical Research in Ohio." *National Genealogical Society Quarterly*, Vol. 75, No. 2, June 1887.

OKLAHOMA

■ NORMAN
(Metropolitan Oklahoma City Area)

B'nai B'rith Hillel Foundation Student Center
494 Elm
Norman, Oklahoma
(405) 321-3703
The staff will attempt to answer limited questions.
The library houses:

- A complete set of the *Southwest Jewish Chronicle*

■ OKLAHOMA CITY

Division of Vital Statistics
State Department of Health
P.O. Box 53551
N.E. 10th and Stonewall
Oklahoma City, Oklahoma 73152
There is a charge for certified copy. A stamped, self-addressed envelope is required. Write for the "Application for Search and Certified Copy" of either birth or death certificates.

- State birth and death records
Oklahoma birth and death records statewide since 1908 under permissive rather than mandatory legislation. As a result, many of the births and deaths were not recorded. Since 1917, registration has been required.

There is no centralized collection of these records in Oklahoma.

Oklahoma County Historical Society
Museum of the Unassigned Lands
4300 North Sewell Boulevard
Oklahoma City, Oklahoma 73118
(405) 521-1889
Primarily a display museum (little reference material available).

The Oklahoma Historical Society
Wiley Post Historical Building
2100 N. Lincoln
Oklahoma City, Oklahoma 73105
(405) 521-2491
Professional genealogists on staff.
Each query must be specific about the type of information diesired and must give the full name, approximate date, and place of residence of the individual on whom data is sought. A legal size, self-addressed, stamped envelope should accompany each inquiry. There is no research fee.
Genealogical questions requiring extensive research cannot be answered by mail.
There is a charge for xerox materials, prints from the microfilm reader/printer, and postage handling.
The Society does not make its materials available through interlibrary loan, but will undertake to fill orders if specific pages are cited.

- Houses the collection of the Oklahoma Genealogical Society in their Genealogy library
- Oklahoma City Directories from 1889

The Metropolitan Library System
131 Dean A. McGee Avenue
Oklahoma City, Oklahoma 73102
(405) 235-0571
Reference librarians will answer telepbone questions, although none are professional genealogists.

- Houses the genealogy collection of the City–County Public Library
- Oklahoma City Directory eollection from 1906
- Addresses of the county clerks (to obtain marriage records since 1907)

The France Room (4th floor)
Resources for responding to written inquiries are limited. Fees for research and photocopying. Materials are available through interlibrary loan.

- Houses the library's Oklahoma Collection

Newspaper
Southwest Jewish Chronical
314-B Robinson
Oklahoma City, Oklahoma 73102
The Jewish quarterly (since 1929).

Synagogues
Emanuel Synagogue [Traditional]
Fonded in 1904.
Has its own Emanuel Hebrew Cemetery, prior to which they used a portion of Fairlawn Cemetery, which Temple B'nai Israel had consecrated for its use.

Temple B'nai Israel [Reform]
Founded in 1903.
Provides for Jewish burials in the Jewish sections of Fairlawn Cemetery and Memorial Cemetery.

Funeral Home
Hahn-Cook Street & Draper
6006 N. Grand Blvd.
Oklahoma City, Oklahoma 73118

Will respond to written inquiries on a limited basis at no charge.

• Records of the Jewish funerals from 1898

Bibliography

B'nai Emunah: 1916–1966. Tulsa, OK: B'nai Emunah, 1966.

Engelhardt, L. "Growing Up Jewish in Oklahoma." *Oklahoma Monthly*, October 1979.

Falk, R. M. *A History of the Jews of Oklahoma*, 1946. (Rabbinical Thesis submitted in partial fulfillment of the requirements for the Degree of Rabbi at HUC).

Temple Israel: Family Album. Tulsa, OK: Temple Israel, 1984.

Tobias, H. J. *The Jews in Oklahoma.* Norman, OK: University of Oklahoma Press, 1980.

Wilson, T. P. *Wheeling Carts Round the World: The Career of Sylvan N. Goldman.* Norman, OK: University of Oklahoma Press, 1978.

OREGON

■ PORTLAND

The Center for Health Statistics
1400 S.W. Fifth Avenue
Portland, Oregon 97201
(503) 229-5895

Fee for record or search. Birth and death records are not made public for 100 years. Birth records are restricted to the registrant, a member of the immediate family, legal representative, or legal guardian.

• Births in Oregon since 1903 (not public until after 100 years)
• Deaths in Oregon since 1903 (not public until after 100 years)
• Marriages in Oregon since 1906
• Divorces in Oregon since 1925

Jewish Historical Society of Oregon
6651 Southwest Capitol Highway
Portland, Oregon 97219
(503) 246-9844

Archives open by appointment. No charge for written replies (exceptions include copying large amount of information).
Archive includes:

• Documents (letters, manuscripts, and minute books of local Jewish institutions)
• Memorabilia
• Photographs
• Over 130 tapes and transcripts of oral histories
• *The Jewish Review* (complete run)
• Papers that predate *The Jewish Review* (small and incomplete series)

The Jewish Review
6800 S.W. Beaverton-Hillsdale Highway
Suite C
Portland, Oregon 97225
(503) 292-4913 and 292-4933

Multnomah County Library
Literature and History Department
801 S.W. 10th Avenue
Portland, Oregon 97205-2597
(503) 223-7201

Will respond to brief written inquiries, although unable to perform in-depth research. Small fees for copying materials.

• *The Jewish Tribune* files (1900–1919)
• *The Scribe* files (1919–1953)
• *The Jewish Review* (1956 to present)
• City directories since 1865 (except 1919, 1942, 1945–1949, 1951, 1966, and 1984)
• Census records for the state of Oregon (1852–1910)
• Local history books
• Various genealogical works pertaining to Oregon and Washington

The Oregon Historical Society
1230 S.W. Park Avenue
Portland, Oregon 97205
(503) 222-1741

The Oregon Historical Society Research Library is a private library open to the public at no charge. Most material available through interlibrary loan.

Genealogical and historical research services available at modest fees, which are outlined in a sheet entitled "Research Assistance-Policy & Fees," which is available upon request.

• *American Hebrew News* files (1893–1900)
• City directories (1863–1989 except for 1919, 1942, 1945–1949, 1951 and 1966)
• U.S. federal census for the state of Oregon (1850, 1860, 1870, 1880, 1900, and 1910)

The Society published *The Jews of Oregon: 1850–1950* by Steven Lowenstein.

• Extensive index (includes all names of persons mentioned in the book or shown in photographs)
• Large and helpful bibliography

Synagogues
Congregation Beth Israel
1931 N.W. Flanders
Portland, Oregon 97209
(503) 222-1069

Will attempt to respond to written inquiries, at no charge.
Archives consist of:

• Programs
• Bulletins
• Photos
• Newspapers
• Minutes
• Membership lists to at least 1970
• Burials at their cemetery (since 1900); access to these records not allowed

Congregation Neveh Shalom
2900 S.W. Peaceful Lane
Portland, Oregon 97201
(503) 246-8831

Access to archives by request, through the synagogue office. Limited requests answered.

Neveh Shalom is the result of the merger of Ahavai Sholom (founded 1869) and Neveh Zedek (founded 1893). Although merged, two separate cemeteries with complete records are maintained.

Ahavai Sholom records:

- Board minutes (1884 on, with the exception of 1928–1932)

Neveh Zedek records:

- *Chronicle* (congregation's bulletin, from 1953); complete file
- *Following a River* (1989), congregational history recounts of past 120 years

Other congregations, over 40 years old:

Kesser Israel
136 S.W. Meade
Portland, Oregon 97201
(503) 277-5999

Shaarei Torah Congregation
920 N.W. 25th Avenue
Portland, Oregon 97210
(503) 226-6131

Archives date back to September 1979. Inquiries in the form of letters to the editor are welcome.

Bibliography
Lowenstein, S. *The Jews of Oregon: 1850–1950.* Portland: Jewish Historical Society of Oregon, 1988.

Toll, W. *The Making of an Ethnic Middle Class: Portland Jewry Over Four Generations.* Albany, NY: State University of New York Press, 1982.

PENNSYLVANIA

■ ELKINS PARK
(Philadelphia Metropolitan Area)

Reform Congregation
Keneseth Israel Archives
Old York and Township Line Roads
Elkins Park, Pennsylvania 19117
(215) 887-8700

Archives contain birth, marriage and death records (will not answer letters of inquiry).

Publication: *90th Anniversary Record,* 1937, 12 pages; *Its First Hundred Years: 1847–1947,* 1950, 1 volume; *1847–1972,* 1972, 4 pages.

■ GREENTREE
(Pittsburgh Metropolitan Area)

Family History Center
46 School Street
Greentree, Pennsylvania 15242
(412) 921-2115

■ HARRISBURG

Pennsylvania Historical and Museum Commission
William Penn Memorial Museum and Archives Bldg.
Box 1026
Harrisburg, Pennsylvania 17108
(717) 783-9873

Holdings include microfilm copies of records concerning Pennsylvania Jewish congregations that responded to the Western Pennsylvania survey. (See p. 120 for further description.)

■ NEW CASTLE

Pennsylvania Department of Health
P.O. Box 1528
New Castle, Pennsylvania 16103
or
101 South Mercer Street
New Castle, Pennsylvania 16103

Births from 1906 to present; deaths from 1906 to 1965.

■ PHILADELPHIA

Annenberg Research Institute
420 Walnut Street
Philadelphia, Pennsylvania 19106
(215) 238-1290

Annenberg Research Institute is a postdoctoral research institution devoted to Judaic and Near Eastern Studies. It is the successor to Dropsie College and is an institution of theological and nondenominational character. Especially rich in Esoterica Judaica dating from the last century. The institute holds over 100,000 volumes relating to Judaic and Near Eastern Studies, including:

- Most Jewish journals and old newspapers
- Yizkor books
- Ancient and medieval manuscripts
- Rare printed books from the 15th and 16th centuries
- Archival materials
- Archaeological artifacts

The Documentation Center has as its goal the acquisition and storage of copies of all available records (communal archives, tombstones, etc.) from Jewish communities in countries where few or no Jews remain today.

The library will transfer these materials (as well as Hebrew and other relevant manuscripts) to a computerized database, which scholars anywhere in the world will be able to reach and use by means of standard telecommunications.

City Archives of Philadelphia
401 N. Broad St. #942
Philadelphia, Pennsylvania 19108
(215) 686-1580

The City Archives does answer simple letters of inquiry (no research fee); however, it cannot handle extended genealogical research.

Note: When requesting birth or death records, state on the application that the records are for genealogical research to insure that you receive complete forms of the certificates. The complete form includes the parents' names, ages, place of birth, and names of the registrar and certifier.

Unlike some other states, Pennsylvania does not permit self-search of the records because of their confidentiality. All searches must be done by the staff except those records prior to 1915. Books, microfilm, three readers available.

Marriage/divorce records, and birth/death records prior to 1906 are not available from the Division of Vital Statistics. In most cases, they may be obtained from the courthouse in the county where the event occurred.

The City Archives and Related Municipal Records contain the following:

- Birth and death certificates, July 1, 1860–June 30, 1915:
  1. With date: Prior to July 1, 1915, write to:

Department of Records
Room 401, City Hall Annex
Philadelphia, Pennsylvania 19107

  2. With date: After July 1, 1915, write to:

Department of Health
P.O. Box 1528
New Castle, Pennsylvania 16103

  3. Without date, locate personally, room 522 (not after 1903 for birth certificate)
- Cemetery records: 1803–1860
- City directories: 1785–1930; 1935–1936
- Deeds 1683–1863; after 1863 go to Room 153, City Hall, Philadelphia 19107
- Marriage Records: indexed, 1865–1885; post-1885: Orphans Court, Room 413, City Hall
- Naturalization Records
  1. WPA index of all records (1794–1880)
  2. County court records, 1881–1897, 1913–1930
- Tax Records: 1769–1854
  Post-1912:

Records Storage
401 N. Broad St.
Philadelphia, Pennsylvania 19108

- Wills: Name index, 1682 to present

Register of Wills, Room 185
City Hall
Philadelphia, Pennsylvania 19107

The Archive does not have specifically Jewish records, but it holds records of Philadelphia Jewish hospitals among its doctors' returns. There is also some information on religion and marriage.

The Genealogical Society of Pennsylvania
1300 Locust Street
Philadelphia, Pennsylvania 19107
(215) 545-0391
and

The Historical Society of Pennsylvania
(215) 732-6200
There is an annual membership fee. Letters of

inquiry are answered on a limited basis. The collection contains the following, specifically relating to Jewish genealogical research:

- Records of Mikveh Israel Jewish Congregation, Philadelphia
- Records of Rodeph Shalom Congregation, Philadelphia
- Tombstone inscriptions from the Jewish cemetery, Ninth & Spruce, Philadelphia

The library also includes a large collection of books, genealogies, manuscripts, newspapers, and other detailed records for the genealogist.

Gratz College Library
Old York Road & Melrose Avenue
Melrose Park, Pennsylvania 19126
(215) 635-7304

The Gratz College Library serves the community of Greater Philadelphia by circulating books to community members on a deposit basis. Visitors to Gratz are welcome to use the library.

The library houses a comprehensive research collection of more than 35,000 volumes of Judaica and Hebraica. Its collection is especially strong in the subject areas of Bible, Rabbinics, Jewish philosophy, medieval and modern Hebrew literature, Yiddish literature, Jewish history, Holocaust studies, American Jewish literature, and Jewish education.

- Large collection of books on Jewish genealogy, many of which are rare and out of print
- Monographs
- Yizkor (memorial) volumes
- Relevant journal articles
- Index to Jewish periodicals
- Index of articles on Jewish studies
- Extensive retrospective periodical files
- More than 100 current periodicals in Hebrew, English, and Yiddish, from the United States, Israel, Great Britain, and Latin America
- Comprehensive works on Jewish history
- The Holocaust Oral History Archive. The archive is collecting testimony from Holocaust survivors now living in Philadelphia. Founded in 1980, the archive houses the largest collection of testimony in the area, gathered from more than 600 survivors

Various encyclopedias housed in the library include

- *Encyclopaedia Hebraica*
- *Encyclopaedia Judaica*
- *Encyclopedia Jüdisches Lexikon*
- *The Jewish Encyclopedia*
- *The Universal Jewish Encyclopedia*

National Museum of American Jewish History
Independence Mall East
55 North Fifth Street
Philadelphia, Pennsylvania 19106
(215) 923-3811

No research fee; donations accepted; will answer letters of inquiry. Contains:

- A number of early directories from New York and Philadelphia
- A Philadelphia mohel's register (early 19th century)

- Philadelphia documents, family histories, and manuscripts

National Archives Middle Atlantic Branch
9th and Market Streets
Philadelphia, Pennsylvania 19107
Room 1350
(215) 597-3000

Serves Delaware, Pennsylvania, Maryland, Virginia and West Virginia. Open to the public, self-service. Small fee for microfilm and paper copies.

Records of U.S. District Courts, U.S. Court of Appeals for third and fourth Circuits, U.S. Army Corps of Engineers, U.S. Navy. They do not have state and local court records. Partial holdings include:

Naturalization Petitions

Eastern District (Philadelphia)	Index: 1795–1951; Petitions 1790–1930
Western District (Pittsburgh)	Index: 1820–1906
Middle District (Scranton and Harrisburg)	Index: 1901–1984
Baltimore & Wilmington, Maryland	Index: 1797–1951

Passenger Lists
Indexes to Passenger Arrival Lists:

Philadelphia
Name Index 1800–1906
Soundex Index 1883–1948
Book Index by date 1906–1926
Baltimore
Name Index 1833–1866
Soundex Index Federal list 1820–1897
Soundex Index 1897–1952
Galveston
Name Index 1896–1951
Name Index 1906–1951
Name Index 1820–1874
Gulf Ports (Atlantic and Gulf Ports) supplemental

Passenger Arrival Lists:

Philadelphia	1800–1882; 1883–1945
Baltimore	1891–1948 (earlier arrival lists in Washington)
Galveston	1891–1948

Philadelphia Records of Special Board of Inquiry, Immigration & Naturalization Service. Interrogations of arrivals on health and legal grounds, 1893–1909.

Census Records: 1790–1910, including two reels from 1890 Soundex for census years: 1880, 1900, 1910.

Civil War Records 1861–1865. Indexes for Union from Maryland, Delaware, Pennsylvania, West Virginia, and Confederate soldiers from Maryland and Virginia.

Revolutionary War Records 1775–1783. Military records and Pension Files of Revolutionary War soldiers.

Clerk of Orphans Court
Division of the Court of Common Pleas
City Hall, Room 415, Marriage Records
Philadelphia, Pennsylvania 19107
Record Room Number: (215) 686-2830

Records may be used without fee or time limit; however, all printing is done by the staff. Microfilm research is normally limited to five records per day.

Marriage records since 1885 (WPA compilation covers 1885–1942). After 1942, entry is handwritten, divided into sections by first name (male column on left, female on the right), not in alphabetical order, divided into one-year intervals. There is one volume for each letter of the alphabet.

All Orphans Court records include minors (guardianships), incompetencies, trust funds, decedents, and dockets. All documents still exist on paper as well as microfilm.

Many of the more recent forms (around 1900) give both parents' occupations, addresses, place of birth, etc.

Request forms can be obtained by mail from City Hall. You are required to furnish the name of the husband and wife (include maiden name), and date and place of marriage. Either a certified or an uncertified copy may be obtained for a fee. (Ask for all the forms in the marriage record.)

Philadelphia City Hall
Register of Wills
Room 185
Philadelphia, Pennsylvania 19107
(215) 686-6250

- Wills: 1642 to present
- Administrations: 1960 to present

Indexes, microfilm, and microfiche may be used without fee or time limit and are open to the public. Staff must get films for you. Original documents must be ordered ahead of time. Fees depend on whether material is certified or uncertified.

Written requests accepted. Include full name of deceased and year of death. Address letter to the attention of the Clerk of Wills and Administration. You will receive a postcard stating findings. You are free to come in and scrutinize or simply send a check.

City Hall of Philadelphia
Department of Records Registry
Room 163, Index Room for Deeds and Mortgages
Philadelphia, Pennsylvania 19107
(215) 686-2294

Index books, microfilms, and microfiche open to the public; staff will explain procedures to get you started. Finding aids include microfilm and microfiche readers.

All index books and microfilms of grantees and grantors and mortgages from 1683 to present. Also assignments, releases, notaries, powers of attorneys, deeds, and satisfactions.

With the name of a property owner and a year (bought or sold) you can look up the proper microfilm in the microfilm index drawer and find a book and page number. With this you can order a microfiche in Room 153 to find your deed or mortgage. Indexes are filed by year and alphabetically by last initial. There are separate drawers for grantors, grantees, and mortgages.

Recent records are still in books.

City Hall of Philadelphia
Department of Records Registry
Room 153, Deeds and Mortgages
Philadelphia, Pennsylvania 19107
(215) 686-2296

- Records of deeds from the colonial period to date
- Records of mortgages 1736 to date

Index books, microfilms, and microfiche open to the public; staff assists in getting the material for you. Finding aids include multiple microfilm and microfiche readers.

Fees depend on whether material is certified or uncertified. Staff takes no requests—self-research only. All printing performed by staff. There is staff to look up information on a computer to access book and page numbers for you to order microfiche for your research.

Free Library of Philadelphia
Logan Square
Philadelphia, Pennsylvania 19103
(215) 686-5396

Social Science and History Department, 2nd Floor

This department houses a fine genealogical collection of indexes, books, and other sources in a special section of shelves. Ask the staff for assistance in locating these and individual family genealogies. Many titles are in closed stacks. Ask reference desk for copy of *Researching Your Family History, Social Science and History Department*. It will assist you in your search. At this same desk, order reverse directories. There is a fifteen-minute wait. They are received in the Literature Department across the hall. This department also contains the Map Department.

Map Department

Offers atlases, gazetteers, globes, maps, books such as *Wards of Philadelphia* going back to 1800s. Area of specialization is Philadelphia, Pennsylvania, Northeastern, and Middle Atlantic states. They will help you find the ward of an address so you can research it in the U.S. census.

Newspaper and Database Center, 2nd Floor (next door to Social Science)

City directories 1785–1936 on microfilm are listed alphabetically by name, occupation, address, and in later years, spouse. Later directories also list by occupations such as butchers, grocers, and tailors. Research is self-service. Printing is performed by staff.

Newspapers are on microfilm and hard copy dating back approximately to the 1860s. Examples: *The Public Ledger, Inquirer, Bulletin,* and *The Philadelphia Record*. A manual lists holdings.

Government Publications, 1st Floor

Philadelphia census on microfilm, 1790–1910, with the exception of 1890, which was destroyed by fire. Microfilm readers and printers. Self-service.

Index for Philadelphia naturalization records 1789–1880, giving names and dates where these documents can be found, e.g., National Archives.

Book index to Pennsylvania census up to 1860.

United States District Court
Eastern District of Pennsylvania
U.S. District Court House
Independence Mall West
601 Market Street
Philadelphia, Pennsylvania 19106
(215) 597-7731

Naturalization Division: Room 2625, 2nd Floor

No research fee. Office answers letters or phone calls of inquiry. Name and approximate year helps; if not, they can check all indexes.

This office provides dates, names, and petition numbers of naturalizations, which researchers may then use to obtain a naturalization petition either from the National Archives Middle Atlantic Branch of Philadelphia, or here, if later than 1965. The indexes may also provide ages, name change, certificate number, when filed, when admitted, and sometimes, addresses.

Card indexes for naturalizations from 1795 to present, open to the public. They are filed alphabetically by "new name," sometimes "old name." They are broken down by years: 1795–1905; 1905–1926; 1926–1953; 1953–present.

Indexes and petitions are for those naturalized in the Philadelphia Eastern District Court of Pennsylvania, and Circuit Court. For copies of records of the Supreme Court of Pennsylvania, write to:

Pennsylvania Historical and Museum Commission
P.O. Box 1026
Harrisburg, Pennsylvania 17120

Records of the Supreme Court of Pennsylvania (a fee is charged—do not send money; they will bill you). Their records cover the period 1794–1868 (primarily petitions), and contain the following information: person's name, country of former allegiance, and date of naturalization. The commission also has an index to naturalization papers from 1794 to 1824 and 1842–1868 (two volumes).

This office holds the actual paper documents for naturalization petitions from 1965 to present. All previous petitions are at the National Archives, 9th and Market Street, Philadelphia.

Immigration Division: Room 1321, 1st Floor
(215) 597-7934 to order forms (recording)
(215) 597-3961 recording for information

Call or write for forms to verify immigrant's records. Each application requires a fee. Request Form G641 to verify information, Forms G639/G652 for Freedom of Information and Privacy Act forms.

You can try ordering a copy of the alien's photograph. If they have it, they will mail it to you.

Philadelphia Jewish Archives Center at the Balch Institute
18 South 7th Street
Philadelphia, Pennsylvania 19106
(215) 925-8090

No research fee. There is a fee per name to search the immigration records.

The Philadelphia Jewish Archives Center is an educational institute for the collection, preservation, and display of the public and private records of the Jewish community of the Philadelphia area. The collection contains the following, specifically relating to Jewish family history:

- Hebrew Immigration Aid Society (HIAS) Records, Records of Arrivals to Philadelphia port, aided by HIAS, 1884–1921

- Passage Order Books. Rosenbaum Bank, 1894–1921. Lipschutz Bank, 1923–1948
- Unidentified volume, 1907–1910
- Jewish Family Service, 1822–1973
- Family papers
- Beneficial associations
- Related genealogical subject files and reference works
- Philadelphia Workmen's Circle records, mostly in Yiddish, cover the district-level activity between 1931 and 1938. A guide to this collection is available
- Trans-Atlantic steamship books
- Pictures

Newspapers

Jewish Exponent
226 South 16th Street
Philadelphia, Pennsylvania 19102

Jewish Times of the Greater Northeast
103-A Tomlinson Road
Huntingdon Valley, Pennsylvania 19006

Synagogues

Congregation B'nai Abraham
521–27 Lombard Street
Philadelphia, Pennsylvania 19147

Congregation Rodeph Shalom
615 North Broad Street
Philadelphia, Pennsylvania 19123
(215) 627-6747
No research fee or membership fee. Letters of inquiry are answered

- Philadelphia marriage book from the 19th century
- Burial records of congregation
- Some family histories

Publication: *The History of Rodeph Shalom Congregation: 1802–1926,* 155 pages (1926).

Har Zion Temple
Hagys Ford at Hollow Roads
Penn Valley, Pennsylvania 19072
Publication: *Light from Our Past: 25th Anniversary,* 50 pages (1958).

Oxford Circle Jewish Community Center
Algon and Unruh Avenues
P.O. Box 11487
Philadelphia, Pennsylvania 19111
Publication: *Our 35th Year,* 1985, 25 pages.

Reform Congregation
Keneseth Israel Archives
(See Elkins Park)

Cemeteries (Philadelphia Metropolitan Area)
Adath Jeshurun Cemetery
1855 Bridge Street
Philadelphia, Pennsylvania 19124
(215) 743-2524

Chevra Bikur Cholem Cemetery
1853 Bridge Street
Philadelphia, Pennsylvania 19124
(215) 745-5338

Har Jehuda Cemetery
8400 Lansdowne Ave.
Upper Darby, Pennsylvania 19026
(215) 789-2104

Har Nebo Cemetery
Oxford Avenue & Benner Street
Philadelphia, Pennsylvania 19111
(215) 535-1530

Haym Salomon Memorial Park
200 Moores Road
Frazer, Pennsylvania 19355
(215) 877-1142

Hebrew Mutual Cemetery
Cemetery Lane and Kingsessing Avenue
Philadelphia, Pennsylvania 19142

King David Memorial Park
3594 Bristol Road
Bensalem, Pennsylvania 19020
(215) 464-4747

Mikve Israel Cemetery
Spruce Street between 8th and 9th Streets on north side of street; historical site
1114 Federal Street
Market Street at 55th Street
Philadelphia, Pennsylvania 19139

Montefiore Cemetery
Church Road and Borbeck Street
Rockledge, Pennsylvania 19111
(215) 742-5200

Mount Carmel Cemetery
Frankford and Cheltenham Avenue
Philadelphia, Pennsylvania 19135
(215) 289-0939

Mount Jacob Cemetery
141 Bartram Avenue
Glenolden, Pennsylvania 19036
(215) 726-8633

Mount Lebanon Cemetery
1200 Bartram Avenue
Collingdale, Pennsylvania 19023
(215) 729-7400

Mount Sharon Cemetery
East Springfield Road
Springfield, Pennsylvania 19064
(215) 543-8900

Mount Sinai Cemetery
Bridge and Cottage Streets
Philadelphia, Pennsylvania 19124
(215) 535-5274

Roosevelt Memorial Park
Old Lincoln Highway
Trevose, Pennsylvania
(215) 673-7500

Shalom Memorial Park
Pine & Byberry Roads
Philadelphia, Pennsylvania 19115
(215) 673-4600

Crescent Burial Park
Route 130 and Westfield Avenue
Pennsauken, New Jersey 08110
(609) 662-6313

Funeral Homes
Berschler Funeral Chapels, Inc.
4300 North Broad Street
Philadelphia, Pennsylvania 19140
(215) 329-2900
5341 State Highway 38
Pennsauken, New Jersey 08109
(609) 665-2900

Goldstein's Funeral Directors, Inc.
6410 North Broad Street
Philadelphia, Pennsylvania 19126
(215) 927-5800

Joseph Levine & Son, Inc.
7112 North Broad Street
Philadelphia, Pennsylvania 19126
(215) 927-2700

Rosenberg's Raphael Sacks Memorial Chapel, Inc.
4720 North Broad Street
Philadelphia, Pennsylvania 19141
(215) 455-0551, 455-0100

Bibliography
Friedman, M. *Jewish Life in Philadelphia 1830–1940.* Philadelphia: ISHI Publications, 1983.
_____. *Jewish Life in Philadelphia 1940–1985.* Ardmore, PA: Seth Press Inc. 1986.
Morais, H. S. *The Jews of Philadelphia.* Philadelphia: The Levytype Co., 1894.
Souvenir Book of Congregation Agudath Israel of Darby & Collingdale, Tenth Anniversry, 1931. Philadelphia: Congregation Agudath Israel.
Wolf, E., II, and Whiteman, M. *The History of the Jews of Philadelphia from Colonial Times to the Age of Jackson.* Philadelphia: The Jewish Publication Society of America, 1957.

■ PITTSBURGH

Carnegie Library of Pittsburgh
4400 Forbes Avenue
Pittsburgh, Pennsylvania 15213
(412) 622-3131 Main telephone number
(412) 622-3114 Information and reference
(412) 622-3154 Pennsylvania Room/History

The Pennsylvania Room holds a vast collection of Western Pennsylvania historical materials, including census rolls, city directories (incomplete set), and passenger records.

The Pittsburgh Room includes the WPA cemetery index project, old *Jewish Criterions* listing members of synagogues, contributors to many organizations, a section of local Judaica including local history, Jewish family books and archival material, card file of indexes to obit notices in several local newspapers (does not include the Jewish papers), published indexes to some local court records which includes relevant data.

City of Pittsburgh
State Office Building, Room 512
300 Liberty Avenue
Pittsburgh, Pennsylvania 15222
(412) 565-5114

From 1906 to present.

City County Building
Marriage Records Department
Grant Street
Pittsburgh, Pennsylvania 15219
(412) 355-4177

There is a minimal research fee for letter inquiries, provided the following information is given: man's name, woman's maiden name, year of marriage.

Marriage/divorce records (1885 to present) are indexed in huge bound volumes by male/female and time period. Original records on microfilm can be personally researched (no fee).

Clerk of Court
Courthouse, Room 114
Pittsburgh, Pennsylvania 15219
(412) 355-5378

- Index to naturalizations (also at National Archives in Philadelphia)
- Naturalizations from 1950 to present (note: records incomplete)

Hillman Library
University of Pittsburgh Campus
Forbes Avenue and Bigelow Boulevard
Pittsburgh, Pennsylvania 15260
(412) 624-4434 (Reference Section)

This library has a Judaica and genealogy section consisting of materials relating to organizations such as United Jewish Appeal and B'nai B'rith as well as small shuls.

Archives of Industrial Society [3rd floor of Hillman Library, phone: (412) 624-4430] contains materials relating mainly to local labor organizations (cigar and needle trades which were virtually all Jewish).

World War I draft records on microfilm.

Holocaust Center of Greater Pittsburgh
242 McKee Place
Pittsburgh, Pennsylvania 15213
(412) 682-7111

Full-service educational resource center. Library (printed and audio-visual), programs include teacher training, curriculum development, speaking engagements, exhibits, production of educational materials, communitywide programs with other organizations, annual Holocaust remembrance programs, writing contest, consultations, and on-site exhibit.

Archive collection (1897 to present), documentation of eyewitness testimonies.

Historical Society of Western Pennsylvania
4338 Bigelow Boulevard
Pittsburgh, Pennsylvania 15213
(412) 681-5533

The society has a library and archives, which constitute one of the finest collections of historical and genealogical material in the area, including an almost complete series of Pittsburgh city directories as well as other towns in Western Pennsylvania. The Western Pennsylvania historical reference collection covers the colonial period, the American Revolution, the Civil War, and the early twentieth century.

The Genealogical Section

- Family histories and genealogies
- Heraldry and lineage books of heraldry organizations

Newspaper Section

- Bound copies of Pittsburgh and other Western Pennsylvania communities' newspapers
- Periodicals include journals from other historical and genealogical societies

Archives

- Papers of Western Pennsylvania families and individuals, business and civic organizations and county records up to the end of the nineteenth century
- Extensive map and picture collection including individuals, buildings and historic scenes
- "Grandmothers, Mothers & Daughters," an oral history study (completed in 1978) of ethnicity, mental health, and continuity of three generations of Jews, Italians, and Slavic American women in Pittsburgh. Contains transcripts and audio cassette tapes of interviews
- Irene Kaufman Settlement of Pittsburgh scrapbooks (1922–1936)

Family History Center
(See Greentree, p. 117)

National Council of Jewish Women
1620 Murray Avenue
Pittsburgh, Pennsylvania 15217
(412) 421-6118

Historical records of the Pittsburgh Jewish community and extensive oral history project.

Jewish Home for the Aged
4724 Browns Hill Road
Pittsburgh, Pennsylvania 15217
(412) 683-7929

Oral history project called "Roots and Branches."

Register of Wills
Court of Common Pleas
City County Building
Pittsburgh, Pennsylvania 15219
(412) 355-4188

Birth/death records from 1870 to 1905.

Letters of inquiry are answered (fee). Requests must include name of the individual you are researching, place of birth, year of birth, and parents' names.

Early death records are indexed for city and county on microfilm, which may be viewed in the City–County Building. Birth and death records not required prior to 1906. *Note:* Family History Library has microfilmed records, which appear to be more complete.

Rodef Shalom Temple
4905 Fifth Avenue
Pittsburgh, Pennsylvania 15203
(412) 621-6566

The congregation maintains the Lippman Library, the Glick Library, and Rabbinic Library, whose combined holdings exceed 10,000 volumes (including bound volumes of the *Jewish Chronicle*, and *Criterion*, which contain birth, marriage, and death notices).

Western Pennsylvania Genealogical Society
4338 Bigelow Boulevard
Pittsburgh, Pennsylvania 15213
(412) 681-5533

Note: Housed in the same building as Historical Society of Western Pennsylvania.

No research fee. Letters of inquiry are answered. There is a membership fee.

Newspaper

Jewish Chronicle
5600 Baum Boulevard
Pittsburgh, Pennsylvania 15203
(412) 687-1000

Funeral Homes

Ralph Schugar
5509 Center Avenue
Pittsburgh, Pennsylvania 15213
(412) 621-8282

Blank Brothers
3222 Forbes Avenue
Pittsburgh, Pennsylvania 15213
(412) 682-4000

Burton Hirsch
2704 Murray Avenue
Pittsburgh, Pennsylvania 15217
(412) 521-2600

H. Samson
537 Neville Street
Pittsburgh, Pennsylvania 15213
(412) 621-8000

Bibliography

Feldman, J. S. *The Early Migration and Settlement of Jews in Pittsburgh, 1754–1894.* Pittsburgh: United Jewish Federation of Pittsburgh and the Pittsburgh Council of B'nai Brith, 1959.

———. *The Jewish Experience in Western Pennsylvania: A History, 1755–1945.* Pittsburgh: The Historical Society of Western Pennsylvania, 1986.

Pine, K. *The Jews in the Hill District of Pittsburgh, 1910–1940: A Study of Trends.* Pittsburgh: University of Pittsburgh.

The Pittsburgh Jewish Community Book. 1924.

Pittsburgh Jewish Society Book. Compiled, arranged, and published by Jewish Criterion, early 20th century.

Pittsburgh Tri-State Pinkas, Jewish National Fund of America, Pittsburgh Council, and Tri-State Region. 1948.

Taylor, M. "The Jewish Community of Pittsburgh. Sample Study" [thesis]. January 1941.

TEXAS

■ AUSTIN

Bureau of Vital Statistics
Texas Department of Health
1100 West 49th Street
Austin, Texas 78756
(512) 458-7451

Birth/death certificates: The state asked the county clerks to record and send these records to the state in 1903. The state did not make it a law to do so until 1921. Even then, many births and deaths were not recorded until as late as the 1930s or even 1940s. Some records can be found at the county clerk's office in the county of birth or death, but not at the state level.

Marriage certificates: The state does not have these records until January 1966. For marriages contracted previous to that date, contact the county clerk in the county where the marriage took place.

Divorce certificates: The state does not have these records until January 1968. For divorce information previous to that date, contact the district clerk in the county where the divorce took place.

Eugene C. Barker Texas History Center
Sid Richardson Hall 2.101
The General Libraries
University of Texas at Austin
Austin, Texas 78713
(512) 471-5961 or (512) 471-1741

The center serves as the single most important resource center in existence for the study of historical development of the state of Texas. In addition, the center's extensive holdings in Southern, Western, and Southeastern history make it one of the best regional historical research repositories in the nation. Its book, map, newspaper, photographic, archival, and manuscripts resources constitute literally a treasure for anyone desiring to know more about these regions.

- A wide variety of books in the collection
- Articles on Jewish life in Texas from regional periodicals
- The following Jewish newspapers: *San Antonio Jewish Weekly; Texas Jewish Post* (Fort Worth); *Jewish Herald Voice* (Houston); *Texas Judaean Outlook* (Waco); *The Texas Jewish Press* (San Antonio); *University Jewish Voice* (Austin)
- *Manuscript Collection*
Contains the organizational records of the Texas Jewish Historical Society founded in 1980 to collect, publish, and preserve Jewish history in all areas of Texas and Texas life. Records consist of videotapes of annual meetings, programs, newsletters, and membership enrollment cards.

Places: Bruceville and Marshall, Texas

Subjects: Banks and banking; Hebrew Benevolent Society; Jewish Institute for Medical Research; Jews and Judaism; Ladies Hebrew Benevolent Society; Law, Practice of; Texas Jewish Histrocial Society; Union of American Hebrew Congregations; Women.

Photograph subjects: Texas Jewish Historical Society

Cohen (Henry) Papers, 1851, 1881–1951
Henry Cohen (1863–1952), Rabbi of the Temple B'nai Israel in Galveston, Texas, was influential in religious and social welfare activities in Texas, especially in the fields of prison reform, hospitals, schools, and immigration.
Contains records from the Ladies Hebrew Benevolent Society from Victoria, 1879–1901. The series on local history contains research on Jewish settlement throughout the state. Of note is a file on correspondence and specifications from the Union of American Hebrew Congregations to construct a camp in Bruceville. Jewish family histories and genealogies form another series in which an 1838 marriage license was granted to Albert Moses Levy and Claudinia V. Gervais by the Republic of Texas. Additions to collections are made periodically

Perry Castaneda Library
University of Texas at Austin
P.O. Box P
University Station
Austin, Texas 78713
Genealogy-related material includes extensive collection of Yizkor books.

Texas State Library and Archives
1201 Brazos Street
Box 12927
Capitol Station
Austin, Texas 78711
Genealogy collection: (512) 463-5463. The research collection emphasizes genealogical material on the

South, because most Texans had ancestors who lived in the southern states. The staff will do limited research, using indexes to answer mail requests.

The collection includes:

- Available census schedules for all states from 1790 through 1910, enhanced by a large collection of printed census indexes and Soundexes
- Yearly tax rolls of each county through 1976
- Material on family histories, marriage indexes, cemetery indexes, county histories, and the indexes to Texas birth and death certificates, located at the Texas Bureau of Vital Statistics, covering 1903 through 1973, and "probate" or delayed birth indexes covering approximately 1880 through 1940

Reference Division: (512) 463-5455.

- Maintains a library for the public and serves as a regional depository in Texas for the United States Government documents
- Houses a permanent depository collection of Texas state documents
- Materials include biographical reference works, atlases, gazetteers, almanacs, and current telephone directories, including various Jewish biographical works and periodicals

Archives Division: (512) 463-5480.

- Houses the permanently valuable, noncurrent records of the Texas government:
  Republic records for the Texas Revolution
  Texas state troop muster rolls and confederate pensions for the Civil War
  Muster rolls for the various ranger organizations from 1836 to 1900
  Old telephone directories and old city directories dating to the 19th century

Local Records Division: (512) 463-5478.

- Preserves records originated at the city and county level, including a microfilmed county-by-county inventory which lists the type and date for the record and the depository for each county with complete address and telephone information
- Has the finding aid, which may be purchased from the Local Records Division

■ BEAUMONT

Jefferson County Historical Commission
P.O. Box 4025
Beaumont, Texas 77704
(409) 835-8701

■ COLUMBUS

Nesbitt Memorial Library
529 Washington Street
Columbus, Texas 78934
(409) 732-3392

Will do research on Jewish families in area for a nominal fee.

■ DALLAS/FORT WORTH

City of Dallas
Bureau of Vital Statistics
City Hall
Dallas, Texas 75201
(214) 670-3092

The bureau provides certified copies of birth and death certificates on file in their office:

- Births back to 1910
- Deaths back to c.1887

For records filed prior to that time, see Dallas County Clerk.

Documents can be obtained by mail. It is also helpful to indicate the reason for requesting the document and applicant's relationship to the registrant. Whether requesting copies by mail or in person (write for fee schedule), the following information is required: (birth certificates) full name, date of birth, father's full name, mother's full maiden name, hospital or place of birth; (death certificates) full name, date of death, place of death.

Dallas County Clerk
Dallas County Records Building
500 Main Street
Dallas, Texas 75202
Write for a fee schedule.

- Records for births and deaths within Dallas city limits, as well as those outside the city limits but within Dallas County
- All marriage records for Dallas County (The full names of both persons are required.)

The Dallas Historical Society
Hall of State Building
Box 26038
Dallas, Texas 75226
(214) 421-5136

The society does not have staff available to respond to written inquiries. The Research Center of the society is currently closed due to the impending renovation of the Hall of State Building. Its collections are at present in storage.

- Photos
- Diaries
- Journals

Dallas Jewish Archives
7900 Northaven Road
Dallas, Texas 75230
(214) 739-2737

The archives actively seeks acquisitions, either by gift or long-term loan, of materials depicting Jewish life in Dallas, past and present. These acquisitions include:

- Photographs
- Oral histories
- Letters
- Documents
- Scrapbooks
- General memorabilia and artifacts

The archives also tapes and maintains the memories of long-time Jewish residents in an ongoing oral history program.

Funeral Home
Sparkman-Hillcrest Funeral Home
7405 West Northwest Highway
Dallas, Texas 75225

Newspaper
Texas Jewish Post
11333 North Central Expressway #213
Dallas, Texas 75243
(214) 692-7283
Published weekly.

Synagogues
Congregation Shearith Israel
9401 Douglas
Dallas, Texas 75225
(214) 361-6606
The synagogue is over 100 years old and maintains one of two Jewish cemeteries.

Temple Emanu-El
8500 Hillcrest Road
Dallas, Texas 75225
(214) 368-3613
The synagogue is over 100 years old and maintains the other Jewish cemetery.

■ GALVESTON

Rosenberg Library
2310 Sealy Avenue
Galveston, Texas 77550
(409) 763-256
Contains special collections on:

- Texas history
- Art
- Maps
- U.S. and state documents
- Maritime history
- Galveston passenger lists

■ HOUSTON

City of Houston
4580 Wayside Drive
Houston, Texas 77087
(713) 6440-0208
Birth/death certificates. Write for fee schedule. Certificates will be released only to immediate family members; identification is required.

Harris County Clerk
Bureau of Vital Statistics
P.O. Box 1525
Houston, Texas 77251
Marriage records since 1836. Write for fee schedule.

Houston Public Library
500 McKinney
Houston, Texas 77002
(713) 224-5441
(713) 236-1313 (quick reference requests)

- Texas and local history
- Archives and manuscripts
- Oral histories
- Biblical Information Center Microfilm

The library contains information on the following newspapers:

Houston Chronicle: since 1901—Biblical Information Center; since 1940s—microfiche; subject collection—clippings

Houston Post: 1885–1900—Texas Room; since 1901—Biblical Information Center; index since 1976; photo collection of *Houston Post* mainly for last thirty years—direct-name index

Houston Press: 1914–1964—Biblical Information Center

Telegraph & Texas Registrar 10/10/1835–10/22/1856 (1854–56 some issues missing). Newspaper was published in Columbus and Harrisburg before it moved to Houston

Houston Weekly Telegram 1860–1870, scattered issues; complete 1879–1880

Houston Daily Post 1880–1881, scattered issues

Galveston Daily News 1865–1900

Other Galveston newspapers, 1838–1871 not complete

Also extensive collection of other newspapers in other towns for late 19th century.
Archival collection (on Jewish subjects):

- National Council of Jewish Women—collection of publications and newsletters
- Leopold Meyer Collection—from early 1900s, letters, correspondence scrapbooks
- Congregation Beth Israel (oldest congregation in Texas)—back to late 19th century, financial minutes, correspondence
- Ray Kay Daily Collection—clippings, correspondence, pamphlets, circulars of Jews in Houston, 1912–1970s
- Index of Texas obituaries 1835–1885

Humanities section: Bound copies of *Jewish Herald-Voice* newspaper 1937–present

Clayton Library
Center for Genealogical Research
5300 Caroline
Houston, Texas 77004
(713) 524-0101
The collection contains:

- Compiled family histories, county histories, state and county records, church records, lineages of various patriotic societies
- Books on methods of research
- Large collection of microfilm, microfiche, and microcards

- Most available federal population census schedules, military records, county records, and rate books
- Galveston steamship records

Council of Jewish Survivors of Nazi Holocaust
P.O. Box 771205
Houston, Texas 77215

Family History Center
Houston Branch
1101 Bering Drive
Houston, Texas 77057
(713) 785-2105

Newspaper
Jewish Herald–Voice
P.O. Box 153
Houston, Texas 77001
(713) 630-0391

A weekly American–Jewish newspaper published every Thursday since its establishment in 1908.

Funeral Home
Levy Funeral Directors
2010 Chetwood
Houston, Texas 77081
(713) 529-6179

■ LIBERTY

State of Texas Archives
Sam Houston Regional Library & Research Center
P.O. Box 989
Liberty, Texas 77575
(409) 336-7097

Citizenship records, 1838–1921, for Southeast Texas, including Beaumont.

Bibliography
Bell, D. "West of Hester Street: A Chronical of Jewish Immigration Through the Port of Galveston." *Southwest Review*, Vol. 3, p. 70, Spring 1985.
Cohen, A. N. *The Centenary History of Congregation Beth Israel of Houston Texas 1854–1954.* Houston, privately published, 1954.
Cohen, H., Lefkowitz, D., and Frisch, E. *Early Jewish Settlements in Texas: One Hundred Years of Jewry in Texas.* Dallas, privately published for the Texas Centennial, 1936.
Evans, E. *The Provincials: A Personal History of the Jews in the South.* New York: Atheneum, 1976.
Fierman, F. S. *Guts and Ruts: The Jewish Pioneer on the Trail in the American Southwest.* New York: Ktav, 1985.
_____. *Roots and Boots: From Crypto-Jew in New Spain to Community Leader in the American Southwest.* Hoboken, NJ: Ktav, 1987.
Goodspeed, W. A. *A History of Texas: Memorial and Genealogical Record of Southwest Texas.* Privately published, 1894.
Harris, L. A., Jr. *Merchant Princes: An Intimate History of Jewish Families Who Built Great Department Stores.* New York: Harper & Row, 1979.
Kielman, C. V. *The University of Texas Archives: A Guide to the Historical Manuscripts Collections in the University of Texas Library.* Austin: University of Texas Press, 1967.
Lefkowitz, D. "The Jews of Texas." In *East Texas: Its History and Its Makers,* ed. T.C. Richardson, vol. 1, chap. 24. New York: Lewis, 1940.
Maas, E. *Jews in Houston.* Houston Center for the Humanities, National Endowment for the Humanities. Fred R. von der Menden, Series Editor. 1982.
Marcus, J. R. *Early American Jewry. 1–2:* Philadelphia: Jewish Publication Society, 1951–1953.
Marinbach, B. *Galveston: Ellis Island of the West.* Albany, NY: State University of New York Press, 1983.
Marks, M. *Life with Mama & Papa: Estelle and Herman Meyer of Galveston.*
Ornish, N. *Pioneer Jewish Texans.* Dallas: Texas Heritage Press, 1990.
Stern, M. H. *Americans of Jewish Descent.* Cincinnati: Hebrew Union College Press, 1960.
_____. *First American Jewish Families: 600 Genealogies 1954–1977.* Cincinnati: American Jewish Archives, 1978.
Winegarten, R., and Schechter, C. *Deep in the Heart: The Lives and Legends of Texas Jews.* Austin, TX: Eakin Press, 1990.
Wolf, S., and Levy, L. E. *The American Jew as Patriot, Soldier and Citizen.* Philadelphia: Levytype; New York: Brentano, 1895.

The following are available at Hebrew Union College Library, Cincinnati, Ohio:

Articles:

- Data published by the late Rabbi Henry Cohen of Galveston in two articles in Publications of the American Jewish Historical Society and in his essay in a souvenir pamphlet prepared for the 1936 Texas Centennial Exposition, entitled *One Hundred Years of Jewry in Texas.* The articles are name-filled, and probably provide as good a source as any for any genealogist's search for early Texas Jewish ancestry.
- Cohen, Henry, in Publications of the American Jewish Historical Society. Vol. 2 (1894) pp. 139–156, "Settlement of the Jews of Texas." Vol. 4 (1896) pp. 9–19, "The Jews in Texas."

Periodicals:

- *Jewish Monitor,* founded 1914 by G. Fox and L. Morris. Fort Worth-Dallas, 1914–1930

Congregational and Communal Histories:

- Beaumont, Temple Emanuel; golden jubilee pamphlet. Beaumont, 1950, 4 pp.
- Castroville, Ruth Curry Lawlor, The Story of Castroville. Castroville, 1951
- Corpus Christi, Temple Beth El; History of the Jewish Community. (25th anniversary). Corpus Christi, 1957
- Dallas, Congregation Shearith Israel, 1884–1934 (50th anniversary history). Dallas, 1934
- Temple Emanu-El; 75th Anniversary. Dallas
- El Paso, Mr. Sinai; 30th Year. El Paso, 1928
- 50th Year. El Paso, 1948
- Temple Tidings (monthly bulletin), 1917, Houston, Anne Nathan Cohen, Congregation Beth Israel; The Centenary History. Houston, 1954
- Congregation Adath Yeshurun; 50th Anniversary. Houston, 1941
- San Antonio, Beth El; 70th Anniversary. San Antonio, 1944
- Diamond Jubilee. San Antonio, 1949
- Announcements (monthly bulletin)

UTAH

■ SALT LAKE CITY

■ INTRODUCTION TO FAMILY HISTORY LIBRARY

Family History Library
35 North West Temple Street
Salt Lake City, Utah 84150

The Family History Library (formerly known as the Genealogical Library), operated by the Church of Jesus Christ of Latter-day Saints (Mormon church or LDS church), is one of the largest genealogical facilities in the world. The library has acquired the world's largest collection of genealogical information (over 250,000 volumes). It maintains a collection of microfilmed genealogical source material from around the world. Its holdings include over 1.7 million rolls of microfilm that it began to acquire in 1938. The collection includes records of value for genealogical research for all ethnic groups, including Jews.

The library is located in downtown Salt Lake City directly west of Temple Square. The library is open to the public. You may use the records and resources of the library without charge. Free two-hour parking is available one-half block north of the Library. All-day parking is available at lots within two blocks of the library. The library is open Monday 7:30 a.m. to 6:00 p.m., Tuesday through Friday 7:30 a.m. to 10:00 p.m., and Saturday 7:30 a.m. to 5:00 p.m.

■ JEWISH COLLECTIONS AT THE FAMILY HISTORY LIBRARY
Daniel Schlyter

The Family History Library, among its other genealogical material, has an excellent collection of records pertaining to both American and European Jews. These records have been acquired at various archives and repositories throughout the world. Many are not accessible anyplace else. Some of these materials are not unique to this library. Many of the American materials such as census records, naturalization records, passenger lists, and such are available at the National Archives and its regional branches. Many of the microfilms of Jewish vital records from Poland are available at the Central Archive for the History of the Jewish People in Jerusalem. But nowhere else in the world will you find such easy access to so many genealogical sources—all in one place.

If you can't travel to Salt Lake City you can still have access to the Family History Library's collection. In addition to the main library in Salt Lake City, the church maintains over 1,500 family history centers (formerly called branch genealogical libraries) throughout the world. These are small facilities, usually located in Mormon church buildings and staffed by local volunteers. They provide local access to the Family History Library Catalog and most of the microfilms and microfiches of the main library. These family history centers order films and fiches from Salt Lake City or from any of several microfilm order centers.

In 1938 the LDS Church initiated a program of microfilming records of genealogical value from throughout the world. This was done to give LDS members access to the records needed to identify their ancestors. The program has expanded each year as archivists of record repositories throughout the world have become aware of this undertaking and recognized its value. Upon request, and according to planned schedules, the LDS Church microfilms records at no cost to the repository. A positive copy of the microfilmed records is donated to the repository for the privilege of microfilming.[1]

In addition to the microfilm collection, the Library's shelves hold tens of thousands of the world's printed family genealogies, past and current genealogical periodicals, and published histories of towns, counties, states, and countries. There are also thousands of genealogical guidebooks, directories, locality finding aids, and other books which help researchers to locate and use the original source materials in the collection.

The Family History Library is a nonprofit institution, supported primarily by tithing funds of the LDS Church. The library is open to the public, and there is no fee for using its research facilities.[2]

You can get a list of the family history centers in your area, by writing to the library in Salt Lake City, to the attention of the Correspondence Section. The Correspondence Section will also answer genealogical questions if they can be answered briefly. But the staff cannot do research for you. When asking questions, please be brief and give specific names, dates, and places.

Catalogs

You can determine whether the library has specific records by using the Family History Library Catalog™ This catalog is on microfiche and you can use it at the main library or at any of the family history centers. Although the catalog is also on compact disc at many centers, the following instructions relate to the catalog on microfiche.

Locality catalog. Records that pertain to specific localities are listed in the locality section of the catalog. The locality microfiche have yellow headings. There is a separately numbered set of microfiche cards for each country. The first entry on each microfiche appears in the upper left corner of the fiche. Use this as a reference point to determine which fiche contains the specific locality you want.

Entries in the locality section are arranged according to levels of jurisdiction from largest to smallest. For each country, records about the country are listed first under the name of the country. Following the national records, each county or province is listed alphabetically. Records that were kept on a county or provincial level are listed under the county heading. For example, records about the province of Galicia in Austria are listed under AUSTRIA, GALIZIEN.

Records for specific localities within each county are listed in alphabetical order after the county-level records. Thus, records of Kraków, such as Jewish vital records or a local history, are listed under AUSTRIA, GALIZIEN, KRAKOW.

At the beginning of the group of microfiche for each country, you will find "see" references. They direct you to the form in which the entry will appear in the catalog.

Example:
MŁAWA → POLAND, WARSZAWA, MŁAWA

These references can be used almost like a gazetteer of the country. However, "see" references are made only for those localities presently included in the catalog, and not for all possible locations.

In some cases, borders have changed over the years, and the town your ancestor lived in may have been in different countries at different periods of time. For most countries in these cases, the locality section of the catalog includes references under each of the countries the town has been part of.

For example, you can look up the records of Posen, Germany (now Poznań, Poland) under:

GERMANY, PREUSSEN, POSEN, POSEN
or
POLAND, POZNAN, POZNAN

Surname Catalog. Use the surname section of the catalog to determine whether the Family History Library has a published family history of your Jewish family. Surnames are listed alphabetically. The library has comparatively few Jewish family histories, compared to histories of Christian families.

Subject Catalog. The subject section of the catalog lists topical subjects and indicates what the library has on each subject. Subjects of interest to Jewish genealogists might be JEWS—UNITED STATES, JEWS—NEW YORK, JEWS—POLAND, JEWS—HISTORY, and JEWS—BIOGRAPHY.

Author/Title Catalog. Use the author/title section of the catalog if you already know the author or title of a particular book and want to find out whether the Family History Library has a copy of the book. Authors and titles are interfiled.

Ancestral File™. Ancestral File is a family-linked computer file containing genealogies contributed to the Family History Department since 1979. It is available on compact disk at the main library and at most family history centers. You can personally search this file for free to see if anyone has already contributed information about your family. If you have access to a personal computer, you can preserve and share your own genealogy and help build Ancestral File by contributing your family information on a diskette (Using Personal Ancestral File™ or another computer program that is Ancestral File certified). Send a diskette containing a copy of your information to the Family History Department, Ancestral File Operations Unit, 50 East North Temple Street, Salt Lake City, Utah 84150. There is not fee for processing the information.

Sources at the Family History Library: United States

Civil Vital Records. The Family History Library has microfilmed vital records for many areas of the United States. These are listed in the locality section of the catalog for the place your ancestor lived under the heading VITAL RECORDS. If the library does not have the vital records you need, then you can write for information. For records under county control, write to the county courthouse for information. Many vital records are in the custody of state offices. Addresses are in "Where to Write for Vital Records: Births, deaths, marriages, and divorces," which is available in many libraries or by writing:

Superintendent of Documents
U.S. Government Printing Office
Washington, D.C. 20402

Census Records. The Family History Library has microfilmed copies of United States census records from 1790 through 1910.

The United States has conducted censuses every 10 years since 1790 (see also National Archives pp. 29–31). Census records are on microfilm in the National Archives, National Archives branches, the LDS Family History Library, and other genealogical libraries. They may also be found in state archives and in public and university libraries.

Census information beginning with 1920 is confidential. However, the government will release information to you on your parents and direct-line ancestors. To request this information, write for *Form BC-600*.

Application for Search of Census Records is available from:

Bureau of Census
Pittsburg, Kansas 66762

Some state censuses, such as those for New York, are available at the FHL through 1925.

Naturalization Records. The Family History Library has microfilmed naturalization records from many areas of the United States.[3] The records, especially those dated after 1906, may provide information on nativity and immigration. The Library's collection includes mostly naturalization applications, from 1790 to 1930, from county and federal courts. See also National Archives, pp. 28–42, and Chapter 1, Immigration and Naturalization.

Passenger Arrival Records. The Family History Library has copies of over 9,000 microfilms of passenger arrival records from the National Archives. The following is a list of the major ports and years for which records are available. The approximate number of immigrants admitted from 1820 to 1920 is in parentheses after the name of the city. The film numbers of these records are most easily found in the locality section of the Family History Library Catalog under [STATE], [COUNTY], [CITY]—EMIGRATION AND IMMIGRATION.

- *New York City* (23,960,000)
  Indexes 1820–1846, 1897–1943
  Lists 1820–1942
- *Boston* (2,050,000)
  Indexes 1848–1891, 1902–1920
  Lists 1820–1874, 1883–1935
- *Baltimore* (1,460,000)
  Indexes 1920s–1952, 1833–1866
  Lists 1820–1920
- *Philadelphia* (1,240,000)
  Indexes 1800–1906, 1883–1948
  Lists 1800–1916
- *New Orleans* (710,000)
  Indexes 1820–1850, 1853–1952
  Lists 1820–1920

The library also has microfilmed copies of U.S. passport applications (1795–1921) and Canadian-U.S. border crossings (1895–1952). Many of these immigration records provide genealogical details such as birthdate and birthplace.

Other U.S. Sources. In addition to copies of land, probate, vital, and other records from over 2,000 county courthouses, the Family History Library has records of special interest to Jewish genealogists. These include files of the Hebrew Immigrant Aid

Society, Hebrew Union College Library, and Russian consular offices.

Sources at the Family History Library: Europe

Historians estimate that during the nineteenth century more than eighty-five percent of the world's Jews lived in Europe (most of these resided in Poland and Russia). Thus, most Jewish family trees can be traced to Europe within a few generations.

To begin genealogical research in Europe, you will need the exact locality or congregation from which your ancestor came. You can then determine what records are available for that locality.

Consular records. Russian consular records from 1860 to the 1920s were left behind in Washington, D.C., by the czarist government. These records include records dealings with Russian emigrants in the United States, such as passport and visa applications, correspondence, banking records, legal certifications, and individual case files. They include thousands of dealings with American Jews of Russian origin. The Family History Library microfilmed the collection at the National Archives in a joint project with the Jewish Genealogical Society of Greater Washington, which indexed the material. The index has been published and is available at many public libraries. This is *The Russian Consular Records and Index Catalog* (New York: Garland, 1987; available on microfilm at family history centers on film no. film 1,605,681).

Hamburg Passenger Lists. Many Jews from central and eastern Europe on their way to America departed through the port of Hamburg, Germany. Beginning in 1850, port officials in Hamburg began keeping a record of passengers. This list of passengers included information on age, occupation, and place of origin for all passengers. This makes the Hamburg passenger lists an excellent source for genealogical research. The lists are indexed and may help you find your ancestor's place or origin. Whereas the passenger lists of Bremen, the other leading German port, have been destroyed, the records of Hamburg are easily accessible for research. The Family History Library has microfilms of the Hamburg passenger lists for 1850 through 1934 (see Appendix D).

Jewish Records. For some countries, the Family History Library is an excellent source of Jewish records. You must use the Family History Library Catalog in order to find specific records or books. Jewish records of birth, marriage, and death are cataloged under the specific locality and the heading JEWISH RECORDS. Materials about Jews, such as Jewish histories or memorial books, are cataloged under the heading MINORITIES. The following paragraphs describe the records found from various countries and indicate in general what records are available at the Family History Library.

Austria. Before the World War I, the Austrian Empire included areas now in the Republic of Austria, Czechoslovakia, Italy, Poland, Yugoslavia, and the Soviet Union. Austrian Jews were required to keep vital records beginning in 1788, but they rarely complied with this law until the mid-19th century.

For Austria, the Family History Library has books and microfilms of detailed maps and gazetteers of the Austro-Hungarian Empire. These can help you locate the exact place in Austria from which your ancestors came and determine what country it is in now. As far as actual Jewish vital records go, the library has only a few such records from the area of former Austrian Galicia (which is now part of Poland).

Britain. The modern Jewish community in England dates from 1656. London had congregations of both Sephardic and Ashkenazic Jews, but Portuguese Sephardic Jews predominated until the 19th century.

Synagogue records date from the end of the 17th century. These were written in Portuguese and Yiddish. Marriage records seem to be complete, but many births were not recorded. The Family History Library has microfilmed synagogue records from Britain.

Civil registration of all births, deaths, and marriages was introduced to Britain in 1837. The Family History Library has microfilmed the index to these civil registration records. The actual civil registers, however, are available only in England.

Czechoslovakia. Czechoslovakia was created in 1918 from parts of Austria-Hungary, including the Czech-speaking provinces of Bohemia and Moravia from Austria and the Slovak speaking northern counties of Hungary. In these areas, most records of Jewish births, marriages, and deaths date only from the early 1800s.

During World War II, Jewish records from throughout Bohemia and Moravia were centralized in Prague. Records from the formerly Hungarian area of Slovakia were gathered to Bratislava and Czechoslovakia. These records have not been microfilmed by the Family History Library, but are readily accessible through research services in Czechoslovakia.

If your ancestor was from the area formerly governed by Austria (Bohemia, Moravia, Silesia), write to:

Czech Ministry of Interior and Environment
Archivní Správa
Dr. Milady Horákové 133
166 21 Praha 6
Czechoslovakia

If your ancestor was from the area formerly governed by Hungary (Slovakia), write to:

Slovak Ministry of Interior and Environment
Archivná Správa
Križková 7
811 04 Bratislava
Czechoslovakia

The archival administration will arrange for searches of records (such as birth, marriage, and death registers). They will send your request for research to the appropriate archive in Czechoslovakia. Qualified archival researchers there will do the actual research, and they will send you a report of the research done. With rare exceptions, the only records available for genealogical research by mail are parish registers [*matriky*] of births, marriages, and deaths. Other records, such as land records and census records, exist and you can use them for research if you visit the archives yourself, but they are difficult to access by writing.

France. Napoleon began civil registration of all births, marriages, and deaths in France, including Jews, in 1792. French civil registration records of births, deaths, and marriages have been microfilmed by the Family History Library for some departments (counties) of France. Eventually records of all departments will be microfilmed. For those areas not yet microfilmed, you may write to the local departmental archive and hire a researcher. Some French records of particular interest to Jewish researchers are listed in Appendix I, p. 177.

Germany. The former German Empire was divided into East and West Germany, Poland, France, and the Soviet Union. Civil registration of Jewish births, deaths, and marriages began at various times in different parts of the empire. Some places began keeping records on Jews in the early and mid-19th century. The registration was not consistent throughout Germany, however, until 1875.

The Family History Library has microfilmed many German Jewish records in Germany and in Poland, and is continually adding to the collection. Jewish documents and congregational records from Germany are also available in some institutions in Israel and the United States. The most current and accurate listing of the library's German holdings is The Family History Library Catalog. The listing in Appendix J (pp. 178–194) is as of 1985.

Hungary. Modern Hungary is much smaller now than it was before the World War I. The former kingdom of Hungary included areas now in Czechoslovakia, the Soviet Union, Romania, Yugoslavia, and Austria. The Family History Library has filmed all available Jewish records in possession of modern Hungary up to 1895. These include birth, marriage, and death records of individual Jewish communities and the 1848 Jewish census for several old Hungarian counties, some of which are now in Czechoslovakia and the U.S.S.R. The most current and accurate listing of the library's Hungarian holdings is the Family History Library Catalog. The listing in Appendix K (pp. 195–201) is as of 1985.

The Netherlands. Many marranos, including numerous wealthy and prominent merchants, settled in the Netherlands in the 1500s and 1600s as refugees of the Spanish Inquisition. In the Netherlands, many reconverted to Judaism. These Spanish and Portuguese Jews were later joined by Ashkenazim fleeing anti-Semitism in less tolerant nations of Western and Eastern Europe.

Genealogies have been compiled for many Jewish families in The Netherlands. The following organizations have many such genealogies and will answer correspondence:

Netherlands Joods Familienarchief
Amsteldijk 67
Amsterdam
The Netherlands

Centraal Bureau voor Genealogie
Postbus 11755
2502 AT's-Gravenhage
The Netherlands

Valuable historical and genealogical articles were published in *Studia Rosenthaliana: Journal for Jewish Literature and History in The Netherlands,* published by the University Library of Amsterdam. It is indexed in the International Index of Periodicals found in most libraries.

After 1811, Jewish births, marriages, and deaths in the Netherlands were included with other religious groups in local civil registers. Prior to this, each congregation was responsible for its own records. The Family History Library has filmed all Dutch civil registers up to 1882 and some as late as 1912. Some early congregational records have also been filmed.

Poland. Prior to 1918, Poland as we know it today was divided between Austria, Russia, and German Prussia. After 1945, areas of eastern Poland became part of the Soviet Union.

The earliest registration of Polish Jews was in the former Austrian territory of Galicia in 1787, but it was not enforced until the mid-19th century. The Family History Library has very few Jewish microfilmed records from the Austrian area of Poland. The Duchy of Warsaw, which later constituted the Russian territory of Poland, began civil registration in 1808. At first, Jews were included in Catholic civil registers. After 1826, separate civil registers were kept for Jews. In areas under German rule, Jews were required to prepare transcripts of vital records beginning in the early 1800s. The Family History Library has an extensive microfilm collection of Jewish vital records from the former Russian and German areas of Poland, making it a significant resource for Jews with ancestry in these areas. The most current and accurate listing of the library's Polish holdings is the Family History Library Catalog. The listing in Appendix L (pp. 202–215) is as of 1985.

Polish records that have been microfilmed are available only up to about 1870. You can obtain information regarding records not filmed and still in Poland by writing to the headquarters of the Polish State Archives.

Naczelna Dyrekcja Archiwów Państwowych
ul. Dluga 6 s.p. 1005
00-950 Warszawa
Poland

History of the Jews in Russia and Poland, by S. M. Dubnow, is of interest to Jews whose ancestry comes from Poland or Russia. It is translated from Russian by I. Friedlander (Philadelphia: The Jewish Publication Society of America, 1916; European Collection 940 F2d—FHL film no. 1183537 item 2).

Romania. Modern Romania consists of territories with varied historical backgrounds. The old Romanian principalities of Wallachia and Moldavia were under Turkish domination until the mid-1800s. The area of Transylvania was under Austro-Hungarian rule until 1918. Civil registration of births, marriages, and deaths was introduced in the Romanian principalities in the 1830s, but it is not clear when Jewish communities began keeping records. In the former Hungarian area of Transylvania, Jewish registers began in the 1830s and 1840s.

The Family History Library has no Jewish records from Romania. If preserved, such records may now be in the Romanian State Archives. Write to the archives in Romanian or French. The address is as follows:

Archivelor Statului din Republica Romania
Bucuresti, Sect. VI
Bdul Gh. Gheorgiu-Dej nr. 29
Romania

It is possible some records could be in Israel or some other Jewish collection outside Romania.

Soviet Union. The Soviet Union includes most of the historical Russian empire. Much of former Austrian Galicia is now in the Soviet Union. Much of the Polish areas of the old Russian empire became part of Poland in 1918, but in 1945 the eastern parts of Poland were ceded to the Soviet Union.

Many Jews trace some ancestral lines to areas now in the Soviet Union. Since the 1918 Revolution, births, deaths, and marriages have been registered in local offices of the U.S.S.R. Ministry of Internal Affairs. Prior to 1918, the Russian Empire had no government offices to keep vital records. In most cases, Jews carefully avoided keeping records that might later be used against them. Some city governments kept vital records of Jews, beginning in the mid-19th century. The records that were kept have been preserved in Soviet archives. But research in Soviet archives is still restricted, and the records are not yet accessible for on-site genealogical research.

Although a handful of Jewish records have been microfilmed in Polish archives, the Family History Library has not microfilmed any Jewish records in the Soviet Union. Because of this, you must rely on alternate sources. Among these are limited synagogue and vital records presently in Israel, Western Europe, or the United States; memorial books; and family traditions. As this volume goes to press, there are dramatic changes taking place in the Soviet Union. The National Genealogical Society is presently working with Soviet archival officials to establish a Soviet American Genealogical Archive Service. Developments in this area will be reported in the newsletters of the various Jewish Genealogical Societies.

Other countries. The Family History Library has materials of interest to Jewish genealogists from many countries of the world not listed here, including Jewish vital records from some localities in Western Europe not noted above. For specific holdings, consult the Family History Library Catalog available at the Family History Library and at family history centers.

Notes

1. Each year, more than 100 million new pages of historical documents are added to the Family History Library's worldwide collection of microfilms.
2. The library has over 500 microfilm and microfiche readers, and more than 50 computer workstations.
3. The records, especially those dated after 1906, may provide information on nativity and immigration. The library's collection includes mostly naturalization applications, from 1790 to 1930, from county and federal courts.

■ JEWISH RECORDS ON MICROFILM IN THE FAMILY HISTORY LIBRARY
John Henry Richter

A variety of Jewish records have been filmed for the Genealogical Society of Utah's microfilming project, which intends to collect communal and parish records from all over the world. This is for the benefit of LDS church members wishing to trace their ancestors so they may be sealed as families eternally. In the process, thousands of Jewish records were also filmed. These films include not only records of birth, marriage, and death, but also many historical documents, correspondence, tax records, and lists of taxpayers, cemetery lists, and other historically valuable papers. Most of the documents are registers started at the time government authorities required Jewish communities to keep their vital statistics. Generally, records of communities that were no longer active were placed in

the custody of regional or state archives, and it is by unexpected good fortune that so many of these records and documents have survived the ravages of World War II.

While a substantial number of the communal records were filmed under contract with the Genealogical Society of Utah, some of the German records were filmed between 1937 and the end of the war (right up to April of 1945) by the Reischsamt fuer Sippenforschung under orders issued by Heinrich Himmler. Candidates for admission to his elite organization, the SS (Schutz-Staffeln) had to prove their "Aryan" ancestry to the sixth generation. He decided to microfilm available Jewish records to check applicants' veracity in cases of doubt. While the original documents seem to have been destroyed, the set of film negatives was found after the occupation of Germany. A copy of the set was given to the Central Archives for the History of the Jewish People in Jerusalem. Another set of these films was acquired by the Genealogical Society of Utah.

The Family History Library makes their collection available to researchers in local Family History Centers and at their main Library in Salt Lake City. It may be well to explain what you can expect to find. The periods covered by the records vary greatly. Most of them cover life cycle events between 1800 and 1900, but a remarkably large number start in the 1700s and even earlier, and extend, in some cases, to 1939 and even later. It is relatively easy to trace a family through four and more generations, although one ought not to expect "complete" information in the case of every record. The records were filmed "as they were," with errors and corrections (and sometimes with just the errors) in a multitude of handwritings, some less legible than others. In some cases, the filming is poor. In other cases, it is clear that the production was done with great care (especially when the Society supervised the filming), repeatedly filming pages that were hard to read. Since many records were quite old at the time of the filming, the copy is only as good as the condition of the original—which means considerable variation in the quality of the images. There are no indexes for most records.

The information one can expect to find can be minimal or surprisingly complete. Birth records usually give the names of both parents. Records of marriages list the names of the parents of the couple and the place of their residence. Unfortunately, most death records give just the name of the deceased, his age and address, cause of death (sometimes, the name of the attending physician) and the date of burial. It will not mention the names of survivors (widow or widower, children). Frequently, these records will include information on the occupation or business of the person involved. Another record often found in Germany is a list of community members (including members of all congregations in the case where a community has more than one), since the responsibility for recording personnel changes fell on the civil community, not on any particular synagogue. These membership lists are priceless, since they represent, in fact, a census of the Jewish population of the town. They give the full names of all family members, their occupations, their ages, and their addresses. Sometimes, they give other information of value, such as place of birth (or of the town from which they came), status of citizenship, etc. Cemetery lists are also available, alas not very often. They allow access to information on relatives, aside from giving at least the date of death and the location of the grave. Community correspondence often contains information on the elected leaders, rabbis, and other synagogue employees, quite aside from the historical record that such documents reveal.

Those who venture to examine the documents must keep in mind that most of them were kept by well-meaning but not always attentive clerks. Dates are sometimes found to be wrong, names are often misspelled—if not altogether reporting the wrong first name—and on occasion, a birth or a death is recorded twice—in different months. More troublesome than possible errors is the fact that some clerks write more legibly than others. The records are generally handwritten in the local language.

In all my contacts with officials of the Family History Library and its branch libraries, I have found them invariably kind and helpful. Loan arrangements are made through the local or regional branch library nearest your home for a very nominal fee per reel. The branch libraries now have the entire catalog of the Library on compact disk and microfiche, which will help anyone to find the records of any locality already microfilmed. The film project is continuing, and additional records are added to the catalog as soon as they are cataloged.

Bibliography
Cerny, J., and Elliott, W., eds. *The Library: A Guide to the LDS Family History Library.* Salt Lake City: Ancestry, Inc., 1988.

Modified from *Avotaynu,* Vol. II, No. 1, 1986.

VIRGINIA

■ NORFOLK

Bureau of Vital Statistics
Health Department
City of Norfolk
401 Colley Avenue
Norfolk, Virginia 23507

Circuit Court
City Hall
City of Norfolk
100 St. Paul's Boulevard
Norfolk, Virginia 23510

Old Dominion University
Archives and Manuscript Collection
Norfolk, Virginia 23508

Sargeant Memorial Room
Norfolk Public Library
301 E. City Hall Avenue
Norfolk, Virginia 23510

Holocaust Survivors
Ruth Fekete
7924 Chesapeake Boulevard
Norfolk, Virginia 23518

Renewal Magazine (published quarterly)
Reba Karp, editor
UJF Virginia News
P.O. Box 9776
Norfolk, Virginia 23505
(804) 489-8040

■ RICHMOND

Congregation Beth Ahabah
Museum and Archives
1109 West Franklin Street
Richmond, Virginia 23220
(804) 353-2668

The archives are accessible to individual researchers and have an extensive collection of communal, synagogue, and family records, artifacts, photographs, and many other items.

- At least 237 family names in the files of the archives (as of December 1986)
- Over 6,000 books, 20,000 documents, and 500 photographs

The archives include a set of the local Jewish press:

- *The Reflector* published by the Jewish Community Federation of Richmond
- *The Jewish News,* published by the local Lubavitch organization

The Beth Ahabah Museum featured exhibits of artifacts related to the Ezekiel and the Hutzler families of Richmond and published comprehensive brochures in connection with each exhibit.

The Virginia State Library
Eleventh Street and Capitol Square
Richmond, Virginia 23219-3491
(804) 786-2305

The library staff tries to respond to written inquiries if they are specific, but does not undertake research. However, it will furnish, upon request, a list of professional genealogists acquainted with the State Library's holdings.

The library's Publication Branch provides a complete list of the State Library's genealogical and historical publications, as well as reference works, bibliographies, and archival guides.
Holdings include:

- Census records (1810–1880, 1900, 1910)
- Census indexes (1810–1850, 1880, 1900, 1910)
- Tax records from 1782 (personal property and land tax lists—unindexed)
- Virginia Military records, including Civil War
- Land Office records (land patents and grants)
- Richmond city directories: 1819, 1850–1852,

1855–1856, 1858–1860, 1866, 1869, 1870–1889, 1891–1944, 1946–1951, 1953 to the present
- Birth, marriage, and death records from 1853; discontinued around the turn of the century, and beginning again around 1914

The Virginia Historical Society
The Boulevard at Kensington Avenue
Richmond, Virginia 23221
(804) 358-4901

Individual inquiries are answered at no charge. Admission is free. Collection includes:

- Richmond city directories: 1850 to date
- Manuscript records of some Jewish families

The Museum of the Confederacy
1201 East Clay Street
Richmond, Virginia 23219
(804) 649-1861

The library is open by appointment only. Requests received through the mail are answered. Limited to events and personages of the Confederacy (1861–1865).

Rabbi Myron Berman
Temple Beth El
3330 Grove Avenue
Richmond, Virginia 23221
(804) 355-3564; 359-2119

The historian of the Jewish community of Richmond. He will respond to written inquiries.

Funeral Homes
Joseph W. Bliley
3d and Marshall Streets
Richmond, Virginia 23219
(804) 649-0511

Bennett Funeral Home
3215 Cutshaw Avenue
Richmond, Virginia 23230
(804) 359-4481

Bibliography
Berman, M. *Richmond's Jewry, 1769–1976*. Charlottesville, VA: The University Press of Virginia, 1979.
Eakin, F. E. *Richmond Jewry: Fulfilling the Promise*. The Museum and Archives Trust, 1986.
Ezekiel, H. T., and Lichtenstein, G. *The History of the Jews of Richmond from 1769 to 1917*. Richmond, VA: Herbert T. Ezekell, 1917.

WASHINGTON

■ BELLEVUE

Washington State Jewish Historical Society
4398 Somerset Boulevard SE
Bellevue, Washington 98006

The Jewish Archives Project of the Historical Society is a joint effort with the University of Washington Libraries in Seattle, and all records are maintained by Manuscripts and University Archives, University of Washington Libraries, in Seattle, Washington.

■ SEATTLE

Manuscripts and University Archives, FM-25
University of Washington Libraries
Seattle, Washington 98195

In reply to written inquiries, the library is able to check only a limited number of sources. It does not do actual research for requesters, and recommends that a local genealogist be engaged if extensive research needed.

- *The Jewish Transcript* (the only relevant item which is on microfilm and available through interlibrary loan)
- *Jewish Voice*, a predecessor

The Pacific Northwest Collection includes:

- Seattle city directories
- Early county histories

The Manuscripts Collection contains:

- Jewish archives for the Seattle area (little of significance to genealogists)

Seattle Genealogical Society
1331 Third Avenue
Seattle, Washington 98104
Will recommend experienced local genealogists.

Seattle Public Library
1000 Fourth Avenue
Seattle, Washington 98104
(206) 625-2665

Staff time is very limited for responding to correspondence, but the library has a special genealogy section and program.

- *Jewish Transcript* (which is available also through the University of Washington Libraries)
- Polk's Seattle city directories (1889–1985)

Jewish Family Service
1214 Boylston Avenue
Seattle, Washington 98101
(206) 447-3240

Founded in 1892, this organization maintains case files on all clients served.

Seattle Department of Vital Statistics
King County Department of Public Health
1300 Public Safety Building
610 Third Avenue (at James Street)
Seattle, Washington 98104
(206) 587-2768

To obtain copies of birth and death records, the following is required: the name of the person, date of birth, place of birth, mother's maiden name, and father's name. To obtain copies of a death record, the following is required: name of the deceased, place of death and date of death (need not be exact).

Marriage Records
King County Administration Building
500 Fourth Avenue
Seattle, Washington 98104
Write for forms of application for copies of their records.

Newspaper
The Jewish Transcript
1904 Third Ave. #510
Seattle, Washington 98101
(206) 624-0136
Semi-monthly newspaper published by the Jewish Federation of Greater Seattle.

Cemeteries
Bikur Cholim Machzikay Hadath
operated by Congregation Bikur Cholim
5145 South Morgan
Seattle, Washington 98118
(206) 723-0970

Herzl Memorial Park
operated by Herzl Ner Tamid Congregation
P.O. Box 574
Mercer Island, Washington 98040
(206) 232-8555

Hills of Eternity Cemetery
(Independent)
6th West and West Raye Street
Seattle, Washington 98119
(206) 283-1166

Seattle Sephardic Brotherhood Cemetery
operated by
Sephardic Bikur Holim Congregation
6500 52d Avenue South
Seattle, Washington 98118
(206) 723-3028

Mr. Isaac Maimon
4825 So. Spencer
Seattle, Washington 98118
Mr. Maimon is in charge of the old archives of the congregation.
The synagogue possesses a record that starts in 1913. Almost everyone who is buried in the two Sephardic cemeteries is on record.

Funeral Directors
Bonney-Watson Funeral Directors
Mr. Ed Wahl, President
1732 Broadway
Seattle, Washington 98122
(206) 322-0013

Bibliography
Genealogical Resources in Washington State: A Guide to Genealogical Recors Held at Repositories, Government Agencies and Archives. The Washington State Archives, P.O. Box 9000, Olympia, Washington 98504.

WISCONSIN

■ HALES CORNERS
(Milwaukee Metropolitan Area)

Family History Center
9600 West Grange Avenue
Hales Corners, Wisconsin 53130
(414) 425-4182

■ MADISON

The Bureau of Health Statistics
P.O. Box 309
Madison, Wisconsin 53701
The reference staff will respond to written questions. The research they are prepared to do is usually limited to searches of census records, obituary, and biographical files.

- Birth, death, marriage, and divorce records for Milwaukee and all Wisconsin cities
- A complete set of *Milwaukee Leader* (also known as *Milwaukee Post* and *Milwaukee New Leader*) from 1911 to 1942

Items available through interlibrary loan may be obtained by arrangement with your local library.

The State Historical Society of Wisconsin
815 State Street
Madison, Wisconsin 53706
(608) 262-3266
- Microfilms of the births, marriages, and deaths recorded in Wisconsin before October 1, 1907 (incomplete and may only be used at the library)

Microfilmed and available for interlibrary loan:

- 1905 Wisconsin state census (the only state census to list all the members of a household by name)
- A county-by-county index for this census is available for nearly all counties.
- Indexes to the U.S. censuses (1820–1870) for the area that is now Wisconsin
- 1820–1870 censuses for Wisconsin
- 1900 and 1910 U.S. censuses for Wisconsin and the Soundex for the 1900 census.

The 1910 census and the Soundex indexes to the 1880 and 1900 censuses do not circulate on interlibrary loan.

The State Archives
(housed in the Historical Society building)

- Manuscript copies of the Wisconsin state censuses:
  1836, 1838, 1842, 1846, 1847, 1855, 1875, 1885, and 1895
  Please note that they extend twenty-five years beyond the available federal censuses. These censuses (which have not been indexed) have been microfilmed and are available for inter-library loan.
- Many biographical sketches in the histories of Wisconsin counties and communities (indexed)
- Several thousand selected obituaries (indexed)
- The papers of Rabbi Joseph L. Baron, who served the Milwaukee and Wisconsin Jewish community for over thirty years

Newspaper
The Reporter
310 North Midvale Boulevard
No. 325
Madison, Wisconsin 53705

■ MILWAUKEE

The Jewish Family and Children's Service
1360 North Prospect Avenue, 3d Floor
Milwaukee, Wisconsin 53202
(414) 273-6515

- Records of Jewish resettlement in Milwaukee (mainly the post World War I period). Records may not be removed from the office nor are photos or copies of records permitted.

If you require access to resettlement records, advance communication with the agency is necessary.

The Golda Meir Library of the University of Wisconsin
Milwaukee Campus
2311 East Hartford Avenue
P.O. Box 604
Milwaukee, Wisconsin 53201

- Jewish Family and Children's Service records (1867 to 1973)
- Case records (1892 to 1899) are restricted and closed.
- Files of several prominent local families: Horwitz family papers (1911–1955); Lizzie Black Kander papers (1875–1960), Joseph L. Baron papers (1910–1960)

The Milwaukee County Genealogical Society
P.O. Box 27326
Milwaukee, Wisconsin 53227

Milwaukee Public Library
The Local History Room
814 West Wisconsin Avenue
Milwaukee, Wisconsin 53233
(414) 278-3074

There is no charge for research service. The staff is also able to recommend a local researcher for more extensive work.

- *Milwaukee Leader* (with title changes) (1911 to 1942)
- *Wisconsin Jewish Chronicle* since 1955 (complete set)

Manuscript collection includes:

- Hebrew Relief Society minute books (1867–1898)
- Erwin C. Rhodes papers (1921–1977). Longtime publisher of the *Wisconsin Jewish Chronicle*

Family History Center
(See Hales Corners)

Register of Deed
901 North Ninth Street
Milwaukee, Wisconsin 53233
(414) 278-4002

Costs are the same as above. They do not have copies of divorce records.

Funeral Home
Goodman–Bensman Funeral Home
4750 North Santa Monica Boulevard
Milwaukee, Wisconsin 53211

Since the 1920s they have conducted 90 to 95 percent of all Jewish funerals.

Bibliography

Congregation Emanu-El 1869–1919: Golden Anniversary. 1919.

Hecht, S. *Congregation Emanu-El. Ten Years . . .* 1898.

Leuchter, S., ed. *Guide to Wisconsin Survivors of the Holocaust.* State Historical Society of Wisconsin.

Levitats, I. *The Story of the Milwaukee Jewish Community.* Bureau of Jewish Education (mimeo), 1954.

Nauen, L., ed. *Guide to the Wisconsin Jewish Archives at the State Historical Society Wisconsin.* 1974.

Swichkow, L. J., and Gartner, L. P. *The History of the Jews of Milwaukee.* Philadelphia: Jewish Publication Society, 1963.

Chapter 3

CANADA: GUIDE TO INSTITUTIONAL RESOURCES ARRANGED BY CITY

Scott E. Meyer and Alan Spencer, Editors

INTRODUCTION: SOURCES FOR THE STUDY OF JEWISH FAMILY HISTORY IN CANADA

Lawrence F. Tapper

Jewish family historians will discover that a large number of sources are available to them in public and private archival repositories across Canada.

Many family historians begin their research at the National Archives of Canada (NA) in Ottawa, Ontario. The NA, in addition to being the official repository for the records of the government of Canada, also acquires and preserves the papers of individuals and organizations that have made important contributions to the growth and development of Canadian society. Over the years, the NA has acquired many valuable collections relating to the immigration and settlement of Jews in Canada.

The following select list of collections in the custody of the Manuscript Division will be of special interest to Jewish genealogists:

- The minute books (1911–1935) of the Hebrew Free Loan Association, Montreal
- The administrative records and case files (1863–1977) of the Jewish Family Services of the Baron de Hirsch Institute, Montreal
- The microfilmed records of the Canadian Jewish Congress, Western Division (1923–1950), found within the Jewish Historical Society of Western Canada Collection
- Funeral records of Benjamin's Park Memorial Chapel, Toronto (1930–1980), Chesed Shel Emes Chapel, Winnipeg (1946–1969), and Steeles-College Memorial Chapel, Toronto (1949, 1951–1975)
- The microfilmed nominal case files (1898–1922) of the thousands of Jewish immigrants found in the LI-RA-MA Imperial Russian Consular Records Collection

Researchers should also be aware that much information will be found in the national records of major Jewish organizations preserved in the NA. These records include those of B'nai B'rith Canada, Canadian Zionist Federation, Hadassah-WIZO Organization of Canada, Jewish National Fund of Canada, and the Jewish Labour Committee of Canada. Most of the records found in these collections are contemporary and will only be of interest to researchers compiling biographical information about their relatives, as well as a record of their communal activities.

For a more detailed description and listing of Jewish collections at the NA, researchers are advised to consult *Archival Sources for the Study of Canadian Jewry,* by Lawrence F. Tapper (see Bibliography). For a free copy and for further information about Jewish history in Canada, write to:

Canadian Jewish Archives Program
Ethnic Archives
Manuscript Division
National Archives of Canada
395 Wellington Street
Ottawa, Ontario, Canada K1A 0N3

Genealogical records created by federal government agencies are the responsibility of the NA's Government Archives Division.

Researchers should write, giving specific details, to:

Genealogical Section
Public Programs Branch
National Archives of Canada
395 Wellington Street
Ottawa, Ontario, Canada K1A 0N3

Information about census records, which are now open until 1891 and passenger shipping lists for all Canadian ports of entry, including the biggest, Quebec City (1865–1919), are available. In addition to sending researchers a free copy of *Tracing Your Ancestors in Canada,* the Genealogical Section will suggest appropriate sources and conduct a limited amount of research for genealogists.

Researchers should also consult the *Union List of Manuscripts in Canadian Repositories.* This publication, regularly updated, is a complete listing and location of manuscripts and collections found in Canadian archival institutions, and will help researchers identify sources that might be of interest.

Another important source for genealogists is synagogue records. The NA has microfilmed records of Holy Blossom Temple, Toronto (1856–1969) and Shaarey Zedek Synagogue, Winnipeg (1889–1983). Researchers should note that, although congregational records are usually kept by synagogues themselves, some have been transferred to various local Jewish community archives across Canada. For a complete and current listing of synagogues in Canada, consult the *National Synagogue Directory 1984–*

1985, published by the National Religious Department of the Canadian Jewish Congress (CJC) in Montreal.

The Jewish press in Canada is an excellent source for the study of Jewish family history. Canada has produced many fine Anglo-Jewish and Yiddish newspapers, many of which have been microfilmed and are available on interlibrary loan from the National Library of Canada (NL), the NA, the Jewish Public Library of Montreal (JPL), and the CJC. These include *The Jewish Times* (1897–1909), *Canadian Jewish Times* (1909–1914), *Canadian Jewish Chronicle* (1914–1966), *Canadian Jewish Review* (1921–1966), *Canadian Jewish News* (established 1960), and the *Jewish Standard* (established 1931). The CJC *Inter-Office Information Bulletins* (1946–1978) provide an historical and chronological record of the community, and also contain biographical information about many Jewish leaders within the community. The NL also has a complete collection of all city and telephone directories published in Canada.

In addition to preserving the dormant records of the CJC, the CJC National Archives is also responsible for the safe care and custody of the national office records of the Jewish Colonization Association (established 1907), the United Jewish Relief Agencies of Canada, and the Jewish Immigrant Aid Services of Canada (JIAS) (established 1919). Together these collections contain thousands of personal case files of Jewish immigrants and farmers. For a further discussion of the collections and inventories describing them, researchers should see *Avotaynu*, Vol. III, No. 2, Spring 1987, as well as Zachary Baker's article, "Immigration Records at the National Archive" (later in this chapter). For further information, researchers should write to:

CJC National Archives
1590 Docteur Penfield Avenue
Montreal, Quebec, Canada H3G 1C5

The best sources for genealogical studies of the Ontario Jewish community and Metropolitan Toronto in particular are available at:

CJC Ontario Region Archives
4600 Bathurst Street
Willowdale, Ontario, Canada M2R 3V2

Many valuable synagogue, landsmanshaftn, and dormant communal records are located here, including those of the Toronto Hebrew Benevolent Society and the CJC Central Region, as well as photographs and oral histories of pioneers. Researchers should also consult Dr. Stephen Speisman's book, *The Jews of Toronto* (see Bibliography and Zachary Baker's review, p. 000).

JIAS
4600 Bathurst Street
Suite 325
Willowdale, Ontario, Canada M2R 3V3

JIAS Central Region case files (1935–present).

(See Dr. Rolf Lederer's article "JIAS Records—Toronto," in *Avotaynu*, Vol. II, No. 3, October 1986, p. 15.)

RECORDS OF IMMIGRATION ACROSS THE CANADIAN BORDER

The U.S. National Archives recently accessioned a group of passenger arrival records on microfilm from the Immigration and Naturalization Service. As the films are inspected and preservation copies are made, these new records are being made available as microfilm publications. Included among them are records of immigrants crossing the Canadian border during the period 1895–1954.

During most of the nineteenth century, no law required passenger arrival records to be kept for persons entering the United States by land from Canada. The Immigration Act of 1891 created an administrative structure that established the first immigration inspection stations along the Canadian border.

Immigration Via Canada

The first United States immigration inspector stationed at Montreal estimated that roughly 40 percent of the passengers arriving in Canada were actually bound for the United States. The majority crossed the border at Sault Ste. Marie and Detroit, Michigan. The Dominion of Canada was encouraging immigration, and Canadian steamship companies and railway lines were cooperating by offering low transportation rates. These low fares encouraged many people bound for the United States to travel through Canada.

Four major shipping lines were engaged in the passenger traffic between Europe and the east coast of Canada. The Beaver and Dominion Lines sailed from Liverpool to Quebec and Montreal. The Allen Mail Line traveled the same route with an additional stop in Glasgow.

The fourth passenger line, the Hansa Line, also traveled between Liverpool and Quebec and Montreal, but, unlike the others, Hansa ships picked up passengers in Antwerp and Hamburg. The Hansa Line, in connection with the Canadian Pacific Railway, offered passage to the United States through Canada to many potential immigrants who would have been denied direct passage under the 1891 immigration law which barred paupers, polygamists, and persons suffering from certain diseases.

Joint Inspection System

By 1895 the United States and Canada had established a system of joint inspection. The Canadian shipping companies signed agreements to manifest passengers in transit to the United States on American immigration lists. These passengers could be inspected by United States officials on arrival in a Canadian port. U.S. commissioners of immigration were located at Quebec, Halifax, and Montreal in the east and in Vancouver and Victoria in the west.

Travel to the United States through Canada meant that the immigrant underwent two separate inspections by American immigration officials. Because immigrant inspectors boarded trains as they crossed the border, often during the night, lawful immigrants and alien visitors who had already been inspected in a Canadian port were issued cards or certificates which they surrendered to the immigration inspector at the border. The immigration inspector annotated the certificates with the date of arrival and sent them to the district office. Since the passenger lists were kept by the district headquarters in Montreal, the border inspectors had no manifest to check against the certificates. They produced their own monthly lists of arrivals by railway. These monthly lists were also forwarded to the district office where they were bound into volumes.

To keep track of Canadians entering through various border ports, individual card manifests were created. The card manifest recorded the same information about each person as the passenger list. The immigration officers also used the manifest cards for non-Canadians to serve as an index to the passenger lists.

Quota Act

World War I brought tighter restrictions on border crossing, a system of passport-permits, and visas. But Congress did not pass a truly restrictive immigration law until 1921. This law set a 3 percent quota on the number of persons of any nationality who could enter the United States, based on the 1910 census. Originally passed as a temporary measure, the 3 percent quota was extended to 1924 and was replaced that year by a 2 percent quota based on the 1890 census. The Immigration Act of 1924 also provided permanent pre-embarkation examination of aliens and the issuance of visas. Having created a restriction that would lead to increased illegal immigration, Congress also created the first Canadian border patrol.

Canada came to play an even more important role in immigration after the passage of the quota act. As late as 1929 no quotas were placed on natives of North America. Furthermore, the quotas were based on national origin and not on place of birth. Hence, by immigrating to Canada and becoming a Canadian resident, an individual could then immigrate to the United States without being subject to the quota system.

INS District 1

When it was created in 1909, District 1 of the Immigration Service, headquartered in Montreal, encompassed the entire Canadian border. By 1924, District 1 included all of Maine, Vermont, New Hampshire, New York, and Sault Ste. Marie, Michigan. Additional districts had been created at Detroit, Michigan, Winnipeg, Manitoba, Spokane, Washington, and Seattle, Washington, which had subports in Vancouver and Victoria, British Columbia.

Immigrants who entered Canada through District 1, Montreal and Quebec, were reported statistically in District 1 regardless of where they crossed the border.

The procedures followed in a typical immigration case were as follows: An immigrant arrived at Quebec by steamer with an immigration visa. The purser had listed him on a sheet manifest with the number of his headtax guarantee and the number of his visa. The immigrant was given a certificate of identity, and its serial number was entered on the manifest and on his visa. His passport was stamped.

At the frontier the immigrant gave up his immigration visa and his certificate of identity. His passport was endorsed to show admission. His certificate of identity was endorsed at the bottom to show the time, place, and manner of entry and sent to Montreal for filing. At Montreal it was compared with the carbon copy on file and pasted into a book. The books were filed in numerical order.

If verification of landing was required for any purpose, a clerk went directly to the manifest, if the immigrant gave the name of the steamer and the date of arrival, or to the card index of arrivals. The manifest showed the number of the certificate of identity. The clerk then retrieved the book and verified the time, place, and manner of entry. The immigrant's records were retained in the records of District 1.

The St. Albans Records

District 1 headquarters were moved to St. Albans, Vermont, where the records were microfilmed by the Immigration and Naturalization Service in the early 1950s. The paper copies were destroyed after filming. The microfilmed copies of the St. Albans records that are being made available by the National Archives are the first records to document fully the passage of immigrants across the Canadian border into the United States.

The St. Albans records consist of five series of records available as five microfilm publications. M1461, *Index (Soundex) to Canadian Border Entries Through the St. Albans, Vermont, District, 1895–1924*, is composed of the individual card manifests arranged according to the Soundex code. Each card represents an abstract of the information found on the original passenger manifest or, in the case of Canadian residents, what would have appeared on a manifest. The cards also serve as an index to the manifests for non-Canadians. This publication includes the names of people who crossed the border in Washington, Montana, Michigan, New York, North Dakota, and Minnesota—all along the United States–Canada border. Covering the same time period is M1462, *Alphabetical Index to Canadian Border Entries Through Small Ports in Vermont, 1895–1924*.

M1463, *Index (Soundex) to Entries into the St. Albans, Vermont, District Through Canadian Pacific and Atlantic Ports, 1924–52*, provides the same information as the earlier index for entries across the border in New York, New Hampshire, Maine, Vermont, and Sault Ste. Marie, Michigan.

The actual passenger lists are reproduced in two series. M1464, *Manifests of Passengers Arriving in the St. Albans, Vermont, District Through Canadian Pacific and Atlantic Ports, 1895–1954*, provides two types of lists. The traditional passenger lists on United States immigration forms are found, as well as monthly lists of aliens crossing the border on trains. These monthly lists are arranged by port and thereunder by railway. There is also a smaller publication of manifests, M1465, *Manifests of Passengers Arriving at the St. Albans, Vermont, District Through Canadian Ports, 1929–49*.

Reprinted from the *NGS Newsletter*, Vol. 13, No. 2, March–April 1987.

BOOK REVIEW: *Jews of Toronto*

Zachary M. Baker

Stephen A. Speisman. *The Jews of Toronto: A History to 1937*. Toronto: McClelland and Stewart, 1979.

Stephen A. Speisman, author of *The Jews of Toronto*, is a professional historian who not only uses the type of primary sources to which genealogists often turn, but as director of the Archives of the Toronto Jewish Congress and the Canadian Jewish Congress, Central Region (Ontario), he is also responsible for having created the sort of information center to which Jewish genealogists in many other communities only dream of having access. The Toronto Jewish Archives are in part a byproduct of Dr. Speisman's local historical research and serve as a repository for documentation that might otherwise have been lost—institutional records, individual collections, photographs, and other memorabilia. The Toronto Jewish archives are located in the building that houses Toronto's Jewish Federation, adjoining the local Jewish Community Centre (4600 Bathurst St., Willowdale, Ontario, Canada M2R 3V2).

The Jews of Toronto is an exemplary contribution to the by now venerable genre of Jewish community historiography. Communities from Indianapolis to the Bronx have been subjected to the scrutiny of trained scholars. Speisman's book is the first to present an in-depth survey of a major Canadian Jewish community. The dynamic and growing Jewish community of metropolitan Toronto numbers some 130,000 souls, now constituting the largest Jewish community in Canada's largest conurbation (3 million+). In recent decades the community has absorbed tens of thousands of immigrants from the Soviet Union, Israel, South Africa, the United States, and—yes—the Province of Quebec.

Toronto is not Canada's oldest Jewish community; the laurels in that department fall to Montreal, which was one of only half a dozen North American Jewish communities to be established before 1776—the others being Newport, New York, Philadelphia, Charleston, and Savannah. The origins of the Toronto community date only to 1832, with the arrival there of the Montreal merchant Arthur Wellington Hart.

For decades thereafter, the community, composed then primarily of German-Jewish immigrant merchants, remained tiny, though over time it acquired the accoutrements of all organized Jewish communities. The Hebrew Congregation was founded in 1849 and was succeeded in 1856 by the Toronto Hebrew Congregation (Sons of Israel), now known as the Holy Blossom Temple. Charitable and fraternal organizations, such as the Toronto Hebrew Ladies Sick and Benevolent Society, founded in 1868, and the Canada Lodge of B'nai B'rith, founded in 1875, also came into existence during these formative decades. According to the 1881 census, 534 Jews resided in Toronto, a figure that in due course was to increase dramatically. By 1901 the Jewish population had grown to 3,090; there were 18,237 Jews in Toronto in 1911, and the community nearly doubled again in size to 34,619, in 1921, a record of truly remarkable growth in a relatively brief time frame.

As in the United States, the post-1881 Jewish immigration to Toronto originated in Eastern Europe, primarily (in Toronto's case) from the Polish provinces of czarist Russia. As elsewhere, many Toronto Jews earned their livelihoods in the needle trades; others became peddlers, storekeepers, wholesalers, or worked in various salvage trades (rags and metal). The area of densest Jewish settlement during this period was the downtown neighborhood known as The Ward; nearby was the picturesque Kensington Market dis-

trict. Today, visitors to this quarter will see little obvious evidence of its former Jewish character, beyond a few delicatessens, clothing and fur stores, and synagogues. On the other hand, the restaurants, in what is now Toronto's vast Chinatown, are well worth a trip down bygone paths.

The first era of mass immigration witnessed the burgeoning of communal organizations, landsmanshaftn, synagogues, and charities, all of which receive ample coverage in Speisman's study. He also discusses the reaction of gentile Torontonians to the sudden presence in their midst of the first significant settlement of non-English speaking immigrants, who were not even Christians at that. Toronto's reputation, largely justified, as a homogeneous city of prim Scots Presbyterians was to persist until after World War II when masses of Italians, Greeks, Portuguese, Ukrainians, Chinese, West Indians, and South Asians arrived, irrevocably changing the city's face. One of the ways in which devout Presbyterians reacted to the early Jewish presence in the city was to establish the Toronto Jewish Mission, in 1894. An entire chapter in Speisman's book is devoted to Protestant missionary activities among Jews and to the response of Toronto Jews to these conversionist crusades.

Philanthropy, religious trends, cultural and educational developments, and political movements within the Jewish community also are accorded ample treatment, as are class conflicts such as arose during the 1912 Eaton's factory strike. At that time, the T. Eaton Company (now best known as a trans-Canadian department store chain) was the largest single employer of Jews in Toronto. Like other immigrant Jewish communities, Toronto possessed a Yiddish daily, the *Hebrew Journal*, published from 1911 until 1969. The city was also a regular stop on the Yiddish theatrical circuit.

As the decades passed, Toronto's Jews experienced many of the same trends in communal organization as affected American Jewish communities. The federation concept, for example, took root in October 1916, with the formation of the Federation of Jewish Philanthropies. In 1923, Orthodox Jews banded together to form a kehillah for the primary purpose of regulating kashruth in Toronto. A similar, more ambitious kehillah experiment had been launched in New York in 1908; like its New York counterpart, which folded in 1922, the Toronto kehillah eventually collapsed (1939). Torontonians also played an active role in the creation of the "parliament" of Canada's Jews, the Canadian Jewish Congress founded in 1919.

Speisman leaves off his study in 1937, the year that saw the establishment of the United Jewish Welfare Fund of Toronto. This was an amalgamation of the Federation of Jewish Philanthropies, the Jewish Centre and Talmud Torah, the United Palestine Fund, the Joint Distribution Committee, the overseas relief organizations, the Old Folks' Home, Mizrachi, ORT, the Hebrew Free Loan Society, and the local office of Canadian Jewish Congress. The creation of this umbrella organization constitutes a benchmark in the maturation of the Toronto Jewish community, which then and subsequently would confront the challenges posted by local anti-Semitism, the Holocaust, the establishment of the State of Israel, and the large-scale postwar influx of displaced persons.

Today Toronto is one of the most dynamic and successful middle-sized Jewish communities on this continent. It has achieved a high level of integration with its surroundings without sacrificing its own religious, educational, and philanthropic obligations. Two of Toronto's postwar mayors, a recent chairman of the Metro Toronto board, leaders of all three party caucuses in the Ontario provincial legislature, and numerous Toronto-area Members of Parliament and Federal cabinet ministers have been Jewish. The contemporary Toronto Jewish community is the worthy heir of the immigrant community described so well in *The Jews of Toronto*. Speisman's book is a lucid, well-written, and inclusive survey of the first century of this important community's flowering.

Excerpted from *Avotaynu*, Vol. III, No. 2, Spring 1987.

BOOK REVIEW: *Archival Sources for Canadian Jewry*
Rolf Lederer

Archival Sources for the Study of Canadian Jewry by Lawrence F. Tapper, text in English (96p) and French (101p), with French text on inverted pages.

Despite the modest and perhaps dry title, this booklet, an update of a 1978 work, contains a wealth of information pertaining to Jewish life in Canada.

The main body of the publication contains 150 entries from the Manuscript Division (Canadian Jewish Archives Programme), detailing the content for each entry. The holdings cover a wide spectrum of organizations and individuals, prominent and lesser known, in Canadian Jewish life: Canadian Zionist Federation, Ottawa Vaad Hair, and so on.

Of particular interest to genealogists are the records of the following: Benjamin's Park Memorial Chapel (Toronto, established 1922); Chesed Shel Emes Chapel (Winnipeg, established 1930); Congregation Shaarey Zedek (Winnipeg, established 1889); Congregation Shearith Israel (Montreal, established 1768—Spanish and Portuguese Synagogue); Jewish Family Services of the Baron de Hirsch Institute (Montreal, contains cemetery records and case files); Steeles College Memorial Chapel (Toronto, established 1927); Temple Anshe Shalom (Hamilton, established 1863).

Also available are the *Canadian Jewish Chronicle* (1912–1966), and the L1-RA-MA, Imperial Russian Consular Records 1898–1922, the acronym referring to the three Russian consular officials who provided consular services at the beginning of the twentieth century and for a few years after the revolution. There are over 10,000 files of immigrants, many Jewish, from the Montreal, Toronto and Vancouver offices.

Smaller sections of the booklet include a sketchy history of Jewish life in Canada from 1760 and a bibliography listing major works pertaining to the history of the Jewish Community in Canada. A National Library project, *A Bibliography of Canadian Jewry*, is in progress. Also listed are major Jewish newspapers and those of Canadian Jewish studies.

Readers are advised that passenger ship lists and federal census records are available in the Government Archives Division. The National Archives Division is located at 395 Wellington Street, Ottawa, Ontario, K1A 0N3. Prior to their visit, researchers should contact Lawrence Tapper, the archivist respon-

sible for the Canadian Jewish Archives Programme. Some portions of the holdings are on microfilm and may be borrowed through the inter-library loan programme.

In short, this is a valuable little booklet with many useful references and is a must for anyone researching Canadian sources.

Reprinted from *Avotaynu*, Vol. IV, No. 2, Spring 1988.

BRITISH COLUMBIA

◼ VANCOUVER

City of Vancouver Archives
1150 Chestnut Street
Vancouver, British Columbia, Canada V6J 3J9
(604) 736-8561

The City Archives does have Voters' Lists from 1886 to present, City Directories from 1887 to present and collections of private manuscript holdings indexed by surname. Certainly Jewish families figure among these records. Unfortunately, the staff is unable to do detailed research by mail, but will answer simple inquiries. Collections are open to the public.

Division of Vital Statistics
Wills Registry
800 Hornby Street
Vancouver, British Columbia, Canada V8Z 2C5

Vital Statistics representatives will tell you only if and where a will has been probated. There is a charge for this information.

The Jewish Historical Society of British Columbia
950 West 41st Avenue
Vancouver, British Columbia, Canada V5Z 2N7
(604) 266-3529

The Society is very active, collects photographs and manuscripts, and publishes a newsletter, *The Scribe*, with accounts of Jewish pioneer families from the region. The Executive Director of the Society is Cyril E. Leonoff, author of *Pioneers, Peddlers and Prayer Shawls—the Jewish Communities in British Columbia and the Yukon* (Sono Nis Press, Victoria, 1978).

Publications of the JHS contain a great deal of personal and family data of interest to genealogists. Research services are available through this office.

Vancouver Public Library
750 Burrard Street
Vancouver, British Columbia, Canada V6Z 1X5

The library has British Columbia directories dating back to 1860 with some gaps in earlier years and the index to the British Columbia census of 1881. It does not have a collection of genealogical records.

It has Vancouver papers back to 1886, and its Sociology Division holds the *Jewish Western Bulletin*.

Staff will respond to written inquiries, with charges made for extensive searches and photocopies.

Newspaper
The Jewish Western Bulletin
3268 Heather Street
Vancouver, British Columbia, Canada V5Z 3K5
(604) 879-6575

Letters to the Editor for genealogical enquiries are accepted up to a maximum of 250 words.

Complete sets of *The Bulletin* are in the "Bulletin" offices.

Synagogues
Congregation Beth Israel
4350 Oak Street
Vancouver, British Columbia, Canada V6H 2N4
(604) 731-4161

Congregation Schara Tzedeck
3476 Oak Street
Vancouver, British Columbia, Canada V6H 2L8
(604) 736-7607

Congregation Beth Israel now has its own cemetery. The older Congregation Schara Tzedeck also maintains a Chevra Kadisha. Both congregations have indicated they will try to respond to requests for information regarding membership, marriages, deaths, etc.

■ VICTORIA

Division of Vital Statistics
1515 Blanchard Street
Victoria, British Columbia, Canada V8W 3C8

Birth, death, and marriage records dating back to 1872 are maintained. The charge for each certificate or photocopy (including one three-year search) is $15.00. Search only, over a 3-year period or less, is $15.00. Payment is to be made in Canadian funds by certified check or money order payable to the Minister of Finance. A Form of Application for Service, which is required, is obtainable from the above address.

A lawyer or registered genealogist, acting on behalf of a qualified applicant (a relative), must include the consent of their client to release family information.

The Jewish Historical Society of British Columbia
Legislative Library, Parliament Buildings
Victoria, British Columbia, Canada V8V 1X4

MANITOBA

■ WINNIPEG

The Jewish Historical Society of Western Canada
402-365 Hargrave Street
Winnipeg, Manitoba, Canada R3B 2K3
(204) 942-9299 or (204) 942-4822

Services: The archival holdings of documents and manuscripts are stored at the Provincial Archives of Manitoba, which are open to the public at regular office hours. Reading room at the Provincial Archives.

Office of the Society provides a reading room. Copies of records are provided on request. Written inquiries are also handled, generally without charge, but this depends on the amount of information requested and the time required to gather it.

History and scope: Founded in Winnipeg in 1968. The society is dedicated to the objectives of gathering, recording, preserving, and presenting the history of the Jewish people of Western Canada, their religious and cultural heritage, and their contributions to the growth and development of Western Canada. The society engages in a continuous program of acquiring new documents, photographs, memorabilia, and artifacts.

Holdings: Approximately 150 linear feet of documentation on Jewish life and activities in Western Canada, from the 1880s to the present; forty-seven boxes of files from the Canadian Jewish Congress and Jewish Immigration Aid, beginning 1919; 4,500 prints and negatives; 380 tapes of oral history interviews totaling approximately 380 hours; three 16mm films; small collection of artifacts and memorabilia.

Processing and accessibility: Cataloging and finding aids are carried out by Jewish Historical Society. There is a card index, with classification as to name, geographic location, and subject.

Use of a very small part of the records is restricted. Permission must be obtained from the society to research the collection of documents and manuscripts housed at the Provincial Archives of Manitoba.

Jewish Public Library
1725 Main Street
Winnipeg, Manitoba, Canada R2Y 1Z4
(204) 338-4048

Books in Yiddish, Hebrew, Russian, and English dealing with all aspects of Jewish life (though no significant collections of specifically genealogical material).

The Provincial Archives of Manitoba
200 Vaughan Street
Winnipeg, Manitoba, Canada R3C 1T5
(204) 945-3971

Its records since 1870 are concerned with the Province of Manitoba and is of interest for Jewish genealogical research of the Winnipeg area.

- Census returns list all members of the household
- The Henderson Directory for the City of Winnipeg (since 1876)
- Municipal records
  - Council minute books
  - Voters' lists
  - Muster rolls (Military District #10)
  - Photographs
  - Individual papers
- Business records and documents
- Individual Jewish family papers

The Recorder
Office of Vital Statistics
Department of Health and Social Development
104 Norquay Building
401 York Avenue
Winnipeg, Manitoba, Canada R3C 0P8

Five-year searches conducted for transcript or verification. Write for a fee schedule.

- Birth, marriage, and death records for the province of Manitoba since 1882

A letter of application must be submitted containing the following information:

Birth—full name, parents' full name, date, address
Marriage—full names of bride and groom, date, address
Death—full name of deceased, date, address

The Registrar
Land Title Office
405 Broadway Avenue
Winnipeg, Manitoba, Canada R3C 3L6
Land records.

Surrogate Court
210 Woodsworth Building
405 Broadway Avenue
Winnipeg, Manitoba, Canada R3C 3L6
Wills and probate records (indexed) since 1871. Information is accessible to the general public and a search of the records can be made for a fee. Photocopies of estate documents are also available for a fee. Write for fee schedules.

Winnipeg Jewish Community Council
370 Hargrave Street
Winnipeg, Manitoba, Canada R3B 2K1
(204) 943-0406
Representatives can indicate available resources in the Jewish community.

Winnipeg Public Library
251 Donald Street
Winnipeg, Manitoba, Canada R3C 3P5
(204) 986-6450
Books are available for use in the library, and in most cases for interlibrary loan. (Census material cannot be sent out on interlibrary loan.) There is no charge for this service.

Newspaper
The Jewish Post and News
117 Hutchings Street
Winnipeg, Manitoba, Canada R2X 2Y4
(204) 694-3332
A weekly English language newspaper serving the Winnipeg Jewish community.

Synagogues
Ashkenazi Congregation (Orthodox)
297 Burrows Avenue
Winnipeg, Manitoba, Canada R2W 1Z7
(204) 589-1517

Beth Israel (Conservative)
1007 Sinclair Street
Winnipeg, Manitoba, Canada R2Y 3J5
(204) 582-2353

B'nai Abraham (Orthodox)
235 Enniskillen Avenue
Winnipeg, Manitoba, Canada R2Y 0H5
(204) 339-9297

Chevurat Tefile—Fellowship of Prayer (Orthodox)
459 Hartford Avenue
Winnipeg, Manitoba, Canada R2Y 0X7
(204) 338-9451

Chevra Mishnayes (Orthodox)
700 Jefferson Avenue
Winnipeg, Manitoba, Canada R2Y 0P6
(204) 338-8503

Herzlia—Adas Yeshurun (Orthodox)
620 Brock Street
Winnipeg, Manitoba, Canada R3N 0Z4
(204) 489-6262 & 489-6668

Lubavitch Centre (Orthodox)
2095 Sinclair Street
Winnipeg, Manitoba, Canada R2Y 3K2
(204) 339-8737 & 339-4756

Resh Pine (Conservative)
123 Matheson Avenue
Winnipeg, Manitoba, Canada R2W 0C3
(204) 589-6306

Shaarey Zedek (Conservative)
561 Wellington Crescent
Winnipeg, Manitoba, Canada R3M 0A5
(204) 452-3711

Talmud Torah—Beth Jacob (Orthodox)
427 Matheson Avenue
Winnipeg, Manitoba, Canada R2W 0E1
(204) 589-5345

Temple Shalom (Reform)
1077 Grant Avenue
Winnipeg, Manitoba, Canada R3M 1Y6
(204) 453-1625
Staff will aid in the facilitation of genealogical research. There is no fee for their services. It may be difficult for the staff to respond to some written requests in a timely fashion; however, researchers may visit the premises.

Many Temple documents are housed on site, including burial records.

Temple Shalom's congregational archives are stored on microfilm at the Manitoba Public Archives and the Jewish Historical Society in Winnipeg. Permission to view the microfilmed material must be obtained through the Temple.

Funeral Home
Chessed Shel Emes Chapel
1023 Main Street
Winnipeg, Manitoba, Canada R2W 3P9
(204) 582-5088
Archives contain the name of deceased, age, date of death, date of burial as well as burial place. Will respond to written requests at no charge.

NOVA SCOTIA

■ SYDNEY

Head, Records Control
Citizenship Registration Branch
Secretary of State
P.O. Box 7000
Sydney, Nova Scotia, Canada B1P 6G5

Records start in 1939 (earlier records are described as "sketchy" and offer very little genealogical information). However, from 1969 onward, parent's names and spouse names are also included in their records. Since 1977, the newspaper clipping relating to a particular funeral or obituary is also included, and since 1986 everything can be accessed by computer.

ONTARIO

■ DOWNSVIEW
(Toronto Metropolitan Area)

Funeral Home
Benjamins Park Memorial Chapel
2401 Steele Avenue W.
Downsview, Ontario, Canada M3J 2P1
(416) 663-9060

Will answer inquiries.

■ ETOBICOKE
(Toronto Metropolitan Area)

Family History Center
95 Melbert Street
Etobicoke, Toronto, Ontario, Canada M9C 3P8
(416) 621-4607

■ MARKHAM
(Toronto Metropolitan Area)

Toronto Records Center
7131 Woodbine
Markham, Ontario, Canada L3R 1A3
(416) 475-1471

Banking records since 1885.

■ OTTAWA

Canadian Jewish Archives Programme
Manuscript Division
National Archives of Canada
395 Wellington Street
Ottawa, Ontario, Canada K1A 0N3

Curatorial Section
Manuscript Division
National Archives of Canada
395 Wellington Street
Ottawa, Ontario, Canada K1A 0N3

Genealogical Unit
References Services Section
Reference and Researchers Services Division
National Archives of Canada
395 Wellington Street
Ottawa, Ontario, Canada K1A 0N3

Ottawa Jewish Historical Society
151 Chapelk Street
Ottawa, Ontario, Canada K1N 7Y2

Services: For access to archival holdings, see next paragraph. Copies of records provided on request. Written inquiries handled without charge.

History and scope: The OJHS was founded in 1966, but did not become active until 1971. In the early 1970s it began to collect and preserve congregational records, manuscripts, synagogue records, and the general archival material of the Jewish community of Ottawa. It also began to collect tapes and photographs. In 1983, with a move to larger premises, an archival repository was created at 151 Chapel Street, where the bulk of the community archives are preserved. Limited facilities for researchers are available as well as photocopying at a nominal charge. A smaller collection of rare minute books and manuscripts is preserved with the Public Archives of Canada (7 linear feet) at 395 Wellington Street, Ottawa. These archives are open to the public on a twenty-four-hour basis, and their facilities are at the disposal of researchers who have obtained access to the holdings from the OJHS.

Holdings: Over 41 linear feet of records. A large collection of photographs, originals and copies, as well as slides and 1 film.

Select list of record groups of special importance and interest:

- Marriage Registers: 1899–1946
- Agudath Achim Congregation—minutes, constitution, bylaws, cemetery records: 1902–1955
- Adath Jeshurun Congregation—minutes, correspondence, etc.: 1892–1956
- Ottawa Vaad Ha'ir—financial records correspondence, reports: 1912–1957
- Ottawa Free Loan Association—financial statements, reports: 1939–1952
- Ottawa Hebrew Benevolent Society—correspondence reports, accounts, relief registration, etc.
- Jewish Immigrant Aid Society of Canada, Ottawa Branch—correspondence, aid accounts

Processing and accessibility: About one-third of the holdings are fully processed. The collections deposited with the Public Archives have been cataloged and are accessible through finding aids MG 28 1 190.

The use of the entire collection is restricted. Permission must be obtained from the Vaad Ha'ir or the society itself.

Pension Searches
Statistics Canada
Jean Talon Bldg.
Section B1 East-34
Tunney' Pasture
Ottawa, Ontario, Canada K1A 0T6

Public Archives of Canada
395 Wellington Street
Ottawa, Ontario, Canada K1A 0N3
(613) 995-5138 (General inquiry)

Reading rooms are open to registered researchers and accredited students. Consultant services are also offered during regular office hours on weekdays.

The Public Archives of Canada was founded in 1870 and is a research institution that acquires all significant archival material "of every kind, nature and description" relating to all aspects of Canadian life and to the development of Canada.

The collection is readily accessible to all serious researchers and a trained staff provides service. Researchers must register in order to utilize the facilities. All inquiries are welcome.

The Public Archives is separated into eight divisions:

- Manuscript Division Federal Archives Division (Formerly Public Records Division)
- Public Archives Library
- Machine Readable Archives Division
- National Map Collection
- Picture Division
- National Photography Collection
- National Film, Television and Sound Division
- Manuscript Division

The Manuscript Division has custody of all nonprinted textual papers received from individuals and corporate organizations. The major collections received from Jewish persons and organizations are described in a 51-page booklet, *A Guide to Sources for the Study of Canadian Jewry* by Lawrence F. Tapper, available through the National Ethnic Archives, Manuscript Division. The bilingual publication lists bibliographical sources as well as the major Jewish collections of the Manuscript Division.

Several other valuable booklets and publications are offered by the Public Archives of Canada to aid in discovering your roots. *Tracing Your Ancestors In Canada* by Patricia Kennedy and Janine Roy of the Manuscript Division is a revised (March 1983) edition that lists and describes the holdings of the Manuscript Division in general (which can contain Jewish immigration information).

Guide to the Reference Room of the Manuscript Division by Judith Cummings discusses the reference tools researchers need to locate archival material of interest to them.

Researchers may telephone or write requesting information on services, holdings, or policies of the division. In addition, the Reference Room provides an oral reference service through a genealogical consultant and a research consultant. The genealogical consultant furnishes information on archival sources for the study of family history; the research consultant disseminates information on archival sources for all other topics of research related to the Manuscript Division.

Staff of the Division, including Reference Room staff, is available for consultation.

Fees for each of these booklets and information about any publications produced by the Public Archives of Canada can be obtained by writing directly to:

Information Services
Public Archives of Canada
395 Wellington Street
Ottawa, Ontario, Canada K1A 0N3
(613) 996-1473

There are currently 13 sections under the direction of the Manuscript Division that focus on specific interests of researchers. Of particular value to researchers of Jewish genealogy is the National Ethnic Archives section of the Public Archives, which is responsible for documentation concerning Canada's multicultural heritage that is *not* British, French, or native in origin. It acquires papers and records of individuals and organizations from these ethnocultural communities and copies of relevant documentation in foreign countries.

Reading Room
Room 225-N
House of Commons
Ottawa, Ontario, Canada K1A 0A9

Russian Archives Program
National Ethnic Archives
Manuscript Division
Public Archives of Canada
395 Wellington Street
Ottawa, Ontario, Canada K1A 0N3
(613) 996-7453

Russian Consulate Records In Canada: The LI-RA-MA Collection (M030 E406) includes files on over 12,000 prerevolutionary Russian immigrants to Canada, half or more of whom, it can be assured, were Jewish. Records are from 1900 to 1922.

The Canadian Consular Records consist of two series: about 11,000 nominal case files on individuals and some 5,000 subject files that deal with such matters as estates and inheritances, deportations, charities, military recruitment, family breakdowns, criminal activities, and interment of Russians among other topics of interest.

The nominal files contain a great deal of genealogical data such as personal documents (photographs, birth certificates, passports, affidavits and family correspondence). The files often contain questionnaires (usually in Russian, though sometimes in English) that describe the immigrant's personal history, including his age, ethnic origin, religion, marital status, place of birth or Russian residence, date of departure from Russia or arrival in Canada, port of entry, places of residence after immigration, military service, relatives, and dependents.

National Ethnic Archives also includes the complete files of two Toronto Jewish Funeral Homes and the records of B'nai Brith Canada.

■ THORNHILL
(Toronto Metropolitan Area)

Funeral Home
Steeles College Memorial Chapel
350 Steeles Avenue W
Thornhill, Ontario, Canada L4J 1A1
(416) 881-6003

Will answer inquiries.

Document from the Leizer Teper File (MG 30, E-406) of the Imperial Russian Consular Records Collection (Courtesy of National Archives of Canada)

The Steeles College Memorial records officially start in 1927 and assistance can be provided if one can identify the exact date of burial.

An article relating to the history of Steeles Memorial Chapel appeared in *The Jewish Standard*.

The National Public Archives in Ottawa has microfilmed the records in existence (up to approximately 1985) and these are now part of the collection in Ottawa.

■ TORONTO

Archives of Ontario
77 Grenville St.
Toronto, Ontario, Canada M7A 2R9
(416) 965-4030

No research fee; no membership fee. Primarily original source material. Will reply to letters briefly but no extensive research is carried out by the staff. People do their own research or hire professional researchers.

Holdings include records regarding:

- Decennial Census Records: microfilm copies 1851–1881. Index available (alphabetical by township)
- Canadian Jewish Institutions
- Personal documents

- Small individual collections (including genealogies), correspondence
- Newspaper clippings and photographs
- Last wills and testaments
- Probate records of the Supreme Court of Ontario
- Land records
- Incomplete holdings of pre-1869 birth, marriage, and death records
- Cemetery records
- Military and draft records

Toronto Records Center (see Markham, p. 144).

Metropolitan Central Reference Library of Toronto
789 Yonge Street
Toronto, Ontario, Canada M4W 8G8
Canadian History Department
(416) 928-5254
Genealogy (416) 928-5275

Telephone and city directories.
Toronto newspapers.

The Multicultural History Society of Ontario
3 Queen's Park Crescent East
Toronto, Ontario, Canada M5S 2C3
(416) 525-4621/4607

For publications, newspapers, and oral tapes regarding ethnics in Canada.

Museum and Archives
Toronto Board of Education
155 College Street
Toronto, Ontario, Canada M5T 1P6
(416) 591-8202

No research fee or membership fee. Letters of inquiry answered.

Student registration information (registers, cards), particularly for the period 1880–1925. These records give details of name, birthday, address, parents' names and occupations, etc., for children of Toronto's Jewish community. This is particularly true of records kept by schools located in the downtown core area of Toronto, where the city's Jewish population first settled upon its arrival in Toronto. Most of these schools are now closed and their records have been deposited in the board's archives.

Access to records of persons still living is only with their consent.

For deceased persons, access may be granted to descendants.

Mail inquiries must include name of school attended, as these files are arranged by name of school, not name of pupil. More complicated searches of these records must be conducted by researchers in person.

The pupil registration files, particularly those of the late nineteenth and early twentieth centuries are used extensively by Toronto's Jewish community for the purpose of genealogical research, as many of the city's early Jewish families came to Toronto from parts of Europe where birth, marriage, etc., records were not kept, or are not today readily available.

- Manuscripts—1847 to present
  The manuscript collection (approximately 600 linear feet) includes holdings of official records of

the Toronto Board of Education and of the school boards of annexed municipalities. Materials include board and committee minutes, correspondence, records of individual schools, attendance and enrollment records, and officials' diaries
- Administrative records (7,000 linear feet)
- Publications—1859 to present
  Board publications (approximately 850 files)
- Press clippings
- Pictures—1859 to present
- Textbooks—1850 to present
- Artifacts—1860s to present

In addition, many of Toronto's schools, which are still active, have holdings of student records that date back to the late nineteenth century. The Archive staff can direct inquiries to these schools.

- Artifacts—The Staff also offers advice on the storage and preservation of historical materials to those principals and school librarians responsible for school archives.

Registrar General of Ontario
Government Public Service Complex
Second Floor
MacDonald Block
Queens Park
Toronto, Ontario, Canada M7A 1Y5
(416) 965-1687

Vital statistics records for Toronto and the province of Ontario. Copies of records can be obtained by the individuals immediately concerned, or by their next of kin. Write for fee schedule. Civil registration began July 1, 1869.

John T. Robarts Research Library
The University of Toronto
130 St. George St.
Toronto, Ontario, Canada M5S 1A1
(416) 978-5275

Collection includes over 300 Yizkor books.

Supreme Court of Ontario
145 Queens Street West
Toronto, Ontario, Canada M5H 2N7

Name changes, wills, and probate records.

Toronto Jewish Congress/ Canadian Jewish Congress
Ontario Region Archives
The Archives of the Jewish Community
(see Willowdale)

Cemetery
Pape Avenue Cemetery
311 Pape Avenue
Toronto, Ontario, Canada

Consisting of approximately 200 stones still extant; first used in the 1850s, majority of burials around the turn of the century and into the 1920s.

■ WILLOWDALE
(Toronto Metropolitan Area)

The Archives of the Jewish Community
Toronto Jewish Congress/
Canadian Jewish Congress
Ontario Region Archives
4600 Bathurst Street
Willowdale, Ontario, Canada M2R 3V2
(416) 635-2883

The archives is open by appointment only, to all interested individuals and organizations. Inquiries answered if possible.

The Archives, a cooperative service of Toronto Jewish Congress and Canadian Jewish Congress Ontario Region, was established in 1973 as the Canadian Jewish Congress Central Region Archives. It is responsible for the collection and preservation of material recording the history of Jews in Ontario:

- Minutes of Jewish organizations (including synagogues and landsmanschaftn)
- Organizational correspondence and personal papers
- Notebooks, diaries, financial and cemetery records
- Passports
- Naturalization certificates
- Wedding contracts
- Deeds
- Books
- Newspapers
  Approximately thirty Jewish newspapers (though only few of which are useful for genealogy). Dr. Stephen Speisman, Archivist, would like all enquiries for newspaper information directed to him
- Magazines, bulletins

Canadian Jewish Congress Ontario Region Archives
4600 Bathurst Street
Willowdale, Ontario, Canada M2R 3V2

The Jewish Colonization Association of Canada
Records concerning the immigration of Jews and their settlement on agricultural colonies in Alberta, Saskatchewan, Manitoba, Ontario, and Quebec (1906 to 1978). Inventory available.

Jewish Immigrant Aid Services of Canada
4600 Bathurst Street
Suite 325
Willowdale, Ontario, Canada M2R 3V3
(416) 630-6481

A national agency providing immigration and settlement services to Jewish immigrants to Canada.

Contains administrative and statistical reports, correspondence with governmental and community organizations worldwide, thousands of case records, photographs, and field reports. Inventory available.

Staff can provide genealogical information to identifiable relatives. Inquiries should be marked "Genealogical Request." Records begin in 1922, with some occasional records 1922–1935.

Documents pertain to daily functions of the organization and include minutes of board meetings and details of annual meetings. Small collection of photographs. Case files: complete from 1935 until the present. Alphabetically arranged records of all persons helped by JIAS Toronto. Information is often of a biographical nature.

Pictorial Material:

- Photographs
- Films
- Paintings
- Blueprints
- Microfilm

Tape Recordings:

- Interviews
- Important events

Artifacts:

- Clothing
- Religious articles
- Furniture
- Memorabilia

Oral Histories: A program of tape recorded memoirs is maintained. Average long-time Jewish residents of the Province, as well as prominent individuals, are interviewed.

Special Programs: The Archives sponsors tours of Jewish districts in the Province, lectures on Ontario Jewish history, converts and other cultural events related to the past.

Publications: From time to time, technical handbooks and finding aids are published.

Albert J. Latner
Jewish Public Library
4600 Bathurst Street
Willowdale, Ontario, Canada M2R 3V3
(416) 635-2996

Holdings include a few books on Jewish genealogy. Will try to answer letters of inquiry. No set research fee.

QUEBEC

■ CÔTE SAINT LUC

Raymond Whitzman
5787 McAlear
Côte Saint Luc, Quebec, Canada H4W 2H3
(514) 489-4094

This small group meets on an occasional basis to discuss matters of mutual interest. Mr. Whitzman has done extensive research into the history of Jewish families in Canada's Atlantic provinces (New Brunswick, Newfoundland, Nova Scotia, Prince Edward Island) and can be of assistance to researchers seeking information on family members residing

there, as well as in Quebec—both Montreal and outlying regions.

■ HULL
(Ottawa Metropolitan Area)

Place Du Portage
Phase IV
Hull, Quebec, Canada K1A 0J9
(819) 997-2911

Post-1908 passenger lists are in the possession of the Canada Employment and Immigration Commission's Records of Entry Unit, which is housed in the Place du Portage; however, access to post-1910 records is *only* granted with the permission of the immigrant or on proof of his or her death.

Query Response Centre
Employment and Immigration Canada
10th Floor, Place du Portage, Phase IV
Hull, Quebec, Canada K1A 0J9

Secretary of State Department
Government of Canada Immigration
Citizenship Registration Branch
15 Eddy Street
Hull, Quebec, Canada K1A 0M5
(819) 997–0055

Naturalization records are available through the Secretary of State at the above address, but there are two hitches:

1. The original records created before 1917 were destroyed in a fire, leaving only an index (which lists heads of families only, together with their residential addresses, occupations, and other information).

2. Post-1917 records do exist on microfilm, but with few exceptions, only the naturalized immigrant may have access to these documents.

■ MONTREAL

Archives Nationales Du Quebec
100 est rue Notre-Dame
Montreal, Quebec, Canada H2Y 1C1
(514) 873-3064

These archives house the vital records for Montreal up to 1881. The collection also contains the following specifically relating to Jewish genealogical research: "Registre Conlernant Les Personnes de Religion Juive 1832–1889."

Canadian Jewish Congress
National Archives
1590 Avenue du Docteur Penfield
Montreal, Quebec, Canada H3G 1C5
(514) 931-7531

Jewish Public Library
5151 chemin de la Côte Ste-Catherine
Montreal, Quebec, Canada H3W 1M6
(514) 735-6535

The Jewish Public Library celebrated its 75th birthday in 1989. This unique community-supported

Judaica lending library has over 100,000 volumes in its collections—in English, French, Yiddish, and other languages—comprising the largest Judaica library in Canada and one of the ten largest Judaica collections in North America. For genealogists, the sections of greatest interest are the JPL's Jewish Canada collection (where achievements of hundreds of individual Canadian Jews in all fields of endeavor are documented), the Ephemeral collection (housing some 450 Yizkor books, along with Holocaust survivors' lists and other scarce pamphlets and books), and the general reference collection.

Readers have access to a full range of books and journals documenting all facets of Jewish history, religion, literature, and culture.

Montreal Public Library
Central Branch
Ville de Montreal
Service des activties culturelles
Division des bibliotheques
1210 rue Sherbrooke Est
Montreal, Quebec, Canada H2L 1L9
(514) 872-5923

This facility possesses a valuable collection of Montreal city directories, Who's Who compendiums, local historical materials, plus microfilms of Quebec City passenger lists and Canadian censuses (only through 1871).

Federal Archives Division (formerly the Public Archives Division) preserves extensive documentation on the Canadian Jewish community to be found in the official records of the government of Canada. Information pertaining to immigration can be located in the various record groups, such as, RG76 (Immigration Branch), RG15 (Department of Interior), and RG26 (Department of Citizenship and Immigration). Other record group data is also available. Please address all inquiries of this nature to the Montreal Public Library.

Montreal Holocaust Memorial Centre,
5151 chemin de la Côte Sainte Catherine
Montreal, Quebec, Canada H3W 1M6
(514) 735-2386

Founded in 1979, the Centre includes both permanent and temporary exhibition galleries and a sanctuary for contemplation, remembrance, and prayer. Group visits may be organized by appointment. The Centre cooperates closely with local Holocaust survivor organizations, in support of their commemorative activities.

Palais Du Justice (Courthouse)
Archives d'etat civil
1 rue Notre Dame Est
Montreal, Quebec, Canada H2Y 1B6
(514) 873-3062

Vital records since 1881 can be searched for a fee. Notarial records, including wills, marriage contracts, orphan records, deeds and others are also on file at the Palais du Justice.

Funeral Homes
Paperman & Sons
5605 Côte des Neiges
Montreal, Quebec, Canada H3T 1Y8
(514) 733-7101

Paperman & Sons is the principal Jewish funeral home in Montreal. It responds to requests for information concerning the dates of death, and places of burial of individuals in Montreal.

Chesed Shel Emes
935 Beaumont
Montreal, Quebec, Canada H3N 1W3
(514) 273-3211

This is a second Jewish funeral home, which primarily serves the Montreal Hasidic community.

Jewish Genealogical Resources in Montreal
Zachary M. Baker

For French Canadians, Montreal and the province of Quebec are a genealogist's paradise. Parish registers dating from the seventeenth century are intact and available to the millions of people throughout North America who trace their descent to a colonial population that stood at a mere 20–30,000 settlers by 1720, when immigration to New France dried up. The careful record keeping of the colony and, later, the province has resulted in a bonanza for genealogists fortunate enough to be descended from the eighteenth century *habitants* and the fabled *voyageurs* who explored so much of the interior of this continent.

By contrast, Jews are relative latecomers to Quebec and Canada. True, there has been a continuous Jewish presence in Quebec since the British conquest (1759), but until the twentieth century, the Jewish population of Canada was infinitesimal, in absolute terms. The large-scale emigration of German, Bohemian, Hungarian, and Lithuanian Jews from the 1840s through the 1870s virtually bypassed Canada.

During the great era of Jewish mass immigration and throughout the twentieth century, there has been a great deal of cross-border traffic. Many American Jews are descended from immigrants who landed at the ports of Halifax and Quebec City, or who lived for a time in Montreal, Toronto, or other Canadian cities. Conversely, many Canadian Jews settled first in Boston, New York, or Philadelphia before proceeding to Montreal, Toronto, or Winnipeg.

For Jewish genealogists seeking information on their Canadian ancestors, the usual range of sources needs to be consulted: vital records, immigration records, and, to a lesser extent, census records (Canadian census files currently are open only through 1881). Some of these records are available in Ottawa, through various agencies of the federal Canadian government.

Vital Records. In Canada, as elsewhere, vital records can be located by consulting local sources. In Quebec, the registration of births, marriages, and deaths is traditionally a clerical responsibility, with duplicate copies of the necessary certificates filed by the priest, pastor, or rabbi at regional courthouses. It is not unheard of for clerics to neglect their mandated duty to keep and file such records, which can cause problems both for the individual seeking to verify his or her birth (for example, for insurance purposes) and for the genealogist.

Central library. The Salle Gagnon houses a valuable collection of Montreal city directories, *Who's Who* compendiums, local historical materials, plus microfilms of Quebec City passenger lists and Canadian censuses.

Jewish Community Organizations. According to the 1981 census, approximately 102,000 Jews reside in Montreal, down from 116,000 in 1971. The community is heterogeneous, including some 20,000 French-speaking Sephardim of North African origin (most Ashkenazim have adopted English as their primary language) and large numbers of relatively recently arrived Hungarian, Soviet, Israeli, and even Ethiopian Jews. In part due to the historical circumstance of being a predominantly English-speaking religious minority living within a French-speaking and Catholic society, Montreal's Jews have developed some of the strongest communal institutions to be found in any North American community. These include hospitals, clinics, social agencies, community centers (Jewish Ys), theatrical ensembles (including the still active Yiddish Drama Group), housing projects for the elderly, schools, fraternal orders, national organizations, and, of course, synagogues—most of them Orthodox. The Jews of Montreal have also supported a large community library and a major community archive, both of which serve as repositories for the history of Quebec and Canadian Jewry. Founded in 1919, the Canadian Jewish Congress (CJC) is an umbrella organization representing the collective interests of Canadian Jewry. Since 1934 CJC's National Archives have endeavored to document Canadian Jewish history, through collecting and arranging the institutional archives of important national and local Jewish organizations and through publishing monographs reflecting these collections' holdings. CJC staff have recently (1986) concluded a project designed to create finding aids to the following collections:

The Jewish Colonization Association (JCA) collection, which includes correspondence, individual case files, administrative, financial, and legal records, agricultural and real estate surveys, photographs and miscellaneous documentation relating to Jewish agricultural colonization in Canada. Material in the JCA archives dates from 1904; of most obvious relevance to genealogists are series CB (administrative files dealing with immigration problems from 1904 to 1959) and CC (nominal lists of Jewish refugees coming to Canada from Liverpool in 1906–07 and from Bucharest in 1924–25). The finding aid to the JCA collection includes an index of clients. By and large, the collection is open to researchers, but research must be carried out on site.

Jewish Immigrant Aid Service of Canada (JIAS) collection. Founded in 1919 and incorporated in 1922, JIAS—like HIAS in the United States—sought to facilitate the legal entry of Jews to Canada and to aid them in their acclimatization to the country. From 1920 to the present, JIAS has assisted almost 150,000 Jewish immigrants to Canada. The JIAS collection of noncurrent records covers the period from 1919 to 1975 and includes correspondence, individual case files, naturalization and citizenship records, reports, statistical documents, financial records, publications, and miscellaneous documentation. The most voluminous series within the JIAS collection are CA (numbered case and subject files, 1920–51, on all immigrants processed by JIAS during this period; 46 linear meters) and E (social service case files, 1948–75; 37 linear meters). A nominal index to the case files for the entire JIAS collection exists and is kept for reference purposes at JIAS offices (5151, chemin de la Côte Sainte Catherine, Montreal, Quebec H3W 1M6), rather than as part of CJC's JIAS collection. Access to the JIAS collection is restricted and is determined solely by JIAS (which in this respect retains control over its archives). Because many of the case files cover individuals who are still alive, the information contained in them is considered sensitive and of a confidential nature. *United Jewish Relief Agencies of Canada* (UJRA) collection. Founded in 1938 as the amalgamation of several Jewish refugee assistance agencies, the UJRA had as its initial, wartime mission the provision of material, moral, and political sustenance to Jewish evacuees, escapees, and interned refugees from Austria and Germany, including over 2,000 German-Jewish refugees who were deported to Canada from Great Britain in 1940 and interned in Canada as enemy aliens. After the war the UJRA took part in international relief efforts on behalf of displaced persons and participated in the tracing service that was set up to help reunite the families of Holocaust survivors. The UJRA collection consists of correspondence, individual case files, administrative, overseas relief and financial records, and other types of documentation. Access to personal case files is restricted and likely to remain so for some time to come.

Bibliography

Brown, M. G. *Jew or Juif? Jews, French Canadians, and Anglo–Canadians, 1759–1914.* Philadelphia: The Jewish Publication Society, 1987.

Canadian Jewish Congress. *Canadian Jews in World War II.* 2 vols. Montreal: 1947–1948. Vol. 1, *Decorations,* Vol. 2, *Casualties.*

Chiel, A. A. *Jewish Experiences in Early Manitoba.* Winnipeg: Jewish Publications, 1955.

Cohen, Z., ed. *Canadian Jewry, Prominent Jews of Canada: A History of Canadian Jewry.* Toronto: Canadian Jewish Historical Publishing, 1933.

Fox, C. L., ed. *Hundert Yor Yidishe und Hebreyishe Literatur in Kanade.* Montreal: Ch. L. Fox Book Committee, 1980.

Gottesmann, E., and Bookman, M., ed. *Who's Who in Canadian Jewry.* Montreal: Central Rabbinical Seminary of Canada, 1965.

Gutkin, H. *Journey into Our Heritage.* Toronto: Lester and Orpen Dennys, Ltd., 1980.

Hart, A. D., ed. *The Jews in Canada: A Complete Record of Canadian Jewry from the Days of the French Regime to the Present Time.* Toronto/Montreal: Jewish Publications, 1926.

Lipsitz, E. Y., ed. *Canadian Jewish Women of Today: Who's Who of Canadian Jewish Women.* Downsview, Ont.: J.E.S.L. Educational Product, 1983.

————. *Canadian Jewry Today: Who's Who in Canadian Jewry.* Downsview, Ontario: J.E.S.L. Educational Products, 1989.

Rome, D., Nevsky, J., and Obermeir, P., comp. *Les Juifs du Quebec.* Quebec: Institut Québecois de Recherche sur La Culture, 1981.

Rosenberg, L. *Canada's Jews: A Social and Economic Study of the Jews in Canada.* Montreal: Canadian Jewish Congress, 1939.

Rosenberg, S. E. *The Jewish Community in Canada.* 2 vols. Toronto: McClelland and Stewart, 1970–1971.

Sack, B. G. History of the *Jews in Canada from the Earliest Beginnings to the Present Day.* Montreal: Harvest House, 1965.

Speisman, S. A. *The Jews of Toronto: A History to 1937.* Toronto: McClelland and Stewart, 1979.

Tapper, L. F. *Archival Sources for the Study of Canadian Jewry.* Ottawa: National Archives of Canada, 1987.

Jewish Genealogical Societies throughout the World

These organizations do not usually have an office, and correspondence is usually sent in care of the Society's president or newsletter editor. The following are subject to change as new officers of the societies are elected.

Arizona, Phoenix/Mesa: Arizona Jewish Historical Society-Historical Committee; Carlton Brooks; 720 West Edgewood Ave., Mesa, Arizona 85210.

Arizona, Tucson: Arizona Jewish Historical Society-Historical Committee; Gates Weisberg; 5490 N. Paseo Pescado, Tucson, Arizona 85718.

California, Los Angeles: Jewish Genealogical Society of Los Angeles: Norma Arbit; P.O. Box 25245, Los Angeles, CA 90025.

California, Orange County: Jewish Genealogical Society of Orange County; Michelle Sandler; 11751 Cherry Street, Los Alamitos, California 90720.

California, Sacramento: Jewish Genealogical Society of Sacramento; Judith Persin; P.O. Box 661767, Sacramento, California 95866.

California, San Diego: Jewish Genealogical Society of San Diego; Carol J. Baird; 255 South Rios Avenue, Solana Beach, California 92075.

California, San Francisco: San Francisco Bay Area Jewish Genealogical Society; Armand S. Cohn; 921 South El Camino Real, San Mateo, California 94402.

Connecticut: Jewish Genealogical Society of Connecticut; Gertrude Singer Ogushwitz; 19 Storrs Heights Road, Storrs, Connecticut 06268.

Florida, Broward County: Jewish Genealogical Society of Broward County; Bernard Kouchel; 1859 N. Pine Island Road #128, Ft. Lauderdale, Florida 33324.

Florida, Miami: Jewish Genealogical Society of Greater Miami; Linda Hoffman; 9370 SW 88th Terrace, Miami, Florida 33176.

Florida, Orlando: Jewish Genealogical Society of Central Florida; Gene Starn; P.O. Box 520583, Longwood, Florida 32752.

Illinois, Chicago Area: Jewish Genealogical Society of Illinois; Scott E. Meyer; 818 Mansfield Court, Schaumburg, Illinois 60194.

Illinois/Indiana: Illiana Jewish Genealogical Society; Sharon Grauer Blitstein; 3033 Bob-O-Link Rd., Flossmoor, Illinois 60422; (708) 957-4598.

Kentucky, Louisville: Jewish Genealogical Society of Louisville; c/o Israel T. Nammani Library; 3360 Dutchmans Lane, Louisville, Kentucky 40205.

Maryland, Baltimore: Genealogy Department, Jewish Historical Society of Maryland; Virginia R. Duvall; 15 Lloyd Street, Baltimore, Maryland 21202.

Massachusetts, Boston: Jewish Genealogical Society of Boston; Sara Schafler; 1501 Beacon Street #501, Brookline, Massachusetts 02146.

Michigan, Detroit: Jewish Genealogical Society of Michigan; Bruce Finsilver; 4987 Bantry Drive, West Bloomfield, Michigan 48322.

Nevada, Las Vegas: Jewish Genealogical Society of Las Vegas, Nevada; Carole Montello; P.O. Box 29342, Las Vegas, Nevada 89126.

New Jersey: Jewish Genealogical Society of North Jersey; Evan Stolbach; 1 Bedford Road, Pompton Lakes, New Jersey 07442.

New Mexico, Santa Fe: Genealogy and Family History Committee; New Mexico Jewish Historical Society; Steven J. Gitomer; 1428 Miracerros South, Santa Fe, New Mexico 87501.

New York, Buffalo: Jewish Genealogical Society of Greater Buffalo; Muriel Selling; 174 Peppertree Drive #7, West Amherst, New York 14228.

New York, Capital District: Jewish Genealogical Society of Capital District; Morris Gerber; 55 Sycamore Street, Albany, New York 12208.

New York, Long Island: Jewish Genealogy Society of Long Island; Les Goldschmidt; 37 Westcliff Drive, Dix Hills, New York 11746.

New York, New York: Jewish Genealogical Society, Inc.; Michael Brenner; P.O. Box 6398, New York, New York 10128.

North Carolina, Raleigh: Jewish Genealogy Society of Raleigh; Chava Katibian; 8701 Sleepy Creek Dr., Raleigh, North Carolina 27612.

Ohio, Cleveland: Jewish Genealogical Society of Cleveland; Arlene Blank Rich; 996 Eastlawn Dr., Highland Heights, Ohio 44143.

Ohio, Cincinnati: Operation Ancestree; c/o Morris Fogel; 1580 Summit Road, Cincinnati, Ohio 45237.

Ohio, Dayton: Jewish Genealogical Society of Dayton; Dr. Leonard Spialter; 2536 England Ave., Dayton, Ohio 45406.

Oregon, Portland: Jewish Genealogical Society of Oregon; Raymond Rowe; 7335 SW Linette Way, Beaverton, Oregon 97007.

Pennsylvania, Philadelphia: Jewish Genealogical Society of Philadelphia; Jon E. Stein; 332 Harrison Ave., Elkins Park, Pennsylvania 19117.

Pennsylvania, Pittsburgh: Jewish Genealogical Society of Pittsburgh; Julian Falk; 2131 Fifth Ave., Pittsburgh, Pennsylvania 15219.

Texas, Houston: Jewish Genealogical Society of Houston; Susan King; P.O. Box 980126, Houston, Texas 77098.

Utah, Salt Lake City: Jewish Genealogical Society of Salt Lake City; Thomas W. Noy; 3510 Fleetwood Drive, Salt Lake City, UT 84109.

Washington, D.C.: Jewish Genealogy Society of Greater Washington; Rita Margolis; P.O. Box 412, Vienna, Virginia 22183.

Societies outside of the United States:

Canada, Montreal: Jewish Genealogical Society of Montreal; Raymond Whitzman; 5787 McAlear Avenue, Côte St. Luc, Quebec, Canada H4W 2H3.

Canada, Toronto: Jewish Genealogical Society of Toronto; Dr. Rolf Lederer; P.O. Box 446, Station "A", Willowdale, Ontario, Canada H2N 5T1.

France: Cercle de Genealogie Juive; Nicole Langlois-Cerf; 219 Grande Rue, 92380 Garches, France.

Israel: Israel Genealogical Society; Ester Ramon; 50 Harav Uziel Street, 96425 Jerusalem, Israel.

Netherlands: Vereniging Nederlandse Kring voor Joodse Genealogie; S. Van Son; Secretariaat, da Costalaan 21, 3743 HT Baarn, The Netherlands.

Switzerland: Schweizerische Vereinigung für Jüdische Genealogie; Rene Loeb; POB 876 CH-8021 Zurich, Switzerland.

United Kingdom: Family History Workshop of the Museum of the Jewish East End (London's Museum of Jewish Life); Coordinator, David Jacobs; Sternberg Centre, 80 East End Road, London N3 2SY England.

Directory of Jewish Historical Societies and Related Agencies of North America

■ UNITED STATES

Arizona

Arizona Jewish Historical Society—Phoenix Chap.
2211 E. Highland Avenue, No. 112
Phoenix, Arizona 80516-4833
(602) 957-7507

Arizona Jewish Historical Society—Southern Chap.
4210 E. 4th Place
Tucson, Arizona 85711
(602) 325-3750

California

Southern California Jewish Historical Society
6505 Wilshire Boulevard, Suite 905
Los Angeles, California 90048
(213) 852-1234 Ext. 3207

Western Jewish History Center of the Judah L. Magnes Museum
2911 Russcll Street
Berkeley, California 94705
(415) 849-2710

Western States Jewish History
2429 23rd Street
Santa Monica, California 90405
(213) 450-2946

Colorado

Rocky Mountain Jewish Historical Society
Center for Judaic Studies
University of Denver
Denver, Colorado 80208-0292
(303) 871-2961

Connecticut

Charter Oak Temple Restoration Association
21 Charter Oak Avenue
Hartford, Connecticut 06106
(203) 249-1207

Jewish Historical Society of Greater Bridgeport
4200 Park Avenue
Bridgeport, Connecticut 06604
(203) 366-5864

Jewish Historical Society of Greater Hartford
335 Bloomfield Avenue
West Hartford, Connecticut 06117
(203) 236-4571

Jewish Historical Society of New Haven, Inc.
169 Davenport Avenue
New Haven, Connecticut 06519
(203) 787-3183

Jewish Historical Society of Waterbury
359 Cooke Street
Waterbury, Connecticut 06710
(203) 755-1114

Stamford Jewish Historical Society
JCC, Box 3326
Newfield Avenue at Vine Road
Stamford, Connecticut 06905
(203) 329-9174

Delaware

Jewish Historical Society of Delaware
101 Garden of Eden Road
Wilmington, Delaware 19810
(302) 656-8558

District of Columbia

Jewish Historical Society of Greater Washington
701 Third Street, N.W.
Washington, D.C. 20001
(301) 881-0100

Georgia

Southern Jewish Historical Society
Valdosta State College, Box 179
Valdosta, Georgia 31698
(912) 333-5350

Hawaii

Levinson Hawaii Jewish Archives
c/o Temple Emanu-El
2550 Pali Highway
Honolulu, Hawaii 96717
(808) 988-2068

Illinois

Chicago Jewish Archives
618 S. Michigan Avenue
Chicago, Illinois 60605
(312) 922-9012 Ext. 904

Chicago Jewish Historical Society
618 S. Michigan Avenue
Chicago, Illinois 60605
(312) 663-5634

Indiana
Indiana Jewish Historical Society, Inc.
203 W. Wayne Street
Central Building, No. 310
Fort Wayne, Indiana 46802
(219) 422-3862

Louisiana
Louisiana Jewish Historical Society
6227 St. Charles Avenue
New Orleans, Louisiana 70118
(504) 861-3693

Maryland
Jewish Historical Society and Archives of
Howard County, Maryland
5403 Mad River Lane
Columbus, Maryland 21044
(301) 992-7992

Jewish Historical Society of Annapolis,
Maryland, Inc.
5 Sampson Place
Annapolis, Maryland 21401
(301) 268-4887

Jewish Historical Society of Maryland, Inc.
Jewish Heritage Center
15 Lloyd Street
Baltimore, Maryland 21202
(301) 732-6400

Massachusetts
Berkshire Jewish Archives Council
75 Mountain Drive
Pittsfield, Massachusetts 01201
(413) 443-6731

North Shore Jewish Historical Society
31 Exchange Street, Suite 27
Lynn, Massachusetts 01901
(617) 593-2386

Michigan
Jewish Historical Society of Michigan
29699 Southfield Road, Suite 217
Southfield, Michigan 48076
(313) 661-1642

Minnesota
Minnesota Jewish Historical Society
Jewish Studies Department
Hamline University
St. Paul, Minnesota 55104
(612) 641-2407

Missouri
St. Louis Jewish Archives
Saul Brodsky Jewish Community Library
12 Millstone Campus Drive
St. Louis, Missouri 63146

Nebraska
Nebraska Jewish Historical Society
333 S. 132nd Street
Omaha, Nebraska 68154
(402) 334-8200 Ext. 277

New Jersey
Association of Jewish Genealogy Societies
1485 Teaneck Road
Teaneck, New Jersey 07666
(201) 837-2700

Jewish Historical Society of Central Jersey
380 De Mott Lane
Somerset, New Jersey 08873
(201) 873-2000

Jewish Historical Society of North Jersey
1 Pike Drive—Goldman Judaica Library
Wayne, New Jersey 07470

Jewish Historical Society of Trenton
999 Lower Ferry Road
Box 7249
Trenton, New Jersey 08628
(609) 883-9550

New Mexico
New Mexico Jewish Historical Society
P. O. Box 15598
Santa Fe, New Mexico 87506

New York
Jewish Historical Committee, Historical
Society of Rockland County
P. O. Box 131C
Monsey, New York 10952-0131
(914) 425-2274

Jewish Historical Society of New York, Inc.
8 West 70th Street
New York, New York 10023
(212) 861-5452

Jewish Historical Society of Staten Island
159 Fields Road
Staten Island, New York 10314
(718) 698-2036

Orthodox Jewish Archives of Agudath Israel
84 William Street, #1200
New York, New York 10038
(212) 797-9000

Southern Tier Jewish Historical Society
c/o Broome County Jewish Federation
500 Clubhouse Road
Attn: Prof. Lance J. Sussman, Director
Binghamton, New York 13903

North Dakota

Jewish Historical Project of North Dakota
P. O. Box 2431
Fargo, North Dakota 58102
(701) 237-6901

Ohio

Cleveland Jewish Archives
Western Reserve Historical Society
10825 E. Boulevard
Cleveland, Ohio 44106
(216) 721-5722

Columbus Jewish Historical Society, Inc.
1175 College Avenue
Columbus, Ohio 43209
(614) 237-7686

Oklahoma

Oklahoma Jewish Archives Project
Fenster Museum of Jewish Art
1223 E. 17th Place
Tulsa, Oklahoma 74120
(918) 582-3732

Oregon

Jewish Historical Society of Oregon
6651 S. W. Capitol Highway
Portland, Oregon 97219
(503) 246-9844

Pennsylvania

Jewish Archival Survey
c/o Historical Society of Western Pennsylvania
4338 Bigelow Boulevard
Pittsburgh, Pennsylvania 15213

National Museum of American Jewish History
55 North Fifth Street
Philadelphia, Pennsylvania 19106
(215) 923-3811

Philadelphia Jewish Archives Center at the Balch Institute
18 South 7th Street
Philadelphia, Pennsylvania 19106
(215) 925-8090 Ext. 23

Rhode Island

Rhode Island Jewish Historical Association
130 Sessions Street
Providence, Rhode Island 02906
(401) 331-1360

Society of Friends of Touro Synagogue
85 Touro Street
Newport, Rhode Island 02840
(401) 847-4794

Tennessee

Archives of Jewish Federation of Nashville and Mid. TN
801 Percy Warner Boulevard
Nashville, Tennessee 37205
(615) 356-7170

Jewish Historical Society of Memphis and Mid-South
163 Beale Street
Memphis, Tennessee 38103
(901) 682-3023

Texas

Dallas Jewish Archives
7900 Northaven Road
Dallas, Texas 75230
(214) 739-2737 Ext. 261

Texas Jewish Historical Society
P.O. Box 50501
Austin, Texas 78763
(512) 479-6840

Virginia

Peninsula Jewish Historical Society
33 Ensign Spence
Williamsburg, Virginia 23185
(804) 253-0345

Washington

Washington State Jewish Historical Society
2031 Third Avenue
Seattle, Washington 98121
Attn:
(206) 443-1903

Wisconsin

Wisconsin Jewish Archives
State Historical Society of Wisconsin
816 State Street
Madison, Wisconsin 53706
(608) 262-3338

■ CANADA

Alberta

History & Archives Committee
c/o Jewish Community Council of Calgary
1607 90th Avenue S.W.
Calgary, Alberta, Canada T2V 4V7
(403) 253-8600

History and Archives Committee
c/o Jewish Community Council of Edmonton
7200 156th Street
Edmonton, Alberta, Canada T5R 1X3
(403) 487-5120

British Columbia

Jewish Historical Society of British Columbia
950 West 41st Avenue
Vancouver, British Columbia V5Z 2N7
(604) 261-8101

Manitoba

Jewish Historical Society of Western Canada, Inc.
365 Hargrove Street, Suite 404
Winnipeg, Manitoba, Canada R3B 2K3

Ontario

Canadian Jewish Historical Society
4600 Bathurst Street
Willowdale, Ontario, Canada M2R 3V2
(416) 635-2883

Ottawa Jewish Historical Society
c/o Jewish Community Center
151 Chapel Street
Ottawa, Ontario, Canada K1N 7Y2
(613) 232-7306

Toronto Jewish Historical Society
4600 Bathurst
Willowdale, Ontario, Canada M2R 3V2
(416) 635-2883

Windsor Jewish Community Council Archives Committee
1641 Quellete
Windsor, Ontario, Canada N8X 1K9
(519) 966-2044

Quebec

Canadian Jewish Congress Archives
1590 Avenue Docteur Penfield
Montreal, Quebec, Canada H3G 1C5
(514) 931-7531

Jewish Historical Society of Montreal
4903 Lacombe Avenue
Montreal, Quebec, Canada 43W 1R8
(514) 737-8480

Saskatchewan

History and Archives Committee
Beth Jacob Synagogue
1640 Victoria Avenue
Regina, Saskatchewan, Canada
(306) 527-8643

History and Archives Committee
c/o Jewish Community Center of Saskatoon
715 McKinnon Avenue
Saskatoon, Saskatchewan, Canada
(306) 343-7023

Appendix C

Federal Archives and Record Centers— Naturalizations in Federal Courts (Record Group 21)

See "Immigration Records in Federal Court Records," p. 3.

State	FARC	Declarations of Intention	Naturalization Petitions	Depositions	Oaths of Allegiance	Records and Certificates	Citizenship Orders	Case Files	Court Comments
AL	Atlanta	1855–1929	1906–1929				1914–1932	1910–1914	For military personnel 1948, 1942–1946
AK	Seattle	1900–1929				1882–1912		1903–1911	Northern Dist. Index 1853–1867
AZ	Los Angeles	1882–1912	1864–1912			1915–1923	1929–1955	1912–1914	
		1915–1966	1915–1965						
CA	San Francisco	1923–1938	1923–1938	1906–1957					Eastern Dist.
		1917–1956	1928–1956						(Sacremento); for military personnel 1944–1945
	Los Angeles	1887–1951	1887–1942				1926–1931, 1938–1954		Central Dist. (Los Angeles); Index 1887–1931; for military personnel 1918, 1942–1946; petitions for repatriation 1922–1952
		1941–1955	1883–1906			1883–1906			Superior Court of San Diego (now Southern Dist.) Index 1853–1958; for military personnel 1918–1919; petitions for repatriation 1936–1955
			1906–1956						
CO	Denver	1876–1949	1876–1949			1876–1949			District Court
CT	Boston	1911–1955				1842–1902			Circuit Court
		1906–1911				1896–1906*			New Haven City Court
		1907–1923				1907–1924			Hartford City Court
						1875–1892			

State	FARC	Declarations of Intention	Naturalization Petitions	Depositions	Oaths of Allegiance	Records and Certificates	Citizenship Orders	Case Files	Court Comments
CT	Boston	1928–1939 1900–1906 1898–1910				1907–1939 1893–1906			Meriden City Court Ansonia City Court Common Pleas, New Haven County District Court Circuit Court
DE	Philadelphia	1845–1902	1845–1910						
DC	NARS National Archives Record Service	1802–1903 (unbound) 1818–1865 (abstracts) 1866–1906 (volumes)				1824–1906	1824–1906		Index 1802–1909; contents of intentions vary from year to year
FL	Atlanta	1867–1948	1875–1948			1875–1948			Southern Dist. (Key West); for military 1943–1948 (Miami) Hearings 1941–1948
		1913–1948	1913–1948			1907–1926 (Stubs) 1913–1948			
GA	Atlanta	1913–1948	1906–1948						North Dist. (Atlanta); military 1918–1924 Circuit Court minutes 1903–1906
HI	San Francisco	1900–1926	1902–1959			1907–1961			Military 1918–1921; dockets 1901–1943
IL	Chicago	1872–1903 1906–1964	1906–1961				1873–1903 1925–1954		North Dist. (Chicago); bef. 1871, lost in fire; military 1918–1926
		1906–1911 1903–1950	1906–1911 1906–1943			1856–1903			Circuit Court Southern Dist. (Springfield)
IL	Chicago	1856–1902 1907–1951	1908–1954			1862–1903 1919–1926 (Stubs) 1887	1929–1957		Circuit Court (Peoria) Overseas naturalizations, 1943–1955
IN	Chicago	1906–1948	1908–1945			1918–1925			Southern Dist. (Indianapolis); military 1918 Northern Dist. (Hammond)
IA	Kansas City	1906–1921 1853–1874							Incl. roll 1857–1865 for Ct. at Des Moines
KS	Kansas City	1915–1964 1919–1920 1918–1956 1906–1942	1915–1967 1922–1964 1930–1955 1902–1967			1916–1929 1918–1928	1937–1966		Western Dist. (Alexandria) (Opelousas) (Shreveport)
LA	Ft. Worth	1898–1903 1906–1910 1906–1911	1911–1919 1838–1961 1906–1911	1908–1927	1876–1898 1863–1898	1837–1840	1930–1955 1929–1956		Eastern Dist. hearings 1926–1929 Circuit Court (Baton Rouge)

State	FARC	Declarations of Intention	Naturalization Petitions	Depositions	Oaths of Allegiance	Records and Certificates	Citizenship Orders	Case Files	Court Comments
ME	Boston	1832–1911				1790–1906			District Court
MD	Philadelphia	1903–1952				1792–1944			Circuit Court Index 1797–1853; minutes 1790–1911 (on microfilm, m931, 7 rolls)
		1796–1906				1796–1906			
MA	Boston	1798–1945				1790–1945			District Court Index, 1790–1911; military 1919
		1845–1911				1845–1911			Circuit Court Index, 1845–1906
MI	Chicago	1856–1906	1837–1941						Eastern Dist. (Detroit) Circuit Court
		1874–1906	1837–1906	1911–1918					Western Dist. (Marquette) Index 1887–1909 (Grand Rapids)
		1887–1909							
MN	Kansas City	1907–1928				1915–1929	1929–1960		Military 1918, 1945; overseas petitions 1947–1954
		1859–1962	1875–1961			1909–1918			
MS	Atlanta		1907–1941			1906–1940			Eastern Dist. (St. Louis)
MO	Kansas City	1916–1924	1916–1924			1907–1929			Western Dist. (Jefferson City)
						1906–1926			
MT	Seattle	1894–1902	1910–1929			1894–1903			Territory journals of proc. 1868–1889
									District Court (Butte) incl. indexes
		1924	1926			1926			(Great Falls)
		1892–1929	1907–1927			1900–1927 (Stubs)	1894–1906		(Helena) Final records in equity 1899–1917
		1891–1893				1891–1898			Circuit Court incl. indexes
NE			1908–1956						District Court (Fallon)
NV	San Francisco	1877–1951	1907–1949			1877–1906			District Court (Reno)
		1853–1944							
NH	Boston	1849–1898							Incl. index 1841–1872; list of persons 1870–1894; 1790–1850 records among term papers
NJ	New York					1838–1906			Index @ Dist. Court
NM	Denver	1882–1917	1906–1917			1907–1911			

State	FARC	Declarations of Intention	Naturalization Petitions	Depositions	Oaths of Allegiance	Records and Certificates	Citizenship Orders	Case Files	Court Comments
NY	New York	1824–1940				1824–1906			Southern Dist. (New York City) minutes 1789–1841 (microfilm m886, 9 rolls)
		1845–1911							Circuit Court minutes 1790–1841 (microfilm m854, 3 rolls)
		1865–1929				1865–1929			Eastern Dist. (Brooklyn)
									WPA photocopies, card index, 1792–1906 (Record Group 85)
									NY Genealogical and Biographical Record 97(1966) and succeeding vols: "Naturalizations in Federal Courts, NY District, 1790–1928," by Mrs. Edward J. Chapin
NC	Atlanta	1939–1947	1926–1948						
ND	Kansas City	1892–1906							
OH	Chicago	1855–1891	1855–1903			1907–1918			Northern Dist. (Cleveland) Index 1855–1903 (Toledo)
		1906–1943				1856–1880			
		1875–1929	1906–1929			1907–1926			(Cincinnati and Columbus) Index, 1852–1905
		1906–1956				1852–1905			
OK	Ft. Worth			1918–1935			1868–1897		Correspondence, notices 1909–1960, and lists of persons applying
OR	Seattle	1859–1962	1868–1970			1907–1926			District Court Indexes 1859–1970; military 1918
		1906–1911	1877–1912						Circuit Court Indexes 1870–1912
PA	Philadelphia	1795–1951	1795–1951						Eastern Dist. (Philadelphia) Indexes 1795–1951
		1815–1911	1790–1911						Circuit Court Indexes 1790–1911 some minutes on microfilm: District Court (m987); Circuit Court (m932)
		1910–1927							Middle District (Scranton)
		1845–1935	1820–1915						Western District (Pittsburgh)

State	FARC	Declarations of Intention	Naturalization Petitions	Depositions	Oaths of Allegiance	Records and Certificates	Citizenship Orders	Case Files	Court Comments
RI	Boston	1901–1921				1842–1844 1888–1906 1907–1945 (Stubs) 1846–1884 1893–1901 1904 1906			Circuit Court records on microfilm (m987) for 1801–1802 Circuit Court
SC	Atlanta	1906–1912 1921–1922	1906–1917 1919–1929						Eastern District (Charleston) military 1918–1924; indexes 1790–1906 to minute books (Columbia)
VT	Boston	1910							
VA	Philadelphia	1859–1917 1855 1864–1896	1855 1864–1896 1907–1917			1855 1864–1896			Eastern District Western District (Abingdon). Records for both are scanty
WA	Seattle	1890–1950	1906–1950	1908–1957 1911–1953		1907–1925 (Stubs)		1892–1906 (minors) 1890–1906 (adults)	Eastern District (Spokane) Western District (Seattle) Statements of fact 1911–1914
		1907–1957	1913–1919			1912–1952 1896–1900	1929–1959		(Tacoma) military 1918–1919; oversea petitions 1954–1955; repatriations 1919–1943
		1892–1906 1854–1859 1889–1910	1906–1928	1868–1924		1890–1904 1889–1906 (and stubs) 1897–1906 (minors)			Circuit Court (Tacoma) King County Court
		1876–1973	1906–1974	1896–1929		1890–1906 1907–1927 (Stubs)	1929–1975		Snohomish Court Repatriations 1939–1955
		1883–1974	1906–1974	1884–1907	1940–1964	1907–1924	1930–1974	1891–1905 (adults) 1903–1906 (minors)	Thurston Court

State	FARC	Declarations of Intention	Naturalization Petitions	Depositions	Oaths of Allegiance	Records and Certificates	Citizenship Orders	Case Files	Court Comments
WI	Chicago	1902–1904 1920–1921 (Superior) 1870–1900 (LaCrosse) 1876–1920	1910–1918			1910–1913			Western District (Madison) Dockets 1855–1884
New England	National Archives Record Service								WPA photocopies and card index (record 85): Connecticut, Maine, Massachusetts, New Hampshire, Rhode Island; some cards for New York and Vermont; Soundex cards
NY	National Archives Record Service					Certificate to U.S. Attorney for review, for Civil Service Examinations 1905–1906			Record Group 146. New York State only

Hamburg Passenger Lists—Register of Microfilm Numbers at the Family History Library, Salt Lake City, Utah

See "Hamburg Passenger Lists," pp. 9–12.

Fifteen-Year Index 1856–1871

Names included	Film number
AAB, Georg—BREYER, Adam	884668
BREYTSPAAK, Eliza H.—FICK, Ludwig	884669
FICK, Maria—HARTZKE, August	884670
HARUNG, Fridolin—KATZ, Salomon	884671
KATZ, Samuel—LEWIN, And.	884672
LEWIN, August—NEUER, Genofeva	884673
NEUFELD, Joseph—RISTOW, Friedr.	884674
RISTOW, H. F. W.—SCHWASSENGEWER, H.	884675
SCHWARTZ, Abrah.—VOLKMANN, A. F. W.	884676
VOLKMANN, Aug.—ZYNDLER, Mathilde	884677

Direct indexes. It is important to note that these direct lists do not include ships with fewer than 25 passengers.

Volume	Type	Time Period	Film Number
—	Direct Index	1850–1854	No index is needed. The lists are alphabetical. Go directly to the Direct Lists section of this register on page #.
Bd 1	Direct Index	1855–1856	473070 item 1*
Bd 2	Direct Index	1857–1858	473070 item 2*
Bd 3	Direct Index	1859–1861	473071 item 1*
Bd 4	Direct Index	1862–1863	473071 item 2*
Bd 5	Direct Index	1864–1865	473072 item 1*
Bd 6	Direct Index	1866	473072 item 2*
Bd 7	Direct Index	1867–1868 Aug	473073*
Bd 8	Direct Index	1868 Aug–1869 Oct	473074 item 1*
Bd 9	Direct Index	1869 Oct–1871 Oct	473074 item 2*
Bd 10	Direct Index	1871 Oct–1872 Dec	473075*
Bd 11	Direct Index	1873 Jan–1874 Jun	473076
Bd 12	Direct Index	1874 Jun–1875 Dec	473077
Bd 13	Direct Index	1876 Jan–1878 Sep	473078
Bd 14	Direct Index	1878 Sep–1880 May	473079 item 1
Bd 15	Direct Index	1880 May–Sep	473079 item 2
Bd 16	Direct Index	1880 Sep–1881 May	473080 item 1
Bd 17	Direct Index	1881 May–Nov	473080 item 2
Bd 18	Direct Index	1881 Nov–1882 May	473081 item 1
Bd 19	Direct Index	1882 May–Sep	473081 item 2
Bd 20	Direct Index	1882 Oct–1883 May	473082 item 1
Bd 21	Direct Index	1883 May–Oct	473082 item 2
Bd 22	Direct Index	1883 Oct–1884 Apr	473083
Bd 23	Direct Index	1884 Apr–Aug	473084 item 1
Bd 24	Direct Index	1884 Sep–1885 May	473084 item 2
Bd 25	Direct Index	1885 May–Dec	473085
Bd 26	Direct Index	1886 Jan–Jun	473086 item 1
Bd 27	Direct Index	1886 Jul–Oct	473086 item 2
Bd 28	Direct Index	1886 Oct–1887 May	473087 item 1
Bd 29	Direct Index	1887 May–Oct	473087 item 2

Volume	Type	Time Period	Film Number
Bd 30	Direct Index	1887 Oct–1888 Apr	473088 item 1
Bd 31	Direct Index	1888 Apr–Jun	473088 item 2
Bd 32	Direct Index	1888 Jul–Dec	473089
Bd 33	Direct Index	1889 Jan–Jun	473090
Bd 34	Direct Index	1889 Jun–Dec	473091
Bd 35	Direct Index	1890 Jan–May	473092
Bd 36	Direct Index	1890 May–Aug	473093 item 1
Bd 37	Direct Index	1890 Sep–Dec	473093 item 2
Bd 38	Direct Index	1891 Jan–Apr	473094 item 1
Bd 39	Direct Index	1891 Apr–Jul	473094 item 2
Bd 40	Direct Index	1891 Jul–Sep	473095 item 1
Bd 41	Direct Index	1891 Sep–1892 Jan	473095 item 2
Bd 42	Direct Index	1892 Jan–Apr	473096 item 1
Bd 43	Direct Index	1892 Apr–Jun	473096 item 2
Bd 44	Direct Index	1892 Jun–Aug	473096 item 3
Bd 45	Direct Index	1892 Aug–1893 Mar	473097
Bd 46	Direct Index	1893 Apr–Jun	473098
Bd 47	Direct Index	1893 Jul–Nov	473099
Bd 48	Direct Index	1893 Nov–1894 Jun	473100
Bd 49	Direct Index	1894 Jun–Nov	473102 item 1
Bd 50	Direct Index	1894 Nov–1895 Jun	473102 item 2
Bd 51	Direct Index	1895 Jun–Nov	473103
Bd 52	Direct Index	1895 Nov–1896 Jun	473104
Bd 53	Direct Index	1896 Jun–1897 Feb	473105
Bd 54	Direct Index	1897 Mar–Oct	473106
Bd 55	Direct Index	1897 Nov–1898 Aug	473107 item 1
Bd 56	Direct Index	1898 Aug–1899 Mar	473107 item 2
Bd 57	Direct Index	1899 Mar–Jun	473108
Bd 58	Direct Index	1899 Jun–Oct	473109
Bd 59	Direct Index	1899 Oct–1900 Mar	473110
Bd 60	Direct Index	1900 Mar–May	473111
Bd 61	Direct Index	1900 May–Jul	473112
Bd 62	Direct Index	1900 Jul–Nov	473113 item 1
Bd 63	Direct Index	1900 Nov–1901 Apr	473113 item 2
Bd 64	Direct Index	1901 Apr–Jun	473114 item 1
Bd 65	Direct Index	1901 Jun–Sep	473114 item 2
Bd 66	Direct Index	1901 Oct–1902 Jan	473115 item 1
Bd 67	Direct Index	1902 Feb–Mar	473115 item 2
Bd 68	Direct Index	1902 Apr–May	473116 item 1
Bd 69	Direct Index	1902 May–Jul	473116 item 2
Bd 69A	Direct Index	1902 Aug–Oct	473117 item 1
Bd 70	Direct Index	1902 Nov–1903 Feb	473117 item 2
Bd 71	Direct Index	1903 Mar–Apr	473118
Bd 72	Direct Index	1903 May–Jun	473119
Bd 73	Direct Index	1903 Jun–Aug	473120
Bd 74	Direct Index	1903 Sep–Dec	473121
Bd 75	Direct Index	1904 Jan–Mar	473122 item 1
Bd 76	Direct Index	1904 Apr–May	473122 item 2
Bd 77	Direct Index	1904 Jun–Jul	473123 item 1
Bd 78	Direct Index	1904 Aug–Sep	473123 item 2
Bd 79	Direct Index	1904 Oct–Nov	473124 item 1
Bd 80	Direct Index	1904 Dec	473124 item 2
Bd 81	Direct Index	1905 Jan–Feb	473125 item 1
Bd 82	Direct Index	1905 Feb–Mar	473125 item 2
Bd 83	Direct Index	1905 Apr–May	473125 item 3
Bd 84	Direct Index	1905 Jun–Jul	473126 item 1
Bd 85	Direct Index	1905 Aug–Sep	473126 item 2
Bd 86	Direct Index	1905 Oct–Dec	473126 item 3

Volume	Type	Time Period	Film Number
Bd 87	Direct Index	1906 Jan–Feb	473127 item 1
Bd 88	Direct Index	1906 Mar–Apr	473127 item 2
Bd 89	Direct Index	1906 May–Jun	473127 item 3
Bd 90	Direct Index	1906 Jul–Aug	473128 item 1
Bd 91	Direct Index	1906 Sep–Oct	473128 item 2
Bd 92	Direct Index	1906 Nov–Dec	473128 item 3
Bd 93	Direct Index	1907 Jan–Feb	473129 item 1
Bd 94	Direct Index	1907 Mar–Apr	473129 item 2
Bd 95	Direct Index	1907 May–Jun	473130 item 1
Bd 96	Direct Index	1907 Jun–Aug	473130 item 2
Bd 97	Direct Index	1907 Sep–Nov	473131 item 1
Bd 98	Direct Index	1907 Nov–1908 Apr	473131 item 2
Bd 99	Direct Index	1908 Apr–Sep	473132 item 1
Bd 100	Direct Index	1908 Sep–Dec	473132 item 2
Bd 101	Direct Index	1909 Jan–Apr	473133 item 1
Bd 102	Direct Index	1909 Apr–Jun	473133 item 2
Bd 103	Direct Index	1909 Jun–Sep	473134
Bd 104	Direct Index	1909 Sep–Nov	473135
Bd 105	Direct Index	1909 Nov–1910 Feb	473136 item 1
Bd 106	Direct Index	1910 Feb–Apr	473136 item 2
Bd 107	Direct Index	1910 Apr–Jun	473136 item 3
Bd 108	Direct Index	1910 Jul–Sep	473137 item 1
Bd 109	Direct Index	1910 Sep–Oct	473137 item 2
Bd 110	Direct Index	1910 Oct–Nov	473137 item 3
Bd 111	Direct Index	1910 Nov–Dec	473137 item 4

• Beginning in 1911 the Indirect Index is included with the Direct Index.

Volume	Type	Time Period	Film Number
Bd 112	Direct Index	1911 Jan–Apr	473138
Bd 113	Direct Index	1911 Apr–Jul	473139
Bd 114	Direct Index	1911 Jul–Sep	473140
Bd 115	Direct Index	1911 Sep–Dec	473141
Bd 116	Direct Index	1911 Dec–1912 Mar	473142 item 1
Bd 117	Direct Index	1912 Mar–May	473142 item 2
Bd 118	Direct Index	1912 May–Jul	473143 item 1
Bd 119	Direct Index	1912 Jul–Oct	473143 item 2
Bd 120	Direct Index	1912 Oct–Nov	473144 item 1
Bd 121	Direct Index	1912 Nov–1913 Feb	473144 item 2
Bd 122	Direct Index	1913 Feb–Apr	473145 item 1
Bd 123	Direct Index	1913 Apr	473145 item 2
Bd 124	Direct Index	1913 May	473145 item 3
Bd 125	Direct Index	1913 May–Jun	473146 item 1
Bd 126	Direct Index	1913 Jun	473146 item 2
Bd 127	Direct Index	1913 Jun–Jul	473146 item 3
Bd 128	Direct Index	1913 Jul–Aug	473147 item 1
Bd 129	Direct Index	1913 Aug	473147 item 2
Bd 130	Direct Index	1913 Sep	473147 item 3
Bd 131	Direct Index	1913 Sep–Oct	473148 item 1
Bd 132	Direct Index	1913 Oct–Nov	473148 item 2
Bd 133	Direct Index	1913 Nov–Dec	473149
Bd 134	Direct Index	1914 Jan–Mar	473150 item 1
Bd 135	Direct Index	1914 Mar–Apr	473150 item 2
Bd 136	Direct Index	1914 Apr–May	473150 item 3
Bd 137	Direct Index	1914 May–Jun	473151 item 1
Bd 138	Direct Index	1914 Jun–Jul	473151 item 2
—	Direct Index	1914 Aug–1919	Not available because of the War (WWI)

• Beginning in 1920 the indexes are fully alphabetical

Volume	Type	Time Period	Film Number
Kartei/Cards	Direct Index	1920 A – L	536487
Kartei/Cards	Direct Index	1920 M – Z	543435
Kartei/Cards	Direct Index	1921 A–BENDER, M.	543436
Kartei/Cards	Direct Index	1921 BENDER, S. – FEINTUCH, Max	543437
Kartei/Cards	Direct Index	1921 FEINTUCH, Mendel – HÖVEL	543438
Kartei/Cards	Direct Index	1921 HOF – KORRATH	536488
Kartei/Cards	Direct Index	1921 KORSCH – NAVARDY	536489

Volume	Type	Time Period	Film Number
Kartei/Cards	Direct Index	1921 NAVARRO – SIEVERS, Walter	536490
Kartei/Cards	Direct Index	1921 SIEVERS, Wilhelm – TRIPF	536491
Kartei/Cards	Direct Index	1921 TRIPLETT – Z	536492
Kartei/Cards	Direct Index	1922 A – BAUMANN, H.	536493
Kartei/Cards	Direct Index	1922 BAUMANN, I. – DENGLER, N.	536494
Kartei/Cards	Direct Index	1922 DENGLER S. – GERLACH	536495
Kartei/Cards	Direct Index	1922 GERLAND – HOHENADEL	536496
Kartei/Cards	Direct Index	1922 HOHENBERGER – KOHL, Anna	536497
Kartei/Cards	Direct Index	1922 KOHL, Augusta – MANTHA, A.	536498
Kartei/Cards	Direct Index	1922 MANTHA, J. – PELSMANN, F.	536499
Kartei/Cards	Direct Index	1922 PELSMANN, J. – SELLMER, H.	536500
Kartei/Cards	Direct Index	1922 SELLMER, L. – STEF, N.	536501
Kartei/Cards	Direct Index	1922 STEFAN, B. – WHITE, F.	536502
Kartei/Cards	Direct Index	1922 WHITE, G. – Z	536505
Bd 139–140	Direct Index	1922 28–30 Dec	473045
Bd 139–140	Direct Index	1923 A – G	473152
Bd 141–142	Direct Index	1923 H – L	473153
Bd 143–144	Direct Index	1923 M – S	473154
Bd 145–146	Direct Index	1923 SCH – Z	473155
Bd 147–148	Direct Index	1924 A – K	473156
Bd 149–150	Direct Index	1924 L – Z	473157
Bd 151–152	Direct Index	1925 A – K	473158
Bd 153–154	Direct Index	1925 L – Z	473159
Bd 155–156	Direct Index	1926 A – H	473160
Bd 157–158	Direct Index	1926 J – S	473161
Bd 159	Direct Index	1926 SSH – Z	473162
Bd 160–162	Direct Index	1927 A – M	473163
Bd 163–164	Direct Index	1927 N – Z	473101
Bd 165–166	Direct Index	1928 A – J	473164
Bd 167–168	Direct Index	1928 K – S	473165
Bd 169	Direct Index	1928 SCH – Z	473166
Bd 169A	Direct Index	1929 2 Jan–14 Mar A – Z	473166
Bd 170	Direct Index	1929 15 Mar–Dec A – L	473167
Bd 171	Direct Index	1929 15 Mar–Dec M – Z	473168
Bd 172	Direct Index	1930 A – K	437169
Bd 173	Direct Index	1930 L – Z	437170
Bd 174–175	Direct Index	1931	437171
Bd 176	Direct Index	1932	473172
Bd 177	Direct Index	1933	473173
Bd 178	Direct Index	1934	473174

*See also Fifteen Year Index (1856-1871)

Each volume (Bd) of Direct Lists for 1850–1854 is arranged alphabetically by the first letter only of the head of household's surname, and no index is required for this time period.

Volume	Type	Time Period		Including Film Number
Bd 1	Direct Lists	1850 Mar–Dec	A – Z	470833 item 1
Bd 2	Direct Lists	1851 Mar–Dec	A – Z	470833 item 2
Bd 3	Direct Lists	1852 Feb–Jul	A – Z	470834 item 1
Bd 4	Direct Lists	1852 Jul–Dec	A – Z	470834 item 2
Bd 5	Direct Lists	1853 Jul–1854 13 Apr	A – Z	470835
Bd 6	Direct Lists	1854 15 Apr–Dec	A – Z	470836
Bd 7	(There is no Volume 7)			

The remaining direct lists for 1855–1934 are arranged approximately by ship departure date. To find a particular passenger, you must first determine a date and page number by using the direct indexes.

Volume	Type	Time Period	Film Number
Bd 8	Direct Lists	1855 Jan–Nov	470838 item 1
Bd 9–10	Direct Lists	1856 Feb–Dec	470838 item 2
Bd 11	Direct Lists	1857 Feb–Dec	470839
Bd 12	Direct Lists	1858 Mar–Nov	470840 item 1
Bd 13	Direct Lists	1859 Feb–Nov	470840 item 2
Bd 14	Direct Lists	1860	470841 item 1
Bd 15	Direct Lists	1861	470841 item 2
Bd 16	Direct Lists	1862	470842
Bd 17	Direct Lists	1863	472894
Bd 18	Direct Lists	1864	472895
Bd 19	Direct Lists	1865	472896
Bd 20	Direct Lists	1866	472897
Bd 21	Direct Lists	1867	472898
Bd 22	Direct Lists	1868	472899
Bd 23	Direct Lists	1869	472900
Bd 24	Direct Lists	1870	472901
Bd 25	Direct Lists	1871	472902
Bd 26	Direct Lists	1872 Jan–Jun	472903
Bd 27	Direct Lists	1872 Jul–Dec	472904
Bd 28	Direct Lists	1873 Jan–Jun	472905
Bd 29	Direct Lists	1873 Jul–Dec	472906
Bd 30–31	Direct Lists	1874	472908
Bd 32	Direct Lists	1875	472908
Bd 33	Direct Lists	1876	472909
Bd 34	Direct Lists	1877	472910
Bd 35	Direct Lists	1878	472911
Bd 36	Direct Lists	1879	472912
Bd 37	Direct Lists	1880 Jan–Jun	472913
Bd 38	Direct Lists	1880 Jul–Dec	472914
Bd 39–40	Direct Lists	1881 Jan–Jun	472915
Bd 41–42	Direct Lists	1881 Jul–Dec	472916
Bd 43	Direct Lists	1882 Jan–Mar	472917
Bd 44	Direct Lists	1882 Apr–Jun	472918
Bd 45–46	Direct Lists	1882 Jul–Dec	472919
Bd 47–48	Direct Lists	1883 Jan–Jun	472920
Bd 49–50	Direct Lists	1883 Jul–Dec	472921
Bd 51–52	Direct Lists	1884 Jan–Jun	472922
Bd 53	Direct Lists	1884 Jul–Dec	472923
Bd 54	Direct Lists	1885 Jan–Jun	472924
Bd 55	Direct Lists	1885 Jul–Dec	472925
Bd 56	Direct Lists	1886 Jan–Jun	472926
Bd 57	Direct Lists	1886 Jul–Dec	472927
Bd 58	Direct Lists	1887 Jan–Jun	472928
Bd 59	Direct Lists	1887 Jul–Dec	472929
Bd 60	Direct Lists	1888 Jan–Apr	472930
Bd 61	Direct Lists	1888 May–Jun	472931
Bd 62	Direct Lists	1888 Jul–Dec	472932
Bd 63	Direct Lists	1889 Jan–Jun	472933
Bd 64–65	Direct Lists	1889 Jul–Dec	472934
Bd 66–67	Direct Lists	1890 Jan–Jun	472935
Bd 68	Direct Lists	1890 Jul–Sep	475678
Bd 69	Direct Lists	1890 Oct–Dec	475679
Bd 70–71	Direct Lists	1891 Jan–Apr	475680
Bd 72–74	Direct Lists	1891 May–Jul	475681
Bd 75	Direct Lists	1891 Aug–Sep	475682
Bd 76	Direct Lists	1891 Oct–Dec	475683
Bd 77–78	Direct Lists	1892 Jan–Apr	475684
Bd 79–80	Direct Lists	1892 May–Jun	475685
Bd 81	Direct Lists	1892 Jul–Sep	475686
Bd 82	Direct Lists	1892 Sep–Dec	472936
Bd 83–84	Direct Lists	1893 Jan–Jun	472937
Bd 85–86	Direct Lists	1893 Jul–29 Dec	472938
Bd 87	Direct Lists	1893 Dec–1894 Jun	472939
Bd 88	Direct Lists	1894 Jul–Dec	472940
Bd 89	Direct Lists	1895 Jan–Jun	472941
Bd 90–91	Direct Lists	1895 Jul–Dec	472942
Bd 92–93	Direct Lists	1896 Jan–Jun	472943
Bd 94	Direct Lists	1896 Jul–Sep	472944
Bd 95	Direct Lists	1896 Oct–Dec	472945
Bd 96	Direct Lists	1897 Jan–Jun	472946
Bd 97	Direct Lists	1897 Jul–Dec	472947
Bd 98	Direct Lists	1898 Jan–Jun	472948
Bd 99–100	Direct Lists	1898 Jul–Dec	472949
Bd 101	Direct Lists	1898 31 Dec–1899 Mar	472950
Bd 102–103	Direct Lists	1899 Apr–Jun	472951
Bd 104	Direct Lists	1899 Jul–Aug	472952
Bd 105–106	Direct Lists	1899 Sep–Dec	472953
Bd 107–108	Direct Lists	1900 Jan–Mar	472954
Bd 109–110	Direct Lists	1900 Apr–May	472955
Bd 111–112	Direct Lists	1900 Jun–Aug	472956
Bd 113	Direct Lists	1900 Aug–Sep	472957
Bd 114–115	Direct Lists	1900 Oct–Dec	472958
Bd 116–117	Direct Lists	1901 Jan–Mar	472959
Bd 118–119	Direct Lists	1901 Apr–May	472960
Bd 120–122	Direct Lists	1901 Jun–Aug	472961
Bd 123–124	Direct Lists	1901 Sep–Oct	472962
Bd 125–126	Direct Lists	1901 Nov–Dec	472963
Bd 127–128	Direct Lists	1902 Jan–Feb	472964
Bd 129–130	Direct Lists	1902 Mar–Apr	472965
Bd 131–132	Direct Lists	1902 May–Jun	472966
Bd 133–135	Direct Lists	1902 Jul–Sep	472967
Bd 136–138	Direct Lists	1902 Oct–Dec	472968
Bd 139–140	Direct Lists	1903 Jan–Feb	472969
Bd 141–142	Direct Lists	1903 Mar–Apr	472970
Bd 143–144	Direct Lists	1903 May–Jun	472971
Bd 145–147	Direct Lists	1903 Jul–Sep	472972
Bd 148–150	Direct Lists	1903 Oct–Dec	472973
Bd 151–153	Direct Lists	1904 Jan–Mar	472974
Bd 154–155	Direct Lists	1904 Apr–May	472975
Bd 156–158	Direct Lists	1904 Jun–Aug	472976
Bd 159–160	Direct Lists	1904 Sep–Nov	472977
Bd 161	Direct Lists	1904 Dec	472978
Bd 162–164	Direct Lists	1905 Jan–Mar	472979
Bd 165–166	Direct Lists	1905 Apr–May	472980
Bd 167–169	Direct Lists	1905 Jun–Aug	472981
Bd 170–172	Direct Lists	1905 Sep–Nov	472982
Bd 173	Direct Lists	1905 Dec	472983
Bd 174–175	Direct Lists	1906 Jan–Feb	472984
Bd 176–177	Direct Lists	1906 Mar–Apr	472985
Bd 178–180	Direct Lists	1906 May–Jul	472986
Bd 181–182	Direct Lists	1906 Aug–Sep	472987
Bd 183–184	Direct Lists	1906 Oct–Nov	472988
Bd 185	Direct Lists	1906 Dec	472989
Bd 186–187	Direct Lists	1907 Jan–Feb	472990
Bd 188–189	Direct Lists	1907 Mar–Apr	472991
Bd 190	Direct Lists	1907 May	472992
Bd 191–192	Direct Lists	1907 Jun–Jul	472993
Bd 193–194	Direct Lists	1907 Aug–Sep	472994
Bd 195	Direct Lists	1907 Oct	472995
Bd 196–197	Direct Lists	1907 Nov–Dec	472996
Bd 198–200	Direct Lists	1908 Jan–May	472997
Bd 201–203	Direct Lists	1908 Jun–Sep	472998
Bd 204–206	Direct Lists	1908 Oct–Dec	472999
Bd 207–208	Direct Lists	1909 Jan–Mar	473000
Bd 209–211	Direct Lists	1909 Apr–Jun	473001
Bd 212–214	Direct Lists	1909 Jul–Sep	473002
Bd 215–216	Direct Lists	1909 Oct–Nov	473003
Bd 217	Direct Lists	1909 Dec	473004
Bd 218–220	Direct Lists	1910 Jan–Mar	473005
Bd 221–222	Direct Lists	1910 Apr–May	473006
Bd 223–225	Direct Lists	1910 Jun–Aug	473007
Bd 226–227	Direct Lists	1910 Sep–Oct	473008
Bd 228–229	Direct Lists	1910 Nov–Dec	473009
Bd 230–232	Direct Lists	1911 Jan–Mar	473010
Bd 233–235	Direct Lists	1911 Apr–Jun	473011
Bd 236–238	Direct Lists	1911 Jul–Sep	473012
Bd 239	Direct Lists	1911 Oct	473013
Bd 240–241	Direct Lists	1911 Nov–Dec	473014
Bd 242–243	Direct Lists	1912 Jan–Mar	473015
Bd 244–246	Direct Lists	1912 Apr–May	473016
Bd 247–248	Direct Lists	1912 Jun–Jul	473017
Bd 249–250	Direct Lists	1912 Aug–Sep	473018
Bd 251–252	Direct Lists	1912 Oct–Nov	473019

Volume	Type	Time Period	Film Number	Volume	Type	Time Period	Film Number
Bd 253	Direct Lists	1912 Dec	473020	Bd 371	Direct Lists	1929 Sep	473780
Bd 254–255	Direct Lists	1913 Jan–Feb	473021	Bd 372	Direct Lists	1929 Oct	473781
Bd 256–257	Direct Lists	1913 Mar–Apr	473022	Bd 373–374	Direct Lists	1929 Nov–Dec	473782
Bd 258–259	Direct Lists	1913 May	473023	Bd 375–376	Direct Lists	1930 Jan–Feb	473783
Bd 260–261	Direct Lists	1913 Jun	473024	Bd 377–378	Direct Lists	1930 Mar–Apr	473784
Bd 262–263	Direct Lists	1913 Jul	473025	Bd 379	Direct Lists	1930 May	473785
Bd 264–265	Direct Lists	1913 Aug	473026	Bd 380	Direct Lists	1930 Jun	473786
Bd 266–267	Direct Lists	1913 Sep	473027	Bd 381	Direct Lists	1930 Jul	473787
Bd 268–269	Direct Lists	1913 Oct	473028	Bd 382	Direct Lists	1930 Aug	473790
Bd 270–272	Direct Lists	1913 Nov–Dec	473029			(first week only)	
Bd 273–274	Direct Lists	1914 Jan–Feb	473030		Direct Lists	Aug–Sep 1930	unavailable at
Bd 275–276	Direct Lists	1914 Mar–Apr	473031				FHL
Bd 277–279	Direct Lists	1914 May–Jun	473032	Bd 383	Direct Lists	1930 Sep	473788
Bd 280	Direct Lists	1914 Jul–Aug	473033	Bd 384	Direct Lists	1930 Oct	437789
—	Direct Lists	1914 Aug–1919	Not available	Bd 385	Direct Lists	1930 Nov–Dec	473791
			because of the	Bd 386–388	Direct Lists	1931 Jan–Mar	473792
			War (WWI)	Bd 389–390	Direct Lists	1931 Apr–May	473793
Bd 281	Direct Lists	1920	473034	Bd 391	Direct Lists	1931 Jun	473794
Bd 282	Direct Lists	1921 Jan–Jun	473035	Bd 392	Direct Lists	1931 Jul	473795
Bd 283	Direct Lists	1921 Jun–Aug	473036	Bd 393	Direct Lists	1931 Aug	473796
Bd 284	Direct Lists	1921 Aug–Oct	473037	Bd 394	Direct Lists	1931 Sep	473797
Bd 285	Direct Lists	1921 Oct–Dec	473038	Bd 395–396	Direct Lists	1931 Oct–Nov	473798
Bd 286	Direct Lists	1922 Jan–Apr	473039	Bd 397	Direct Lists	1931 Dec	473799
Bd 287	Direct Lists	1922 15	473040	Bd 398–39	Direct Lists	1932 Jan–Feb	484973
		Apr–10 Jun		Bd 400	Direct Lists	1932 Mar	473800
Bd 288	Direct Lists	1922 Jun–Jul	473041	Bd 401–402	Direct Lists	1932 Apr–May	473801
Bd 288A	Direct Lists	1922 Aug–Oct	473042	Bd 403–404	Direct Lists	1932 Jun–Jul	473802
Bd 289	Direct Lists	1922 Sep–Oct	473043	Bd 405	Direct Lists	1932 Aug	473803
Bd 290	Direct Lists	1922 Sep–Nov	473044	Bd 406	Direct Lists	1932 Sep	473804
Bd 291	Direct Lists	1922 Nov–Dec	473045	Bd 407	Direct Lists	1932 Oct	473805
Bd 292–293	Direct Lists	1923 Jan–Feb	473046	Bd 408–409	Direct Lists	1932 Nov–Dec	473806
Bd 294	Direct Lists	1923 Mar	not available	Bd 410–412	Direct Lists	1933 Jan–Mar	473807
Bd 295	Direct Lists		473047	Bd 413–414	Direct Lists	1933 Apr–May	473808
Bd 296–297	Direct Lists	1923 May–Jun	473048	Bd 415–416	Direct Lists	1933 Jun–Jul	473809
Bd 298–300	Direct Lists	1923 Jun–Jul	473049	Bd 417	Direct Lists	1933 Aug	473810
Bd 301–303	Direct Lists	1923 Aug–Sep	473050	Bd 418	Direct Lists	1933 Sep	473811
Bd 304–306	Direct Lists	1923 Sep–Oct	473051	Bd 419	Direct Lists	1933 Oct	473812
Bd 307–309	Direct Lists	1923 Nov–Dec	473052	Bd 420–421	Direct Lists	1933 Nov–Dec	473813
Bd 310–311	Direct Lists	1924 Jan–Feb	473053	Bd 422–423	Direct Lists	1934 Jan–Feb	473814
Bd 312–313	Direct Lists	1924 Mar–Apr	473054	Bd 424–425	Direct Lists	1934 Mar–Apr	473815
Bd 314	Direct Lists	1924 May	473055	Bd 426–427	Direct Lists	1934 May–Jun	473816
Bd 315–316	Direct Lists	1924 Jun–Jul	473056	Bd 428	Direct Lists	1934 Jul	473817
Bd 317–318	Direct Lists	1924 Aug–Sep	473057	Bd 429	Direct Lists	1934 Aug	473818
Bd 319–321	Direct Lists	1924 Oct–Dec	473058	Bd 430–431	Direct Lists	1934 Sep–Oct	473819
Bd 322–323	Direct Lists	1925 Jan–Apr	473059	Bd 432–433	Direct Lists	1934 Nov–Dec	473820
Bd 324–325	Direct Lists	1925 Apr–Jul	473060				
Bd 326–327	Direct Lists	1925 Jul–Sep	473061				
Bd 328	Direct Lists	1925 Sep–Oct	473062				
Bd 329–330	Direct Lists	1925 Oct–Dec	473063				
Bd 331–333	Direct Lists	1926 Jan–Mar	473064				
Bd 334–335	Direct Lists	1926 Apr–May	473065				
Bd 336–337	Direct Lists	1926 Jun–Jul	473066				
Bd 338–339	Direct Lists	1926 Aug–Sep	473067				
Bd 340–342	Direct Lists	1926 Oct–Dec	473068				
Bd 343	Direct Lists	1927 Jan–Mar	473069				
Bd 344	Direct Lists	1927 Mar–Apr	473175				
Bd 345	Direct Lists	1927 Apr–Jun	473176				
Bd 346	Direct Lists	1927 Jun–Jul	473177				
Bd 347	Direct Lists	1927 Jul–Aug	473178				
Bd 348	Direct Lists	1927 Aug–Oct	473179				
349–350	Direct Lists	1927 Oct–Dec	473180				
Bd 351–353	Direct Lists	1928 Jan–Mar	473181				
Bd 354–355	Direct Lists	1928 Apr–May	473182				
Bd 356–357	Direct Lists	1928 Jun–Jul	473183				
Bd 358	Direct Lists	1928 Aug	473184				
Bd 359	Direct Lists	1928 Sep	473185				
Bd 360	Direct Lists	1928 Oct	473186				
Bd 361–362	Direct Lists	1928 Nov–Dec	473187				
Bd 363–364	Direct Lists	1929 Jan–Feb	473188				
Bd 365–366	Direct Lists	1929 Mar–Mar	473189				
Bd 367	Direct Lists	1929 May	473190				
Bd 368	Direct Lists	1929 Jun	473777				
Bd 369	Direct Lists	1929 Jul	473778				
Bd 370	Direct Lists	1929 Aug	473779				

Indirect Indexes

The indirect lists and indexes first began to be kept in June of 1854. Each volume (Bd) of indirect indexes for 1855–1910 is arranged alphabetically by the first letter only of the head of household's surname.

Volume	Type	Time Period	Film Number
—	Indirect Index	1854 June–Dec	No index is needed. The lists are alphabetical. Go directly to the Indirect Lists section of this register.
Bd 1	Indirect Index	1855–1865	1049068 item 1
Bd 2	Indirect Index	1866–1871	1049068 item 2
Bd 3	Indirect Index	1872–1873	1049068 item 3
Bd 4	Indirect Index	1874–1879	1049084
Bd 5	Indirect Index	1880–1881 Mar	1049085 item 1
Bd 6	Indirect Index	1881 Apr–Dec	1049085 item 2
Bd 7	Indirect Index	1882 Jan–1883 Sep	1049069 item 1
Bd 8	Indirect Index	1883 Oct–1885 Oct	1049069 item 2
Bd 9	Indirect Index	1885 Nov–1886 Jun	1049070 item 1
Bd 10	Indirect Index	1886 Jul–Sep	1049070 item 2
Bd 11	Indirect Index	1886 Oct–1887 Aug	1049093 item 1

Volume	Type	Time Period	Film Number
Bd 12	Indirect Index	1887 Sep–1888 May	1049093 item 2
Bd 13	Indirect Index	1888 May–Dec	1049092 item 1
Bd 14	Indirect Index	1889	1049092 item 2
Bd 15	Indirect Index	1890 Jan–Aug	1049091 item 1
Bd 16	Indirect Index	1890 Sep–Dec	1049091 item 2
Bd 17	Indirect Index	1891 Jan–Jul	1049090 item 1
Bd 18	Indirect Index	1891 Jul–Dec	1049090 item 2
Bd 19	Indirect Index	1892 Jan–Jul	1049089 item 1
Bd 20	Indirect Index	1892 Jul–1894 Dec	1049089 item 2
Bd 21	Indirect Index	1895–1903	1049088 item 1
Bd 22	Indirect Index	1904–1906	1049088 item 2
Bd 23	Indirect Index	1907	1049087 item 1
Bd 24	Indirect Index	1908–1909	1049087 item 2
Bd 25	Indirect Index	1910	1049087 item 3

• Beginning in 1911 the indirect indexes are included with the direct indexes.

The first volume (Bd) of indirect lists for June to December 1854 is arranged alphabetically by the first letter only of the head of household's surname, and does not require an index. The remaining indirect lists 1855–1910 are arranged approximately by ship departure date. To find a particular passenger you must first determine a date and page number by using the indirect indexes.

Volume	Type	Time Period	Film Number
Bd 1	Indirect Lists	1854 Jun–Dec A – Z	1049001 item 1
Bd 2	Indirect Lists	1855	1049001 item 2
Bd 3–4	Indirect Lists	1856–1857	1049002
Bd 5–8	Indirect Lists	1858–1861	1049003
Bd 9–10	Indirect Lists	1862–1863	1049004
Bd 11	Indirect Lists	1864	1049005
Bd 12	Indirect Lists	1865	1049006
Bd 13	Indirect Lists	1866	1049007
Bd 14	Indirect Lists	1867	1049008
Bd 15	Indirect Lists	1869	1049009
Bd 16	Indirect Lists	1870	1049010
Bd 17–18	Indirect Lists	1871	1049011
Bd 19	Indirect Lists	1872 Mar–Jul	1049012
Bd 20	Indirect Lists	1872 Aug–Dec	1049013
Bd 21	Indirect Lists	1873 Jan–Apr	1049014
Bd 22	Indirect Lists	1873 May–Aug	1049015
Bd 23	Indirect Lists	1873 Sep–Dec	1049016 item 1
Bd 24	Indirect Lists	1874 Jan–Mar	1049016 item 2
Bd 25–26	Indirect Lists	1874 Apr–Sep	1049017
Bd 27	Indirect Lists	1874 Oct–Dec	1049018 item 1
Bd 28	Indirect Lists	1875 Jan–Jun	1049018 item 2
Bd 29	Indirect Lists	1875 Jul–Dec	1049019 item 1
Bd 30	Indirect Lists	1876 Jan–Jun	1049019 item 2
Bd 31	Indirect Lists	1876 Jul–Dec	1049071
Bd 32–33	Indirect Lists	1877	1049072
Bd 34	Indirect Lists	1878 Jan–Jun	1049073
Bd 35	Indirect Lists	1878 Jul–Dec	1049020
Bd 36–37	Indirect Lists	1879	1049021
Bd 38	Indirect Lists	1880 Jan–Apr	1049074
Bd 39	Indirect Lists	1880 May–Aug	1049075

Volume	Type	Time Period	Film Number
Bd 40	Indirect Lists	1880 Sep–Dec	1049022
Bd 41	Indirect Lists	1881 Jan–Mar	1049023
Bd 42	Indirect Lists	1881 Apr	1049024
Bd 43	Indirect Lists	1881 May	1049025
Bd 44–45	Indirect Lists	1881 Jun–Sep	1049026
Bd 46	Indirect Lists	1881 Oct–Dec	1049076
Bd 47–48	Indirect Lists	1882 Jan–Mar	1049077
Bd 49–50	Indirect Lists	1882 Apr–Jun	1049027
Bd 51	Indirect Lists	1882 Jul–Sep	1049028
Bd 52	Indirect Lists	1882 Oct–Dec	1049029
Bd 53–54	Indirect Lists	1883 Jan–Jun	1049030
Bd 55–56	Indirect Lists	1883 Jul–Dec	1049031
Bd 57	Indirect Lists	1884 Jan–Apr	1049032
Bd 58	Indirect Lists	1884 Apr–Jul	1049033
Bd 59	Indirect Lists	1884 Jul–Dec	1049034
Bd 60–61	Indirect Lists	1885 Jan–Jun	1049035
Bd 62	Indirect Lists	1885 Jul–Sep	1049036
Bd 63	Indirect Lists	1885 Sep–Dec	1049037
Bd 64	Indirect Lists	1885 Dec–1886 Mar	1049038
Bd 65	Indirect Lists	1886 Apr–Jun	1049039
Bd 66	Indirect Lists	1886 Jul–Sep	1049040
Bd 67	Indirect Lists	1886 Oct–Dec	1049041
Bd 68–(69)	Indirect Lists	1887 Jan–30 Jun	1049042
Bd 70	Indirect Lists	1887 30 Jun–Sep	1049078
Bd 71	Indirect Lists	1887 Oct–Dec	1049079
Bd 72–73	Indirect Lists	1888 Jan–Apr	1049043
Bd 74	Indirect Lists	1888 May–Jun	1049044
Bd 75	Indirect Lists	1888 Jul–Sep	1049045
Bd 76	Indirect Lists	1888 Oct–Dec	1049046
Bd 77	Indirect Lists	1889 Jan–Mar	1049047
Bd 78	Indirect Lists	1889 Apr–Jun	1049048
Bd 79	Indirect Lists	1889 Jul–Sep	1049049
Bd 80	Indirect Lists	1889 Oct–Dec	1049050
Bd 81–82	Indirect Lists	1890 Jan–Apr	1049051
Bd 83	Indirect Lists	1890 May–Jun	1049080
Bd 84–85	Indirect Lists	1890 23 Jun–Oct	1049081
Bd 86	Indirect Lists	1890 Oct–Dec	1049052
Bd 87–88	Indirect Lists	1891 Jan–Apr	1049053
Bd 89–90	Indirect Lists	1891 May–Jun	1049054
Bd 91–92	Indirect Lists	1891 Jul–Aug	1049055
Bd 93	Indirect Lists	1891 Sep	1049056
Bd 94–96•	Indirect Lists	1891 Oct–Dec	1049057
Bd 96•–100	Indirect Lists	1891 Dec–1892 Apr	1190477
Bd 100–101	Indirect Lists	1892 5 Apr–May	1049058
Bd 102–103	Indirect Lists	1892 Jun–Jul	1049059
Bd 104–105	Indirect Lists	1892 Aug–Dec	1049060
Bd 106–107	Indirect Lists	1893–1894	1049061
Bd 108	Indirect Lists	1895	1049062
Bd 109–110	Indirect Lists	1896	1049063
Bd 111–112	Indirect Lists	1897–1898	1049064
Bd 113–115	Indirect Lists	1899–1903	1049065
Bd 116	Indirect Lists	1904	1049082
Bd 117–118	Indirect Lists	1905–1906	1049083
Bd 119–120	Indirect Lists	1909–1910	1049066
Bd 121–122	Indirect Lists	1909–1910	1049067

• Beginning in 1911 the indirect lists are included with the direct lists

*Bd 96 (Dec 1981) is filmed in two parts on two microfilm rolls.

Aerial Photos in the National Archives— Cartographic and Architectural Branch, Washington, D.C.

See "Still Pictures Research" (The National Archives—District of Columbia), p. 40.

Ahrenfeld
Alexandria
Alt Kyschau
Alt-Postyal (Malojaroslawetz Vtoroy)
Anton
Anyksciai
Ashford
Audierne

Baden
Balzer (Golyj Karamysch)
Baranow-Sandomierski
Bakshty
Bedzin
Beresina
Berezdov
Bialystock
Blazowa
Borisov
Brezovica
Brody
Buczacz
Butrimonys
Byuten

Cairo
Certizne
Chelm
Cherkassy
Chernovtsky
Chervon (Igumen)
Chinteni
Chorostkow
Chwarzenko
Cib/Cheb
Czarny Oslawa
Czernilawa
Czestochowa

Demidovka
Dinkel/Tarlykowka
Divin
Dobinka
Donnhof (Vysokoje)
Dreispitz (Baranovka)
Dukstas (Duksht)
Dzh'ginskoye
Duniloviche/Dunalivitch

Ejsiskes
Enders
Erlenbach
Essex

Fischer (Pavlovka)
Frankfort (Jewish Cemetery)

Gajdobra
Galka
Gattung/Zug
Gawluszowice
Gnadendorf
Gobel/Grjasnocha
Golshany
Graf/Krotojarowka
Grechikhino
Grimm
Grjasnocha/Gobel
Grodno
Gronau
Grunda Gorna
Guldendarf/Krasnoselka

Hammermühle
Herzog
Hoffnungstal
Holstein
Hotzel
Huck
Hussenbach

Iveniec

Jablonowke
Jagodnaja Poljana
Jaslo
Jastrabie
Johannestal
Jos-Fotal (Skripalova)
Josephstal

Kaltanenai
Kalvariya
Kamenka
Kamennaya Mogila
Kamments Podolsky
Kamyschin
Karaul 'no-Buyerachnoye
Karlsbad
Karlsruhe
Katharinenstadt
Katharinental
Kaunas/Kovno
Kepno
Khotin
Kiev
Klcinwerder
Klimontow
Kobrin
Kobyl'nik

Koehler
Kolkhoe-Vorms
Konotop
Korcyzna
Korsuv/Korsow
Kovel/Kowel
Kovno/Kaunas
Kozhan-Gorodok
Kraft
Krakow
Kraslava
Krasnik
Kratzke
Krivojar
Kromolow
Krukenica
Kukkus
Kupil
Kutter/Karamysh
Kwasnikowa

Lagisza
Lancut
Landau
Lauwe/Jablonowke
Lekek
Lendava
Lengyel
Lichtental/Svetlodolinsk
Lida
Loyev
Lubaczow
Lubience
Lublin
Lucke
Lukanowice
Lvov

Magierow
Makarow
Malojaroslawetz Vtory
Maraiental
Malowidz
Marienfeld
Martynowka
Matkow
Merkel/Makarowka
Messer
Metline
Miller
Mir
Mlinov
Mstibuv/Mscibow
Mucsi
Myadel

Naxos
Nemetska-Khaginka
Niedzica
Neu-Arzis/Wischniski
Neu Obermonjou/Nowokrinowka
New Paleschken
Ney-Galka
Nisko
Norka
Nov Topowka
Novoya Ushitsa

Oberdorf
Ober-Monjou
Ogulim

Olyka
Ostrovu Mare
Ostrowec
Ostrozec
Ostrzeszou

Pevkos
Pilica
Piryatin
Podgornoye
Ponieman
Porto Farina
Preuss/Krasopolje
Priluki
Privolnoje/Warenburg
Proskurov
Przasnysz
Pukivichi

Radul
Rafraf
Rava Russka
Rechitsa
Reinwald
Rezina
Rohrbach
Rosenberg
Rosental
Rostov-on-Don
Rudnik
Rybal'skoye
Rzeszow

Samolusksowce
Sanok
Schaefler
Schimpf
Schtscherbakowka
Schultz/Lugowaja
Schwab
Seirijai/Serei
Semenovka
Semenowka
Schedrin
Shepetovka
Sieniawa
Skalat
Skatowke/Straub
Skvira/Skwiea
Slubice
Smolnik
Sompolno
Sosnowice
Speyer
Splawnucha
Starobino
Starogard Gianski
Stephen
Stepnoje/Stahl
Stonehenge
Storozhinets
Straub
Streshin
Stryj
Suchostaw/Sukhostav
Sudilkov/Sudilkow
Sulz
Svedasai

Tarutino
Teplitz

Ternoka
Ternopol/Tarnopol
Tetiyev/Tetiev
Timisora
Tiuste/Towste
Tripoli
Troskana
Tscherbakowa/Scherbakova
Tschon
Tula

Ukmerge
Utena

Vasilkov
Vero Vets/Wierzbowiec
Vilnius/Vilna/Wilno
Vinogradnoye
Vitebsk
Vitunj
Vladimir-Volynskiy
Vollmer

Volma
Voloka
Walter
Warenburg
Warka
Wickerau
Wielun
Wierzbowiec
Wieruszow
Wittman/Solotoje
Wloclawek
Wolfenbuttel
Worms/Vernoye
Yezczhany
Zarki
Zablotow
Zarnowice
Zavod
Zbehnov
Zelenopol'ye
Zhitomer
Zvenigordka

Listing of Town Plans, U.S.S.R.— Geography and Map Division, Library of Congress, Washington, D.C.

See "Geography and Map Division," (Library of Congress—District of Columbia), pp. 46–47. Note: This listing is directly from the index in Drawer 9 and is not in strict alphabetical order due to name changes (Leningrad/St. Petersburg) or spelling variations (Schitomir/Zhitomir).

Akhtyrka
Alapajewsk
Alma-Ata
Arkhangel
Arkhangelska
Archangelsk
Armavir
Artemovskiy
Astrakhan
Astrachan

Daku
Baldone
Pillau/Ballau
Batum
Bauska
Beketowka
Belaya Tserkov
Belenko
Belomorsk/Soroka
Berdichev
Biuro Bakinskoi
Blagoveshchenska
Bobruisk/Bobruysk
Borissow/Borisov
Brjansk
Brzesc/Brest
Brzezany

Tscheljabinsk
Cherkassy
Chernigovka
Czernowitz/Cernauti
Chernovtsy
Chita

Daugavpils
Dneprodzerzhinsk
Dnjepropetrowsk
Druck
Dunaburg
Dzaudzikau

Ekaterinburza
Engels

Fastov
Frunse/Pischpek

Gaissin
Glavnyi

Blusk
Golenki
Gomel/Gomelia
Gorkij
Gorlowka
Gorodka
Grodekovo
Grodno
Grosnyj/Grossnyi
Grozny
GurevaGumbinnen

Haapsalu/Hapsal

Ippolitovka
Irkutsk/Irkutska
Islauzas
Iwanowo

Jelgava/Mitau
Mitauschen

Kalinin
Kalugi/Kaluga
Kamenets Podolskiy/Kamensk
Kamyshlova
Kazan
Kemeri
Khabarovsk
Kharkov
Cherson/Kherson
Maoka
Khorly
Khotin
Kiev
Kiew
Kirow
Kirowabad/Kirowograd
Kirowsk
Kischinew/Chisinau
Kobeljaki
Kobryn
Kokhvytsi
Kolomna
Kolomyya
Kolpino
Koningsberg
Konotop
Kowno/Kaunas
Korosten
Kostroma
Kowel
Kraskino
Krasnodar
Krasnoe
Krasnoiarska/Krasnoyarsk

Krasnoufimska
Kremenchug
Krivogo-Roga/Kriwoj-Rog
Kronstadt
Kropotkin
Kuresaare
Kursk
Kujbyschew/Kuibyschew
Kutais/Kutaisi

Ladozhskaya
Leningrad/St. Petersburg
Libau/Liepaja
Likhoi
Lipetsk
Lubny
Lvov/Lwow/Lemberg

Machatsch
Magadan
Magnitogorska/Magnitogorsk
Makeyevka
Manzovka and Monastyrischche
Mariupol
Maykop
Medyn
Melitopol
Memel
Michalpol/Mikhaylovka
Michurinsk
Millerowo
Minsk
Mogilev/Mohilev
Mogilev-Podolskiy
Mogzon
Morosowskaja
Moskva/Moscow
Mosyr
Murmansk

Nadezhdinska
Naro-Fominsk
Narwa/Narva
Naseleniia
Nikel/Niddeli
Nikolaiew/Nikolajew/Nikolayev
Nikolayevsk/Khabarovskiy Kray
Nomme (vicinity of Tallin)
Novolitovskoya
Novorossiiska/Noworossijsk
Novosibirsk
Novo-Ukrainka
Nowgorod
Nowotscherkassk/Novocherkassk
Sulitsa-Nova

Objekten
Oczakov/Oczakow
Odessa
Okeanskaya and Sedanka
Omsk/Omskii
Onega
Orel
Orenburg
Orsha/Orscha
Ostrog/Ostrogoshsk
Otschemtschiry

Parnu
Pavlovsk
Pawlograd

Pensa
Permi
Pervomaysk
Peterhof/Petergofe
Petropavlovskom
Petrovka
Pinsk
Pleskau
Podolsk
Polozk/Polotsk
Poltava/Poltawa
Poti
Priluki
Primorskaya
Prokopevska
Pskov
Pjatigorsk/Pyatigorsk

Rawa
Razdolnoye
Riga
Rjasan
Rogachev
Romny
Roslavlia/Roslavl
Rostov/Rostow
Rschew
Rybinsk

Salska
Samarkand
Samary/Samara
Sambek
Samtredia
Samur
Saranska
Saratova
Semipalatinsk
Serdobska
Sergeyevka
Serpukhov
Sestroretsk
Sevastopol/Sebastopol
Shakhty
Shkotovo, Smolyaninovo & Romanovka
Schostka
Sigulda
Simferopol
Sinelnikovo
Slavyanka
Smela
Smolensk
Ssotschi
Sochi
Spassk-Dalniy
Ssalzy
Stalingrad
Stalino
Stanislau/Stanislawow
Staraja
Sravropol
Strugi Krassnyje
Suchan
Sumy
Sungach
Sverdlovsk
Syktyvkara

Tafuin
Taganrog

Tallinn
Tambov
Tartu
Tashkent
Ternopol
Tiflis/Tbilisi
Tikhoretsk
Tilsit
Tomsk
Toroptsa
Tula

Ufa/Ufy
Upravlenie
Uglovaya
Uljanowsk
Uman
Uzhorod

Valgamaa
Valki
Verkhoturia
Verkhneudinsk
Viljandi
Vindava
Vinnitsa
Vitebsk
Vladimir
Vladivostok
Volgograd
Volotskoi

Voronezh
Voroshilovsk
Vozdvizhenka
Voznesensk
Vyborg
Vyshnevolotskoi

Wilna/Vilna
Windau/Ventspils
Wjasma
Winniza
Wolmar
Wologda/Vologda
Woronesh

Iakutsk
Yaroslavl/Jaroslawl
Jelez
Yelets
Eniseiska
Erivani
Yalta/Ialta/Jalta
Yereva/Erewan/Eriwan

Saporoshje/Zaporozh
Zhdanov
Schitomir/Zhitomir
Zhmerinka
Zlatousta
Slatoust

Listing of Town Plans, Poland— Geography and Map Division, Library of Congress, Washington, D.C.

See "Geography and Map Division" (Library of Congress, District of Columbia), p. 47.

Angeburg

Baranowicze
Bartoszyce
Bedzin
Bialystok
Bielsko
Brzeg
Brzesc/Brest
Bytom

Chelm
Chmielnil
Chorzow
Cracow/see Krakow
Czeladz
Czestochowa

Deutsch Krone
Dziergon

Elblag

Gdansk
Gdynia
Gizycko
Gliwice/Bleiwitz
Glubczyce
Grudziadz
Grupa
Grybow

Jaroslaw
Jaslo
Jaworzyna

Karpacz
Katowice
Ketrzyn
Kielce
Kolobrzeg
Koscierzyna
Koszalin
Kowel—see Kovel (USSR)
Krakow

Leczyca
Legnica
Lodz
Lowicz
Lubiniec
Lublin
Lvov

Malbork
Mikolow
Mystowice

Nowe Siolkowice
Nysa
174

Odolanow
Olsztyn
Opole
Orzysz
Ostroda
Ozorkow

Piotrkow
Plock
Podebice
Polanow
Prabuty
Przemysl
Pszczyna
Pulawy
Pultusk

Rabka
Radom
Rembertow
Rowne—see Rovno (USSR)
Rumja
Rybnik
Rzeszow

Siedlce
Skierniewice
Sopot
Sosnowiec
Spala
Siolkowice
Stargard Szcjecinski
Szczecin
Strzegom
Swiebodzice
Swinemunde
Szozytno
Szprotawa

Tarnow
Tarnowskie Gory
Tomaschow
Torun

Walbrzych
Warsaw
Wloctawek
Wieliczka
Wilno—see Vilna (USSR)
Wroclaw/Breslau
Wrzeszcz

Zabrze
Zakopane
Zielona Gora
Zlotow
Zory
Zyrardow

Genealogical Resources in the New York Metropolitan Area— Table of Contents

See "Book Review: *Genealogical Resources in the New York Metropolitan Area*" (New York City/New Jersey), pp. 79–80.

▮ NEW YORK CITY

Manhattan

Agudath Israel of America, Orthodox Jewish Archives
American Gathering of Jewish Holocaust Survivors
American Jewish Joint Distribution Committee
Board of Elections, Manhattan Borough Office
Bund Archives of the Jewish Labor Movement
City Clerk's Office, Marriage License Bureau
City Register's Office
Civil Court of the City of New York
County Clerk's Office, State Supreme Court, New York County
   Division of Old Records
Hadassah—The Women's Zionist Organization of America, Archives
Hebrew Union College—Jewish Institute of Religion, Klau Library
HIAS (Hebrew Immigrant Aid Society), Location Department
Jewish Theological Seminary of America
   Archives of Conservative Judaism
   Library, Archives and Rare Book Room
Leo Baeck Institute, Library—Archives
New York Academy of Medicine, Library
New York City Department of Health, Bureau of Vital Records
New York City Department of Records and Information Services
   Municipal Archives
   Municipal Reference and Research Center
New York Genealogical and Biographical Society, Library
New York Historical Society, Library and Manuscript Room
New York Public Library
   Annex
   Central Research Library
      General Research Division
      Jewish Division
      Map Division
      Miriam and Ira D. Wallach Division of Art, Prints and Photographs
      Slavic and Baltic Division
      U.S. History, Local History and Genealogy Division and Microforms Division
   Performing Arts Research Center at Lincoln Center
   Schomburg Center for Research in Black Culture

New York University, Elmer Holmes Bobst Library
   Tamiment Institute Library and Robert F. Wagner Labor Archives
Research Foundation for Jewish Immigration, Archives
Surrogate's Court, Record Room
U.S. District Court—Southern District of New York, Naturalization Division
Yeshiva University
   Archives
   Gottesman Library of Hebraica-Judaica
YIVO Institute for Jewish Research
   Archives
   Library
Young Men's & Young Women's Hebrew Association (92nd Street "Y"), Archives

Bronx

Board of Elections
Bronx County Historical Society, Theodore Kazimiroff Research Library and Archives
City Clerk's Office, Marriage License Bureau
City Register's Office
Civil Court of the City of New York
County Clerk's Office—State Supreme Court
Surrogate's Court, Record Room

Brooklyn

Board of Education
Board of Elections
Brooklyn Historical Society, Library
Brooklyn Public Library
   Business Library
   Central Library
Center for Holocaust Studies, Documentation and Research
City Clerk's Office, Marriage License Bureau
City Register's Office
Civil Court of the City of New York
County Clerk's Office—State Supreme Court
Sephardic Community Center, Sephardic Archives
Surrogate's Court
U.S. District Court—Eastern District of New York, Naturalization Division

Queens

Board of Elections
City Clerk's Office, Marriage License Bureau
City Register's Office
Civil Court of the City of New York
County Clerk's Office—State Supreme Court
Queens Borough Public Library, Long Island Division

Queens College, Historical Documents Collection
Surrogate's Court

Staten Island

Board of Elections
City Clerk's Office
Civil Court of the City of New York
County Clerk's Office—State Supreme Court
Staten Island Historical Society
Staten Island Institute of Arts and Sciences
Surrogate's Court

■ OUTSIDE NEW YORK CITY

Albany

New York State Education Department, Office of Cultural Education
  New York State Archives and Records Administration
  New York State Library
New York State Health Department, Vital Records Section, Genealogy Unit

Nassau County

County Clerk's Office
Surrogate's Court

Suffolk County

County Clerk's Office
Surrogate's Court

Westchester County

County Clerk's Office
  Westchester County Archives
Surrogate's Court

■ NEW JERSEY

Trenton

New Jersey State Department of Health, Bureau of Vital Statistics
New Jersey Department of State, Division of Archives and Records Management
  New Jersey State Archives
New Jersey State Library, New Jersey Reference Services
Superior Court of New Jersey

Bergen County

County Clerk's Office
Department of Parks, Division of Cultural and Historic Affairs, Historical Archives
Surrogate's Court

Essex County

County Clerk's Office
County Register's Office

New Jersey Historical Society, Library
Newark Public Library, New Jersey Reference Division
Surrogate's Court
U.S. District Court, New Jersey—Naturalization Section

Hudson County

Chancery Court
County Clerk's Office
County Register's Office
Surrogate's Court

■ NATIONAL ARCHIVES AND RECORDS ADMINISTRATION

National Archives, Northeast Region

■ FAMILY HISTORY CENTERS (LDS)

■ APPENDICES

Appendix A: Bibliography of Eastern European Memorial (Yizkor) Books
Appendix B: Application Forms for Genealogical Records
  B-1 Marriage License—New York City Marriage License Bureau
  B-2 Birth Record—New York City Department of Health, Bureau of Vital Records
  B-3 Death Record—New York City Department of Health, Bureau of Vital Records
  B-4 Birth Record—New York City Municipal Archives
  B-5 Death Record—New York City Municipal Archives
  B-6 Marriage Record—New York City Municipal Archives
  B-7 General Information & Application for Genealogical Services, New York State Department of Health
  B-8 Vital Record—New Jersey State Department of Health
  B-9 Vital Records Request—New Jersey State Archives
Appendix C: Soundex Code Systems
Appendix D: New York Public Library Annex—Foreign Telephone Directories
Appendix E: New York Public Library Microforms Division—City Directories (Other than NYC)
Appendix F: New York Public Library Annex—Selected U.S. and Foreign Newspapers
Appendix G: New York Area Jewish Cemeteries

This Table of Contents is reprinted from a guide published by the Jewish Genealogical Society, Inc., P.O. Box 6398, New York, NY 10128, edited by Estelle M. Guzik.

French-Jewish Records at the Family History Library, Salt Lake City, Utah

See "Jewish Collections at the Family History Library" (Utah), pp. 130–131.

Civil registration officially began in France in 1791. Records of most communities actually begin within two to four years of that date. Jewish vital records of birth, marriage, and death were included in these civil registers along with those of Christians. French Jews received full civil rights in 1799 and were compelled to take family names in 1808.

To locate vital records in the library collection, check the Family History Library Catalog on microfiche or compact disk.

Other Records	Film Number
Miscellaneous records pertaining to Jews in Alsace	1,069,946 item 2
Jewish census material of Alsace, 1780	1,071,766 item 3
Census of the Jews of Alsace, 1784 (arranged alphabetically by locality)	1,071,438 item 1
Register of the Jews of Alsace, 1808 (adoption of surnames)	1,070,259

For the towns of Balbronn, Bassemberg, Birkenwald, Bischheim, Bischoffsheim, Bitschhoffen and Walck (La), Boesenbiesen, Bolsenheim, Bouxwiller, Buswiller, Dambach-le-Ville, Dauendorf, Dehlingen, Dettwiller, Diebolsheim, Dossenheim, Duppigheim, Epfig, Ettendorf, Fegersheim, Fouchy, Froeschwiller, Gersheim, Goersdorf, Gunstett, Haegen, Harskirchen.

For the towns of Haguenau,   1,070,260
Herrlisheim, Hochfelden, Hoenheim, Ingenheim, Ingwiller, Itterswiller, Krautergersheim, Kuttolsheim, Krtzenhausen, Lalaye, Langensoultzbach, Lauterbourg, Lembach, Lichtenberg, Mackenheim, Marckolsheim, Marmoutier.

For the towns of Matzenheim,   1,070,261
Minversheim, Mittelhausen, Mommenheim, Mulhausen, Muttersholtz, Mutzig, Neuwiller-les-Saverne, Niederbronn-les-Bains, Niedernai, Oberbronn, Oberlauterbach, Obernai, Oberschaeffolsheim, Odratzheim, Offwiller.

For the towns of Osthoffen, Osthouse,   1,070,262
Ottrot, Pfaffenhoffen, Quatzenheim, Reichshoffen, Riedseltz, Ringendorf, Romanswiller, Rosenwiller, Rosheim, Rotheim, Rothbach, Sarre-Union, Saverne, Schaffhouse-sur-Zorn, Scharrachbergheim, Scherwiller, Schirrhoffen, Schwenheim, Schwindratzheim, Sélestat, Stotzheim.

For the towns of Strasbourg, Struth, Surbourg, Tieffenbach, Uttenheim, Valff, Waltenheim, Weinbourg, Weiterswiller, Westhoffen, Westhouse, Wingersheim. 1,070,263

German-Jewish Records at the Family History Library, Salt Lake City, Utah

See "Jewish Collections at the Family History Library" (Utah), p. 131.

Listed below are the 2,159 microfilm numbers of Jewish vital statistics records designated as "Germany" in the possession of the Family History Library as of the October 1985 catalog. A current catalog is available at Family History Centers. The Family History Library Catalog is available on compact disk and on microfiche. Each entry contains town name, abbreviation of province, a legend describing the documents, year represented, and microfilm number.

Abbreviation of provinces:

AN-Anhalt
BA-Baden
BR-Braunschweig
BY-Bayern
EL-Elsass-Lothringen
HA-Hamburg
HE-Hessen
HO-Preussen, Hohenzollern
HN-Preussen, Hessen-Nassau
LI-Lippe
LU-Lubeck
ME-Mecklenburg-Schwerin
MS-Mecklenburg-Strelitz
OS-Preussen, Ostpreussen
PH-Preussen, Hannover
PN-Preussen, Posen
PO-Preussen, Pommern
PR-Preussen, Rheinland
PS-Preussen, Brandenburg
PW-Preussen, Westfalen
SA-Preussen, Sachsen
SC-Preussen, Schlesien
SG-Sachsen, Coburg-Gotha
SH-Preussen, Schleswig-Holstein
SL-Schaumburg-Lippe
SM-Sachsen-Meiningen
SN-Sachsen
SW-Sachsen-Weimar-Eisenach
TH-Thuringen
WA-Waldeck
WP-Preussen, Westpreussen
WU-Wurttemberg

Nature of the material:

B Births
M Marriages
D Deaths
V Divorces
Cem Cemetery
Cen Census
Cir Circumcisions

Fam Family names
I/O Incoming and outgoing Jews
Nam Acquisition of new names
Sch School Records

Dates are represented in one of four ways. If there is a single year, the information is for that year only. If the two years are separated by a comma (1823,1855), then only those two years are represented. If there are two years separated by a slash (1823/1855), then the records are inclusive of those years with a significant number of years missing within the time period. If there are two years separated by a dash (1823–1855), then the records are inclusive of all the years or the vast majority of the years are represented. Abbreviations with years: Ab, about; ca, circa.

If a town is not represented on the list, do not assume there are no Jewish records for the town. What is shown below is a listing of only those records classified as "Jewish Records." It is possible that the town of interest has other records such as church records, land records, or civil registrations that include information about the Jews of the town. It is wise to check the catalog at a local LDS branch library to see if other records of the town exist.

In addition, small towns may be part of the records for the major town in the area. For example, the 1826 census of Jews in Gunzenhausen includes the town of Cronheim (which is not even noted on the LDS microfiche index).

Some towns, primarily in the Baden area, have more than one microfilm number for the same set of vital statistics. This is because these towns often recorded Jewish births, marriages and deaths in (1) the civil register, (2) synagogue, and (3) parish register.

Abterode	HN	BMD	1808-1809	800,125
Abterode	HN	BMD	1810-1811	800,126
Abterode	HN	BMD	1812	800,127
Achern	BA	BMD	1810-1869	1,054,984
Achern	BA	BD	1865-1868	1,054,984
Adelsberg	BY	BMD	1811-1875	1,190,994
Adelsheim	BA	BMD	1810-1870	1,055,114
Adelsheim	BA	BMD	1810-1870	1,335,031
Adelsheim	BA	BMD	1812-1854	1,192,020
Adelsheim	BA	BMD	1847-1912	1,192,021
Aidhausen	BY	BMD	1811-1875	1,190,994
Alikendorf	AN	BMD	1801,1803	1,185,003
Alikendorf	AN	BMD	1832-1849	1,185,003
Allendorf (Lumda)	HE	BMD	1822-1875	870,522
Allendorf (Werra)	HN	Nam	1823-1846	809,994
Allenstein	OS	BMD	1847-1874	1,334,557
Allersheim	BY	BMD	1811-1875	1,190,994
Alsbach (Kr Bensheim)	HE	BMD	1791-1808	1,340,364
Alsfeld	HE	BD	1801-1807	1,336,897

Place	Region	Type	Years	Number	Place	Region	Type	Years	Number
Alt Landsberg	PS	B	1847-1874	1,184,462	Augsberg	BY	Fam	1555-1731	580,432
Altdorf	BA	BMD	1810-1870	1,186,409	Augsberg	BY	Fam	1565-1802	580,431
Alten Buseck	HE	BMD	1809-1822	870,527	Augsberg	BY	Fam	1570-1701	580,436
Alten Buseck	HE	BMD	1823-1875	870,522	Augsberg	BY	Fam	1702-1722	580,437
Alten Buseck	HE	BMD	1828-1875	870,540	Augsberg	BY	Fam	1732-1743	580,433
Altenburg	HN	BMD	1824-1852	817,495	Augsberg	BY	Fam	1733-1750	580,438
Altenstadt	HE	BMD	1824-1852	1,194,056	Augsberg	BY	Fam	1743-1745	580,434
Altenstadt	HE	BMD	1824-1852	1,273,150	Augsberg	BY	Fam	1745-1802	580,435
Altenstadt	HE	BMD	1824-1870	870,523	Augsberg	BY	Fam	1751-1760	580,439
Altenstadt	HE	BMD	1826-1870	870,535	Augsberg	BY	Fam	1761-1772	580,440
Altenstadt	HE	BMD	1853-1861	1,273,149	Augsberg	BY	Fam	1773-1804	580,441
Altenstadt	HE	BMD	1853-1875	1,273,150	Augsberg	BY	Fam	1805-1817	580,442
Altenstadt	HE	BMD	1861-1875	1,194,057	Aurich	PH	B	1782-1931	1,272,913
Altenstadt (Schwaben)	BY	Fam	1756-1869	1,344,023	Aurich	PH	D	1782-1935	1,272,913
Altenstadt (Schwaben)	BY	M	1819-1890	1,344,023	Aurich	PH	M	1844-1904	1,272,913
Altenstadt (Schwaben)	BY	BD	1849-1894	1,344,023	Babstadt	BA	BMD	1810-1870	1,334,584
Alzenau	BY	BMD	1811-1825	1,190,994	Bad Durkheim	BY	Nam	?	587,617
Angelturn	BA	BMD	1810-1869	1,055,279	Badbergen	PH	BMD	1844-1874	1,272,916
Angelturn	BA	BMD	1826-1870	1,192,020	Baden (Baden-Baden)	BA	BMD	1809-1821	1,055,197
Angerburg	OS	BMD	1847-1874	1,198,247	Baden (Baden-Baden)	BA	BMD	1822-1833	1,055,198
Angerburg	OS	B	1849-1874	1,335,310	Baden (Baden-Baden)	BA	BMD	1834-1843	1,055,199
Annaberg	SN	D	1900-1936	1,184,462	Baden (Baden-Baden)	BA	BMD	1844-1853	1,055,200
Ansbach	BY	Cen	1826	1,190,988	Baden (Baden-Baden)	BA	BMD	1854-1862	1,055,201
Ansbach	BY	Cen	1826	1,190,989	Baden (Baden-Baden)	BA	BMD	1863-1869	1,055,202
Ansbach	BY	Nam	1859-1861	1,190,974	Bahn	PO	BMD	1848-1874	1,334,562
Apolda	TH	BMD	1817-1838	1,184,485	Bahnbrucken	BA	BMD	1806-1869	1,056,123
Apolda	TH	B	1838-1858	1,184,482	Baiertal	BA	BMD	1811-1870	1,192,021
Apolda	TH	M	1838-1858	1,184,484	Baldenburg	WP	BMD	1812-1847	1,334,561
Apolda	TH	D	1838-1858	1,184,487	Ballenstedt	SA	B	1824-1871	1,184,463
Apolda	TH	M	1857-1893	1,184,484	Ballenstedt	SA	M	1828-1862	1,184,463
Apolda	TH	M	1857-1893	1,184,485	Ballenstedt	SA	D	1828-1864	1,184,463
Apolda	TH	D	1858-1906	1,184,488	Bamberg	BY	B	?	536,187
Apolda	TH	B	1859-1904	1,184,483	Baranowitz	SC	BMD	1810-1870	879,598
Apolda	TH	Nam	1872-1939	1,184,486	Baranowitz	SC	BMD	1810-1874	879,596
Apolda	TH	M	1894-1906	1,184,485	Baranowitz	SC	BMD	1812-1870	879,596
Argenau	PN	BMD	1815-1847	719,220	Barchfeld (Werra)	HN	BD	1849-1874	809,959
Arneburg	SA	BMD	1815-1849	1,334,570	Barntrup	LI	BMD	1825-1875	1,334,575
Arnsberg	PW	BMD	1847-1874	1,271,454	Bartenstein	OS	D	1852-1938	1,184,377
Arnstein	BY	BMD	1811-1874	1,273,451	Barwalde	PO	BMD	1848-1874	1,334,557
Aschendorf	PH	BMD	1844-1874	1,272,913	Barwalde	PS	BMD	1847-1874	1,271,450
Aschenhausen	SW	BMD	1817-1838	1,184,485	Bastheim	BY	BMD	1822-1875	1,194,042
Aschenhausen	SW	M	1838-1858	1,184,484	Battenberg	HN	BMD	1809-1846	809,965
Aschenhausen	TH	Cem	1713-1777	1,184,462	Battenberg	HN	BMD	1847-1862	809,966
Aschenhausen	TH	B	1739	1,184,462	Battenberg	HN	BMD	1862-1874	809,967
Aschenhausen	TH	B	1753-1838	1,184,462	Bauerbach	BA	BMD	1810-1869	1,056,124
Aschenhausen	TH	D	1775-1838	1,184,462	Bauerbach	BA	BMD	1810-1869	1,190,991
Aschenhausen	TH	Cem	1800-1880	1,184,463	Bauerbach	TH	B	1738-1914	1,184,463
Aschenhausen	TH	M	1809-1838	1,184,462	Bauerbach	TH	M	1789-1845	1,184,463
Aschenhausen	TH	BMD	1817-1838	1,184,485	Bauerbach	TH	D	1839-1867	1,184,463
Aschenhausen	TH	B	1838-1858	1,184,482	Bauerbach	TH	B	1939	1,184,463
Aschenhausen	TH	D	1838-1858	1,184,487	Beckum	PW	BMD	1815-1871	1,194,060
Aschenhausen	TH	M	1838-1901	1,184,462	Beerfelden	HE	BMD	1810-1875	68,870
Aschenhausen	TH	M	1838-1917	1,184,462	Beerfelden	HE	BMD	1810-1875	1,194,066
Aschenhausen	TH	B	1838-1919	1,184,462	Beienheim	HE	BMD	1826-1873	870,524
Aschenhausen	TH	M	1857-1893	1,184,484	Beiseforth	HN	BMD	1824-1852	810,924
Aschenhausen	TH	M	1857-1893	1,184,485	Belecke	PW	B	1779-1807	1,052,867
Aschenhausen	TH	D	1858-1906	1,184,488	Belecke	PW	BMD	1808-1874	1,052,867
Aschenhausen	TH	B	1859-1904	1,184,483	Belgard (Persante)	PO	BMD	1813-1847	1,334,563
Aschenhausen	TH	Nam	1872-1939	1,184,486	Belgard (Persante)	PO	BMD	1840-1847	1,334,583
Aschenhausen	TH	M	1894-1906	1,184,485	Belgard (Persante)	PO	BMD	1847-1874	1,334,562
Aschenhausen	TH	M	1904-1927	1,184,463	Belgard (Persante)	PO	BMD	1853-1869	1,184,378
Aschersleben	SA	BM	1809-1815	1,184,463	Belgard (Persante)	PO	BMD	1870-1872	1,184,377
Aschersleben	SA	BMD	1848-1874	1,334,618	Belgard (Persante)	PO	D	1914-1929	1,184,378
Aschendorf	PH	BMD	1844-1874	1,272,913	Bensheim	HE	BMD	1823-1875	1,271,462
Assenheim	HE	BMD	1853-1857	871,590	Bentheim	PH	BMD	1844-1874	1,272,923
Assenheim	HE	BMD	1856-1873	870,527	Berent	WP	B	1813-1847	185,344
Augsberg	BY	Fam	1298-1802	580,429	Berent	WP	B	1813-1892	185,344
Augsberg	BY	Fam	1534-1813	580,443	Berent	WP	BM	1847-1865	742,795
Augsberg	BY	Fam	1550-1756	580,430	Bergen (Kr Hanau)	HN	BMD	1825-1874	811,325

Place	Reg	Type	Years	Film
Bergen (Kr Hanau)	HN	M	1829-1881	70,819
Berkach	TH	B	1831-1875	1,184,463
Berkach	TH	B	1831-1929	1,184,464
Berkach	TH	D	1831-1931	
Berkach	TH	M	1835-1875	1,184,463
Berkach	TH	M	1835-1917	1,184,464
Berkach	TH	D	1837-1875	1,184,463
Berlin	PS	Fam	1812	477,284
Berlin	PS	B	1812-1840	477,280
Berlin	PS	B	1812-1840	477,281
Berlin	PS	B	1812-1840	477,283
Berlin	PS	B	1812-1840	1,271,483
Berlin	PS	B	1812-1841	477,282
Berlin	PS	M	1812-1847	477,288
Berlin	PS	V	1812-1847	477,290
Berlin	PS	D	1812-1847	477,291
Berlin	PS	D	1812-1847	477,292
Berlin	PS	Fam	1812	477,285
Berlin	PS	MD	1813-1840	477,290
Berlin	PS	Fam	1820	477,286
Berlin	PS	Fam	1821-1847	477,287
Berlin	PS	MD	1841-1847	477,289
Berlin	PS	B	1847-1851	477,293
Berlin	PS	B	1847-1853	477,294
Berlin	PS	D	1847-1855	477,304
Berlin	PS	M	1847-1856	477,300
Berlin	PS	M	1847-1872	477,309
Berlin	PS	M	1847-1874	477,308
Berlin	PS	M	1850-1874	477,310
Berlin	PS	B	1853-1861	477,295
Berlin	PS	D	1855-1865	477,305
Berlin	PS	M	1856-1862	477,301
Berlin	PS	B	1859-1866	477,296
Berlin	PS	M	1862-1871	477,302
Berlin	PS	D	1865-1871	477,306
Berlin	PS	B	1866-1869	477,297
Berlin	PS	M	1867-1874	477,304
Berlin	PS	D	1867-1874	477,307
Berlin	PS	B	1869-1873	477,298
Berlin	PS	B	1869-1874	477,299
Berlin	PS	M	1871-1874	477,303
Berlin	PS	B	1873-1874	477,300
Berlinchen	PS	Nam	1736,1746	1,184,378
Berlinchen	PS	Nam	1816	1,184,378
Bernburg	AN	Fam	1809	1,184,464
Bernburg	AN	B	1810-1863	1,184,464
Bernburg	AN	BMD	1828-1875	1,184,465
Bernstadt	SC	B	1847-1887	1,184,378
Bernstadt	SC	BMD	1847-1887	1,184,379
Bernstadt	SC	D	1851-1864	1,184,378
Bernstadt	SC	M	1856-1861	1,184,378
Bernstein (Kr Soldin)	PS	BMD	1825-1874	1,184,379
Berstadt	HE	BMD	1824-1875	870,524
Berwangen	BA	BMD	1804-1850	1,192,020
Berwangen	BA	BMD	1812-1870	1,335,034
Berwangen	BA	BMD	1830-1869	1,186,374
Berwangen	BA	D	1851-1869	1,189,140
Berwangen	BA	D	1851-1869	1,272,362
Bessingen	BR	M	1810	1,334,577
Betsche	PN	BMD	1817-1847	1,335,040
Bettenhausen	HN	BMD	1808-1812	811,338
Betziesdorf	HN	BMD	1849	811,339
Beuern	HE	BMD	1823-1875	870,525
Beuthen (Kr Beuthen)	SC	BMD	1812-1847	1,271,417
Beuthen (Kr Beuthen)	SC	BMD	1812-1847	1,273,452
Beuthen (Kr Beuthen)	SC	D	1840-1940	1,184,405
Beuthen (Kr Beuthen)	SC	BMD	1847-1874	1,273,156
Geuthen (Kr Beuthen)	SC	M	1848-1874	1,271,495
Beuthen (Kr Beuthen)	SC	B	1849-1866	1,335,074
Beuthen (Kr Beuthen)	SC	B	1849-1866	1,335,075
Beuthen (Kr Beuthen)	SC	B	1866-1874	1,194,063
Beuthen (Kr Beuthen)	SC	M	1880-1885	1,184,405
Beuthen (Kr Beuthen)	SC	B	1880-1886	1,184,404
Beuthen (Kr Beuthen)	SC	M	1921-1925	1,184,405
Beuthen (Kr Beuthen)	SC	M	1935-1938	1,184,405
Beuthen	SC	BMD	1847-1874	1,271,490
Bibra	SA	BMD	1838-1937	1,184,466
Bickenbach	HE	Fam	1772-1798	1,340,366
Bickenbach	HE	BM	1780-1792	1,340,366
Biebesheim	HE	B	1761-1890	1,195,352
Biebesheim	HE	M	1796-1805	1,195,352
Biebesheim	HE	D	1798-1800	1,195,352
Bielefeld	PW	BMD	1815-1874	1,335,031
Billigheim	BA	BMD	1810-1870	1,190,992
Binau	BA	BMD	1810-1870	1,190,992
Binau	BA	BMD	1811-1870	1,192,022
Birklar	HE	BMD	1835-1875	870,525
Birnbaum	PN	BMD	1816	1,194,061
Birstein	HN	Nam	1850	813,033
Birstein	HN	Nam	1851-1852	813,035
Birstein	HN	Nam	1853-1856	813,036
Birstein	HN	Nam	1856-1859	813,037
Birstein	HN	Nam	1860-1864	813,038
Birstein	HN	Nam	1865-1868	814,326
Bischhausen	HN	BMD	1808-1812	800,134
Bischofsburg	OS	BMD	1847-1874	1,271,457
Bischofsheim	HN	BD	1851-1867	814,341
Bischwind	BY	BMD	1818-1874	1,273,451
Blomberg	LI	D	1810-1875	1,334,575
Blomberg	LI	M	1827-1868	1,334,575
Blomberg	LI	B	1830-1875	1,334,575
Blomberg	LI	BMD	1839-1875	1,335,027
Blutenam	PN	BMD	1832-1847	719,231
Bocholt	PW	BMD	1822-1874	1,334,619
Bochum	PW	BMD	1822-1841	1,194,060
Bodigheim	BA	BMD	1808-1847	1,056,403
Bodigheim	BA	BMD	1813-1869	1,192,024
Bodigheim	BA	BMD	1848-1870	1,056,404
Boizenburg	ME	BMD	1813-1920	68,935
Bomst	PN	B	1817-1847	1,273,157
Bonfeld	WU	B	1808-1875	1,195,662
Bonfeld	WU	D	1812-1875	1,195,662
Bonfeld	WU	M	1831-1872	1,195,662
Bonn	PR	Nam	1808	1,271,353
Bonnland	BY	BMD	1812-1875	1,194,042
Borek (Kr Koschmin)	PN	BMD	1833-1837	1,273,157
Borghorst	PW	BMD	1822-1875	1,273,449
Bornheim-Brenig	PR	Nam	1808	1,190,993
Boxberg	BA	BMD	1810-1870	1,055,285
Boxberg	BA	BMD	1826-1870	1,192,020
Brackwede	PW	BMD	1814-1847	1,190,971
Brackwede	PW	M	1847-1874	1,190,971
Brackwede	PW	B	1847-1882	1,190,971
Brake	LI	BMD	1810-1875	1,335,027
Brandenburg (Havel)	PS	BMD	1789-1870	1,184,467
Brandenburg (Havel)	PS	BMD	1863-1874	1,334,618
Bratz	PN	BMD	1847	807,873
Braunschweig	BR	BMD	1808-1814	958,059
Braunschweig	BR	BMD	1812-1868	1,273,155
Breitenau	HN	BMD	1808-1810	800,135
Breitenau	HN	BMD	1808-1812	800,136
Breitenbach	HN	BD	1838-1863	815,013
Breitenbach	HN	B	1849/1867	815,011
Breslau	SC	Cem		1,184,403
Breslau	SC	Fam	?	1,184,404
Breslau	SC	Cir	1743-1813	1,184,403
Breslau	SC	B	1760-1840	1,184,379
Breslau	SC	Cem	1761-1856	1,184,402

Breslau	SC	B	1766-1812	1,184,384		Burstadt	HE	BMD	1823-1875	1,271,458
Breslau	SC	M	1772-1773	1,184,384		Butow	PO	B	1812-1847	1,334,558
Breslau	SC	M	1772-1812	1,184,389		Butow	PO	BMD	1840-1874	1,190,931
Breslau	SC	D	1780-1874	1,184,402		Butthart	BY	BMD	1835-1874	1,273,451
Breslau	SC	M	1784-1796	1,184,385		Butzbach	HE	BMD	1810-1850	870,528
Breslau	SC	Fam	1791	1,184,403		Butzbach	HE	BMD	1851-1860	870,529
Breslau	SC	D	1791-1812	1,184,390		Butzbach	HE	BMD	1861-1865	870,530
Breslau	SC	M	1797-1811	1,184,386		Butzbach	HE	BMD	1866-1875	870,531
Breslau	SC	Cem	18??-19??	1,184,401		Butzow	ME	BMD	1813-1898	68,935
Breslau	SC	M	1804-1812	1,184,387		Cadolzburg	BY	Cen	1826	1,190,988
Breslau	SC	B	1804/1846	1,184,380		Cadolzburg	BY	Cen	1826	1,190,989
Breslau	SC	B	1812-1820	1,271,412		Caldern	HN	BMD	1810-1867	815,196
Breslau	SC	D	1813-1859	1,184,391		Calvorde	BR	BD	1738-1889	949,296
Breslau	SC	D	1815-1827	1,184,392		Cammin (Krst	PO	BMD	1814-1874	1,273,145
Breslau	SC	B	1825,1847	1,184,384		Cammin)				
Breslau	SC	B	1827-1838	1,184,381		Cammin (Krst	PO	BMD	1848-1874	1,334,556
Breslau	SC	M	1832-1847	1,184,388		Cammin)				
Breslau	SC	B	1838-1846	1,184,382		Carolath	SC	BMD	1847-1874	1,335,031
Breslau	SC	M	1846-1847	1,184,387		Cassel (Stkr Cassel)	HN	BMD	1808-1810	839,331
Breslau	SC	M	1846-1847	1,184,389		Cassel (Stkr Cassel)	HN	BD	1848-1867	839,331
Breslau	SC	B	1846-1872	1,184,383		Castrop	PW	BMD	1818-1826	936,716
Breslau	SC	B	1847	1,184,383		Christburg (Kr Stuhm)	WP	BMD	1847-1875	1,334,558
Breslau	SC	D	1860-1874	1,184,393		Coblenz	PR	Nam	1808	1,271,265
Breslau	SC	M	1873-1930	1,184,389		Coblenz	PR	Nam	1808	1,334,543
Breslau	SC	Cem	1889-1898	1,184,400		Coln	PR	Nam	1817-1844	1,334,585
Breslau	SC	M	1903-1938	1,184,390		Corbach	WA	BMD	1833-1853	841,277
Breslau	SC	D	1910-1921	1,184,394		Corbach	WA	BD	1859-1875	841,277
Breslau	SC	D	1914-1927	1,184,395		Coswig	AN	D	1800-1878	1,184,468
Breslau	SC	D	1914-1927	1,184,396		Coswig	AN	B	1828-1868	1,184,468
Breslau	SC	D	1918-1926	1,184,397		Coswig	AN	M	1836-1865	1,184,468
Breslau	SC	D	1928-1940	1,184,398		Cothen	AN	Fam	1760-1820	1,185,004
Breslau	SC	D	1928-1940	1,184,399		Cothen	AN	B	1820-1871	1,185,003
Breslau	SC	Nam	1932-1939	1,184,403		Cothen	AN	D	1820-1875	1,185,004
Breslau	SC	B	1933-1939	1,184,384		Crainfeld	HE	BMD	1838-1875	1,334,570
Brieg (Stkr Brieg)	SC	B	1794-1798	1,184,407		Crivitz	ME	BMD	1813-1877	1,184,468
Brieg (Stkr Brieg)	SC	M	1809-1874	1,184,405		Cronheim	BY	BMD	1801-1810	1,042,637
Brieg (Stkr Brieg)	SC	B	1809-1874	1,184,407		Crossen (Oder)	PS	Cem	1825-1836	1,184,406
Bricg (Stkr Brieg)	SC	D	1810-1874	1,184,406		Crossen (Oder)	PS	Nam	1844	1,184,406
Brieg (Stkr Brieg)	SC	MD	1847-1874	1,190,996		Crossen (Oder)	PS	Cem	1860-1955	1,184,406
Brilon	PW	BMD	1809-1874	1,194,053		Czempin	PN	Cem	1833-1843	1,184,406
Broel (Ag Broel)	ME	BMD	1787-1903	68,935		Daber (Kr Naugard)	PO	BMD	1839-1867	1,334,556
Brokeln	BR	Fam	1773-1893	949,296		Damgarten	PO	B	1812-1875	1,185,012
Brokeln	BR	BMD	1809-1810	949,343		Damgarten	PO	BMD	1855-1869	1,190,932
Bromberg (Krst)	PN	Fam	1833-1843	1,271,466		Danzig	WP	Cem	18??	1,184,407
Bromskirchen	HN	BMD	1823-1846	815,014		Danzig	WP	D	18??	1,184,410
Brunnau	BY	BMD	1852-1875	1,194,042		Danzig	WP	Nam	1814	1,184,410
Bublitz	PO	BMD	1812-1859	1,190,925		Danzig	WP	M	1837-1847	1,184,407
Bublitz	PO	B	1816-1818	1,184,406		Danzig	WP	B	1839-1847	1,184,407
Bublitz	PO	MD	1818	1,184,406		Danzig	WP	B	1847-1850	742,680
Bublitz	PO	BMD	1847-1874	1,190,924		Danzig	WP	D	1847-1883	1,184,407
Buchen	BA	BMD	1810-1842	1,056,406		Danzig	WP	M	1848-1851	742,684
Buchen	BA	BMD	1843-1870	1,056,407		Danzig	WP	Fam	1848-1906	1,184,409
Buchenau	HN	B	1825-1881	815,764		Danzig	WP	M	1851-1855	742,685
Buchholz	SN	D	1900-1936	1,184,462		Danzig	WP	B	1852-1854	742,680
Buer	PH	BMD	1845-1874	1,272,958		Danzig	WP	D	1852-1855	742,780
Buhl	BA	B	1810-1856	1,057,185		Danzig	WP	M	1853-1857	742,686
Buhl	BA	D	1811-1870	1,057,187		Danzig	WP	B	1854-1857	742,681
Buhl	BA	M	1812-1869	1,057,186		Danzig	WP	D	1855-1859	742,781
Buhl	BA	B	1857-1869	1,057,186		Danzig	WP	M	1857-1859	742,687
Bunde	PH	D	1844-1896	1,257,051		Danzig	WP	B	1857-1862	742,682
Bunde	PH	B	1844-1924	1,257,051		Danzig	WP	D	1859-1864	742,782
Bunde	PH	BMD	1859-1860	1,187,668		Danzig	WP	M	1860-1863	742,688
Bunzlau	SC	Cem	1840-1933	1,184,406		Danzig	WP	M	1860-1863	742,777
Bunzlau	SC	Cem	1840-1933	1,184,406		Danzig	WP	B	1861-1864	742,683
Buren (Krst Buren)	PW	BMD	1847-1874	1,334,614		Danzig	WP	M	1862-1863	742,778
Buren (Krst Buren)	PW	BMD	1851-1865	1,271,454		Danzig	WP	B	1864-1865	742,684
Burg Grafenrode	HE	BMD	1851-1875	870,526		Danzig	WP	M	1864-1865	742,779
Burgholzhausen	HE	BMD	1823-1875	870,526		Danzig	WP	D	1864-1865	742,783
Burkhardfelden	HE	BMD	1823-1874	870,526		Danzig	WP	D	1889-1940	1,184,408

Danzig	WP	B	1905-1939	1,184,407	Dresden	SN	Nam	1899	1,184,480
Dargun	ME	BMD	1813-1874	1,184,468	Dresden	SN	I/O	1899	1,184,481
Darmstadt	HE	M	1788-1790	1,190,506	Drossen	PS	BMD	1813-1899	1,184,410
Darmstadt	HE	BD	1788-1800	1,190,506	Drove	PR	Nam	1808	1,334,577
Darmstadt	HE	M	1788-1807	1,190,506	Duhren	BA	BMD	1811-1870	1,192,007
Darmstadt	HE	BD	1800-1808	1,190,506	Duhren	BA	BMD	1818-1865	1,273,451
Darmstadt	HE	BMD	1823-1872	870,524	Duisburg	PR	BMD	1847-1874	1,336,811
Darmstadt	HE	BM	1823-1875	870,532	Duren (Krst Duren)	PR	Nam	1808	1,190,966
Darmstadt	HE	D	1823-1875	870,533	Eberbach	BA	BMD	1816-1870	1,192,007
Daubringen	HE	BMD	1826-1875	870,534	Eberbach	BA	BMD	1816-1874	1,194,065
Deisel	HN	BMD	1810-1811	816,450	Eberbach	BA	BMD	1818/1866	1,184,005
Demmin	PO	BMD	1847-1874	1,334,559	Eberbach	BA	BMD	1867-1870	1,184,053
Dertingen	BA	BMD	1810-1836	1,190,975	Eberbach	BA	BMD	1867-1870	1,184,338
Dertingen	BA	BMD	1837-1869	1,190,990	Eberstadt	BA	BMD	1808-1835	1,056,410
Detmold	LI	BMD	1809-1875	1,271,461	Eberstadt	BA	BMD	1811-1864	1,192,023
Detmold	LI	BMD	1809-1875	1,273,155	Eberstadt	BA	BMD	1836-1870	1,056,411
Detmold	LI	M	1813-1871	1,334,576	Eberstadt	HE	BMD	1781-1807	1,190,527
Detmold	LI	D	1815-1873	1,334,576	Eberstadt	HE	BMD	1823-1873	871,592
Detmold	LI	B	1818-1874	1,334,576	Ebsdorf	HN	M	1810	816,480
Dettensee	HO	BMD	1820-1888	1,190,955	Ebsdorf	HN	Nam	1811	816,480
Dettensee	HO	Fam	1820-1888	1,190,955	Ebsdorf	HN	D	1852-1910	816,480
Deutsch Krone	WP	BMD	1812-1847	1,271,456	Ebsdorf	HN	B	1855	816,480
Deutsch Krone	WP	D	1847-1874	1,273,147	Eckardroth	HN	BD	1826-1874	816,480
Deutsch Krone	WP	BM	1847-1874	1,335,039	Eckardroth	HN	M	1864-1873	816,480
Diedelsheim	BA	B	1812-1869	1,192,007	Egeln	SA	BD	1867-1874	1,184,482
Dielmissen	BR	BMD	1808-1812	949,340	Egeln	SA	M	1870	1,184,482
Dielmissen	BR	BMD	1810-1813	949,317	Egelsbach	HE	BMD	1844-1869	870,534
Dielmissen	BR	BMD	1810-1813	1,334,577	Ehrstadt	BA	BMD	1811-1870	1,192,024
Diersburg	BA	BD	1813-1869	1,192,008	Ehrstadt	BA	BMD	1817-1865	1,335,035
Diersburg	BA	M	1813-1870	1,192,006	Ehrsten	HN	BMD	1808-1810	806,721
Diersburg	BA	B	1860-1820	1,192,006	Eichstetten	BA	BMD	1810-1825	1,194,052
Diez	HN	B	1817-1850	1,335,025	Eichstetten	BA	BMD	1826-1848	1,334,568
Dinkelsbuhl	BY	Cen	1826	1,190,988	Eichstetten	BA	B	1843-1870	1,192,009
Dinkelsbuhl	BY	Cen	1826	1,190,989	Eichstetten	BA	BMD	1849-1869	1,190,970
Dirschau	WP	BMD	1828-1848	743,206	Eichstetten	BA	Fam	1851-1870	1,192,009
Dobberschutz	PN	BMD	1817-1864	1,273,157	Eimeldingen	BA	BMD	1821/1862	1,192,016
Domitz	ME	D	1812-1844	1,184,481	Eisenach	TH	BMD	1817-1838	1,184,485
Domitz	ME	B	1812-1899	1,184,481	Eisenach	TH	B	1838-1858	1,184,482
Domitz	ME	M	1813-1871	1,184,481	Eisenach	TH	M	1838-1858	1,184,484
Domitz	ME	BD	1847-1848	1,185,013	Eisenach	TH	D	1838-1858	1,184,487
Domitz	ME	M	1894	1,184,481	Eisenach	TH	M	1857-1893	1,184,484
Dornberg	BA	BMD	1810-1870	1,056,409	Eisenach	TH	M	1857-1893	1,184,485
Dornigheim	HN	BD	1811	832,395	Eisenach	TH	D	1858-1906	1,184,488
Dornum	PH	M	1815-1831	1,257,052	Eisenach	TH	B	1859-1904	1,184,483
Dornum	PH	D	1815-1906	1,257,052	Eisenach	TH	Nam	1872-1939	1,184,486
Dornum	PH	B	1822-1911	1,257,052	Eisenach	TH	M	1894-1906	1,184,485
Dornum	PH	BMD	1844-1872	1,257,052	Eiterfeld	HN	M	1853-1874	817,246
Dornum	PH	M	1844-1893	1,257,052	Elben	HN	BMD	1808-1812	806,721
Dossenheim	BA	BMD	1810-1870	1,188,011	Elbing	WP	BMD	1812-1871	742,026
Dossenheim	BA	BMD	1820-1869	1,052,370	Elgershausen	HN	BMD	1808-1812	806,722
Dramburg	PO	B	1779-1827	1,184,410	Ellrich	SA	Fam	1750-1908	1,184,489
Dramburg	PO	D	1808-1838	1,184,410	Ellrich	SA	D	1820-1869	1,184,489
Dramburg	PO	M	1818-1820	1,184,410	Ellrich	SA	BMD	1825-1869	1,334,568
Dramburg	PO	B	1839-1847	1,184,410	Ellrich	SA	B	1876-1884	1,184,489
Dramburg	PO	BMD	1839-1874	1,184,410	Ellrich	SA	D	1876-1886	1,184,489
Dreissigacken	TH	B	1811-1870	1,184,481	Elmshagen	HN	BD	1860	817,247
Dreissigacken	TH	D	1812-1869	1,184,481	Elnhausen	HN	B	1849-1867	817,248
Dresden	SN	Nam	?	1,184,479	Emden	PH	BMD	1816-1876	1,257,052
Dresden	SN	BMD	1786-1835	1,184,473	Emden	PH	BMD	1844-1856	1,258,184
Dresden	SN	Nam	1786-1864	1,184,471	Emden	PH	BMD	1844-1866	1,258,191
Dresden	SN	BMD	1786-1875	1,184,474	Emden	PH	M	1844-1868	1,258,192
Dresden	SN	BMD	1786-1890	1,184,474	Emden	PH	BMD	1865	1,258,184
Dresden	SN	Nam	1790-1824	1,184,472	Emden	PH	D	1924-1925	1,257,052
Dresden	SN	BM	1835-1864	1,184,471	Emden	PH	B	1924-1926	1,257,052
Dresden	SN	B	1865-1890	1,184,475	Emmendingen	BA	BMD	1810-1819	1,334,584
Dresden	SN	D	1865-1894	1,184,477	Emmendingen	BA	D	1811-1869	1,192,011
Dresden	SN	M	1865-1910	1,184,476	Emmendingen	BA	BM	1811-1870	1,192,010
Dresden	SN	B	1891-1910	1,184,476	Emmendingen	BA	BMD	1820-1832	1,334,618
Dresden	SN	D	1894-1910	1,184,478	Ems	HN	D	1801	1,195,227

Epfenbach	BA	MD	1842-1870	1,192,036	Fordon	PN	BMD	1835-1840	814,573
Eppingen	BA	BMD	1811-1870	1,186,384	Fordon	PN	B	1841-1851	814,573
Eppingen	BA	BMD	1811-1870	1,192,025	Fordon	PN	B	1849	814,574
Eppingen	BA	BMD	1811-1870	1,335,034	Fordon	PN	D	1849-1888	814,575
Erbstadt	HN	B	1852	817,228	Fordon	PN	B	1850-1852	814,575
Erfurt	SA	Fam	1800-1910	1,184,490	Fordon	PN	M	1852	814,575
Erfurt	SA	Fam	1810-1900	1,184,490	Forth	BY	BMD	1815-1875	1,273,449
Erfurt	SA	BMD	1817-1838	1,184,485	Frankenau	HN	BMD	1808-1813	817,498
Erfurt	SA	Cem	1818-1878	1,184,489	Frankenberg	HN	BMD	1808-1812	817,501
Erfurt	SA	B	1838-1858	1,184,452	Frankenstein	SC	Cem	18??-19??	1,184,411
Erfurt	SA	M	1838-1858	1,184,484	Frankershausen	HN	BMD	1863-1902	71,247
Erfurt	SA	D	1838-1858	1,184,487	Frankfurt (Main)	HE	D	1849-1868	817,483
Erfurt	SA	BM	1847-1869	1,184,489	Frankfurt (Oder)	PS	Fam	1760-1840	1,184,491
Erfurt	SA	Cem	1856-1878	1,184,489	Frankfurt (Oder)	PS	Nam	1776	1,184,491
Erfurt	SA	M	1857-1893	1,184,484	Frankfurt (Oder)	PS	D	1810-1870	1,184,492
Erfurt	SA	M	1857-1893	1,184,485	Frankfurt (Oder)	PS	M	1820-1846	1,184,491
Erfurt	SA	D	1858-1906	1,184,488	Frankfurt (Oder)	PS	D	1831-1841	1,184,491
Erfurt	SA	B	1859-1904	1,184,483	Frankfurt (Oder)	PS	BMD	1847-1863	584,092
Erfurt	SA	D	1863-1865	1,184,489	Frankfurt (Oder)	PS	BMD	1864-1878	584,093
Erfurt	SA	Nam	1872-1939	1,184,486	Frauenburg	OS	Cem	?	1,184,411
Erfurt	SA	Cem	1878-1887	1,184,489	Fraustadt	PN	BMD	1817-1840	1,271,451
Erfurt	SA	D	1879-1898	1,184,490	Freiburg	BA	BMD	1845-1870	1,192,011
Erfurt	SA	M	1894-1906	1,184,485	Freienwalde	PS	BMD	1813-1850	1,184,492
Erksdorf	HN	BMD	1808-1861	860,106	Freienwalde	PS	Cem	1937	1,184,492
Erksdorf	HN	B	1856-1874	817,259	Freren	PH	BMD	1844-1889	1,336,559
Erksdorf	HN	D	1856/1869	817,259	Freystadt	WP	D	1893-1930	1,184,413
Erlangen	BY	Cen	1826	1,190,988	Friedberg	HE	BMD	1828-1838	870,536
Erlangen	BY	Cen	1826	1,190,989	Friedberg	HE	BMD	1839-1873	870,537
Erlbach	BY	Cen	1826	1,190,988	Friedeberg	PS	D	1794-1913	1,184,493
Erlbach	BY	Cen	1826	1,190,989	Friedrichstadt	SH	BMD	1847-1875	1,201,809
Ermetzhofen	BY	BMD	1815-1867	1,194,042	Frielendorf	HN	B	1790-1868	828,533
Ernsthausen	HN	B	1856-1873	817,260	Frielendorf	HN	M	1829-1871	828,500
Ernsthausen	HN	D	1859/1873	817,260	Friesenheim	BA	BMD	1813-1870	1,192,012
Erzhausen	HE	BMD	1822-1872	870,535	Fritzlar	HN	BMD	1801-1812	828,534
Eschelbach	BA	BMD	1811-1870	1,192,024	Fritzlar	HN	B	1824-1871	828,534
Eschershausen	BR	Fam	1763-1876	949,296	Frohnhausen	HN	B	1822-1828	828,535
Eschershausen	BR	Fam	1809	1,190,954	Frohnhausen	HN	D	1828	828,535
Eschershausen	BR	B	1810	949,329	Furstenberg	PS	B	1840-1871	1,184,494
Eschershausen	BR	B	1810	1,334,577	Furstenberg	PW	BMD	1850-1874	1,194,060
Eschollbrocken	HE	BMD	1809-1875	871,592	Furth	BY	Nam	1817-1827	1,190,974
Eschwege	HN	BMD	1808-1812	806,724	Gadebusch	ME	BMD	1793-1922	68,935
Eschwege	HN	BMD	1825-1930	071,178	Gailingen	BA	BMD	1810-1850	1,335,030
Esens	PH	D	1845-1938	1,257,052	Gailingen	BA	BMD	1851-1869	1,190,990
Esens	PH	B	1846-1936	1,257,052	Gandersheim	BR	Fam	1775-1852	949,296
Ettenheim	BA	BMD	1814-1831	1,186,413	Gandersheim	BR	BMD	1810-1813	1,334,577
Ettenheim	BA	BMD	1832-1870	1,186,414	Gandersheim	BR	BMD	1853-1896	1,196,137
Eubigheim	BA	BMD	1810-1829	1,055,291	Garbenteich	HE	BD	1825-1875	870,537
Eubigheim	BA	BMD	1830-1870	1,055,292	Gardelgen	SA	Cem	1932-1935	1,184,494
Fechenheim (Frank-furt)	HN	D	1849-1868	817,483	Garnsee	WP	Cem	?	1,184,411
					Garrin	PO	Nam	1561	1,273,138
Felsberg (b Cassel)	HN	BMD	1824-1852	817,495	Gebweiler	EL	Nam	1792-1862	736,254
Feodenheim	BA	BMD	1810-1860	1,238,463	Gebweiler	EL	Nam	1792-1892	734,519
Festenberg	SC	D	1812-1818	1,184,411	Gebweiler	EL	D	1793-1806	736,262
Festenberg	SC	BMD	1819-1874	1,184,411	Gebweiler	EL	M	1793-1820	734,525
Feuchtwangen	BY	Cen	1826	1,190,988	Gebweiler	EL	M	1805-1806	736,253
Feuchtwangen	BY	Cen	1826	1,190,989	Gebweiler	EL	B	1805-1821	734,520
Feudenheim	BA	BMD	1810-1860	1,238,463	Gebweiler	EL	D	1807-1825	736,263
Feudenheim	BA	BMD	1810-1870	1,271,209	Gebweiler	EL	M	1820-1840	736,253
Feudenheim	BA	BMD	1860-1870	1,238,464	Gebweiler	EL	M	1821-1839	736,259
Flatow (Krst Flatow)	WP	Fam	?	1,184,411	Gebweiler	EL	B	1822-1833	734,521
Flatow (Krst Flatow)	WP	BMD	1813-1846	1,184,410	Gebweiler	EL	D	1826-1838	736,264
Flehingen	BA	BMD	1810-1832	1,056,137	Gebweiler	EL	B	1834-1842	734,522
Flehingen	BA	BMD	1810-1869	1,192,026	Gebweiler	EL	D	1839-1852	736,265
Flehingen	BA	BMD	1833-1869	1,056,213	Gebweiler	EL	M	1840-1857	736,260
Floss	BY	BMD	1813-1838	1,194,062	Gebweiler	EL	B	1843-1852	734,523
Fordon	PN	M	1820-1851	814,573	Gebweiler	EL	B	1853-1862	734,524
Fordon	PN	B	1823-1834	814,573	Gebweiler	EL	D	1853-1862	736,266
Fordon	PN	BMD	1823-1848	814,574	Gebweiler	EL	Nam	1853-1872	736,255
Fordon	PN	D	1823-1851	814,574	Gebweiler	EL	M	1858-1862	736,261

Place	Reg	Type	Years	Film	Place	Reg	Type	Years	Film
Gebweiler	EL	B	1863-1872	774,488	Glogau	SC	Nam	1812	1,184,415
Gebweiler	EL	M	1863-1872	774,489	Glogau	SC	B	1812-1850	1,184,416
Gebweiler	EL	D	1863-1872	774,490	Glogau	SC	Cem	1818-1893	1,184,418
Gedern	HE	BD	1824-1875	870,538	Glogau	SC	BMD	1820-1847	1,184,416
Gehaus	TH	BMD	1817-1838	1,184,485	Glogau	SC	BD	1821-1864	1,184,416
Gehaus	TH	BMD	1820-1838	1,184,494	Glogau	SC	Sch	1862-1895	1,184,418
Gehaus	TH	B	1838-1858	1,184,482	Glogau	SC	B	1864-1870	1,184,416
Gehaus	TH	M	1838-1858	1,184,484	Glogau	SC	B	1864-1938	1,184,418
Gehaus	TH	D	1838-1858	1,184,487	Glogau	SC	D	1864-1938	1,184,418
Gehaus	TH	BMD	1838-1937	1,184,495	Gnesen	PN	BMD	1840-1841	1,271,464
Gehaus	TH	M	1857-1893	1,184,484	Gnesen	PN	BMD	1840-1847	719,426
Gehaus	TH	M	1857-1893	1,184,485	Gnoien	ME	B	1813	1,184,496
Gehaus	TH	D	1858-1906	1,184,488	Gnoien	ME	D	1813-1815	1,184,496
Gehaus	TH	B	1859-1904	1,184,483	Gnoien	ME	BMD	1833-1911	1,184,496
Gehaus	TH	Nam	1872-1939	1,184,486	Gochsheim	BA	B	1806-1869	1,056,215
Gehaus	TH	M	1894-1906	1,184,485	Gochsheim	BA	MD	1806-1869	1,056,216
Gehrden	PH	B	1767-1877	1,184,495	Gochsheim	BA	BMD	1812-1865	1,192,030
Gehrden	PH	D	1839-1879	1,184,495	Goldberg	ME	BMD	1814-1916	68,935
Geisa	TH	BMD	1817-1838	1,184,485	Gollnow	PO	BMD	1815-1847	1,271,450
Geisa	TH	B	1838-1858	1,184,482	Gollnow	PO	M	1847-1874	1,194,052
Geisa	TH	M	1838-1858	1,184,484	Gollnow	PO	BD	1847-1874	1,271,450
Geisa	TH	D	1838-1858	1,184,487	Gollnow	PO	Fam	1860-1934	1,184,417
Geisa	TH	M	1857-1893	1,184,484	Gollub	WP	BMD	1808-1819	812,349
Geisa	TH	M	1857-1893	1,184,485	Gollub	WP	BMD	1819-1825	812,350
Geisa	TH	D	1858-1906	1,184,488	Gollub	WP	BMD	1826-1840	812,351
Geisa	TH	B	1859-1904	1,184,483	Gollub	WP	BMD	1826-1850	812,352
Geisa	TH	Nam	1872-1939	1,184,486	Gollub	WP	BMD	1851-1859	812,353
Geisa	TH	M	1894-1906	1,184,485	Gollub	WP	BMD	1858-1865	812,354
Geismar	HN	BMD	1851-1874	828,698	Gondelsheim	BA	B	1808-1869	1,056,219
Gelnhausen	HN	M	1823-1833	828,721	Gondelsheim	BA	MD	1808-1869	1,056,220
Gelsungen	HN	BMD	1824-1852	817,495	Gondelsheim	BA	BMD	1811-1870	1,192,030
Gembitz (Kr Mogilno)	PN	BMD	1832-1847	719,219	Gorlitz	SC	Cem	1850-1940	1,184,417
Gemmingen	BA	BMD	1811-1870	1,192,027	Gorlitz	SC	BMD	1864-1932	1,184,418
Gemmingen	BA	BMD	1811-1870	1,273,448	Gossfelden	HN	MD	1824-1883	831,642
Gemmingen	BA	BMD	1813-1829	1,186,385	Gotha	TH	B	1870-1907	1,184,496
Gemmingen	BA	BMD	1830-1870	1,186,387	Gotha	TH	Cem	1870-1940	1,184,496
Genin	LU	BMD	1828-1875	492,312	Graben	BA	BMD	1812-1869	1,271,337
Gensungen	HN	BMD	1811	806,645	Grabow (Ag Grabow)	ME	BD	1835-1925	1,184,496
Georgenhausen	HE	BD	1828-1875	870,538	Grabow (Ag Grabow)	ME	Nam	1868-1873	1,184,497
Gernrode	AN	BMD	1828-1871	1,184,495	Grafenhausen	HE	BMD	1823-1872	870,539
Gernsbach	BA	D	1811-1869	1,192,013	Gratz (Krst Gratz)	PN	D	1817-1837	1,271,465
Gernsbach	BA	M	1811-1870	1,192,012	Grebenstein	HN	B	1727-1811	831,658
Gernsbach	BA	BMD	1815-1869	1,188,124	Grebenstein	HN	BMD	1808	806,646
Geseke	PW	Fam	1756-1808	1,052,059	Grebenstein	HN	M	1827-1881	831,658
Giessen	HE	B	1809-1822	870,538	Grebenstein	HN	D	1827-1887	831,658
Giessen	HE	B	1809-1875	801,155	Greding	BY	Cen	1826	1,190,988
Giessen	HE	MD	1823-1873	801,155	Greding	BY	Cen	1826	1,190,989
Giessen	HE	BMD	1825-1875	871,590	Greene	BR	BD	1809	1,334,577
Gilgenburg	OS	BMD	1847-1874	1,271,459	Greene	BR	BMD	1809,1812	949,334
Glatz	SC	D	1832-1940	1,184,414	Grcetsiel	PH	BD	1815-1817	1,257,052
Glauberg	HE	BMD	1841-1852	1,194,056	Greifenberg	PO	BMD	1815-1847	1,190,946
Glauberg	HE	BMD	1841-1852	1,273,150	Greifenberg	PO	BMD	1848-1874	1,194,051
Glauberg	HE	BMD	1841-1870	870,539	Griesheim	HE	BMD	1778-1875	1,190,956
Gleicherwiesen	TH	BMD	1831-1937	1,192,013	Griesheim	HE	BD	1823-1872	870,541
Gleicherwiesen	TH	Fam	1831-1937	1,192,013	Groningen	SA	Nam	1731-1813	1,184,497
Gleiwitz	SC	Cem	1800	1,184,414	Groningen	SA	B	1733-1815	1,184,497
Gleiwitz	SC	BMD	1812-1847	875,339	Gross Bieberau	HE	BMD	1576-1679	1,190,548
Gleiwitz	SC	BMD	1812-1847	1,335,024	Gross Bieberau	HE	BMD	1800-1846	1,190,546
Gleiwitz	SC	D	1812-1874	1,194,054	Gross Bieberau	HE	BMD	1801-1807	1,190,547
Gleiwitz	SC	D	1812-1874	1,194,055	Gross Bieberau	HE	B	1808-1818	1,190,547
Gleiwitz	SC	V	1812-1874	1,194,055	Gross Bieberau	HE	M	1808-1824	1,190,545
Gleiwitz	SC	M	1812-1874	1,271,453	Gross Bieberau	HE	D	1808-1844	1,190,560
Gleiwitz	SC	B	1812-1874	1,334,567	Gross Bieberau	HE	M	1824-1877	1,190,560
Gleiwitz	SC	B	1812-1874	1,334,612	Gross Bieberau	HE	B	1825-1900	1,190,559
Gleiwitz	SC	D	1847-1849	875,339	Gross Bieberau	HE	BMD	1827-1875	870,540
Gleiwitz	SC	B	1858-1861	875,339	Gross Bieberau	HE	D	1837-1904	1,190,559
Gleiwitz	SC	BMD	1858-1861	1,335,024	Gross Bieberau	HE	D	1844-1875	1,190,559
Gleiwitz	SC	Cem	1903-1940	1,184,414	Gross Bieberau	HE	BM	1847-1875	1,190,545
Gleiwitz	SC	D	1910-1939	1,184,414	Gross Gerau (Kreis)	HE	BMD	1808-1822	870,534

Gross Strehlitz	SC	MD	1828-1919	1,184,417	Halberstadt	SA	BMD	1801-1825	1,184,499
Gross Strehlitz	SC	B	1850-1910	1,184,417	Halberstadt	SA	D	1825	1,184,499
Gross Wartenberg	SC	Cem	1820-1867	1,184,417	Halberstadt	SA	M	1829	1,184,499
Gross Wierau	SC	Cem	Ab1820	1,184,417	Halberstadt	SA	BMD	1830-1850	1,184,499
Gross Wierau	SC	Cem	1820-1867	1,184,417	Halberstadt	SA	B	1843	1,184,499
Grossalsleben	AN	BMD	1801-1803	1,184,497	Halberstadt	SA	BMD	1844	1,184,500
Grossalsleben	AN	BMD	1801,1803	1,185,003	Halberstadt	SA	Nam	1844-1929	1,185,002
Grossalsleben	AN	BMD	1832-1848	1,184,497	Halberstadt	SA	Nam	1852-1879	1,184,500
Grossalsleben	AN	BMD	1832-1849	1,185,003	Halle	BR	BMD	1808-1812	1,334,577
Grosseichholzheim	BA	BMD	1810-1870	1,055,117	Halle	PW	BMD	1815-1874	1,194,064
Grosseichholzheim	BA	BMD	1811-1869	1,192,029	Hamburg	HA	B	1781-1811	1,190,978
Grossen Buseck	HE	BMD	1809-1822	870,527	Hamburg	HA	B	1811-1815	1,190,978
Grossen Buseck	HE	BMD	1823-1875	870,522	Hamburg	HA	B	1816-1829	1,335,029
Grossen Buseck	HE	BMD	1828-1875	870,540	Hamburg	HA	B	1816-1865	1,335,030
Grossen Linden	HE	BD	1823-1875	870,541	Hamburg	HA	B	1830-1840	1,190,978
Grosseneder	PW	BMD	1815-1821	1,051,557	Hamburg	HA	B	1841-1851	1,335,028
Grosseneder	PW	B	1858-1870	1,053,270	Hamburg	HA	B	1852-1860	1,335,029
Grossenenglis	HN	BMD	1808-1812	806,664	Hamburg	HA	B	1861-1865	1,335,029
Grossmuhlingen	AN	B	1778-1828	1,184,497	Hameln	PH	BMD	1853-1874	1,194,066
Grossmuhlingen	AN	D	1796-1828	1,184,497	Hanau	HN	B	1866-1869	832,416
Grossmuhlingen	AN	BMD	1828-1871	1,184,497	Harderode	BR	BD	1809-1810	1,334,577
Grossropperhausen	HN	BMD	1828-1874	853,749	Hardheim	BA	BMD	1810-1832	1,056,421
Grotzingen	BA	BMD	1811-1820	1,190,897	Hardheim	BA	BMD	1833-1850	1,056,422
Grotzingen	BA	BD	1811-1869	1,192,027	Hardheim	BA	BMD	1851-1870	1,056,423
Grotzingen	BA	BMD	1811-1869	1,192,028	Haren	PH	BMD	1844-1875	1,336,569
Grotzingen	BA	BMD	1821-1830	1,271,268	Harmuthsachsen	HN	BMD	1808-1809	806,668
Grotzingen	BA	BMD	1831-1840	1,334,528	Harmuthsachsen	HN	BMD	1810-1812	806,652
Grotzingen	BA	BMD	1841-1850	1,334,535	Hattingen	PW	BD	1847-1874	582,546
Grotzingen	BA	BMD	1851-1860	1,273,303	Hattingen	PW	M	1851-1873	582,546
Grotzingen	BA	BMD	1861-1869	1,334,549	Hatzbach	HN	BD	1856-1874	832,419
Gruningen	HE	BMD	1823-1875	870,542	Haynau	SC	Cem	1888-1936	1,184,419
Grusen	HN	MD	1810-1811	832,004	Heeghelm	HE	BD	1860-1866	870,544
Gudensberg	HN	BMD	1808-1812	806,662	Heepen	PW	BMD	1814-1847	1,190,971
Gudensberg	HN	M	1867-1874	832,395	Heepen	PW	M	1847-1874	1,190,971
Gunzenhausen	BY	Cen	1826	1,190,988	Heepen	PW	B	1847-1882	1,190,971
Gunzenhausen	BY	Cen	1826	1,190,999	Hehlen	BR	Fam	1773-1893	949,296
Gustrow	ME	BMD	1813-1935	68,935	Hehlen	BR	BMD	1808-1812	949,340
Gutersloh	PW	BMD	1815-1874	1,335,040	Hehlen	BR	BMD	1809-1810	949,343
Guttentag (St)	SC	D	1846-1880	1,184,419	Hehlen	BR	BMD	1809-1810	1,334,577
Guttstadt	OS	D	1846-1937	1,184,419	Heidelberg	BA	BMD	1810-1870	1,188,142
Guxhagen	HN	BM	1825-1852	832,395	Heidelberg	BA	BMD	1822/1870	1,188,145
Guxhagen	HN	B	1848-1859	832,395	Heidelsheim	BA	BMD	1814-1870	1,056,377
Haag	BA	BMD	1867-1870	1,184,061	Heidelsheim	BA	BMD	1814-1870	1,192,028
Habitzheim	HE	BMD	1823-1875	870,542	Heidenheim	BY	Cen	1826	1,190,988
Hadmersleben	SA	Nam	1731-1813	1,184,497	Heidenheim	BY	Cen	1826	1,190,989
Hadmersleben	SA	B	1733-1815	1,184,497	Heiligenstadt	SA	BMD	1815-1874	1,271,490
Hagenburg	SL	B	1841-1875	1,271,402	Heiligenstadt	SA	BMD	1816-1842	1,185,002
Hagenburg	SL	D	1842-1875	1,271,402	Heiligenstadt	SA	BMD	1843-1847	1,335,035
Hagenburg	SL	M	1848-1873	1,271,402	Heiligenstadt	SA	BMD	1848-1874	1,185,003
Hagenow	ME	B	1813-1883	1,184,498	Heilsbronn	BY	Cen	1826	1,190,988
Hagenow	ME	D	1813-1937	1,184,498	Heilsbronn	BY	Cen	1826	1,190,999
Hagenow	ME	M	1819-1859	1,184,498	Heinebach	HN	BMD	1809-1810	806,657
Hagenow	ME	M	1871-1935	1,184,498	Heinsheim	BA	BMD	1812-1869	1,192,029
Hagenow	ME	B	1900?	1,184,498	Heldenbergen	HE	BMD	1809-1837	1,190,953
Hahnlein	HE	BMD	1823-1872	870,543	Heldenbergen	HE	Fam	1820	1,335,026
Hahnlein	HE	B	1746-1809	1,195,087	Heldenbergen	HE	BMD	1823-1875	870,544
Hahnlein	HE	M	1787-1809	1,195,087	Heldenbergen	HE	B	1837-1875	1,190,953
Hahnlein	HE	D	1796-1808	1,195,087	Heldenbergen	HE	MD	1838-1875	1,335,026
Hainchen	HE	BMD	1830-1852	1,194,056	Helmarshausen	HN	D	1827-1889	832,422
Hainchen	HE	BMD	1830-1852	1,273,150	Helmarshausen	HN	B	1827-1893	832,422
Hainchen	HE	BMD	1830-1870	870,544	Helmarshausen	HN	M	1830-1873	832,422
Hainstadt	BA	BMD	1810-1839	1,056,419	Helmstedt	BR	BMD	1810-1813	1,194,063
Hainstadt	BA	BMD	1840-1870	1,056,420	Helmstedt	BR	Fam	1847-1874	949,296
Halberstadt	SA	BMD	1761-1807	1,184,498	Helmstedt	BR	BMD	1847-1874	1,194,063
Halberstadt	SA	Nam	1762	1,185,001	Herbstein	HE	BMD	1857-1872	870,544
Halberstadt	SA	Fam	1784	1,184,500	Herlehausen	HN	BMD	1808-1813	806,659
Halberstadt	SA	Nam	1790	1,185,002	Herrieden	BY	Cen	1826	1,190,988
Halberstadt	SA	Fam	1791	1,184,500	Herrieden	BY	Cen	1826	1,190,989
Halberstadt	SA	Fam	1800-?	1,185,001	Heubach	HN	D	1826-1873	832,452

Heubach	HN	B	1826-1878	832,452	Immenroda	TH	M	1831-1913	1,185,003
Heubach	HN	M	1827-1870	832,452	Immenroda	TH	D	1831-1924	1,185,003
Heuchelheim	HE	BMD	1824-1875	870,545	Insterburg	OS	BD	1857-1862	1,184,419
Hildburghausen	TH	Sch	1826-1875	1,185,003	Iserlohn	PW	BMD	1822-1842	1,335,031
Hildburghausen	TH	BMD	1836-1922	1,185,003	Ittlingen	BA	BMD	1814-1869	1,192,032
Hildmannsfeld	BA	BMD	1810-1870	1,057,396	Ittlingen	BA	BMD	1814-1869	1,273,448
Hilsbach	BA	BMD	1801-1869	1,192,029	Ittlingen	BA	BMD	1815-1834	1,186,388
Hintersteinau	HN	BM	1837-1874	833,862	Ittlingen	BA	BMD	1835-1870	1,186,389
Hintersteinau	HN	D	1838-1870	833,862	Jarotschin	PN	Fam	1810-1879	1,271,464
Hirschberg	SC	Cem	1886-1938	1,184,419	Jastrow	WP	BMD	1816-1839	1,184,420
Hirschhorn	HE	BMD	1823-1875	1,190,986	Jastrow	WP	D	1830	1,184,421
Hochhausen	BA	BMD	1812-1869	1,192,030	Jastrow	WP	BMD	1840-1847	1,184,421
Hochst	HE	BMD	1826-1852	1,194,056	Jauer	SC	Fam	Ab1819	1,184,423
Hochst (Kr Bodingen)	HE	BMD	1826-1870	870,545	Jauer	SC	Cem	1806-1939	1,184,422
Hochst (Odenwald)	HE	BMD	1822-1875	1,190,979	Jauer	SC	BMD	1815-1840	1,184,422
Hochst(a/d Nidder)	HE	BMD	1826-1852	1,194,056	Jauer	SC	BMD	1840-1863	1,184,422
Hochst(a/d Nidder)	HE	BMD	1826-1852	1,273,150	Jemgum	PH	B	1816-1883	1,257,052
Hochstadt (Kr Hanau)	HN	D	1825-1867	833,863	Jemgum	PH	M	1819-1882	1,257,052
Hochstadt (Kr Hanau)	HN	M	1825-1873	833,863	Jemgum	PH	D	1822-1883	1,257,052
Hochstadt (Kr Hanau)	HN	B	1827/1867	833,863	Jemgum	PH	D	1933	1,257,052
Hockenheim	BA	M	1814-1866	1,273,451	Jemgum	PH	B	1935	1,257,052
Hockenheim	BA	B	1846-1870	1,134,585	Johlingen	BA	BMD	1810-1869	1,271,329
Hofgeismar (Krst)	HN	M	1809	833,824	Johlingen	BA	BMD	1810-1869	1,271,330
Hofgeismar (Krst)	HN	BMD	1810-1813	833,824	Josbach	HN	B	1856-1874	834,165
Hofgeismar (Krst)	HN	D	1827-1903	833,824	Julich	PR	Nam	1808	1,334,572
Hofgeismar (Krst)	HN	M	1828-1889	833,824	Kaiserslautern	BY	Cem	?	536,484
Hofgeismar (Krst)	HN	M	1869-1872	833,825	Kaldern	HN	BMD	1810-1867	815,196
Hohe	BR	BMD	1809	957,306	Kallies	PO	BMD	1778-1848	1,334,572
Hohe	BR	Fam	1809	1,190,954	Kallies	PO	BMD	1847-1874	1,334,575
Hohenhausen	LI	BMD	1809-1875	1,190,983	Kalme	BR	BMD	1809-1812	949,710
Holzhausen	HN	BM	1811	851,356	Kamen	PW	Nam	1751-1801	1,190,967
Holzhausen	HN	BD	1856-1873	851,356	Kamen	PW	BMD	1822-1874	1,190,967
Holzhein	HE	BMD	1823-1875	870,545	Kamen	PW	Nam	1846	1,190,967
Holzminden	BR	Fam	1808	1,190,954	Kamen	PW	Fam	1874	1,190,967
Holzminden	BR	BMD	1808-1812	949,340	Kanth	SC	I/O	1823-1869	1,334,473
Holzminden	BR	B	1809	949,708	Kanth	SC	B	1812-1924	1,184,423
Holzminden	BR	BMD	1809	1,334,577	Kanth	SC	M	1823-1862	1,334,473
Holzminden	BR	Fam	1839-1876	949,296	Kanth	SC	I/O	1823-1869	1,334,473
Homburg (Pfalz)	BY	Nam	1808	1,334,572	Kanth	SC	M	1823-1920	1,184,423
Homburg	HN	Fam	1750-1824	1,273,154	Kanth	SC	B	1824-1872	1,334,473
Hoof (b Cassel)	HN	BD	1849-1860	834,010	Kanth	SC	D	1828-1874	1,334,473
Horden	BA	D	1811-1869	1,192,013	Kanth	SC	D	1828-1937	1,184,423
Horden	BA	M	1811-1870	1,192,012	Karlsruhe	BA	Cen	1809	1,180,442
Horn	LI	BMD	1837-1876	1,334,575	Karlsruhe	BA	BMD	1810-1865	1,256,447
Hornburg	BR	BMD	1808-1814	949,708	Karlsruhe	BA	BMD	1865-1869	1,192,484
Hornburg	BR	Fam	1839-1876	949,296	Katscher	SC	BMD	1812-1874	1,335,040
Horrenbach	BA	BMD	1810-1820	1,055,294	Kattowitz	SC	D	1825-1939	1,184,426
Hottenberg	HE	BMD	1809-1822	870,546	Kattowitz	SC	B	1860-1936	1,184,423
Hoym	AN	BMD	1828-1880	1,185,003	Kattowitz	SC	Nam	1868-1897	1,184,428
Huffenhardt	BA	BMD	1811-1869	1,192,046	Kemnade	BR	BMD	1809	957,306
Huffenhardt	BA	BMD	1847-1869	1,192,030	Kemnade	BR	BMD	1809-1812	949,710
Hundsfeld (Kr Ols)	SC	BMD	1812-1857	1,184,419	Kemnade	BR	Fam	1810	1,190,954
Hundsfeld (Kr Ols)	SC	Cem	1868-1923	1,184,419	Kempen	PN	BD	1825	742,975
Hungheim	BA	BMD	1816-1834	1,055,122	Kempen	PN	BMD	1825/1835	742,975
Hungheim	BA	BMD	1816-1870	1,334,617	Kempen	PN	BMD	1836-1841	742,976
Huttengesass	HN	B	1840-1877	834,021	Kempen	PN	BMD	1842-1844	742,977
Huttengesass	HN	BMD	1840-1877	834,021	Kieferstadtel	SC	Cir	1806-1865	1,184,428
Huttengesass	HN	D	1842-1876	834,021	Kieferstadtel	SC	Cem	1831-1893	1,184,428
Huttengesass	HN	M	1843-1877	834,021	Kiel	SH	BMD	1841-1874	1,334,544
Iba	HN	BMD	1808-1812	806,638	Kirchardt	BA	BMD	1816-1869	1,192,032
Iba	HN	BMD	1808-1812	806,689	Kirchardt	BA	B	1821-1841	1,192,033
Iburg	PH	BMD	1869-1871	1,272,976	Kirchardt	BA	BMD	1833/1870	1,192,048
Ihringen	BA	BMD	1811-1870	1,192,014	Kirchen	BA	BMD	1811-1838	1,192,015
Ilvesheim	BA	BMD	1810-1870	1,238,454	Kirchen	BA	M	1839-1869	1,192,016
Ilvesheim	BA	BMD	1810-1870	1,271,220	Kirchen	BA	BD	1839-1870	1,192,015
Ilvesheim	BA	BMD	1810-1870	1,271,221	Kirchhain (b Cassel)	HN	BMD	1810-1812	841,263
Immenhausen	HN	BMD	1808-1812	806,638	Kirchhain (b Cassel)	HN	BMD	1856-1874	841,263
Immenroda	TH	Nam	1831	1,185,003	Kirn (Nahe)	PR	Nam	1808-1843	1,190,970
Immenroda	TH	B	1831-1899	1,185,003	Kirtorf	HE	BMD	1809-1823	870,546

Town	Reg	Type	Years	Film	Town	Reg	Type	Years	Film
Kladam	WP	Fam	1799-1810	1,184,440	Koslin	PO	Cem	1835-1935	1,184,431
Kladam	WP	Fam	1799-1810	1,184,441	Koslin	PO	BMD	1841-1847	1,184,430
Kladam	WP	BMD	1815-1847	1,184,439	Koslin	PO	BMD	1847-1874	1,334,583
Kleinalsleben	AN	BMD	1801,1803	1,185,003	Krakow	ME	BMD	1813-1874	68,935
Kleinalsleben	AN	BMD	1832-1849	1,185,003	Krakow	ME	B	1813-1874	1,185,004
Kleineichholzheim	BA	BMD	1808-1870	1,192,031	Krakow	ME	D	1813-1883	1,185,004
Kleineichholzheim	BA	BMD	1810-1870	1,190,996	Krakow	ME	Fam	1819	1,185,004
Kleineichholzheim	BA	D	1846-1870	1,192,035	Krakow	ME	M	1845-1873	1,185,004
Konig	HE	BMD	1823-1874	1,334,585	Krappitz	SC	BMD	1819-1847	1,190,961
Konigheim	BA	BMD	1810-1870	1,271,488	Krautheim	BA	BMD	1810-1849	1,055,296
Konigsbach	BA	BMD	1810-1869	1,190,972	Krautheim	BA	BMD	1850-1870	1,055,297
Konigsbach	BA	BMD	1811-1869	1,192,031	Krautheim	BA	BMD	1851-1870	1,047,435
Konigsberg	OS	BMD	1809-1871	1,184,428	Kremmen	PS	BMD	1813-1849	1,185,004
Konigsberg	OS	BMD	1811-1874	1,184,427	Kremmen	PS	V	1819	1,185,004
Konigsberg	OS	D	1837-1846	491,525	Kreuzburg	SC	BD	1813-1815	890,725
Konigsberg	OS	D	1846-1866	1,184,430	Kreuzburg	SC	BMD	1830-1855	1,184,431
Konigsberg	OS	D	1846-1868	491,526	Kriewen	PN	BMD	1835-1847	743,099
Konigsberg	OS	M	1847-1851	491,510	Krojanke	WP	BMD	1800-1863	1,184,432
Konigsberg	OS	B	1847-1852	475,875	Kropelin	ME	BMD	1810-1840	1,185,004
Konigsberg	OS	M	1847-1852	476,220	Kropelin	ME	BMD	1817-1898	068,935
Konigsberg	OS	D	1847-1857	491,521	Kroppenstedt	SA	Fam	1731-1813	1,184,497
Konigsberg	OS	BD	1850-1874	479,093	Kroppenstedt	SA	B	1733-1815	1,184,497
Konigsberg	OS	M	1851-1855	491,511	Krotoschin	PN	BMD	1825-1841	743,091
Konigsberg	OS	B	1852-1857	585,589	Krotoschin	PN	BMD	1842-1847	743,092
Konigsberg	OS	M	1852-1858	491,518	Kurnik	PN	M	1817-1834	742,003
Konigsberg	OS	M	1852-1874	585,590	Kurnik	PN	D	1834-1840	1,194,062
Konigsberg	OS	M	1856-1859	491,512	Kurnik	PN	Nam	1840-1847	1,194,061
Konigsberg	OS	D	1858-1864	491,522	Kustrin	PS	BD	1815-1849	1,334,576
Konigsberg	OS	B	1858-1871	585,590	Kyritz	PS	BM	1812-1908	1,190,966
Konigsberg	OS	B	1859	475,875	Kyritz	PS	D	1815-1936	1,190,966
Konigsberg	OS	M	1859-1867	491,519	Laage	ME	BMD	1813-1907	68,935
Konigsberg	OS	B	1860/1865	475,876	Ladenburg	BA	BMD	1810-1870	1,238,445
Konigsberg	OS	M	1863-1864	491,513	Ladenburg	BA	BMD	1810-1870	1,271,357
Konigsberg	OS	M	1865-1866	491,514	Ladenburg	BA	BMD	1812-1870	1,192,034
Konigsberg	OS	D	1865-1870	491,523	Lage	LI	BMD	1809	1,271,461
Konigsberg	OS	M	1867-1868	491,515	Lage	LI	BMD	1809	1,273,155
Konigsberg	OS	D	1867-1880	1,184,429	Lage	LI	BMD	1810-1875	1,334,576
Konigsberg	OS	M	1868-1874	491,520	Lage	LI	BMD	1870-1875	1,271,461
Konigsberg	OS	B	1868/1874	491,509	Lage	LI	BMD	1870-1875	1,273,155
Konigsberg	OS	M	1869-1870	491,516	Lahr	BA	B	1858-1869	1,192,016
Konigsberg	OS	M	1871-1872	491,517	Lampertheim	HE	BMD	1805-1875	1,271,457
Konigsberg	OS	D	1871-1874	491,524	Lampertheim	HE	BMD	1823-1875	1,271,458
Konigsberg	OS	M	1873-1877	475,877	Landau	BY	BMD	1784-1790	488,361
Konigsberg	OS	Nam	1910-1918	491,508	Landau	BY	Nam	1808	488,361
Konigshofen	BA	BMD	1810-1824	1,273,452	Landeck	SC	Cem	1922-1934	1,184,432
Konigshutte	SC	D	1867-1940	1,184,430	Landeshut	SC	Cem	1800-1938	1,184,432
Konigslutter	BR	Fam	1872-1874	949,296	Landeshut	SC	I/O	1812-1848	1,184,432
Konin (Kr Samter)	PN	M	1815	741,998	Landeshut	SC	B	1812-1863	1,184,432
Konin (Kr Samter)	PN	BMD	1826-1845	741,998	Landeshut	SC	B	1816-1842	1,184,432
Konin (Kr Samter)	PN	BMD	1846/1853	741,999	Landeshut	SC	M	1827-1852	1,184,432
Konin (Kr Samter)	PN	BMD	1855/1865	742,000	Landeshut	SC	M	1832-1840	1,184,432
Konin (Kr Samter)	PN	BMD	1866	1,191,093	Landeshut	SC	Fam	1839-1842	1,184,432
Konin (Kr Samter)	PN	BMD	1869-1874	1,191,094	Landeshut	SC	D	1881-1938	1,184,432
Konstadt	SC	BD	1835-1890	1,184,431	Landeshut	SC	Nam	1906-1913	1,184,432
Konstanz	BA	BMD	1863-1869	870,274	Landgenselbold	HN	D	1849-1868	841,286
Korb	BA	Fam	1747	1,055,123	Landsberg	SC	Nam	1843	1,184,432
Korb	BA	BMD	1808-1870	1,055,123	Landsberg	SC	D	1843-1844	1,184,432
Korb	BA	BMD	1810-1870	1,190,996	Lang Gons	HE	BMD	1809-1875	870,546
Koschmin	PN	BMD	1811-1812	742,946	Langen Bergheim	HE	BMD	1853-1870	870,546
Koschmin	PN	D	1818-1836	1,194,062	Langendiebach	HN	B	1826-1867	841,285
Kosel (Krst Kosel)	SC	BMD	1810-1812	1,184,406	Langendiebach	HN	D	1826-1874	841,285
Kosel (Krst Kosel)	SC	BMD	1812-1846	1,190,954	Langendiebach	HN	M	1830-1870	841,285
Kosel (Krst Kosel)	SC	BMD	1821-1825	1,184,406	Langendorf	SC	Nam	1762-1820	1,184,433
Kosel (Krst Kosel)	SC	BMD	1821-1828	1,184,406	Langendorf	SC	B	1810-1857	1,184,432
Kosel (Krst Kosel)	SC	M	1879-1895	1,184,406	Langendorf	SC	M	1828-1851	1,184,434
Kosel (Krst Kosel)	SC	D	1908-1917	1,184,406	Langendorf	SC	I/O	1845	1,184,434
Koslin	PO	Fam	1800	1,184,430	Langendorf	SC	Nam	1877-1889	1,184,434
Koslin	PO	BMD	1812-1846	896,086	Langenselbold	HN	B	1827-1868	841,286
Koslin	PO	BMD	1813-1847	1,334,576	Langsdorf	HE	BMD	1823-1875	870,546

Lathen	PH	D	1845-1888	1,336,739	Luckenwalde	PS	Cem	1833-1922	1,185,004
Lathen	PH	B	1845-1891	1,336,739	Ludwigslust	ME	B	1817-1910	1,185,004
Lathen	PH	M	1848-1885	1,336,739	Ludwigslust	ME	M	1827-1895	1,185,004
Lauberg	HE	BMD	1841-1852	1,194,056	Ludwigslust	ME	D	1827-1913	1,185,004
Lauenburg	PO	Nam	1829	1,184,433	Ludwigslust	ME	BMD	1827-1920	68,935
Lauenburg	PO	BMD	1829-1846	1,184,433	Magdeburg	SA	BMD	1800-1903	1,190,885
Lauenburg	PO	Cem	1844-1936	1,184,433	Magdeburg	SA	D	1815-1837	1,185,005
Lauenburg	PO	Cem	1844-1936	1,184,434	Magdeburg	SA	BMD	1815-1874	1,271,215
Lauf	BY	Cen	1826	1,190,988	Magdeburg	SA	BMD	1815-1874	1,271,216
Lauf	BY	Cen	1826	1,190,989	Magdeburg	SA	D	1817-1939	1,185,005
Laurahutte	SC	I/O	1856-1862	1,184,434	Magdeburg	SA	B	1829-1830	1,185,004
Laurahutte	SC	M	1880	1,184,434	Magdeburg	SA	D	1829-1832	1,185,004
Leer	PH	BMD	1842-1939	1,257,052	Magdeburg	SA	M	1830	1,185,004
Lehrensteinsfeld	WU	B	1745-1866	1,346,084	Magdeburg	SA	D	1908-1934	1,185,005
Leidenhofen	HN	B	1850-1862	841,290	Mainz	HE	Nam	1808	1,271,217
Leidenhofen	HN	D	1859-1866	841,290	Mainz	HE	Nam	1835-1888	1,271,196
Leihgestern	HE	BMD	1823-1875	870,547	Mainzlar	HE	BMD	1827-1875	870,549
Leimen	BA	BMD	1810-1870	1,188,237	Malchin	ME	B	1813-1879	1,185,006
Leimen	BA	BMD	1812-1869	1,192,035	Malchin	ME	BMD	1813-1884	68,936
Lemgo	LI	BMD	1810-1875	1,271,461	Malchin	ME	D	1813-1884	1,185,006
Lemgo	LI	BMD	1810-1875	1,273,155	Malchin	ME	M	1814-1876	1,185,006
Leobschutz	SC	D	1818-1937	1,184,434	Malchin	ME	Fam	1819	1,185,006
Leschnitz	SC	Cem	1855-1933	1,184,378	Malchow (Ag Malchow)	ME	D	1812-1891	1,185,006
Lessen	WP	BMD	1824/1860	1,184,434	Malchow (Ag Malchow)	ME	B	1813-1895	1,185,006
Lessen	WP	B	1861-1885	1,184,434	Malchow (Ag Malchow)	ME	M	1814-1877	1,185,006
Leutershausen	BA	BMD	1811-1869	1,192,035	Malchow (Ag Malchow)	ME	BMD	1860	1,185,013
Leutershausen	BY	Cen	1826	1,190,988	Mannheim	BA	BMD	1805-1807	1,190,898
Leutershausen	BY	Cen	1826	1,190,989	Mannheim	BA	BMD	1805-1814	1,238,457
Leverkusen	PR	BMD	1808	176,106	Mannheim	BA	BMD	1808-1809	1,190,899
Lich	HE	BMD	1822-1875	870,547	Mannheim	BA	BMD	1810-1816	1,190,901
Lichtenau	BA	BMD	1812-1870	1,192,016	Mannheim	BA	BMD	1810-1860	1,238,463
Lichtenau	BA	BMD	1812-1870	1,200,597	Mannheim	BA	BMD	1810-1870	1,272,109
Lichtenberg	HE	BMD	1849-1864	870,548	Mannheim	BA	BMD	1815-1859	1,238,458
Liebenau (b Cassel)	HN	D	1827-1885	841,299	Mannheim	BA	BMD	1817-1827	1,190,902
Liebenau (b Cassel)	HN	B	1828-1888	841,299	Mannheim	BA	BMD	1828-1841	1,190,903
Liebenau (b Cassel)	HN	M	1880-1884	841,299	Mannheim	BA	BMD	1842-1852	1,271,362
Liebenwalde	PS	Cem	1826-1900	1,185,004	Mannheim	BA	BMD	1853-1859	1,271,363
Liedolsheim	BA	BMD	1823-1861	1,192,036	Mannheim	BA	BMD	1860-1865	1,271,364
Liegnitz	SC	Nam	1812-1850	1,184,436	Mannheim	BA	BMD	1860-1870	1,238,459
Liegnitz	SC	Cem	1814-1939	1,184,436	Mannheim	BA	BMD	1860-1870	1,238,464
Liegnitz	SC	BMD	1855-1940	1,184,435	Mannheim	BA	BMD	1866-1870	1,271,365
Lindach	BA	BMD	1823-1866	1,185,189	Mansbach	HN	M	1825-1868	843,660
Lindheim	HE	BMD	1823-1869	870,548	Marburg	HN	B	1849-1864	801,069
Lindheim	HE	BMD	1830-1852	1,194,056	Marburg	HN	D	1849-1869	801,069
Lindheim	HE	BMD	1830-1852	1,273,150	Mardorf (Kr Homberg)	HN	BD	1859-1873	846,196
Lipperode	LI	BMD	1809-1875	1,190,933	Marienburg	WP	BMD	1847-1865	742,802
Lipperode	LI	BMD	1809-1875	1,190,983	Marienwerder	WP	Cem	1833-1932	1,184,441
Lohne	HN	BMD	1808-1812	806,617	Marisfeld	SM	Sch	1843-1888	1,185,006
Lohra	HN	B	1810-1869	841,302	Marisfeld	TH	B	1768-1876	1,185,006
Lohra	HN	D	1852-1868	841,302	Marisfeld	TH	D	1827-1876	1,185,006
Lollar	HE	BMD	1815-1874	870,549	Marisfeld	TH	B	1837-1875	1,185,007
Lorrach	BA	Fam	1728-1869	1,238,141	Marisfeld	TH	Sch	1840-1876	1,185,007
Lorrach	BA	Fam	1767	1,271,416	Marisfeld	TH	Sch	1843-1888	1,185,006
Lorrach	BA	Fam	1827-1867	1,192,015	Marisfeld	TH	M	1848-1874	1,185,006
Lorrach	BA	BMD	1827-1867	1,192,018	Marisfeld	TH	M	1848-1874	1,185,007
Lowen	SC	BM	1815-1835	1,184,436	Marisfeld	TH	D	1848-1875	1,185,007
Lowen	SC	I/O	1825-1823	1,184,436	Marisfeld	TH	Fam	1868	1,185,007
Lowen	SC	D	1825-1835	1,184,436	Marisfeld	TH	M	1876-1909	1,185,007
Lowen	SC	Nam	1836	1,184,436	Marisfeld	TH	B	1876-1919	1,185,007
Lowen	SC	Nam	1837-1850	1,184,437	Marisfeld	TH	D	1876-1936	1,185,007
Lowen	SC	Cem	1882-1934	1,184,437					
Lowenberg	SC	Cem	1815-1932	1,184,437	Markisch Friedland	WP	Nam	1799-1810	1,184,440
Lublinitz	SC	D	1820-1900	1,184,437	Markisch Friedland	WP	Nam	1799-1810	1,184,441
Lubtheen	ME	Fam	Ca1850	1,185,004	Markisch Friedland	WP	BMD	1815-1847	1,184,439
Lubtheen	ME	B	1826-1877	1,185,004	Markobel	HN	BD	1849-1866	846,198
Lubtheen	ME	D	1883-1900	1,185,004	Markt	BA	BD	1821-1862	1,192,016
Lubz	ME	BMD	1813-1895	68,935					
Lubz	ME	B	1815-1907	1,185,004					
Lubz	ME	D	1816-1872	1,185,004					

Markt	BA	M	1839	1,192,016	Munchen	BY	Cem	?	1,272,273
Marlow	ME	BMD	1814-1866	68,936	Munchen	BY	B	1812-1875	1,272,271
Marlow	ME	D	1814-1866	1,185,007	Munchen	BY	D	1816-1845	1,272,272
Marlow	ME	B	1814-1868	1,185,007	Munchen	BY	M	1826-1864	1,272,271
Marlow	ME	M	1815-1873	1,185,007	Munchen	BY	D	1844-1876	1,272,273
Meckesheim	BA	BMD	1811-1869	1,192,036	Munchen	BY	M	1864-1940	1,272,272
Meckesheim	BA	BMD	1812-1869	1,188,241	Munster	PW	Nam	1801-1874	1,053,297
Mecklenburg-Schwerin	ME	BMD	1858-1865	1,185,013	Munzesheim	BA	BMD	1811-1870	1,192,033
Mecklenburg-Schwerin	ME	I/O	1912-1932	1,185,013	Muschenheim	HE	BMD	1835-1875	870,551
Mecklenburg-Schwerin	ME	I/O	1926-1933	1,185,007	Nakel	PN	BMD	1823-1867	715,115
Meimbressen	HN	M	1815-1873	848,666	Nakel	PN	Nam	1833-1835	1,184,443
Meimbressen	HN	B	1827-1889	848,666	Nakel	PN	BD	1848-1874	715,114
Meiningen	TH	B	1789-1838	1,192,045	Nakel	PN	M	1854-1867	715,114
Meiningen	TH	MD	1825-1838	1,192,045	Namslau	SC	D	1812-1842	1,184,443
Meiningen	TH	BMD	1839-1875	1,192,045	Namslau	SC	BM	1812-1847	1,184,443
Meiningen	TH	Fam	1850-1870	1,185,008	Namslau	SC	BM	1817-1832	1,184,443
Meiningen	TH	M	1862-1937	1,185,008	Namslau	SC	Cem	1914-1918	1,184,443
Meiningen	TH	BD	1867-1937	1,185,008	Naumburg (b Cassel)	HN	BMD	1808-1812	810,506
Melbach	HE	BMD	1826-1872	870,550	Neckar Steinach	HE	BMD	1824-1875	1,190,984
Melsungen	HN	BMD	1824-1852	810,924	Neckarbischofsheim	BA	BMD	1811-1874	1,334,619
Menzingen	BA	BMD	1800-1869	1,192,034	Neckarbischofsheim	BA	BMD	1841-1870	1,192,037
Menzingen	BA	B	1845-1869	1,056,385	Neckarzimmern	BA	BMD	1811-1869	1,192,036
Meppen	PH	BMD	1844-1877	1,272,992	Neidenstein	BA	MD	1842-1870	1,192,036
Merchingen	BA	BMD	1811-1870	1,055,127	Neisse	SC	B	1809-1928	1,184,443
Merchingen	BA	BMD	1811-1870	1,190,995	Neisse	SC	D	1813-1930	1,184,444
Merzhausen	HN	D	1811	801,306	Neisse	SC	M	1814-1928	1,184,444
Merzhausen	HN	D	1824-1866	801,306	Neisse	SC	I/O	1914-1938	1,184,444
Merzhausen	HN	BMD	1828-1883	801,306	Nesselroden	HN	BMD	1808-1812	810,509
Meseritz	PN	M	1817-1820	1,184,442	Netra	HN	BMD	1808-1812	810,509
Meseritz	PN	BMD	1817-1834	1,271,415	Netzwalde	PN	BMD	1823/1844	719,149
Meseritz	PN	B	1817-1840	1,184,442	Neubukow	ME	BM	1813-1876	1,185,010
Meseritz	PN	D	1835-1841	1,184,442	Neuenbrunslar	HN	BMD	1824-1852	817,495
Meseritz	PN	BMD	1835-1847	1,271,181	Neuenhaus	PH	M	1843-1869	1,336,576
Meseritz	PN	BMD	1847-1875	1,196,136	Neuenhaus	PH	D	1843-1873	1,336,576
Meseritz	PN	BMD	1847-1875	1,196,137	Neuenhaus	PH	B	1844-1880	1,336,576
Messel	HE	BMD	1823-1872	870,550	Neukalen	ME	BMD	1813-1875	68,936
Michelbach	WU	BM	1808-1872	1,195,662	Neukalen	ME	D	1813-1875	1,185,010
Michelbach	WU	M	1808-1872	1,195,662	Neukalen	ME	MD	1824-1875	1,185,010
Michelbach	WU	Fam	1810-1841	1,195,662	Neukirchen	HN	BD	1849-1875	849,086
Michelbach	WU	BMD	1863-1875	1,195,662	Neumarkt	SC	B	1818-1848	1,184,444
Michelbach	WU	M	1863-1875	1,195,662	Neumarkt	SC	Cen	1841	1,184,444
Michelbach	WU	D	1864-1875	1,195,662	Neumarkt	SC	M	1841-1847	1,184,444
Michelfeld	BA	BMD	1811-1870	1,192,032	Neumittelwalde	SC	B	1868-1883	1,184,441
Miechowitz	SC	M	1880,1885	1,184,442	Neumittelwalde	SC	Cem	1870-1906	1,184,444
Mingolsheim	BA	BMD	1811-1869	1,056,272	Neunstetten	BA	BMD	1813-1870	1,192,037
Mittelsinn	BY	B	1826-1830	801,307	Neustadt	ME	Fam	1811-1869	1,185,010
Mittelsinn	BY	D	1826-1855	801,307	Neustadt	ME	M	1870-1871	1,185,010
Mittelsinn	BY	M	1827-1829	801,307	Neustadt	ME	B	1870-1876	1,185,010
Mixstadt	PN	BD	1836-1840	746,949	Neustadt	ME	D	1874-1875	1,185,010
Mixstadt	PN	BMD	1841-1846	746,949	Neustadt (a/d Warthe)	PN	D	1820-1836	1,273,157
Momberg	HN	B	1856-1873	801,308	Neustadt	SC	I/O	1812-1824	1,184,444
Momberg	HN	D	1856-1873	801,309	Neustadt	SC	D	1816-1939	1,184,444
Muhlbach	BA	BMD	1812-1870	1,192,033	Neustadt	SC	B	1833-1874	1,184,444
Muhlbach	BA	BMD	1812-1870	1,273,377	Neustadt	SC	I/O	1838-1842	1,184,444
Muhlhausen	SA	B	1725-1935	1,185,009	Neustadtgodens	PH	BMD	1815-1874	1,257,053
Muhlhausen	SA	Cem	1808-1938	1,185,009	Neustettin	PO	Cem	1788-1870	1,184,444
Muhlhausen	SA	D	1809-1933	1,185,009	Neustettin	PO	Fam	1788-1870	1,184,444
Muhlhausen	SA	BMD	1809-1936	1,185,008	Nieder Eschbach	HE	BMD	1827-1875	870,551
Muhlhausen	SA	M	1812-1934	1,185,009	Nieder Mockstadt	HE	BMD	1823-1866	870,552
Muhlhausen	OS	Cem	1873-1938	1,185,009	Nieder Mockstadt	HE	BMD	1824-1847	1,194,056
Muhlheim	HE	Nam	1835-1875	1,185,009	Nieder Mockstadt	HE	BMD	1824-1847	1,273,149
Mulheim (Ruhr)	PR	B	1811	1,336,817	Nieder Mockstadt	HE	BMD	1824-1852	1,273,150
Mulheim (Ruhr)	PR	D	1822-1874	1,336,817	Nieder Mockstadt	HE	BMD	1847-1852	1,273,149
Mulheim (Ruhr)	PR	B	1823-1874	1,336,817	Nieder Ramstadt	HE	BMD	1823-1872	870,551
Mulheim (Ruhr)	PR	M	1825-1847	1,336,817	Niederklein	HN	BM	1809-1812	849,121
Mullheim	BA	BMD	1810-1870	1,192,017	Niederklein	HN	BD	1856-1871	849,122
Mullheim	BA	Cen	1812	1,192,017	Niedermeiser	HN	BMD	1808-1810	810,504
Mullrose	PS	D	1817-1831	1,185,009	Niederntudorf	PW	B	1643-1732	1,050,181
Mumling-Grumbach	HE	BMD	1825-1875	1,334,585	Niederrodenbach	HN	BD	1849-1867	850,173

Nordeck	HN	B	1850-1856	850,175	Ostfriesland	PH	Nam	1939	1,257,595
Nordeck	HN	D	1851-1869	850,176	Ostringen	BA	BMD	1810-1869	1,056,288
Nordeck	HN	D	1852-1856	50,175	Ostrowo	PN	Fam	1836-1838	1,271,464
Nordeck	HN	B	1853-1866	850,176	Ottenstein	BR	Fam	1768-1876	949,296
Norden	PH	B	1812-1874	1,257,053	Ottenstein	BR	Fam	1809	1,190,954
Norden	PH	M	1812-1884	1,257,053	Ottenstein	BR	BMD	1809-1813	958,004
Norden	PH	D	1812-1888	1,257,053	Otterstadt	BY	Nam	18??-19??	1,257,999
Norden	PH	M	1845-1884	1,257,053	Ottrau	HN	D	1824-1853	850,229
Norden	PH	D	1853-1874	1,257,053	Ottrau	HN	B	1824-1873	850,229
Nordenburg	OS	BMD	1848-1874	1,198,172	Ottrau	HN	D	1853,1868	850,229
Nordhausen	SA	Fam	1829-1830	1,185,010	Ottrau	HN	D	1872-1873	850,229
Nordhausen	SA	BMD	1830-1882	1,185,010	Padberg	PW	BMD	1804-1826	1,053,252
Nordhorn	PH	M	1845-1896	1,336,580	Paderborn	PW	Nam	1808-1894	1,269,996
Nordhorn	PH	D	1845-1933	1,336,580	Paderborn	PW	Nam	1810-1818	1,200,539
Nordhorn	PH	B	1847-1925	1,336,580	Pakosch	PN	BMD	1823-1847	719,232
Nurnberg	BY	Cen	1808-1840	1,334,620	Papenburg	PH	BMD	1864-1876	1,336,732
Nurnberg	BY	B	1857-1875	1,271,418	Parchim	ME	BMD	1813-1934	1,185,010
Nurnberg	BY	M	1857-1875	1,271,419	Parchim	ME	Nam	1936	1,185,010
Nurnberg	BY	D	1857-1875	1,271,420	Pasewalk	PO	D	1865-1906	1,185,010
Nurnberg	BY	Nam	1859-1861	1,190,974	Penzlin (Ag Penzlin)	ME	BMD	1814-1915	068,936
Nussloch	BA	BMD	1810-1870	1,188,251	Perleberg	PS	BMD	1812-1899	1,185,010
Ober Asphe	HN	B	1737-1810	828,635	Pfaffen Beerfurth	HE	BMD	1868-1874	870,555
Ober Asphe	HN	D	1804-1818	828,635	Pforzheim	BA	BMD	1810-1870	1,192,038
Ober Asphe	HN	BMD	1826-1847	850,177	Pforzheim	BA	BMD	1857-1869	1,190,972
Ober Erlenbach	HE	Nam	1875	870,553	Pfungstadt	HE	BMD	1823-1872	870,555
Ober Klingen	HE	BMD	1852-1875	870,553	Plau	ME	B	1813-1897	1,185,011
Ober Ramstadt	HE	B	1734-1763	1,197,101	Plau	ME	BMD	1813-1917	68,936
Ober Ramstadt	HE	Nam	18??	1,197,101	Plau	ME	D	1814-1913	1,185,011
Ober Ramstadt	HE	BMD	1823-1872	870,552	Plau	ME	M	1815-1889	1,185,011
Ober Seemen	HE	BMD	1826-1875	870,553	Plau	ME	Fam	1819	1,185,011
Ober Wollstadt	HE	BMD	1841-1857	870,553	Plaue	TH	D	18??-1920	1,185,011
Oberaula	HN	B	1824-1866	850,198	Plaue	TH	BMD	1825-1875	1,185,011
Oberaula	HN	D	1825-1863	850,198	Pleschen	PN	Nam	1834-1836	1,190,960
Oberaula	HN	D	1849-1850	850,199	Pleschen	PN	BMD	1835-1847	752,629
Oberaula	HN	B	1850	199	Pleschen	PN	D	1837-1839	1,190,960
Oberaula	HN	D	1850-1851	199	Pless	SC	BMD	1847-1874	1,184,446
Oberaula	HN	M	1858-1872	850,198	Pohl-gons	HE	B	1798-1807	1,195,311
Oberaula	HN	M	1867-1870	850,196	Pohl-gons	HE	D	1804	1,195,311
Obergrombach	BA	BMD	1811-1869	1,056,278	Pohl-gons	HE	M	1806	1,195,311
Obervorschutz	HN	BMD	1808-1812	810,517	Polzin	PO	D	1858-1936	1,184,446
Oberzell	HN	M	1826-1874	850,223	Potsdam	PS	Cem	1745-1933	1,185,011
Oberzell	HN	B	1826-1875	850,223	Potsdam	PS	Cem	1800-?	1,185,012
Oberzell	HN	D	1826-1878	850,223	Potsdam	PS	BMD	1810-1863	1,185,011
Obornik	PN	Nam	1835-1839	1,194,061	Potsdam	PS	Cem	1838-1939	1,185,012
Ockershausen	HN	B	1849-1868	850,224	Potsdam	PS	D	1906-1936	1,185,011
Ockershausen	HN	D	1850-1869	850,224	Prenzlau	PS	Fam	1843-1846	1,185,015
Odenheim	BA	BMD	1810-1869	1,056,284	Prenzlau	PS	D	1844-1940	1,185,015
Ohlau	SC	BMD	1817/1888	1,184,445	Preussisch Stargard	WP	B	1812-1874	414,467
Ohlau	SC	Cem	1818-1933	1,184,445	Preussisch Stargard	WP	D	1812-1939	414,468
Ols	SC	BMD	1812-1859	1,184,444	Preussisch Stargard	WP	M	1813-1874	414,468
Ols	SC	I/O	1812-1859	1,184,444	Preussisch Stargard	WP	M	1848-1874	414,468
Ols	SC	Cem	1830-1930	1,184,444	Preussisch Stargard	WP	Cem	1848-1904	1,184,446
Oppeln	SC	BMD	1812-1907	1,184,445	Preussisch Stargard	WP	D	1848-1904	1,184,446
Oppeln	SC	I/O	1822-1874	1,184,445	Preussisch Holland	OS	Cem	1825-1907	1,184,446
Oppeln	SC	I/O	1929-1938	1,184,445	Preussisch Holland	OS	D	1825-1907	1,184,446
Oranienburg	PS	D	1815-1839	1,185,010	Priemhausen	PO	B	1833-1837	1,190,966
Orlinghausen	LI	BMD	1848-1875	1,335,027	Pyritz	PO	Cen	1853	1,184,446
Orschweier	BA	BMD	1819/1870	1,186,615	Randegg	BA	BMD	1810-1869	1,273,450
Ortenburg	HE	BMD	1831-1875	870,554	Rappenau	BA	BMD	1813-1869	1,192,037
Ortenburg	HE	BMD	1834-1875	870,555	Rastenburg	OS	BMD	1813-1874	1,184,447
Osnabruck	PH	D	1844-1914	1,336,729	Rathenow	PS	BMD	1812-1847	1,334,618
Osnabruck	PH	B	1845-1880	1,336,729	Rathenow	PS	B	1848-1874	1,334,618
Osnabruck	PH	M	1852-1880	1,336,729	Ratibor	SC	M	1814-1862	1,184,449
Osterberg	BY	B	1849-1875	1,344,023	Ratibor	SC	B	1815-1847	1,184,449
Osterberg	BY	D	1849-1895	1,344,023	Ratibor	SC	D	1865-1930	1,184,448
Osterkappelen	PH	M	1809	1,336,731	Ratibor	SC	Cem	1888-1940	1,184,447
Osterkappelen	PH	B	1810	1,336,731	Rauischholzhausen	HN	BM	1811	851,356
Osterode	OS	BMD	1865-1936	71,081	Rauischholzhausen	HN	BD	1856-1873	851,356
Ostfriesland	PH	Nam	1723-1939	1,257,051	Rauschenberg	HN	BD	1856-1874	851,403

Rehna	ME	D	1813-1882	1,185,012	Rothenkirchen	HN	M	1811-1812	855,680
Rehna	ME	M	1814-1872	1,185,012	Ruckingen	HN	BD	1849-1868	855,680
Rehna	ME	BMD	1814-1882	68,936	Rudigershagen	SA	BMD	1818-1820	1,185,019
Rehna	ME	Fam	1819	1,185,012	Rudigershagen	SA	BMD	1832-1835	1,185,012
Rehna	ME	B	1856-1871	1,185,012	Rudigershagen	SA	M	1834-1866	1,185,012
Reichenbach	SC	Cem	1830-1930	1,184,449	Rudigershagen	SA	D	1834-1871	1,185,012
Reichenbach	SC	Nam	1889-1901	1,184,449	Rudigershagen	SA	B	1834-1874	1,185,012
Reilingen	BA	BMD	1811-1869	1,192,038	Rugenwalde	PO	B	1846-1861	1,184,450
Reinheim	HE	BMD	1823-1875	870,556	Ruttershausen	HE	BMD	1823-1875	870,557
Reiskirchen	HE	BMD	1823-1875	870,556	Sachsenflur	BA	BMD	1841-1866	1,055,304
Reitberg	PW	M	1810-1852	1,185,230	Sagan	SC	D	Ab1865	1,184,450
Rennertshausen	HN	BMD	1835-1846	851,405	Sagan	SC	Cem	1841-1937	1,184,450
Rheinbischofsheim	BA	BMD	1810-1843	1,192,019	Sagan	SC	Cem	1915-1918	1,184,450
Rheinbischofsheim	BA	BMD	1810-1869	1,256,663	Salmunster	HN	B	1835-1875	855,827
Rheinbischofsheim	BA	BMD	1844-1870	1,192,018	Salmunster	HN	M	1848-1873	855,827
Rheinland	PR	Nam	1808	1,190,930	Salmunster	HN	D	1849-1891	855,827
Rhina	HN	BMD	1811-1812	851,409	Salzuflen	LI	BMD	1809-1875	1,271,461
Rhoden	WA	BMD	1833-1858	1,184,449	Salzuflen	LI	BMD	1809-1875	1,273,155
Rhoden	WA	B	1859-1874	1,184,449	Sandersleben	AN	BMD	1795-1877	1,185,012
Ribnitz	ME	B	1812-1875	1,185,012	Sandhausen	BA	BMD	1810-1870	1,188,254
Richelsdorf	HN	BMD	1808-1812	810,525	Sandhausen	BA	BMD	1840-1857	1,192,039
Richelsdorf	HN	D	1851-1907	860,568	Sandhausen	BA	M	1858-1868	1,192,039
Richelsdorf	HN	M	1852-1912	860,568	Santomischel	PN	BMD	1817-1839	1,184,450
Richen	BA	BMD	1810-1869	1,186,397	Santomischel	PN	BMD	1817-1839	1,190,958
Richen	BA	BMD	1810-1870	1,273,377	Santomischel	PN	Nam	1834-1853	1,190,958
Riesenburg	WP	BMD	1823-1874	1,184,449	Schenklengsfeld	HN	M	1870-1874	858,003
Riesenburg	WP	B	1920	1,184,449	Schieder	LI	BMD	1809-1875	1,335,027
Rietberg	PW	M	1810-1852	1,185,230	Schiffelbach	HN	BD	1856	858,004
Rimbach	EL	Nam	1808	1,069,535	Schiffelbach	HN	D	1866,1868	858,004
Rimbach (Odenwald)	HE	BMD	1823-1858	870,556	Schildberg	PN	BMD	1835-1846	747,832
Rimbach (Odenwald)	HE	BMD	1831-1875	851,971	Schildesche	PW	BMD	1814-1847	1,190,971
Robel	ME	MD	1813-1874	1,185,012	Schildesche	PW	M	1847-1874	1,190,971
Robel	ME	B	1814-1915	1,185,012	Schildesche	PW	B	1847-1882	1,190,971
Roddenau	HN	D	1856-1874	851,409	Schlichtingsheim	PN	Nam	1756	1,184,450
Rodgen (Kr Giessen)	HE	BMD	1827-1855	870,557	Schlichtingsheim	PN	BMD	1819-1840	1,271,450
Rodigershagen	SA	BMD	1818-1820	1,185,019	Schlichtingsheim	PN	BMD	1819-1840	1,271,451
Rodigershagen	SA	BMD	1832-1835	1,185,012	Schlichtingsheim	PN	BMD	1835-1837	1,184,450
Rodigershagen	SA	MD	1834-1871	1,185,012	Schlichtingsheim	PN	M	1840-1843	1,184,450
Rogasen	PN	B	1817/1835	752,799	Schlichtingsheim	PN	M	1859	1,184,450
Rogasen	PN	BMD	1840-1847	752,800	Schloppe	WP	Fam	1750	1,184,450
Rohrbach (Heidelberg)	BA	BMD	1812-1869	1,192,039	Schluchtern	BA	BMD	1810-1869	1,192,040
Rohrbach (Sinsheim)	BA	BMD	1812-1870	1,192,039	Schluchtern	BA	BMD	1810-1869	1,194,076
Rohrenfurth	HN	BMD	1838-1852	851,410	Schluchtern	HN	BMD	1811-1812	811,120
Rollshausen	HN	B	1846-1863	853,745	Schluchtern	HN	M	1826-1874	850,223
Rollshausen	HN	D	1856-1866	853,745	Schluchtern	HN	MD	1826-1874	860,501
Rommelhausen	HE	BMD	1853-1870	870,557	Schluchtern	HN	B	1826-1875	850,223
Rosenberg	BA	BMD	1812-1869	1,055,132	Schluchtern	HN	D	1826-1878	850,223
Rosenberg	SC	BMD	1812-1847	1,184,449	Schluchtern	HN	B	1845-1874	860,501
Rosenberg	SC	I/O	1815-1847	1,184,449	Schluchtern	HN	M	1856-1857	858,026
Rosenberg	SC	I/O	1815-1847	1,184,450	Schluchtern	HN	M	1863-1871	858,030
Rosenberg	SC	D	1891-1938	1,184,449	Schluchtern	HN	M	1870	858,030
Rosenberg	WP	B	1847-1874	904,700	Schmalkalden	HN	BM	1824-1894	1,185,013
Rosenberg	WP	BMD	1847-1874	1,198,521	Schmalkalden	HN	D	1825-1921	1,185,013
Rosenthal (b Cassel)	HN	M	1808-1812	853,769	Schmalkalden	HN	Nam	1840	1,185,013
Rosenthal (b Cassel)	HN	M	1849-1867	853,760	Schmalkalden	HN	D	1849-1872	860,506
Rosenthal (b Cassel)	HN	M	1851	853,763	Schmalkalden	HN	B	1849-1874	860,506
Rossdorf	HE	BMD	1823-1872	870,543	Schonholthausen	PW	B	1804-1808	1,238,094
Rossdorf	HN	D	1856/1859	853,771	Schonholthausen	PW	D	1818	1,238,094
Rossdorf	HN	B	1857/1860	853,771	Schonholthausen	PW	B	1820	1,238,094
Rossdorf	HN	D	1868-1869	853,771	Schoningen	BR	BMD	1808-1812	958,254
Rossdorf	HE	M	1808-1875	868,405	Schoningen	BR	BMD	1818-1875	1,334,576
Rossdorf	HE	BMD	1823-1872	870,543	Schoningen	BR	BMD	1818-1876	949,296
Rossow (Dosse)	ME	BMD	1814-1845	68,936	Schonlanke	PN	BMD	1815-1834	1,190,959
Rostock	ME	BMD	1839-1874	68,936	Schonlanke	PN	B	1817-1847	1,184,451
Rotenburg (Fulda)	HN	M	1827/1832	853,783	Schonlanke	PN	D	1823-1847	1,184,451
Rotenburg (Fulda)	HN	M	1849-1874	853,780	Schonlanke	PN	M	1825-1847	1,184,451
Rotenburg (Fulda)	HN	M	1862-1872	853,778	Schonlanke	PN	BMD	1835-1847	1,190,975
Rotenburg (Fulda)	HN	M	1869-1874	853,788	Schonstadt	HN	B	1864-1865	860,511
Roth (Kr Biedenkopf)	HN	BMD	1824-1874	855,679	Schonstadt	HN	D	1866	860,511

Place	Region	Type	Years	Film
Schotmar	LI	BMD	1809-1875	1,335,027
Schrecksbach	HN	BD	1849-1874	860,512
Schriesheim	BA	BMD	1810-1870	1,257,316
Schriesheim	BA	BMD	1810-1870	1,271,255
Schriesheim	BA	BMD	1811-1869	1,192,040
Schrimm	PN	BMD	1817-1847	758,361
Schulitz	PN	BMD	1823-1847	719,152
Schwaan	ME	BMD	1813-1883	68,936
Schwaan	ME	BD	1813-1883	1,185,013
Schwaan	ME	M	1816-1858	1,185,013
Schwabach	BY	Nam	1813/1846	1,190,968
Schwabach	BY	Nam	1817-1827	1,190,974
Schwalenberg	LI	BMD	1809-1875	1,190,983
Schwarza	SA	BMD	1825-1875	1,185,013
Schwarzach	BA	BMD	1810-1870	1,057,395
Schwarzenborn	HN	D	1824-1872	860,517
Schwarzenborn	HN	B	1824-1874	860,517
Schwedt	PS	Fam	1750-1815	1,185,013
Schwedt	PS	B	1775-1809	1,185,013
Schwedt	PS	D	1812-1860	1,185,013
Schwedt	PS	BMD	1812-1860	1,190,968
Schweidnitz	SC	BMD	1854-1875	1,184,451
Schweinsberg	HN	BMD	1809-1812	860,535
Schweinsberg	HN	B	1856-1872	860,535
Schweinsberg	HN	D	1856-1874	860,535
Schwerin	ME	D	1849-1869	1,185,014
Schwerin	ME	B	1852-1875	1,185,014
Schwerin	ME	M	1856-1874	1,185,014
Schwerin	PN	BM	1808-1817	1,184,452
Schwerin	PN	D	1808-1844	1,184,454
Schwerin	PN	BMD	1817-1835	1,184,452
Schwerin	PN	B	1835-1838	1,184,452
Schwerin	PN	M	1836-1847	1,184,454
Schwerin	PN	Nam	1838-1862	1,190,959
Schwerin	PN	B	1839-1846	1,184,453
Schwerin	PN	D	1845-1847	1,184,455
Schwerin	PN	B	1847	1,184,454
Schwerin	PN	D	1875-1918	1,184,455
Seckmauern	HE	BMD	1844-1874	1,194,045
Seebach	BY	Nam	1808-1810	587,607
Seelow	PS	D	1800-1876	1,185,014
Sennfeld	BA	BMD	1811-1869	1,055,135
Sennfeld	BA	BMD	1811-1870	1,192,042
Sennfeld	BA	Fam	1855-1866	1,192,041
Siemianowitz	SC	I/O	1856-1862	1,184,434
Siemianowitz	SC	M	1880	1,184,434
Sierenz	EL	Nam	1808	783,352
Sindolsheim	BA	BMD	1810-1870	1,055,137
Sindolsheim	BA	BMD	1812-1870	1,192,041
Sinsheim	BA	BMD	1812-1870	1,192,041
Sodel	HE	BMD	1823-1861	870,557
Sogel	PH	BMD	1845-1891	1,336,739
Sohrau	SC	D	1837-1879	1,184,456
Soldin	PS	BMD	1833-1847	1,184,456
Sontra	HN	BMD	1808-1809	811,128
Sontra	HN	BMD	1810-1811	811,129
Sontra	HN	BMD	1812	811,128
Sontra	HN	B	1820-1825	860,568
Sontra	HN	M	1827-1909	860,568
Sontra	HN	D	1827-1934	860,568
Spachbrocken	HE	BMD	1823-1875	870,559
Spangenberg	HN	BMD	1808-1810	810,872
Spangenberg	HN	BMD	1808-1812	810,873
Speckswinkel	HN	BMD	1808-1861	860,106
Sprottau	SC	I/O	1813-1845	1,184,456
Sprottau	SC	BMD	1813-1847	1,184,456
Sprottau	SC	Fam	1816	1,184,456
Sprottau	SC	Cem	1817-1933	1,184,456
Sprottau	SC	D	1817-1933	1,184,456
Staden	HE	BMD	1823-1852	1,273,149
Staden	HE	BMD	1823-1852	1,273,150
Staden	HE	BMD	1823-1870	870,557
Stadtlengsfeld	TH	B	1720-1813	1,185,014
Stadtlengsfeld	TH	MD	1809-1813	1,185,014
Stadtlengsfeld	TH	BMD	1817-1838	1,184,485
Stadtlengsfeld	TH	BMD	1817-1838	1,185,015
Stadtlengsfeld	TH	Fam	1823	1,185,017
Stadtlengsfeld	TH	B	1838-1858	1,184,482
Stadtlengsfeld	TH	M	1838-1858	1,184,484
Stadtlengsfeld	TH	D	1838-1858	1,184,487
Stadtlengsfeld	TH	BMD	1838-1875	1,185,016
Stadtlengsfeld	TH	Cem	1840-1936	1,185,017
Stadtlengsfeld	TH	D	1845-1931	1,185,017
Stadtlengsfeld	TH	M	1857-1893	1,184,484
Stadtlengsfeld	TH	M	1857-1893	1,184,485
Stadtlengsfeld	TH	D	1858-1906	1,184,488
Stadtlengsfeld	TH	B	1859-1904	1,184,483
Stadtlengsfeld	TH	Nam	1872-1939	1,184,486
Stadtlengsfeld	TH	M	1894-1906	1,184,485
Stadtoldendorf	BR	Fam	1774-1876	949,296
Stadtoldendorf	BR	BMD	1809	957,306
Stadtoldendorf	BR	Fam	1809	1,190,954
Staedtel	SC	M	1810-1852	1,184,456
Staedtel	SC	B	1810-1870	1,184,456
Staedtel	SC	D	1812-1873	1,184,456
Stammheim	HE	BMD	1826-1852	1,273,150
Stammheim	HE	BMD	1826-1870	870,558
Stammhein	HE	BMD	1826-1852	1,273,149
Stargard	PO	Nam	1761	1,184,456
Stargard	PO	BMD	1812-1849	1,190,966
Stassfurt	SA	Cem	1874-1902	1,185,017
Staufenberg	HE	BMD	1829-1846	870,558
Stavenhagen	HE	BMD	1848-1867	68,936
Stebbach	BA	D	1811-1869	1,192,046
Stebbach	BA	BM	1811-1870	1,192,042
Stebbach	BA	BMD	1813-1869	1,194,076
Stebbach	BA	BMD	1813-1870	1,186,401
Steinach	BY	BMD	1812-1895	1,190,994
Steinbach	HE	BMD	1825-1875	870,558
Steinberg	HE	BMD	1824-1875	870,560
Steinfurth	HE	BMD	1863-1872	870,558
Steinheim	PW	BMD	1803-1825	1,057,959
Steinsfurt	BA	BMD	1813-1869	1,192,043
Stendal	SA	BMD	1816-1846	1,334,570
Stendal	SA	BMD	1847-1874	1,271,459
Stendal	SA	Nam	1852-1880	1,185,017
Sterbfritz	HN	BMD	1826-1874	860,133
Sternberg	ME	B	1806-1890	1,185,017
Sternberg	ME	D	1824-1937	1,185,017
Sternberg	ME	M	1838-1870	1,185,017
Sternberg-Barntrup	LI	BMD	1809-1875	1,335,027
Sterzhausen	HN	BD	1849-1865	860,134
Stettin	PO	Nam	1841-1847	1,184,457
Stettin	PO	D	1845-1849	1,184,457
Stettin	PO	Nam	1850-1880	1,184,457
Stettin	PO	BD	1854-1874	1,184,458
Stettin	PO	M	1901-1939	1,184,458
Stockheim	HE	BMD	1837-1875	870,559
Stolberg	PR	Nam	1808	1,334,572
Stolberg (Harz)	SA	BMD	1809-1847	1,334,573
Stollhofen	BA	BMD	1809-1870	1,057,400
Stolp	PO	BMD	1813-1848	1,334,572
Stolp	PO	BMD	1840-1847	1,334,580
Stolp	PO	BMD	1840-1875	1,334,580
Storkow	PS	Nam	1818-1848	1,273,304
Strelitz	MS	D	1760-1923	1,185,018
Strelitz	MS	Cem	1820-1888	1,185,018
Striegau	SC	BD	1850-1939	1,184,458

Striegau	SC	Cem	1850-1939	1,184,458	Viernheim	HE	BMD	1823-1875	1,271,458
Stuhm	WP	Cem		1,184,458	Volkershausen	SW	BMD	1818-1875	1,185,021
Sudlohn	PW	BMD	1819-1847	1,049,389	Volkershausen	TH	BMD	1817-1838	1,184,485
Suhl	SA	BMD	1817-1838	1,184,485	Volkershausen	TH	BMD	1818-1875	1,185,021
Suhl	SA	B	1838-1858	1,184,482	Volkershausen	TH	B	1838-1858	1,184,482
Suhl	SA	M	1838-1858	1,184,484	Volkershausen	TH	M	1838-1858	1,184,484
Suhl	SA	D	1838-1858	1,184,487	Volkershausen	TH	D	1838-1858	1,184,487
Suhl	SA	M	1857-1893	1,184,484	Volkershausen	TH	M	1857-1893	1,184,484
Suhl	SA	M	1857-1893	1,184,485	Volkershausen	TH	M	1857-1893	1,184,485
Suhl	SA	D	1858-1906	1,184,488	Volkershausen	TH	D	1858-1906	1,184,488
Suhl	SA	B	1859-1904	1,184,483	Volkershausen	TH	B	1859-1904	1,184,483
Suhl	SA	Nam	1872-1939	1,184,486	Volkershausen	TH	Nam	1872-1939	1,184,486
Suhl	SA	M	1894-1906	1,184,485	Volkershausen	TH	M	1894-1906	1,184,485
Sulz	EL	Fam	1925	1,071,437	Vollmerz	HN	B	1780-1887	858,305
Sulze (Ag Sulze)	ME	BMD	1815-1904	68,936	Vollmerz	HN	D	1826-1884	858,305
Sulze (Ag Sulze)	ME	BD	1815-1904	1,185,018	Vollmerz	HN	M	1828-1882	858,305
Tangermunde	SA	BMD	1815-1846	1,334,570	Vorden	PW	BMD	1808-1814	1,185,212
Tangermunde	SA	Nam	1820-1860	1,185,018	Wachenbuchen	HN	BD	1849-1869	858,305
Tarnowitz	SC	BMD	1847/1870	877,402	Waldbreitbach	PR	BMD	1828-1847	1,190,979
Tarnowitz	SC	B	1813-1855	1,184,458	Waldbreitbach	PR	BD	1857-1874	1,190,979
Tarnowitz	SC	D	1813-1871	1,184,458	Waldenburg	SC	BMD	1934-1938	1,184,461
Tarnowitz	SC	D	1817-1885	1,184,459	Waldhausen	BA	BMD	1810-1870	1,057,175
Tarnowitz	SC	M	1824-1854	1,184,458	Walldorf	TH	BMD	1818-1875	1,185,021
Tarnowitz	SC	D	1895-1901	1,184,460	Walldorf	TH	Nam	1827,1829	1,185,022
Tempelburg	PO	BD	1829-1852	1,184,460	Walldorf	TH	B	1839-1925	1,185,021
Tessin (Ag Tessin)	ME	BMD	1813-1885	1,185,018	Walldorf	TH	M	1839-1932	1,185,022
Teterow	ME	B	1813-1880	1,185,018	Walldorf	TH	D	1839-1938	1,185,022
Teterow	ME	M	1814-1864	1,185,018	Walldorf	TH	B	1872-1873	1,185,022
Thann	EL	Nam	1808	764,708	Walldorf	TH	Cem	1881-1938	1,185,022
Themar	TH	Fam	1820-1920	1,185,018	Walldurn	BA	BMD	1816-1869	1,334,583
Themar	TH	B	1876-1938	1,185,018	Wanfried	HN	BMD	1808-1812	859,944
Tirschtiegel	PN	Nam	1834-1848	1,184,460	Wankheim	WU	BMD	1778-1875	1,190,991
Tost	SC	D	1841-1872	1,184,461	Warburg	PW	BMD	1809-1822	1,273,148
Tost	SC	M	1886	1,184,461	Warburg	PW	BMD	1822-1847	1,335,036
Trachenberg	SC	Cem	?	1,184,461	Waren	ME	B	1813-1886	1,185,023
Trebbin (Kr Teltow)	PS	Nam	1692-1812	1,185,020	Waren	ME	M	1814-1881	1,185,023
Trebbin (Kr Teltow)	PS	I/O	1700-1800	1,185,020	Waren	ME	D	1814-1889	1,185,023
Trebbin (Kr Teltow)	PS	Nam	1742-1800	1,185,020	Waren	ME	Nam	1843-1871	1,185,023
Trebbin (Kr Teltow)	PS	Nam	1801	1,185,019	Warendorf	PW	BMD	1816-1848	1,190,961
Tremessen	PN	BMD	1832-1847	719,242	Warendorf	PW	BMD	1822-1849	1,334,613
Treysa	HN	B	1824-1902	858,243	Warin	ME	BMD	1815-1876	1,185,023
Trier	PR	Nam	1808	1,190,930	Warin	ME	M	1815-1876	1,185,023
Tumringen	BA	Fam	1827-1867	1,192,015	Warstein	PW	M	1806-1807	1,053,248
Tumringen	BA	Fam	1827-1870	1,192,018	Warstein	PW	B	1819	1,053,248
Uffholz	EL	Nam	1784-1788	759,597	Warstein	PW	D	1824	1,053,248
Uffholz	EL	Nam	1808-1811	759,597	Wasserlos	BY	BMD	1811-1825	1,190,994
Ulrichstein	HE	B	1746-1835	1,201,598	Watzenborn	HE	BMD	1824-1875	870,560
Ulrichstein	HE	Cir	1769-1796	1,201,598	Weckensheim	HE	BMD	1836-1872	870,560
Ulrichstein	HE	BM	1797-1808	1,201,598	Weener	PH	BMD	1844-1939	1,257,053
Ulrichstein	HE	D	1798-1806	1,201,598	Weener	PH	BMD	1859-1860	1,187,668
Ulsen	PH	BMD	1844-1875	1,336,744	Wegeleben	SA	Nam	1731-1813	1,184,497
Ungedanken	HN	BMD	1808-1812	810,880	Wegeleben	SA	B	1733-1815	1,184,497
Unrukstadt	PN	BMD	1817-1874	1,184,461	Wehrda (Kr Marburg)	HN	B	1849-1866	859,948
Unrukstadt	PN	Nam	1848,1834	1,334,579	Weiler	BA	BMD	1811-1869	1,192,043
Untergrombach	BA	BMD	1815-1869	1,056,392	Weimar	TH	BMD	1817-1838	1,184,485
Unterschupf	BA	BMD	1811-1869	1,192,043	Weimar	TH	B	1838-1858	1,184,482
Unterschupf	BA	BMD	1813-1870	1,055,313	Weimar	TH	M	1838-1858	1,184,484
Usenborn	HE	BMD	1829-1875	870,559	Weimar	TH	D	1838-1858	1,184,487
Uttrichshausen	HN	BMD	1837-1873	858,246	Weimar	TH	M	1857-1893	1,184,484
Vacha	SW	B	1813-1916	1,185,021	Weimar	TH	M	1857-1893	1,184,485
Vacha	SW	D	1818-1876	1,185,019	Weimar	TH	D	1858-1906	1,184,488
Vacha	SW	D	1839-1920	1,185,021	Weimar	TH	B	1859-1904	1,184,483
Vacha	SW	M	1840-1899	1,185,021	Weimar	TH	Nam	1872-1939	1,184,486
Vacha	TH	B	1815-1875	1,185,019	Weimar	TH	M	1894-1906	1,184,485
Vacha	TH	M	1840-1899	1,185,021	Weingarten	BA	BMD	1810-1824	1,271,329
Vandsburg	WP	BMD	1825-1847	719,323	Weingarten	BA	BMD	1810-1869	1,271,330
Varenholz	LI	BMD	1809-1875	1,190,983	Weingarten	BA	BMD	1824-1869	1,271,328
Veldhausen	PH	B	1743-1824	1,336,745	Weinheim	BA	BMD	1811-1869	1,192,044
Veldhausen	PH	BMD	1843-1874	1,336,745	Weissenfels	SA	D	1883-1937	1,185,023

Weiterstadt	HE	BMD	1823-1872	870,561	Wolfenbuttel	BR	BMD	1808-1810	1,334,577
Wenings	HE	BMD	1834-1875	871,590	Wolfenbuttel	BR	BMD	1808-1814	958,025
Wenzen	BR	M	1812	1,334,577	Wolferode	HN	BD	1856-1873	864,624
Werne	PW	M	1822-1865	1,190,961	Wolfhaugen	HN	BMD	1808-1810	810,895
Werne	PW	B	1822-1873	1,190,961	Wollenberg	BA	BMD	1811-1869	1,192,046
Werne	PW	D	1822-1875	1,190,961	Wollin	PO	BMD	1813-1874	1,334,576
Westheim	BY	BMD	1820-1876	1,190,961	Worlitz	AN	BMD	1838-1844	1,185,023
Wettolsheim	EL	B	1719-1793	1,069,533	Worms	HE	Nam	1808,1824	1,335,027
Wettolsheim	EL	Nam	1808	1,069,533	Worms	HE	Nam	1832	1,335,027
Wieschowa	SC	BD	1847-1848	877,421	Wreschen	PN	Fam	1834	1,190,958
Wiesloch	BA	BMD	1811-1824	1,192,043	Wreschen	PN	M	1859-1860	1,186,460
Wieszcyczyn	PN	BMD	1832-1847	719,244	Wreschen	PN	D	1867-1869	1,186,460
Wilatowen	PN	BMD	1832-1847	719,244	Wriezen	PS	BMD	1813-1847	1,334,573
Willingshausen	HN	M	1793-1812	864,610	Wriezen	PS	Fam	1824-1834	1,185,023
Willingshausen	HN	BD	1849-1873	864,610	Wriezen	PS	BMD	1839-1847	1,185,023
Wimpfen	HE	BMD	1813-1833	1,334,574	Wronke	PN	Nam	1832,1835	1,184,461
Wimpfen	HE	BMD	1838-1874	1,334,574	Wronke	PN	Nam	1842	1,184,461
Windecken	HN	BMD	1825-1874	864,611	Wusterhausen	PS	BMD	1814-1874	1,185,023
Windecken	HN	BD	1849-1869	864,611	Zabrze	SC	Cem	1873-1940	1,184,419
Winzenheim	EL	Nam	1808	764,668	Zabrze	SC	Cem	1882-1926	1,184,419
Wittelsberg	HN	BMD	1849-1865	868,036	Zanow	PO	BMD	1848-1874	1,190,970
Wittenburg	ME	BMD	1813-1877	68,936	Zduny (Kr Krotoschin)	PN	MD	1818-1846	765,799
Wittenheim	EL	Nam	1808	764,856	Zduny (Kr Krotoschin)	PN	D	1835-1847	765,799
Wittmund	PH	D	1723-1930	1,257,054	Zeitlofs	BY	BMD	1812-1875	1,335,039
Wittmund	PH	B	1804-1882	1,257,054	Zerbst	AN	BMD	1781-1933	1,185,024
Wittmund	PH	M	1844-1872	1,257,054	Ziegenhain	HN	M	1848-1866	868,684
Wittmund	PH	D	1844-1875	1,257,054	Ziegenhain	HN	B	1849-1873	868,694
Wittstock	PS	Cem	1806-1907	1,185,023	Zimmersrode	HN	BMD	1809-1812	868,618
Wixhausen	HE	BMD	1823-1872	871,591	Zuntersbach	HN	BMD	1827-1875	868,618
Wohnbach	HE	BMD	1823-1875	871,591	Zwingenberg	BA	BMD	1823-1866	1,185,169
Wolbeck	PW	BMD	1822-1879	1,190,955	Zwingenberg	HE	B	1732-1805	1,340,367
Woldenburg	PS	M	1770-1854	1,184,461	Zwingenberg	HE	B	1808	1,340,369
Woldenburg	PS	B	1778-1800	1,184,461	Zwibrucken	BY	Nam	1808	1,334,573
Woldenburg	PS	D	1795-1854	1,184,461					
Woldenburg	PS	B	1807-1854	1,184,461					
Wolfenbuttel	BR	Fam	1775-1852	949,296					

Reprinted from *Avotaynu*, Vol. III, No. 1, Winter 1987.

Hungarian-Jewish Records at the Family History Library, Salt Lake City, Utah

See "Jewish Collections at the Family History Library" (Utah), p. 131.

Listed below are the microfilm numbers for the Jewish vital statistic records designated as Hungary in the possession of the Family History Library as of October 1985. The current Family History Library Catalog is available on microfiche and on compact disk at LDS Family History Centers.

Each entry contains town name, abbreviation of county, a legend describing the nature of the documents, year(s) represented, and microfilm number.

Abbreviation of counties:

AT	Abauj-Torna
BA	Baranya
BE	Bekes
BI	Bihar
BB	Bacs-Bodrog
BO	Borsod
CN	Csanad
CS	Csongrad
ES	Esztergom
FE	Fejer
GY	Gyor
HA	Hajdu
HE	Heves
JA	Jasz-Nagy-Kun-Szolnok
KO	Komarom
MO	Moson
NO	Nograd
PE	Pest-Pilis-Solt-BB Kis-Kun
SA	Saros
SO	Somogy
SP	Sopron
ST	Szatmar
SZ	Szabolcs
TO	Tolna
VA	Vas
VE	Veszprem
ZA	Zala
ZE	Zemplen

Nature of Material

B	Births
M	Marriages
D	Deaths
BI	Birth index
MI	Marriage Index
DI	Death Index
Cen	Census
Fam	Family Register

Important Note! There was a census of Jews in 1848 of which only the following counties survive. The number in parentheses is the microfilm number.

(718823) Baranya, Bekes, Bihar, Csanad, Csongrad, Esztergom, Fejer, Gyor, Hajdu, Komarom, Szolnok, Krasso, Kraszna, Maramaros, Moson and Szabolca.
(719825) Tolna.
(719826) Trencsen, Turocz, Ung.
(719827) Vas, Veszprem.
(719828) Zala.

Dates are represented in one of four ways. If there is a single year, the information is for that year only. If the two years are separated by a comma (1823,1855), only those two years are represented. If there are two years separated by a slash (1823/1855), the records are inclusive of those years with a significant number of years missing within the time period. If there are two years separated by a dash (1823–1855), the records are inclusive of all the years, possibly with minor exceptions.

There have been a substantial number of town name changes in the past 150 years. The list has references for each name. For example, the town of Keresztes is also shown as Mezokeresztes and Beharkeresztes. The exception is Budapest. All prior names are listed as "Budapest" only.

If a town is not represented on the list, do not assume there are no Jewish records for the town. What is shown below is a listing of only those records classified as Jewish Records. It is possible that the town of interest has other records, such as civil records. For example, there were a great number of censuses in Hungary during the 19th century. It is wise to check the catalog at a local Family History Center to see if other records of the town exist.

Aba	FE	BMD	1800-1895	642,794
Abaujszanto	BO	BMD	1842-1888	642,726
Abaujszanto	BO	BMD	1888-1895	642,727
Abony	PE	BMD	1837-1895	642,846
Acs	KO	BMD	1868-1895	642,837
Adand	SO	BMD	1845-1895	642,880
Adony	FE	BMD	1850-1885	642,794
Ajak	SZ	BMD	1876-1895	642,900
Akaszto	PE	BD	1883-1890	642,848
Albertirsa	PE	BMD	1847-1895	642,848
Almosd	BI	BMD	1852-1885	642,750
Alpar	PE	BD	1883-1885	642,849
Alsodabas	PE	BMD	1850-1895	642,851
Alsohahot	ZA	BMD	1871-1895	642,946
Anarcs	SZ	BMD	1876-1895	642,900

Apagy	SS	BMD	1849-1886	642,900	Bojt	BI	BMD	1876-1886	642,753
Apostag	PE	BMD	1825-1895	642,849	Bolcske	TO	BMD	1846-1885	642,924
Asszonyfa	GY	BMD	1853-1885	642,847	Boldogasszony	MO	BMD	1835-1895	700,859
Aszod	PE	B	1837-1895	642,849	Bolyok	BO	BMD	1867-1895	642,777
Aszod	PE	MD	1856-1895	642,849	Bonyhad	TO	BMD	1851-1895	642,923
Bacsbokod	BB	BMD	1858-1885	642,728	Budaabrany	SZ	BMD	1867-1884	642,759
Baja	BB	B	1853-1885	642,728	Budapest (Buda)	PE	B	1820-1895	642,991
Baja	BB	D	1853-1877	642,729	Budapest (Buda)	PE	M	1823-1885	642,991
Baja	BB	M	1853-1895	642,729	Budapest (Buda)	PE	D	1831-1895	642,992
Baja	BB	D	1877-1895	642,730	Budapest (Buda)	PE	BM	1876-1895	642,993
Baja	BB	B	1886-1895	642,729	Budapest (Buda)	PE	M	1886-1895	642,992
Bajai District	BB	BMD	1886-1895	642,730	Budapest (Kobanya)	PE	BM	1876-1895	642,993
Baka	SZ	BMD	1876-1885	642,916	Budapest (Kobanya)	PE	D	1885-1895	642,993
Bakonszeg	BI	BMD	1876-1885	642,750	Budapest (Obuda)	PE	B	1802-1885	642,994
Bakonyszentkiraly	VE	B	1840-1884	642,940	Budapest (Obuda)	PE	BI	1803-1895	642,997
Baksa	BA	Cen	1850	642,741	Budapest (Obuda)	PE	Fam	1850	642,997
Baksa	BA	B	1851-1895	642,741	Budapest (Obuda)	PE	D	1851-1873	642,995
Baksa	BA	D	1851-1879	642,741	Budapest (Obuda)	PE	DI	1851-1895	642,997
Baksa	BA	M	1851-1889	642,741	Budapest (Obuda)	PE	M	1851-1895	642,995
Balassagyarmat	NO	B	1850-1878	642,841	Budapest (Obuda)	PE	D	1874-1895	642,996
Balassagyarmat	NO	BMD	1850-1880	642,840	Budapest (Obuda)	PE	B	1886-1895	642,995
Balassagyarmat	NO	D	1850-1867	642,841	Budapest (Obuda)	PE	BMD	1889-1895	642,997
Balassagyarmat	NO	M	1850-1895	642,841	Budapest (Pest)	PE	B	1836-1851	642,961
Balassagyarmat	NO	D	1886-1895	642,841	Budapest (Pest)	PE	BI	1836-1874	642,986
Balatonboglar	SO	B	1768-1883	642,880	Budapest (Pest)	PE	D	1836-1846	642,976
Balatonfokajar	VE	BMD	1815-1895	642,940	Budapest (Pest)	PE	DI	1836-1884	642,988
Balatonfured	ZA	BMD	1863-1895	642,945	Budapest (Pest)	PE	M	1836-1859	642,973
Balkany	SZ	BMD	1845-1862	642,900	Budapest (Pest)	PE	MI	1836-1879	642,987
Balkany	SZ	BMD	1853-1895	642,901	Budapest (Pest)	PE	D	1847-1860	642,977
Balmazujvaros	HA	BMD	1876-1895	642,807	Budapest (Pest)	PE	M	1848-1866	642,985
Ban	BA	BMD	1851-1895	642,732	Budapest (Pest)	PE	B	1851-1862	642,962
Baracska	FE	BD	1842-1872	642,794	Budapest (Pest)	PE	M	1851-1871	642,974
Baracska	BB	BMD	1853-1885	642,731	Budapest (Pest)	PE	D	1861-1867	642,978
Barand	BI	BM	1877-1895	642,750	Budapest (Pest)	PE	B	1863-1867	642,963
Bataszek	TO	BMD	1851-1895	642,922	Budapest (Pest)	PE	B	1868-1871	642,964
Bataszek	TO	Fam	1851-1870	642,922	Budapest (Pest)	PE	D	1868-1875	642,979
Batmonostor	B	BMD	1854-1884	642,731	Budapest (Pest)	PE	M	1871-1885	642,990
Batorkeszi	ES	BMD	1834-1867	642,791	Budapest (Pest)	PE	M	1871-1888	642,975
Battonya	CN	BMD	1851-1895	642,780	Budapest (Pest)	PE	B	1872-1876	642,965
Becske	NO	BMD	1856-1882	642,841	Budapest (Pest)	PE	B	1872-1895	642,990
Bedo	BI	BMD	1880-1885	642,750	Budapest (Pest)	PE	BI	1875-1892	642,987
Bekes	BE	B	1851-1895	642,742	Budapest (Pest)	PE	B	1876-1879	642,966
Bekes	BE	MD	1855-1895	642,742	Budapest (Pest)	PE	D	1876-1878	720,185
Bekescsaba	BE	B	1820-1885	642,743	Budapest (Pest)	PE	B	1879-1882	642,967
Bekescsaba	BE	BMD	1832-1895	642,744	Budapest (Pest)	PE	D	1879-1883	642,980
Bekescsaba	BE	MD	1850-1895	642,745	Budapest (Pest)	PE	MI	1880-1895	642,988
Bekescsaba	BE	B	1881-1895	642,745	Budapest (Pest)	PE	B	1882-1886	642,968
Bekesszentandras	BE	BMD	1850-1885	642,745	Budapest (Pest)	PE	D	1884-1886	642,981
Beled	SP	BMD	1836-1895	642,897	Budapest (Pest)	PE	DI	1885-1895	642,989
Belsbocs	BO	B	1864-1885	642,765	Budapest (Pest)	PE	MD	1885	642,986
Bercel	SZ	BMD	1854-1895	642,916	Budapest (Pest)	PE	B	1886-1888	642,969
Bercel	NO	BMD	1884-1888	642,841	Budapest (Pest)	PE	D	1886-1888	642,982
Beregboszormeny	BI	BMD	1877-1885	642,751	Budapest (Pest)	PE	M	1888-1895	642,976
Berencs	SZ	BMD	1886-1895	642,916	Budapest (Pest)	PE	B	1889-1890	642,970
Berettyoszentmarton	BI	BMD	1878-1895	642,751	Budapest (Pest)	PE	D	1889-1892	642,983
Berettyoujfalu	BI	BMD	1846-1895	642,752	Budapest (Pest)	PE	B	1890-1892	642,971
Besenyod	SZ	BMD	1849-1885	642,902	Budapest (Pest)	PE	D	1890-1895	642,990
Bezded	SZ	BMD	1876-1885	642,916	Budapest (Pest)	PE	B	1892-1894	642,972
Bezi	GY	BMD	1839-1885	642,803	Budapest (Pest)	PE	D	1892-1894	642,984
Bicske	FE	BMD	1886-1895	642,795	Budapest (Pest)	PE	B	1894-1895	642,973
Biharkeresztes	BI	BMD	1877-1892	642,753	Budapest (Pest)	PE	D	1895	642,985
Biharnagybajom	BI	BMD	1845-1895	642,753	Budszentmihaly	SZ	BM	1856-1895	642,917
Bihartorda	BI	BMD	1877-1886	642,753	Budszentmihaly	SZ	D	1862-1895	642,917
Biharugra	BI	BMD	1877-1885	642,753	Cece	FE	BMD	1844-1895	642,795
Bikity	BB	BMD	1858-1885	642,728	Cegled	PE	BMD	1850-1895	642,850
Bocs	BO	B	1864-1885	642,765	Celldomolk	VA	BMD	1877-1895	642,933
Bodrogkeresztur	ZE	BMD	1827-1895	642,952	Cinkota	PE	BMD	1878-1882	642,851
Bogat	SZ	BMD	1851-1885	642,913	Csaba	BO	BMD	1851-1895	624,094
Boglar	SO	B	1768-1883	642,880	Csabrendek	ZA	B	1771-1895	642,945

Place	County	Type	Years	Film
Csabrendek	ZA	BMD	1828-1895	642,946
Csatalja	BB	BMD	1853-1885	642,731
Csecse	NO	BMD	1850-1895	642,841
Csege	HA	BMD	1873-1885	642,763
Csenger	ST	D	1851-1895	642,919
Csenger	ST	B	1886-1895	642,919
Csepreg	SP	BMD	1886-1895	642,898
Csokmo	BI	BMD	1854-1895	642,754
Csongrad	CS	BMD	1841-1895	642,781
Csorna	SP	BMD	1850-1895	642,898
Csurgo	SO	B	1776-1895	642,881
Csurgo	SO	BMD	1848-1895	642,882
Csurgo	SO	D	1856-1895	642,882
Csurgo	SO	M	1856-1895	642,881
Dabas	PE	BMD	1850-1895	642,851
Darda	BA	BMD	1851-1895	642,732
Darvas	BI	BMD	1877-1895	642,754
Dautova	BB	BMD	1853-1894	642,731
Davod	BB	BMD	1853-1894	642,731
Debrecen	HA	B	1856-1895	642,807
Debrecen	HA	M	1856-1895	642,808
Debrecen	HA	D	1859-1895	642,808
Debrecen	HA	BMD	1870-1895	642,808
Debrecen	HA	Cen	1870	722,262
Debrecen	HA	Cen	1870	722,263
Debrelen	HA	Cen	1848	719,823
Derecske	BI	BMD	1871-1895	642,755
Derzs	ST	M	1876-1885	642,920
Devavanya	JA	BMD	1846-1895	642,827
Diosgyor	BO	BMD	1859-1895	642,765
Doge	SZ	BMD	1886-1895	642,902
Dombovar	TO	B	1851-1895	642,924
Dombovar	TO	M	1874-1895	642,924
Dombovar	TO	D	1886-1895	642,924
Dombrad	SZ	BMD	1876-1895	642,902
Domony	PE	BMD	1840-1884	642,851
Domsod	PE	BMD	1876-1882	642,851
Dunafoldvar	TO	BMD	1851-1895	642,925
Dunafoldvar	TO	BMD	1852-1895	642,926
Dunapataj	PE	BMD	1850-1895	642,852
Dunapentele	FE	BMD	1843-1895	642,795
Dunaujvaros	FE	BMD	1843-1895	642,795
Ecser	PE	BD	1869-1883	642,852
Eger	HE	BM	1840-1895	642,815
Eger	HE	D	1850-1895	642,816
Egyek	HA	BMD	1873-1885	642,809
Encsencs	SZ	BMD	1871-1885	642,902
Enying	VE	BMD	1845-1895	642,941
Eperjes	SA	Cen	1848	719,823
Ercsi	FE	BMD	1882-1895	642,796
Erdobenye	ZE	BMD	1840-1895	642,952
Erdotelek	HE	BMD	1876-1885	642,816
Erk	HE	BD	1876-1885	642,816
Erpatak	SZ	BMD	1870-1885	642,902
Esztar	BI	BMD	1877-1895	642,756
Esztergom District	ES	B	1828-1895	642,791
Esztergom District	ES	D	1833-1895	642,792
Esztergom District	ES	M	1835-1872	642,791
Esztergom District	ES	BMD	1872-1875	642,792
Esztergom District	ES	M	1872-1895	642,792
Fadd	TO	BMD	1850-1886	642,927
Farmos	PE	BD	1878-1895	642,852
Fehergyarmat	ST	BMD	1851-1895	642,919
Felsodabas	PE	BMD	1850-1895	642,851
Felsohahot	ZA	BMD	1871-1895	642,946
Felsojozsa	HA	BMD	1886	642,757
Felsomindszent	BA	BMD	1851-1880	642,733
Felsopenc	NO	BMD	1862-1880	642,843
Fenyeslitke	SZ	BMD	1874-1895	642,902
Foldes	HA	BMD	1863-1895	642,809
Fulek	NO	BMD	1856-1895	642,842
Furta	BI	BMD	1877-1895	642,756
Fuzesabony	HE	BMD	1876-1886	642,816
Fuzesgyarmat	BE	BMD	1879-1885	642,746
Gaborjan	BI	BMD	1877-1895	642,756
Galgagyork	PE	BMD	1848-1895	642,852
Gara	B	B	1857-1882	642,731
Gara	B	M	1860-1879	642,731
Gara	B	D	1861-1885	642,731
Gata	MO	BMD	1835-1895	700,874
Gava	SZ	BMD	1854-1895	642,902
Gelse	SZ	B	1850-1885	642,913
Gelse	SZ	MD	1866-1885	642,913
Gemzse	SZ	BMD	1852-1882	642,902
Geszt	BI	BMD	1878-1885	642,756
Gesztered	SZ	BMD	1852-1895	642,902
Gige	SO	BMD	1862-1885	642,883
Godollo	PE	BMD	1851-1895	642,853
Godollo District	PE	B	1838-1885	642,854
Godollo District	PE	MD	1851-1885	642,854
Gonc	AT	BMD	1850-1882	642,728
Gorbo-belecska	TO	BMD	1851-1895	642,930
Gyoma	BE	BMD	1862-1895	642,746
Gyomore	GY	BMD	1841-1895	642,803
Gyomro	PE	BD	1871-1880	642,854
Gyon	PE	BMD	1859-1872	642,854
Gyongyos	HE	B	1846-1863	642,818
Gyongyos	HE	B	1846-1876	642,816
Gyongyos	HE	D	1846-1895	642,818
Gyongyos	HE	M	1846-1895	642,817
Gyongyos	HE	Cen	1848	719,823
Gyongyos	HE	D	1851-1863	642,818
Gyongyos	HE	BMD	1864-1878	642,819
Gyongyos	HE	B	1876-1895	642,817
Gyongyos	HE	BMD	1879-1895	642,820
Gyongyos	HE	MD	1881-1895	642,818
Gyongyosmellek	SO	B	1848-1885	642,883
Gyongyosmellek	SO	D	1848-1895	642,883
Gyongyosmellek	SO	M	1857-1885	642,883
Gyonk	TO	B	1831-1895	642,927
Gyonk	TO	MD	1851-1895	642,927
Gyor	GY	BMD	1846-1895	642,804
Gyor	GO	Cen	1848	719,823
Gyorasszonyfa	GY	BMD	1853-1885	642,847
Gyorszentmarton	GY	BMD	1850-1895	642,847
Gyorsziget	GY	BMD	1840-1895	642,805
Gyula	BE	BMD	1863-1895	642,747
Gyulahaza	SZ	BMD	1878-1895	642,902
Hahot	ZA	BMD	1871-1895	642,946
Hajdubagos	BI	BMD	1877-1885	642,757
Hajduboszormeny	HA	BMD	1861-1895	642,757
Hajdudorog	HA	BMD	1851-1895	642,809
Hajduhadhaz	HA	BMD	1856-1895	642,809
Hajdunanas	HA	BMD	1851-1895	642,810
Hajdusamson	HA	BMD	1845-1895	642,811
Hajduszoboszlo	HA	BMD	1826-1895	642,812
Hajduszovat	HA	BMD	1853-1895	642,813
Hajduszovat	HA	BMD	1876-1895	642,757
Hatvan	HE	BMD	1850-1895	642,821
Hedervar	GY	BMD	1858-1885	642,806
Hegykozszentimre	BI	BMD	1869-1877	642,757
Hejocsaba	BO	BMD	1851-1895	642,766
Hencida	BI	BMD	1877-1895	642,757

Hidasd	BA	BMD	1851-1895	642,739	Kiscell	VA	BMD	1877-1895	642,933
Hidasd	BA	BMD	1875-1884	642,731	Kiskoros	PE	M	1811-1895	642,857
Hidasd District	BA	Fam	1850	642,731	Kiskoros	PE	B	1821-1885	642,858
Hodasz	ST	BMD	1876-1885	642,919	Kiskoros	PE	BMD	1842-1895	642,858
Hodmezovasarhely	CS	BM	1844-1895	642,782	Kiskoros	PE	D	1851-1885	642,858
Hodmezovasarhely	CS	D	1844-1876	642,782	Kiskoros	PE	B	1866-1885	642,857
Hodmezovasarhely	CS	B	1846-1895	642,783	Kiskunfelegyhaza	PE	BMD	1851-1895	642,860
Hodmezovasarhely	CS	M	1849-1895	642,783	Kiskunhalas	PE	BMD	1851-1895	642,859
Hodmezovasarhely	CS	D	1850-1895	642,783	Kiskunmajsa	PE	BMD	1850-1895	642,860
Hodmezovasarhely	CS	Fam	1855,1857	642,782	Kisleta	SZ	BMD	1876-1885	642,903
Hodmezovasarhely	CS	D	1877-1895	642,783	Kismarja	BI	BMD	1877-1886	642,758
Hogyesz	TO	BMD	1842-1895	642,928	Kismarton	SP	BMD	1833-1895	700,794
Hogyesz District	TO	BMD	1842-1883	642,929	Kistelek	CS	B	1859-1880	642,783
Hogyesz District	TO	BMD	1851/1894	642,928	Kistelek	CS	MD	1877-1879	642,783
Hosszupalyi	BI	BMD	1877-1885	642,757	Kisujszallas	JA	BMD	1851-1895	642,831
Hugyaj	SZ	BMD	1870-1885	642,902	District				
Ibrony	SZ	BMD	1852-1880	642,913	Kisvarda	SZ	B	1851-1895	642,905
Irsa	PE	BMD	1847-1895	642,848	Kisvarda	SZ	BMD	1851-1885	642,904
Ivandarda	BA	BMD	1851-1895	642,732	Kisvarda	SZ	M	1851-1895	642,906
Izsak	PE	BMD	1843-1895	642,854	Kisvarda	SZ	D	1852-1895	642,906
Janoshaza	VA	BMD	1850-1895	642,933	Kisvarda	SZ	BM	1886-1895	642,904
Jarmi	ST	BMD	1806-1885	642,919	Kisvarda	SZ	D	1886-1895	642,905
Jaszapati	JA	BMD	1878-1889	642,827	Kisvarsany	SZ	BMD	1876-1885	642,918
Jaszbereny	JA	B	1851-1895	642,827	Kobanya	PE	BM	1876-1895	642,993
Jaszbereny	JA	MD	1851-1895	642,828	Kobanya	PE	D	1885-1895	642,993
Jaszbereny District	JA	B	1851-1895	642,829	Koka	PE	BMD	1877-1895	642,861
Jaszbereny District	JA	BMD	1851-1895	642,830	Kokad	BI	BMD	1877-1885	642,758
Jaszkerekegyhaza	PE	B	1863-1885	642,857	Komadi	BI	BMD	1877-1885	642,758
Jaszsag District	JA	D	1854-1885	642,831	Komoro	SZ	BMD	1881-1895	642,907
Jaszsag District	JA	M	1862-1885	642,831	Konyar	BI	BMD	1879-1885	642,758
Jaszsag District	JA	B	1877-1885	642,830	Kopsceny	MO	BMD	1835-1895	700,871
Jaszszentandras	JA	B	1886-1888	642,831	Kormend	VA	BMD	1841-1895	642,934
Jeke	SZ	BMD	1886-1891	642,902	Kormend	VA	B	1851-1895	642,933
Jozsa	HA	BMD	1886	642,757	Korosladany	BE	BMD	1879-1885	642,747
Kaba	HA	BMD	1835-1895	642,757	Korosnagyharsany	BI	BMD	1877-1885	642,758
Kaba	HA	BMD	1876-1895	642,813	Korosszakal	BI	BMD	1877-1885	642,758
Kabold	SP	BMD	1833-1895	700,788	Korosszegapati	BI	BMD	1877-1895	642,758
Kadarkut	SO	BMD	1851-1885	642,883	Koszeg	VA	BMD	1851-1895	642,935
Kajaszo	FE	BMD	1813-1895	642,796	Kotegyan	BI	BMD	1879-1885	642,758
Kajaszoszentpeter	FE	BMD	1813-1895	642,796	Kovagoors	ZA	BMD	1847-1895	642,948
Kakad	BI	BMD	1877-1885	642,758	Kulsobocs	BO	B	1864-1885	642,765
Kallosemjen	SZ	BMD	1870-1895	642,902	Kunhegyes District	JA	BMD	1857-1895	642,832
Kalocsa	PE	BMD	1850-1895	642,856	Kunmadaras	JA	BMD	1855-1895	642,832
Kalocsa	PE	BMD	1850-1895	642,855	Kunszentmarton	JA	B	1857-1895	642,832
Kantorjanosi	ST	M	1876-1885	642,919	District				
Kanyar	SZ	BMD	1888-1895	642,916	Kunszentmiklos	PE	BMD	1855-1895	642,861
Kapolcs	ZA	BMD	1867-1895	642,947	Lajtakata	MO	BMD	1835-1895	700,874
Kapolnasnyek	FE	BMD	1777-1895	642,797	Lakompak	SP	BMD	1833-1895	700,801
Kaposmero	SO	B	1861-1884	642,883	Laskod	SZ	BMD	1886-1895	642,907
Kaposmero	SO	M	1875-1876	642,883	Lengyeltoti	SO	BMD	1846-1895	642,887
Kaposmero	SO	D	1876-1877	642,883	Lepseny	VE	B	1863-1885	642,941
Kaposvar	SO	B	1771-1895	642,884	Lorinci	NO	BMD	1850-1895	642,843
Kaposvar	SO	BMD	1844-1877	642,885	Losoncz	NO	B	1850-1885	642,843
Kaposvar	SO	BMD	1844-1895	642,886	Losoncz	NO	B	1850-1895	642,842
Kaposvar	SO	D	1851-1885	642,884	Losoncz	NO	BMD	1850-1865	642,843
Kaposvar	SO	M	1851-1895	642,884	Losoncz	NO	D	1884-1885	642,843
Kaposvar	SO	D	1886-1895	642,885	Lovasbereny	FE	BMD	1764-1895	642,797
Kapuvar	SP	BMD	1879-1895	642,899	Mad	ZE	BMD	1827-1895	642,952
Karad	SO	B	1881-1885	642,887	Mada	SZ	D	1851-1895	642,914
Karasz	SZ	BMD	1876-1895	642,913	Mada	SZ	BM	1880-1895	642,914
Karcag District	JA	BMD	1856-1895	642,831	Madaras	JA	BMD	1855-1895	642,832
Kecskemet	PE	BMD	1832-1895	642,857	Magocs	BA	BMD	1833-1895	642,734
Kekcse	SZ	BMD	1886-1895	642,902	Magocs	BA	BMD	1851-1886	642,733
Kemecse	SZ	BMD	1875-1895	642,903	Magy	SZ	BMD	1852-1884	642,907
Kerekegyhaza	PE	B	1863-1885	642,857	Magyargencs	VA	BMD	1893-1895	642,935
Keresztes	BO	BMD	1851-1895	642,767	Magyarhomorog	BI	BMD	1877-1885	642,758
Keresztes	BI	BMD	1877-1892	642,753	Mako	CN	BMD	1833-1895	642,780
Keszthely	ZA	BMD	1852-1895	642,947	Mandok	SZ	BMD	1850-1885	642,907
Kisber	KO	BMD	1868-1895	642,838	Mandok	SZ	BMD	1850-1895	642,908

Mandok	SZ	B	1886-1895	642,907	Nagyrabe	BI	BMD	1875-1895	642,759
Mandok	SZ	MD	1886-1895	642,908	Nagysimonyi	VA	BMD	1851-1895	642,936
Marcali	SO	B	1774-1895	642,887	Nagyszalonta	BI	B	1854-1895	642,761
Marcali	SO	M	1807-1895	642,887	Nagyszalonta	BI	D	1854-1876	642,761
Marcali	SO	BMD	1845-1895	642,888	Nagyszalonta	BI	M	1855/1895	642,761
Marcali	SO	D	1851-1895	642,888	Nagyszombat	??	Cen	1848	719,823
Mateszalka	ST	BMD	1863-1895	642,920	Nagyteteny	PE	B	1760-1895	642,865
Mezobereny	BE	BMD	1879-1895	642,747	Nagyteteny	PE	M	1820-1895	642,865
Mezocsat	BO	BMD	1851-1895	642,767	Nagyteteny	PE	BMD	1851-1895	642,866
Mezogyan	BI	BMD	1878-1885	642,758	Nagyteteny	PE	D	1851-1895	642,865
Mezokeresztes	BO	BMD	1851-1895	642,767	Nagyvarsany	SZ	BMD	1876-1885	642,918
Mezokovesd	BO	BMD	1851-1895	642,768	Nagyvazsony	VE	BMD	1842-1895	642,941
Mezoladany	SZ	M	1858	642,908	Nemesdomolk	VA	BMD	1877-1895	642,933
Mezoladany	SZ	B	1876-1885	642,908	Nemesszalok	VA	BMD	1875-1888	642,936
Mezoladany	SZ	D	1878-1885	642,908	Nemetkeresztur	SP	BMD	1827-1895	700,836
Mezopeterd	BI	BMD	1877-1884	642,759	Nemetujvar	VA	BMD	1841-1895	700,702
Mezoszilas	VE	BMD	1854-1885	642,932	Nyirabrany	SZ	BMD	1867-1884	642,759
District					Nyiracsad	SZ	BMD	1863-1895	642,910
Mezoszilasve	VE	BMD	1841-1895	642,943	Nyiradony	SZ	BMD	1871-1885	642,759
Mezotur	JA	BMD	1850-1895	642,832	Nyirbator	SZ	BMD	1845-1895	642,911
Mihalydi	SZ	BMD	1850-1885	642,915	Nyirbator	SZ	BMD	1851-1895	642,912
Mihalyfa	ZA	BMD	1866-1895	642,948	Nyirbogat	SZ	BMD	1851-1885	642,913
Mikepercs	HA	BMD	1886	642,759	Nyirderzs	ST	M	1876-1885	642,920
Mindszent	BA	BMD	1851-1880	642,733	Nyiregyhaza	SZ	BMD	1866-1895	642,913
Mindszent	CS	BMD	1851-1895	642,784	Nyirgelse	SZ	B	1850-1885	642,913
Miskolc	BO	B	1836-1883	642,772	Nyirgelse	SZ	MD	1866-1885	642,913
Miskolc	BO	B	1838-1881	642,769	Nyiribrony	SZ	BMD	1852-1880	642,913
Miskolc	BO	Cen	1848	719,823	Nyirkarasz	SZ	BMD	1876-1895	642,913
Miskolc	BO	D	1851-1882	642,775	Nyirlugos	SZ	BMD	1870-1885	642,913
Miskolc	BO	M	1851-1895	642,774	Nyirmada	SZ	M	1851-1895	642,914
Miskolc	BO	D	1871-1895	642,771	Nyirmada	SZ	BD	1880-1895	642,914
Miskolc	BO	M	1871-1875	642,770	Nyirmeggyes	ST	BMD	1853-1895	642,921
Miskolc	BO	BMD	1879-1886	642,770	Nyirmihalydi	SZ	BMD	1850-1885	642,915
Miskolc	BO	B	1882-1895	642,770	Nyirtass	SZ	BMD	1852-1895	642,915
Miskolc	BO	M	1882-1888	642,770	Ocsod	BE	BMD	1850-1886	642,748
Miskolc	BO	D	1883-1895	642,776	Odombovar	TO	B	1851-1895	642,924
Miskolc	BO	B	1884-1895	642,773	Odombovar	TO	M	1874-1895	642,924
Miskolc	BO	M	1889-1895	642,771	Odombovar	TO	D	1886-1895	642,924
Modor	??	Cen	1848	719,823	Okany	BI	BMD	1877-1885	642,759
Mohacs	BA	Fam	1850	642,735	Okecske	PE	BMD	1851-1895	642,872
Mohacs	BA	BMD	1851-1895	642,735	Olahapati	BI	BMD	1877-1882	642,759
Monor	PE	BMD	1835-1895	642,861	Olaszilszka	ZE	BMD	1841-1895	642,953
Monor	PE	BMD	1837-1895	642,862	Onod	BO	BMD	1851-1895	642,777
Monostorpalyi	BI	BMD	1889-1895	642,759	Opalyi	ST	BMD	1874-1885	642,921
Mor	FE	BMD	1841-1895	642,798	Orladany	SZ	M	1858	642,908
Moson	MO	BMD	1835-1895	601,568	Orladany	SZ	B	1876-1885	642,908
Mosonmagyarovar	MO	BMD	1835-1895	601,568	Orladany	SZ	D	1878-1885	642,908
Muraszombat	VA	BMD	1835-1895	642,935	Oroshaza	BE	BMD	1874-1895	642,747
Nadudvar	HA	BMD	1850-1895	642,813	Oroszvar	MO	BMD	1835-1895	601,569
Nagyabony	PE	BMD	1837-1895	642,846	Ozd	BO	BMD	1867-1895	642,777
Nagyatad	SO	BM	1851-1895	642,888	Pacsa	ZA	BMD	1838-1895	642,950
Nagyatad	SO	D	1851-1877	642,888	Paks	TO	B	1830-1893	642,929
Nagyatad	SO	D	1860-1895	642,889	Paks	TO	BMD	1852-1895	642,931
Nagyatad	SO	BMD	1861-1895	642,889	Paks	TO	BMD	1887-1895	642,929
Nagybajom	BI	BMD	1845-1895	642,753	Pand	PE	BMD	1860-1895	642,867
Nagybajom	SO	BMD	1856-1895	642,889	Pap	SZ	BMD	1878-1894	642,915
Nagybajom	SO	BMD	1856-1895	642,890	Papa	VE	BMD	1848-1895	642,942
Nagydobos	ST	BMD	1859-1885	642,920	Papos	ST	BMD	1874-1885	642,921
Nagyecsed	ST	BMD	1856-1885	642,920	Paszto	HE	BMD	1833-1895	642,822
Nagyharsany	BI	BMD	1877-1885	642,758	Patahaza	GY	BMD	1839-1844	642,806
Nagykallo	SZ	BMD	1844-1895	642,909	Patroha	SZ	BMD	1852-1895	642,915
Nagykanizsa	ZA	BMD	1835-1895	642,949	Pecel	PE	BMD	1859-1884	642,867
Nagykata	PE	B	1851-1895	642,862	Pecs	BA	Cen	1848	719,823
Nagykata	PE	MD	1851-1885	642,862	Pecs	BA	BM	1851-1895	642,736
Nagykata	PE	BMD	1859-1895	642,863	Pecs	BA	D	1851-1895	642,737
Nagykoros	PE	BMD	1834-1895	642,864	Pecs	BA	B	1860-1895	642,737
Nagyleta	BI	BMD	1875-1895	642,759	Pecs	BA	MD	1860-1895	642,738
Nagymarton	SP	BMD	1833-1895	700,813	Pecs District	BA	BMD	1851-1885	642,738
Nagyoroszi	NO	BMD	1850-1895	642,843	Pecs District	BA	BMD	1864-1888	642,739

Place	Co.	Type	Years	Film	Place	Co.	Type	Years	Film
Pecsvarad District	BA	Fam	1850	642,731	Szalard	BI	B	1852-1895	642,761
Pecsvarad District	BA	BMD	1851-1895	642,739	Szalard	BI	M	1862/1885	642,761
Penc	PE	BMD	1862-1880	642,843	Szalard	BI	D	1885-1895	642,761
Peteri	PE	BMD	1877-1880	642,867	Szanto	AT	BMD	1842-1888	642,726
Petervasara	HE	BMD	1851-1895	642,823	Szanto	AT	BMD	1888-1895	642,727
Petnehaza	SZ	BMD	1852-1895	642,915	Szarvas	BE	BMD	1850/1895	642,748
Pilis	PE	BD	1877-1880	642,867	Szarvas	BE	BMD	1871-1895	642,749
Pilisvorosvar	PE	BMD	1819-1895	642,867	Szecseny	NO	BMD	1850-1885	642,844
Pincehely	TO	BMD	1851-1895	642,930	Szeged	CS	BM	1844-1895	642,787
Piricse	SZ	BMD	1877-1885	642,916	Szeged	CS	BMD	1844-1851	642,785
Pocsaj	BI	BMD	1852-1895	642,759	Szeged	CS	D	1844-1877	642,787
Polgar	SZ	BMD	1853-1895	642,916	Szeged	CS	BI	1850-1895	642,786
Polgar	SZ	BMD	1854-1895	642,814	Szeged	CS	B	1852-1885	642,785
Pomaz	PE	BMD	1851-1895	642,868	Szeged	CS	MD	1852-1885	642,786
Poroszlo	HE	BMD	1850-1895	642,823	Szeged	CS	B	1871-1885	642,786
Puspokladany	HA	BMD	1854-1895	642,814	Szeged	CS	BM	1871-1885	642,788
Pusztakovacsi	SO	B	1867-1877	642,890	Szeged	CS	D	1874-1885	642,786
Pusztatold	BI	BMD	1877-1884	642,763	Szeged	CS	D	1874-1885	642,788
Racadony	FE	BMD	1850-1885	642,794	Szeged	CS	D	1878-1895	642,788
Racalmas	FE	BMD	1877-1885	642,799	Szeged	CS	BM	1886-1895	642,786
Rackeve	PE	BMD	1862-1895	642,869	Szeghalom	BE	B	1895	642,749
Rajka	MO	BMD	1835-1895	601,569	Szegkalom	BE	M	1888	642,749
Regoce	BK	BMD	1853-1885	642,731	Szekelyhid	BI	BI	1831-1880	642,762
Retkozberencs	SZ	BMD	1886-1895	642,916	Szekelyhid	BI	BMD	1851-1895	642,762
Revfalu	GY	BMD	1839-1844	642,806	Szekesfehervar	FE	BMD	1845-1843	642,800
Rigyica	BK	BMD	1853-1885	642,731	Szekesfehervar	FE	BMD	1776-1895	642,802
Rohonc	VA	BMD	1834-1895	700,726	District				
Sajokazinc	BO	BMD	1867-1895	642,778	Szendro	BO	BMD	1851-1895	642,779
Sajoszentpeter	BO	BMD	1851-1895	642,778	Szentandras	BE	BMD	1850-1885	642,745
Salgotarjan	NO	BMD	1874-1895	642,844	Szentendre	PE	BMD	1853-1895	642,870
Samson	HA	BMD	1845-1895	642,811	Szentes	CS	B	1849-1895	642,789
Sap	BI	BMD	1877-1886	642,760	Szentes	CS	MD	1850-1895	642,790
Sarand	BI	BMD	1877-1885	642,760	Szentes	CS	BMD	1852-1895	642,789
Sarbogard	FE	BMD	1843-1895	642,799	Szentgotthard	VA	BMD	1886-1895	642,937
Sarkad	BI	BMD	1853-1895	642,760	Szentgrot	ZA	BMD	1828-1832	642,951
Sarkadkeresztur	BI	BMD	1877-1895	642,760	Szentgyorgy		Cen	1848	719,823
Sarospatak	ZE	BMD	1833-1895	642,953	Szentgyorgyabrany	SZ	BMD	1867-1884	642,759
Sarretudvari	BI	BMD	1877-1895	642,760	Szentlorinc	BA	Cen	1850	642,741
Sarvar	VA	B	1851-1885	642,936	Szentlorinc	BA	BMD	1851-1895	642,741
Sarvar	VA	MD	1851-1895	642,937	Szentlorinckata	PE	BMD	1878-1895	642,870
Sarvar	VA	BMD	1882-1895	642,936	Szentmartonkata	PE	BMD	1875-1895	642,870
Sarvar	VA	B	1886-1895	642,937	Szentmihaly	SZ	BM	1856-1895	642,917
Satoraljaujhely	ZE	B	1827-1850	642,955	Szentmihaly	SZ	D	1862-1895	642,917
Satoraljaujhely	ZE	B	1851-1895	642,954	Szcntpeterszeg	BI	BMD	1878-1895	642,763
Satoraljaujhely	ZE	MD	1851-1874	642,954	Szenttamas	ES	BMD	1833-1879	642,792
Satoraljaujhely	ZE	MD	1851-1895	642,955	Szenttamas	ES	BMD	1880-1895	642,793
Satoraljaujhely	ZE	BMD	1856-1885	642,955	Szerencs	ZE	BMD	1827-1895	642,958
Satoraljaujhely Distrct	ZE	BMD	1841-1885	642,956	Szerep	BI	BMD	1877-1886	642,763
					Szigetvar	SO	B	1842-1895	642,893
Satoraljaujhely District	ZE	BMD	1886-1895	642,957	Szigetvar	SO	BMD	1842-1895	642,894
					Szigetvar	SO	MD	1851-1895	642,893
Sege	HA	BMD	1873-1885	642,763	Szil	SO	BMD	1846-1895	642,892
Sellye	BA	BMD	1881-1885	642,739	Szil	SO	BMD	1850-1895	642,891
Siklos	BA	BMD	1851-1895	642,740	Szilasbalhas	VE	BMD	1841-1895	642,943
Simonyi	VA	BMD	1851-1895	642,936	Szilasbalhas District	VE	BMD	1854-1885	642,932
Siofok	VE	B	1865-1877	642,943					
Somberek	BA	BMD	1851-1895	642,739	Szilsarkany	SP	BMD	1881-1895	642,899
Somogvszil	SO	BMD	1846-1895	642,892	Szirak	NO	BMD	1850-1895	642,845
Somogvszil	SO	BMD	1850-1895	642,891	Szolnok	JA	BMD	1833-1895	642,833
Sopron	SP	Cen	1848	719,823	Szolnok District	JA	BMD	1850-1895	642,834
Sopron	SP	BMD	1867-1895	642,899	Szombathely	VA	BMD	1850-1895	642,938
Sopronkeresztur	SP	BMD	1827-1895	700,836	Szombathely	VA	BMD	1850-1895	642,939
Soroksar	PE	BMD	1850-1895	642,869	Szovat	HA	BMD	1853-1895	642,813
Sumeg	ZA	BMD	1876-1895	642,950	Szovat	HA	BMD	1876-1895	642,757
Szabadszallas	PE	BMD	1858-1895	642,870	Szugy	NO	BMD	1850-1895	642,845
Szabolcsbaka	SZ	BD	1876-1885	642,916	Tab	SO	Fam	1819-1852	642,896
Szabolcsveresmart	SZ	BMD	1886-1895	642,916	Tab	SO	BMD	1845-1895	642,896
Szakal	BI	BMD	1877-1885	642,758	Tab	SO	BMD	1847-1895	642,895
Szakolca		Cen	1848	719,823	Tab District	SO	BMD	1851-1885	642,932

Tab District	SO	BMD	1870-1885	642,896	Turkeve	JA	BMD	1851-1895	642,836
Tallya	ZE	BMD	1827-1895	642,959	Udvari	BI	BMD	1877-1895	642,760
Tapiobicske	PE	BMD	1863-1895	642,871	Ugra	BI	BMD	1877-1885	642,753
Tapiosag	PE	BMD	1860-1895	642,871	Ujfeherto	SZ	BMD	1844-1895	642,918
Tapiosuly	PE	BMD	1877-1886	642,871	Ujfeherto	SZ	BMD	1852-1895	642,917
Tapioszecso	PE	BMD	1855-1895	642,871	Ujkecke	PE	BMD	1851-1895	642,872
Tapioszele	PE	BMD	1823-1895	642,871	Ujpest	PE	D	1850-1895	642,875
Tapioszentmarton	PE	BD	1881-1895	642,872	Ujpest	PE	B	1851-1892	642,873
Tapolca	ZA	BMD	1828-1895	642,950	Ujpest	PE	M	1851-1885	642,874
Tarcal	ZE	BMD	1827-1895	642,959	Ujpest	PE	BMD	1872-1890	642,875
Tass	PE	BMD	1833-1895	642,870	Ujpest	PE	M	1886-1895	642,875
Tass	SZ	BMD	1852-1895	642,915	Ujpest	PE	B	1892-1895	642,874
Tata	KO	BMD	1868-1895	642,839	Ujvikek	BB	Cen	1848	719,823
Teglas	HA	BMD	1857-1895	642,763	Ullo	PE	BMD	1877-1885	642,875
Temesvar		Cen	1848	719,823	Uny	ES	B	1822-1871	642,793
Tepe	BI	BMD	1877-1885	642,763	Uny	ES	D	1852-1865	642,793
Tet	GY	BMD	1840-1895	642,806	Uny	ES	M	1854-1864	642,793
Tetetlen	HA	BMD	1886-1895	642,763	Uri	PE	BMD	1878-1880	642,875
Tetszentkut	GY	BMD	1840-1895	642,806	Vac	PE	BMD	1846-1895	642,878
Tinnye	PE	BMD	1769-1885	642,872	Vac	PE	B	1853-1895	642,876
Tiszabercel	SZ	BMD	1854-1895	642,916	Vac	PE	MD	1853-1895	642,877
Tiszabezded	SZ	BMD	1876-1895	642,916	Vac	PE	B	1874-1885	642,876
Tiszabo District	JA	BMD	1850-1895	642,834	Vac	PE	B	1886-1895	642,877
Tiszacsege	HA	BMD	1873-1885	642,763	Vamospercs	HA	BMD	1876-1886	642,763
Tiszadada	SZ	B	1886-1895	642,916	Vancsod	BI	BMD	1877-1895	642,763
Tiszafoldvar	JA	BMD	1856-1895	642,834	Varosszalonak	VA	BMD	1841-1895	700,744
District					Varsany	SZ	BMD	1876-1885	642,918
Tiszafured	HE	BMD	1840-1895	642,824	Vaskut	BK	B	1884-1888	642,731
Tiszafured District	HE	BMD	1851-1888	642,825	Vaskut	BK	D	1884-1885	642,731
Tiszakanyar	SZ	BMD	1888-1895	642,916	Vaskut	BK	M	1885	642,731
Tiszakecske	PE	BMD	1851-1895	642,872	Vasvar	VA	BMD	1851-1895	642,939
Tiszalok	SZ	BMD	1877-1895	642,916	Vekerd	BI	DMD	1070-1095	042,703
Tiszaszentimre	JA	BMD	1850-1895	642,835	Veresmart	SZ	BMD	1886-1895	642,916
District					Verpelet	HE	Fam	1781-1855	642,825
Tiszaszentmarton	SZ	BD	1876-1886	642,917	Verpelet	HE	B	1851-1874	642,825
Tiszavasvari	SZ	BM	1856-1895	642,917	Verpelet	HE	D	1851-1895	642,826
Tiszavasvari	SZ	D	1862-1895	642,917	Verpelet	HE	M	1852-1895	642,826
Toalmas	PE	BMD	1868-1895	642,872	Verpelet	HE	B	1875-1895	642,826
Tokaj	ZE	BMD	1827-1895	642,959	Vertes	BI	BMD	1846-1895	642,764
Tolcsva	ZE	BMD	1821-1895	642,960	Veszprem	VE	BMD	1836-1890	642,944
Tolcsva	ZE	BMD	1847-1851	642,959	Veszprem	VE	B	1851-1895	642,943
Tolcsva	ZE	B	1851-1883	642,959	Veszprem District	VE	BMD	1886-1895	642,944
Told	BI	BMD	1877-1884	642,763	Vitka	ST	BMD	1862-1885	642,921
Tolna	TO	BMD	1851-1895	642,932	Vorosvar	PE	BMD	1819-1895	642,867
Torda	BI	BMD	1877-1886	642,753	Votokom	PE	BMD	1821-1885	642,854
Torokszentmiklos	JA	BMD	1850-1895	642,836	Zalaegerszeg	ZA	BMD	1835-1895	642,951
Torokszentmiklos	JA	M	1850-1885	642,835	Zalalovo	ZA	BMD	1830-1895	642,951
Torokszentmiklos	JA	D	1851-1885	642,835	Zalaszentgrot	ZA	BMD	1828-1832	642,951
Torokszentmiklos	JA	B	1886-1895	642,835	Zombor		Cen	1848	719,823
Tortel	PE	BD	1881-1885	642,872	Zsadany	BI	BMD	1877-1885	642,764
Totgyork	PE	BMD	1848-1895	642,852	Zsaka	BI	BMD	1877-1895	642,764
Totkomlos	BE	BMD	1872-1885	642,749	Zsambek	PE	BMD	1841-1895	642,879
Trenscen		Cen	1848	719,823					
Tunyog	ST	B	1871-1885	642,921					
Tunyogmatolcs	ST	B	1871-1885	642,921					

Reprinted from *Avotaynu*, Vol. IV, No. 1, Winter 1988.

Polish-Jewish Records at the Family History Library, Salt Lake City, Utah

See "Jewish Collections at the Family History Library" (Utah), p. 131.

Listed below are the 1,735 microfilm numbers of Jewish vital statistics records for Poland in the possession of the Family History Library as of the October 1985 catalog. The current Family History Library Catalog, available at Family History Centers on microfiche or compact disk, contains additional entries for recent acquisitions. Each entry contains town name, abbreviation of province, a legend describing the documents, years represented, and microfilm number.

Abbreviation of provinces:

BI	Bialystock
BY	Bydogszcz
GD	Gdansk
KA	Katowice
KI	Kielce
KO	Koszalin
KR	Krakow
LO	Lodz
LU	Lublin
LW	Lwow
OL	Olsztyn
OP	Opole
PO	Pozan
RZ	Rzeszow
SZ	Szczecin
WA	Warszawa
WR	Wroclaw
ZI	Zielona Gora

Nature of the material:

B	Births
M	Marriages
D	Deaths
V	Divorces
Fam	Family names
Cem	Cemetery records
Cen	Census
I/O	Incoming and outgoing Jews
Mil	Military records
Nam	Acquisition of new names
Sch	School records

Dates are represented in one of four ways. If there is a single year, the information is for that year only. If there are two years separated by a dash (1823–1855), then the records are inclusive for those years. If there are two years separated by a slash (1823/1855) then the records are inclusive for those years with a significant number of years missing within the time period. If the two years are separated by a comma (1823,1855) then only those two years are represented.

If a town is not represented on the list, do not assume there are no Jewish records for the town. What is shown below is a listing of only those records classified as "Jewish Records." It is possible that the town of interest has church records, land records, or civil registrations that include information about the Jews of the town. It is wise to check the catalog at a local Family History Center to see if other records of the town exist.

In addition, small towns may be part of the records for the major town in the area. For example, records for the major town of Lomza indicate that they also include the towns of Dobrzyjalowo, Gal, Kalinowo, Lomzyca, Ostrowki, Piatnica, Pniewo, Podgorz, Wyludzin, and Wyrziki.

Most Jewish vital statistics records were not isolated from Christian records until the 1820s. Therefore if the town in question does have Jewish records, there are almost certainly pre-1820 Jewish records among the church records or civil registrations. It will be necessary to go to a branch library to get these microfilm numbers.

Aleksandrow Lodzki	LO	BMD	1826-1844	678,740
Aleksandrow Lodzki	LO	BMD	1845-1857	678,741
Aleksandrow Lodzki	LO	BMD	1858-1865	678,742
Aleksandrow Lodzki	LO	BMD	1866-1870	766,346
Aleksandrow Lodzki	LO	BMD	1871-1875	1,189,025
Aleksandrow Lodzki	LO	BMD	1876	1,189,026
Andrzejewo	WA	BMD	1808-1819	808,606
Andrzejewo	WA	BMD	1814-1820	808,607
Andrzejewo	WA	BMD	1819-1825	808,608
Andrzejewo	WA	BMD	1826-1836	810,589
Andrzejewo	WA	BMD	1826-1838	808,614
Andrzejewo	WA	BMD	1838-1859	810,590
Andrzejewo	WA	BMD	1839-1850	808,615
Andrzejewo	WA	BMD	1851-1859	808,616
Annopol	LU	BMD	1826/1855	681,139
Babiak	PO	BMD	1826-1859	810,118
Babimost	ZI	B	1817-1847	1,273,157
Babimost	ZI	Fam	1847-1899	474,924
Babimost	ZI	Fam	1848-1916	474,931
Bakalarzewo	BI	BMD	1826/1841	746,481
Bakalarzewo	BI	BMD	1842/1864	746,482
Bakalarzewo	BI	BMD	1866-1877	1,191,984
Bakalarzewo	BI	BMD	1878	1,191,273
Bakalarzewo	BI	BMD	1879	1,191,274
Banie	SZ	BMD	1848-1874	1,334,562
Baranow	LU	BMD	1827-1855	681,154
Baranow	LU	BMD	1856/1875	681,155
Baranow	LU	BMD	1879-1905	681,156
Baranowice	KA	BMD	1810-1870	879,598
Baranowice	KA	BMD	1810-1874	879,597
Baranowice	KA	BMD	1812-1870	879,596

Barglow Dworny	BI	B	1869-1871	1,191,274	Bilgoraj	LU	BM	1868-1869	1,201,149
Barglow Dworny	BI	BMD	1869/1882	1,191,276	Bilgoraj	LU	BMD	1870-1873	1,201,150
Barglow Dworny	BI	B	1871-1882	1,191,275	Biskupice	LU	BMD	1826-1855	689,827
Barglow Dworny	BI	D	1874-1881	1,191,277	Biskupice	LU	D	1829-1862	689,828
Barlinek	SZ	Cen	1736,1746	1,184,378	Biskupice	LU	B	1852-1861	689,828
Barlinek	SZ	Cen	1816	1,184,378	Biskupiec	OL	BMD	1847-1874	1,271,457
Barlinek	SZ	Cen	1847-1853	544,649	Blaszki	PO	BMD	1826-1867	588,121
Bartoszyce	OL	D	1852-1938	1,184,377	Blaszki	PO	B	1871-1893	127,713
Barwice	KO	BMD	1848-1874	1,334,557	Blaszki	PO	BMD	1892/1939	127,716
Bedkow	LO	BMD	1826-1846	681,063	Blaszki	PO	MD	1899-1910	127,715
Bedzin	KA	BMD	1826-1830	766,055	Blaszki	PO	B	1899-1921	127,714
Bedzin	KA	BMD	1831-1844	766,056	Blaszki	PO	B	1922-1939	127,715
Bedzin	KA	BMD	1845-1856	766,057	Bledzew	ZI	Fam	1839-1888	474,923
Bedzin	KA	BMD	1857-1859	766,058	Bobolice	KO	BMD	1812-1859	1,190,925
Belchatow	LO	BMD	1824/1843	681,038	Bobolice	KO	BMD	1816-1818	1,184,406
Belchatow	LO	BMD	1844-1851	681,039	Bobolice	KO	BMD	1847-1874	1,190,924
Belchatow	LO	BMD	1852-1860	681,040	Bobrowniki	WA	BMD	1826-1828	689,496
Belchatow	LO	BMD	1861-1865	681,041	Bobrowniki	WA	BMD	1829-1833	702,431
Belchatow	LO	BMD	1873-1874	1,189,029	Bobrowniki	WA	BMD	1834-1850	702,432
Belzyce	LU	BMD	1826-1842	681,163	Bobrowniki	WA	BMD	1851-1858	702,433
Belzyce	LU	MD	1826-1859	681,166	Bodzanow	WA	BMD	1826-1850	729,202
Belzyce	LU	BMD	1843-1849	681,164	Bodzanow	WA	BMD	1851-1865	729,203
Belzyce	LU	BMD	1850-1854	681,165	Bodzanow	WA	BMD	1866-1872	1,201,495
Belzyce	LU	BMD	1855-1864	681,167	Bodzanow	WA	BMD	1873-1879	1,201,496
Belzyce	LU	BMD	1866-1868	767,802	Bodzentyn	KI	BMD	1869-1870	1,192,415
Biala	LU	BMD	1826-1831	681,203	Bodzentyn	KI	BMD	1869-1874	1,192,416
Biala	LU	D	1826-1858	681,207	Bogoria	KI	BMD	1826-1847	813,072
Biala	LU	M	1826/1848	681,206	Bogoria	KI	BMD	1848-1865	588,927
Biala	LU	BMD	1832-1836	681,204	Bogoria	KI	BMD	1866-1877	1,199,823
Biala	LU	B	1836-1864	681,205	Boleslawiec	LO	BMD	1826-1838	681,099
Biala	LU	BMD	1845-1857	681,208	Boleslawiec	WR	Cem	1840-1933	1,184,406
Biala	LU	BMD	1858-1865	681,209	Bolimow	LO	BMD	1826-1858	681,111
Biala Podlaska	LU	BMD	1845/1851	1,199,950	Borek Wielkopolski	PO	BMD	1833-1837	1,273,157
Biala Podlaska	LU	BMD	1853-1864	1,199,951	Brodnica	BY	B	1823-1897	544,875
Biala Podlaska	LU	BMD	1865-1873	1,199,952	Brodnica	BY	BMD	1840-1847	808,142
Biala Podlaska	LU	BMD	1874-1877	1,201,147	Brojce	ZI	BM	1847	807,873
Biala Rawska	LO	BMD	1826-1868	681,070	Brok	WA	BMD	1826-1856	808,604
Bialobrzegi	KI	BMD	1866-1873	1,201,343	Brok	WA	BMD	1857-1865	808,605
Bialobrzegi	KI	BMD	1874-1877	1,201,344	Brzeg	OP	B	1794/1874	1,184,407
Bialogard	KO	BMD	1812-1846	896,086	Brzeg	OP	M	1809-1874	1,184,405
Bialogard	KO	BMD	1813-1847	1,334,563	Brzeg	OP	D	1810-1874	1,184,406
Bialogard	KO	BMD	1813-1847	1,334,576	Brzeg	OP	MD	1847-1874	1,190,996
Bialogard	KO	BMD	1840-1874	1,334,583	Brzesko	KR	BM	1849-1886	948,419
Bialogard	KO	BMD	1847-1874	1,334,562	Brzeziny	LO	BMD	1826-1844	689,703
Bialogard	KO	BMD	1853-1869	1,184,378	Brzeziny	LO	BMD	1845-1856	689,704
Bialogard	KO	BMD	1870-1872	1,184,377	Brzeziny	LO	BMD	1857-1865	689,705
Bialogard	KO	D	1914-1929	1,184,378	Brzeziny	LO	BMD	1866-1870	766,370
Bialy Bor	KO	BMD	1812-1847	1,334,561	Brzeziny	LO	BMD	1872-1874	1,192,287
Bialystok	BI	BMD	1835/1860	747,735	Brzeziny	LO	BMD	1874-1876	1,192,288
Bialystok	BI	BMD	1861-1863	747,736	Brzeziny	LO	BMD	1877	1,199,884
Bialystok	BI	BMD	1864-1865	747,737	Brzeznica-nowa Osada	LO	BMD	1826-1848	689,720
Bialystok	BI	BM	1866	1,191,933					
Bialystok	BI	MD	1866/1878	1,191,934	Brzeznica-nowa Osada	LO	BMD	1849-1864	689,721
Bialystok	BI	BMD	1870-1873	1,191,935					
Bialystok	BI	BMD	1873-1878	1,191,936	Burzenin	LO	BMD	1826-1864	689,741
Bialystok	BI	BM	1878	1,191,937	Bychawa	LU	BMD	1826-1855	689,851
Bialystok	BI	BMD	1878-1880	1,191,364	Bychawa	LU	D	1836-1844	689,852
Bialystok	BI	MD	1927-1939	1,186,442	Bychawa	LU	BMD	1845-1854	689,853
Biecz	RZ	BD	1850-1868	753,059	Bychawa	LU	BMD	1848-1873	1,201,223
Bielawy	LO	BMD	1826-1841	681,078	Bychawa	LU	BM	1852-1875	1,201,222
Bielawy	LO	BMD	1842-1855	681,079	Bychawa	LU	BMD	1864-1875	1,201,224
Bielsk	WA	BMD	1826-1850	729,200	Bychawa	LU	BMD	1869/1877	1,201,225
Bielsk	WA	BMD	1851-1865	729,201	Bydgoszcz	BY	Fam	1833-1845	1,271,466
Bielsk	WA	BMD	1866-1870	1,201,495	Bytom	KA	BMD	1812-1847	1,271,417
Bielsk Podlaski	BI	BMD	1835	1,191,937	Bytom	KA	BMD	1812-1847	1,273,452
Bierun Nowy	KA	BMD	1847-1870	864,953	Bytom	KA	BMD	1847-1874	1,273,156
Bierutow	WR	BMD	1847-1887	1,184,378	Bytom	KA	M	1848-1874	1,271,495
Bierutow	WR	BMD	1847-1887	1,184,379	Bytom	KA	B	1849-1866	1,335,074
Biezun	WA	BMD	1857-1858	702,625	Bytom	KA	B	1849-1866	1,335,075

Bytom	KA	B	1866-1874	1,194,063	Ciepielow	KI	BMD	1826-1856	813,909
Bytom	KA	MD	1867/1940	1,184,405	Ciepielow	KI	BMD	1857-1865	813,910
Bytom	KA	B	1880-1886	1,184,404	Ciepielow	KI	BMD	1866-1870	1,192,418
Bytom Odrzanski	ZI	BMD	1847-1874	1,271,490	Ciepielow	KI	BMD	1871-1873	1,192,419
Bytow	KO	BMD	1812-1847	1,334,558	Ciepielow	KI	BMD	1874-1877	1,201,344
Bytow	KO	BMD	1840-1874	1,190,931	Czaplinek	KO	BD	1829-1852	1,184,460
Ceglow	WA	BMD	1826-1836	702,434	Czemierniki	LU	BMD	1810/1855	723,592
Charzyno	KO	Cen	1561	1,273,138	Czemierniki	LU	BMD	1858/1877	1,201,242
Checiny	KI	BMD	1866-1868	1,192,416	Czempin	PO	Cem	?-?	1,184,406
Checiny	KI	BMD	1869-1873	1,192,417	Czersk	WA	BMD	1826-1836	723,683
Checiny	KI	BMD	1874-1877	1,192,418	Czerwinsk	WA	BMD	1826/1865	689,633
Chelm	LU	D	1823	702,696	Czestochowa	KA	BMD	1826-1840	875,326
Chelm	LU	D	1823	1,201,231	Czestochowa	KA	BMD	1841-1851	875,327
Chelm	LU	B	1826-1828	702,674	Czestochowa	KA	BMD	1852-1859	875,328
Chelm	LU	BMD	1828	702,680	Czestochowa	KA	BMD	1860-1865	875,329
Chelm	LU	BMD	1828	1,201,229	Czestochowa	KA	BMD	1866-1871	1,191,843
Chelm	LU	BMD	1843-1847	702,672	Czestochowa	KA	BMD	1872-1876	1,191,844
Chelm	LU	BMD	1848-1854	702,673	Czestochowa	KA	BMD	1877	1,191,845
Chelm	LU	M	1851-1861	702,674	Czlopa	KO	Fam	1750-?	1,184,450
Chelm	LU	D	1853-1866	702,696	Czyzew Osada	BI	BMD	1826-1838	808,614
Chelm	LU	D	1853-1866	1,201,231	Czyzew Osada	BI	BMD	1839-1850	808,615
Chelm	LU	BMD	1855-1859	1,201,229	Czyzew Osada	BI	BMD	1851-1859	808,616
Chelm	LU	BMD	1855-1860	702,680	Czyzew Osada	BI	BMD	1860-1865	747,701
Chelm	LU	B	1857-1864	702,674	Czyzew Osada	BI	BMD	1866-1875	1,199,529
Chelm	LU	BMD	1859-1869	1,201,230	Czyzew Osada	BI	BMD	1876-1880	1,191,361
Chelm	LU	BMD	1861-1869	702,681	Dabie	PO	BMD	1826-1849	810,675
Chelm	LU	M	1861-1874	1,201,231	Dabie	PO	BMD	1850-1865	810,676
Chelm	LU	B	1864-1874	1,201,232	Dabie	PO	BMD	1866	1,201,435
Chelm	LU	D	1866-1874	1,201,232	Dabie	PO	BMD	1867-1875	1,201,436
Chelm	LU	BMD	1870	1,201,231	Dabrowno	OL	BMD	1847-1874	1,271,459
Chelm	LU	BMD	1870-1884	702,682	Daleszyce	KI	BMD	1826-1846	729,025
Chelm	LU	BMD	1873	1,201,233	Daleszyce	KI	BMD	1847-1865	729,026
Chelm	LU	BMD	1874	1,201,232	Daleszyce	KI	BMD	1866-1870	1,192,419
Chelm	LU	BMD	1875-1882	1,201,233	Darlowo	KO	B	1846-1861	1,184,450
Chelm	LU	BMD	1885-1888	702,683	Dobiegniew	ZI	BMD	1770/1854	1,184,461
Chelm	LU	BMD	1889-1894	702,684	Dobra	SZ	BMD	1839-1867	1,334,556
Chelm	LU	BMD	1894	702,684	Dobre Miasto	OL	D	1846-1937	1,184,419
Chelm	LU	BMD	1895-1898	702,685	Dobrodzien	KA	Cem	1846-1880	1,184,419
Chelm	LU	BMD	1899-1901	702,686	Dobrzyca	PO	BMD	1817-1864	1,273,157
Chelm	LU	BMD	1902-1904	702,687	Drawsko Pomorskie	KO	BMD	1779/1874	1,184,410
Chelm	LU	BMD	1905/1909	702,688	Drobin	WA	BMD	1826-1846	729,204
Chelm	LU	BMD	1910-1913	702,689	Drobin	WA	BMD	1847-1864	729,205
Chelm	LU	M	1914	702,675	Drobin	WA	BMD	1866-1879	1,201,496
Chelm	LU	BD	1915	702,679	Dubienka	LU	BMD	1826-1839	729,418
Chelm	LU	B	1923-1925	702,675	Dubienka	LU	BMD	1840-1852	729,419
Chelm	LU	D	1924-1927	702,679	Dubienka	LU	BMD	1853-1864	729,420
Chelm	LU	M	1924-1936	702,679	Dubienka	LU	BMD	1866-1874	1,201,253
Chelm	LU	B	1926-1929	702,676	Dzialoszyce	KI	BMD	1810-1820	588,908
Chelm	LU	BMD	1930-1931	702,690	Dzialoszyce	KI	BMD	1821-1827	588,909
Ceglm	LU	B	1931,1936	702,677	Dzialoszyce	KI	B	1826-1856	588,913
Chelm	LU	BMD	1932-1933	702,691	Dzialoszyce	KI	BM	1826-1864	814,603
Chelm	LU	BMD	1934	702,692	Dzialoszyce	KI	MD	1826-1864	814,604
Chelm	LU	BMD	1935	702,693	Dzialoszyce	KI	BMD	1849-1865	814,605
Chelm	LU	BMD	1937	702,694	Dzialoszyn	LO	BMD	1828-1837	702,383
Chelm	LU	B	1937,1939	702,678	Dzierzgon	GD	BMD	1847-1875	1,334,558
Chelm	LU	BMD	1938	702,695	Dzierzoniow	WR	Cem	1830-1930	1,184,449
Chmielnik	KI	BMD	1876-1877	1,192,418	Elblag	GD	BMD	1812-1871	742,026
Chojnow	WR	Cem	1888-1936	1,184,419	Filipow	BI	BMD	1829-1855	746,504
Choroszcz	BI	V	1883/1913	1,186,451	Filipow	BI	BMD	1856-1865	746,505
Chorzele	WA	BMD	1826-1841	723,213	Filipow	BI	BMD	1866-1869	1,191,984
Chorzele	WA	BMD	1842-1854	723,214	Filipow	BI	BMD	1870-1877	1,191,985
Chorzele	WA	BMD	1855-1863	723,215	Filipow	BI	BMD	1873/1879	1,191,274
Chorzow	KA	Cem	1867-1940	1,184,430	Firlej	LU	B	1826	1,201,320
Choszczno	SZ	BMD	1847-1853	544,649	Firlej	LU	BMD	1826-1831	729,183
Ciechanow	WA	BMD	1826-1841	702,466	Fordon	BY	BMD	1820-1851	814,573
Ciechanow	WA	BMD	1842-1851	702,467	Fordon	BY	BMD	1823-1851	814,574
Ciechanow	WA	BMD	1852-1865	702,468	Fordon	BY	BMD	1849-1888	814,575
Ciechanowiec	BI	BMD	1839/1870	1,191,937	Frampol	LU	BMD	1871-1875	1,201,321
Ciechanowiec	BI	BMD	1847/1935	1,186,427	Frombork	OL	Cem		1,184,411

Place	Region	Type	Years	Number
Gardeja	GD	Cem	?-?	1,184,411
Gdansk	GD	Fam	1814	1,184,410
Gdansk	GD	BMD	1837/1939	1,184,407
Gdansk	GD	B	1847-1854	742,680
Gdansk	GD	M	1848-1851	742,684
Gdansk	GD	Fam	1848-1906	1,184,409
Gdansk	GD	M	1851-1855	742,685
Gdansk	GD	D	1852-1855	742,780
Gdansk	GD	M	1853-1857	742,686
Gdansk	GD	B	1854-1857	742,681
Gdansk	GD	D	1855-1859	742,781
Gdansk	GD	M	1857-1859	742,687
Gdansk	GD	B	1857-1862	742,682
Gdansk	GD	D	1859-1864	742,782
Gdansk	GD	M	1860-1863	742,688
Gdansk	GD	M	1860-1863	742,777
Gdansk	GD	B	1861-1864	742,683
Gdansk	GD	M	1862-1863	742,778
Gdansk	GD	B	1864-1865	742,684
Gdansk	GD	M	1864-1865	742,779
Gdansk	GD	D	1864-1865	742,783
Gdansk	GD	D	1889-1940	1,184,408
Gdansk	GD	Cem	19XX	1,184,407
Gebice	BY	BMD	1832-1847	719,219
Gliwice	KA	Cem	1800	1,184,414
Gliwice	KA	BMD	1812-1847	1,335,024
Gliwice	KA	BMD	1812-1861	875,339
Gliwice	KA	D	1812-1874	1,194,054
Gliwice	KA	D	1812-1874	1,194,055
Gliwice	KA	M	1812-1874	1,271,453
Gliwice	KA	B	1812-1874	1,334,567
Gliwice	KA	B	1812-1874	1,334,612
Gliwice	KA	BMD	1858-1861	1,335,024
Gliwice	KA	Cem	1903-1940	1,184,414
Glogow	ZI	Cen	1812	1,184,415
Glogow	ZI	BMD	1812/1938	1,184,416
Glogow	ZI	Cem	1818-1893	1,184,416
Glowno	LO	BMD	1812-1833	702,417
Glowno	LO	BMD	1834-1843	702,418
Glowno	LO	BMD	1844-1853	702,419
Glowno	LO	BMD	1854-1865	702,420
Glowno	LO	BMD	1866-1870	767,085
Glowno	LO	BMD	1871-1826	1,192,278
Glubczyce	OP	D	1818-1937	1,184,434
Glusk	LU	BMD	1826/1894	808,075
Glusk	LU	BMD	1834-1836	808,076
Glusk	LU	BMD	1853-1872	1,201,325
Glusk	LU	BMD	1873-1877	1,201,326
Gniewkowo	BY	BMD	1815-1847	719,220
Gniewoszow	KI	BMD	1857-1867	1,201,344
Gniewoszow	KI	BMD	1868-1877	1,201,345
Gniezno	PO	BMD	1840-1841	1,271,464
Gniezno	PO	BMD	1840-1847	719,426
Goleniow	SZ	BMD	1815-1847	1,271,450
Goleniow	SZ	M	1847-1874	1,194,052
Goleniow	SZ	BD	1847-1874	1,271,450
Goleniow	SZ	Fam	1860-1934	1,184,417
Golina	PO	BMD	1826-1838	719,441
Golina	PO	BMD	1840/1862	719,442
Golina	PO	BMD	1866-1870	1,201,460
Golub-dobrzyn	BY	BMD	1808-1819	812,349
Golub-dobrzyn	BY	BMD	1819-1825	812,350
Golub-dobrzyn	BY	BMD	1826-1840	812,351
Golub-dobrzyn	BY	BMD	1826-1850	812,352
Golub-dobrzyn	BY	BMD	1851-1859	812,353
Golub-dobrzyn	BY	BMD	1858-1865	812,354
Gora Kalwaria	WA	BMD	1826-1847	723,681
Gora Kalwaria	WA	BMD	1848-1859	723,682
Gorzkow	LU	BMD	1826-1846	808,092
Gorzkow	LU	BMD	1847-1855	808,093
Gorzkow	LU	BMD	1856-1870	767,825
Gorzkow	LU	BMD	1875	1,201,328
Gorzow Slaski	OP	D	1843-1844	1,184,432
Gowarczow	KI	BMD	1826-1840	716,402
Gowarczow	KI	BMD	1841-1859	716,403
Grabowiec	LU	BMD	1826-1836	808,189
Grabowiec	LU	BMD	1837-1854	808,190
Grabowiec	LU	BMD	1855-1865	808,191
Grabowiec	LU	BMD	1866-1867	767,826
Grabowiec	LU	BMD	1867-1875	1,201,332
Grajewo	BI	BMD	1834/1857	747,019
Grajewo	BI	BMD	1871-1873	1,199,529
Grajewo	BI	BMD	1874-1875	1,199,530
Grajewo	BI	BMD	1876-1879	1,191,361
Grajewo	BI	BMD	1880	1,191,362
Granica	KI	BMD	1857-1867	1,201,344
Granica	KI	BMD	1868-1877	1,201,345
Grocholice	LO	BMD	1826-1845	723,499
Grocholice	LO	D	1827-1830	767,091
Grocholice	LO	BMD	1831-1869	767,091
Grodzisk Mazowiecki	WA	BMD	1810	1,199,884
Grodzisk Mazowiecki	WA	BMD	1810/1865	1,199,885
Grodzisk Mazowiecki	WA	BMD	1865-1876	1,199,886
Grodzisk Mazowiecki	WA	BMD	1877	1,199,887
Grodzisk Wielkopolski	PO	D	1817-1837	1,271,465
Grojec	WA	DMD	1820-1836	723,673
Grojec	WA	BMD	1826/1842	723,674
Grojec	WA	BMD	1843-1857	723,675
Grojec	WA	BMD	1858-1864	723,676
Gryfice	SZ	BMD	1815-1847	1,190,946
Gryfice	SZ	BMD	1848-1874	1,194,051
Horodlo	LU	BMD	1826-1854	807,824
Hrubieszow	LU	BMD	1826-1838	807,844
Hrubieszow	LU	BMD	1839-1840	807,845
Hrubieszow	LU	BMD	1841-1846	807,739
Hrubieszow	LU	BMD	1847-1852	807,740
Hrubieszow	LU	BMD	1853-1859	807,741
Hrubieszow	LU	BMD	1860-1865	807,742
Hrubieszow	LU	BMD	1866-1867	767,828
Ilza	KI	BMD	1850-1861	714,995
Ilza	KI	BMD	1862-1865	714,996
Ilza	KI	BMD	1866-1870	1,192,419
Ilza	KI	BMD	1871-1875	1,192,420
Ilza	KI	BMD	1876	1,201,345
Ilza	KI	BMD	1877	1,201,346
Izbica	LU	BMD	1826-1846	807,755
Izbica	LU	BMD	1847-1858	807,756
Izbica	LU	BMD	1859-1864	767,830
Izbica Kujawska	PO	BMD	1810/1835	741,831
Izbica Kujawska	PO	BMD	1836-1852	741,832
Izbica Kujawska	PO	BMD	1853-1865	741,833
Jablonka Koscielna	BI	BMD	1826/1865	747,702
Jablonka Koscielna	BI	BMD	1838/1888	1,186,444
Jablonka Koscielna	BI	BMD	1866/1871	1,199,530
Jablonka Swierczewo	BI	BMD	1838/1888	1,046,484
Janow Podlaski	LU	BMD	1826-1839	807,766
Janow Podlaski	LU	BMD	1840-1843	807,767
Janow Podlaski	LU	BMD	1844-1865	807,768
Janow Podlaski	LU	BMD	1866-1869	937,498
Janowiec	LU	BMD	1817-1841	813,880
Janowiec	LU	BMD	1842-1857	813,881
Jarczow	LU	BMD	1827-1850	813,882

Jarczow	LU	BMD	1851-1865	813,883	Kepno	PO	BMD	1825/1835	742,975
Jarczow	LU	BMD	1866-1870	937,498	Kepno	PO	BMD	1836-1841	742,976
Jarocin	PO	BMD	1810-1879	1,271,464	Kepno	PO	BMD	1842-1847	742,977
Jastrowie	KO	BMD	1816-1839	1,184,420	Ketrzyn	OL	BMD	1813-1874	1,184,447
Jastrowie	KO	D	1830	1,184,421	Kielce	KI	BMD	1868-1872	1,192,420
Jastrowie	KO	BMD	1840-1847	1,184,421	Kielce	KI	BMD	1873-1877	1,192,421
Jawor	WR	Cem	1806-1939	1,184,422	Kietrz	OP	BMD	1812-1874	1,335,040
Jawor	WR	BMD	1815-1863	1,184,422	Kisielice	OL	D	1893-1930	1,184,413
Jawor	WR	Fam	1819	1,184,423	Kleczew	PO	BMD	1866-1868	1,191,082
Jelenia Gora	WR	Cem	1886-1938	1,184,419	Kleczew	PO	BMD	1869-1870	1,191,083
Jezow	LO	BMD	1826-1860	723,535	Klimontow	KI	BMD	1826-1839	809,129
Jezow	LO	BMD	1861-1865	723,536	Klimontow	KI	BMD	1840-1853	809,130
Jezow	LO	BMD	1866-1870	767,101	Klimontow	KI	BMD	1854-1861	809,131
Jezow	LO	BMD	1871-1876	1,257,770	Klimontow	KI	BMD	1861-1870	1,199,823
Jozefow (bilgoraj)	LU	BMD	1826-1843	813,893	Klimontow	KI	BMD	1862-1865	809,132
Jozefow (bilgoraj)	LU	BMD	1844-1863	813,894	Klimontow	KI	BMD	1866-1874	1,199,825
Jozefow Nad Wisla	LU	BMD	1825-1845	813,895	Klimontow	KI	BMD	1867-1870	1,199,824
Jozefow Nad Wisla	LU	BMD	1846-1862	813,896	Klimontow	KI	BMD	1875-1878	1,199,826
Jozefow Nad Wisla	LU	B	1863	905,146	Klobuck	KA	BMD	1826-1860	879,546
Jozefow Nad Wisla	LU	BMD	1866-1868	905,146	Klobuck	KA	BMD	1856-1864	879,547
Kalisz	PO	BMD	1809-1820	743,141	Klobuck	KA	BMD	1859-1877	1,199,680
Kalisz	PO	BMD	1821-1828	743,142	Klodawa	PO	BMD	1826-1831	743,000
Kalisz	PO	BMD	1829-1837	743,143	Klodawa	PO	BMD	1832-1858	743,001
Kalisz	PO	BMD	1838-1845	743,144	Klodawa	PO	BMD	1859-1865	743,002
Kalisz	PO	BMD	1846-1851	743,145	Klodawa	PO	BMD	1866-1877	1,191,084
Kalisz	PO	BMD	1852-1857	743,146	Klodzko	WR	D	1832-1940	1,184,414
Kalisz	PO	BMD	1858-1861	743,147	Kluczbork	OP	BMD	1830-1855	1,184,431
Kalisz	PO	BMD	1862-1865	743,148	Klukowo	BI	M	1934,1936	1,186,445
Kalisz	PO	BMD	1866-1868	1,191,074	Klwow	KI	BMD	1851-1860	718,961
Kalisz	PO	BMD	1869-1874	1,191,075	Klwow	KI	BMD	1866-1874	1,192,421
Kalisz	PO	BMD	1875-1876	1,199,926	Klwow	KI	BMD	1875-1877	1,201,346
Kalisz	PO	BMD	1877	1,199,927	Kock	LU	BMD	1826-1842	813,989
Kalisz Pomorski	KO	BMD	1778-1848	1,334,572	Kock	LU	BMD	1843-1858	813,990
Kalisz Pomorski	KO	BMD	1847-1874	1,334,575	Kock	LU	BMD	1859-1865	813,991
Kaluszyn	WA	BMD	1826-1832	702,435	Kock	LU	BMD	1867-1870	905,156
Kaluszyn	WA	BMD	1833-1840	702,436	Koden	LU	BMD	1826-1841	813,999
Kaluszyn	WA	BMD	1841-1846	702,437	Koden	LU	BMD	1843-1854	814,000
Kaluszyn	WA	BMD	1847-1852	702,438	Kolbiel	WA	BMD	1826-1838	702,445
Kaluszyn	WA	BMD	1853-1859	702,439	Kolbiel	WA	BMD	1854	702,445
Kaluszyn	WA	BMD	1860-1863	702,440	Kolo	PO	BMD	1825-1840	741,979
Kaluszyn	WA	BMD	1864-1865	702,441	Kolo	PO	BMD	1841-1854	741,980
Kamien Pomorski	SZ	BMD	1814-1874	1,273,145	Kolo	PO	BMD	1855-1865	741,981
Kamien Pomorski	SZ	BMD	1848-1874	1,334,556	Kolo	PO	BMD	1866-1869	1,191,087
Kamienna Gora	WR	Cem	1800-1938	1,184,432	Kolo	PO	BMD	1869-1877	1,191,088
Kamienna Gora	WR	I/O	1812-1848	1,184,432	Komarow	LU	BMD	1826-1842	813,874
Kamienna Gora	WR	B	1812-1863	1,184,432	Komarow	LU	BMD	1843-1860	813,875
Kamienna Gora	WR	M	1827-1852	1,184,432	Komarow	LU	BMD	1861-1865	813,876
Kamienna Gora	WR	Cen	1839-1842	1,184,432	Komarow	LU	BMD	1866-1870	905,158
Kamienna Gora	WR	D	1881-1938	1,184,432	Koniecpol	KI	BMD	1826-1842	730,078
Kamionka	LU	BMD	1826-1865	813,843	Koniecpol	KI	BMD	1844-1855	730,079
Karczew	WA	BMD	1826-1841	702,442	Konin	PO	M	1815	741,998
Karczew	WA	BMD	1842-1864	702,443	Konin	PO	BMD	1826-1845	741,998
Karczew	WA	BMD	1842-1872	702,444	Konin	PO	BMD	1846-1853	741,999
Kargowa	ZI	BMD	1817-1874	1,184,461	Konin	PO	BMD	1855/1865	742,000
Kargowa	ZI	Fam	1834,1848	1,334,579	Konin	PO	BMD	1866	1,191,093
Kartuzy	GD	Fam	1848-1873	475,222	Konin	PO	BMD	1869-1874	1,191,094
Katowice	KA	D	1825-1939	1,184,426	Konskie	KI	BMD	1826-1836	716,412
Katowice	KA	D	1850-1939	1,184,425	Konskie	KI	BMD	1837-1845	716,415
Katowice	KA	B	1860-1936	1,184,423	Konskie	KI	BMD	1846-1859	716,416
Katowice	KA	Fam	1868-1897	1,184,428	Konskie	KI	BMD	1857-1863	716,413
Katowice	KA	D	1869-1934	1,184,424	Konskie	KI	BMD	1860-1865	716,607
Katy Wroclawskie	WR	BMD	1812/1937	1,184,423	Konskie	KI	BMD	1864-1865	716,414
Katy Wroclawskie	WR	I/O	1823-1869	1,334,573	Konskie	KI	BMD	1866-1868	1,192,421
Katy Wroclawskie	WR	BMD	1824-1874	1,334,573	Konskie	KI	BMD	1869-1877	1,192,422
Kazanow	KI	BMD	1828-1857	730,310	Konskowola	LU	BMD	1826/1844	715,368
Kazanow	KI	BMD	1859-1877	1,201,346	Konskowola	LU	BMD	1845/1863	715,369
Kazimierz Dolny	LU	BMD	1826-1841	813,859	Konskowola	LU	BMD	1866-1870	905,160
Kazimierz Dolny	LU	BMD	1842-1848	813,860	Konstantynow	LO	BMD	1832-1851	730,171
Kazimierz Dolny	LU	BMD	1863	813,860	Lodzki				

Konstantynow Lodzki	LO	BMD	1852-1865	730,172		Krapkowice	OP	BMD	1819-1847	1,190,961
Konstantynow Lodzki	LO	BMD	1868-1870	767,113		Krapkowice	OP	BMD	1819-1848	1,184,431
Konstantynow Lodzki	LO	BMD	1871-1874	1,257,354		Krapkowice	OP	BD	1820-1843	890,725
						Krasniczyn	LU	BMD	1826-1836	715,450
Konstantynow Lodzki	LO	BMD	1875-1876	1,257,355		Krasnik	LU	B	1629-1670	995,812
Konstantynow Nad Bugi	LU	BMD	1826-1854	715,358		Krasnik	LU	BD	1735-1747	995,812
						Krasnik	LU	M	1735-1790	995,813
Koprzywnica	KI	BMD	1857-1858	809,133		Krasnik	LU	B	1735-1810	995,812
Kornik	PO	BMD	1817-1847	742,003		Krasnik	LU	D	1781-1818	995,813
Kornik	PO	D	1834-1840	1,194,062		Krasnik	LU	D	1826-1847	715,443
Kornik	PO	Fam	1840-1847	1,194,061		Krasnik	LU	B	1826-1849	715,440
Koronowo	BY	B	1847-1874	813,169		Krasnik	LU	M	1826-1870	715,442
Koscierzyna	GD	BM	1847-1865	742,795		Krasnik	LU	D	1847-1867	715,444
Koscierzyna	GD	Fam	1847-1873	474,721		Krasnik	LU	B	1850-1865	715,441
Koscierzyna	GD	Fam	1873-1919	474,715		Krasnobrod	LU	BMD	1827-1846	715,421
Kosow	WA	BMD	1827/1844	808,908		Krasnobrod	LU	BMD	1847-1857	715,422
Kosow	WA	BMD	1845-1862	808,909		Krasnopol	BI	BMD	1836/1862	746,651
Koszalin	KO	Fam	1800	1,184,430		Krasnopol	BI	BMD	1866/1875	1,191,985
Koszalin	KO	BMD	1812-1846	896,086		Krasnystaw	LU	BMD	1826/1851	715,438
Koszalin	KO	BMD	1813-1847	1,334,576		Krasnystaw	LU	BMD	1852-1860	715,439
Koszalin	KO	Cem	1835-1935	1,184,431		Krasnystaw	LU	BMD	1868-1870	905,162
Koszalin	KO	BMD	1840-1874	1,334,583		Kromolow	KA	BMD	1826-1835	879,569
Koszalin	KO	BMD	1841-1847	1,184,430		Kromolow	KA	BMD	1836-1854	879,570
Kozienice	KI	MD	1810-1811	729,351		Krosno Odrzanskie	ZI	Cem	1825/1955	1,184,406
Kozienice	KI	BMD	1826-1830	729,351		Krosno Odrzanskie	ZI	Cen	1844	1,184,406
Kozienice	KI	B	1826-1830	729,354		Krotoszyn	PO	BMD	1825-1841	743,091
Kozienice	KI	BMD	1826/1841	729,355		Krotoszyn	PO	BMD	1842-1847	743,092
Kozienice	KI	BMD	1831-1838	729,352		Krylow	LU	BMD	1826-1840	715,463
Kozienice	KI	BD	1831/1845	729,356		Krylow	LU	BMD	1841-1859	715,464
Kozienice	KI	BMD	1839-1852	729,353		Krysk	WA	BMD	1808-1815	689,597
Kozienice	KI	M	1842-1859	729,357		Krysk	WA	BMD	1815-1825	689,598
Kozienice	KI	BMD	1847/1861	729,358		Krysk	WA	BMD	1826-1841	689,599
Kozienice	KI	BMD	1849-1858	729,359		Krysk	WA	BMD	1842-1854	689,600
Kozienice	KI	BMD	1859-1863	729,360		Krysk	WA	BMD	1855-1865	689,601
Kozienice	KI	BMD	1864-1865	1,201,346		Krysk	WA	BMD	1866-1876	1,191,921
Kozienice	KI	BMD	1866-1875	1,201,347		Krzepice	KA	BMD	1830-1847	879,559
Kozienice	KI	BMD	1876-1877	1,201,348		Krzepice	KA	BMD	1848-1865	879,560
Kozle	OP	BMD	1810/1828	1,184,406		Krzepice	KA	BMD	1866-1874	1,199,692
Kozle	OP	BMD	1812-1846	1,190,954		Krzepice	KA	BMD	1875-1877	1,199,693
Kozle	OP	M	1879-1895	1,184,406		Krzeszow	RZ	BMD	1854-1874	1,199,826
Kozle	OP	D	1908-1917	1,184,406		Krzeszow	RZ	BMD	1871-1877	1,199,827
Kozmin	PO	BMD	1811-1812	742,946		Krzeszow Gorny	LU	BMD	1826-1834	718,678
Kozmin	PO	D	1818-1836	1,194,062		Krzywin	PO	BMD	1835-1847	743,099
Kozuchow	ZI	M	1849-1873	896,080		Kuczbork	WA	BMD	1826/1865	702,639
Krajenka	KO	BMD	1800-1863	1,184,432		Kurow	LU	BMD	1828/1847	718,699
Krajenka Chelmno	BY	Fam	1829-1832	495,967		Kurozweki	KI	BMD	1875-1878	1,199,827
Krakow	KR	M	1798-1816	718,918		Kutno	LO	BMD	1808-1812	730,039
Krakow	KR	B	1798-1819	718,912		Kutno	LO	BMD	1813-1816	730,040
Krakow	KR	D	1811/1828	718,922		Kutno	LO	BMD	1817-1821	730,041
Krakow	KR	D	1816-1819	718,912		Kutno	LO	BMD	1822-1828	730,042
Krakow	KR	M	1817-1829	718,919		Kutno	LO	BMD	1829-1833	730,043
Krakow	KR	B	1820-1829	718,913		Kwidzyn	GD	Sch	1812-1827	496,157
Krakow	KR	D	1829-1838	718,923		Kwidzyn	GD	Sch	1814-1860	496,166
Krakow	KR	B	1830-1836	718,914		Kwidzyn	GD	Fam	1818-1824	496,013
Krakow	KR	M	1830-1839	718,920		Kwidzyn	GD	Sch	1827-1828	496,158
Krakow	KR	B	1837-1843	718,915		Kwidzyn	GD	Sch	1829-1832	496,159
Krakow	KR	D	1839-1847	718,924		Kwidzyn	GD	Sch	1832-1835	496,160
Krakow	KR	M	1840-1852	718,921		Kwidzyn	GD	Cem	1833-1932	1,184,441
Krakow	KR	B	1844-1850	718,916		Kwidzyn	GD	Sch	1835-1837	496,161
Krakow	KR	D	1848-1854	741,914		Kwidzyn	GD	Sch	1837-1840	496,162
Krakow	KR	B	1851-1855	718,917		Kwidzyn	GD	Sch	1837-1843	496,163
Krakow	KR	BMD	1871-1875	1,201,163		Kwidzyn	GD	Sch	1843-1848	496,164
Krakow	KR	B	1874-1876	1,201,162		Kwidzyn	GD	Sch	1848-1854	496,165
Krakow	KR	BMD	1876-1877	1,201,163		Kwidzyn	GD	Mil	1852	495,963
Krakow	KR	BMD	1877	1,201,164		Kwieciszewo	BY	BMD	1832-1847	719,231
Krapkowice	OP	BMD	1812/1907	1,184,445		Ladek Zdroj	WR	Cem	1922-1934	1,184,432
						Lasin	BY	BMD	1824/1885	1,184,434
						Lask	LO	BMD	1827-1831	808,471
						Lask	LO	BMD	1832-1841	808,472

Lask	LO	BMD	1842-1850	808,473	Lowicz	LO	BMD	1861-1868	767,136
Lask	LO	BMD	1851-1859	808,474	Lowicz	LO	BMD	1867-1870	767,137
Lask	LO	BMD	1859-1865	808,475	Lowicz	LO	BMD	1872	1,191,730
Lask	LO	BMD	1866-1869	767,128	Lozdzieje	BI	BMD	1827-1854	746,680
Laszczow	LU	BMD	1827-1844	718,748	Lubartow	LU	BMD	1826-1842	718,719
Laszczow	LU	BMD	1845-1854	718,749	Lubartow	LU	BMD	1843-1854	718,720
Laszczow	LU	BMD	1855-1865	718,750	Lubartow	LU	BMD	1855-1865	718,721
Laszczow	LU	BMD	1866-1869	905,178	Lubartow	LU	BMD	1866-1868	905,168
Latowicz	WA	BMD	1827/1836	702,446	Lublin	LU	BMD	1826-1830	702,740
Lebork	GD	Fam	1829	1,184,433	Lublin	LU	D	1826-1840	702,738
Lebork	GD	BMD	1829-1846	1,184,433	Lublin	LU	BMD	1826-1840	723,564
Lebork	GD	Cem	1844-1936	1,184,433	Lublin	LU	M	1826-1846	702,737
Lebork	GD	Cem	1844-1936	1,184,434	Lublin	LU	B	1830/1842	702,735
Leczna	LU	BMD	1826-1835	718,760	Lublin	LU	BMD	1831-1837	702,741
Leczna	LU	BMD	1836-1846	718,761	Lublin	LU	BMD	1838-1841	702,742
Leczna	LU	BMD	1846-1855	718,762	Lublin	LU	BMD	1841-1853	723,565
Leczyca	LO	BMD	1817/1824	767,130	Lublin	LU	D	1841/1850	702,739
Legnica	WR	Fam	1812-1850	1,184,436	Lublin	LU	BMD	1842-1843	702,743
Legnica	WR	Cem	1814-1939	1,184,436	Lublin	LU	B	1843-1846	702,736
Legnica	WR	BM	1855-1940	1,184,435	Lublin	LU	BMD	1844-1845	702,744
Legnica	WR	D	1855-1940	1,184,436	Lublin	LU	BMD	1846-1847	702,745
Lelow	KI	BMD	1873-1876	1,199,693	Lublin	LU	BMD	1848-1849	702,746
Lelow	KI	BMD	1877	1,199,694	Lublin	LU	BMD	1849-1851	702,747
Lesnica	OP	Cem	1855-1933	1,184,378	Lublin	LU	BMD	1852-1853	702,748
Lewin Brzeski	OP	BMD	1815-1836	1,184,436	Lublin	LU	BMD	1854-1855	702,749
Lewin Brzeski	OP	Fam	1836-1850	1,184,437	Lublin	LU	BMD	1854-1864	723,566
Lewin Brzeski	OP	Cem	1882-1934	1,184,437	Lublin	LU	BMD	1856	702,750
Lezajsk	RZ	D	1826-1866	766,021	Lublin	LU	BMD	1857	702,751
Lipsko	KI	BMD	1826-1850	813,919	Lublin	LU	BMD	1858-1859	723,560
Lipsko	KI	BMD	1837	723,731	Lublin	LU	BMD	1860-1861	723,561
Lipsko	KI	BMD	1851-1858	813,920	Lublin	LU	BMD	1862-1863	723,562
Lipsko	KI	BMD	1866-1867	1,192,422	Lublin	LU	BMD	1864	723,563
Lipsko	KI	BMD	1868-1874	1,192,423	Lublin	LU	BMD	1865	905,172
Lipsko	KI	BMD	1875-1877	1,201,348	Lublin	LU	BMD	1866	905,173
Lisow	KI	BMD	1810-1836	723,731	Lublin	LU	BMD	1867	905,174
Lisow	KI	BMD	1837-1859	723,732	Lublin	LU	BMD	1868-1869	905,175
Lodz	LO	BMD	1826-1847	809,427	Lubliniec	KA	D	1820-1900	1,184,437
Lodz	LO	BMD	1848-1858	809,428	Lukow	LU	BMD	1826-1835	743,174
Lodz	LO	BMD	1859-1862	809,429	Lukow	LU	BMD	1836-1847	743,175
Lodz	LO	BMD	1863-1865	809,430	Lukow	LU	BMD	1848-1860	743,176
Lodz	LO	BMD	1866-1868	767,143	Lukow	LU	BMD	1861-1865	743,177
Lodz	LO	BMD	1869-1870	767,144	Lukow	LU	BMD	1866-1868	905,182
Lodz	LO	BMD	1871-1872	1,191,746	Lutomiersk	LO	BMD	1826-1833	810,239
Lodz	LO	BMD	1873-1874	1,191,747	Lutomiersk	LO	BMD	1834-1844	810,240
Lodz	LO	BMD	1875-1877	1,191,748	Lutomiersk	LO	BMD	1845-1859	810,241
Lodz	LO	BMD	1877	1,191,749	Lutomiersk	LO	BMD	1860-1865	810,242
Lomazy	LU	BMD	1826-1837	718,770	Lutomiersk	LO	BMD	1866-1868	767,124
Lomazy	LU	BMD	1838-1854	718,771	Lwow	LW	B	1814-1837	905,274
Lomza	BI	BMD	1827-1838	747,709	Lwowek Slaski	WR	Cem	1815-1932	1,184,437
Lomza	BI	BMD	1839/1853	747,710	Magnuszow	KI	BMD	1826-1839	729,040
Lomza	BI	BD	1846/1858	747,711	Magnuszow	KI	BMD	1858-1869	1,201,348
Lomza	BI	MD	1852/1864	747,712	Magnuszow	KI	BMD	1876	1,201,348
Lomza	BI	BMD	1857/1875	1,199,533	Malbork	GD	B	1847-1865	742,802
Lomza	BI	B	1859-1864	747,713	Malbork	GD	MD	1847-1865	742,803
Lomza	BI	BMD	1863/1872	747,714	Malogoszcz	KI	BMD	1826-1843	814,645
Lomza	BI	BMD	1865/1872	1,199,530	Malogoszcz	KI	BMD	1844-1864	814,646
Lomza	BI	BMD	1867/1875	1,199,531	Malogoszcz	KI	BMD	1865-1867	1,192,423
Lomza	BI	BMD	1869-1873	1,199,532	Markuszow	LU	BMD	1826/1846	743,200
Lomza	BI	BMD	1876-1880	1,191,362	Michow	LU	BMD	1826/1855	742,876
Losice	WA	BMD	1829-1841	811,236	Miechowiec	KA	M	1880,1885	1,184,442
Losice	WA	BMD	1844-1860	811,237	Miedzyborz	WR	B	1868-1883	1,184,441
Lowicz	LO	BMD	1808-1811	811,066	Miedzyborz	WR	Cem	1870-1906	1,184,444
Lowicz	LO	BMD	1811-1817	811,067	Miedzychod	PO	BMD	1816	1,194,061
Lowicz	LO	BMD	1818-1823	811,068	Miedzyrzec Podlaski	LU	BMD	1826-1835	742,870
Lowicz	LO	BMD	1824-1825	811,069	Miedzyrzec Podlaski	LU	BMD	1836-1840	742,871
Lowicz	LO	BMD	1826-1843	811,070	Miedzyrzec Podlaski	LU	BMD	1841-1847	742,872
Lowicz	LO	BMD	1826/1832	1,199,884	Miedzyrzec Podlaski	LU	BMD	1848-1854	742,873
Lowicz	LO	BMD	1844-1859	811,071	Miedzyrzec Podlaski	LU	BMD	1855-1860	742,874
Lowicz	LO	BMD	1860-1865	811,072	Miedzyrzec Podlaski	LU	BMD	1861-1865	742,875

Miedzyrzec Podlaski	LU	BMD	1866-1868	905,191	Nur	WA	BMD	1846-1859	811,052
Miedzyrzecz	ZI	BMD	1817-1834	1,271,415	Nysa	OP	B	1809-1928	1,184,443
Miedzyrzecz	ZI	BMD	1817/1841	1,184,442	Nysa	OP	MD	1809-1930	1,184,444
Miedzyrzecz	ZI	BMD	1835-1847	1,271,481	Oborniki	PO	BMD	1835-1839	1,194,061
Miedzyrzecz	ZI	Fam	1846-1875	474,926	Okuniew	WA	BMD	1826/1837	689,634
Miedzyrzecz	ZI	BMD	1847-1875	1,196,136	Olawa	WR	BMD	1817/1888	1,184,445
Miedzyrzecz	ZI	BMD	1847-1875	1,196,137	Olawa	WR	Cem	1818-1933	1,184,445
Miedzyrzecz	ZI	Fam	1848-1903	474,929	Olesnica	WR	BMD	1812-1859	1,184,444
Miejsce	OP	BMD	1810/1873	1,184,456	Olesno	OP	BMD	1812-1847	1,184,449
Mikstat	PO	BMD	1836-1846	746,949	Olesno	OP	I/O	1815-1847	1,184,449
Minsk Mazowiecki	WA	BMD	1826-1845	702,447	Olesno	OP	I/O	1815-1847	1,184,450
Minsk Mazowiecki	WA	BMD	1846-1855	702,448	Olesno	OP	D	1891-1938	1,184,449
Miroslawiec	KO	Fam	1799-1810	1,184,440	Olkusz	KR	BMD	1827-1840	875,262
Miroslawiec	KO	Fam	1799-1810	1,184,441	Olkusz	KR	BMD	1841-1857	875,263
Miroslawiec	KO	BMD	1815-1847	1,184,439	Olkusz	KR	B	1853-1860	923,473
Mlawa	WA	BMD	1823-1847	702,504	Olkusz	KR	BMD	1858-1870	923,473
Mlawa	WA	BMD	1848-1859	702,505	Olsztyn	OL	BMD	1847-1874	1,334,557
Mlawa	WA	BMD	1860-1865	702,506	Opatow	KI	BMD	1835-1845	809,163
Mlynary	OL	Cem	1873-1938	1,185,009	Opatow	KI	BMD	1843-1855	809,164
Mogielnica	KI	BMD	1874-1877	1,201,348	Opatow	KI	BMD	1854-1865	809,165
Mogielnica	KI	BMD	1877	1,201,349	Opoczno	KI	BMD	1866-1868	1,192,424
Mogielnica	WA	BMD	1826-1842	723,668	Opoczno	KI	BMD	1869-1874	1,192,425
Mogielnica	WA	B	1836-1860	723,673	Opole	OP	BMD	1812-1907	1,184,445
Mogielnica	WA	BMD	1843-1858	723,669	Opole	OP	Cem	1816-1918	1,184,445
Mogielnica	WA	BMD	1859-1865	723,670	Opole Lubelskie	LU	D	1826-1850	747,889
Mogielnica	WA	BMD	1860-1864	723,673	Opole Lubelskie	LU	M	1826-1851	747,888
Mokobody	WA	BMD	1827/1860	808,846	Opole Lubelskie	LU	B	1826-1854	747,887
Mokotow	WA	BMD	1827-1842	1,234,567	Orla	BI	BMD	1836-1866	1,191,940
Mordy	WA	BMD	1826-1845	808,853	Osieciny	BY	BM	1826-1852	530,227
Mordy	WA	BMD	1846/1858	808,854	Osieciny	BY	D	1826-1892	530,227
Mosina	PO	B	1835-1836	746,967	Osieciny	BY	M	1826-1931	530,226
Mstow	KA	BMD	?-?	1,199,703	Osieciny	BY	B	1826-1934	530,225
Mstow	KA	BMD	1826-1858	864,928	Osieciny	BY	D	1917-1938	530,227
Mszczonow	WA	BMD	1826-1844	723,427	Osno	ZI	BMD	1813-1899	1,184,410
Mszczonow	WA	BMD	1845-1854	723,428	Ostrow Mazowiecka	WA	BMD	1826-1837	808,429
Mszczonow	WA	BMD	1855-1865	1,199,887	Ostrow Mazowiecka	WA	BMD	1837-1843	808,430
Mszczonow	WA	BMD	1866-1876	1,199,888	Ostrow Mazowiecka	WA	BMD	1841-1845	808,431
Mysliborz	SZ	BMD	1833-1847	1,184,456	Ostrow Mazowiecka	WA	BMD	1843/1848	808,432
Myslowice	KA	B	1847-1866	864,943	Ostrow Mazowiecka	WA	BMD	1847/1859	808,434
Myslowice	KA	BMD	1847-1870	864,946	Ostrow Mazowiecka	WA	BMD	1849/1854	808,433
Myslowice	KA	M	1849-1860	864,944	Ostrow Mazowiecka	WA	BMD	1856/1865	808,435
Myslowice	KA	M	1859-1863	864,945	Ostrow Wielkopolski	PO	Fam	1836-1838	1,271,464
Nadarzyn	WA	BMD	1827-1828	1,199,888					
Nadarzyn	WA	BMD	1832-1849	1,199,889	Ostrzeszow	PO	BMD	1835-1846	747,832
Nadarzyn	WA	BMD	1850-1867	1,199,745	Ozarow	KI	BMD	1826-1849	809,166
Nadarzyn	WA	BMD	1868-1874	1,199,746	Ozarow	KI	BMD	1844-1857	809,167
Naklo Nad Notecia	BY	BMD	1823-1867	715,115	Ozorkow	LO	M	1872,1883	1,186,428
Naklo Nad Notecia	BY	Cen	1833-1835	1,184,443	Ozorkow	LO	M	1923	1,046,468
Naklo Nad Notecia	BY	BMD	1848/1874	715,114	Pabianice	LO	MD	1831/1862	714,498
Namyslow	OP	BMD	1812-1847	1,184,443	Pabianice	LO	BMD	1850-1865	714,499
Namyslow	OP	Cem	1914-1918	1,184,443	Pabianice	LO	BMD	1866-1870	768,013
Nowe Miasto Pilica	LO	BMD	1826-1836	588,562	Pabianice	LO	BMD	1871-1874	1,191,880
Nowe Miasto Pilica	LO	BMD	1837-1854	588,563	Pacanow	KI	BMD	1875-1877	1,192,425
Nowe Miasto Pilica	LO	BMD	1856-1865	768,005	Pajeczno	LO	BMD	1826-1837	716,008
Nowe Miasto Pilica	LO	BMD	1874-1877	1,201,349	Pajeczno	LO	BMD	1838-1865	716,009
Nowe Miastro Warta	PO	BMD	1817-1836	1,273,157	Pajeczno	LO	BMD	1866-1870	766,015
					Pakosc	BY	BMD	1823-1847	719,232
					Parczew	LU	BD	1825/1853	747,900
					Paslek	OL	Cem	1825-1907	1,184,446
Nowogrod	BI	BMD	1826/1846	747,715	Pelczyce	SZ	BMD	1825-1874	1,184,379
					Piaseczno	WA	D	1829	723,683
Nowogrod	BI	MD	1847/1864	747,716	Piaseczno	WA	BMD	1833-1836	723,683
Nowogrod	BI	BMD	1857-1871	1,199,533	Piaski	LU	BMD	1826-1837	748,070
Nowogrod	BI	BMD	1867/1886	1,199,534	Piaski	LU	BMD	1838-1855	748,071
Nowogrod	BI	BMD	1876/1880	1,191,362	Pilica	KR	BMD	1826-1835	875,273
Nowy Korczyn	KI	BMD	1826-1839	1,192,423	Pilica	KR	B	1826-1850	875,276
Nowy Korczyn	KI	BMD	1849/1876	1,192,424	Pilica	KR	M	1826-1863	875,277
Nur	WA	BMD	1826-1845	811,051	Pilica	KR	BMD	1836-1846	875,274
					Pilica	KR	D	1836-1865	875,278

Pilica	KR	BMD	1847-1857	875,275	Plonsk	WA	BMD	1853/1863	689,624
Pilica	KR	B	1850/1865	875,277	Plonsk	WA	BMD	1864-1865	689,625
Pilica	KR	BMD	1858-1870	923,477	Plonsk	WA	BMD	1865/1870	1,191,987
Pinczow	KI	BMD	1608-1810	716,155	Plonsk	WA	BMD	1868/1873	1,191,988
Pinczow	KI	BMD	1810-1827	716,163	Plonsk	WA	BMD	1872	1,191,989
Pinczow	KI	BMD	1811-1814	716,156	Poddebice	LO	M	1857-1858	1,186,433
Pinczow	KI	BMD	1815-1820	716,157	Polaniec	KI	BMD	1826-1836	588,928
Pinczow	KI	BMD	1821-1825	716,158	Polaniec	KI	BMD	1837-1860	588,929
Pinczow	KI	BMD	1826-1828	716,159	Polaniec	KI	BMD	1861-1865	588,930
Pinczow	KI	BMD	1828-1838	716,164	Polaniec	KI	BMD	1866-1873	1,199,827
Pinczow	KI	BMD	1830-1841	716,160	Polaniec	KI	BMD	1874-1877	1,199,828
Pinczow	KI	BMD	1839-1847	716,165	Polczyn Zdroj	KO	Cem	1858-1936	1,184,446
Pinczow	KI	BMD	1842-1851	716,161	Prabuty	OL	BMD	1823-1874	1,184,449
Pinczow	KI	BMD	1848-1850	716,166	Prabuty	OL	B	1920	1,184,449
Pinczow	KI	BMD	1851-1864	716,167	Praszka	LO	BMD	1826-1851	715,837
Pinczow	KI	BMD	1852-1865	716,162	Praszka	LO	BMD	1852-1865	715,838
Pinczow	KI	BMD	1862-1863	1,192,425	Praszka	LO	BMD	1866-1867	768,026
Pinczow	KI	BMD	1865-1871	1,192,426	Praszka	LO	BMD	1869-1870	1,199,716
Pinczow	KI	BMD	1866/1870	1,192,358	Pruchnik	RZ	B	1834-1870	766,039
Pinczow	KI	BMD	1870-1875	1,192,359	Prudnik	OP	Nam	1812-1824	1,184,444
Pinczow	KI	BMD	1871-1875	1,192,427	Prudnik	OP	B	1833-1874	1,184,444
Pinczow	KI	BMD	1875-1877	1,192,360	Prudnik	OP	D	1861-1939	1,184,444
Piotrkow Trybunalski	LO	BMD	1808-1810	715,786	Przasnysz	WA	BMD	1826-1837	702,526
					Przasnysz	WA	BMD	1838-1848	702,527
Piotrkow Trybunalski	LO	BMD	1810-1816	715,787	Przasnysz	WA	BMD	1849-1857	702,528
					Przasnysz	WA	BMD	1858-1865	702,529
Piotrkow Trybunalski	LO	BMD	1816-1821	715,788	Przedborz	KI	BMD	1826-1834	719,103
					Przedborz	KI	BMD	1835-1846	719,104
Piotrkow Trybunalski	LO	BMD	1821-1824	715,789	Przedborz	KI	BMD	1847-1856	719,105
					Przedborz	KI	BMD	1857-1865	719,106
Piotrkow Trybunalski	LO	BMD	1824-1830	715,790	Przedborz	KI	BMD	1866	1,192,427
					Przedborz	KI	BMD	1867-1871	1,192,428
Piotrkow Trybunalski	LO	BMD	1831-1838	715,804	Przemocze	SZ	Fam	1761	1,184,456
					Przemocze	SZ	BMD	1812-1849	1,190,966
Piotrkow Trybunalski	LO	BMD	1839-1846	715,805	Przerosl	BI	BMD	1827-1852	747,007
					Przerosl	BI	BMD	1853-1865	747,008
Piotrkow Trybunalski	LO	BMD	1847-1853	715,806	Przerosl	BI	BMD	1866-1877	1,191,985
					Przerosl	BI	BMD	1878-1879	1,191,274
Piotrkow Trybunalski	LO	BMD	1854-1858	715,807	Przybyszew	KI	BMD	1826-1834	723,683
					Przyrow	KA	BMD	1826-1846	875,468
Piotrkow Trybunalski	LO	BMD	1858-1864	715,808	Przyrow	KA	BMD	1847-1858	875,469
					Przyrow	KA	BMD	1859-1873	1,199,718
Piotrkow Trybunalski	LO	BMD	1864-1869	768,023	Przyrow	KA	BMD	1874-1877	1,199,719
					Przysucha	KI	BMD	1826-1839	718,969
Piotrkow Trybunalski	LO	BMD	1864-1873	1,191,757	Przysucha	KI	BMD	1840-1854	718,970
					Przysucha	KI	BMD	1854-1863	718,971
Plawno	LO	BMD	1826-1842	715,816	Przysucha	KI	BMD	1869-1877	1,201,349
Plawno	LO	BMD	1843-1863	715,817	Przytyk	KI	BMD	1826-1842	729,068
Plawno	LO	BMD	1864-1865	715,818	Przytyk	KI	BMD	1826-1864	729,066
Plawno	LO	BMD	1866-1870	768,052	Przytyk	KI	D	1840-1862	729,067
Plawno	LO	BMD	1871-1873	1,191,758	Przytyk	KI	BMD	1843-1850	729,069
Pleszew	PO	Fam	1834-1839	1,190,960	Przytyk	KI	BMD	1851-1859	729,070
Pleszew	PO	BMD	1835-1847	752,629	Przytyk	KI	BMD	1860-1862	1,201,349
Plock	WA	BMD	1808-1816	729,206	Przytyk	KI	BMD	1863-1877	1,201,350
Plock	WA	BMD	1815-1825	729,207	Pszczew	ZI	BMD	1817-1847	1,335,040
Plock	WA	BMD	1826-1836	730,201	Pszczew	ZI	Fam	1877-1918	474,925
Plock	WA	BMD	1837-1844	730,202	Pszczyna	KA	BMD	1847-1874	1,184,446
Plock	WA	BMD	1845-1852	730,203	Puck	GD	Fam	1812-1855	474,720
Plock	WA	BMD	1853-1859	730,204	Puck	GD	Fam	1857-1920	474,714
Plock	WA	BMD	1860-1863	730,205	Pulawy	LU	BM	1838/1866	753,304
Plock	WA	M	1864-1869	1,201,498	Punsk	BI	BMD	1833-1865	747,764
Plock	WA	D	1864-1875	1,201,498	Punsk	BI	BMD	1866-1875	1,191,986
Plock	WA	D	1864-1875	1,201,499	Punsk	BI	BMD	1878-1879	1,191,274
Plock	WA	B	1865-1866	1,201,496	Pyrzyce	SZ	Cen	1853	1,184,446
Plock	WA	B	1866-1872	1,201,497	Pyzdry	PO	BMD	1826-1845	752,757
Plonsk	WA	BMD	1826-1840	689,635	Pyzdry	PO	BMD	1846-1865	752,758
Plonsk	WA	BMD	1841-1847	689,636	Pyzdry	PO	BMD	1866-1868	1,191,311
Plonsk	WA	BMD	1848-1852	689,637	Pyzdry	PO	BMD	1869-1877	1,191,312
Plonsk	WA	BD	1852/1870	1,191,932	Raciaz	WA	BMD	1826-1846	730,163

Place	Region	Type	Years	Film No.
Raciaz	WA	BMD	1847-1856	811,222
Raciaz	WA	BMD	1857-1865	811,223
Raciaz	WA	BMD	1866-1872	1,191,025
Raciaz	WA	BMD	1873-1875	1,191,026
Raciborz	OP	BM	1814-1862	1,184,449
Raciborz	OP	D	1865-1930	1,184,448
Raciborz	OP	Cem	1888-1940	1,184,447
Radom	KI	BMD	1827-1844	716,127
Radom	KI	BMD	1845-1848	716,128
Radom	KI	BMD	1848-1852	716,129
Radom	KI	BMD	1852-1858	716,130
Radom	KI	BMD	1859-1862	716,131
Radom	KI	BMD	1862-1865	716,132
Radom	KI	BMD	1866	1,201,350
Radom	KI	BMD	1866-1877	1,201,351
Radom	KI	BMD	1870-1875	1,201,352
Radom	KI	BMD	1876-1877	1,201,353
Radomsko	LO	BMD	1826-1840	718,597
Radomsko	LO	BMD	1841-1856	718,598
Radomsko	LO	BMD	1857-1865	718,599
Radomsko	LO	BMD	1866-1870	768,054
Radomsko	LO	BMD	1871-1872	1,191,763
Radoszyce	KI	BMD	1826-1841	719,332
Radoszyce	KI	BMD	1842-1850	719,333
Radoszyce	KI	BMD	1851-1859	719,334
Radoszyce	KI	BMD	1866-1869	1,192,428
Radoszyce	KI	BMD	1871-1873	1,192,429
Radzanow	WA	BMD	1824-1825	702,836
Radzanow	WA	BMD	1826/1847	702,837
Radzanow	WA	BMD	1848-1862	702,838
Radzilow	BI	BMD	1826-1847	747,020
Radzilow	BI	BMD	1878	1,191,362
Radzyn Podlaski	LU	BMD	1826/1846	753,330
Radzyn Podlaski	LU	BMD	1837-1847	753,331
Radzyn Podlaski	LU	BMD	1848/1863	753,332
Rajgrod	BI	BMD	1826-1850	747,021
Rawa Mazowiecka	LO	BMD	1809/1823	718,609
Rawa Mazowiecka	LO	BMD	1824/1839	718,610
Rawa Mazowiecka	LO	BMD	1841-1852	718,611
Rawa Mazowiecka	LO	BMD	1853/1862	718,612
Rawa Mazowiecka	LO	BMD	1865-1866	768,029
Rawa Mazowiecka	LO	BMD	1869-1873	1,191,764
Rejowiec	LU	B	1826-1852	753,346
Rejowiec	LU	BMD	1826/1859	753,347
Rejowiec	LU	M	1837-1859	753,346
Rogozno	PO	BMD	1817/1839	752,799
Rogozno	PO	BMD	1840-1847	752,800
Rozprza	LO	BMD	1826-1850	718,796
Rozprza	LO	BMD	1851-1865	718,797
Rozprza	LO	BMD	1866-1870	768,031
Rozprza	LO	BMD	1871-1872	1,191,765
Rutki	BI	BMD	1850-1860	747,724
Rychwal	PO	BMD	1826-1855	752,823
Ryczywol	KI	BMD	1826-1857	1,201,353
Ryczywol	KI	BMD	1857-1875	1,201,354
Ryczywol	KI	BMD	1876-1877	1,201,355
Rynarzewo	BY	BMD	1823/1844	719,149
Rypin	BY	BMD	1808-1820	715,061
Rypin	BY	BMD	1820/1826	715,062
Rypin	BY	BMD	1827-1841	715,063
Rypin	BY	BMD	1842-1850	715,064
Rypin	BY	BMD	1851-1858	715,065
Rypin	BY	BMD	1859-1865	715,066
Sandomierz	KI	BMD	1826-1837	809,134
Sandomierz	KI	BMD	1832/1870	1,199,828
Sandomierz	KI	BMD	1838-1844	809,141
Sandomierz	KI	BMD	1845-1851	809,142
Sandomierz	KI	BMD	1852-1865	809,136
Sandomierz	KI	BMD	1866-1873	1,199,829
Sandomierz	KI	BMD	1874-1875	1,199,830
Sarnaki	WA	BMD	1836-1847	810,575
Sarnaki	WA	BMD	1848/1858	810,576
Secemin	KI	BMD	1826-1845	716,107
Secemin	KI	BMD	1846-1865	716,108
Secemin	KI	BMD	1866-1869	1,192,429
Sejny	BI	BMD	1826/1865	747,778
Sejny	BI	BMD	1866-1875	1,191,986
Sereje	BI	BMD	1826-1856	752,589
Seroczyn	WA	BMD	1841/1859	808,635
Sianow	KO	BMD	1848-1874	1,190,970
Siedlce	WA	BMD	1828/1840	808,645
Siedlce	WA	BMD	1841-1844	808,646
Siedlce	WA	BMD	1845/1857	808,647
Siedlisko	ZI	BMD	1847-1874	1,335,031
Siedliszcze	LU	BMD	1827,1829	753,411
Siemianowice Slaskie	KA	I/O	1856-1862	1,184,434
Siemianowice Slaskie	KA	M	1880	1,184,434
Siennica	WA	BMD	1826-1836	702,449
Sienno	KI	BMD	1826-1844	813,931
Sienno	KI	BMD	1845-1855	813,932
Sienno	KI	BMD	1856-1865	813,933
Sienno	KI	BMD	1866-1873	1,192,429
Sienno	KI	BMD	1874-1877	1,201,355
Sierpc	WA	BMD	1826-1837	730,159
Sierpc	WA	BMD	1838-1852	730,160
Sierpc	WA	BMD	1853-1863	730,161
Sierpc	WA	BMD	1864-1865	730,162
Sierpc	WA	BMD	1866-1873	1,191,026
Sierpc	WA	BMD	1873-1879	1,191,027
Skarszewy	GD	Fam	1871-1919	475,222
Skicrniewice	LO	BMD	1826-1845	743,266
Skierniewice	LO	BMD	1846-1865	743,267
Skierniewice	LO	BMD	1866	768,040
Skierniewice	LO	BMD	1867	1,191,774
Skierniewice	LO	BMD	1868-1875	1,191,775
Skulsk	PO	BMD	1826/1865	752,879
Skwierzyna	ZI	BMD	1808-1838	1,184,452
Skwierzyna	ZI	BMD	1808/1847	1,184,454
Skwierzyna	ZI	Fam	1838-1862	1,190,959
Skwierzyna	ZI	B	1839-1846	1,184,453
Skwierzyna	ZI	D	1845-1847	1,184,455
Skwierzyna	ZI	D	1875-1918	1,184,455
Slawatycze	LU	BM	1847/1876	753,441
Slesin	PO	BMD	1826-1855	752,880
Slupca	PO	BMD	1869-1875	1,191,407
Slupsk	KO	BMD	1813-1848	1,334,572
Slupsk	KO	BMD	1840-1875	1,334,580
Smoszewo	WA	BMD	1809-1812	689,628
Sniadow	BI	BMD	1808,1832	996,527
Sniadow	BI	BMD	1826/1838	747,725
Sniadow	BI	BMD	1839-1848	747,726
Sniadow	BI	BMD	1849/1864	747,727
Sniadow	BI	BMD	1867-1868	1,199,534
Sniadow	BI	BMD	1869-1873	1,199,535
Sniadow	BI	BMD	1876-1878	1,191,362
Sniadow	BI	BMD	1879-1880	1,191,363
Sniadow	PO	BMD	1867-1868	1,199,534
Sniadow	PO	BMD	1869-1875	1,199,535
Sniadow	PO	BMD	1876-1878	1,191,362
Sniadow	PO	BMD	1879-1880	1,191,363
Sobkow	KI	BMD	1810-1853	715,872
Sobkow	KI	BMD	1854-1865	715,873
Sobkow	KI	BMD	1866-1876	1,192,430
Sobota	LO	BMD	1826-1865	743,026
Sochocin	WA	BMD	1826-1849	689,626
Sochocin	WA	BMD	1850-1859	689,627

Sochocin	WA	BMD	1860-1879	1,191,989	Swierze	LU	BMD	1826/1865	766,278
Sokolow Podlaski	WA	BMD	1827-1838	809,156	Sycow	WR	Cem	1820-1867	1,184,417
Sokolow Podlaski	WA	BMD	1839-1846	809,157	Szadek	LO	BMD	1826-1854	747,923
Sokolow Podlaski	WA	BMD	1847-1855	809,158	Szczebrzeszyn	LU	BMD	1825-1839	755,509
Sokolow Podlaski	WA	BMD	1856-1864	809,159	Szczebrzeszyn	LU	BMD	1840-1850	755,510
Sokoly	BI	BMD	1826/1865	747,741	Szczebrzeszyn	LU	BMD	1851-1860	755,511
Sokoly	BI	BMD	1847/1930	1,046,485	Szczebrzeszyn	LU	BMD	1861-1865	755,512
Sokoly	BI	BMD	1867/1878	1,191,940	Szczebrzeszyn	LU	BMD	1866-1870	904,319
Sokoly	BI	BMD	1880	1,191,362	Szczecin	SZ	Fam	1841-1847	1,184,457
Sokoly-nowosiolki	BI	BMD	1840/1910	1,186,448	Szczecin	SZ	D	1845-1849	1,184,457
Solec Kujawski	BY	BMD	1823-1847	719,152	Szczecin	SZ	Fam	1850-1880	1,184,457
Sompolno	PO	BMD	1826/1847	758,352	Szczecin	SZ	BD	1854-1874	1,184,458
Sompolno	PO	BMD	1848-1865	758,353	Szczecin	SZ	M	1901-1939	1,184,458
Sompolno	PO	BMD	1866-1877	1,191,414	Szczecinek	KO	Cem	1788-1870	1,184,444
Sosnicowice	KA	Cir	1806-1865	1,184,428	Szczekociny	KI	BMD	1826-1843	716,115
Sosnicowice	KA	Cem	1831-1893	1,184,428	Szczekociny	KI	BMD	1826-1846	1,199,732
Srem	PO	BMD	1817-1847	758,361	Szczekociny	KI	BMD	1847-1852	1,199,733
Sroda Slaska	WR	B	1818-1848	1,184,444	Szczekociny	KI	BMD	1867-1877	1,199,734
Sroda Slaska	WR	Cen	1841	1,184,444	Szczepankowo	BI	M	1820-1821	747,727
Sroda Slaska	WR	M	1841-1847	1,184,444	Szczercow	LO	BMD	1826/1847	747,932
Stanislawow	WA	BMD	1826-1836	702,450	Szczercow	LO	BMD	1848-1865	747,933
Stargard Szczecinski	SZ	Cen	1761	1,184,456	Szczercow	LO	BMD	1866-1870	760,113
					Szczercow	LO	BMD	1871-1874	1,191,787
Stargard Szczecinski	SZ	BMD	1812-1849	1,190,966	Szczuczyn	BI	BMD	1826/1853	747,022
					Szczuczyn	BI	BMD	1850-1860	747,023
Starogard Gdanski	GD	B	1812-1874	414,467	Szczuczyn	BI	BMD	1861-1865	747,024
Starogard Gdanski	GD	BMD	1812-1939	185,355	Szczuczyn	BI	BMD	1866/1879	1,199,535
Starogard Gdanski	GD	MD	1812-1939	414,468	Szczuczyn	BI	BMD	1870-1879	1,199,536
Starogard Gdanski	GD	Fam	1847-1862	474,723	Szczuczyn	BI	BMD	1876-1879	1,191,363
Starogard Gdanski	GD	Cem	1848-1904	1,184,446	Szlichtyngowa	ZI	Cem	1763-1936	1,184,412
Starogard Gdanski	GD	Fam	1862-1870	474,724	Szlichtyngowa	ZI	D	1802-1833	1,184,411
Starogard Gdanski	GD	Fam	1882-1903	474,717	Szlichtyngowa	ZI	BD	1802-1833	1,184,412
Starogard Gdanski	GD	Fam	1904-1920	474,718	Szlichtyngowa	ZI	BMD	1811-1876	1,184,413
Staszow	KI	BMD	1866-1872	1,199,830	Szlichtyngowa	ZI	M	1817-1833	1,184,412
Staszow	KI	BMD	1873-1877	1,199,831	Szlichtyngowa	ZI	BMD	1817-1840	1,271,450
Staszow	WA	BMD	1826-1836	588,931	Szlichtyngowa	ZI	BMD	1817-1840	1,271,451
Staszow	WA	BMD	1837-1850	588,932	Szlichtyngowa	ZI	BMD	1835-1843	1,184,450
Staszow	WA	BMD	1851-1856	588,933	Szlichtyngowa	ZI	BMD	1835-1847	896,081
Staszow	WA	BMD	1857-1865	588,934	Szlichtyngowa	ZI	D	1838-1840	1,184,412
Stawiszyn	PO	BMD	1826-1865	764,034	Szlichtyngowa	ZI	D	1859	1,184,450
Stopnica	KI	BMD	1875-1877	1,192,430	Szprotawa	ZI	BMD	1811-1847	1,184,456
Strykow	LO	BMD	1826-1835	747,973	Szprotawa	ZI	I/O	1813-1845	1,184,456
Strykow	LO	BMD	1836-1853	747,974	Szprotawa	ZI	Cem	1817-1933	1,184,456
Strykow	LO	BMD	1854-1865	747,975	Szrensk	WA	BMD	1809-1816	702,854
Strykow	LO	BMD	1866-1870	768,049	Szrensk	WA	BMD	1817-1823	702,855
Strzegom	WR	BMD	1850-1839	1,184,458	Szrensk	WA	BMD	1826-1843	702,856
Strzelce Krajenskie	ZI	D	1794-1913	1,184,493	Szrensk	WA	BMD	1845-1868	702,857
Strzelce Krajenskie	ZI	BMD	1847-1853	544,649	Szrensk	WA	BMD	1848-1868	702,858
Strzelce Opolskie	OP	BMD	1828-1919	1,184,417	Sztum	GD	Cem	?-?	1,184,458
Sulechow	ZI	BMD	1813-1874	1,334,572	Szydlowiec	KI	BMD	1826-1843	716,419
Sulejow	LO	BMD	1826-1842	747,995	Szydlowiec	KI	BMD	1844-1852	716,420
Sulejow	LO	BMD	1843/1865	747,996	Szydlowiec	KI	BMD	1853-1861	716,421
Sulejow	LO	BMD	1866-1870	760,106	Szydlowiec	KI	BMD	1859/1869	1,201,355
Sulmierzyce	LO	BMD	1826-1855	748,109	Szydlowiec	KI	BMD	1862-1865	716,422
Sulmierzyce	LO	BMD	1856-1865	748,110	Szydlowiec	KI	BMD	1870-1877	1,201,356
Sulmierzyce	LO	BMD	1866-1870	760,108	Tarczyn	WA	BMD	1808/1851	723,671
Sulmierzyce	LO	BMD	1871-1872	1,191,784	Tarczyn	WA	BMD	1852-1859	723,672
Suraz	BI	BMD	1870/1914	1,186,429	Tarlow	KI	BMD	1826-1851	813,946
Susz	OL	B	1847-1874	904,700	Tarlow	KI	BMD	1852-1865	813,947
Suwalki	BI	BMD	1826/1834	752,618	Tarlow	KI	BMD	1866-1868	1,192,430
Suwalki	BI	BMD	1835-1840	752,619	Tarlow	KI	BMD	1869-1873	1,192,431
Suwalki	BI	BMD	1842-1847	752,620	Tarnow	KR	BD	1808/1855	742,702
Suwalki	BI	BMD	1848-1854	752,621	Tarnow	KR	BD	1849-1870	948,420
Suwalki	BI	BMD	1856-1861	752,622	Tarnow	KR	MD	1849-1870	948,422
Suwalki	BI	BMD	1862-1865	752,623	Tarnow	KR	B	1863-1870	948,421
Suwalki	BI	BMD	1866	1,191,986	Tarnowskie Gory	KA	BMD	1813-1871	1,184,458
Suwalki	BI	BMD	1866-1877	1,199,520	Tarnowskie Gory	KA	BMD	1847-1870	877,402
Suwalki	BI	BMD	1878-1879	1,191,274	Tarnowskie Gory	KA	D	1871-1885	1,184,459
Swidnica	WR	BMD	1854-1875	1,184,451	Tarnowskie Gory	KA	D	1895-1901	1,184,460

Tczew	GD	BMD	1828-1848	743,206	Warka	WA	BMD	1873	1,201,356
Tczew	GD	Fam	1882-1919	475,221	Warka	WA	BMD	1874-1877	1,201,357
Terespol	LU	BMD	1826-1834	756,981	Warszawa	WA	BMD	1826-1830	689,510
Terespol	LU	BMD	1835-1843	756,982	Warszawa	WA	BMD	1826-1844	689,524
Terespol	LU	BMD	1844-1854	756,983	Warszawa	WA	BMD	1828-1829	689,511
Tomaszow Lubelski	LU	BMD	1826-1836	757,366	Warszawa	WA	BMD	1830-1831	689,512
Tomaszow Lubelski	LU	BMD	1837-1845	757,367	Warszawa	WA	BMD	1832-1833	689,513
Tomaszow Lubelski	LU	BMD	1847-1850	757,368	Warszawa	WA	BMD	1834-1836	689,514
Tomaszow Lubelski	LU	BMD	1851-1855	757,369	Warszawa	WA	BMD	1834-1838	689,517
Tomaszow Lubelski	LU	BMD	1856-1861	757,370	Warszawa	WA	BMD	1835-1837	689,515
Tomaszow Lubelski	LU	BMD	1862-1869	757,371	Warszawa	WA	BMD	1837	689,516
Tomaszow Lubelski	LU	BMD	1870	904,324	Warszawa	WA	BMD	1837-1844	689,525
Tomaszow Mazowiecki	LO	BMD	1830-1845	747,938	Warszawa	WA	B	1838-1841	689,521
					Warszawa	WA	BMD	1839	689,518
Tomaszow Mazowiecki	LO	BMD	1846-1857	747,939	Warszawa	WA	BMD	1840	689,519
					Warszawa	WA	BMD	1841	689,520
Tomaszow Mazowiecki	LO	BMD	1858-1865	747,940	Warszawa	WA	BMD	1842	689,522
					Warszawa	WA	BMD	1843	689,523
Tomaszow Mazowiecki	LO	BMD	1866-1870	760,115	Warszawa	WA	BMD	1843-1845	689,526
					Warszawa	WA	BMD	1843-1846	689,527
Tomaszow Mazowiecki	LO	BMD	1871-1872	1,191,788	Warszawa	WA	BMD	1846-1847	689,557
					Warszawa	WA	BMD	1847	689,528
Torun	BY	Fam	1818	496,009	Warszawa	WA	BMD	1847	689,529
Toszek	KA	D	1841-1872	1,184,461	Warszawa	WA	B	1847-1854	689,535
Toszek	KA	M	1886	1,184,461	Warszawa	WA	BMD	1848-1849	689,530
Trzcianka	PO	BMD	1815-1834	1,190,959	Warszawa	WA	BMD	1851	689,531
Trzcianka	PO	BMD	1817-1847	1,184,451	Warszawa	WA	BMD	1851	689,532
Trzcianka	PO	BMD	1835-1847	1,190,975	Warszawa	WA	D	1851-1853	689,536
Trzcianne	BI	BV	1871/1919	1,186,454	Warszawa	WA	BMD	1852	689,533
Trzciel	ZI	Fam	1834-1848	1,184,460	Warszawa	WA	BMD	1852-1853	689,534
Trzemeszno	BY	BMD	1832-1847	719,242	Warszawa	WA	BMD	1853-1856	689,539
Turobin	LU	BMD	1826-1842	757,404	Warszawa	WA	BMD	1854-1855	689,537
Turobin	LU	BMD	1843-1850	757,405	Warszawa	WA	BMD	1855	689,538
Turobin	LU	BMD	1851-1860	757,406	Warszawa	WA	BMD	1857	689,540
Turobin	LU	BMD	1861-1869	904,327	Warszawa	WA	BMD	1857	689,541
Tuszyn	LO	BMD	1826-1848	747,955	Warszawa	WA	B	1857-1860	689,542
Tuszyn	LO	BMD	1849-1865	747,956	Warszawa	WA	BMD	1858-1859	689,543
Tuszyn	LO	BMD	1866-1872	760,119	Warszawa	WA	BMD	1860	689,544
Tuszyn	LO	BMD	1871-1872	1,191,789	Warszawa	WA	BMD	1860	689,545
Twardogora	WR	D	1812-1818	1,184,411	Warszawa	WA	BMD	1860	689,546
Twardogora	WR	BMD	1819-1874	1,184,411	Warszawa	WA	BMD	1861	689,547
Tykocin	BI	BMD	1826/1844	747,742	Warszawa	WA	BMD	1862-1863	689,548
Tykocin	BI	BMD	1829/1934	1,186,457	Warszawa	WA	B	1862-1863	689,550
Tykocin	BI	BMD	1839/1856	747,743	Warszawa	WA	BM	1862-1864	689,549
Tykocin	BI	BMD	1847/1863	1,186,455	Warszawa	WA	BMD	1863-1864	689,552
Tykocin	BI	BMD	1857-1864	747,744	Warszawa	WA	BMD	1863-1866	689,551
Tykocin	BI	BMD	1859/1904	1,186,456	Warszawa	WA	BMD	1864-1865	689,554
Tykocin	BI	BMD	1866	1,191,940	Warszawa	WA	BMD	1864-1866	689,553
Tykocin	BI	B	1867-1873	1,191,940	Warszawa	WA	BMD	1865	689,556
Tykocin	BI	BMD	1868-1874	1,191,941	Warszawa	WA	BMD	1865-1866	689,555
Tykocin	BI	BMD	1874-1876	1,191,942	Warta	LO	BMD	1809-1815	753,084
Tyszowce	LU	BMD	1826-1828	766,304	Warta	LO	BMD	1815-1824	753,085
Tyszowce	LU	BMD	1829-1843	766,305	Warta	LO	BMD	1825-1832	753,086
Tyszowce	LU	BMD	1844-1860	766,306	Warta	LO	BMD	1833-1850	753,087
Tyszowce	LU	BMD	1861-1869	766,307	Warta	LO	BMD	1851/1858	753,088
Tyszowce	LU	BMD	1870	904,328	Wasilkow	BI	BMD	1818/1933	1,186,458
Uchanie	LU	BMD	1826-1844	766,425	Wasosz	BI	BMD	1840-1865	747,025
Uchanie	LU	BMD	1845-1864	766,426	Wasosz	BI	BMD	1866-1875	1,199,536
Ujazd	LO	B	1826-1865	748,077	Wasosz	BI	BMD	1878	1,191,363
Ujazd	LO	BMD	1826-1865	748,078	Wawolnica	LU	D	1826-1870	761,160
Ujazd	LO	BMD	1866-1870	760,121	Wawolnica	LU	B	1851-1899	761,160
Ujazd	LO	BMD	1876	1,191,789	Wawolnica	LU	M	1854-1890	761,160
Walbrzych	WR	BMD	1934-1938	1,184,461	Wegorzewo	OL	BMD	1847-1874	1,198,247
Walcz	KO	BMD	1812-1847	1,271,456	Wegorzewo	OL	B	1849-1874	1,335,310
Walcz	KO	D	1847-1874	1,273,147	Wegrow	WA	B	1826-1848	811,273
Walcz	KO	BM	1847-1874	1,335,039	Wegrow	WA	BMD	1826/1848	810,101
Warka	WA	BMD	1826-1841	723,677	Wegrow	WA	BMD	1838/1853	810,102
Warka	WA	BMD	1842-1854	723,678	Wejherowo	GD	Fam	1848-1873	474,722
Warka	WA	BMD	1855-1859	723,679	Wejherowo	GD	Fam	1882-1912	474,716

Wejherowo	GD	Fam	1913-1919	474,719	Wolbrom	KR	BMD	1831-1838	923,370
Widawa	LO	BMD	1826-1850	753,103	Wolbrom	KR	BMD	1842-1847	923,369
Widawa	LO	BMD	1852-1865	753,104	Wolbrom	KR	B	1845-1859	876,799
Widawa	LO	BMD	1866-1870	760,130	Wolbrom	KR	BMD	1848-1855	923,370
Widawa	LO	BMD	1871-1875	1,191,794	Wolbrom	KR	M	1852-1863	876,799
Wiecbork	BY	BMD	1825-1847	719,323	Wolbrom	KR	BMD	1856-1866	923,371
Wiejsieje	BI	BMD	1840-1853	752,634	Wolbrom	KR	BMD	1867-1870	923,372
Wieliszew	WA	BMD	1808-1817	689,647	Wolczyn	OP	BD	1835-1890	1,184,431
Wieliszew	WA	BMD	1818-1825	689,648	Wolin	SZ	BMD	1813-1874	1,334,576
Wieliszew	WA	BMD	1826-1841	689,649	Wroclaw	WR	Fam	?-?	1,184,404
Wieliszew	WA	BMD	1842-1858	689,650	Wroclaw	WR	Cem	1743/1939	1,184,403
Wieliszew	WA	BMD	1859-1865	689,651	Wroclaw	WR	B	1760-1804	1,184,379
Wielowies	KA	Fam	1762-1820	1,184,433	Wroclaw	WR	Cem	1761-1856	1,184,402
Wielowies	KA	B	1810-1857	1,184,432	Wroclaw	WR	B	1766-1812	1,184,384
Wielowies	KA	M	1828-1851	1,184,434	Wroclaw	WR	B	1766/1847	1,184,384
Wielowies	KA	Fam	1845/1889	1,184,434	Wroclaw	WR	M	1772-1773	1,184,384
Wielun	LO	BMD	1826/1853	753,121	Wroclaw	WR	M	1772-1812	1,184,389
Wielun	LO	BMD	1854-1865	753,122	Wroclaw	WR	M	1772/1930	1,184,389
Wielun	LO	BMD	1866-1870	760,136	Wroclaw	WR	D	1780-1874	1,184,402
Wieniawa	LU	BMD	1826-1840	723,564	Wroclaw	WR	M	1784-1796	1,184,385
Wieniawa	LU	BMD	1841-1853	723,565	Wroclaw	WR	Fam	1791	1,184,403
Wieniawa	LU	BMD	1854-1864	723,566	Wroclaw	WR	D	1791-1812	1,184,390
Wieniawa	LU	BMD	1865-1869	905,176	Wroclaw	WR	M	1797-1811	1,184,386
Wieszowa	KA	BD	1847-1848	877,421	Wroclaw	WR	Cem	1800-1900	1,184,401
Wilczyn	PO	BMD	1827/1858	764,452	Wroclaw	WR	M	1804-1812	1,184,387
Wiskitki	WA	BMD	1826-1845	723,429	Wroclaw	WR	B	1804-1846	1,184,380
Wiskitki	WA	BMD	1846-1854	723,430	Wroclaw	WR	B	1812-1820	1,271,412
Wiskitki	WA	BMD	1856-1865	1,199,746	Wroclaw	WR	V	1812-1857	1,184,419
Wiskitki	WA	BMD	1866-1877	1,199,747	Wroclaw	WR	BMD	1812-1857	1,184,419
Wislica	KI	BMD	1826-1846	588,922	Wroclaw	WR	D	1813-1859	1,184,391
Wislica	KI	BMD	1847-1865	588,923	Wroclaw	WR	D	1815-1827	1,184,392
Wislica	KI	BMD	1866-1875	1,192,431	Wroclaw	WR	B	1827-1838	1,184,381
Wisnicz	KR	BM	1814-1870	936,648	Wroclaw	WR	M	1832-1847	1,184,388
Wisznice	LU	B	1826-1849	761,187	Wroclaw	WR	B	1838-1846	1,184,382
Wizajny	BI	BMD	1829-1832	752,653	Wroclaw	WR	M	1846-1847	1,184,387
Wizajny	BI	BMD	1833-1848	752,654	Wroclaw	WR	M	1846-1847	1,184,389
Wizajny	BI	BMD	1851-1865	752,655	Wroclaw	WR	B	1846-1872	1,184,383
Wizajny	BI	BMD	1866/1874	1,199,521	Wroclaw	WR	B	1847	1,184,384
Wizajny	BI	BMD	1877-1879	1,191,274	Wroclaw	WR	D	1860-1874	1,184,393
Wizna	BI	BMD	1828-1836	747,728	Wroclaw	WR	Cem	1868-1923	1,184,419
Wizna	BI	BMD	1838-1865	747,729	Wroclaw	WR	M	1873-1930	1,184,389
Wizna	BI	BMD	1868-1873	1,199,536	Wroclaw	WR	M	1887-1898	1,184,389
Wizna	BI	BMD	1876,1878	1,191,363	Wroclaw	WR	Cem	1889/1898	1,184,400
Wloclawck	BY	M	1929	1,186,459	Wroclaw	WR	M	1903-1919	1,184,389
Wlodawa	LU	D	1826-1836	761,193	Wroclaw	WR	M	1903-1938	1,184,390
Wlodawa	LU	B	1844-1848	761,192	Wroclaw	WR	D	1910-1921	1,184,394
Wlodawa	LU	M	1846-1859	761,192	Wroclaw	WR	D	1914-1927	1,184,395
Wlodawa	LU	B	1851-1865	761,193	Wroclaw	WR	D	1914-1927	1,184,396
Wloszczowa	KI	BMD	1823-1857	716,122	Wroclaw	WR	D	1918-1926	1,184,397
Wloszczowa	KI	BMD	1858-1865	716,149	Wroclaw	WR	D	1928-1940	1,184,398
Wloszczowa	KI	BMD	1866-1875	1,192,432	Wroclaw	WR	D	1928-1940	1,184,399
Wloszczowa	KI	BMD	1876	1,924,433	Wroclaw	WR	B	1933-1939	1,184,384
Wodynie	WA	BMD	1826-1839	808,665	Wronki	PO	Fam	1832/1842	1,184,461
Wodzislaw	KI	BMD	1826-1834	715,885	Wrzesnia	PO	Fam	1834	1,190,958
Wodzislaw	KI	BMD	1835-1844	715,886	Wrzesnia	PO	M	1859-1860	1,186,460
Wodzislaw	KI	BMD	1845-1858	715,887	Wrzesnia	PO	D	1867-1869	1,186,460
Wodzislaw	KI	BMD	1859-1865	715,888	Wschowa	ZI	Cem	1763-1936	1,184,412
Wodzislaw	KI	BMD	1867-1875	1,192,433	Wschowa	ZI	Fam	1800	1,184,413
Wodzislaw	KI	BMD	1876-1877	1,192,436	Wschowa	ZI	D	1802-1833	1,184,411
Wohyn	LU	BMD	1826-1842	761,208	Wschowa	ZI	BMD	1802/1840	1,184,412
Wohyn	LU	BMD	1844-1864	767,001	Wschowa	ZI	BMD	1811-1876	1,184,413
Wojslawice	LU	BMD	1826/1850	767,024	Wschowa	ZI	BMD	1817-1840	1,271,450
Wojslawice	LU	BMD	1851-1870	767,025	Wschowa	ZI	BMD	1817-1840	1,271,451
Wolanow	KI	BMD	1826-1858	716,441	Wschowa	ZI	BMD	1838	896,082
Wolanow	KI	BMD	1860-1877	1,201,357	Wschowa	ZI	Fam	1840-1899	1,184,413
Wolborz	LO	BMD	1826-1846	753,174	Wschowa	ZI	Fam	1847	1,184,412
Wolborz	LO	BMD	1847-1856	753,175	Wschowa	ZI	Fam	1890-1919	474,930
Wolborz	LO	BMD	1857-1867	760,149	Wylatowo	BY	BMD	1832-1847	719,244
Wolbrom	KR	BMD	1826-1841	923,368	Wysokie	LU	B	1820	771,631

Place				
Wysokie	LU	BMD	1826-1836	771,631
Wysokie Mazowiekie	BI	BMD	1826/1848	747,730
Wysokie Mazowiekie	BI	BMD	1834/1890	1,186,440
Wysokie Mazowiekie	BI	D	1848-1880	1,186,438
Wysokie Mazowiekie	BI	BMD	1849/1865	747,731
Wysokie Mazowiekie	BI	M	1859/1911	1,046,472
Wysokie Mazowiekie	BI	BMD	1866/1875	1,199,537
Wysokie Mazowiekie	BI	BMD	1872/1936	1,186,439
Wysokie Mazowiekie	BI	BMD	1876/1879	1,191,363
Wysokie Mazowiekie	BI	BMD	1898/1910	1,186,441
Wyszogrod	WA	BMD	1826-1835	730,206
Wyszogrod	WA	BMD	1836-1844	730,207
Wyszogrod	WA	BMD	1845-1851	730,208
Wyszogrod	WA	BMD	1850-1865	730,211
Wyszogrod	WA	BMD	1852-1858	730,209
Wyszogrod	WA	BMD	1859-1865	730,210
Wyszogrod	WA	BMD	1866-1873	1,201,499
Wyszogrod	WA	BMD	1875-1879	1,201,500
Zabkowice Slaskie	WR	Cem	18??-19??	1,184,411
Zabrze	KA	Cem	1873-1940	1,184,419
Zabrze	KA	M	1882-1883	1,184,461
Zagan	ZI	Cem	1841-1937	1,184,450
Zagorow	PO	BMD	1826-1843	765,779
Zagorow	PO	BMD	1844-1865	765,780
Zaklikow	LU	BMD	1826-1862	771,637
Zakroczym	WA	BMD	1825-1831	689,628
Zakroczym	WA	BMD	1832-1844	689,629
Zakroczym	WA	BMD	1845-1850	689,630
Zakroczym	WA	BMD	1851-1857	689,631
Zakroczym	WA	BMD	1858-1863	689,632
Zakroczym	WA	BMD	1868-1876	1,191,911
Zambrow	BI	BMD	1842-1847	747,732
Zambrow	BI	BMD	1848-1865	747,733
Zambrow	BI	BMD	1867-1874	1,199,537
Zambrow	BI	BMD	1875	1,199,538
Zambrow	BI	BMD	1876-1880	1,191,363
Zamosc	LU	BMD	1826-1830	755,697
Zamosc	LU	B	1832-1843	771,650
Zamosc	LU	BMD	1832/1852	771,651
Zamosc	LU	MD	1852/1865	755,697
Zaniemysl	PO	BMD	1817-1839	1,184,450
Zaniemysl	PO	BMD	1817-1839	1,190,958
Zaniemysl	PO	Fam	1834-1853	1,190,958
Zareby Koscielne	WA	BMD	1836/1845	810,610
Zareby Koscielne	WA	BMD	1846-1859	810,611
Zareby Koscielne	WA	BMD	1874-1875	1,191,363
Zareby Koscielne	WA	BMD	1876-1880	1,191,364
Zarki	KA	BM	1826-1829	1,199,847
Zarki	KA	BMD	1826-1848	1,199,848
Zarki	KA	BMD	1849/1860	1,199,849
Zarki	KA	BD	1859/1874	1,199,850
Zarki	KA	BMD	1875-1878	1,199,851
Zarnow	KI	BMD	1826-1853	718,949
Zarnow	KI	BMD	1854-1865	718,950
Zarnow	KI	BMD	1866-1873	1,192,434
Zarnowiec	KR	BMD	1811-1824	876,803
Zarnowiec	KR	BMD	1825	876,804
Zarnowiec	KR	BMD	1826-1833	876,807
Zarnowiec	KR	BMD	1826/1857	876,809
Zarnowiec	KR	BMD	1834-1852	876,808
Zarnowiec	KR	MD	1839/1870	876,810
Zarnowiec	KR	BMD	1858-1868	923,375
Zawichost	KI	BMD	1826-1838	809,137
Zawichost	KI	BMD	1839-1850	809,138
Zawichost	KI	BMD	1851-1858	809,139
Zawichost	KI	BMD	1859-1864	809,140
Zawichost	KI	BMD	1865-1866	1,199,831
Zawichost	KI	BMD	1867-1877	1,199,832
Zawichost	KI	BMD	1877	1,199,833
Zdunska Wola	LO	BMD	1826/1854	753,220
Zdunska Wola	LO	BMD	1850-1865	753,221
Zdunska Wola	LO	BMD	1866-1867	760,161
Zdunska Wola	LO	BMD	1867	1,201,135
Zdunska Wola	LO	BMD	1868-1872	1,201,136
Zdunska Wola	LO	BMD	1873-1874	1,201,137
Zduny	PO	MD	1818-1847	765,799
Zgierz	LO	BMD	1826-1846	753,243
Zgierz	LO	BMD	1847-1859	753,244
Zgierz	LO	BMD	1860-1865	753,245
Zgierz	LO	BMD	1866-1870	760,165
Zgierz	LO	B	1871-1878	1,201,141
Zgierz	LO	MD	1871-1880	1,201,142
Zgorzelec	WR	Cem	1850-1940	1,184,417
Zgorzelec	WR	BMD	1864-1932	1,184,418
Zloczew	LO	BMD	1826-1830	766,318
Zloczew	LO	BMD	1831-1858	766,319
Zloczew	LO	BMD	1859-1865	766,320
Zloczew	LO	BMD	1866	760,168
Zloczew	LO	BMD	1867-1872	1,201,143
Zlotow	KO	Fam	?-?	1,184,411
Zlotow	KO	BMD	1813-1846	1,184,410
Zmigrod	WR	Cem	?-?	1,184,461
Zolkiewka	LU	BMD	1827-1849	753,996
Zolkiewka	LU	BMD	1850-1860	753,997
Zolkiewka	LU	BMD	1861-1870	904,337
Zory	KA	D	1837-1879	1,184,456
Zuromin	WA	BMD	1808-1825	702,523
Zuromin	WA	BMD	1829-1845	702,524
Zuromin	WA	BMD	1846-1865	702,525
Zwolen	KI	BMD	1826-1833	716,373
Zwolen	KI	BMD	1834-1851	716,374
Zwolen	KI	BMD	1852-1858	716,375
Zwolen	KI	BMD	1859-1865	716,376
Zwolen	KI	BMD	1866	1,201,357
Zwolen	KI	BMD	1867-1877	1,201,358
Zychlin	LO	B	1903-1913	1,186,461

Reprinted from *Avotaynu,* Vol. II, No. 1, 1986.

National Archives Regional Branches and Federal Records Centers

See "The National Archives" (District of Columbia), pp. 28–42.

■ NATIONAL ARCHIVES REGIONAL BRANCHES

California
Pacific Sierra Region
1000 Commodore Drive
San Bruno, California 94066
(415) 876-9009

Pacific Southwest Region
24000 Avila Road, P.O. Box 6719
Laguna Niguel, California 92677-6719
(714) 643-4220

Colorado
Rocky Mountain Region
Building 48, Denver Federal Center
Denver, Colorado 80225
(303) 236-0818

District of Columbia
Central Information Division
National Archives
Washington, DC 20408
(202) 523-3220

Georgia
Southeast Region
1557 St. Joseph Avenue
East Point, Georgia 30344
(404) 763-7477

Illinois
Great Lakes Region
7358 South Pulaski Road
Chicago, Illinois 60629
(312) 581-7816

Massachusetts
New England Region
380 Trapelo Road
Waltham, Massachusetts 02154
(617) 647-8100

Missouri
Central Plains Region
2312 East Bannister Road
Kansas City, Missouri 64131
(816) 926-7271

New Jersey
Northeast Region
Building 22-Military Ocean Terminal
Bayonne, New Jersey 07002
(201) 823-7252

Pennsylvania
Mid-Atlantic Region
9th and Market Streets
Philadelphia, Pennsylvania 19107
(215) 597-3000

Texas
Southwest Region
501 West Felix Street, P.O. Box 6216
Fort Worth, Texas 76115
(817) 334-5525

Washington
Pacific Northwest Region
6125 Sand Point Way NE
Seattle, Washington 98115
(206) 526-6507

■ FEDERAL RECORDS CENTERS

California, San Francisco
1000 Commodore Drive
San Bruno, California 94066
(415) 876-9003

California, Los Angeles
24000 Avila Road
Laguna Niguel, California 92677
(714) 643-4220

Colorado, Denver
P.O. Box 25307
Bldg. 48, Denver Federal Center
Denver, Colorado 80225
(303) 236-0804

District of Columbia
Washington National Records Center
Washington, DC 20409
(301) 763-7000

Georgia, Atlanta
1557 St. Joseph Avenue
East Point, Georgia 30344
(404) 763-7476

Illinois, Chicago
7358 South Pulaski Road
Chicago, Illinois 60629
(312) 353-0164

Massachusetts, Boston
380 Trapelo Road
Waltham, Massachusetts 02154
(617) 647-8745

Missouri, Kansas City
2312 East Bannister Road
Kansas City, Missouri 64131
(816) 926-7271

Missouri, St. Louis
National Personnel Records Center
9700 Page Boulevard
St. Louis, Missouri 63132
(314) 263-7201

New York, Bayonne, NJ
Bldg. 22, Military Ocean Terminal
Bayonne, New Jersey 07002
(201) 823-7161

Ohio, Dayton
3150 Springboro Road
Dayton, Ohio 45439
(513) 225-2878

Pennsylvania, Philadelphia
5000 Wissahickon Avenue
Philadelphia, Pennsylvania 19144
(215) 951-5588

Texas, Fort Worth
Box 6216
Fort Worth, Texas 76115
(817) 334-5515

Washington, Seattle
6125 Sand Point Way NE
Seattle, Washington 98115
(206) 526-6501

Biographical Sketches of Contributors

Zachary M. Baker is head librarian of the YIVO Institute for Jewish Research (New York). He has served as contributing editor of *Toledot* and *Avotaynu* and written for other genealogical publications. His *Bibliography of Eastern European Memorial Books* has been published in three separate editions.

Michael Brenner is currently president of the Jewish Genealogical Society of New York. Born in the Bronx, New York, in 1935, he has been actively searching his family history since 1975. He has used the LDS library and National Archives extensively, concentrating on Polish vital records and immigration records.

Marsha Saron Dennis, a professional genealogist, traces families for individuals and for attorneys settling estates. She has published articles in *Avotaynu*, *Dorot*, and *Heritage Quest*. Since 1980, she has published her own family's newsletter, *SaroNews*, and she was editor of *Dorot* in 1989. Ms. Dennis served on the Executive Council of the Jewish Genealogical Society of New York, for eight years, four as vice president. She also serves as genealogical consultant to the Lower East Side Tenement Museum.

Arlene H. Eakle is president and founder of The Genealogical Institute, Salt Lake City; she has been a professional genealogist for more than 25 years.

Dr. Eakle was also the first American genealogist to receive the highest award given by the Institute of Heraldic and Genealogical Studies, Canterbury, England (1988). The Julian Bickersteth Memorial Medal is for notable and outstanding contributions to family history education.

A prolific writer with more than 30 titles on her publications list, she is general editor with Johni Cerny of the award-winning *The Source: A Guidebook for American Genealogy* (1984), and author of three chapters (Census Records, Court and Probate Records, and Tracking Immigrant Origins). The American Library Association recognized *The Source* as one of the 10 Best Reference Works of 1984.

Eli Grad is a Contributing Editor of *Search* and is President Emeritus and former Dean of Faculty at Hebrew College in Brookline, Massachusetts. He has also served as editor of *The Judaica Post* and is a former president of the National Council of Jewish Education.

Arthur Kurzweil is Vice President of Jason Aronson, Inc., and is Editor-in-chief of The Jewish Book Club. He is author of *From Generation to Generation: How to Trace Your Jewish Genealogy and Personal History* (Schocken Books) and *My Generations: A Course in Jewish Family History* (Behrman House). He lives in Brooklyn, New York, with his wife and three children. He is co-editor of the three-volume *Encyclopedia of Jewish Genealogy* with Miriam Weiner.

Rolf A. Lederer is a psychiatrist and co-founder and current president of the Jewish Genealogical Society of Toronto. He is Canadian corresponding editor for *Avotaynu*, as well as the author of genealogical articles for other publications, including the *Canadian Jewish Times* and *Shem Tov*. Dr. Lederer also lectures on genealogical themes.

Scott E. Meyer is the associate editor of *Search, International Journal for Researchers of Jewish Genealogy*. He served as consulting editor of the second edition of *A Translation Guide to 19th-Century Polish-Language Civil-Registration Documents* (by Judith R. Frazin) and is president of the Jewish Genealogical Society of Illinois. Mr. Meyer's thoughts on the subject of Jewish genealogy have appeared in various publications in the field. In addition to teaching and lecturing on Jewish genealogy, he is certified by the Board of Jewish Education of Metropolitan Chicago and has taught religious school courses for over 15 years. Mr. Meyer is co-editor of the Guides to Institutional Resources in the United States and Canada of *The Encyclopedia of Jewish Genealogy*.

Sybil Milton is senior resident historian at the United States Holocaust Memorial Museum, Washington, D.C.

John Henry Richter, born in Vienna, Austria in 1919, and educated at the University of California, Berkeley, has held library positions with the Library of Congress (1950–1956), and the University of Michigan (1956–1982). Special interests include Prussia and Bohemia (ancestral families), selected Berliner families, and rabbinical genealogy. He has been a contributor to *Avotaynu* and *Search, International Journal for Researchers of Jewish Genealogy*. Mr. Richter's latest study, "From the Rhineland to Wisconsin," traces the ancestry and descendants of a number of Jewish pioneer merchant families who settled in Wisconsin (1850–1880) (unpublished).

Daniel M. Schlyter, born in California in 1949, now resides in Salt Lake City. He is an accredited genealogist (Poland and Czechoslovakia). He has been a European reference consultant at the Family History Library since 1978, specializing in Eastern European, German, and Jewish research, and a member of the Polish Genealogical Society (on board of directors since 1984). He has lectured at numerous genealogical seminars, and is the author of numerous articles on Eastern European Genealogical research and the following books: *A Gazetteer of Polish Adjectival Place-names* (1980), *Handbook of Czechoslovak Genealogical Research* (1985), and *Mecklenburg: Genealogical Outline and Gazetteer* (1989). Mr. Schlyter is the co-author of *Sources for Genealogical Research in the Soviet Union* (1983), with Kahlile Mehr, and *Greek Genealogical Research* (1988), with Lica Catsakis Bywater.

Jürgen Sielemann, born in Bevensen, Germany in 1944, received his senior staff diploma to become an archives' official in 1969. Since that time, he has been a referent at the Department of Genealogy and Biography at the Hamburg State Archives. His duties include genealogical and biographical research for legal claims and scientific and private purposes and compilation of the history of religious minorities, principally the records of the Jewish communities of Hamburg, Altona, and Wandsbek in the Hamburg State Archives.

His publications (in German) include: "The History of the Monastery of Cismar" (Grömitz, 1972); "Luis Vernet: A Hamburg Citizen First Settler on the Falkland Islands" (Hamburg, 1982); "Family Research Facilities in Hamburg State Archives" (Hamburg, 1985); and editing the "Memorial Book for the Jewish Victims of National Socialism in Hamburg."

Alan Spencer is a charter member of the Jewish Genealogical Society of Illinois and a former director of the organization. He is also the founder and editor of *Search, International Journal for Researchers of Jewish Genealogy.* Mr. Spencer was among those actively involved in the formation of the Association of Jewish Genealogical Societies. His biography appears in *Who's Who in the Midwest, Personalities of America, Directory of Distinguished Americans, The International Directory of Distinguished Leadership,* and *Who's Who in Entertainment.* Mr. Spencer is co-editor of the Guides to Institutional Resources in the United States and Canada of *The Encyclopedia of Jewish Genealogy.*

Lawrence Tapper is the staff archivist responsible for the preservation and acquisition of records of national significance relating to the Jewish community in Canada at the National Archives of Canada in Ottawa. He is currently compiling and editing a biographical index of the Canadian Jewish community from Canadian Jewry's first Anglo-Jewish newspaper *The Jewish Times,* 1897–1909.

Miriam Weiner, born in California, resides in Secaucus, New Jersey. Her syndicated column, "Roots and Branches," is published in over 90 Anglo-Jewish periodicals. She received her B.A. from SUNY Albany (1986) in Historical Studies (Modern Judaic History and the Holocaust). She was the first certified Jewish Genealogist (1985) by the Board for Certification of Genealogists in Washington, D.C., and Ms. Weiner lectures on Jewish genealogy and Holocaust research under the auspices of the B'nai B'rith Lecture Bureau and U.J.A. Speakers Bureau. She is consultant to the Museum of Jewish Heritiage in New York, as well as being the Former Executive Director of the American Gathering of Jewish Holocaust Survivors in New York. Ms. Weiner is author of numerous articles and reference guides on Jewish genealogy, Sephardic resources, and Holocaust research, and she is coordinator of "Routes to Roots" Genealogy Tours offered by ISRAM Travel in New York City. She is co-editor of the three-volume *Encyclopedia of Jewish Genealogy* with Arthur Kurzweil.

Suzan Fisher Wynne began her career in genealogical research by tracing her own family history in 1977. She published three books and organized one family reunion as a result. She is a founder of the Jewish Genealogy Society of Greater Washington. She also served as a JGSGW board member, newsletter editor, program chairman for the 1982 Summer Seminar, and program consultant for the 1988 Summer Seminar. She is currently vice president of AJGS. She has been a professional genealogist since 1983.

INDEX